Also by Arlene Croce

GOING TO THE DANCE (1982)

AFTERIMAGES (1977)

THE FRED ASTAIRE & GINGER ROGERS BOOK (1972)

Sight Lines

ARLENE CROCE

Sight Lines

ALFRED · A · KNOPF

NEW YORK

1 9 8 7

This Is a Borzoi Book
Published by Alfred A. Knopf, Inc.

Most of the articles in this book were originally published
in The New Yorker.

Owing to limitations of space, all other acknowledgments
for permission to reprint previously published material will
be found following the index.

Library of Congress Cataloging-in-Publication Data

Croce, Arlene. Sight lines.

Includes index.
1. Dancing—New York—New York (City)—Reviews.
2. Dancing—United States—Reviews.   I. Title.
GV1624.5.N4C78   1987   793.3'2'097471   87-45433
ISBN 0-394-56164-3

Manufactured in the United States of America
First Edition

All of the articles in this book were first published in
The New Yorker, with the following exceptions:
"Edward Villella" was written for an exhibition of
photographs at the United States Military Academy,
West Point. "Le Mystère Baryshnikov" appeared in a
Christmas issue of French *Vogue* edited by Mikhail
Baryshnikov. Part 1 of "Edwin Denby" combines
portions of articles previously written for *Dance
Magazine* and *Harper's* with the text of a memorial
tribute delivered at the Museum and Library of the
Performing Arts, Lincoln Center. A version of this
tribute was published in *Ballet Review*.

Acknowledgments

I wish to acknowledge the contribution to this book made by two superb editors at *The New Yorker*, Susan Moritz and Ann Goldstein. To William Shawn, who supported and encouraged a "Dancing" column from the very beginning, my everlasting thanks.

I thank Robert Greskovic, most charitable of colleagues, for continuing to share with me his files, his technical knowledge of dance, and his expert recall of events.

My gratitude also goes to the people who did their best to make sure that critics had sight lines—principally Leslie Bailey and Maitland McDonagh of New York City Ballet, Bob Pontarelli and Elena Gordon of American Ballet Theatre, Rima Corben of the Joffrey, Winnie Sampson of Dance Theatre of Harlem, Ellen Lampert and Susan Spier at Brooklyn Academy of Music, the staff of Shirley Herz Associates, Virginia Donaldson at Kennedy Center, Matt Hessburg at Wolf Trap, and Ellen Jacobs, Stephen Adler, Max Eisen, Mark Goldstaub, Meg Gordean, Alan Hale, Marilynn LeVine, and Audrey Ross, who represented companies and attractions too numerous to mention.

Contents

CELEBRATIONS

Sight Lines

Back Home Again
in Emerald City

At a moment when shows like *Dancin'* and *42nd Street* and *Sophisticated Ladies* are featuring wall-to-wall dance with hardly any book, postmodern dance is giving up some of its conceptual austerity and bringing in story lines—not boy meets girl, but not Oedipus meets Jocasta, either. The new storytelling forms, as employed by Twyla Tharp and Kenneth Rinker and Marta Renzi, have the ambiguity of contemporary song lyrics. And as a parallel to the tap-dance revival on Broadway we have a fair number of postmoderns tapping away in lofts and school gyms. Some of these dancers abjure music; others are feeling their way toward jazz, trying to devise a new version of the specialty jazz dance of the forties. A few daring choreographers, combining two major trends of the moment, are trying to fashion tap narratives. *Wave*, the longest and most ambitious of these attempts, ran for several weeks this summer at the La Mama annex, billed as A *Tap-Dance Melodrama*. The characters neither spoke nor sang, but they certainly did dance; in between the waltz clogs, the jazz fugues, and the percussive rumbas, they tapped out their dilemmas and disagreements in the manner of Fred and Ginger in "I'll Be Hard to Handle." Actually, *Wave* itself was pretty hard to handle for the first ten minutes or so. But thanks to the inventiveness of the choreographer, Gail Conrad, what might have been a two-hour study in monomania turned out to be a rounded lyrical experience—a book musical with aspirations, which it largely fulfilled, toward allegory.

The story, conceived by Conrad, was an episodic affair set in comic-strip Suburbia. Enter the Maid, pursued by the Lodger. A Mother who is obsessed with shopping expeditions, a Father who has retreated into solitaire, an adolescent Son filled with macho uncertainty are unexpectedly joined by a Long-Lost Daughter, who has run away to sea. The daughter is the herald of change, which in the form of a tidal wave made of painted muslin breaks right into the living room and disrupts everybody's life. The main point of *Wave*, though, is that the family's pattern isn't altered by the tides that wash over it from the world outside. The shock is absorbed and the household rituals go on: the maid's exercise ritual, the father's card-game ritual, the mother's shopping ritual. There are various quarrel rituals. An unvarying meal ritual performed with folded napkins makes a perfect theme number. At the end of the show, the characters have changed their routine to the extent of wearing swimming tubes and putting their furniture up on stilts, and the daughter is gone again. At cocktail time, the family celebrates the anniversary of its rescue with a "wave ritual"—the mother flings a drink in her family's faces and everyone assumes a scared pose. Otherwise, life is the same as before.

Wave is not as bluntly schematic as all this may make it sound. It putters along amiably, even diffidently. There is no moral pressure in Conrad's view of the family and none in her performance as the daughter. She wears her sailor hat while her mother wants her to wear a flowered cloche, but that's how mothers and daughters are. The daughter's other emblems are a steamer trunk and a huge anchor, dragged along behind, like the weight of experience. From the way these props are manipulated, we can infer the exact degree of tension in her relations with the rest of the family. But Conrad doesn't set herself above the others, and we hardly notice when she takes her leave. Home life in all its repetitious buzz and distraction is the subject of *Wave*, and at the end there it stands, shakily intact, innocent and unaccused. The main business is surviving.

As a satire of middle-class values, *Wave* has some of the genial tackiness of Rosalyn Drexler's 1964 play *Home Movies*. The clunky symbolism and the cultivatedly amateurish production stem, perhaps, from Conrad's association with various experimental performance groups that got their start in the sixties. The influence of sixties avant-garde theatre, though, isn't as strong as the aura of thirties and forties populism. Maybe the tap dancing just naturally evokes that period; maybe Gail Conrad means to awaken certain slumbering motifs from the heyday of movie musicals and restage them in the perspective of her own generation. The wave is like the tornado in *The Wizard of Oz*, but the heroine's direction is reversed, and so are her priorities. It's as if her home had turned into Oz. The prelude to *Wave* introduces the cast in slickers, in the tradition of *Singin' in the Rain* and *The Hollywood Revue of 1929*, and the printed program carries spoofing character descriptions like the title cards in silent-film comedies: "The Lodger—A three-time divorcé who prefers other people's homes. . . . The Mother—Former Miss Montana who won her husband in a card game." The word "melodrama" in the show's subtitle cements the link to another era. However, it signifies more than Conrad's reliance on genre situations. Characters in melodrama are not affected by their experiences. In the perspective of *Wave*, melodrama is truer to life than drama is. A more contemporary, sixties-derived word for the melodrama inherent in life is "ritual."

Tap dancing is strangely appropriate to the ritual-ridden lives that *Wave* deals with. As we watch the show, the pattern of changeless change begins to lock together at different points in the action, and the dances seem to reinforce the pattern. We soon see that the dances, especially the ensembles, *are* the pattern; they're the essence of routine. (In tap parlance, the words "essence" and "routine" have special meanings.) But before we see a pattern we must see a shape. Gail Conrad's ability to mold dynamic shapes in space sets her apart from all the other young tap choreographers, whose work, like the work of the jazz hoofers of the forties, is emphatically acoustic. Jazz dancing in this tradition is related to jazz drumming. Conrad's field isn't jazz—it's musical comedy, which is to say drama. Like Astaire's, her emphasis is kinetic-acoustic, and her rhythm is based on high-contrast, unpredictable phrase patterns. A dramatic rhythm. And the whole body dances, not just the feet.

Tap dancing makes sharp and abrasive character relationships more fun than, say, modern dance does, but it must work harder to establish dramatic terms that we can believe in. As a dramatic instrument, tap's main enemy is the deadly equilibrium that sets in through the constant beat of the feet on the floor. Conrad offsets this by heightening the plasticity of the figure as it dances. She keeps the arms lively and the thrust of the legs as clearly defined as the action of the feet; she stresses mid-body torsion and a balanced line. All this makes an appealing visual parallel to the sound of the taps; it confirms and extends the acoustical evidence. In movies, tap dancing worked the other way around: the sound underlined what the picture told us. Tap has more impact on the stage, but it still needs a bilateral presence to have a dramatic impact. The positions the body takes as it moves must correspond more than functionally to the rhythm of the feet. Out of this correspondence, there develops a sense of character and situation. In hack choreography, the development is speeded up so that it can be grasped at an elementary level of perception, and it makes the human body into a caricature. In Conrad's choreography, the characterizations come more gradually and last longer. The mother's first dance, a wonderfully ferocious workout to Kurt Weill's "Alabama Song," doesn't reduce her to one characteristic—ferocity. It characterizes ferocity in terms of Cheryl Wawro, the dancer. Cheryl Wawro has a large, leonine head, which doesn't quite go with her pinup body; she looks like a blond female warrior. With her flaring and inscrutable facial expressions and her extraordinary qualities of rhythm and attack, she creates a complex character—one whose threatening nature is accepted by everybody but her. She lives for pattern; the set and costume designers (Franco Colavecchia and Naimy Hackett) have matched her print dress to an upholstered chair. With a pancake hat mashed against the side of her head, she marches around carrying her stack of packages or she leads the napkin ritual, a terrorist of the breakfast nook.

Cheryl Wawro, who has also performed as a unicyclist, is physically so imposing that she naturally commands the stage. Another choreographer might have played up the physicality, but Conrad's dances let Wawro breathe; her command *is* natural. I saw Wawro perform again, later in the summer, in a concert given by Andrea Levine, and although Wawro dominated, Levine's uninflected, four-square sequences and hard-driving style didn't bring up her lustre. Levine seems to be living out a fantasy about being a tap dancer, but Wawro really is one. Gail Conrad is, too, and in *Wave* she should have made as strong an impression, by reason of her technique. But her performance as the errant daughter was withdrawn—generous of spirit but a bit absent of mind. Her large eyes had the listening look that I associate with the pure tap dancer. Strange to say, Conrad may be a bit too pure to perform in her own shows.

The father is described in the program by the single word "Retired," and that about sums up Tony Scopino's performance. Scopino is a smoothly routined dancer whose professionalism comes to seem an expression of the father's disengagement. The noncommittal, easygoing surface is broken twice: once when he reprimands the son for chasing the maid, and again in a duet with Conrad, when he shows a twinkle of sympathy with his daughter. (The head of a household with both a maid and a lodger, he goes around in an undershirt. In spite of their suburban setting, the characters are a "Moon Mullins" jumble of lower-middle-class city types.) To judge from the way she casts her shows, Conrad isn't as interested in good tappers as she is in good dancers—people who can move their bodies. Given this talent, she seems to be able to turn anyone into a tap dancer, and to design flattering and stylish choreography. Anthony Peters has a muscular, hockey player's body, but he's a dancer by any standard. As the teenage son, who dances with taps on his sneakers, he's required to hold back much of his force, which colors his solidity with tentative rebellion and makes him the most endearing character in the show. Rotund, oily-pated Steven Albert, as the lodger, looks as though he could do more than partner Muriel Favaro, who has too much business as the antic maid and overplays *that*. These two characters hold up the start of the action and then turn out to be marginal, which in a cast of six seems like an indulgence; the show needs to integrate its world. Conrad doesn't always distinguish between crucial and diversionary material, and she mixes so many unmixable elements in so laid-back a style that at times we don't know how to take things. The confusion was reflected in the reviews. Next to the Royal Ballet's *Isadora*, *Wave* got the worst notices of the season; it was the tap experiment that failed. "The Alabama Song" was the moment when the show clicked for me, and as a *dance* show, not just a tap show, it went on to become fascinating. But, as with other Conrad productions—there has been one a year since 1978—it was a while before I was seeing the whole pattern I was meant to see.

Some of the structural clumsiness may have had to do with the heterogeneous music—a grab bag of classical and pop, big-band swing and salsa, European folk music, movie soundtracks, and modern jazz. A rapid-clip version of the waltz from *Eugene Onegin* came out a waltz clog and sounded like a hornpipe. Conrad worked wonders with this motley score, and she had it arranged for a small orchestra and played live, which did impose a certain unity, but in spite of her best efforts it sounded provisional. Yet what's a choreographer to do? A commissioned score would have smoothed out the continuity, but what living composer would have provided such a variety of rhythmic cues, such fertile dance terrain as Weill and Tchaikovsky, Nino Rota and Dave Brubeck put together? Then, too, a makeshift score enhances the modest scale and homemade flavor of the show. A lot of avant-garde theatre toys with the pretense of putting on a performance in a garage, but Conrad is a born tinkerer who really can whip up a production number out of nothing. For the flood, which forms the climax of *Wave*, she divides the stage into lanes with ropes and buoys, and has her troupe of dancers cross and recross in single-file shuffles, gradually advancing all the way downstage, where they are beached. It's a long scene, studded with variations, and it goes on to some two hundred and twenty repeats of a salsa vamp. One feels that if Conrad had ordered up this music it wouldn't have sounded very different.

In this number, which is performed by the extended company—the six principals plus some "suburban boat people"—Conrad heads straight for the doldrums of tap and pulls off a tour de force. Although the flood number is as pure tap as the show ever gets, it still isn't exhibition tap. (And the dancers, who come in all shapes and sizes and with all levels of training, aren't exhibition dancers.) It reminded me of cave drawings or nature studies in primitive art where natural movement is depicted demoniacally as pattern. In a succession of dance shapes, to a pattern of dance sounds, the flood ritual passed through many waters—rapids, whirlpools, channels. Strange to think that a form as prosaic as tap dancing can be touched by primitive magic. —*September 14, 1981*

Oh, That Pineapple Rag!

When choreographers take real life as their subject, they usually take it in the abstract. Literal intentions are almost always suicidal; even when they succeed they generally don't succeed at a high level, and the choreographer is accused of trying to think, as if cogitation and choreography were mutually antagonistic. Twyla Tharp's newest work, *The Catherine Wheel*, which she is showing at the Winter Garden, manages to be literal and abstract at the same time, so that the turn of a thought and its realization in dance are more often than not presented together. But they are also presented in separate systems that are elaborately cross-referenced. Tharp's use of semi-abstract mime and semi-literal dance is one such system. She also uses the straight varieties of dance and mime, an array of props and costumes, a sophisticated and highly theatrical rock score by David Byrne, and the ingenious stage technology of Jennifer Tipton and Santo Loquasto. *The Catherine Wheel* is schematically overloaded, but then Tharp tends to be excessive. She's like a juggler piling Pelion on Ossa on Mount Saint Helens on the tip of her nose. When the elements are harmoniously integrated, as in *Deuce Coupe* and *Push Comes to Shove*, we get magic. When the overload collapses, as it did in last year's *When We Were Very Young*, we get cacophony. *The Catherine Wheel* holds together. Unlike *When We Were Very Young*, which was a playlet with dances, it is a multilevel poetic fantasy that discharges its deepest meanings through music and dance. On one level, it is a reworking of *When We Were Very Young*: some of the characters from that piece are back doing some of the same things; Tharp seems determined to reduce the American nuclear family to a pile of smoked turkeys. This time, though, she zips through her catalogue of abuse, adds a twist of scalawag comedy and a suite of social dances through the ages, and gets on with the main objective of the show, which is to enlarge the turkey story to the dimensions of a fable. It's a little like interleaving the *National Enquirer* with *The Golden Bough*, but Tharp does it, and brings it off as an uncluttered, intensively lyrical experience. And keeps it going for eighty minutes without interruption.

The Catherine Wheel is so completely systematized that although it encloses a story about the modern world, it is always and only about itself. From time to time, lyrics are sung to the music which seem to relate to the action. For instance:

> *Well the bride bride and the groom*
> *Run in a circle around their house*
> *They're goin' out they're comin' in*
> *Inside a circle around their house.*

That's about as explicit as the lyrics ever get, and we do see a bride and groom. Yet at no time are the words used as a functional element in the staging. They're in dream language to begin with, and then, as part of the processed studio sound that makes up Byrne's taped score, they're largely unhearable. When a word drifts out of the sonic haze, it strikes us as pre-articulate speech—closer to the sources of pain and emotion than normal speech is. The cryptic sound goes with the various pieces of primitive machinery which Loquasto has fashioned out of what look like scraps from a Victorian bicycle shop. The wheels turn but they don't go anywhere. Another contraption, which is lowered from the flies, has a use that may be guessed from its retractable prongs: it is a torture rack. One may with cause think of St. Catherine impaled on her wheel or of Lear's "I am bound upon a wheel of fire, that mine own tears do scald like molten lead." But one isn't given time to ponder wheel symbolism, or even wheel nonsymbolism; there's more going on. *The Catherine Wheel* has wheels within wheels.

It also has pineapples. The wheel is a perfect symbol for the spectacle that has been devised by Twyla Tharp and her collaborators; the music, the décor and props, the costumes, the lighting, the staging, and the choreography are spokes radiating meaning from the hub of conception. And when the wheel spins and gives off sparks, it really is a pyrotechnical accomplishment. The pineapple is not a self-referential symbol; it's more in the nature of what Alfred Hitchcock used to call the MacGuffin. In Hitchcock's movies, what people chased after—secret formulas or uranium ore in wine bottles—was the MacGuffin, and, as Hitchcock told François Truffaut, the meaning of the MacGuffin is always beside the point. "The only thing that really matters is that in the picture the plans, the documents, or secrets must seem to be of vital importance to the characters." In *The Catherine Wheel*, the characters worship pineapples; they need and want and love pineapples, they steal pineapples, make sacrifices of pineapples. At the start of the show, a cluster of pineapples glows through the gloom like a Christmas tree, like the tree of the knowledge of good and evil, like the burning bush. A vestal virgin (Sara Rudner) extracts one fruit; it brains a coy bridegroom (Tom Rawe). So we witness the fall of man, the rages and quarrels, the cretinous offspring (Katie Glasner, Raymond Kurshals), acts of brutality and of bestiality. A furry dog (Christine Uchida) is sexually abused; later she kills her tormentor. A monster mother (Jennifer Way) pimps for her daughter. A young poet (John Carrafa) shows some interest in the girl but he'd rather sleep with a pineapple. A pineapple isn't the Holy Grail; it isn't sex or money or power, although at different times it seems to be those things, and if you think it looks like a grenade it is that thing as well. It's an absurdist symbol, a symbol of absurdity, and a dumb device all at once. It's active, whereas the wheel symbolism is passive; pineapples, and not wheels, turn the plot and at the same time turn our minds to thoughts of illusion and degradation, of slavishness and cultishness and obscene greed. The pineapple is Tharp's pretext for showing us the harsh and depressing world we live in. As the frenzy reaches its climax and tapers off, Rudner, as the priestess, returns bearing a golden wheel with a pineapple at the hub, and the inner and outer thought systems of the ballet are merged; at least, they're meant to be. But, like the "sacrifice of the pineapple" that occurred a moment before, the moment of the merger is largely a mystifying one. In the sacrifice scene (Tharp calls it "The Leader Repents"), Rudner takes her precious pineapple, now reduced to a bag of (Styrofoam) chunks, and shoves it—literally impales it over and over on the torture rack. Although the scene is repeated many times and played alongside another "loop," of the monster family at its most Jukes-like, we don't get a chance to sort out the meanings or to relate the two scenes. We haven't drunk deep enough of the pineapple—we've been too busy discarding hypotheses—to know that it is capable of dying for our sins.

The last quarter of the ballet is a dance apotheosis of astonishing beauty and power. Tharp's title for it is "The Golden Section," and it rises like an Atlantis from the murk of the pineapple world, transforming it into a paradise of new feelings and visionary exploits. Tharp's abrupt alchemy substituting harmony for chaos is almost painful in its honesty. It's as if she were substituting art for life, knowing that no solution to the palpable terrors she has invoked is possible. Art, less than a solution yet more than a consolation, offers terms she can settle for; it's the great alternative to the dilemma of life, the only other reality that isn't death. "The Golden Section" is the classical "white" ballet, with all its implications of redemption intact. In the old ballets, though—*Giselle* and *La Bayadère* and *Swan Lake*—death was the condition of redemption. In "The Golden Section," the dancers are dressed not as incorporeal figures in white tulle but as acrobats in gold tights, launching themselves against a honey-gold backdrop. The characters of the previous scene return transformed and dance wonderfully, and the choreography reaches supersonic speeds as it passes from one prodigious episode to the next, until suddenly, in the middle of a leap, the lights go out. The dance ends in midair, which is to say it does not end. "The Golden Section" is a glimpse of infinity; it's a celestial version of those moments of Tharpian continuity in other works (like *Baker's Dozen*) when the dance leaves the stage and returns, having continued behind the scenes. Tharp keeps the energy level climbing and the invention flowing, but she doesn't create a compulsive, inhumanly brilliant atmosphere, as she did in last year's *Brahms' Paganini*. "The Golden Section" seems to rise effortlessly above the negotiations of virtuosity and to ride along in a kind of relaxed ecstasy. For the first time, Twyla Tharp attains grandeur.

The world of *The Catherine Wheel*, half in darkness, half in light, has the completeness of Elizabethan cosmogony and the aura of myth. The rude mechanicals and their swinish and sleazy existence, the supernatural priestess and her entourage, the innocents (the Poet, the Pet, the hysterical Maid danced by Shelley Washington) occupy their classic positions as forms of life and dramatic counterweights. And in "The Golden Section," when they dance, dance, dance, they are all one race, neither gods nor human beings but the gilded beasts of the Greek fables. The ballet is a running frieze of stags and hinds and winged colts, with some broncos and circus ponies cut into the herd. It's a Circean transformation, and as an image it's true to the rough, inarticulate nature of the parable that precedes it. For all its polished surfaces and moments of blinding lucidity, *The Catherine Wheel* is an experience of mute sensations; we look and wonder, and are lifted we know not how, and at the end our blood is changed.

But to say that the experience is mute is not to say that it is incoherent. No; feeling about in the dark, we are able to sense and then grasp with conviction the relationship of things, and whether we accept pineappleism as mystical wisdom or tactical whimsy we are bound to follow the pattern it imposes—we can't get lost. The climate of Twyla Tharp's best work has usually been so Spartan that the plush fancies of *The Catherine Wheel* are overdazzling at first, and one may be inclined to mistrust them. But you could strip away the symbolical apparatus; you could cancel Tipton's shadows and scrims, her shimmering blacks and ashen grays and warm golds; you could delete Loquasto's fierce little engines, and even his forest of poles, through which the whole first section of the piece is danced, and stage the work, as Tharp often staged her early dances, in a school gym. And still the piece would work, on the strength of its current of rhythm. The choreography has no trouble sustaining rhythmic tension over an improbably long span of time; the flat-out driving attack of "The Golden Section" only accelerates the excitement—Tharp has been in high gear right along.

Byrne's music is the first rock score to pull solid weight in a theatrical-dance context. It has real rhythm, not just a beat. The deficiencies of rock as dance music were noticed long ago by Paul Draper, who pronounced it "rhythmically more arid than the Sahara," and went on to define rhythm as "visual or aural patterns which live within the framework of the beat and the time." Byrne's brand of concert rock must, I suppose, be accorded the status of serious music. Its werewolf-and-charnel-house sound imagery is not the kind of seriousness I care for, but there is no doubt that working with Tharp has sharpened Byrne's sensitivity to the variety of pulse and mood a dance score has to have. The horrendous chill that I take to be characteristic of Byrne's music—it is there in his records with the Talking Heads as well—is perfectly suited to the dark side of Tharp's world, where dads rape dogs, devils writhe in women's bodies, and public assassins creep in the shadows. In "The Golden Section," the brilliant metallic clang of the music is appropriately circusy; then it changes into a choir sweetly chanting

Oh I don't understand
Oh it's not just a sound
Oh I don't understand
It doesn't matter at all.

For a thinking choreographer's comment on the world, *The Catherine Wheel* is strangely precognitive. One would have to go back to Paul Taylor's *Orbs* to find a work of comparable scale, purity, and charm. But even Taylor did not attempt an uninterrupted dance epic. Nor did he use a commissioned score. *The Catherine Wheel* is a major event in our theatre.   —*October 12, 1981*

Connections: Taylor and Tharp

In Paul Taylor's *House of Cards*, Bettie de Jong has another of those Bettie de Jong mime parts that place her firmly at the center of events yet mysteriously outside them. The title role in *Big Bertha* may have been the prototype of these disquieting impersonal instruments of fate, which de Jong has played ever since. The rehearsal mistress in *Le Sacre du Printemps (The Rehearsal)* is a high-key version of the role; the central figure in the slow movement of *Esplanade* is low key. Although de Jong's presence in *Esplanade* magnetizes the action without exactly controlling it, we still are unsettled by her, and "the shepherdess" or "the sheltering mother"—however we may privately characterize her role in this section—is the most benign variation on the de Jong character up to now. As Big Bertha, the clockwork doll that drove the other characters to their doom, de Jong was malevolent; in *Le Sacre* she was inscrutable. In *House of Cards*, though, she's inscrutable in a different way; we just don't know who she's supposed to be or why she has to be there. The rehearsal mistress is so neatly jigsawed into the pattern of *Le Sacre* that we may not notice how marginal the role really is—it's the most tenuous of Taylor's jokes in this piece. But the fact that de Jong is also the rehearsal mistress of the Paul Taylor Dance Company seems to be all there is behind her role in *House of Cards*; she seems to be making a guest appearance as a performer.

The piece, a highly tentative affair, deals in a Taylorishly oblique way with culture and the arts in Paris at the time of the music, which is Darius Milhaud's *La Création du Monde* (1923). De Jong's role is as static as one might imagine an Ida Rubinstein role of the same period to be, and her costume, by Cynthia O'Neal, seems designed to inhibit her even further: a stiff flaring jacket over a long skirt that maintains its bulky silhouette no matter how de Jong moves—or, rather, is moved. For although she makes the commanding Big Bertha gestures that dictate what the rest of the cast does, she is most often a passive figure, constantly being lifted and carried idol-like, or en cortège, or with straddling legs as the others pass beneath her. In her gown and her turban sprouting egret feathers, she's a period reference, while the others are neutrally clad in formal renditions of everyday dancewear. Her link to the period is clear when she's being obeyed or "celebrated"; then we see her as an all-powerful society hostess or patroness. But when she's a fallen statue we don't know what toppled her. Perhaps Taylor intended a lament for lost times and for lost ladies like Misia Sert. He doesn't follow the scenario of Milhaud's ballet, although he casts a sidelong glance at it now and then, and de Jong could be a parallel to the totems worshipped in the "tribal" dances of the old ballet. As iconography, the role is clear enough. Psychologically and structurally, it's opaque.

That de Jong's presence isn't as well integrated with the surrounding action as other de Jong roles have been is a real flaw. Yet it's also characteristic of the way the piece has been made. *House of Cards* (the title may be telling us something) is exceedingly fragile in construction, full of loose hinges and unmoored conceits. Nothing really holds together. The dancers are introduced to the mournful and sluggish "up from the slime" music at the beginning. As they roll one by one out of a revolving huddle in the dark, they groggily sketch out "period" identities that range from the broadly familiar (Linda Kent as a Charleston dancer) to the obscure (Karla Wolfangle as a marionette). These bits are like an orchestra tuning up, but the piece goes on being bits; it's always building up to a breakdown. Maybe that's why de Jong is there—as a focal point around which to assemble the sparse motifs and the discontinuities of the score. As Misia Sert or Lady Ripon or whoever, she's at her most obviously focal in the frantic group dances of the party scenes, but the focus she provides keeps dissipating, just as the groups do. At the end, everyone goes off single file, as if to affirm the linear, noncollective nature of the action we have just witnessed.

The fragmentation in *House of Cards* might be unbearably baffling if there weren't a strong foundation to support it. As often happens with Taylor, the foundation is the music. There isn't a moment of choreography that isn't musically justified; there isn't an image that doesn't have *some* light shining behind it. When we connect the dots of light, we begin to see *House of Cards* as one of a series of recent pieces in which Taylor seems to be meditating on historic eras of dance. From *Images* to *Profiles* to *Le Sacre*, similarities can be traced which incorporate two lines of descent—from historic American modern dance and from the era of the Ballets Russes. *House of Cards*, set to a renowned jazz ballet by a European composer (which was originally produced in Paris by Ballets Suédois), concentrates on the taste of the twenties for particular kinds of colloquial art. Not only the Afro-Americanisms of Milhaud's score are here, along with fragments of his scenario (the Adam and Eve figures are retained by Taylor and danced by Christopher Gillis and Ruth Andrien); we also find imitations of *Petrushka* and *Parade* and *Les Biches*—all ballets to which street songs, café Dixieland, tea dances, and bal musette in one form or another made decisive contributions. There is the Hostess from *Les Biches*; here, in Karla Wolfangle's puppet, is Petrushka, maybe

Pulcinella, maybe even the Joker in *Jeu de Cartes*; Gillis and Andrien are also the acrobats in *Parade*—a ballet that for Taylor seems to be a key source of ideas. With its looseleaf impressions of a chaotic scene, *House of Cards* may be distantly modelled on the "vaudeville" structure of *Parade*. (And did not the Chinese Conjuror in that ballet find his way into Taylor's *Sacre*?) It follows from these precedents that Taylor's choreography for Milhaud's music is inspired mainly by the parody Charlestons and tangos in the score. Where most settings of this music ignore the colloquialisms or render them as straight demonstrations, Taylor gives us the chivied Charlestons, the tormented tangos of his own invention. When he comes to the miasmic interlude following the party, he stages a dazed morning-after scene as a slow-motion tumbling act for two men (Gillis and Daniel Ezralow). If the method invokes the music hall by way of Pilobolus, yet there's madness in it. Scott Fitzgerald's ghost is not far off.

House of Cards isn't major Taylor—it's an omelette by a master chef with a piece of eggshell stuck in it. The de Jong role is pardonable, but, like the pineapple in Twyla Tharp's *The Catherine Wheel*, it causes more confusion than it is really worth. Alternating Taylor evenings at the Brooklyn Academy of Music with Tharp evenings at the Winter Garden, I came this season to have a new respect for the links between these two marvellous artists—links that Tharp's dramatic emergence a decade ago had obscured. At that time, one saw only the novelty in Tharp; dances like *The Fugue* and *Eight Jelly Rolls* made Taylor look mustily old-fashioned. Today, in such a piece as *The Catherine Wheel*, with its analogous systems of meaning and effect, Tharp seems very close to Taylor. The concept of *The Catherine Wheel* owes much to his *Orbs* and *American Genesis*. How strange that in the same season Taylor should have commissioned Mimi Gross's scenery for *House of Cards*—a strip of painted canvas which unrolls during the dance in the manner of the graffiti strips in *Deuce Coupe*. And that his dancers should be costumed by Mrs. O'Neal in the variations on practice dress that Santo Loquasto introduced in *Sue's Leg*. Tharp doesn't compose like Taylor; although she once danced in Taylor's company, there is no way one could mistake one of her dances for one of his. But her choreography is like his in its seamless continuity and elasticity of phrase. I heard Tharp compared this season with Jiří Kylián—the comparison was meant as the highest kind of praise—for her non-stop rhythm and pursuit of a dramatic subject, not only in *The Catherine Wheel* but in *Short Stories*. But I find that Kylián's rhythm isn't really non-stop and that he doesn't use it in support of drama, as Tharp does. His line is full of breaks, which the dancers push themselves through, and his drama is pictogrammatic statements that spell out emotions. Kylián's roots lie in Central European modern dance and his impetus in the current revival of that tradition on the Continent and in England. Taylor and Tharp inherited the miscellaneous legacy of American dance at a time—the fifties and sixties—when it was flowing with riches. Martha Graham, Cunningham and Cage, and the School of American Ballet were all at separate peaks of power and influence. A lively student could leap from peak to peak. Taylor eventually positioned himself at the end of the line that stretches through

Graham back to Denishawn and Denishawn's contemporaries. He is the sentinel of modernity and, as his recent recherché work shows, its keenest and most delicate analyst. There is in *House of Cards* an avidity for the past but also an unwillingness to probe beyond the barrier of retrospection. Taylor isolates a few motifs and monuments and hangs them up for scrutiny. The only conclusion he draws is a sighing "They don't look like much now, do they?" He's resigned to the vulnerability of history—history as a house of cards.

Tharp has always been an eclectic choreographer. Her omnivorous sweep tosses aside self-contradictions and mows down categorical shalt-nots. I don't see how anyone can resist the electric crackle of *Short Stories*—especially the first part, which so finely calibrates degrees of relaxation and tension that drama becomes a creation of pure rhythm. Is Tharp returning the dance theatre to psychologically paraphrasable movement? Is *The Catherine Wheel* her *Clytemnestra*? I don't think so. Her movement isn't an exorcism of words, as Graham's was; it's movement for which words don't exist. In *Short Stories*, some teen-agers at a dance quarrel almost for the sake of quarrelling. The jealousies and rivalries the quarrelling engenders aren't a byproduct of a social evening, they're the whole point of it. I see this and say this easily enough, yet the ritual as Tharp stages it is inexplicable; one really doesn't know why these things happen. We see the inarticulate rage and, at the same time, the strategies that keep it going. Then we see one girl who seems to take it all seriously—who becomes the victim from whose viewpoint the story is told. The switch from the general to the particular, from omniscient to subjective narration, is only one of Tharp's achievements. Another is her control of our comprehension of the words of the rock song she uses as accompaniment. Supertramp's "Lover Boy" is played twice; the first time it's just background, but the second time it applies cuttingly in every note and syllable to a single person. Whether the girl (Mary Ann Kellogg) is raped or murdered, whether she dies an actual or a spiritual death are questions that are transcended by the reality of an individual drama. Compared with this piercing vignette, the second part of *Short Stories*, set to a Bruce Springsteen song, is only an effective treatment of the same theme—quarrelling—among grownups.

In *The Catherine Wheel*, the family scenes are all done allegro-staccato and reprised legato by the chorus. The antiphonal effect is gradually narrowed until, just before they disappear, family and chorus are down to echoes being batted back and forth in two spotlights. The staccato attack is a metaphor for irritation; it's used in gobs of literal Me Tarzan–You Jane pantomime, in on-the-beat dancing of all kinds, in sexual brawls timed like the wrestling on TV. The only explanation I can think of for that strange moment when Jennifer Way as the Mother tap-dances across the stage and exits is that it's the most staccato—the most irritating—thing she can do at that point. When the Mother and the Father (Tom Rawe) are momentarily reconciled, they do a ballroom duet that is all adagio swoops. And in one of the most extraordinary scenes in the whole show the frightened little Maid, played by Shelley Washington, does a Kathakali-like mime solo in which she proceeds with slow and deliberate care through an extensive catalogue of ferocious grimaces; the timing makes our hair stand on end. The grimacing solo that Sara Rudner executes at top speed is completely different in effect. In writing about *The Catherine Wheel* two weeks ago, I characterized Rudner's role as that of a vestal virgin or goddess. She's also the evil genius of the show, a kind of kinetic Bettie de Jong who directs its grand design without regard for moral consequences; all that matters is the flow of energy. The interesting thing is that the moral consequences are shown: bad and good are depicted as coexisting forces arbitrated by chance. The almost Oriental equanimity that Tharp shows is quite different from Taylor's American-puritan view of good and evil, but what other two choreographers could be discussed in these terms? Some observers of *The Catherine Wheel* were upset by the fact that there's no way out of the impasse of existence; they missed the outcome of a catharsis that could have elevated the lyrical coda called "The Golden Section" to a point beyond wish fulfillment. It seems to me that the catharsis is there in the rhythm. The transition from the fallen world to the celestial regions occurs first of all in the music, with its lengthening and steadily broadening crescendo. Meanwhile, the pulse of the stage action has diminished to a terse rondo pattern—two patterns, in fact, which pit the family and the chorus against each other as twin points of jabbing intensity. When the stage picture finally changes from black to gold, there's a wonderful catch-up effect as the dancers enter on the new momentum the music has created.

Tharp showed two other new pieces this fall, neither on the level of *The Catherine Wheel* or *Short Stories*. *Uncle Edgar Dyed His Hair Red* is the title Dick Sebouh, a California octogenarian, gave to his synthesizer score. Tharp's choreography is as charming as the music; it consists of two duets and a trio performed for the most part in double unison on both sides of a scrim. *Assorted Quartets* is another set of exercises and sketches, half in silence and half in time to the country fiddling of Gina McNather, who appeared onstage in a long black dress and a plump auburn braid. *Assorted Quartets* contains the kind of roughhouse material that Tharp later used so explosively in *Short Stories* and the family scenes of *The Catherine Wheel*, but the tone is genial. Since there have been complaints about Tharp's violence this season, it seems fair to cite this work in rebuttal, along with Susanne K. Langer's observation that "the feeling in a work of art is something the artist *conceived* as he created the symbolic form to present it, rather than something he was undergoing and involuntarily venting in an artistic process." *Assorted Quartets* is much more than a footnote to the towering works it was seen with, and I trust it isn't its comparatively sanguine temper that makes me want to overlook it critically this time. This is the season, after all, that has shown Tharp entering a new phase. Next to what she's doing now, *Assorted Quartets* looks all too Bennington, and *Uncle Edgar* looks more so.

—*October 26, 1981*

Maximizing Minimalism

St. Cecilia's music, Auden wrote, made "sounds so entrancing the angels dancing came out of their trance into time again." Something like that has happened to Laura Dean, to music of her own making. In *Tympani*, impelled by "notes tremendous from her great engine," her six dancers, in their regulation silk pajamas, behave remarkably like a dance company, and not a religious sect. As a composer, Dean has been somewhat of a pedant. As a choreographer, minimalist by persuasion, she has made movement seem elementary rather than elemental. And because of the monastic air of concentration her dancers give off when they are counting out their ritual steps it has been tempting to see her relation to them as that of a guru enforcing a Gurdjieff-like discipline. *Tympani*, scored for kettledrums and two pianos, might seem methodical bombast coming from anyone else; coming from Dean, it is a release. The entrancing (or *de*trancing) percussiveness jars her rigid metrics into rhythmic configurations. She comes out of the trance of timelessness into time as dancers know it.

Tympani was given at the Brooklyn Academy of Music this month for the first time in New York. It marks a break with the temporal suspensions in Dean's music which, translated into choreography, produced a kind of inanimate, benumbed trance-dancing. The choreography for *Tympani*, while it contains nothing new in step or gesture, is flowingly articulate in a way that provides the minimalist vocabulary with a whole new foundation. The dancing is more active; it moves by phrases rather than by steps; it is concerned less with hypnotic repetition than with transition and contrast. Even the ever-regular domineering drumbeat—Dean remains devoted to a steady pulse—seems more resilient. There are passages of complex syncopation that call out with a kind of licentious delight. Yet the over-all effect isn't one of complexity. Dean has established this new feeling of freshness and variety without violating the cardinal simplicity of her style or its contemplative calm.

One can overstate the influence on Dean of Eastern dance forms and meditative rituals. (Dean herself, in certain of her dances, has overstated it.) Compared with Indian, Balinese, or African rhythm, Dean's rhythm has been remarkably uninflected. Her "Hindu" torso and arms, her use of extended dervishlike spinning are colorful adaptations, like sitars in rock bands. What Dean does is in fact completely Western and contemporary in its point of origin; her time sense is probably more powerfully influenced by the exoticism of the disco than by a sympathy with the East. The pretense of a mystique, which I have found so discomforting in Dean's work, has been greatly reduced in *Tympani*. One didn't have to be a co-religionist to enjoy the dancing. That this striking demystification should coincide with a new rhythmic vitality is perhaps not accidental. The secular appeal of *Tympani* is based on a quality of rhythmic differentiation very unlike the static divisions of "head" dance. Dean is suddenly more danceable, but then so is rock the minute it stops pretending never to have heard of jazz.

Choreographers of the rock generation have a monolithic view of rhythm, which many of them have exploited in overregulated, symmetrical choreography of great sparsity, performed, as a rule, in silence or to a metronomic beat. Now that music is back, one looks for signs of rhythmic fertility, and one doesn't often find them. Dean could be achieving a breakthrough, and possibly Charles Moulton is on the verge of one, too.* Twyla Tharp, this generation's standard-bearer, abandoned silence and minimalism a decade ago; she has recently risen to a new height of rhythmic awareness. But Kenneth Rinker's experiments with the composer Sergio Cervetti, which began so promisingly, have become increasingly dim. Rinker's *Generation Pieces: 168*, performed last month at Dance Theatre Workshop, was slack and muddled except for an ensemble workout to "Rock Around the Clock." I took nothing home from Marta Renzi's concert at the same place a few evenings before. (Renzi seems uninterested in dramatizing in her choreography her own strengths as a dancer, which include musicality.) For her company's first appearance in the Brooklyn Academy opera house, Trisha Brown, who seldom uses music, collaborated this season with Robert Ashley on *Son of Gone Fishin'*. The sound was bouncy, but the dancing, without Brown onstage often enough to augment it, was bewilderingly small-featured and textureless.

Perhaps it is too early to tell whether or not a revolution is at hand. Only last year, Laura Dean's concert in Brooklyn featured the gruelling, incense-steeped *Music* and drove the audience from the theatre. This year's program was cheered, even though it included the 1976 composition *Dance*, which for me was nearly as stifling as *Music*. Dean may have scheduled this 1976 work in order to show how far she'd come since: the difference between it and *Tympani* was the difference between sand painting and stone sculpture. And the sand was measured out in grains. For an overture, the two-piano score to *Night* was played. In this very successful piece, done last season for the Joffrey Ballet, Dean anthologized some of her best routines and avoided the extremes she'd been promoting with her own company. From the adroit presentation of her material in *Night*, Dean has gone on to a new freedom of construction. I find *Tympani* most exciting when passages of counterpoint are in full play against counterpoint in the music, but even when Dean is sticking to her old method of executing one pattern at a time she seems to be able to turn succession into progression, so that the dance grows upon its effects and doesn't subside under them. She has understood, too, how the pace of events can be independent of the tempo, and that is just about the largest

* *Postscript 1987*: See page 63. Dean's breakthrough has been in terms of audience response. Her subsequent work hasn't continued the advances of *Tympani*, and I now think I overrated the significance of the piece. It contains only as much complexity as Dean's audience seems willing to take.

understanding anyone is showing right now of the still engaging possibilities of minimalist form.

The Joffrey is celebrating its silver anniversary, at the City Center, but there isn't much cause for congratulation in its latest acquisitions: two undistinguished imports from the European repertory and a new Gerald Arpino ballet. There are no additions to the honorable series of Joffrey restorations, but *Cakewalk, Les Patineurs, A Wedding Bouquet, Parade,* and *The Green Table* are all on view, and Tharp's *Deuce Coupe II* and Dean's *Night* are in good shape. Ballets like these two are the nearest the Joffrey's dancers ever get to advanced material and contemporary expression. (Arpino's ballets are typically punched out for a sensation-hungry audience; the new one, *Light Rain,* is no exception.) The Joffrey is now having to compete with American Ballet Theatre in the search for new choreography, and the new regime at A.B.T. is even hiring the non-ballet choreographers whom formerly only Robert Joffrey had the daring to enlist. Joffrey's solution this season—to bring in another Jiří Kylián piece—was as much a gamble as producing *Swan Lake* would have been. Even though *Transfigured Night* represents Kylián at his heaviest and wettest and isn't likely to please people who respond to *Return to the Strange Land,* such is Kylián's popularity that the ballet is automatically a hit.

But what could have governed the choice of John Cranko's brutal and ineffectual *The Taming of the Shrew?* Reputation again? The ballet isn't even good slapstick. The pacing is panicky, and the jokes aren't developed. In the second act, when Petruchio instructs his servants to pretend to be grotesque and deformed monsters so as to frighten Kate, we get a few seconds of amusement from the different examples of grotesquerie and deformity which Petruchio sets forth and which the four servants imitate. Then Kate comes in and sees them and reacts to them all at once, and the fun is over. Four servants, one reaction: is that a *joke?* Maybe deformity jokes are better off dropped, but Cranko was insensitive enough to introduce one, and it was his insensitivity as a humorist and a dramatist that kept him from seeing how it could have been used to illuminate a Kate who is human underneath her shrewishness and a worthy object of desire to Petruchio. This Kate, who might have reacted sympathetically to the first gargoyle but not sympathetically to all four, is a funnier as well as a more touching Kate than Cranko knew how to create. The failure of the ballet is a failure of human sympathy; the weak choreography is irrelevant. As it happens, the Kate-Petruchio choreography was constructed for the narrowly acrobatic talents of Marcia Haydée and Richard Cragun, which is why it lends itself neither to wit nor to lyricism. The part of Kate is also notably uglifying; I saw Beatriz Rodriguez, who if she wasn't very funny wasn't ugly, either. Gregory Huffman, in the equally trying role of Petruchio, managed the swagger without the boorishness that is *its* pitfall.   —*November 16, 1981*

Pilobolism

On a hot, humid morning last summer, as the members of Pilobolus Dance Theatre were rehearsing at their studio in rural Connecticut, there was a thunderstorm, and the dancers rushed gratefully out into the rain, throwing themselves down in the wet grass, leaping and shouting. The rain stopped, but they stayed outside all day, muddily improvising movements for a new piece of choreography, begun the day before. Yesterday, nothing they tried had worked; today, everything worked. The whole episode is commemorated in *Day Two*, which I saw, along with several other excellent recent pieces, at the McCarter Theatre in Princeton, one of the stops on the company's fall tour. Pilobolus pieces customarily begin in group improvisation and are edited into shape. *Day Two* does not literally reproduce the terms in which it was created or anything of the circumstances except for the thunderstorm, which was captured on tape and is used as an overture. Every move in the piece had a spontaneous origin, but the final version is a logical development in a controlled series of metaphors. Only at the very end, after the curtain calls have begun, is there a relapse into literalism, when the dancers, who are all but nude, fling themselves one after another into fantastic body slides through puddles of water sloshed across the stage. Here is one of the giddiest events that occurred on Day Two, as the company went dripping back into the studio. The effect on a stage, coming after a piece that has already surprised us so often, is one of raw shock.

Part of the shock comes from the precision of the calculation behind it. The slides are a completely unnecessary folly, yet the minute they start we know how exactly right they are and how wrong they'd have been had we been given them an instant sooner. Their unreasoning logic puts the piece into perspective, and it also puts Pilobolus into perspective. *Day Two* is one of those compositions of theirs—like *Untitled* and parts of *Monkshood's Farewell*—that mingle beauty and absurdity in the intensest degrees, so that we are constantly caught between laughter and pain. This feeling of being impaled on a perception is allied to the curiously intellectual emotion that one feels at the ballet. It seems to be the unique function of ballet style to fuse the rational and the irrational. Without being a ballet company, without claiming much in the way of a legitimate dance style, Pilobolus does something quite similar: it gives us the logic of fantasy. Because fantasy logic does not run on alternating currents, there's never a moment in the dance when we can respond in simple, clear-cut terms. The fusion generates a deeper and more complicated emotion than we can easily express. At the ballet, one keeps seeing the lyricism of mechanics, the naturalness of artifice, the spontaneity of a plan, the random schematics of what, if one could reduce poetry to philosophy, one would call empiricism. The image before us is uncommonly like the real world, so uncommonly that the resemblance seems merely accidental. The dialectical process at Pilobolus may not be as complex as the process of classical ballet (and Pilobolus hardly ever seems accidentally brilliant), but it's just as clean. When the slides begin at the end of *Day Two*, they magnify one side—the crazy side—of what we've been watching to such a degree that there's nothing to do but laugh and scream. Up to this moment, the meanings in the dance had been focussed in the perceptual. The slides—it doesn't seem possible to travel thirty feet in an inch of water, yet it happens—are pure physics: a pure demonstration of the law of motion. This is factual reality, and it's the one clear-cut absurdity in the entire piece.

Pilobolus choreography has by tradition been a group effort; the name-studded choreography credits in the company's programs are invariably lists of the original casts. The method of collaboration, which was actually impractical, reflected the company's early preoccupation with itself as a performing commune with equal shares in the creative process. Although the substance of *Day Two* was group-generated, Moses Pendleton, who does not appear in the piece and who may have gained some advantage from the fact, was the editor-choreographer. As in most Pilobolus works, the material is organized in related sections, like a rock album, but it's not as bitsy as *Monkshood's Farewell* and it's a lot dancier than *Untitled*. The music is by the extremely popular David Byrne and Brian Eno (excerpts from *My Life in the Bush of Ghosts*, *Remain in Light*, and *Another Green World*). The Byrne-Eno sound has qualities of ambiguity, dissociation, and theatricality which could easily overwhelm a dance. But except for the opening section it turns out to be the perfect kind of sound for the things that go on in *Day Two*. When the dancing began, I thought it looked and felt too light. The Pilobolian birds and beasts, pecking and stalking, were deer-park creatures, and the song "Houses in Motion" has a slugging beat and a wail more appropriate to a dog pound. In the next section, the problem vanishes, never to return. Over and over, four men on their knees perform contrapuntal variations on touching their heads to the ground, then straightening up. From a crouch, they progress to an upright kneel, then to a standing pose. The changes come each time on one count, and the process of bending and straightening continues unpredictably; it's like trying to follow the hammers in a piano as the music ascends in pitch. (When the dance shifts to profile, it's like a change in key.) This male quartet has the charm of an elegant vaudeville act; the clever dynamics have to have been the invention of Pendleton, who has to have seen the male quartet in Paul Taylor's *Cloven Kingdom*. But Pendleton may also have been referring to the evolution of the Pilobolus company from a monklike male foursome to a sextet (emphasis on the first syllable) including two women. In *Day Two*, when two women enter and break up the quartet the atmosphere immediately becomes more problematic.

At first, nothing happens: the dancers run through some quick-action mumbo-jumbo, the gestures more or less standard to Pilobolus (some of them are based on the cleaning up after the downpour); all turn into a browsing herd in the tall grass of *Shizen*. After a blackout, we get to the heart of the piece and the heart of Pilobolus—those mutations and permutations in which anatomy becomes metaphysics. The girls hang from the men's bodies like infants, like succubi; changing position slowly, as if in their sleep, they turn into shameful growths. Their victims waddle desolately. In the next part, the men carry the women between them on poles, which they raise and lower like piston rods. Seated or slung on the rod, each woman rotates her body around it in ornamental poses, pedalling in air. The poles become the spokes of a turning wheel, and the wheel slows, a ponderous carrousel. The poles are braced vertically on the floor, and as the men grasp them hand over hand the women ride up on the men's arms. Through all the pole stuff (and there's much more) and the plain and fancy partnering, the object is illusion—either the imagistic kind or the mechanistic kind in which weights and balances are unthinkably displaced. Two men are crouched one over the other, their feet pressed together sole to sole. The supine man balances the other, then gradually straightens his knees; even more gradually, the other stands erect. At the climax of all this, the stage floor—actually, the marly covering it—suddenly starts to buckle and heave, and the dancers disappear. The "waters" rise and cover all, then subside, leaving a cluster of survivors. They turn into amphibious reptiles, then into beasts with monstrous wingspreads. In slow motion, as the lights dim out, they fly away. The great sliding scene is, of course, in the nature of an encore; it's not part of the Darwinian scenario. The slides are done standing, sitting, and sprawling; the last one is performed by Robert Faust, who spins endlessly on the tip of his spine as the curtain drops.

Faust, a powerfully built acrobat, is one of the new members of the company. I had not seen him before; nor had I seen Carol Parker, Peter Pucci, or Cynthia Quinn. They were all as pliant and as committed, physically and mentally, as the elder-generation Piloboli who were on hand, Moses Pendleton and Michael Tracy, and as Jamey Hampton, who joined the company in 1978. (Hampton, recuperating from a shoulder injury, performed two of his three roles on the program; his place in *Day Two* was taken by Daniel Ezralow, of the Paul Taylor Company.) There's a slightly different physical tone to the company these days, which comes from the beautifully stretched and seasoned dancers' bodies of Parker, Pucci, and Quinn. Faust has the muscularity of a wrestler. In *The Empty Suitor*, he takes the role of the pregnant derelict, created by Jonathan Wolken. He's seedier, less debonair than Wolken, and in his long black coat he looks mountainous. When the woman pops out of his buttonhole, she seems to be his scruffy little daughter, not the fantasy mistress whom Wolken beamed his lascivious eye upon. *The Empty Suitor*, with its top hats and sticks, its park bench and crumpled newspapers all compressed into Magritte-style dream imagery, is one of the few non-pastoral repertory items this country-based company owns. Michael Tracy's nightmare solo, in which he dances to "Sweet Georgia Brown" while trying to keep control of his hat, his stick, and his footing atop a flotilla of rolling tubes, stops the show.

Moses Pendleton, one of the company's founders and one of the authors of its style, has an apparently limitless capacity for orchestrating that style to suit different subjects. *Bonsai*, another of his pieces, is quintessentially Pilobolian-pastoral, even though he made it originally for another company. It begins awesomely, with two men standing erect and very slowly bringing from their shoulders to the floor two women who are also standing erect. The four dancers then come together and, moving as one, create the base out of which the forms suggested by the title begin to spread and flower and change into other forms. Permutation is organic; growth is strictly controlled. Pendleton's command is such that we follow the sense of a change even when our view of it is partly inhibited by the lighting or by its taking place on the floor. Pilobolus style has fascinated a large public for ten years. The reason, I think, is that it is perfectly clear and aboveboard in the way it gets its effects. It seems to spring from a sharp-sighted vision of the natural world, and every movement is meant to be looked at; there's no filler for the eye to slip over. Pendleton, in a solo called *Momix* (which is also the name of the small offshoot company he formed last year with Alison Chase), plays with the possibilities of this highly concentrated, maximum-grip surface by deliberately improvising in front of the audience. The tone of the solo, which is done to reggae music, is usually jovial-sinister—it might be subtitled "Pendleton's Merry Pranks"—and it is very, very bitsy; all shimmies, shakes, stops, and starts. You want just one long-ball drive. At Princeton, Pendleton actually started swinging his cane like a golf club, and the transcendent moment almost happened when, too near the wings, he whacked the hell out of an interfering curtain, raising a dust storm.

The company has not played New York since 1977, which is a grievous deprivation. However, as the Princeton engagement ended, plans were being laid for a season at the ANTA Theatre around Christmas.　　　*—November 30, 1981*

Ballet Fantasque

The latest additions to American Ballet Theatre's Balanchine repertory are well chosen: *La Sonnambula*, which no one does well (so legend has it), and *Bourrée Fantasque*, which no one does anymore. I saw them both at the Kennedy Center, in Washington, along with *The Wild Boy*, a new ballet by Kenneth MacMillan, which ought not to be done at all. Another of MacMillan's tales of sex and violence, this one is told in the form of a fable, and MacMillan is no fabulist. *The Wild Boy* stars Mikhail Baryshnikov and Natalia Makarova. *Configurations* is another new piece that was made for Baryshnikov, with Marianna Tcherkassky. The dancers I saw, Kevin McKenzie and Martine van Hamel, seemed not to make any difference to choreography which features the mindlessly methodical swirling-to-music of Choo San Goh, set this time to Samuel Barber's Piano Concerto. The place for Goh's choreography, surely, is the movies. Since it never accumulates an image, the continual dispersal of effects which the movies inflict on classical choreography ought to do it justice, and it would make an ideal background for those scenes in which something is happening onstage while, in the audience, Paul Newman hides from the police.

As an ensemble, A.B.T. looks better and better. The attention that Baryshnikov and his staff are giving to younger members of the company is paying off in performances such as the one I saw of Paul Taylor's *Airs*. When, last season, this piece was first done—and done quite well—by A.B.T., there was some reason to assume that it would not last long. Productions of modern-dance works by ballet companies are usually token attempts to reproduce an alien style and can be abandoned early without disgrace. But just when one might expect A.B.T.'s Taylor experiment to start breaking down, the company put out a second cast, which was, on the whole, better than the first—better at the style, better at cutting loose and enjoying itself. Ballet Theatre's dancers are actually more adept at Taylor than they are at Fokine; I wish they had the kind of musical coaching that could point out the similarities between the two. *Les Sylphides*, a lovable ballet, is still getting the overreverent, uncomprehending treatment that long ago killed it for modern-day audiences. The dancers are more vigorous and more correct than they used to be; their performance of the hallowed choreography bears evidence of step-by-step scrutiny. But without spontaneity—without the kind of crazy pleasure they get out of *Airs*—*Les Sylphides* does not exist.

I wish, too, that more rigorous musical coaching could be given the Balanchine works. *La Sonnambula*, which was acquired last year, and the new *Bourrée Fantasque* are triumphs of production. The first has a fine atmospheric set, by Zack Brown, and pretty period costumes, by Theoni V. Aldredge. The second is an exact replica of the old New York City Ballet production of 1949, with Jean Rosenthal's candelabra backdrop, which the company used on tour, replacing her cartwheel chandelier, which it used at home. The snappy black Karinska costumes, slashed with saffron, ice blue, and cerise, are all there; the girls have their fans, the boys their tams, and nothing is really wrong except that the dancers don't fit inside the music. Chabrier should be their element, but they aren't into it yet. They're attuned more to the piece's situations and its gags, which Balanchine doesn't really develop, than to its musical expression, which he does. The dancers may respond that way because the choreography has very few steps and the music very high spirits. The ballet represents Balanchine in his bewitching Harlequin mood and also at his most thrifty. How much he manages to accomplish with how little! New York City Ballet danced *Bourrée Fantasque* throughout the fifties alongside a simplified *Symphony in C* and a theatrically surefire *La Valse*. For the relatively inexperienced troupe that N.Y.C.B. then was, that trio provided ear training, dance technique, a taste of the French genius, glamorous roles, and—not to be underestimated—applause. One guesses that when *Bourrée Fantasque* was being made Balanchine set the timings, saying to his charges, "Do these little things for me and you will be a hit." If he didn't actually say it, he didn't need to; the choreography said it for him. And that is how it works now, even with some of the dancers misconceiving their roles. Some who do not include van Hamel in the first movement; she's musical *and* funny, with her fan, her girlish floral headpiece, and her broad, restlessly shifting thighs, though a farther cry from the role's originator, Tanaquil LeClercq, can't be imagined. Her partner, Danilo Radojevic, wisely lets her take the lead; Johan Renvall, in the second cast, keeps pressing himself on Leslie Browne, who has no choice but to react (more and more fretfully). In the two outer movements of the ballet, the ensemble roles are juicy. In the middle movement, the corps of women runs and poses or glides along on point while the principals do all the work. The work is not hard, except for its partnering "lesson," which has the man three times cut into the path of his partner's en-dehors pirouette and complete it in a promenade, his arm around her waist. The subtlety and restraint of the choreography and the wonderful fragrance of the music (the Intermezzo from the opera *Gwendoline*) make this one of Balanchine's tenderest adagios, especially in its "love" passages. Understatement—of necessity, perhaps—is the key, but there is true poetic understatement in the moment when the ballerina, caught in arabesque by her partner, simply lowers her head and brushes the floor with her point, or when she falls headlong into his arms to a sudden hush in the music. Young Susan Jaffe, who has looked wooden to me in her other classical roles, suddenly melted here, yet without losing the firmness of outline and accent that characterize the part.

The third movement, to the "Fête Polonaise," recaptures and extends the brio of the first. The corps makes a running entrance in couples, as in *Theme and Variations*; coryphées swing into huge kicks, pitch themselves forward and back in their partners' arms, and split their legs in high lifts. Finally, the cavalier brings on the mite-size ballerina and flies her highest of all. Ronald Perry's love for his work shines through everything he does, even this hefting role; and Christine Spizzo is the most rapturous of heftees—she cartwheels through the air like a glorified cancan dancer at the Moulin Rouge. From here on, the ballet is all Balanchine pyrotechnics, the formations coming and going like neon against the night. When you think you've seen it all, Chabrier throws another switch and off we go again. The "Fête Polonaise" is really a waltz, drunk with space and surging with color, and Balanchine knows exactly when to hurl his forces into it and when to refrain from competition. At one point, he lets the music build and build while three alternating armies of dancers do nothing more than cross the stage in diagonal run-run-jeté-jeté sweeps. I had not seen the ballet in fifteen years, and it had been an explosive and brilliant memory. It is a revelation to see of what plain material it is really made. Yet all of it—even the coarse-grain parts— is very finely cut. The mere-ness of *Bourrée Fantasque* is a deception.

Maria Callas used to say that she took her dramatic cues from the music. In the most recent biography, she is quoted as saying, "When you want to find how to act onstage, all you have to do is listen to the music." And, she adds, "really listen with your soul and your ears." It is good advice for dancers of Balanchine ballets. Callas, I think, would have understood what Balanchine was up to when he divorced Bellini's plots from Bellini's music and created the ballet that he eventually called *La Sonnambula*. (Actually, the scenario and the musical arrangements were devised for Balanchine by Vittorio Rieti.) In its new context, away from the vacuous libretti that for years exposed it to gross misjudgment and neglect, the transcendent purity of the music is liberated and its intrinsic dramatic power is confirmed. In 1946, when Balanchine and Rieti made their ballet, the bel canto revival that Callas inspired had not yet dawned. It took courage to use this music in support of a *new* story, which, while not as loony as the one that Bellini had used in the opera *La Sonnambula*, was nevertheless a somnambulist fantasy drawn from the Romantic ballet of Bellini's time. (Bellini's opera borrowed its plot from Aumer's ballet *La Somnambule.**) Balanchine's ballet does not have a sleeping girl poised above a water wheel; it has a Poet who, like James in *La Sylphide*, engages a supernatural force. At a masked ball, he encounters a Sleepwalker who has emerged from some secret part of the house, and during a long scene in which she does not once awaken or otherwise acknowledge his presence he dances with her, tantalized at first, then enthralled. When she drifts away, he plunges after her as recklessly as James plunges after the Sylph. Sylph and Sleepwalker symbolize a desire that cannot be consummated in this world; James and the Poet pay for their crime of hubris, but, unlike James, the Poet is vindicated in the end by a gesture that places him beyond the reach of society's judgment. Dead in the arms of his magic beloved, he is translated with her into eternity. The actual depiction of this event on the stage still stirs disbelief. The Sleepwalker carries the body away unaided (which is shock enough); then we see the light of her candle as it travels up the dark tower whence she came, moving from this window to that until it appears by itself above the tower and rises into the sky.

The ballet takes the charges of frivolity, emotional insincerity, and shallowness that were commonly levelled against bel canto and converts them into a dramatic rationale. The life of society as the Poet knows it *is* frivolous, insincere, and shallow. The visual metaphor for this—the masked ball—is borne out in simpering social dances that reach a peak of affectation (and charm) in a grand polacca (to "Son vergin vezzosa" from *I Puritani*). As the entertainment that the host has set out, Rieti arranged a "Bellini" suite of lightweight and somewhat scatty dances, performed not by the guests but by hired professionals. Yet the passion of "Qui la voce" from *I Puritani* and "Ah! non credea mirarti" from *La Sonnambula* also belongs to Bellini, and the passages of shimmering and mournful cantilena which form the basis for the great Sleepwalker-Poet pas de deux and the traumatic finale give the ballet its heart. Social intrigue and theatrical artifice: one feels that the

---

* *Postscript 1987*: The complicated, incident-crammed libretto of the ballet *La Somnambule* (1827) was by the prolific Eugène Scribe. According to an article by Elizabeth Forbes in the Spring 1982 issue of *About the House*, Scribe incorporated several details from a two-act "comédie-vaudeville," also called *La Somnambule*, which he had co-written in 1819; otherwise, the story was new. From a comparison of the scenarios, both of which Miss Forbes recounts in full, it is clear that the earlier work is the real source of the Rieti-Balanchine ballet. Not only does the heroine sleepwalk, she also dances. Other plot elements would appear to have influenced the libretto of *La Sylphide*, which was produced one year after Bellini's opera.

Poet's choice anathematizes all forms of hypocrisy. Against the masquerade, the tunes, and the dances, there is this one cry of the artist and his wound.

The new production has the ball take place in a leafy walled garden with the tower to one side and a bridge running across the top. The candlelight at the end moves out of the tower and is straying somewhat inconclusively along the balustrade as the curtain falls. The suggestion is sometimes made that, for the ending to work, the set must have a second story, so that the Sleepwalker can take the Poet's body somewhere. The point, though, is that she takes it *from* somewhere to nowhere, and that point is not made, either at A.B.T. or at N.Y.C.B., by a follow spot that does nothing but light up features of the set. (The set in use at N.Y.C.B., an ascetic structure with carved stone masks hanging over it, is not even a somewhere.) At the Kennedy Center, when the Sleepwalker's music was first heard I didn't see the light come down the shaft, but it could be that my sight line was bad. Another jarring element was the restyling, by John Taras, of the Blackamoors' pas de deux as a "Danse Exotique," in Balinese-type costumes. The ruse doesn't work; Rieti's rhythm is Gottschalkian, and the dance is blackface minstrelsy. The fourth number in the Divertissement has been restored as a "Danse Gitane" for five women, with choreography also by Taras. Unlike the other dances in the suite, it just doesn't begin to sink in. It might make appropriate background action, like Choo San Goh's stuff.

The way to dance the ballet is the way to dance any Balanchine ballet: follow the music. Victor Barbee has a clear picture of what he wants to project as the Poet—a lord of Romanticism, Manfred or Don Juan—and he approaches the Sleepwalker floridly, as if he were mentally composing an ode. But this interpretation misses what the music tells so clearly—that the hero is at this moment spellbound, struck witless by the vision of a beauty and innocence of which he had only dreamed. The pas de deux is the ballet's one statement of direct emotion. The Poet's inability to stop the Sleepwalker's forward momentum even when he locks his body around hers is a blow to an open heart, but the tragedy isn't shown, because, in fact, Barbee does stop her momentum, dragging her some five or six steps backward before she steps over him and walks on. And his slow backbend when he tries to restrain her should be drawn out to the fullest extent of the crescendo that accompanies it. There was a good moment in Barbee's performance later on: after he stumbled out of the tower and fell to his knees, he looked up in blank astonishment, as if he didn't know what had hit him. This is a Poet who doesn't realize he's broken the rules until it's too late. When I saw Chrisa Keramidas as the Sleepwalker last summer, she was a stick figure, with long points, long hair, and a long nose. As she gathers confidence in the part, she becomes more beautiful and more beautifully rapt. Leslie Browne and Richard Shafer are uncomfortable as the Coquette and the Baron. Balanchine's staging of their scenes *is* quaintly operatic, but it's not strained or tense, and until the climax neither is the music. As Callas says, "Listen with your soul and your ears." The only performer in the ballet who is given license to embellish, both by the trivial nature of the music and by the choreography, is the Harlequin. This Harlequin isn't like the hero of *Harlequinade*; he's crafty and show-wise. Johan Renvall danced and mimed inventively.

Kenneth MacMillan collaborated effectively with the composer Gordon Crosse in *Playground*, produced a couple of years ago by Sadler's Wells Royal Ballet. The choreography, which took character mime to clinical extremes, worked a favorite MacMillan theme, mental disorder. Though it's not a very likable piece, I hope it can be shown here. MacMillan and Crosse don't seem to have come up with much in *The Wild Boy*. The music (which, like the score of *Playground*, was composed separately) constantly imputes meanings to the choreography, and vice versa. The ballet never reveals what it intends by its primitive characters and forest setting. The story—of two men who jointly possess a woman and then capture a wild boy—resembles MacMillan's *Triad* combined with elements of Tudor's *Shadowplay*. The theme of bestiality is pronounced. But MacMillan's treatment of it is disconcertingly bland. In sexual terms, the story is confused. The two men (Kevin McKenzie and Robert La Fosse) may be victims of the depravities of civilization, yet the Wild Boy's downfall comes less through contact with them than through contact with the Woman, whom they have brutalized. MacMillan, the master of the sensationally erotic pas de deux, has here contrived a specimen for Makarova and Baryshnikov which never gets those colored lights going. Maybe MacMillan needs a speedy tempo; this coupling is very slow and very long. And is it the Woman's or the Wild Boy's story that is being told? Our sympathies are attached to him, but she is an innocent, too. How, then, does it happen that sex with the Wild Boy doesn't revive her but only drains him? The moment of truth is reached when the two brutes are made to kiss each other accidentally and fall back in horror at this revelation of homosexuality. It drives the Wild Boy to drink, after which the animals of the forest sniff him disdainfully. Oliver Smith has done a big green jungle set, with looping vines. To judge from Willa Kim's brightly colored tatters, she may have thought she was designing costumes for a nursery tale. As for the dancers, Baryshnikov does everything willingly and lustily; MacMillan gets him into the air in some amazing renversé barrel turns. The next most powerful performance is La Fosse's; of all the young soloists in A.B.T., he shows the greatest improvement. McKenzie, like most of the principal dancers, seems to be nursing a problem. MacMillan has given him a good part. Makarova's part is oddly negative. In Ashton's dances for Stravinsky's *Nightingale*, at the Met, she does little more than show off her ravishing figure, but she has authority.

Star performing at A.B.T. these days is likely to be uneven. Cynthia Gregory and Alexander Godunov do nothing for each other, though they are often teamed. Gregory in *Raymonda* (the divertissements from Acts II and III) and in Robbins's *Other Dances* was all gloss. She seems strong, yet the dancing lacks vitality; instead of a calm center, Gregory has a dead middle. Van Hamel, too, had begun to look a bit tired to me. Her perky *Bourrée Fantasque* was a surprise, and her grand Nikiya in the Shades scene of *La Bayadère* was the old van Hamel, fully restored. As her Solor, she had Patrick Bissell, who never fails, either as partner or as soloist. No, he hasn't cleaned up his style, but is there a young male dancer in the world with a greater generosity toward his partner or a more accurate sense of the shape of a classical variation? In this same *Bayadère*, the dancing of Cheryl Yeager, Deirdre Carberry, and Susan Jaffe as the Shadows was the best this production has seen. In that fact alone may lie the true measure of the progress American Ballet Theatre has made in the past year. *—December 28, 1981*

The Movie Musical
in Books

A few years ago, publishers were bringing out book after book on Broadway shows and Broadway composers. Now they're doing movie musicals, but with nothing like the same grasp of their subject. The movie books that are out now are all conscious tributes to a genre, but only one of them tries to explain what made the musical Hollywood's richest fantasy form, and how it worked. At its best, the musical represented the movies' success at reconciling extreme mass appeal with extreme stylization and elegance of technique. No other genre went so far or failed so often to bring its audience and its art together, but even at their worst the musicals endowed singing and dancing with super-real presence and resources. It was always an improbable dream world that one visited, and it was as accessible to children as to adults. One can't really say that about Broadway musicals until the era of Rodgers and Hammerstein. One can't really say it about the other movie genres, either. (Musicals may, in fact, have made more of an impact on young and impressionable psyches than any other kind of movie.) Can this be the reason that the musical is hardly ever written about in the same serious terms as the gangster film, the Western, the thriller, and the screwball comedy— not to mention the Broadway of Kern and Gershwin and Berlin and Porter and Lorenz Hart? The market for musical memorabilia, expanded by the success of M-G-M's *That's Entertainment*, seems to have called forth a buzz of data, but almost no original research or comment. Most authorities on the form write in a glow of childhood reminiscence. In the America of the movie musicals, they see themselves growing up. Their preferences (the forties over the thirties, the late thirties over the early) give away their ages, and only by their erudition, which may run to maniacal extremes, can we tell how hard they were hit, back there between the newsreel and the coming attractions, by the depth charge of the musical.

Hollywood Musicals, by Ted Sennett (Abrams), is at least a visual bonanza: eight pounds of stills handsomely reproduced in chronological sequence. The text is a stream of mild predictabilities purling between the monuments: Jolson, Lubitsch, Chevalier and MacDonald, Astaire and Rogers, Busby Berkeley and Crosby and Alice Faye and Betty Grable, Shirley Temple and Bojangles, Garland and Rooney, Garland and Kelly, Garland and Minnelli. As the movies get worse, the book gets more magnificent, until it reaches its apotheosis with full-page shots of Audrey Hepburn in those wondrous Beaton gowns which may have been the best part of *My Fair Lady*.

In Clive Hirschhorn's *The Hollywood Musical* (Crown), the stills are not much bigger than Chiclets, but there are over thirteen hundred of them. This is gargantuanism on a different scale of ambition—an attempt to encompass every musical ever made and give more than statistical information about each one. Actually, there is not enough statistical information. The films are laid out year by year, presumably in order of their release, but release and/or production dates are not given. Running times—which are particularly useful to have when one is dealing with television prints—are not given. Time and again, the films are presented in terms of plot rather than of musical numbers. A preface summarizing the historical background of the studio period contains nothing that is not covered in the main text. (For detailed information about the studios' general output, one has to consult *The MGM Story* and *The Warner Bros. Story*—books issued several years ago by Crown in a format similar to that of *The Hollywood Musical*.) A periodic breakdown of trends might have served to unclog the flow of minutiae in the author's capsule commentaries. Sins aside, this is an important reference book for a commercial publisher to have produced. Though readers who aren't addicts will probably prefer Stanley Green's trimmer and tidier package of facts and chatter, *Encyclopaedia of the Musical Film* (Oxford), there is much to be said for a comprehensive survey of an all-but-vanished genre the like of which may never be seen again.

With Hirschhorn to clear away the mist of oblivion, then, it is a pleasure to settle down to Ethan Mordden's *The Hollywood Musical* (St. Martin's)—a solid discussion of the musical as an art form, an evolving stereotype, a commercial product, and a mirror of its times. Mordden, who has published books on American social history, theatre, and music, seems ideally suited to his task. He is erudite but not esoteric, omnivorous but not indiscriminate, enthusiastic but not immature, boldly assertive but not without depth. He writes out of fresh curiosity, without recourse to reminiscence or received ideas, and he asks himself hard questions: What is a musical? When did it get its shape? How do we experience it? Like Tom Wolfe or James Wolcott, Mordden is a nimble essayist who is able to compress in a single image perceptions that might take another writer pages to develop. Toward the end of the book, he demonstrates in one sentence how cultural changes have been accommodated in the musical and how the process— a kind of apostolic succession of personalities—works: "Midler and *The Rose* are, in a sense, the latest event in a history of transformation through stasis: Jolson, in steady helpings, broke the ground for West, while Astaire readied a stage for Kelly, while Chevalier's finesse necessitated the clumsiness of Crosby, and then Garland grew up to connect the aggressiveness of Eleanor Powell with the innocence of Alice Faye, and then Streisand claimed Brice's unplayed cards, dealing in Midler, while Minnelli took over for Garland by right of genes. Nobody changed character from role to role: that's stasis. But each role-player enlarges possibilities in the game." The colloquial dash of the writing is occasionally abridged to a shorthand ("Tyke sings of nice and dances with big") that mimics our primal responses to movies and the way production formulas played upon them.

For a hardhead, Mordden has surprising taste: he likes operetta; he *likes* Rouben Mamoulian. But then he's especially good on the formative years of sound, when Mamoulian flourished. This was Hollywood's Balzac period: the movies were filled with people and places that, once the genre became refined, were seen in musicals no more. Mordden is right when he says that Mamoulian's best film, *Applause*, a story of burlesque, is "as shabby onstage as it is off." But *Dance of Life*, released the same year (1929) by the same studio (Paramount), depicted burlesque just as realistically; I wonder if Mordden has seen it. (He's seen pretty nearly everything—not just the items on the revival circuit but real out-of-the-way stuff, like *Moonlight and Pretzels* and the first *Show Boat*. "I overtrained for this book," he tells us at the outset.) It is hard to see old films that have been forgotten. Three movies that seem to be related are Helen Morgan's *Applause*, Sophie Tucker's *Honky Tonk* (which also had a mother-daughter plot), and *Dance of Life*, which was the film version of the play *Burlesque*. All three were released in 1929, according to Hirschhorn. (Incidentally, for the 1929 film *Melody Lane* Hirschhorn has a still from the 1930 *Puttin' On the Ritz*.) But in what order were they made? Without more specific dates—which Hirschhorn might have provided—the question of precedents and influences can't even be approached. *Burlesque* (1927) may have set off the cycle—if cycle it was. The film version, directed by John Cromwell, starred Hal Skelly, as the drunken "eccentric dancer" he had played on Broadway, and Nancy Carroll, in Barbara Stanwyck's role as his wife. Cromwell, Skelly, Carroll. *Who?* A nice feature of Mordden's book is his sense of justice. He trims some of the excess glory from Judy Garland's reputation and gives it to Alice Faye, who hasn't had enough. The urge to reform gets a little out of hand, though, in an appendix in which the author installs his favorites in a personal Hall of Fame. The fresh sensibility of the book is tarnished by this lapse into clubhouse ritual. But maybe Mordden can't help it; he is a fan, after all.

We think of the musical as a set of fixed formal ideas, but the halcyon era when a musical meant the singing of songs and the dancing of dances was actually a brief span embedded in a history of ill-defined notional experimentation. Even in the great days, there was room for philosophical distinctions such as the one Mordden makes between Astaire's movies and the movies of Eleanor Powell, which were "Powell films rather than dance films: she didn't spread dance all over the screen. *She* danced; the other characters sang, joked, and ran the plot. Powell, too, sang, joked, and plotted, but by focusing on *her* dances as the special things in her films, she eliminated the need for dance as expression of person or story." As James Agee wrote in 1944, "There is no reason, after all, why a movie musical should not be as good as any other sort of movie"—or why a book on movie musicals should not be as good as any other sort of book written for grown-ups. Mordden's, the least lavishly produced of the current crop, and the only one that was written to be read, not only can be read but should be.

—*January 18, 1982*

Starting Over

Dance Theatre of Harlem and Pilobolus are, in their different ways, unique companies; they risk losing more than just strength when their dancers are lured away by other companies or by new ventures—they risk losing profile. Dance Theatre of Harlem has reconstituted itself several times since its establishment, in 1970, by Arthur Mitchell and Karel Shook, and it keeps on having to replace key dancers. Just recently, it lost Mel Tomlinson to New York City Ballet, and that was on top of Ronald Perry's transfer to American Ballet Theatre and Lydia Abarca's defection to *Dancin'* and Hinton Battle's to *Sophisticated Ladies*. Add to this talent drain the fact that the company has no house choreographer apart from Mitchell and you *should* have, in D.T.H., a dancing identity crisis. In reality, you have a formidable institution, organized not around personnel but around clear-cut aesthetic goals. The current season, at the City Center, shows a self-possessed company in confident pursuit of those goals. Whatever else it may have lost, its school has endured test after test, and its ambition is alive.

The Pilobolus "school," an informal and far more precarious affair, is just now entering the critical stage of its first testing period. At the ANTA Theatre, in an engagement that ended last month, we saw the founders ceding their roles to the next generation, proving that a Pilobolus II exists. But this was very much a transitional season. The new members of the company haven't yet created their place in it. The bright new group piece, *Day Two*, is their biggest contribution so far, but perhaps a few solos or duets need to be made before *Day Two* becomes in fact the dawn of a new day for Pilobolus.

Through all its trials and vicissitudes, Dance Theatre of Harlem has stayed a classical company—one that has defined itself more and more distinctively in the tradition of Russian and Russian-derived classicism from early Diaghilev to middle Balanchine. If there is such a style as Afro-Russian, D.T.H. has it; it has had it most conspicuously and enjoyably in *Le Corsaire* and *Paquita*, in last year's revival of *Schéhérazade* and this year's production of *Firebird*, and in such Balanchine ballets as *Agon* and *Bugaku*, where figurative or fantastic elements transform the classical line of the choreography. Wherever the classical line is relatively straight (as in *Concerto Barocco* or *The Four Temperaments*), the dancing is relatively stiff. The Harlem dancers bring a special élan to the hybrid classicism that the Russians used to refer to as demi-caractère. The Spanish Petipa of *Paquita* has become an ensemble showcase. (In earlier years, their Soviet Petipa had the same kind of élan, but that memorable *Corsaire* showed off only two dancers.) It makes one re-ponder—indeed, it makes one relocate—the "usable past" that is available to dancers. In the fun it gets out of dancing these old pieces, D.T.H. confirms its link with tradition and claims its share of a legacy. Our other major black-dominated company, Alvin Ailey American Dance Theatre, used to produce a series called "Roots of the American Dance." The Ailey's connections with those roots grow more tenuous with each passing season. Although Ailey's dance back-ground is much the same as Geoffrey Holder's and Carmen de Lavallade's, it is D.T.H. that puts on the distinguished revivals of the Holder-Lavallade ballets. This season, Virginia Johnson is doing an old de Lavallade solo, *Songs of the Auvergne*. She dances in stocking feet, a trifle uncomfortably, I would imagine, but her technique is more than credible. The Ailey was formed in 1958. Then it may have stood on firm native ground; these days it wades through slush. Ailey's latest ballet, *Landscape*, is one of his periodic hopeful returns to old-school expressionistic modern dance. The choreography shows good form, but the dancers take no pleasure in it; for them *Landscape* is a routine assignment, the zillionth rerun of Ailey's pet patterns. They can't conceal the inanition of expressionistic design; all they can do is punch up the show. The *Paquita* staged for D.T.H. by Alexandra Danilova represents her memory of the Petipa she learned as a girl during the period of Petipa's near-cancellation by Fokine. Structurally, the ballet is still a marvel, but its choreographic details are sparse, especially in allegro. Danilova's *Paquita* is like a handsome Spanish shawl, an heirloom all the more cherishable because it is threadbare. The Harlem dancers can't fill out the bare places, but they do supply a kind of suggestive power; watching them, you see the underlying vitality of the conventions. When you watch *Landscape*, you see only conventions.

And you see only conventions when you watch Valerie Bettis's *A Streetcar Named Desire*. The Bettis piece, done originally in 1952 for a company headed by Mia Slavenska and Frederic Franklin, was revived this season by D.T.H., although its histrionic movement idiom, solemn and slick at the same time, is really as unrevivable as the more decorous expressionistic idiom the Ailey company keeps trying to work in. In *Streetcar*, based on the Tennessee Williams play, the forms that possibly were once signposts of emotion are blank. This makes the ballet doubly inarticulate: deprived not only of Williams's dialogue but also of an expressive vein of movement. And since Bettis sticks close to the Williams scenario and cast of characters, and uses the music that Alex North wrote for the movie, we are constantly being reminded of the things that aren't being portrayed. We don't know why Blanche DuBois (Virginia Johnson) is so nervous or what her affectations stem from or why she gets under Stanley Kowalski's skin. Stanley (Lowell Smith) rapes her in a fit of irritation, and it is a trivial conquest. Blanche is not a threat to him in what she represents; her world and his are concepts that Bettis never succeeds in clarifying, for all her picture hats and bare light bulbs and louvered doors. Yet Bettis has made a discovery of sorts. When you switch off the soundtrack of *Streetcar* and strip the drama of its particulars, it turns into something very like Antony Tudor's *Pillar of Fire*. At the end, Blanche even exits behind the scenery, trailing off into the forever on the arm of her attendant, like Hagar on the arm of her lover. If Bettis had forced the resemblance even further than she already has with her gauzy Tudoresque dream figures—if she could have made dances and gestures through which Hagar-Blanche expressed herself and her situation—we might have had a second-rate *Pillar*, but at least we'd have had a ballet, and not a series of scenes in which the heroine *isn't* saying "Young, young, young man" or "Stella for star!" or "I have always depended on the kindness of strangers."

The new *Firebird* is splendidly done. Geoffrey Holder has placed the action in a Rousseau tropical forest heavy with night-blooming flowers. His Firebird is a red comet against the sky; his Princess and his Maidens are orchidaceous in draped chiffon and streamers. The 1945 suite of dances is staged by John Taras much as Balanchine staged it in 1949, in a style both innocent and suave; there is a salute to Balanchine in the long tremolo exit of the ballerina as, back bent and wings spread, she flutters off on her points into the dark. Elsewhere, the fluid and resourceful steps are Taras's own. The Maidens' round dance reminded me of his Russian bloodlines; the Firebird's solos recalled that he was once ballet master at the Paris Opéra. With its leggy plastique, its preenings and flouncings, the role can only be described as Josephine Baker Petipa, and it is actively enhanced by a lavish plumed headdress and a red-feathered leotard cut high on the hipbones and ending in a fantail ruff. Stephanie Dabney looks great in this costume of Holder's, and she bends and plummets and skims the ground with amazing tensility. An eager performer, Dabney sometimes anticipates her cues and acts too much with her face. But she has speed and softness, and when she trusts herself to be even softer she will give an even finer performance. This production of *Firebird* tries, not very seriously, to separate the ballet from Russian mythology. The Tsarevich (Donald Williams) is called Young Man and is dressed like an intruder from outer space. The Princess is called Princess of Unreal Beauty. Danced in trailing blue chiffon by the five-foot-ten-inch Lorraine Graves, she is all of that. The monsters suggest demons out of Haitian folklore. Kastchei (here Prince of Evil), in a dark polka-dotted dress, alone of the principals makes no impact.

Holder—it has been a Geoffrey Holder season—also revived his *Banda*, a Haitian funeral scene in which vestiges of Catholicism are mixed with voodoo ritual in a swirl of incense and crinoline. The costumes are not the whole show. There is the Dracula-like ghoul Baron Samedi, a hip-rolling lascivious role that once belonged to Holder himself. Donald Williams—the decorative hero of *Firebird*, the placid Mitch of *Streetcar*—dances with a precision that is truly fiendish.

One of the most memorable performing ensembles of the seventies, Pilobolus gained its greatest fame as a sextet—four men and two women—whose harmony lay in exquisitely balanced dissonances. The basic unit was a male quartet, and here, too, dissonances were resolved. Jamey Hampton in Moses Pendleton's roles, Robert Faust in Jonathan Wolken's, and Peter Pucci in Robby Barnett's have been good, but they haven't set up a tetrachord with Michael Tracy, who remains for the most part in his old roles. Pucci and Tracy are at the moment too much alike, physically and temperamentally; they're small, light, and winsome. Hampton is properly gnomic, and so is Faust, but Faust is also a giant—so large he looks out of scale with the others. And there's nothing happening between the men and the women—Carol Parker and Cynthia Quinn, who do the Alison Chase–Martha Clarke roles.

Of course, it is unfair to judge the newcomers in terms they themselves have not set, even though that is exactly what the ANTA performances invited us to do, particularly in the signature group pieces *Monkshood's Farewell* and *Untitled*, and in specialties like *Momix* and *Geode*, which are self-portraits of Pendleton and Barnett. The new people could not quite cast off the shadow of their predecessors; neither were they always free to reinterpret. When they did reinterpret, they were disappointing, with a tendency to broaden and coarsen effects or simply to miss them. In some pieces, the exaggerations must have been irresistible. *Molly's Not Dead*, a country-and-Western number, has a built-in tendency to self-inflate. *Walklyndon*, the oldest item in the repertory, is unmitigated slapstick. But I was startled to see in *Shizen* italicizations that sprang from nothing in the piece and that did it some disservice. *Shizen*, a duet created by Pendleton and Chase, is quiet, unemphatic, imperturbable; it has always been an audience-resistant piece, the opposite of *Walklyndon* and *Molly's Not Dead*. Hampton and Quinn—too conscious, perhaps, of not being Pendleton and Chase—chose to emphasize moments. They didn't need to, nor did they need the big orange spotlight that was thrown on those moments as if to say "This is famous." (The lighting of Neil Peter Jampolis throughout the season was otherwise admirable.) Pilobolus charms audiences as a matter of course; few companies have that kind of magic, and few must be as mindful of the difference between eliciting approval and soliciting it. At the same time, Pilobolus is show biz, and it knows that, too. Among the many awesome balances the older generation used to strike was the balance between high and low taste. They had an infallible instinct, too, when it came to holding the audience within the bounds of that agreement. Pilobolus II, in the working out of its own Pilobolian vision, may find that its greatest challenge is the audience. —*February 1, 1982*

This Space and That Jazz
and These Dancers

It is a misfortune that George Gershwin did not write a ballet. When he died, he was planning his first full-scale composition for dancers, "The Swing Symphony," as part of the score of the movie *The Goldwyn Follies*; his choreographer would have been George Balanchine. And he would presumably have worked with Balanchine the way Tchaikovsky worked with Petipa—filling out musical prescriptions at the behest of one who understood the developed language of dance. In 1970, Balanchine made a Gershwin ballet of sorts out of selections from the composer's 1932 songbook and called it *Who Cares?*—a title that, like the ballet itself, evokes the hedonism and throwaway elegance of the twenties, when American musical comedy was at its peak. *Who Cares?* commemorates Fred Astaire as well as Gershwin; it is made up of dance numbers that express in ballet scale and ballet impetus the tradition of American show dancing at its most imaginative. If Balanchine chose to work with Gershwin's songs rather than his concert pieces, it may have been because it was in the songs that Gershwin most intensely visualized his idea of dance, and it is the social dance—the Charleston, the fox-trot—of his era. Although dance rhythm is always present in his orchestral works and piano pieces, it is subordinate to another stream of visualization. Gershwin isn't seeing dances in his *Rhapsody in Blue* and *An American in Paris* or in his piano concerto. The fact that choreographers persistently attempt this music testifies to its power of kinetic suggestion, but the ballets invariably fail, because Gershwin's kinetic powers are focussed in unstageable visions. He eludes the net of dance, and sets traps for choreographers.

The Piano Concerto in F has provoked two recent ballets. One, by Billy Wilson for the Alvin Ailey company, is in a jazz-wrenched modern-dance idiom; the other is in the sleekly upholstered classicism of Jerome Robbins and New York City Ballet. The most interesting thing about both these ballets is that, in relation to the music, they have no life except when Gershwin refers to dancing, as he does glancingly throughout the first movement and again at the end of the third. His motif is the Charleston, and it goes as quickly as it comes, swallowed up in the throng of motifs by which he sought to depict his subject. Gershwin's original title for the Concerto in F was "New York Concerto," and he does seem to be presenting a city panorama—one far more detailed and grand than he would later present in *An American in Paris*. Neither Wilson nor Robbins seems to have any inkling about New York or its meaning to Gershwin. (It was his home city, and, for this child of Russian-Jewish immigrants, making his way out of the ghetto, it was also his crucible.) What is more important, neither choreographer is able to contrive a substitute for Gershwin's vision—the panorama that he shows us in such concrete scenic and dramatic detail that if he had any visual accompaniment in mind it was surely the motion picture, in which images can be intercut with a comparable velocity. (The concerto was written in 1925, the year not only of the Charleston but of *Potemkin*.) In the Wilson piece, the dancers are scattered like dry leaves by the force of the music. Although Robbins manages to contain a lot of this force, he's irresolute about what he's containing it for. He doesn't seem to want to impose his own construct on the music so much as to keep it from imposing itself on him. The parading chorus of women behind the lovers' pas de deux in the slow movement imparts a sense of continuity, and its mood of drifting ennui is not inappropriate to the music. But Robbins doesn't tell us who these women are. It's not enough for them to be impersonal observers—strangers in the city—especially when they settle down during the principals' most intimate passages and simply stare. Earlier, in the first movement, women and men had crossed the stage in blocklike masses against the soloist's line of direction, and we could see for a moment the drama of the individual and the crowd; and the surge of that opposition, repeating itself to the heartbeat of the music, began to be thrilling. There are not many moments like this. Robbins calls his ballet *The Gershwin Concerto*, but it's not really about the music. It's not an independent choreographic statement, either. It's like most Robbins ballets—its only subject is New York City Ballet.

Robbins has always loved to make pieces about dancers. Beginning with *Dances at a Gathering* and continuing with *Goldberg Variations* and most of the works that followed it (not omitting the sleeper of the Ravel Festival, *Ma Mère l'Oye*), his portraits of dancers have become less generic, more personal. One can really believe of some of his latter-day pieces the statement he made about the personae of *Dances at a Gathering*—that "the dancers are themselves dancing with each other to that music in that space." Coming from almost any other choreographer, this might be taken as a declaration of artistic integrity: the dance is complete in itself and has no need of motivation from the standpoint of characterization or subject matter. Coming from Robbins, it means the opposite—not a disavowal of programmatic content but an affirmation of it. Robbins no doubt believes in the ideal of pure expression; working for the same company as Balanchine, he could not help believing it. But what may be for Balanchine a working hypothesis enabling him to dispense with extraneous references is for Robbins an automatic presumption that *all* references are extraneous—that when, as in *The Gershwin Concerto*, we see Maria Calegari and Darci Kistler dancing with Christopher d'Amboise and Mel Tomlinson we are seeing these dancers in their actual roles as members of New York City Ballet, and nothing else. By these lights, the meanings in a dance are not only internal but nontranscendent; they change when the casting changes. And Robbins is in fact ingenious at exercising the talents of various N.Y.C.B. dancers without giving them roles in which they may transcend their circumstances and take their place in the world—the world, I mean, of art and the imagination. For Robbins, the making of a Gershwin ballet means that certain dancers are seen in circumstances set by Gershwin; they're creatures of the Jazz Age, yes, but this is only a ploy—we're not interested in any of that. The Art Deco attitudes of the female corps keep dissolving; "the past" keeps circling back to the present. When the women stand or sit around watching the principals, they aren't setting Gershwin's scene, they're a ballet company watching onstage instead of from the wings. You almost feel that for them to carry Gershwinesque scene-painting beyond a suggestive daub here and there would be a violation of their rights. The Dance comes first.

I think Robbins is involved in a profound confusion of ends and means, but he's been at it so long that he's succeeded in establishing his constricted world view as a basic reality of ballet life. A Robbins ballet is some other place for the dancers to be besides the world of Balanchine, yet what is a Robbins ballet but a view of the world of Balanchine—or, rather, of the company he has created? *The Gershwin Concerto* does not omit a quotation from *Who Cares?*—of course not, since Gershwin already belongs to this company. I find implausible the habits of the Robbins devotees who don't attend regular performances of New York City Ballet. What do they think he's talking about? But the N.Y.C.B. devotee who isn't interested in Robbins premières puzzles me, too. A new Robbins is, if it is nothing else, a slice of the company's life. One can try and match Robbins's impressions of the dancers against one's own, or—more amusingly—against Balanchine's. And Robbins in repertory provides good muscle-flexing opportunities for aspiring dancers. *Goldberg Variations*, with its profusion of soloist roles, has become, through wholesale annual or semi-annual recasting, a grid for screening aspirants. Robbins will often pinpoint a dancer's quality before Balanchine does; it was he who "spotted" Kyra Nichols, Daniel Duell, Bart Cook, Robert Weiss. In *The Gershwin Concerto*, I think he overestimates Christopher d'Amboise's abilities almost as much as he underrates Mel Tomlinson's. (The former Dance Theatre of Harlem soloist has been given a jiving and strutting role verging on caricature.) The two ballerinas, who are sharply differentiated at the outset, soon become interchangeable. To be sure, Kistler and Calegari are sisters under the N.Y.C.B. skin, but, having stated Kisterlian and Calegaresque themes in his choreography and related them to different themes in the music (red-hot and blue), Robbins apparently feels free not only to intermingle his themes in the second movement but to lose them completely in the third. The two feminine leads, which are the crux of the ballet, wind up as blank as the Merle Park–Jennifer Penney leads in Kenneth MacMillan's *Fin du Jour*. Right at the end, Robbins has the two women change partners; the effect is all but unnoticeable.

Robbins's infatuation with dancers has always been a great strength. But it used to have a poetic dimension. Think of *Afternoon of a Faun*. And, in spite of what he says about it, *Dances at a Gathering* embraces a broader reality than the literal one of dancers dancing. To put it another way, it is possible while watching that ballet and listening to the Chopin music to think of Poland. And the ballet is enhanced, not diminished, by the thought. Robbins, though, seems bent on legendizing dancers in a vacuum. Maybe he agrees with the people out front who adore New York City Ballet as a race of gods. When he sets a role on Dancer X, he almost always gives that audience lots of what it loves about X. But the real revelations about dancers are left to Balanchine. One feels that Robbins is satisfied with this arrangement—that, indeed, he would hear of no other. He seems to enjoy being inside and outside the company at once, being both an observer of New York City Ballet and a shaper of its image. The enjoyment shows in the smooth, untroubled progress of his ballets, in their watchability, in their audience psychology. Robbins doesn't fail; he has hits. The fact that his work is increasingly centered in a mystique does it no harm at the box office. The general public takes Robbins as Robbins; the ballet public takes him as Balanchine's coadjutor as well. And Robbins appears to take himself as Balanchine's foremost disciple. But it's not Balanchine's creative method that Robbins has adopted—it's his creative product.

In *Mozartiana*, Balanchine last year created four variations for Suzanne Farrell which were a redefinition of Farrell, and this year, by putting Peter Martins opposite her in the leading male role, he re-created the pas de deux which follows the variations. He also inserted a program note in the form of a letter from a young Russian émigré, the musicologist Solomon Volkov. It is unlike Balanchine to use a fan letter to plug one of his ballets, and, in any case, Volkov's letter is not remarkably elucidating. I was perplexed until I noticed a key word. "The dance," Volkov writes, "draws the music into a complex counterpoint; *Mozartiana* blossoms." The word is "counterpoint." It is the underlying principle of the climactic section of the ballet, which the ballerina shares with her partner. In the pas de deux, the continuous line of the dance is made out of two bodies moving in counterpoint, and this continuous line moves, as Volkov observed, in counterpoint to the music. Farrell and Martins made the whole thing seem like a conversation in which a subject is discussed without its ever being mentioned and no sentence is finished; the line of contact was respun, ever more fine, at each performance. One Saturday matinée, particularly, when Robert Irving was conducting, it was like seeing the drama of dancing with every nerve exposed. The two great dancers are very great together—incomparable in measured adagio phrases, amazing in allegro. Martins, in dancing a part originally made for Ib Andersen, had to fit himself into tight allegro patterns, and he did it without seeming to have a moment's discomfort and without distorting his royal *profundo* intonation. Balanchine first noticed Martins's gift for speedy, intricate movement when he cast him in *Duo Concertant*, ten years ago; and being in that ballet this season appears to have rejuvenated Farrell. Her whole presence seems refreshed. *Duo* closes with a spotlit vignette about the Poet losing and regaining his Muse. As performed by Farrell and Martins, it is a lovely pendant to *Chaconne*, in which they are glimpsed as Orpheus and Eurydice.

The company put on thoughtful productions of its two new works. Besides *The Gershwin Concerto*, which has a geometric Art Deco backdrop in blue by Santo Loquasto, Martins's revival of *The Magic Flute* has been fitted out with scenery and costumes in the style of eighteenth-century French pastoral prints. The tints are vegetable—pleasantly so in David Mitchell's scenery, excessively so in Ben Benson's costumes. *The Magic Flute* (no connection to Mozart's opera) was first done by the School of American Ballet last spring. In addition to décor, it has acquired an orchestration, by Robert Irving, that does honor to the composer, Riccardo Drigo; also, there are some new dances, in which the tinies of the school participate. The ballet is for children and very young or plausibly young adults. Martins cast Andersen and Helgi Tomasson as the adolescent hero but a last-minute crisis compelled him to dance the part himself at the opening performance. Actually, the only thing wrong with that was that he was too busy looking out for everyone else to concentrate. This is his best ballet. It is theatrically uninhibited and emotionally sincere, and the company is rising to it. Darci Kistler dances the heroine with that unsettling precocity which has marked all her performances up to now. Her mime is on the same level, and mime is not in the N.Y.C.B. line; here she really does have a Merle Park–Jennifer Penney type of role. In the alternate cast, Katrina Killian, guided by the experienced Tomasson, improves on her exuberant school performance. The character mimes are not bad, but the student cast was funnier. Only Florence Fitzgerald, as the mother, is getting the most out of her role at the moment. Ulrik Trojaborg, though, has been handed the role of Oberon and triumphs by getting the *least* out of it. (In the school production, Oberon was a girl.)

Poland. I went out to C. W. Post Center, on Long Island, to see whether Mazowsze, the Polish folk-dance troupe, would actually appear in a subscription series for which it had been booked last fall, and, if so, whether I would recognize it as the company that used to tour the United States in the sixties and seventies with rather more fanfare. The company appeared, unmistakably Mazowsze. The bright young faces were glowing, the costumes—twenty-five complete changes, including shoes, for as many numbers—were knockouts, and the dancing, too, was as I remembered: high-spirited, elegant, occasionally exciting, but not con-sistently what one might have hoped for from Poles. Still, it was a vibrant show, with singing in English as well as in Polish, and with ample opportunity for a friendly audience to demonstrate solidarity. The audience, which was a large one, was no friendlier than it would have been to the Ice Capades. Some people down front, evidently Poles, raised one cheer at some passing patriotic sentiment, and that was it. No response—not even when a song was introduced, in English, as one that was sung "in a time of foreign domination." At the end, after a fairish amount of applause, the audience hurried off to its cars in the freezing dark, and the company, I guess, began packing for the rest of its twelve-week tour. I don't know what kind of reception the dancers have had elsewhere. But the silence on Long Island could only have been a comfort to the government that sent them.

—*February 22, 1982*

Finders Keepers

In *Lost, Found and Lost*, Paul Taylor and Alex Katz meet again, and the result is another amazing theatrical creation—one in which the two men seem not to be seeing eye to eye but to be looking past each other at different views of the world they share. Taylor has returned to some of his early experiments as a choreographer of "found" movement; the dances consist of blandly naturalistic behavior, like standing and walking, or of awkwardly shaped and often convulsive bits of activity that never come together into phrases. But the movement isn't carefully dissected, as in Taylor's famous anti-dance concert of 1957 (which is specifically commemorated here); it is chopped up and strewn around the stage in huge indiscriminate slabs, and the cleaver keeps slashing against the grain. The calm elucidations of the fifties were right for that buttoned-up age, but now, Taylor seems to be saying, disassembled movement is no longer provocative in itself. Randomness and violence have to be part of the anti-pattern.

If Alex Katz had dressed Taylor's dancers in anti-costumes—say, the civilian khakis and flippy skirts he gave to *Diggity* or the bathing suits he gave to *Private Domain*—*Lost, Found and Lost* might not be the consuming experience it is. Instead of the found clothing that goes with found movement, Katz has put the ten dancers into stretch-terry-cloth jump suits, all black and all strategically decorated with sequins. Footwear is also black; some dancers have one colored shoe. This costume is topped off by black close-fitting caps decorated with sequins, and over the caps men and women alike wear black tulle veils. It is a look of high fashion and high androgyny, and the look does not lose its mystery as the piece goes on, because the rough and casual nature of the choreography keeps contradicting it. But on some remote plane the two conceptions meet. There is in both choreography and costume design the semblance of familiarity—an allusiveness to things already seen and known in daily living and in the world of fashion. The collusion and collision of these two worlds is completely unpredictable. If one accepts that it is natural to be fashionable and fashionable to be *au naturel*, *Lost, Found and Lost* is not bewildering to look upon. It is merely fascinating.

Taylor was, in his early period, a prophet of that school of post-modern dance which deals in natural, unconstructed, or minimal movement. A recent PBS show presented old footage from that period, and of one of the dances shown—a duet for two women in which the most noticeable movement is the wind rippling their dresses—Taylor was quoted as saying, "I thought I was making an abstract dance out of natural postures and walking. But when one woman finally walks away, across the stage, she isn't just walking, she's leaving the other. I learned from this that posture and gesture are inseparable." I take this to be a tenet of Taylor's art—one that was ignored by many of the choreographers who came later. When Taylor says that posture and gesture are inseparable—when, in other words, there can be no poses that movement would not qualify and no movement that would not distort the poses—then he is saying that there is no abstraction in dance; dance is intrinsically dramatic. While Taylor went on to see what he could do with this discovery, the postmodernist choreographers came along and tried to continue on the old reductionist principles. And so, for the most part, they continue today. Even when found, natural, or dislocated movement has been built up into a communicable style, there is no attempt at an other than abstract rendition of the material. A recent concert by the talented Nina Wiener was maddening in the way it kept producing inventive movement and bringing it to the not-quite conflagration point of suggestiveness. Wiener, like virtually every other choreographer of her generation, seems determined to take no notice of immanent dramatic themes in her work; either that or she thinks it's enough to just let them lie where they fall (and get kicked around by the dancing). A year or so ago, there was the beginning of a return to dramatic statement in the work of several young choreographers; there was even a name for the trend: "para-narrative dance." But most of it has been implausible. What is the point of *finding* movement if one is going to slap a situation or a personality power play on top of it?

The other big lesson Taylor says he learned from his 1957 concert—which emptied the hall—was that audiences are important. His radical phase occasionally resurfaces, in pieces like *Esplanade*, where the use of simple walking, running, and skipping becomes a joke between him and his audience—painless populism. In *Lost, Found and Lost*, he teases the audience extensively and gets away with it, maybe because we feel that the fundamental absurdity of presenting found movement is on Taylor's mind even as he does present it. The piece has a portentous opening, with the company stretching and milling and the orchestra playing slow, suspended chords. Then suddenly it breaks into "Charmaine," and the dancers are waiting in line to go somewhere offstage. It's the first of many such gags. Dancers in real life spend a lot of time waiting, in unemployment lines, for example. What else do they do? They rehearse; they attempt the idiotic contrivances of their choreographers. They have to do the Frug while performing grands jetés en tournant. And they pose for photographs. Katz's set is a white floorcloth and void that Jennifer Tipton illuminates like a photographer's studio or plunges into blackout. The production elements are high-key, while the dancing is low-key. And over the whole thing Taylor's composer, Donald York, pours a sludge of fifties Muzak—melodies like "Limelight" and "Ebb Tide" and "Red Roses for a Blue Lady" played in the style of Mantovani. When the dance and the design and the music aren't clashing madly, they're patting each other on the back; there are no straight emotions in *Lost, Found and Lost*. But Taylor's attitude seems clear. Although he repeats the 1957 women's duet (with Carolyn Adams and Karla Wolfangle), this time it's only a starting point. Perhaps he means to tell us (perhaps the title has already told us) that movement found in one era can never be found again.

The other première of the Taylor season at the City Center was also on the subject of dance, but *Mercuric Tidings* is an unkinky virtuoso display piece, completely different in style from *Lost, Found and Lost*, and different in intention from *Arden Court* and *Airs*, to name Taylor's other "ballets." *Mercuric Tidings*, in three movements, is *about* ballet as a machine for effects; Taylor seems to have taken the machine apart, examined its inmost intricacies, and reconditioned it as a vehicle for his own company. The most enrapturing of ballet's capacities to him, it would appear, is speed. Taylor makes his dancers fly all through the first movement and then fly again all through the third. The music, two movements taken from Schubert's first two symphonies, does the same thing, and the repetition is deliberate; Taylor has clearly staged it to see how much of a distinction he could make between two congested ensemble compositions in the same tempo of allegro vivace. He tests himself in other ways, fashioning substitutes for pointwork (the women are barefoot), experimenting with lifts (a woman may lift a man), playing with space in the circular and pyramidal formations that ballet espouses. At one point in the third movement, the company separates into two decorative clusters halfway into the wings, leaving the middle of the stage as blank, for the moment, as a tennis court. The second movement, to a slow, sweet Schubert waltz, is Taylor's view of the standard nineteenth-century adagio, with the ballerina and her partner enclosed by a female corps led by a soloist who intervenes in the pas de deux and supplements it in curious ways. This figure—Myrtha, the Lilac Fairy—remains constant, while the lead couple is danced by two and then three different pairs of dancers. Again Taylor restages a situation without repeating his effects, just as ballet repertory does, with Farrell and Martins on one night and McBride and Tomasson on another. Toward the end of the adagio, some men put in a token appearance (Taylor must be remembering the old days of ballet), and all three couples enter and exit together. Myrtha-Lilac is the last to leave, rolling over and over on the floor across the stage. Well, who says it has to be pas de bourrée?

Compared with those of a ballet master, Taylor's technical resources are few. Not only does he surmount that problem, he also makes you see that the weight and grandeur of ballet aren't produced by its technique or its specialized vocabulary. The one quality of the grand style that eludes him, I think, is emotion. The adagio doesn't spell out a real event, and the two outer sections are empty in relation to it. But then Taylor's concern is not style but similitude. *Mercuric Tidings* may not repeal the mechanism of ballet, but it does set it in an astonishing perspective. And you don't have to see the ballet allusions to enjoy the piece. In its scale and sweep of phrase, in its singular palette of invention (based, it would seem, on varieties of pas de chat), this is the most impressive exhibition of technical virtuosity that Taylor has given us up to now. The dancers lash themselves along gallantly and a little fearfully; next season they will be marvellous. The only flaw is Gene Moore's pink costumes, as effulgent as his rose backdrop in *Arden Court*. As the great machine functions—there is never a moment when it is not functioning—it seems to be churning out gobs of strawberry parfait.

It is now the custom to speak of Taylor's burst of creativity as a choreographer since he stopped dancing, in 1974, as if he had shown no comparable creativity before. The revival of *Orbs* this season denies that assumption; so does *Private Domain*, which Taylor keeps in repertory despite the audience's dislike of it. The movement invention in this one piece, which Taylor made in 1969, could furnish six other choreographers with ideas for weeks. And it is *sheer* movement invention, not noticeably reliant upon the musical accompaniment, which is by Iannis Xenakis. In *Orbs*, Taylor forms an uncanny alliance with Beethoven. When he began work on this hour-long piece about the Sun and the other stars, he at first used Vivaldi's *The Four Seasons* and followed the scheme of that music in sections that he called "Venusian Spring," "Martian Summer," "Terrestrial Autumn," and "Plutonian Winter." (Then as now, Taylor's titles spring, like some of his movement motifs, from Martha Graham.) But the choreography was developed to Beethoven's late quartets, which, with their catapulting rhythms, their spaces and silences, and their unexpected, jolting contrasts, lent a powerful impetus to Taylor's brooding exploration of the cosmos. *Orbs*, which had its première in 1966, is about the cycle of our life, the ambivalence of our God, primal energy, birth, and copulation, and death. It was in its time the most ambitious of Taylor's works, the first of those layered allegorical structures in which even now he has no peer. Taylor handles his large themes with a light touch; he never pontificates. In the slapstick scherzo "Terrestrial Autumn," the planets and moons reappear in street clothes as a wedding party; the Sun becomes the preacher, who gets drunk and pinches the women. There may be a bit too much Renaissance spirit-of-man jubilation in this section for some tastes; for me, this is more than offset by the deep sobriety, tenderness, and force of "Plutonian Winter" and its sleep of death.

The designer, Alex Katz, was also under the influence of Graham. His Noguchi-like skeletal set, his leotards and fishtail skirts are regulation Graham-company dress, executed by an artist of imagination. The authentic Katz peeps out in the streetwear of "Terrestrial Autumn" and in the odd design of the Sun's mantle, an affair of Dynel tufts and sequins. The performance by the company was faithful in every detail. As the Sun, a role in which Taylor blazed and thundered, Daniel Ezralow might have been expected to be too light. But Ezralow's focussed power and grand progressions of bodily gesture in the slow movements were as wonderful as his boyish suavity in the allegros. Of the four planets, only Carolyn Adams was there in her original role, and it was her farewell performance. A sad thing to write. With Adams into retirement goes one of our last remaining links to the individualistic older generation of modern dancers. Carolyn Adams seemed to step fully prepared into her roles and to fill them with her personality—the personality of a shy, modest, yet beautifully equipped lyrical dancer. Her spirits were eternally youthful. Would Taylor have created the sprinting, cakewalking Miss B. in *Big Bertha* without her? Would the backward-skittering runs in *Esplanade* have been possible without Adams's spry relevé and seamless rhythm? Yet in *Runes* the same dancer was a model of composure and meticulous nuance. She leaves the company in a phase of accomplishment it would not have reached without her.

The Merce Cunningham season that preceded the Taylor season at the City Center was pretty much Cunningham as usual except for *Gallopade*, a new piece that was unlike anything I have seen since *Antic Meet*. But where *Antic Meet* was pointedly satirical and absurdist in its situations *Gallopade* invented a broad, galumphing kind of humor in the very shape and texture of its movement. It was a self-enclosed Cunningham cartoon, filled with floppy, deranged bodies and eccentric, squabbling sign language that made the company look like earnest cavemen. Cunningham played the crazy uncle or elder of the tribe, hilariously creaky in his joints, ever hopeful in communication. Physical comedy seldom goes higher or spins a finer web than in *Gallopade*. Some of the movements are said to have been based on Cunningham's attempts to compose while recovering from an injury—on found movement of the most personal sort. Other choreographers have presented works rooted in similar experiences, but no one else has ever done a *Gallopade*. The truth of found movement lies in who's looking.

—*May 10, 1982*

The Prince and the Swan

The plague has struck American Ballet Theatre. Of the dozen dancers whom the company bills as principals, half are on the sick list or recently have been on it; four of these are ballerinas. However, just below the top rank one can easily count another dozen soloists who are proving their worth and dependability in important assignments this season. Mikhail Baryshnikov, who is himself among the injured, probably didn't realize, when he decided to build up the talent in the ranks, how soon this policy would have to start paying off. Along with the rest of the audience at the Met, I mourn Baryshnikov's absence. I mourn also Natalia Makarova, who made a few glamorous but weak appearances and then resuccumbed, and Martine van Hamel, who was felled onstage. But through all the cancellations and confusion it has been possible to see some very good dancing. In the first of four *Swan Lakes* I attended, the pas de trois in Act I was given by three of Baryshnikov's "discoveries": Lucette Katerndahl, Christine Spizzo, and Charles Maple. They were all fine. Maple, a promising dancer some years back, had been buried in corps and character roles when Baryshnikov retrieved him. Now he has emerged once more as a classical dancer. Spizzo, perfect in allegro roles, typifies the new clarity and brightness of execution we have been enjoying from the female second echelon. Katerndahl, previously unknown to me, typifies the new strength of the corps de ballet. If Baryshnikov can pull people like her—and Deirdre Carberry and Harriet Clark—out of the corps, he hasn't so much to worry about after all.

In that same *Swan Lake*, Ross Stretton, who is still listed as a soloist, danced his first Siegfried with a refinement that suggested he had been doing it for years. Stretton, as long of limb and lean in profile as an Afghan hound, is a perfect Prince both in our imagination and in his; he seems incapable of an unregal gesture. Kevin McKenzie dances the same role with some of the same fragility and diffidence of manner as Stretton, but where Stretton suggests the retiring aristocrat McKenzie just looks out of it. He doesn't seem to have made a connection to the Prince in his imagination; he's droopy and inattentive to others on the stage, and all his energy—there is an astonishing amount of it—goes into his dancing. Since Baryshnikov revised the production, a new touchstone in the role has emerged in the legato solo with the crossbow. Baryshnikov, who danced Siegfried unforgettably last year, made of the taking up of the crossbow a moment of poignant self-awareness when the young Prince faces his end as a boy and the need to put away childish things. For Baryshnikov, this is the last hunt. For Patrick Bissell, it is the first—the one that fills his mind with intimations of dark opportunity. Fernando Bujones mimes in such splendid isolation, slipping from one diagrammatic pose to another, never taking a step without stretching and arching his feet, that he appears cut off from the human society of the first act. In the second act, he seems to be actively seeking his destiny among the swans and the diversions of pure form. The meaning of this act is planted early in the ballet, in the Prince's relations with his court, and since only the barest essentials are delivered in A.B.T.'s staging, it must be the dancer who conveys the point. Bujones in *Swan Lake* is incapable of conveying anything outside the strict limits of dance, but I was surprised when McKenzie showed a similar incapacity. Surely, like Stretton, he could give us a Sleeping Prince who wakes up.*

Bissell's exhilarating performances could scarcely have been predicted a year ago. With its large-scale naturalness and ease of expression, his dancing was always one of the great sights in classical ballet, but was inclined to be lazy; now it has a new spring and tautness. His acting has acquired depth. Bissell's Siegfried is a high-spirited, democratic prince. He runs on, full of life, protests when his tutor curtsies, grins at the girls, is devout toward his mother, charming to everyone, interested in all that happens. With the crossbow, he seizes control of his fate and for a moment stares into the heart of his mystery. In the second act, his attention shifts from his mystery to Odette's. Her powerlessness brings out his strength; he swears his fidelity, and the gesture is done almost gaily, against the grain of solemn circumstance. In the third act, when he is rude to the princesses

---

* *Postscript 1987*: McKenzie did wake up. He is now one of the company's most authoritative performers of *danseur noble* roles.

(an intrusive note in this production), he is clearly not himself. So much sunny good health and likability should be cloying, but Bissell's golden disposition is as transparently real as his dancing. And he shows no intention of letting audiences spoil him. He never makes a bid, through exaggerated bravura effects, for applause. Too good to be true? One might believe so, except that at his side in *Swan Lake* he had the equally restrained, wonderfully accomplished young French dancer Magali Messac. Messac's Odette-Odile had impressed me earlier, when she danced it opposite Stretton; opposite Bissell she reached a new peak in her career.

Messac's technique is not brilliant, but it is precise. Indeed, I know of no other dancer who combines precision and clarity of nuance with the lambent grace of Magali Messac. Like the great Russo-European ballerinas who once came among us with their lovely feet, their womanly sensuosity, their unstraining sophistication of style, Messac is really very simple and direct. There is nothing excessive in those subtle and fluent details of hers, which color her movement like so many grace notes. When, in the white adagio, she turns toward her prince and pauses in passé on point, the turn and the pause flow into and out of each other: the line flows through the curve of the indented shoulder, the peak of the knee, and the arch of the foot in one sinuous gesture. In the black adagio—adagio is Messac's nature—Odile is soft, so soft that the twisting, violent en-dedans spins between her partner's hands stand out as near-naked moments of force, a baring of fangs rather than a display of technique. For all her fine detail, Messac is a big dancer—big in scale and in spirit. She and Bissell are well matched. Bissell partnered her, and Paul Connelly conducted, with the sympathy that they habitually extend to every ballerina. Still, one couldn't help feeling that Messac had inspired them both. In an age of perilous extremes, she represents the triumph of temperance and just proportions. She avoids the broad slowing down and speeding up of tempos which have distorted other Odettes. (Makarova's legacy, licentiously wielded this season by Makarova herself, hangs heavy over the ballet.) She eschews the swami exit in the second act, which customarily brings down the house, and in the third act, against the tricks and tactics of other ballerinas, she defends the rule of taste.

Susan Jaffe's début as the Swan Queen was an occasion I should like to have applauded, because Jaffe is very young and very American and physically a perfect-looking catalyst for the infusion of the Kirov style. But the débutante was technically immature, with a short range in adagio. She phrased mechanically and mimed on the beat. Jaffe has a striking figure, long legs, an easy open hip, and, below the waist, a clean style; she needs developing if she is not to freeze at a pictorial level of perfection. Baryshnikov has brought her and Robert La Fosse along at the same pace. Technically more expansive than Jaffe, La Fosse is a now-you-see-it-now-you-don't dancer. He has an inertness that can appear lyrical, an opacity that can register as force. I'm afraid I find him something of a cipher, in standard roles as well as new ones.

One of the new pieces, *Great Galloping Gottschalk* (an odd title for a ballet that does not celebrate the composer), looks as though it had been commissioned with orders to play up the younger talent in the company. The choreographer, Lynne Taylor-Corbett, has arranged a suite of dances around such appealing stereotypes as the Tender Lovers, the Woman Alone, and Madcaps (of both sexes). The audience is told just how to look at everybody; outside of that the ballet seems to have no purpose. It adds nothing to what we may already know of the dancers from their appearances in other ballets; Lise Houlton has her tragic distinction, and Danilo Radojevic and Johan Renvall are a pair of crowd-pleasing acrobats, and so on. When the casting is blank, there's not enough going on in the choreography to have an impact. As performed by Jaffe and La Fosse, the little bits of "amusing" fustian that are knitted into the young-lovers pas de deux—bits like the hooking of arms as in a champagne toast—are hardly noticeable, and if you do notice them they're likely to seem an aberration. These hints of an atmosphere may have been intended to invoke something of Gottschalk's period, but the atmosphere isn't sustained in the rest of the ballet. The two roisterers danced by Radojevic and Renvall are conceived in roguish Russian-peasant style, the Two Ivans. And the other "characters," from Houlton's indecisive loner to a giggly trio of girls, are in a slick modern-dance idiom too far below the dancers' capacities. *Great Galloping Gottschalk* is also not great enough for the Met stage. If there is to be a new generation of stars at Ballet Theatre, it needs to be challenged in serious roles on an appropriate scale. I expect the forthcoming production of Merce Cunningham's *Duets* to serve the dancers better on both counts.

—*May 24, 1982*

The Return of the Shades

The Palais des Congrès, at the wrong end of the Bois de Boulogne, is where the airport buses drop their passengers. Above the garages are dozens of shiny boutiques where no one shops; outside are high-rise hotels and office blocks, glass and concrete, dust and desolation. Neither urbia nor suburbia, it's the worst possible introduction to Paris. The Palais also houses the largest theatre—around four thousand seats—in the city. Here, since April 17th, the Kirov Ballet, from Leningrad, has been performing *Swan Lake* and *Giselle* and *Chopiniana* and *La Sylphide*, among other works, on a stage too wide and shallow and to the accompaniment of its own excellent orchestra, which has to be miked. The palatial bleakness, to New Yorkers, recalls the Uris or the Felt Forum. It was strange to be in Paris seeing the ballet at such a place, but the Kirov, with its reputation for bureaucratic intrigue surpassing even that of the Opéra, and with its recent history of scandals and defections, is hardly a distraction from negative modern realities. Things have been pretty quiet since the Panov affair; nevertheless, the company has not ventured in force to any Western capital but Paris since 1970, when it last appeared in London. The Mitterrand government is hospitable, and the company enjoys a lively trade with French ballet—Béjart and Petit for productions of Petipa. Even so, a two-month engagement in Paris is being sustained at half strength; not all the dancers who were announced for the season have appeared, and some who have been left at home are said to be among the most interesting the company has recently developed. Pro-Solidarity demonstrations disrupted the opening-night performance of *Swan Lake*; leafleteers from Amnesty International have kept up a nightly vigil. But there is no feeling of unrest around the company. Outsiders are welcome to observe classes in the large rehearsal rooms below the theatre; interviews are freely granted. Perhaps the remoteness of the neighborhood—remote from the heart of Paris as well as from points East—makes this possible.

How long it has been since the Kirov was seen in New York was borne in on me by a single event: the discovery of a new and gifted young ballerina, who was only three years old when the last New York season took place, in 1964. But this discovery did not dominate my impressions of the company, for the simple reason that the newcomer was not starred in Paris. Altinay Asylmuratova was a name that was spoken—or, more often, misspoken. Other ballerinas were having their day. Barring this one revelation, and the disappointment of seeing two Kirov monuments crumble—the Shades scene and the *Paquita* divertissement—I found the company much as I had remembered it. It is a great company afflicted by isolation. Even in the sixties, it had a tendency to be narrowly ingrown. That tendency has not been remedied by the relatively enlightened policies of the current artistic director, Oleg Vinogradov. Russia is a closed society. Vinogradov may take Western ballets in; he may not let dancers out. Although it is difficult to judge the company's condition on nine performances in a foreign city, the lack of a true contemporary direction was painfully evident. There was no good modern choreography. The swans swam in stagnant waters. The genius of the company lay in its Romantic revivals. But all this was true two decades ago. I make my report, the rest of which will appear next week, hoping that the Kirov's dancers will one day soon see New York again. They need us as much as we need them.

May 26th and 27th. The great revelation of the Kirov's first Western tours, in the early sixties, was the Shades scene from *La Bayadère*. It changed our notion of the Petipa corps de ballet from that of a decorative frame for the principals to that of a participant in the action. In the single-file entrance of the corps and in its ensuing communal rites, Petipa is closer to the true eschatological spectacle of the Romantic ballet than he is thirteen years later in the Vision scene of *The Sleeping Beauty*. Compared with the former ballet, the Vision scene is inspired pastiche—a vision of a vision, like Fokine's *Chopiniana*. The impact of the Kirov's *Bayadère* scene on New Yorkers was of something immemorial; ghosts walked, dead bones rose and sang. I remember the audience in shock at the old Met. I also seem to remember that after we had seen Rudolf Nureyev's staging for the Royal Ballet the Kirov's seemed less wonderful. Nureyev had introduced an exaggerated slow tempo, which raised the hypnotic ritual to a stupor of excitement; he had arranged a more splendid coda and finale. I have not seen this production for some time (Nureyev has recently revived it in London), but Natalia Makarova's staging for American Ballet Theatre is also exaggeratedly slow. The ideal opening tempo is probably somewhere between this and the unwontedly brisk pace at which the Kirov dancers descended the ramp in Paris. To be sure, there were thirty-two of them to be got on, but there was not safety in numbers. Despite the faster clip, quite a few of the protracted balances were seen to wobble. In the subsequent dances, brisk became brusque. The three soloists barrelled through their variations. Olga Chenchikova and, on the following night, Elena Evteyeva picked distractedly at the ballerina role, as if they could afford not to maximize its opportunities; they chewed gristle and threw away meat. The role of Nikiya is not glorious: the two adagios run together make up a blurry image, and the variations contain no felicities of invention comparable to the soloist variations. Nikiya is a hollow assignment that needs to be filled by an adagio technician with some—not too much—allegro twinkle. The contrasts in the role are arrived at through a difference in rhythm. The Kirov ballerinas apply a difference of attack. They are legato technicians, and very monotonous about it, too. Evteyeva, less powerful than Chenchikova, is technically more finely bred. Chenchikova has been spoken of as the company's great new classicist. In the linked adagios, I see a monolithic kind of grandeur but no discernment. In the slow variation that ends in an allegro flourish, instead of lightening or softening her tone she just switches gears. Both women are partnered by Eldar Aliev, who does not dance a solo. It strikes me that the Russians have seen the slightness of the ballerina role and sought to disguise it by suppressing the male variation (which was Chabukiani's interpolation anyway—not *echt* Petipa). The stratagem doesn't work. The remedy for a weak Nikiya is a strong dancer.

A set of modern works comes next. The Kirov is not the first classical company to mistake its direction in contemporary choreography, but it may be the first to base its mistake on the assumption that "classical" and "contemporary" are con- tradictions. There is not the slightest sense of form in two pieces by Boris Eifmann, a young house choreographer—not even the elementary form that orders our sensations so that we may perceive shape, continuity, consequence. About all that's distinguishable is genre. A *Deux Voix* is a porno pas de deux; *Adagio* is one of those nameless-terror pieces in which a sinister group disgorges a soloist, lets him emote nakedly for an hour or two, and returns to pick him up. It is conceivable that a Russian audience sees meaning in these works—sees, for example, a victory over officialdom in the blatant sexuality of the pas de deux and its use of the music of Pink Floyd. And maybe in Russia real feelings are aroused by *Adagio*, and its terror is not nameless after all. I prefer to think that these gratifications exist despite the work and not because of it. Was any good cause ever served by bad art? Eifmann seems to have taken Béjart as his model. In the pas de deux, Galina Mezentseva reproduces to uncomfortable perfection the look of a libidinous hornet which is a specialty of Béjart's danseuses, and in *Adagio* Evgeny Neff dances his Jorge Donn–like role with more conviction than absolutely necessary. Two of Béjart's own works, *Webern Opus 5* and *Bhakti*, are also danced, and are actually made to look good—better, that is, than Béjart's own dancers can make them. In *Webern Opus 5*, Chenchikova wears a white unitard, revealing her retracted pelvis, which diminishes the power of her thighs and makes her upper and lower body look tenuously connected. Chenchikova is scrupulously careful about her footwork, and once you get used to the odd line of her neck and shoulders and her jutting head, which is a Kirov trait, she is also very striking in épaulement. But I find her plastically inexpressive, with no flow-through to relate and enliven the various poses and steps she executes perfectly; she's like a singer with perfect pitch who hasn't learned to project a melody. Instead of fluency, Chenchikova uses the cascading legato she used in the Shades scene. Again, it is attack doing the work of rhythm. But *is* it attack? Is it legato or lethargy?

The most puzzling item on this mixed bill is *Variations on a Theme of the Thirties*, a miniature by another Kirov choreographer, Dmitri Briantsev. The music is by Shostakovich—the light Shostakovich of the ballet scores, which were indeed written in the thirties and denounced for their decadence. Fyodor Lopukhov, one of Shostakovich's choreographers, became an unperson. Later, Lopukhov reflected bitterly, "The thirties were a turning point not only for my personal fate but in the life of Soviet ballet." He meant by that the sanctions imposed by the government on all forms of artistic expression not in line with Socialist realism. Briantsev's little ballet is untranslatable; the two characters, who appear to be a peasant and his girl, may recall a period when lighthearted folkloric comedies were popular and the collective farms could be satirized, as in the Shostakovich-Lopukhov *Bright Stream*. But Briantsev's comic style is in the leaden tradition of Soviet kitsch; the boy is lunkish, the girl a doll-faced twit, and what we are to make of their dancing—their lunging tangos, the grands jetés that he performs while gripping the forward ankle, her incessant pas courus—is never clear.

The portion of the program called "Chorégraphies Anciennes" introduces another puzzle—the everlastingly inscrutable Petipa legacy. There are three Petipa fragments that I have never before seen the Kirov perform: "Grand Pas Classique" from *Carnival in Venice*, to Paganini's music arranged by Pugni; "Pas de Six" from *Esmeralda*, to Drigo's score; and "Divertissement" from *Paquita*, which is almost as renowned a Kirov specialty as "The Shades," and which also has a Minkus score. The program states whose version of Petipa we are seeing in each case, and that is a big help. Agrippina Vaganova, though, is given sole credit for the *Esmeralda* excerpt; Petipa's name doesn't appear at all. This may be true to the facts of authorship; nevertheless, Vaganova's *Esmeralda* turns out to be the most persuasively *ancienne* of all the relics, and the most like Petipa in both shape and substance. But before buckling down to these matters we are given the pleasure of seeing Irina Kolpakova perform with Sergei Berezhnoy a little pas de deux from Offenbach's *Le Papillon* arranged by Pierre Lacotte. Kolpakova's only appearances this season have been in the Romantic revivals and pastiches of the repertory. In her late age—she is now fifty—she has become the queen of sylphs; her grand impalpable style has never seemed more secure. Kolpakova does not offer us illusion in place of a technique that she no longer possesses; she offers us the mysterious extension of that illusion which her technique has always sought to fulfill, even at its height. When Kolpakova lands from a grand jeté and throws up her back leg to make us think she has jumped higher we are instantly pleased by the illusion, and we don't think of the jumping she used to do twenty years ago. Now, as then, the separate facets of her technique are precisely in scale one to another. Like Ulanova at the same age, Kolpakova makes you concentrate on what she does, not on what she doesn't do. She judges every effect, and yet she doesn't shrink or fake in the interests of "style"—she appears to dance with the freedom of the day she was born. Kolpakova refreshes my faith in Kirov ballerina style and its possibilities of expression. The generation just below her—the one that startled New York—is dispersed (Natalia Makarova) or unrepresented in Paris (Alla Sizova, Gabriela Komleva). Evteyeva and Natalia Bolshakova (whom we saw in *Bhakti*) are younger still, and retain some of the qualities of training and expression of their predecessors. But between this level and the next there seems to be a wide gap. The airy flickering variety of Kolpakova and the workmanlike precision of Chenchikova have nothing detectable in common. In an adagio, Kolpakova seems to float; Chenchikova works with mass, volume, cantilevered weight. I suppose there is room for both. But not in my heart.

"Grand Pas Classique" gives us still another of the current ballerinas—Svetlana Efremova, who is all candy floss. I find that by the end of the excerpt she has given me a toothache. Or maybe it's the howlers in the choreography—the ugly anachronistic lifts, the coy and unseemly recapitulations of Aurora's dances in *The Sleeping Beauty*. It is not unlikely that Petipa repeated steps from role to role—all ballet masters do that. But to repeat himself unthinkingly—and to caricature himself—is the way not of a ballet master but of a confused regisseur hoping to recapture some lost essence and settling for literal repetition. (The revival is credited to Nadezha Kranocheyeva.) When Efremova does her variation, four men with lutes appear behind her, recalling not only the four suitors who partner Aurora in the Rose Adagio but also the four friends with lutes who in some productions become involved with the suitors. In "Grand Pas Classique," nobody becomes involved with anybody; the men do some double air turns and that's that. The giveaway is that the music is in fours: would Petipa have passed up such an opportunity? And in the units of choreography you can see double fours repatterned meaninglessly as strings of eights.

A corrective comes in the very next number—*Esmeralda*. Vaganova may have designed it, but she built upon Petipa just as surely as Petipa built upon Perrot (and Saint-Léon and Mazilier and Taglioni). The pas de six is, like the Rose Adagio, a pas d'action. The heroine, partnered by a man she does not love, must dance for the man whom she loves and has lost. Petipa, having made his dance for Virginia Zucchi, demanded of Kchessinskaya, who coveted the role, "You love? You suffer?" The story is drawn from Hugo's *Notre-Dame de Paris*. Esmeralda, the street dancer, is partnered by Gringoire. Not Hugo but Drigo is responsible for the chorus of gypsy girls who dance a perkily irrelevant pas de quatre. (These semi-detached female foursomes—Drigoettes?—turn up also in *Harlequinade* as staged by Balanchine and *The Magic Flute* as staged by Peter Martins.) The high point is the pas de deux, in which Esmeralda's heartbreak, her faltering courage, and, finally, her unquenchable high spirits and love of dancing are depicted. Tambourines, which are played by all hands, are woven into the emotional fabric of the dance. In the pas de deux, a tambourine held over the heroine's head becomes a token of the enforced levity that draws her onward. She grasps the tambourine (arms en haut), bends low in arabesque, and, in a gesture of pride and submission, completes the adagio in a long slow penchée promenade. In the variation, she reaches a peak of euphoria—only to end slumped in dejection. Yes, what a role. And what a dancer. This is Asylmuratova (Ah-sill-moor-*ah*-to-va), and until this moment I had never heard of her, nor had I ever seen what she showed me: emotional highs and lows depicted with the unbroken tension of idyllic lyrical dancing. One doesn't know whether her impulse is musical or dramatic; the sense of consummation, of wholeness and richness, is there before you in everything she does. The other Kirov ballerinas dance on as large a scale, but they don't have her burning vitality or her musical momentum or her range. Asylmuratova can be huge, as in the yawning stretched-through arabesque allongée that she takes on entrance in *Esmeralda*. Or, slipping into épaulée attitude, she can show a delicious Kolpakova-like subtlety. (She slips the forward shoulder farther forward without strain or distortion.) She was born in Kazakhstan. Both her parents and both her mother's parents were dancers, and she was brought up in theatres, which may account for her near-atavistic sense of drama. She began her training at the Kirov school at the age of ten and joined the company at seventeen. Vinogradov predicted jokingly that she would dance *Swan Lake* her first year in the company; her début came this year. In Paris, the week before I arrived, she danced *Swan Lake* unscheduled; it was her second performance of Odette-Odile. Olivier Merlin filed a dithyramb in *Le Monde*, comparing her to Makarova and going on about her Greek nose, cherry mouth, and Circassian sloe eyes. She also had the most gently curved bosom, voluptuous arms, long legs, and the loveliest feet in the world. To people who had not seen her, it sounded like a grab for attention on behalf of a company whose ballerinas up to now had not thrilled Paris. But Asylmuratova is the real thing. And she is a great beauty. I saw her give her Esmeralda performance again; the second time she was slightly broader and twice as wonderful. She was also one of the fiancées in the ballroom act of *Swan Lake*, and she appeared in the corps of *Chopiniana* and *La Sylphide*. That was all I saw of her. In his review, Merlin said that rapid promotion of young dancers is unusual at the Kirov. It isn't in the case of unusual talent. Makarova danced Giselle and Sizova Aurora at twenty-one. But I agree that Asylmuratova is the most prodigiously endowed ballerina the Kirov has shown us in twenty years.

Vinogradov restaged the *Paquita* excerpt, which was danced before a drop

53

portraying the audience at the Maryinsky in the eighteen-eighties. The variations (except the ballerina's) were deleted, the man's role was reduced to partnering, and the "chorale" pas de deux, in which the ballerina's supported poses are echoed and complemented by the unsupported poses of the corps, was as evasively presented as it was in the Makarova version given in New York two years ago. I suspect the great aesthetic divide between Kirov and Western style is over the question of adagio. What the Kirov dances in this *Paquita* pas de deux is not what we would call an adagio—that is, a connected succession of slow movements; it is a succession of fast movements performed in a slow tempo. The time between movements is either filled in with poses until the music catches up or bridged by legato leakages that do not sustain connections so much as they avoid posing. It may be that Petipa's point was to show precisely the difference between dancing and changing poses when he set supported and unsupported versions of the same steps. Whatever he intended, there is little substance here. The confusions in the Makarova version, which was said to derive from the Kirov, tended to diminish the stature of the ballerina. Here she dominates. But, as in "The Shades," she does so at the expense of the other roles. Chenchikova danced with overwhelming strength and authority—especially in her solo, when she knocked off high-attitude en-dedans spins that ended in perfectly controlled hopping arabesques. In the coda, she started turning her fouettés with a triple. I think I see what others mean by calling her a classicist—it's her impeccability in the execution of steps. Tatiana Terekhova, who also danced *Paquita*, is even cleaner than Chenchikova and to my eye more comfortably centered. Unfortunately, she has a hard stage face. One can see the importance of these dancers in the development of Kirov ballerina technique. The great promise of Asylmuratova rests in the fact that she's not a throwback; she incorporates the Chenchikova strain and loops it back to Kolpakova, if not all the way back to Zucchi. —*June 21, 1982*

The Kirov Abroad, Stravinsky at Home

Palais des Congrès, Paris; May 28th, 29th, and 30th: To anyone who has seen American Ballet Theatre's *Swan Lake* recently, the Kirov production is not eccentric. Except in the overture, which begins in a long-drawn-out moan of anguish, the tempos are not slower; they're only *as* slow, and often they're faster. The action is tautly paced; the peak is reached in the last act. Oleg Vinogradov has supervised a freshened version of the Konstantin Sergeyev production that has served the company since the fifties. Igor Ivanov has dressed it well: the swans as they cross the lake are reflected in deep-blue water; the throne room has stone

Gothic arches and tapestries; everywhere, there is light and space. I would like to see the *Sleeping Beauty* that this designer could do. The costumes, by G. Solovieva, are unaffectedly beautiful, with mild references to early German Renaissance painting. (A.B.T.'s late-German Holbein-and-Brueghel look is too plummy.) The show opens badly, with a dozen courtiers doing sautés to the pantomime march, but this is not to be a series of scènes dansantes, like the Bolshoi production. Indeed, one of the most attractive aspects of this *Swan Lake* is its traditionalism; it even eliminates the Prince's slow variation with the crossbow, which years ago the Kirov introduced. The intrusive jester is still there, performing his misshapen grande pirouette after the hazing of the tutor. Of course, there is no Benno, no speech by the Princess Mother about choosing a wife, and no organized hunt. The big ensembles in the first act are both performed by nobles (no peasants) in a sprightly, small-stepping style that suggests sixteenth-century court dance. In the pas de trois, the man's solo opens with three sissonnes battues facing the downstage corner; Evgeny Neff, who danced in all three performances, had to adjust his tombé landing each time. The steps done at A.B.T., no less awkward, are in fact the opening steps of the Third Shade's variation at the Kirov. Wires are constantly crossing in Petipa revivals. Sometimes the crossing is deliberate, like the attitude balance that the Kirov's Odette takes standing on the Prince's thigh at the end of the coda. This is a vestige of the Benno version of the pas de deux; the customary high lift has been transferred by the Kirov to the end of the Black Swan pas de deux. Ah, the fascination of dull detail! The pas de trois, however, is a true mystery. The Kirov attributes it to Petipa, which makes nonsense of Nicholas Sergeyev's claim to have obtained his quite different version—the version adopted by the Royal Ballet—from Stepanov's notation of Petipa. The Kirov program book for the Paris season credits the separate scenes and numbers of *Swan Lake*; Petipa turns out to have contributed two dances—the pas de trois and a mazurka—and part of the Odile-Siegfried pas de deux. A Pavlova exhibition currently at the bookshop La Danse, on the Rue de Beaune, shows a program for a Pavlova performance at Tsarskoye Selo, one of the imperial summer residences, which lists among excerpts from the ballroom scene a "pas d'action" for Odile, Siegfried, Benno, and Rothbart. If this was Petipa's work, when and by whom was the pas de deux constructed? The Kirov credits as the other choreographers Agrippina Vaganova and K. Sergeyev, but the pas de deux, eliminating Benno and most of Rothbart, existed before their time.

These questions would be irrelevant if *Swan Lake* in all its parts and as a whole functioned as well as *Giselle* and *The Sleeping Beauty*. It has come down to us a patchwork, and a patchwork it will probably always be. The Kirov version is the smoothest that one can see; the power of it keeps rising all evening long. The national dances are not a boring interlude before the pas de deux; taken at a tearing pace, they are performed with devotion, and even pleasure. These dances have long been a point of pride with the Kirov, as has the work of the corps in the swan scenes. Kirov swans are more elegant than Bolshoi swans; no other swan corps I know is comparable. The Russian companies possess a collective style for *Swan Lake* which has existed as long as the ballet has. While I admire the Kirov's style as sheer accomplishment, I don't find the emphasis of it very appealing. At the heart of the style is timing. The whole company, from ballerinas down to littlest cygnets, dances a beat behind the orchestra. But this first point of connection to a phrase of music may also be the last. It's as if correct execution of a step mattered more than musical transparency. The efforts of dancers and orchestra to get together take certain ritualistic forms. The orchestra often slows down the end of a number. Odette's variation is played as well as danced legato. But the fidgeting of the corps as it forms up in this act is musically inexcusable—who cares whether they stand pointe tendue back or front? None of the three ballerinas I saw—Olga Chenchikova, Tatiana Terekhova, Galina Mezentseva—was able to make the stylistic prerogatives lovely. (Right behind them were eight young demi-soloists any one of whom might have done the job.) The corps was best in the last act, performing its grand-scale orchestrations of Lev Ivanov's themes. At the end of the Valse Bluette, the dancers walk toward the audience in ranks, their arms around each other's waists, and there is a slowing down that, for once, has a real effect. The Russian dance historian Yuri Slonimsky has described it:

> *Their walk becomes slower and slower until, in accordance with the last measures of the dying-down music, the group of black swans stops on its last drawn-out step, as if throwing to the auditorium a whispered "All has ended."*

Unfortunately, all hasn't; Soviet custom still requires the tearing off of the sorcerer's wing and the lovers united in life.

If I haven't mentioned the men of the company, it's because up to now they haven't done much. In truth, they're not asked to do more than partner, perform their solos in an appropriate style, and, in general, present a good appearance. Sergei Berezhnoy in *Le Papillon*, *Swan Lake*, and *La Sylphide*, Vladimir Petronin in *Paquita* and *Swan Lake*, Vladimir Bondarenko in *Chopiniana*, Eldar Aliev in "The Shades" and *Esmeralda* (also a good Rothbart), and one or two others, whose names in last-minute loudspeaker announcements were unclear to me, did all they were asked. Kirov men are not as rigorously trained as the women. The technical precision of a Nureyev, a Baryshnikov, a Yuri Soloviev is not emulated, though the Baryshnikov "look"—boyish, tousled, angelic—is still popular. Konstantin Zaklinsky took many of the leading roles, and it is easy to see why: he is tall, with exceptionally long and handsome legs, and with some of the Rudi-Misha magnetism. In modern roles, he has a feral power, but in the classics his dancing and deportment are unpolished. Valery Emets is an evidently important dancer whom I didn't get to see enough of. Neff, on the other hand, was all over the place. A rising young man, he looks as if he hadn't the energy to rise much farther. Limpness, translated into Romantic lassitude, was his main quality as Albrecht in *Giselle*.

June 1st: The company has an excellent character dancer in Vadim Gulyayev, whose serenity at the center of Vinogradov's ballet on Gogol's *The Inspector General* was very nearly heroic. The piece is a whirlwind of unrealized conceptions or else of realizations—such as the use of dancers in paper costumes to represent currency or letters—that should never have been conceived. Ninel Kurgapkina, who will be remembered from the American tours, and Natalia Bolshakova appeared as comic ladies, and there was an enormous cast of stomping, storming, reeling, prancing, and mincing actor-dancers in grotesque makeup. I admire Vinogradov's effort to reintroduce narrative into Russian ballet without resorting either to standard mime or to currently popular all-dance formulas. But he chose an impossible vehicle. Words or some form of linguistic expression is essential to *The Inspector General*. Vinogradov may have suspected as much when he constructed the "conversation" in which Gulyayev and another dancer hurl syllables like "ah-*hah*, ah-*hee*" at each other.

June 2nd: *Chopiniana, La Sylphide*. Less than a week *chez* Kirov, and I have fallen into the company's thought patterns. Romantic ballet is one style, classical is another. *Chopiniana, La Sylphide*, and *Giselle* are Romantic; *La Bayadère* is Petipa, hence classical. Whatever they mean by these categories, there is no question that Romantic ballet is home to Kirov dancers. *Chopiniana*, the Fokine pastiche of Romanticism that we know as *Les Sylphides*, is every bit as wonderful as I had remembered. The tempos do not drag; the performance—*spirituel*, not soulful—is vibrant with belief, fantasy, fun. Elena Evteyeva gives her liveliest performance of the week in the mazurka and the waltz pas de deux. A kind of pantomimic suggestiveness lies beneath the skin of these dances. Elena Kondratyenko in the prelude and Tamara Mirzoyan in the waltz brought it out. Would that I could have photographed it and taken it home to Ballet Theatre. Bondarenko's performance had some of the insularity that has long disturbed me in Nureyev's (why do they stand there gazing into their armpit while bien-aimée is dancing?), but I liked his vigor.

Vinogradov was right to acquire the Bournonville *La Sylphide* instead of Pierre Lacotte's mishmash of Taglioni. Apart from a tendency to mime too forcefully, the company's behavior is charmingly correct, and it dances as well as it does in anything else. The production, staged after a version by Elsa-Marianne von Rosen, has been tailored here and there to local taste; if it is un-Danish, it is never dull. Irina Kolpakova's dancing ripples with wit, and the sylphs, more impish than their Danish sisters, are adorable. There are four demis, led by one who in her solo takes some inappropriate développé-balances à la seconde. The program identifies her as Olga Likhovskaya, tomorrow night's Giselle.

· · ·

June 3rd: Olga Likhovskaya turns out to be somebody else. The question is: Just who is she? This is the most boring Giselle I have ever seen, and it's opposite the most anemic Albrecht—Neff. Likhovskaya is young and pretty; she doesn't have the harridan look of Terekhova or Mezentseva or the glacial moon face of Chenchikova. But she has no conception of Giselle beyond the one that seems to have been handed to her, like a text, to study and master. The Kirov ballerinas are apparently expected to play their roles according to a set interpretation; even where you think the flash and fire of individuality could hardly be avoided, they are all alike. I saw three different Odiles stamped from the same mold. And you think of Makarova confined in this prison and then escaping to cut and polish numberless facets of the one or two gems in her native repertory. Likhovskaya is a good girl who has been to Giselle school. In the second act, she takes the damnable legato phrasing so seriously she seems to be moving under water. Well, no matter: the production is marvellous—not in Act I, which plods and temporizes, but in Act II. Let me add one more qualification: what's marvellous is the corps. Giselle originally had two choreographers: Perrot is thought to have done Giselle's dances and her pas de deux with Albrecht; Coralli is generally credited with the Wilis and all that end of things. In Russia, Petipa overhauled the whole ballet, and through the ages it went on being subtly redesigned until it became what it usually is today—a star vehicle, with the roles of Myrta and the Wilis scaled down to a supporting chorus. The Kirov production, which might be called "Coralli's Revenge," restores Myrta and, even more impressively, the Wilis to full dimension. When the Giselle and Albrecht are as uninteresting as they are tonight, the performance can still offer excitement in the staging of the Wilis' dances: in the ghostly materialization out of the night mist of Myrta, in the equally ghostly materialization of the corps, which appears halfway out of the wings wearing bridal veils and pauses there as the veils are whooshed away—an effect accomplished without raising the laugh that has caused it to be deleted from Western productions. (It's a matter of timing; the Kirov also manages a dignified introduction for its dummy Swan Queen at the start of the lakeside scene.) Then there is the excitement of the big waltz over consecrated ground which prepares Giselle's entrance, followed by the concerted sweep of the dances that ensnare first Hilarion and then Albrecht in their fatal web. The diabolical choral symmetry of the choreography is thrilling to behold on the wide stage of the Palais des Congrès. Thirty Wilis, each with an obdurate shoulder, compose a diagonal line as solid as an executioner's wall. And the dramatic sense of the choreography is carried out in the "dialogue" between the principals and the corps. Albrecht is directed to his doom not just by Myrta but by all the Wilis; the slow half turn that waves him up the line is a turn through the shoulder. Then, as Giselle appears, running down the line, it re-forms itself in reverse, as if it had changed its mind. In the Hilarion episode, the corps masses behind him doing fouettés sautés in arabesque, which he clumsily tries to approximate; as in no other production, we actually see the Wilis compelling his moves, and when he collapses and they add the upflung arm that completes the step (we have already seen it in the waltz) it's like a cry of victory.

Some flying effects at the start of the act don't quite work. After her materialization out of the dark, Myrta vanishes, to be flown by wire across the back of the stage; later, when she appears to Albrecht, Giselle is flown in the opposite direction. Likhovskaya and Neff, for all their dullness, manage a persuasive set of apparitions, most effectively climaxed by her launching herself into the slow lift that coincides with the repeat in the melody. Other Kirov touches are traditional—Giselle leaning from her bower to rain lilies on Albrecht's head or reclining in his arms as he carries her tenderly away from the grave. There are some parts of the *Giselle* canon to which the Kirov gives peculiar emphasis. The Wilis, stationed on the sidelines, constantly change their stance, like sentinels, but in one such change they repeat the pas de bourrée from their big dance, unsettling, then resettling, then re-unsettling themselves in a way that looks crazed with exhaustion. Why this restless flexing and shifting of the feet should have expressive effect in *Giselle* when a similar fidgeting in *Swan Lake* has none is something to puzzle over. But then a far greater puzzle is the disparity between the two ballets as the Kirov performs them. *Swan Lake*, for all its handsomeness as a production, is dead—dead in its dance core—and *Giselle* is alive.

June 4th: All Kirov ballerinas are equal, but Mezentseva is more equal than others. Her head juts out farther, her tempos are slower, her legato is gummier than anybody else's. In this *Giselle*, as in her *Swan Lake*, she turns adagio into largo; even her mad scene is slow. In Act II, her points, which seem arched only from the metatarsus down, dig into the stage like claws. But Mezentseva puts on a big face, *souffrant* and semi-blind, and wins big applause. Those feet of hers are an extreme version of the inflexible pointwork one occasionally sees in the corps. One sees, too, consistently bumpy relevés, nothing like the smooth rolling up to or down from point which American dancers cultivate. The "sick" feet may be part of what I love in the *Giselle* corpswork and reject in *Swan Lake*. On second thought—tonight brings me a second thought—the big difference may be in the music. The orchestra produces more emotion in the mad scene than the dancers do. In the second act, it works hand in glove with the corps. The emotion is enormous—Tchaikovskyan. But the corps and the orchestra that carry *Giselle* lag and drag and natter when it comes to the tempos and rhythms of *Swan Lake*. In the second act, they give you the feeling that they want it as much like *Giselle* as possible. The way everybody hits the waltz phrase—with a retard, with a lurch, with a swoon—looks quaint, and quaintness is not the most desirable characteristic in *Swan Lake*. *La Sylphide*, with its charming, tractable score, by Løvenskjold, can aspire to the condition of *Giselle*, but *Swan Lake* is musically light-years beyond them both. Slonimsky, who, along with Vinogradov, was responsible for the present production of *Giselle*, has written books on all three of these ballets which undoubtedly provide clues to their treatment by the Kirov, but the books have yet to be translated.

Performance tradition is so strong in the indisputable masterpiece of the repertory that tonight the ballet again succeeds despite its cast. Zaklinsky plays Albrecht as a heedless, ardent boy; the caddish Albrecht of former days seems to have been banished. But although he performs earnestly, Zaklinsky really doesn't know how to give the role shape and stature. The peasant pas de deux is attractively performed on both nights by Irina Chistyakova, who was thanklessly cast in the Briantsev piece I mentioned last week. The better of her two partners, and one of the most elegant male soloists I have seen all week, is Andrei Garbuz. Why don't the Kirov dancers spot their turns? Tonight's Myrta, Olga Iskanderova, spins herself dizzy for lack of a spot. Jerome Robbins includes a joke about this habit of the Kirov in his *Other Dances*, made for Makarova and Baryshnikov. But without its crotchets the Kirov wouldn't be the Kirov. When a company has as much to show us as this one still has, crotchets can become as significant as any other element of style.

New York State Theater, June 10th: I imagine that nothing New York City Ballet does appears more inward and inexplicable to foreigners than its Stravinsky ballets. N.Y.C.B.'s main crotchets of style are in that Stravinsky beehive it keeps returning to, sometimes making honey, sometimes just buzzing around. This evening, the Stravinsky Centennial Celebration is inaugurated with two trumpeters playing the "Fanfare for a New Theatre," which was composed for the opening of the house, in 1964. Then Jerome Robbins leads on forty-eight little girls in his clever *Circus Polka*, and the orchestra plays *Fireworks*. Finally, the first new work—*Tango*, conceived by Balanchine with a laconic wit that the dancers, Karin von Aroldingen and Christopher d'Amboise, seem unable to get hold of. *Tango*, like *Circus Polka*, reflects Stravinsky the vaudevillian, and *Piano-Rag Music* (the ballets, as is the custom of this company, are named after their music) continues the theme. Peter Martins's choreography is a set of trim acrobatic configurations for Darci Kistler and four men. Kistler, in black satin and rhinestones and with her hank of blond hair swinging, is at her most buoyant and evocative. She reminds you of the intrepid heroines of the musclemen acts, but without the queasiness; she doesn't in the least mind being pulled and hauled about—she thrives on it (Kistler grew up with four brothers who were wrestlers) and gives it style. And, as always, Kistler's sense of style is not imitative; it's her own authentic invention. An amazing performer. Soon afterward—I keep to the premières on the program—Jacques d'Amboise's *Pastorale* re-presents Kistler effectively in quite different terms. But this brief lyrical pas de deux with Christopher d'Amboise might have more impact some other time; the Martins is a tough act to follow. John Taras's *Concerto for Piano and Wind Instruments* is his third and most successful treatment of this score. Its imagery recalls the first version, *Arcade* (1963), in its dual suggestion of the circus and the cloister. Kyra Nichols and Adam Lüders are a chaste couple in white, flanked by the profane forms of Wilhelmina Frankfurt, Peter Frame, and Mel Tomlinson. These three are actually among the lankiest and most llamalike dancers in the company; watching them career through Taras's stride-stretch-strut ensemble sections is a pleasure, like watching an unusually well-matched precision drill team.

June 11th: *Noah and the Flood*. In 1962, much publicity surrounded the collaboration of Stravinsky and Balanchine on a work commissioned by CBS Television. *The Flood*, as it was then called, was billed as a "dance-drama." Staged tonight, in scenery and costumes by the original designer, Rouben Ter-Arutunian, it is much more a drama-oratorio with incidental action and one dance. This dance, a convoluted corps-de-ballet number, is recognizably Balanchinean, but it is unrecognizable as the descriptive action that the scenario identifies as "The Building of the Ark." (Stravinsky wrote that he had visualized the builders as dancers—"the men pulling over their shoulders on imaginary ropes, the women bending, tugging, dragging." Balanchine seems to have cocked an ear and visualized pure-dance scintillation.) The Flood itself, in which some dancers roll invisibly under a black sheet while others are carried along on top of it, is the only passage with the kind of faux-naïf fantasy that Stravinsky appears to have had in mind. The other bits of action, which involve Adam and Eve, Lucifer as a scorpion and then as a thirty-foot serpent, and Noah and his family, who wear dummy heads and mime dialogue spoken by the narrator (John Houseman), do not require the services of a choreographer. Nor does the parade of the animals to the Ark, which is rendered here not by dancers but by dancers carrying cutouts of animals. Robert Craft conducts the performance, which includes members of the New York City Opera Chorus. The fragment called "The Building of the Ark" is reconstructed from CBS tapes, and is typical of Balanchine's serial-music period, which ran intermittently between 1957 and 1966.

June 12th: *Norwegian Moods*. New York City Ballet does not need to import Stravinsky ballets. This production of a Lew Christensen piece that was originally done for San Francisco Ballet salutes an old colleague who, forty-five years ago, was Balanchine's and Stravinsky's first American Apollo. *Norwegian Moods*, a pas de deux, also happens to be a good piece of choreography, structurally unorthodox, rhetorically inventive. Christensen hits off a skittish resemblance in the music to the bridal dances in *Le Baiser de la Fée*. The dancers, who perform glowingly, are Nichol Hlinka and N.Y.C.B.'s *Baiser* hero, Helgi Tomasson.

June 13th: *Elégie*, a viola solo, is danced by Suzanne Farrell alone, in a filmy white dress. Kneeling, she begins what appears to be a conventional dance of mourning but then turns into something unconventional, unforeseen, and perhaps, when it is given again, unrecapturable. Emotionally, the dance is not extreme; it is, for Farrell, rather quiet. And, because it describes a singular more than a general condition, it is also noncathartic; it leaves you hanging. *Elégie* could become a solo version of *Meditation*, which in the great performances Farrell used to give with Jacques d'Amboise was always a singular experience, different each time it was seen.

In *Concerto for Two Solo Pianos*, Peter Martins casts two male soloists—Ib Andersen and Jock Soto—against a female ensemble. If he had stopped there, he might have had an adequate mirror of the music. He might even have produced a copy of the Balanchine-Hindemith *Kammermusik No. 2*, with the ballerina and corps roles sexually reversed. Martins's *Concerto is* like *Kammermusik* in the close identification of the two male leads; they could be two aspects of one man as easily as two men. But Martins also casts Heather Watts between Andersen and Soto, and his use of her determines the shape of the whole ballet. This is the first time I can recall Martins making a ballet that was not exclusively, or even primarily, about its music. Perhaps I should except *Piano-Rag Music*; perhaps also *Calcium Light Night*, Martins's début as a choreographer. (*The Magic Flute*, a story ballet, is generically disqualified from the competition.) *Piano-Rag Music*, for all that it is an accomplished and charming piece of work, is only three minutes long. And if *Calcium Light Night* was about something more than Charles Ives's music, I don't think it was planned that way. The twenty-minute *Concerto* has a conscious dramatic subject, which it projects through the music—a very different thing from letting the music dictate what the drama will be. Watching the *Concerto*, you don't hear the music so much as absorb it. It makes exactly the right sound for every second of what you see, but you aren't directed to listen. Sight and sound come naturally and plausibly together.

This is an impressive advance for a New York City Ballet choreographer to have made, and from the evidence of his choreography I would guess that Martins knows he has made it. He pushes the drama all the way; he makes it uncomfortable for us. Not that it is comfortable to begin with. Here are the men in Stravinskyan split focus, there the tidily metrical, apian corps. Then Heather Watts walks on (shuffles on, really. Has any classical ballerina ever made an entrance like it?), and the drama immediately begins. The choreography for Watts both sums her up and explains her: it takes into account the thorniness that has made some people dislike her as well as the qualities of quick intelligence and serious dedication that have won her respect. Watts has worked very hard these past few years and progressed remarkably as a dancer, and it has changed her temper; she seems more open and genuine, happier to be right where she is, more obliging toward her audience. Yet she hasn't lost the almost bitter honesty that made her original indifference noticeable. Martins's ballet is in part about a destructive kind of honesty in the heroine. In a pas de deux with Andersen, Watts dances in a continual whorl of indecision; no move she makes looks wrong or bad, but she keeps on moving, keeps testing alternatives. You sense her outstripping the man— or his patience—and finally alienating him. A second pas de deux, with Soto, was less intricately fascinating in this première performance, and I am uncertain of the weight of the various solos in the piece as a whole. The female corps is both unnecessary and indispensable. Like the female corps in *Movements for Piano and Orchestra*, its function is to reflect and summarize aspects of the ballerina's role, and the ballerina's role, as Martins has understood it through Watts, is to illuminate a general condition through a process of self-exposure. In the *Concerto*, Watts projects the kind of tension that is felt today by many women. She becomes part of the spectacle of our world and time. The role makes her a star. This uneasy, brilliant ballet is the first substantial work of the Stravinsky Celebration.   —*June 28, 1982*

Names and Places

It is strange that New York, whose dancers are known and admired the world over, should have so few decent dance theatres. I'm made aware of this lack every spring when the School of American Ballet gives its workshop performances in the Juilliard Theater, in Lincoln Center. This small-scale opera house would be perfect for the dozens of little or medium-sized companies that the city has somehow given rise to, but it is unavailable to non-students (more specifically, to non-Juilliard-affiliated students). These companies will presumably find their long-sought showcase in the Joyce, which has just opened downtown. On a bigger scale, the best dance theatre in New York is the opera house at the Brooklyn Academy of Music. The same building contains an excellent small theatre, the Helen Carey Playhouse, and a forbiddingly commodious performing area called the Lepercq Space. (Though it was intended for dance, most companies get swallowed up by it.) The Academy has signed Twyla Tharp to a long-term residency; the arrangement should prove mutually advantageous. Dancers have managed to fit themselves into the swollen spectacle that is Lincoln Center, but it is a fact that both the main theatres there are too big for ballet. The Met is almost too big for anything; however, it is a well-focussed house and, when the lights are down, a warm one. The State Theater is currently undergoing acoustical renewal; one must hope that the results will make it right, at last, for ballet as well as opera. The perennially inadequate City Center remains a dance theatre because, like the Sadler's Wells, in London, it has gained a certain prestige from the uses of adversity, and because, like the Joyce, which is also a subsidized low-rent facility, it is cheap.* As for the various lofts, gyms, churches, garages, and basements that have been converted into performing spaces, not one of them is really satisfactory; where the stage is good, the seating accommodations are apt to be impossible.

Having to perform in improvised spaces has affected the aesthetic as well as the psychology of postmodernist choreographers for the past twenty years. If enough loft people are let into the Joyce, the consequences for postmodern dance could be enormous. But that is an outside possibility; what matters now is the effect the

---

* *Postscript 1987*: Renovation has made the orchestra level of the City Center much more comfortable. But the best seats are still in the front rows of the balcony.

new theatre will have on the fluctuations that postmodern dance is going through at this moment. One of the most critical changes has to do with the decline of novelty, that avant-garde specialty, to the status of a gimmick. A related change reverses the customary relationship of the choreographer's identity to his work. Instead of creating work that reveals an identity, younger postmodern choreographers like Jim Self, Charles Moulton, Bill T. Jones, and Johanna Boyce are constructing personae for themselves that impose meaning on their work. At its worst, as in the work of Bill T. Jones, this practice leads to egotistical domination and manipulation of the audience. At its mildest, as in the work of Self and Moulton, it leads to a kind of befuddled image-mongering. Moulton's career in the past couple of years illustrates the collapse of an idea into a gimmick. His precision ball-passing routines began as an idea about rhythm, but instead of developing it Moulton just became the guy who does precision routines and whose every move is less important than the fact that he makes it. The concerts I've seen Bill T. Jones give—both solo and with his habitual partner, Arnie Zane—have all begun with a conscious display of avant-garde techniques and devices and ended with Jones going wild: haranguing the audience or working himself into an emotional frenzy. He did it again in his latest concert, held in one of the city's most uncongenial basement rooms, the Space at City Center. Jones began by "using the space"; that is, he filled the wide and usually uninhabited forestage with dancers playing ritual games (pretending to race, freezing, falling in clinches to the floor) while the audience was getting seated. Two projectors trained on the back wall flashed the word "Now" alongside a blowup of an old snapshot from Jones's family album. The concert then made its way through more clichés to its inevitable self-induced tizzy, which was accompanied by the whooping and hollering of a female rock trio. Jones, who is black, presents the emotional attitudes of expressionistic black dance in a non-expressionistic postmodern framework. He offers himself to an audience shamelessly as a star, and he provides it with cultural uplift at the same time. He meets the issues—black anger, gay love, anti-nuke fear and trembling—and deflects them with personal charm. His taste is of the corniest: we watch dance-class exercises while a voice purrs "Testing, one, two, three" into a mike, and at some point in the action we are sure to hear this same voice or that of Jones himself singing "I Believe," his theme song of indictment. Jones is the apostle of postmodern pop; he has marched the New Narcissism right into the fever swamps.

Besides being narcissists (the showing of family-album photographs has become a convention), many of the young postmodernists who are now concertizing across the land are not notably talented dancers, and their training is apt to be incomplete. Moulton may be an exception; Jones has enough equipment to get into a Broadway show—maybe not quite enough. It's because of this fundamental deficiency, I suppose, that we are getting so much emphasis on flashy stuntwork, bemusing décors, and personalities. But if a reaction to the older rational and progressive (if minimalistic) methods of movement was inevitable, shouldn't the reaction have been back toward dancing rather than further away from it? The new generation has converted the perennial avant-garde where-do-we-go-from-here crisis into an opportunity for personal manifestos. And this reactionary trend, barely two years old, has probably gained postmodern dance a greater following than two decades of earnest experimentation. These people *are* stars, already. This summer's American Dance Festival, in Durham, North Carolina, is presenting Moulton, Self, and Boyce. Bill T. Jones and Arnie Zane will be part of the Brooklyn Academy's "Next Wave" series this winter. Along with conventional modern-dance troupes and small ballet companies, the Joyce will most likely be opening its doors to avant-garde postmodern dancers. It will be doing so at a time when the avant-garde is facing its most serious threat of extinction—not from without but from within.

The Feld Ballet, which initiated and sponsored the construction of the Joyce Theater, used to appear in the Public Theater, and my first impression of the Joyce was that it looked like a corrected version of the Public, where the audience peers down at the stage, like interns watching an operation. There is no orchestra pit at the Joyce (there wasn't one at the Public), and you sit close to a stage that is nearly twice as wide as it is high. It's so wide that one of the Feld ballets I saw there seemed to separate into two ballets; this was *Circa*, a nymphs-and-satyrs number. The stereoscopic effect may not have been intentional; Feld seemed to be aiming at a frieze. I understand that the proscenium can be made even wider, but anyway the stage is not difficult. By the third ballet, which was much the best part of the program, I had adjusted to its proportions.

Over the Pavement, to music by Charles Ives, develops a curious period atmosphere, and an even more curious character atmosphere, in a way typical of Feld: a few movements of great intensity are repeated over and over. The movements are based on naturalistic behavior, but they're so intensified they seem like parodies. When Feld's method doesn't work, they *are* parodies. When it works, as it does here, the intensification charges our vision, so that the parody turns away from the natural and toward the real. In *Over the Pavement*, seven young toughs in derisory haircuts, their fists jammed into the pockets of their ragged overalls, slump and slouch across the stage in regimented gangs. Linking up in twos and threes, they squat down and hurdle each other; breaking into solos, they buck and heave in the air. Periodically, they retreat to a lighted cell, where they lie exhausted or to try to climb the wall. Though they suggest a mixture of identities—*Nicholas Nickleby* orphans, turn-of-the-century ragamuffins, contemporary punks—the monochromatic movement never wavers, even when they are off the streets and in prison. But after Feld has shown us this life of cyclical degradation he can't break the cycle; the curtain calls are all taken in character—more slouching, more glaring and blinking across the footlights. I guess he wants us to think something like "The ballet's over but the life goes on"; he doesn't trust the ballet to sink in and make the point by itself. Nevertheless, *Over the Pavement* has some of the most cogent movement that Eliot Feld has ever made; its stylistic exaggerations, which seem literary at first, are obsessive and, finally, addictive.

. . .

Jerome Robbins's four-part contribution to New York City Ballet's Stravinsky Centennial Celebration turned out to be much like the celebration as a whole: it was one-quarter serious and successful invention (*Concertino*), one-quarter permutation (*Septet*), and two-quarters padding. The padding consisted of *Ragtime* and *Octet*; they seemed irrelevant not because they were lighthearted but because Robbins had overextended the gags. In *Ragtime*, set to 1920 music, the gag didn't go much beyond the 1920 costumes. Excessive fooling in *Octet* undermined the spirit of the music. Choreographing as much Stravinsky as New York City Ballet has done over the years leads inevitably to a draining of the wells. The celebration's premières featured too many scores of lesser choice to which permutations of greater dances were set. This was true also of last summer's Tchaikovsky Festival, but perhaps it was less obvious. If we feel that Tchaikovsky wrote many more concert compositions to which ballets can be set than Stravinsky did, it's simply because Tchaikovsky's distinctions between ballet and non-ballet music are no longer credible to us and Stravinsky's are. Modern ballet accommodates the non-ballet scores of the nineteenth century, but Stravinsky is himself a modern; you know when he wants a score to be danced, even if it isn't a ballet commission—he gives it feet. Although *Septet*, which he composed four years before *Agon*, seems rooted in the same interest in seventeenth-century dance forms as *Agon*, it isn't a ballet—it isn't for the same reason that *Agon is* a ballet. In a New York City Ballet setting, the music of *Septet* can hardly help referring us to *Agon*; Robbins himself underlines the reference with a male duet that looks like a gloss on the Balanchine one. A Stravinsky series that omits *Pulcinella, Jeu de Cartes, Scènes de Ballet, Danses Concertantes*, and the complete *Baiser de la Fée* as well as the first three ballet classics is straining the proposition, stated in one of the company's souvenir programs, that Stravinsky's music "compels dancing." (In an interview with Dale Harris in *Keynote*, Balanchine recently made the point that few of the great composers have a feeling for dance and fewer still express it in their best work. Because Stravinsky is one of these, he said, "you can have a festival devoted just to him." But why should the festival exclude so many of the *ballets* that are among the best work?)

To N.Y.C.B.'s repertory of Stravinsky ballets—*Agon, Orpheus, Apollo, Duo Concertant, Violin Concerto, Symphony in Three Movements*, the *Baiser* Divertimento, *Rubies, Monumentum, Movements*—the celebration, which numbered twelve premières, added a few lightweight items and two solid pieces of choreography. The Peter Martins ballet *Concerto for Two Solo Pianos*, which I wrote about after its first performance, looked even stronger after its second. Only Jock Soto's performance remains to be integrated. Heather Watts's plum role is pitilessly drawn; it's the full-length portrait for which *Calcium Light Night* was the sketch, and she dances every step unflinchingly. A magnanimous performance. Like Martins, Robbins in his *Concertino* does more than report on the music: he finds analogous movement and builds upon it a further analogy—dancers as circus acrobats, the music as the tightrope they walk. Merrill Ashley, flanked by Sean

Lavery and Mel Tomlinson, has a bisexual role—feminine in the supported adagio, masculine in the sections where she dances on equal terms with the men. (This is another gloss on *Agon*—one that Robbins has devised on his own, with no urging from Stravinsky.) It is a zestful, untrammelled performance. The trio also dances three overlapping solos (to the Three Pieces for Solo Clarinet), in which Lavery is given poetic Pierrot-like attitudes, Tomlinson a vortex of spins with snaking arms, and Ashley rapid perambulations on and off point, alternating with wide leaps around the stage.

On the closing night of the festival, Stravinsky's birthday was celebrated with a vodka toast before the curtain by Balanchine and Lincoln Kirstein, the singing of *Zvezdoliki* (*Le Roi des Étoiles*) by male voices of the New York City Opera Chorus, a performance of *Apollo*, still without its prologue, by Peter Martins, Suzanne Farrell, Kyra Nichols, and Maria Calegari, and the première of *Perséphone*, staged by Balanchine with and primarily for Vera Zorina, and conducted by Robert Craft. The staging, in which Balanchine was also assisted by John Taras, did not disguise the hybrid nature of Stravinsky's "melodrama" (song-drama), or its static quality. The chorus, a monkish assembly cowled in red, sat onstage in two toboggans between and around which nymphs, shades, and, in the final scene, choir boys entered and disposed themselves. The production's visual style, designed by Kermit Love, was a blend of High Episcopalian pageantry and the Tchelitchew of the forties; it was as if time had stopped for Vera Zorina. Surrounded by gauzy nymphs and staglike men with candelabras, Zorina appeared barefoot, lifted her large and still-handsome face to the light, and spoke the Gide poem in her German-tinted French. A little light running and posing prepared the audience for the moments when she would go off and Karin von Aroldingen would appear, wearing a matching peignoir. The most effective of these substitutions occurred beneath Pluto's towering silk batwings. As the dancing Perséphone, von Aroldingen's role was small; Gen Horiuchi's Mercury had the outstanding solo. As Pluto, Tomlinson did his baleful-spider number. Zorina was miked but not the singers, who included Joseph Evans as the high priest Eumolpus, dressed by Love as a choirmaster. The production, and the Stravinsky series as a whole, was mounted in the plastic cylindrical setting devised for the Tchaikovsky Festival by Philip Johnson and John Burgee. The tubes can be active décor or passive environment; low-key lighting, by Ronald Bates, made them a persuasive grotto of stalactites in the Underworld scenes. The evening concluded, like the Stravinsky Festival of 1972, with free shots of vodka for the audience. But ending with Perséphone's return to the Underworld—"*au fond de la détresse humaine*"—brought inescapably to mind the sombre finale (*Adagio Lamentoso*) of the Tchaikovsky Festival.

I visited the Martha Graham company at the City Center to see what had befallen *Primitive Mysteries* and *Dark Meadow* since they were last revived. *Primitive Mysteries*, Graham's masterpiece of the thirties, had Takako Asakawa as the Graham figure, and an ensemble quivering with concentrated energy. The halting walks to and from the wings which divide the three sections of the piece had been restored. It was a performance one could believe in. *Dark Meadow* is an enigmatic work in the best of performances; the corps once again distinguished itself, but Yuriko Kimura, Susan McLain, and Peter Sparling did not penetrate beneath the surface of their roles. I also saw a new work called *Dances of the Golden Hall*, which Graham is said to call her Denishawn ballet. It is exactly that: little Hindu gods and goddesses on pillars, rows of bending acolytes, and blinding gold costumes, by Halston. In fifteen minutes, it releases more incense than an entire program of Denishawn revivals. —*July 12, 1982*

An Underground Classic?

Peer sat and soon was in a half dreaming state, looking out upon it all. The bushes seemed to have shapes half of human sort and half of beastly form. They stood motionless, while the mist rose like a great waving veil. Something like this had Peer seen in a ballet at the theatre, when elfin maidens were represented, whirling and waving with veils of gauze.

HANS CHRISTIAN ANDERSEN, "Lucky Peer"

Andersen's Peer had undoubtedly seen *A Folk Tale*. The details that stuck in Andersen's mind are part of the staging to this day: "Just in front, in the mist, appeared most distinctly a female shape, and it became three, and the three many; they danced hand in hand, floating girls. . . . They danced into the garden and about him; they enclosed him in their circle." In the ballet, the elf-maidens encircle the young squire Ove and make him mad. But they don't encircle the entire ballet with their dark power, as the Wilis do in *Giselle*. The controlling spirits in *A Folk Tale* are the trolls, and the difference makes the ballet a satirical comedy rather than a sinister fantasy. Still, the trolls are fantastic creatures, and it's the element of fantasy that has made *A Folk Tale*, after *La Sylphide*, the most discussed Bournonville ballet. John Frandsen, the conductor who recorded the remarkable score for EMI, writes in the liner notes of impressions that go back to his childhood: "With a mixture of delight and fear [*en blanding af fryd og frygt*] I remember Hartmann's music for the second act." And although *A Folk Tale* has been internationally known only since 1979, when it was discovered by the (largely American) dance press at the Bournonville centennial festival in Copenhagen, something like an atavistic delight and fear lies at the heart of its popularity. If *A Folk Tale* wasn't part of our childhood, we can wish it had been. We can also wish it into existence as a classic of the Romantic ballet, which I don't believe it is or ever was.

The American enthusiasm for Bournonville as applied to questions of dance technique and style, to scholarly inquiry and historical renovation has been demonstrably beneficial, both to the American and to the Danish dance community. But there's a sentimental aspect of our interest, too, in which the Danish ballet appears the reincarnation of a golden age of purity and innocence. This Arcadian vision—not altogether unprompted by the Danes themselves—has reached a new intensity in the cult of *A Folk Tale*, which, born in Copenhagen, gathered steam in Chicago (where two years ago the Royal Danish Ballet presented highlights of the Bournonville festival) and gained official status with the visit, just concluded, of the Danish company to Washington and New York. I call it a cult because a great deal of what is claimed for the ballet in terms of poetic wisdom, psychological insight, and theatrical effectiveness isn't really earned by it. Bournonville himself attributed most of the ballet's success to the music, which besides J. P. E. Hartmann's palpitating second act includes two outer acts of spontaneous and fluent charm by Niels W. Gade, Hartmann's son-in-law. The tingling of the trolls' picks and anvils, which forms a motif throughout the score, the whirlwind dance of the elf-maidens, the roistering drinking song of the trolls, and the lighter-than-air flute solo that accompanies the heroine's dance in their midst: it actually seems true of these and other wonderful musical episodes that once heard they are never forgotten. (The Wedding Waltz, in the third act, which has attained popular fame in Denmark, seems to me the ballet's only trite number.) Like some works of art, some literary masterpieces, and some movies, *A Folk Tale* is endowed with elements of popular myth which one has already partly experienced the appeal of; on encountering one of these works, one has the sense of recapturing some original pleasure. It seems that we have known Lady Macbeth and Scrooge and D'Artagnan and Carmen and the Merry Widow and Gatsby and Franny and Zooey and Astaire and Rogers before we ever met them. So it is with Hilda and Viderik and Diderik and poor, raddled Frøken Birthe in *A Folk Tale*. The ballet is a great Danish cornucopia of benign and perverse primal sensations; the unknown world of the trolls inspires delight and fear in its mysterious concourse with the human world. Even after we see that the trolls are allegorical reconstructions of human beings in their monstrous greed and materialism, even after they've made us laugh, we are still a little afraid of them; the tendency toward Disneyfication in the current production doesn't blight this basic reaction.

That tendency is largely the fault of the décor. For the 1979 revival, Lars Juhl was commissioned. Juhl had designed costumes and scenery for the new *Kermesse at Bruges*, and he used the same artificial, contemporary style for *A Folk Tale*. The flimsiness that is permissible in *Kermesse*, a farce, is deadly in *A Folk Tale*, which needs nineteenth-century magic and realism. The trapdoor out of which the first elf-maiden emerges to become three wasn't available at the Kennedy Center or at the Met. But Juhl's scenery did not do its part. When the earth shook under Ove and the troll hill was supposed to rise on four glowing pillars, all that happened was that a backcloth lifted to reveal another one behind it. Birthe's chamber in Act III could have told us more about the life of this extraordinary character, and it could have been designed to make Hilda's homecoming less precipitate. At nearly every point in the action, Juhl's scenery was saying "Don't believe this." Yet one did.

It is one thing to experience the appeal of A *Folk Tale* and another to applaud it as a ballet masterpiece. It was created in 1854, thirteen years after *Giselle* and thirty-six years before *The Sleeping Beauty*; it contains elements of both ballets and yet it isn't remotely comparable in poetic force to either of them or to any other ballet classic. To seek parallels for the force that is in A *Folk Tale* one must go to opera or theatre or movies, and then the ballet starts to look very small indeed. And this isn't because it is a ballet d'action, with pantomime taking up more time than dance; quite the best part of the show is the second act, in which the only dancing is Hilda's solo and the drunken galop of the trolls. The precision with which dance and mime are woven together to express a meaning makes this scene the heart of the ballet, and the one for which the most serious claims can be made. But Act I is little more than a collection of genre scenes—a set of Romantic ballet tintypes—and Act III is overplotted, with patches of opacity and a hasty dénouement. It also has a dance apotheosis in which the spotlight falls not on any of the central characters but on a troupe of gypsies in a pas de sept. One could take the skeptic's way out and say that A *Folk Tale* was meant only to evoke a general pattern of incident and atmosphere, and not to tell a specific story; but then the second act, with its quite specific situation of the changeling who recognizes her true origins (the heiress of the manor has been switched in her cradle for a troll child), becomes emotionally disproportionate. To see Hilda among the trolls—especially to see Lis Jeppesen among a troll family consisting of Fredbjørn Bjørnsson, Niels Kehlet (or Johnny Eliasen), and Lillian (or Mona) Jensen—is to see theatrical perfection of a sort. Why should it have taken a hundred and twenty-five years to become known outside Denmark? Why, since the forest outing in the first act seems to have influenced the creators of *The Sleeping Beauty*, hasn't the ballet enjoyed even a critical reputation?

The answer to the second question must lie in the Danes' diffidence toward their own repertory. But the answer to why the ballet never became a world classic is buried down there among the trolls. What makes the second act wonderful makes the ballet unmaneuverable as a whole. There really isn't enough dancing; there's just enough to fill out the meaning of the story, and this story simply doesn't find its essential expression in dance. Fantasy in the ballet classics doesn't operate from a story premise anyway. It starts with dance and adds a little situation to fill out some perceptible implication in the dance. And so a libretto grows. Without exception, the nineteenth-century classics that have come down to us have subjects that unlock some part of the secret fascination of dancing—that in a sense explain it, although no explanation ever really suffices. The brilliant, irrational surface of classical dancing is charged with a depth of meaning in respect to a story. The meaning is beyond naming; it is beyond diabolism in *Giselle*, beyond holy plenitude in *La Bayadère*, beyond bondage and immolation in *Swan Lake*. The list of nineteenth-century masterpieces terminates in a list of twentieth-century ones—*Les Sylphides*, *Faune*, *Apollo*, *Serenade*—that grow more and more abstract as the need for story support diminishes. The elves and fairies start packing up their pretexts, and, as the shadow of the Romantic twilight lengthens, the principal emotion of delight and fear gives way to simple awe. In *The Sleeping Beauty* and to a certain extent in *The Nutcracker* we glimpse an earthly paradise that consciously reflects all that dancing tells us of the beauty of our species as well as the need of the nineteenth-century theatre for spectacles of transfiguration and apotheosis. According to the principles of this theatre, the classical ballet subject is one that is carried *in performance*; we can't understand *Swan Lake* simply by reading about it or listening to the music. A *Folk Tale* has, instead of the swans or sylphs or Wilis who by their supernature "explain" the peculiar behavior of classical dancers, trolls. Trolls who behave peculiarly. But this literally earthbound behavior can't be expressed in classical dancing, which means that it can't be sustained as a subject except in the second act, when we see it dramatically contrasted with Hilda's zephyrlike classicism. Human nature is apotheosized in the third act not by Hilda and Ove, the man she has saved, but by the gypsies— free spirits, evidently—who are introduced at the last minute. There is in *A Folk Tale* no spectacle the motive and expression of which must be classical dancing. In all of Bournonville (all that has come down to us), there is no such thing.

Bournonville, we know, was a sophisticated man of the theatre, but he was also a puritan. He stood in clear disapproval of the morbid frenzy of the Romantic ballet. The grand exception, *La Sylphide*, was a remake of an already famous Taglioni vehicle, and in contriving a new version Bournonville seems to have switched the emphasis from the Sylph's erotic mystery to James's transgression of the social code. In *La Sylphide* (which was not included in the United States tour), James is struck down by an evil witch, but the last twist of the knife is reserved to the forces of home and hearth which James himself has tried to strike down; his nemesis is the bland bourgeois disregard of the Romantic impulse. The simplicity of *A Folk Tale* is marred by a moralizing libretto that puts Hilda and human society on the side of Good and the trolls on the side of Evil. It's only in the satirical energy of the troll scenes that the ballet atones for this pompous attitude. (Nothing quite atones for the dragging in of Christian symbolism. Not only is Hilda clean, trustworthy, brave, and classical, but she must also hold up crucifixes; the goblet she gives Ove becomes, quite unnecessarily to his salvation, the Holy Grail.) Bournonville's Romanticism lies in his inexhaustible pursuit of the exotic. Nearly all his subjects were derived from the lore of foreign lands. A *Folk Tale* is the most Danish of his ballets and, in the quality of its lyricism, the darkest. Its themes may have been so familiar to the Copenhagen audience that they didn't need to be integrated and placed in a dramatic perspective, like the themes of *Napoli*. The lack of integration is a weakness one can ascribe to provincialism, but then in *Coppélia*, to which the Danes bring all the brightness of their pragmatic temper, we see a kind of strength that can be ascribed to provincial fortitude.

The Danish *Coppélia* is not a Bournonville ballet. It was imported into Denmark in 1896 and reconceived in Bournonville's style by his successor, Hans Beck. The current production is the second or third by the company's senior Bournonville authority, Hans Brenaa, and it has been mounted by Søren Frandsen in settings of an almost photographic optical brilliance. Barns and meadows glow in the afternoon sun; the attic toolshop of Coppélius practically reeks of wood shavings. The Danes take *Coppélia* very literally, as the story of a cunning peasant's trick on a wise man. Where the Russian-derived versions of the ballet are occupied with dances, the Danish version creates characters. The ear-of-wheat episode, with Swanilda sitting on the girls' knees while she consults their opinion, is followed by an extended argument-flirtation between the two lovers (Delibes's "Thème slave varié") in which they take alternate variations, as if scoring points. The dialogue builds to a climax, but when it bursts into the concluding gavotte the lovers retire and two anonymous "friends" take over the dancing. The intrusion of the gypsies in *A Folk Tale* is more logical; they are there, after all, for the purposes of a divertissement. (If you're missing gypsies in *Coppélia*, hold on; a whole flock of them will arrive to dance the czardas.) The Danes, it seems, have no use for the metaphor of structure. Perhaps they see that the gavotte coda implies some sort of reconciliation for Swanilda and Frantz and they will have none of it.

The rest of the staging is carried out in strict logic. Apart from a huge Danish Pierrot who bangs a drum in the workshop scene, the only dancer we see conspicuously playing a doll is the only one who isn't *meant* to be a doll—Jeppesen as Swanilda playing Coppélia—and whose obviously human movements, therefore, do not disturb our sense of illusion. (Coppélia's dance on the balcony is staged, but in a light so dim we can hardly make it out.) When you add up all the production's idiosyncrasies, the ballet begins to seem as if it must end with Act II, and, in fact, the Act III that the Danes give us is a skimpy epilogue, which omits the Festival of the Bell and the wedding, along with some of Delibes's best music. One has to admire the conviction behind all this. The Danes simply don't feel the reciprocal tug between the image of the doll and the image of the classical dancer which makes *Coppélia* the most ironic of ballet classics. They don't feel it and they don't pretend to. Jeppesen—who is as wonderful here as she is in *A Folk Tale*—acts out a relatively plain story of a woman-into-doll transformation. The subsequent materialization of woman-into-ballerina does not take place. Act III is as much as possible a recapitulation of Act I; it is not the consequence of Act II. Since we haven't seen the dehumanizing side of classicism, we've no need to see the redemptive power of it in a bridal pas de deux. (It may be relevant that, whereas most Coppélias stand primly turned out in first position, Jeppesen's doll spraddles and turns in.) In its caustic realism, this is still a great production. But the structural metaphor—the bonework of *Coppélia*—is missing.

It was a good season for Bournonville at the Met. The company put on pieces it used to think would never play in New York, and they did play, thanks to the dancers, who projected mightily, and to the splendid conductors. The standard suite from *Napoli* was given a series of performances that in brilliance and sheer elation came close to the realm of transcendent metaphor. It was music as wine, dancing as joy.   —*July 19, 1982*

Artists and Models

Ballet Rambert, the renowned British company, appeared for three performances in Brooklyn at the start of a fall tour of North America. The engagement, sponsored by Brooklyn Center for the Performing Arts at Brooklyn College, had to pass for a New York début; from here the company flies west, dips into Mexico, swings north, south, west again, and winds up in Los Angeles just before Thanksgiving. America should take to it. The repertory is carefully mounted, with good designing. It presents the company, which traces its origins backs to 1926, in its third or fourth incarnation: seven ballets, all created since 1980, by three house choreographers who are largely unknown in this country. Born classical, the Rambert has been a modern-dance company since the mid-sixties. The prevailing influences are American. Graham and Ailey show up in the work of Robert North, the artistic director, who is also American. Richard Alston's *Rainbow Ripples* deals successfully with a range of ideas adapted from Merce Cunningham. An eighth ballet, unperformed in Brooklyn, is Paul Taylor's *Airs*. And there are Christopher Bruce's dances in the European tradition that, from Jooss to Kylián, has had a recurrent effect on English ballet.

More striking than any of these derivations, though, is the distinctive English lyricism of the dancing. The Rambert dancers bring this most congenial native gift to a repertory that would otherwise consist of conscientious pastiche and stale incentives to get into character and act. British dancers are instinctual actors, but they are at their greatest when the instinct is sublimated. I suspect that they know it, too, and that the reason for the Rambert's current resurgence is its assertion of lyricism as the mode of sublimation at a time when the Royal Ballet is giving itself over to a kind of sticky metaphoric expressionism. It is the Rambert's stylistic emphasis, not its allegiance to modern dance, that holds real meaning for British dance today. Properly developed, it is what could make the Rambert again into the spearhead company it once was.

At the moment, the Rambert is not yet fully conscious of its capacity for lyrical-dramatic expression. Alston, who has the surest sense of it, is sometimes confused about enforcing it or about his choice of contexts. His version of *Le Sacre du Printemps* is filled with ideas about the historic Nijinsky production, but it's the softest *Sacre* I have ever seen; the Chosen Maiden, with her light, graceful limbs and buttery falls, is a lamb to the slaughter. The paroxysm you expect from the music (here performed in the two-piano reduction) never happens. When the music ends, the ensemble takes a few bars of silence to express its compassion. In North's *Lonely Town, Lonely Street*, we are offered a scene of urban desolation, with loners, lovers, and losers wandering through it to a rock score. Although it is dedicated to the modern-jazz dancer Matt Mattox, the ballet is very like one of those Ailey pieces that seem to come out of a Broadway show. But it doesn't have the flaring-fading tension that Ailey wove into his dances for *Blues Suite* and *Masekela Langage*. We can tell who North's people are, but when his dances get going the patterns are so flat and musically so predictable that they obstruct our view of what's happening. The opposite weakness invades Bruce's *Ghost Dances*. The dances themselves are tautly constructed in relation to the music (a suite of wonderfully insidious folk songs by the South American group Inti-Illimani) but not in relation to the story, which is about how death claimed each of the dancers. In *Das Berliner Requiem*, an excerpt from a long Kurt Weill ballet, Bruce darkens and thickens his movement to stygian viscosity and loses control of it completely. The choreography is a succession of static images: a limp girl held up by four men in greatcoats, four more men in bloody tatters, a zombie chorus. Images like this don't have to move for us to get their meaning, but then why do they try?

It's refreshing to see new choreography that shows quite clearly what the choreographer has been looking at and thinking about. In this country, we are starting to get observant and thoughtful work (from Peter Martins, Peter Anastos, and Daniel Levans, among others) after a long period in which no one seemed to be looking anywhere but into a mirror. If models were used, they were used triflingly. All the Rambert ballets, even the failures, show somebody looking at something and trying to learn from it or adapt its lessons. The whole point of a model, of course, is adaptability. Bruce, trying for nineteen-twenties-style *Expressionismus* in the *Requiem*, is betrayed by the sterility of the idiom. In *Ghost Dances*, he attempts a non-idiomatic remake of *The Green Table*, with three stalwart ghouls instead of one ushering his cast of characters to their doom. Because he hasn't managed to integrate characterization and dance, the company's dance style and the charming music carry what they can of the piece. North's awareness of the company style is less well defined, and he doesn't seem to have assimilated all *his* models, either. *Pribaoutki*, an allegorical work, was meant to leap from one mythical or hallucinatory episode to the next by means of free association, but North's association of Stravinsky's music with Picasso and Martha Graham added up to a very lumpy allegory. I'm not sure I know what Alston saw in Balanchine's *Apollo* that made him produce *Apollo Distraught*, with its vigorous bacchantic women and its three passive and languorous men. The sexual balance suggests Ashton, not Balanchine—specifically, it suggests *Daphnis and Chloe*, and the lush, long scroll-like dance phrases do, too. Apollo is not in Alston's cast. The ballet concerns the god's followers—Apollonians or classical dancers—and the choreography is a meditation on classicism. It is in this ballet that the melting line of the Rambert dancers, their juicy through-the-body movement, has its fullest expression. Without being academically correct in every move and pose, they are phenomenally neat about points of style. With them, one sees clearly what some of our ballet dancers can make us forget—that the object of schooling is dancing.

Why, then, is Apollo distraught? Probably because of the music, a flute concerto by the young English composer Nigel Osborne. Alston has built the ballet to the specifications of the music, and in a program note he describes the concerto's "classical architecture" and speaks of a "tension in the opposition between a contained proportional form and a rather explosive content." Apollo, then, with a Dionysian fire in his belly. One can see that Alston has tried to work out this premise in the choreography, but, like all form-content conceits, it is very hard to illustrate. Frequently, it seems that the tension is between the music and the choreography—that for the sake of his classical constructions Alston is ignoring sections of the music which are fraught with violence, or that for the sake of the music (particularly its supercharged and too-short final movement) he loads the dance with implications of a dramatic nature. However, the piece is enormous fun to watch. You can see it as a landscape crowded with sensation, now bright and pleasant, now dampened by squalls or covered by cloud shapes that balloon and drift and contract slowly or suddenly. You can make out mythical encounters and seasonal escapades in a land of dim Diaghilevian contours. It is a ballet of high combustibility and temperament, and it has a most peculiar force. As a progression of ideas—I mean ideas about dance, not dance ideas—it is highly tentative. Alston is continually testing paradoxes. He uses the ballet to see, for example, how the classical images formed by the body keep their serenity at flying tempos or what happens when a slow tempo is used for a supported adagio danced by men. Most of all, I think, he is interested in contemporary applications of classical ideals. The sex-role reversals may be less an inquiry into weights and balances than an attempt to locate male and female archetypes within the sexually indeterminate universe of the eighties. Even here, though, Alston's choice of music works against him. It rushes every possibility he outlines, and when at the end of the hard-driving last movement the principals collapse to the floor we may feel that it's because the music hasn't given them time to come to a proper conclusion. (It may also be the ballet's only genuine reference to *Apollo*, parodying the "fatigue" ending of the coda.)

Rainbow Ripples gives us Alston in complete command of his material, which is very openly derived from Cunningham. (Alston is similarly unguarded in his *Les Noces* borrowings for *Sacre*. Since Alston's version of *Sacre* is in part a recounting of Nijinsky's themes, the suggestion that many of these themes wound up in his sister's ballet is not misplaced. And the suggestion may have been authorized by Marie Rambert, who assisted Nijinsky in rehearsal and who nurtured Alston's production as one of the last acts of a dazzling career.) Alston studied for several years in New York with Cunningham, and he has caught the silhouettelike clarity of the Cunningham dancer, the complex rhythm, the nervous directional changes that characterize Cunningham's choreography, and a whole body of the master's steps as well. It's fascinating to see a British choreographer do what no American would dare—Alston even uses those rapid relevés in fourth position—and yet not tip over into caricature. But then Alston is spelling out a particular affinity. Cunningham is the most lyrical of modern-dance choreographers, despite his abjuring of music. And Alston doesn't go all the way with his imitation. The score, a collage of words and sentences cleverly broken up and layered to form shafts of sound, is used as an actual base for the choreography. The dances seem to take their spring and impetus and the quality of their energy directly from these sounds, much as if they constituted a musical setting. And then, as a finale, Alston does use a musical setting—the rag "Rainbow Ripples" played on a xylophone (and taped, like all the Rambert's scores except *Sacre*)— and we have the pleasure of seeing the dancing continue without anything being changed but the way we experience it. Alston has an extraordinary ear; he can hear sound as shape. How odd to see this great asset demonstrated in a mock-Cunningham context.

One would think the Rambert's choreographers sophisticated enough craftsmen not to cast themselves as apprentices. It is their decision to let us see them taking risks, testing options, and grooming a company. Whatever comes of the Rambert, it is already, in its current phase, a worthy memorial to its founder.

When Marie Rambert was driven by economics to scale down her forces in the sixties, she turned the bulk of the artistic direction over to Norman Morrice, who oversaw the company's conversion to modern dance (and who now directs the Royal Ballet). Morrice produced the work of the American choreographer Glen Tetley. Between the Rambert and the Netherlands Dance Theatre, which had sponsored him earlier, Tetley was primed for his subsequent conquest of the Continent. He has never enjoyed the same kind of success in the United States. He arrived just when European dance, surfeited with ballet (and ballet costs), wanted an alternative, not too stylistically demanding. Tetley provided it, and he goes on providing it to aspiring companies. In 1979, when the Rambert was under the direction of John Chesworth, it gave the world première of Tetley's full-evening work *The Tempest*, and a year later *The Tempest* was acquired by the Norwegian National Ballet, which chose it for its New York début, at the Brooklyn Academy in mid-October. There are few ballets I would rather avoid than those of Glen Tetley, but I had never seen the Norwegians, and despite my feeling that a Tetley piece was no way to see them I went. I didn't stay. Tetley was evidently bent on producing his answer to the large-scale ballet productions he was originally commissioned to replace back in the sixties. *The Tempest* is done modern-dance style, with stripped-down décor and costumes (no male wears a shirt) and un-dulating seas of China silk. From Loie Fuller to Martha Graham, in whose company Tetley once danced, the roll call of modern-dance signature devices and clichés is sounded. There are trappings from the Noh theatre, which by now must qualify as a Graham outpost. The music, by Arne Nordheim, features male and female solo voices in a manner that recalls Halim El-Dabh's score for *Cly-temnestra*. It is Graham's presence that looms over the stage, not Shakespeare's. Tetley declares his source as openly as any Rambert choreographer. But one would think that Graham and Fuller were contemporaries. Tetley may believe he is making modern art; in fact, his heart is back there in the era of l'Art Nouveau, with empurpled visions of bodies swaying beneath silken waves. The story of Prospero and Ariel and Caliban is rendered in terms of steam-bath decadence; the rest of the story—But I didn't stay for the rest of the story. Except for Ketil Gudim, a powerful Ariel, the Norwegian Ballet dancers looked just strong enough for the linear, insubstantial choreography they were called on to execute.

The Tempest makes a very poor dance subject, notwithstanding the many attempts at adaptation which it seems to have invited. If you can manage to keep the characters straight, you still gain nothing from seeing them danced. Their fate isn't centered in visible acts, like the fate of Romeo and Juliet or Othello or any of the characters in A *Midsummer Night's Dream*. Don't choreographers know what a difficult play this is? (Maybe they think the difficulty lies in trying to cast Ariel and Caliban with actors.)

Eliot Feld, who formed a repertory by doing his own versions of well-known ballets and who was the only young choreographer of his period doing it intelligently, seems to have made the big transition. He now remakes his own work. *Straw Hearts*, which I saw at the Joyce, is a Gay Nineties version of *The Real McCoy*, his Gershwin ballet. The hero is another hat-and-stick man, and he has a pas de deux with a heroine who rambles about on her points not unlike the heroine of Balanchine's *La Sonnambula*; however, Feld's staging—having her repeatedly hooked with the stick, having the stick be an all-purpose prop—is more like his rolling-couch scene in *The Real McCoy*. But Feld has stick mania. And in a trio for men who continually doff their straw hats he has hat mania. The repetitiousness that has become disturbing and destructive in Feld's work had its origin in his obsession with formal consistency. Balanchine's famous remark about what he learned from making *Apollo*—that there are family relations among gestures which impose their own laws—may have affected Feld's idea of composition to the point that where he used to devise familial gestures he now tends to make clones. The straw-hat trio contains the best and worst of Feld's craftsmanship. It is clonish, but it is also familial, a reflection and a parody of the close harmony in the music.

Like so much of Feld's work, *Straw Hearts* is overextended. And the nub of the piece—the man's role—isn't really there. Feld has conceived a boulevardier based on Chaplin (models within models!) whose big moment comes when, to the amazement and delight of a bunch of Florodoras, he dances *four* solos accompanied by a florid trumpet rendition of "Carnival of Venice." In between solos, he has a hat-cane-gloves ritual that the audience adores, but the solos themselves should be filled with spectacular feats, and they're underchoreographed. Gianfranco Paoluzi, who originated Tetley's Ariel with Ballet Rambert, performs admirably here; he's a bantam sharpie, like Feld himself, or like Chaplin, for that matter. He's also a funny mime and strong, clean dancer. But his solos cry out for Baryshnikov and Baryshnikov's steps.   —*November 1, 1982*

Ballerina

The most reasonable alternative to *The Nutcracker* at this time of year is Prokofiev's three-act ballet *Cinderella*, yet it is not often produced, probably because, unlike *The Nutcracker*, it cannot be done cheaply. A small-budget company can put on Tchaikovsky's ballet with a cast of children, assigning the divertissement roles to older students and corps members, and reserving Sugar Plum and her Cavalier for two guest stars who only have to come on once and do a pas de deux. But in *Cinderella* all the roles were meant to be taken by professionals, and the two principals dance continuously. The choreography has to be made from scratch; there are no well-known models to draw from. (Frederick Ashton's production for the Royal Ballet has not been seen in this country since 1967.) And the music has its curious side.

Although Prokofiev's score is popular—after his *Romeo and Juliet*, it is the most popular full-length ballet score written in this century—it is stylistically elusive, an unpredictable blend of romance and satire. Prokofiev is never satirical at the expense of romance, though; you can get away with underplaying—and even undercasting—the ugly stepsisters and the scenes at court, but the love story must be given full value. When Ashton produced *Cinderella* in 1948, he topcast himself and Robert Helpmann as the sisters and carried the ballet to success. Ashton and Helpmann were squarely in the English "dame" tradition, and their slapstick helped put the whole production in perspective as a loving tribute to England's Christmas pantomimes. But for foreign audiences the Royal *Cinderella* hasn't worn well. Because Ashton and Helpmann no longer dance the sisters, the comedy scenes are diminished in force (though not in length), and this shows up the two main characters, who were too straight and too sweet to begin with. In the Kirov *Cinderella* that was seen here in the early sixties, the ugly sisters weren't played by men and weren't very funny, but there was a gallery of cartoon characters—tutors, pages, lackeys, and so forth—who created a hubbub against which the spacious emotion of the love duets achieved a transcendent meaning. Cinderella and her prince were not just precipitated into each other's arms—they were galvanized by love and desire, like Romeo and Juliet.

In no production can I recall Cinderella herself participating in the fun. But she has to be more than a homebody with inexplicable dreams of grandeur; she has to be the kind of girl you can pull for when she goes to the ball. She must *deserve* her glory. Most Cinderellas I've seen have struck me as inhumanly perfect, and have covered themselves with vainglory. It's only that little human lapse of forgetting to leave before twelve that makes them sympathetic. Last month, I saw a new version of *Cinderella*, by a new company, the Chicago City Ballet, with

Suzanne Farrell in the title role. Farrell gets to the humanity of Cinderella in a way no other dancer could. She lets you see that her dreams of grandeur are not about romance and riches but about her own gifts; she's a Cinderella who becomes a ballerina. The choreography, by Paul Mejia (who is Farrell's husband), abets her in the process, so much so that the production seems impossible to stage without her. So far—this was the second annual presentation of the ballet at the Auditorium Theatre—the company hasn't tried to stage it without her, or without Adam Lüders as the prince. For the young members of the Chicago City Ballet, Mejia provides good ballroom and divertissement dances, and to swell the scene he invents an Enchanted Forest with masses of children fluttering about as butterflies and beetles. The Chicago company is lively and well trained, but, as hosts of *Nutcracker* presenters have discovered, nothing guarantees community interest in a production like the presence of small children in the cast. Farrell as the star guaranteed critical interest as well. Mejia, who with Maria Tallchief directs the Chicago City Ballet, may have applied *Nutcracker* formulas, but he hasn't just turned out *Not "The Nutcracker."* Largely because of Farrell, he has a *Cinderella* that is unique.

Farrell could have been all wrong in the role and still have been riveting. At the beginning, barefoot, her hair bound in a scarf, she does look miscast—but in a familiar way, much as if she'd gone back to her country girl in *Don Quixote*, a role that summed up without actually featuring the kinds of commonplace things she has to do here, such as the meditative solo with the broom and the "dialogue" with the caged bird. As she does her chores and as she dances with an Ash Man who has rolled out of the fireplace, fantasizes about a Fairy Godmother, and wanders around being rebuked by the stepsisters, Farrell retains the insular calm of her Dulcinea—the calm of self-possession, not self-absorption. She wins our sympathy by never asking for it. Her despair is seen in the averted pose she assumes sitting a long time apart, her face pressed to the brick wall of the hearth. When she gets to the ball, she dances ravenously, with a hunger to embrace the world. This is the Farrell we know from the third act of *Don Quixote*. In essence, Farrell's Cinderella is a Balanchine creation. Mejia uses the Balanchine Farrell as a matrix, much as Ashton used the English pantomimes. In the ballroom scene, the characteristic Farrell bravura (of *Chaconne* and *Walpurgisnacht Ballet* as well as of *Don Quixote*) is embellished by luxuriant slow backbends, which she executes while kneeling on Lüders's shoulder or recovering from swift spins and super-high battements in his arms. It is a display of personal treasure so abundant that we can't help seeing it, at this point in the ballet, as Cinderella coming into her kingdom.

Mejia's handling of straight narrative and narrative-through-dance is uneven. He overstresses the intervention of the Fairy Godmother (Cynthia Tosh) in the heroine's fortunes but leaves unexplained his doublecasting of Jennifer Barton and Gail Rosenheim as the stepsisters and as Spanish and Ethiopian temptresses in the bazaar scene that describes the prince's global search. He ignores the vexing problem that *Cinderella* always poses, of the discrepancy between the toe shoes that the heroine dances in and the glass slipper that she leaves behind. As in the Kirov production, the hours striking midnight are portrayed by a chorus of children, but without the saccharine antics of the Kirov. Three acts are condensed to two; the shrewish stepsisters in mob-caps occupy much less running time than they might have. Just as the Enchanted Forest derives from A *Midsummer Night's Dream*, the ballroom scene, stripped of its three oranges (in a city that saw the première of *Love for Three Oranges*), owes much to *La Sonnambula* and *La Valse*. As Cinderella arrives, we see her through the tall windows at the back of the set, slowly and apprehensively climbing a steep staircase and peering in upon the lavish scene. It's a moment as lovely, in its way, as the entrance in *Vienna Waltzes*. The scenery, by Steven Rubin, and the costumes, by Ben Benson, enforce a solidly conventional look of storybook fantasy. The show is a hit. But its real Fairy Godmother is Balanchine.

The Imperial Ballet of St. Petersburg in its last flowering produced a pride of ballerinas who, when their days of glory were done, lived on into illustrious old age. Lopokova died only a year ago; Spessivtseva, the last of the great prerevolutionary ballerinas, is still alive. The exception is Pavlova, who amassed the greatest legend of all. She died at fifty, on tour, a blazing comet that had burned itself out. Her death, from pleurisy, was headline news the world over, and she was mourned by a vaster public than any dance star had known before—or has known since. Her millions did not come to her; she came to them, traveling some four hundred thousand miles over six continents. Pavlova was a titan in an age of titans; even so, the facts of her career continue to amaze and appall. She endured the most arduous life a dancer can lead—a life on the road—and the bulk of her touring was composed of one-night stands. A new and valuable book, *Anna Pavlova: Her Life and Art* (Knopf), reprints the itinerary of her North American tour of 1914–15. Keith Money, the author, is good at projecting himself back in time; he writes, "Just to look at it was to recoil with fatigue." *Was?* Here she goes, across the map of America, night after night stopping in a different city. Shrewd and ruthless bookers put her into the biggest halls they could find—three- and four-thousand-seaters—packed them solid, and then shot her on to the next Masonic lodge or Shriners' auditorium. But Pavlova was indefatigable. When after nine months the tour ends in Chicago, her company rests. She herself films *The Dumb Girl of Portici*, goes to the West Coast for more filming, returns to Chicago, and begins a new tour, with the Boston Grand Opera, during which she performs, among other items, the opera on which the film is based. As Money remarks of a later and similar tour, "for the most part it was arrive, unpack, show, pack, travel—all in a twenty-four-hour span."

She did it, he thinks, because her restlessness and avidity gave her no choice. The Russian Empire was crumbling when, in 1909, Pavlova launched her Western career. Had she remained in Russia, she would have faced compulsory retirement at thirty-five, but even if, as in Preobrajenska's case, this rule had been relaxed and she had been allowed to continue, she would have had to deal with the stultifying regime at the Maryinsky. Not only Petipa, the ballet's principal architect and Pavlova's sponsor, but also her teacher Cecchetti had been dismissed, and the creative resources of the rising generation had already been corralled by Diaghilev for an assault on the West. There was a moment when Pavlova might have become the permanent prima ballerina of the Diaghilev company and Nijinsky's partner; Diaghilev let that moment pass. Butterfingers, Money suggests. He also suggests that Pavlova perceived an essential truth about the Diaghilev enterprise—that it was not primarily dedicated to dancing. This attitude betrayed her into some lapses of judgment (she rejected the title role in *Firebird* because she could not hear the dance pulse in the music), but it also fortified her on the missionary course her career took. She became in the world's eyes the absolute classical dancer, the singular representative of the Russian dance academies, the true successor to Taglioni and Elssler, the one and only great ballerina, the Swan.

Pavlova's art was so new in most of the places she went that reviewers and promoters alike had to search out a vocabulary to describe it. In the more sophisticated capitals, she was known as a "Russian" dancer; Isadora Duncan and Maud Allan were "classical"—i.e., "Greek." The word "ballet" meant nothing. When Pavlova arrived in America, her performance was billed as "ocular opera," and Carl Van Vechten wrote his famous laborious description of a traveling arabesque: "With her left toe pointed out behind her, maintaining her body poised to make a straight line with it, she leapt backward step by step on her right foot." Her physical appearance was new, too. For a dancer, she was thought to be unusually tall and thin, and she was not considered beautiful—not "exquisite" or "bewitching," like Adeline Genée. On behalf of her beloved *Giselle*, she fought the accumulated prejudices of her era. A New York reviewer found that "the ballet is just about as interesting to ordinary play goers now as looking over the files of *Godey's Lady's Book* for 1858 might prove." She danced it in London with Nijinsky. "The little jerky 'tunes' are unendurable. No! *Giselle* will not do!" It was the age of modernism, of expressionism, much too wise for the Wilis. "Who could really be alarmed by these nice young ladies in their white ballet-skirts?"

It may have been in response to criticisms like this that Pavlova began presenting her Wilis in Duncan-like draperies. Pavlova, of course, was a great Giselle; she was to Romantic ballet what Callas later became to bel canto, and ultimately Pavlova triumphed. Her votaries stamped *Giselle* with her image, and it dominates the ballet to this day. Money's book, with its wealth of documentation, makes Pavlova credible as a forerunner of the classical revivalism of our time. He dwells on such episodes as the Hippodrome production, in one act, of *The Sleeping Beauty*. This was in 1916, five years before Diaghilev attempted his own, full-length revival in London. Both Pavlova and Diaghilev were forced to dismantle their productions before the runs were up. Pavlova's, a jewel-box fairyland concocted by Bakst, is far less known than the Diaghilev version, also by Bakst. But then much less is known about Pavlova than about Diaghilev and everyone and everything connected with him.

Anna Pavlova: Her Life and Art is an attempt to correct the record. It is an elaborate testimonial to tireless research, to single-mindedness, to connoisseurship of the most involving kind. Money, who has also done a book about Margot Fonteyn, obviously adores Pavlova, and sometimes his scholarly discipline has to strain against an instinct to protect her, to make her be all things good. He cites her sponsorship of two Fokine ballets to prove that her taste in art was not reactionary. (Perhaps only her taste in music? The ballets were to Liszt and the nonentity Spendiarov. She turned down *Le Coq d'Or*, and it was produced by Diaghilev.) He uses her activism in reform movements at the Maryinsky to suggest that she was politically avant-garde. (But later, when Isadora came home Red, Pavlova was enraged.) If she slapped her partners, there must have been a reason. She was not jealous of Nijinsky or any other dancer. She paid her dancers well and gave expensive gifts. She loved children, small animals, and birds, especially swans. Although Money gives the impression of being able to place her accurately on almost every day of her life, he does not pretend to be omniscient. He speculates on her character without subjecting it to analysis. That she was a lonely woman with an enigmatic sex life is something Money accepts. It was her lot. (Victor Dandré, who attached himself to her in Russia and remained until the end, was possibly her husband; if so, Money believes, there was no sexual union to speak of.) The Pavlova legend has always had about it the odor of martyrdom. Her genius, her toil, her power over the multitudes, and her early death seem to spell sacrifice and tragedy. There was sacrifice, perhaps, in dying at fifty. Implored to stop touring, Pavlova would say, "But my company! What will become of them?" Yet most dancers are dead as dancers by that age. What else but dancing could Pavlova have lived for? There was certain tragedy in the thinning repertory that was also her lot. Pavlova's wanderings began when she was twenty-eight; she had already conquered the standard ballerina repertory, had already claimed her signature roles (Giselle, Nikiya in *La Bayadère, Chopiniana*) and her personal vehicles (*The Swan, Autumn Bacchanale*). For the rest of her life, she was not to create another artistic success. Instead, she circled the earth repeating ancient triumphs, adding more dragonflies, more autumn leaves, more bacchantic veils to the diaphanous train of vanity ballets that sustained her. In India, she refreshed herself with Hindu dancing, and she performed awhile with Uday Shankar. But even this was a return of sorts—to *La Bayadère*.

She pushed on: Egypt, Japan, Australia. Money says of her obsession with touring, "Her body and mind were so programmed to this routine that the thought of abandoning it opened up black chasms of the unknown that terrified her more than the remorselessness of further touring." Perhaps it was to distract herself from such thoughts that she waged one of the most intensive personal publicity campaigns of the period. She endorsed face cream, silk stockings, pianos; she gave interviews by the score; she posed for endless photographs, many of which are reproduced in this book with the care one might expect of Money (who is also a photographer) and the Knopf art department. There is not a bad one in the lot. Like Abraham Lincoln's, Pavlova's face is archetypal; it is changing and changeless at the same time. It responds to the lens as inventively as any movie star's, and it burns with inner life right from the start of the book—from the moment, to be exact, that she becomes a dance student. Its expression is irremediably tragic, but not bleakly so. There is pride in the way the head lifts itself above the tapering pedestal of the neck. And what vitality in that neck! How she flaunts it in her "grand" roles and guards it in her coquettish ones! Even in closeup, Pavlova's discipline proclaims her a dancer. She becomes pathetic only in the photographs that were taken in her forties—when she knows the search has ended. In one photograph, she appears to be offering her hands to the camera, and not her face, but her face is caught anyway, wearing a look of grief. In a portrait on the same page, the chronic depression she suffered from is evidently upon her. Money's caption is "By now Pavlova was less inclined to force cheerfulness for the camera's benefit."

What makes the book valuable is that it isn't keyed to Pavlova's gloom. It projects a multifaceted picture: Pavlova as celebrity, sacred monster, symbol of the dance, artist, and star. The woman was fun, and Money has realized it. It takes some slogging to get through his text, but then Pavlova was a slogger. As the details pile up (enormous pains are taken to sort out her for the most part piddling repertory), we begin to sense something of the pain and joy of hard work, the bliss of sheer continuity, that Pavlova must have felt. Wholeness of mind and body must surely have been her salvation. In the fashion photographs, there is no affectation. There is artificiality, to be sure, along with elegance, wit, and style. In the dozens of dance photographs (some, with unretouched points, escaped Pavlova's vigilance), she shows the protean sensibility of performers of her era; she is always creating roles. But, unlike Karsavina or Nijinsky, she does not disappear into them. No matter the role or the circumstance, onstage or off, the eyes look out with an expression that says, "I have found my life."

—*December 20, 1982*

Mostly Mozart

The dancing at New York City Ballet this winter is that of a great institution in a vintage year. It has been possible to see Farrell at her grandest and Ashley (before an injury put her out) at her most incisive. Nichols and Watts, Kistler and Calegari have all outdone themselves, and the way McBride, returning at forty after maternity leave, has been dancing her old roles is a lesson in the unfathomable technique of a star. Among the men, Andersen has become larger and easier; nearly everyone with a chance to improve has seized it. Yet, with all the brilliant, sensitive, and high-spirited performing that has been going on in the diverse ballets of the Balanchine repertory (*Tchaikovsky Piano Concerto No. 2* and *Symphony in Three Movements* and *Who Cares?* and *Donizetti*

Variations and, above all, *Mozartiana*), one still had to go out of town for the major event of the season: to Kennedy Center, in Washington, where American Ballet Theatre last month staged its revival of *Symphonie Concertante*, an old and—as a setting of Mozart—rare Balanchine work, last danced by New York City Ballet in 1952.

Some Balanchine ballets dropped by Balanchine are passed on to other companies, but *Symphonie Concertante* had not been seen in thirty years. It was, however, notated in the late forties and placed in the archives of the Dance Notation Bureau, in New York. American Ballet Theatre's production is based on this score, and on very little else. No one at New York City Ballet remembers anything of the choreography; Balanchine could not help. On his recommendation, Gretchen Schumacher, a Labanotation expert, was sent to transcribe the steps. When she had done so, Diana Adams, who had danced one of the leading roles, advised on matters of style. The result of the experiment—the first of its kind to be performed on a Balanchine ballet—is the emergence from virtual extinction of a small masterpiece.

Symphonie Concertante issues from the same creative impulse that produced Balanchine's great works of the forties. The youthful brio, the large female corps, even some of the step sequences are to be seen in *Symphony in C* (1947), while the most beautiful passages, in which a man supports two women at the same time, may well have developed from the celebrated fourth variation of *Danses Concertantes* (1944)—the pas de trois for Maria Tallchief, Mary Ellen Moylan, and Nicholas Magallanes. Structurally, there is a resemblance to *Concerto Barocco* (1941), where two ballerinas also correspond to two solo instruments. But in the Mozart ballet (to the Sinfonia Concertante for Violin and Viola, K. 364) Balanchine divides the two solo roles equally; one sees and hears two voices in all three movements. Since *Symphonie Concertante* disappeared from the N.Y.C.B. repertory the same year a new Mozart ballet was produced (*Caracole*, later *Divertimento No. 15*), since it even yielded its scenery for a time to the later piece, many of us who hadn't seen it assumed that it had been supplanted or superseded in some way—"ploughed under," to use Lincoln Kirstein's term. Perhaps at the time Balanchine did not have room for two Mozart ballets. But *Divertimento No. 15* no more crowds out *Symphonie Concertante* than the Ricercata in *Episodes* crowds out *Concerto Barocco*.

Balanchine composed the ballet, in 1945, for one performance only, at Carnegie Hall. Two years later, he reproduced it for Ballet Society, and he retained it when Ballet Society became New York City Ballet. The inordinate size of the corps—twenty-two girls—may have made the piece hard to keep in repertory, especially alongside other giant-corps pieces, like *Symphony in C*. The 1945 cast consisted entirely of School of American Ballet students plus Todd Bolender, who had the lone male role. Balanchine, with no company of his own at this time, was not so hard up for dancers that he had to use students. He could have made his ballet on Ballet Russe de Monte Carlo, of which he was then resident choreographer. His choice of students seems to have had an expressive purpose interlaced with a political one. He and Kirstein (who had just got out of the Army) wanted to form a company based on the school. The Carnegie Hall evening, arranged by Kirstein in collaboration with the National Orchestral Association, was somewhat didactically designed. *Symphonie Concertante* was supposed to show a relation between classical ballet and symphonic music. The presence of students in the cast (and the inclusion of Balanchine's *Circus Polka* on the program) suggests the presence of schoolchildren in the audience. There is a certain diagrammatic austerity in the opening movement of the *Symphonie*. It soon disappears, but the air of a graduation exercise—of crisp little drills and ceremonious play—never quite leaves the piece, and although the pas de trois in the Andante accumulates and sustains an erotic tension, it is tension without passion. Compared with the erotic encounters in *Divertimento No. 15*, the patterns are of a Euclidean purity: no lifts, no twists, no embraces—no climaxes, even. Just a steadily shifting con-figuration of weights, lengths, heights, and densities as the three bodies move across the lines of the music. (And what music. Trust Balanchine to find the tenderest, gravest, and most unearthly Mozart.) The poignance in all this is at once strange and familiar. We recognize in the bright image of ceremony one of Balanchine's controlling metaphors, recurrent throughout his work in the forties. And we know this adolescent-reverie mood from the many ballets of his where the man, bracing two or more women as they launch themselves into space, seems to be both dividing and uniting them and to be himself divided, simulta-neously cradled and dragged apart. In *Symphonie Concertante*, the man stays so contentedly long in his bubble of femininity, leaving it only to stand aside and admire it (whereupon the two women immediately partner each other), and never being forced to shatter it by choosing between his two loves, that he may be unique among Balanchine's romantic heroes. As the Andante ends, the trio is enclosed by six attendant women in another bubble, and the whole cortège glides out of sight, its happy illusion intact. The last movement is an energetic Presto, with multiple entrées. The three principals return separately, are reunited and reseparated. The man gets to dance several emphatic solo passages. We are back in the temperate academic climate of the first movement, yet we've never really left it. The innocence and august impersonality of *Symphonie Concertante* are unbrokenly achieved from first to last.

It would be a pleasure to study the ballet for the secret of its integrity. One would need many more showings than the two that A.B.T. gave during its Wash-ington week. And the company needs to dance the ballet many more times, with different casts. As yet, only Patrick Bissell looks right. Boyish and bright-eyed, partnering and dancing with relaxed authority, he dominated both performances. The casting of Cynthia Gregory and Martine van Hamel together is a tribute to the importance of the ballet, but it sheds no light on roles that were obviously designed for youngsters. For really young dancers one may, of course, substitute youthfulness of style, but neither Gregory nor van Hamel has ever exemplified that. And their individual styles don't mesh. The violin and the viola are sisters—in Mozart as well as in Balanchine. Gregory (violin), with her complacent skill, and van Hamel (viola), with her gracious imperturbability, *are* as one in their defeat of any technical challenges their roles may offer. They've cracked the code stepwise, and they have more than enough stamina, but the steps aren't very hard. Phrasing and attack matter more. Gregory's sense of these things was especially inert; van Hamel's more sharply defined musicality saved her. It's an odd sight: here are two of the most robust and accomplished technicians in American ballet, and they're unable to cut through the surface of their roles. There's technique, and then, to be invidious, there's Balanchine technique. The surface of these roles was made to be cut by milk teeth. In 1945, Balanchine was already envisioning another kind of technical sophistication for American dancers.

To see *Symphonie Concertante* is to revisit the forties and re-recognize Balanchine's links, consciously established in one piece after another, to Petipa and nineteenth-century classicism. In the *Symphonie*, he seems at times to be giving us a Russo-American *Konservatoriet*. The corps, formally arrayed in box lines and repeated motifs, is a Petipa corps. (Balanchine's shift from an uncomplicated "echo" corps to a more organic contrapuntal corps seems to have been completed during this decade.) But the heart of the ballet, now as then, is its disclosure of a corner of the Balanchine pleasure garden we haven't seen before. The Andante that takes us there ranges over terrain as far back as *Serenade* (1934) and the *Tchaikovsky Concerto No. 2* (*Ballet Imperial*, 1941) and as far ahead as the 1981 *Mozartiana*; the phrasal exchanges between the two girls are uncannily like the Farrell-Andersen antiphonal pas de deux. And the more likenesses one sees (the more contradictions, also), the less one understands Balanchine's neglect of this work. If he thought it was too "young" for his dancers, why has the School of American Ballet not revived it? Ballet Theatre has done a great service in bringing the ballet back to the stage. But it is a curatorial service that should have been performed by Balanchine's own organization.

As it happened, Washington saw a Balanchine masterpiece while Balanchine's audience in New York was given a disastrous new ballet by Jacques d'Amboise—overlong, incoherent, and filled with inequalities. Mendelssohn music forms the score, piano and orchestral selections bumpily alternating. Solos, pas de deux, ensembles follow no sequential logic; neither do steps. Little girls appear alongside grownups with no place found for them. (Balanchine's use of children from *Nutcracker* to *Mozartiana* is always a clear assignment, never a cute idea.) The piece is called *Celebration* and is dedicated to the teachers and staff of the School of American Ballet. What a way to celebrate! Let *Symphonie Concertante* do the honors.

I seem to want to get to *Mozartiana*. But there's more to reflect on in this curious business of American Ballet Theatre's putting on a former School of American Ballet work (*Symphonie Concertante* is, among other things, *about* the School of American Ballet), not only because of d'Amboise's misfired tribute to the school but because of the New York season a few weeks ago of American Ballet Theatre II, at the Joyce. This is the junior company that acts as a filter for aspirants to A.B.T. and other big companies. It tours a lot, with a repertory ranging from Petipa and Bournonville to commissioned works from all over. It is a likable young group but not a very fresh one stylistically. Compared with what one might see at any annual S.A.B. recital, the technique is fuzzy, with problems of discontinuity between the upper and lower parts of the body. The ballets are for the most part unchallenging, and collectively the dancers look like a reprocessed version of the parent company in the sixties. I know no solution to faded style except new and venturesome choreography. But chances are that even if the junior A.B.T. were lucky enough to find such a thing—or, even more magically, a person who produces such a thing—the senior A.B.T. would snatch it/him/her away.

I was unfamiliar with one of the new pieces on the Joyce programs, Lynne Taylor-Corbett's *Sequels*, and found it a more appealing work than her *Great Galloping Gottschalk*, though in no less regressive an idiom. The appeal lay in the smoother craftsmanship of the choreography and in its accountability; one never asked who *these* people were or why they were doing *those* things—they were Modern Dancers having a Modern Dance Experience. Watching *Sequels* is a matter of adjusting to certain comfortable, limited expectations. When you shop for furniture, you have a furniture experience—you don't expect the store to have helicopters. Maybe someday Lynne Taylor-Corbett will make a daring piece of work. She is doing yet another ballet for the new A.B.T. season. But will it have helicopters?

Balanchine is such a natural Mozartean that the thought occurs: If he keeps only one Mozart ballet in repertory, he may be trying to resist typecasting. In *Mozartiana*, he even places himself at one remove from the composer. *Mozartiana* is Balanchine communicating with Mozart through Tchaikovsky, while in two of the ballet's four sections Tchaikovsky is dealing with Liszt on Mozart and Mozart on Gluck. The musical accretions don't appear to be as important to Balanchine as they may have been when he made his previous versions of this ballet, but he still visualizes a hall of mirrors. The ballet is concerned with reflections and replications. The four little girls to whom Farrell gives religious instruction in the first scene, the four duchesses who resemble both Farrell and the little girls and from whom the artist figure (Victor Castelli) takes his inspiration—all make a harmonious and reverberant setting for the centerpiece pas de deux. Suzanne Farrell and Ib Andersen are queen and consort. (When Peter Martins danced opposite Farrell last year, they were queen and king.) While the queen collects in her *four* variations all the attributes of females half-grown and full-grown that could possibly interest her consort-lover, Castelli is off in another part of the palace painting these attributes into murals (which he signs "Titian"). The interaction of Farrell and Andersen is the process made visible to us of the artist's labor. Andersen and Castelli are, in other words, two halves of the same "maestro" character: artist, consort, lover, replicator. It's as if the hero of *Symphonie Concertante* had split himself in two, the better to deal with *one* woman. Balanchine was forty-one when he made *Symphonie Concertante*; he recently passed his seventy-ninth birthday. Ripeness is all.

The birthday occasion has been marked by the publication, by Eakins Press, of *Choreography by George Balanchine: A Catalogue of Works*. The book includes a chronology of Balanchine's professional activities and lists of his companies' itineraries, of festivals he directed and roles he performed. There is a bibliography of writings by and about him. The most impressive feature is the catalogue itself, which begins with *La Nuit*, to music of Anton Rubinstein, which Balanchine created around 1920 in Petrograd, and ends four hundred and twenty-four entries later with *Variations for Orchestra*, a solo for Farrell to Stravinsky music which trailed last summer's Stravinsky festival by two weeks. Not only ballets are listed but also operas, ballets for operas, opera-ballets, operettas, musical comedies, films, and television shows, among several other kinds of work. Most of my historical information for this article came from this book. From it, I learned, too, of the creation, in 1942, of still another Mozart ballet, *Concierto de Mozart*, for the Ballet of the Teatro Colón, in Buenos Aires. The music was the A-Major Violin Concerto, K.219. The editors have made a serious attempt to keep track of recensions and revisions as ballets travel down the years. Under *Variations for Orchestra*, for example, the reader is reminded of an earlier Farrell solo to the same music, and is informed that the 1982 version was entirely rechoreographed. Since repertory is in constant flux, and since, furthermore, Balanchine is always making changes in his work, one would expect omissions and errors to be unavoidable. But the catalogue is so hawkeyed that the conscientious reader may feel honor bound to keep the record going. (My own first impulse is to add to the note on décor for No. 368, *Who Cares?*: "Terrible new costumes, January 14, 1983.") This prodigious volume is unillustrated save for a frontispiece—a photograph of the choreographer by Tanaquil Le Clercq, who was the original "violin" in *Symphonie Concertante*.   —*February 7, 1983*

Ordinary People

In the time-honored genealogical tradition of modern dance, choreographers are bred from other choreographers. A dancer in one company gets interested in making dances and starts another company, which produces dancers in a different style, some of whom will get interested in making dances. And so it goes: different and yet again different. But not always new and exciting. The tables over the years show a proliferation of companies; they don't show a proliferation of great choreographers. Choreography takes talent of a kind that not even the most accomplished dancers may possess. However, the tables also show that the best choreographers we've had, from Martha Graham to Twyla Tharp, have been electrifying performers; one could bank on that, just as one could bank on the expectation that sooner or later a good portion of our finest dancers would lose their potential simply because they didn't know how to choreograph, even for themselves. The one thing they'd have left was authority. Even though they weren't turning out remarkable dances, they'd still be the best dancers in their own companies—the system of succession compelled them to be, and the system was inviolable. So one would have thought until about a decade ago.

Sometime in the early seventies, the principle of the choreographer-leader fell into disrepute. Performing collectives sprang up which attributed choreography to the group. Ad-hoc performances were arranged by one person who would convene a group, which would then have the option of sticking together or disbanding. There were groups that did stick together and didn't renounce the idea of the choreographer-leader, but the choreographer-leader was no longer invariably the outstanding dancer in the group. He or she was a conceptualist. The time had come when one could no longer identify the key person in an unfamiliar company merely by picking out the best dancer on the floor. (The first time I saw Andy DeGroat's company, I thought Garry Reigenborn was DeGroat.) The anti-star system of the seventies hasn't entirely succeeded in erasing stars, but it has succeeded in erasing dancing as the basis of stardom. By choreography alone—in their capacity or noncapacity as choreographers—we are asked to recognize the stars of today. If the old system was élitist, the new one is emphatically democratist. Under the old system, star performers would produce self-designed choreography, and if it worked for them, frequently it wouldn't work for anybody else. The problem with the new choreography, which looks as though it were designed at computer terminals, is that just about anybody can do it. Untrained dancers and rudimentary modes of expression are concomitants of computer choreography. Where trained dancers are used, as in Jim Self's company, they're kept busy trying to articulate the demands of an inarticulate printout. (The printout may be read in Self's own blurry performing.) It was different when a choreographer had to rationalize his theories of movement on his own body. At least there'd be *one* good performance to watch. Now that the choreographer-dancer-leader has been conceptualized out of existence, one can only watch good dancers struggle or weak dancers triumph.

The anybody-can-do-it school arose in the sixties as a reaction to exclusive personal virtuosity and self-display. This reaction was only partly dance-related. Deeper impulses lay in the countercultural politique, which was formed largely by progressive-school whiz kids trying to get in step with the underprivileged. Paradoxically, the idea of a minimal vocabulary executed by trained or untrained dancers came about just as the shift occurred in social dancing from learned dances to improvisation. In discothèques around the country, "ordinary" people were making art for recreation; in studios, professional dancers were doing Arthur Murray–like box steps. This may explain why the minimalist revolution never attracted much of an audience. Rooted in populist assumptions, it was out of phase with popular feeling. Besides, when ordinary people went to see dance performances they overwhelmingly chose the ballet, where spectacular lyrical dancing flourished. (To understand the dimensions of this rejection, try to imagine opera enjoying a wave of popularity while Barry Manilow and Elton John compete for government grants.)

The new choreography of today broadens and to some extent coarsens the egalitarian sentiments held by the minimalist vanguard of the sixties. Steve Paxton's "people dances" were like the life-size plaster casts of human bodies one began seeing at that time in art galleries. The dances and the sculpture were statements about how people actually move and look as opposed to how they were made to move and look in the theatre and the museum. It must be remembered that a big factor in Pop Art philosophy was the notion of things in unaccustomed places. Putting ordinary people making ordinary movements on a stage was like hanging a picture of a Campbell's Soup can in an art show. The idea was that the location would do the work of transfiguration which persons and objects normally underwent to become artworthy. As the sixties turned into the seventies and Pop Art polemics eased up, it was possible to see fruitful work—choreography that reaffirmed dancing as a natural human act. This accomplishment, though, was independent of prevailing stylistic trends, and it wasn't until later that these trends put their stamp on the era and decided the human temper of the dances that were being done. People dances had given way to structured choreography of a minimal nature. The beat returned to dominate what had seemed to be random movement in unfigured time. And then music came back—music marked not only by a heavy beat but by incessant rhythmic and melodic repetitions. The beat and the repetitions became characteristic of the new postmodern choreography. By the end of the seventies, it seemed that every new choreographer was presiding over some form of mechanized motion. Choo San Goh was doing it in ballet, and Molissa Fenley, following Lucinda Childs and Laura Dean, was doing it in postmodern dance. However one chooses to interpret the original impulse of the sixties—a symptom, a shock of the moment, or something finer and more lastingly significant—it is hardly possible to deny its conversion into a cult in the seventies. The regulating effect that cults have on creativity is well known. What we're seeing now is regulated *material*—literally, sports and games.

In postmodern dance, as the metrics got tighter and the repetitions more insistent a new kind of content evolved—one that superficially resembled the pedestrian tasks that were assigned to dancers by the older choreographers (like Yvonne Rainer's lugging of mattresses and Trisha Brown's manipulation of sticks). Charles Moulton's dancers stood or knelt in static groups and passed balls back and forth in complicated patterns. Or they flipped color squares in the manner of a cheering section in a stadium. These precision games of Moulton's were not—like the "tasks"—designed to reveal something about movement; they were substitutes for movement. As a cheerful naïve form of vaudeville, they were very entertaining, and audiences took to them. But they were only a new version of artists following box-step diagrams. Moulton is not as limited as I have made him sound, and he keeps on experimenting with popular dances and investigating specific dance forms. He's tried tap; he's even tried old-style expressionistic dance. But the results so far have been dry, a little clinical and Teutonic. Moulton's use of old forms highlights the enormous change that has come over the pop sensibility in recent times. The cornerstone of popular American music and dance has been rhythm, and the rhythmic expression of American masters like Astaire and Louis Armstrong and Duke Ellington has been expansive and buoyant. Moulton, like every other member of his generation, doesn't think of rhythm as something that gets larger and lighter; he thinks of it as getting tighter and heavier. In the dances of Johanna Boyce, which seem to have taken a lot from Moulton, minimal style reaches a new low of childishly gleeful overdeterminism. It's tiddly-pom with a vengeance.

Boyce's work, which I've seen quite a lot of lately at Dance Theater Workshop, doesn't just reduce the idea of minimalism—it makes reductionism a whole new principle. It completes the reduction of rhythm to metrics, and of plastic relationships to functional ones, and it goes further: it cuts away the supports of basic bodily gesture—it cuts into the *bone* of dance. The point of minimalism was to clarify and if possible to revitalize basic bodily gesture, but Boyce doesn't bother with basics; she hurls people around and lets the gesture take care of itself. She gets hold of one step combination (say, a hop-skip-jump) and repeats it, varying only number and direction, in a rhythm that gradually becomes deadening. In *Kinscope*, she has her company skip from one end of the piece to the other, throwing and catching and bouncing balls as they go. It sounds like fun, but it's so pressured and rhythmically so unrelenting that it becomes an endurance test—a black-humored marathon. The audience gets into the spirit and, at the end, cheers like the audience at *Rocky* or *Chariots of Fire*; the dancers have come through their ordeal. Team sports have fed choreographers ideas for a long time, but until now no one had thought to convert a sporting event into a dance. As choreographer (or games mistress), Boyce doesn't make the conversion complete. Things get wobbly the minute the dancers have to do two things at once or in two rhythms or speeds. In *Kinscope*, they each have to do an arm-whirling windup before throwing the ball, and very few of them can do it without looking frantic and smearing the movement. The idea of basic gesture, firmly supported from the base of the spine and cleanly delivered, is tossed away as casually as the ball.

It's rare to see so little discrimination brought to bear upon fundamentals. The last time I saw anything as heedless as this was in Molissa Fenley's solo concert last fall (*Eureka*, at Dance Theater Workshop), in which she performed almost continuously at a fairly brisk pace for over an hour. It was almost as naked a sports event as some of Boyce's work. Fenley didn't toss balls, but she did toss off a small repertory of dance steps, bringing to them about as much plastic energy, refinement, and variety of expression as she would have needed to cross a finish line. (Fenley is a runner who believes in working out in gyms instead of taking dance classes.) Like Boyce's, her dynamics are confined to a single choice between fast and slow. But where Fenley tried to create a lyrical impression, waving her arms and flinging back her head (she reminded me of gymnasts who add ballet "finish" to their performance), Boyce seems to value gracelessness and cloddishness. The heavy inflexible rhythms are as deliberate as the tackiness of the costumes she designs, which are mostly shapeless T-shirts and shorts, rendered in a nightmarish assortment of floral prints. She also uses a number of people who aren't dancers, so that the bodies lumber where they might float, and look awkward and vulnerably sexual when stripped (for a nude sequence), unlike dancers' bodies. I have never understood the appeal of unskilled labor in the performing arts; still less do I understand why the unskilled should wish to appear downright stupid. There's a vein of thick-necked truculence through all Boyce's work that I've seen. (I include last year's concert *Incidents*.) In *Out of the Ordinary*, she has her people tape coins onto their shoes and try to tap-dance. They try it for so doggedly long that, again, the audience takes its cue and begins to applaud condescendingly.

Boyce herself is about twenty pounds overweight for a dancer, and if she ever performed with another professional company her bios don't reveal it. Like Fenley and a few others, she seems to have come to New York straight from college and set up shop as a choreographer right away. (Moulton and Self were briefly in Merce Cunningham's company.) I wish I felt that she took more pleasure in her work and wasn't so determined to prove something. I wish, too, that she'd give up her evening-length autobiographical pieces, which come too close to being a form of personal mortification. It's interesting, though, that when Boyce did her solo in the latest of these epics, *With Longings to Realize*, she left the balls and batons and hockey sticks out of it and did a slow, brooding dance with flailings of the arms and little twitches, rather like—wistfully like—one of Merce Cunningham's solos. Was this the real Boyce, and how did it fit in with the clunkiness of all the rest? Boyce may need more time to emerge fully. Just now she's like a physical-education instructor trying to borrow a little status from the dance department.

Postmodern conceptualists are now being asked to create for ballet companies. It's not such an adventure as it might seem. People whose own companies resemble drill teams can easily conceptualize a ballet company in terms of the ballet syllabus and its classifications of steps. The charm of Tharp's 1973 *Deuce Coupe* for the Joffrey Ballet came partly from Tharp's parody of this idea—a parody of conceptualism itself. I'm sorry that the original *Deuce Coupe* had to be replaced by the comparatively straightforward and dull version the company does now, in which almost no sign of self-awareness remains. I looked in vain for signs of self-awareness in *Fire*, Laura Dean's new piece for twelve Joffrey dancers. *Fire* takes a series of by now familiar Dean devices and transposes them more or less even-handedly into ballet terms. It gets nothing from the transposition. Well, one thing: chaînés on point are better to look at than Dean's customary spins. What the experiment proves is that a step is a step is a step; what it may also prove is that Dean has a blind eye for everything but group pattern. In construction, *Fire* is a slow crescendo in which the movement stays off the beat until the climax is reached, then hits the beat hard. (The piece would have been better had it ended at this point; instead it has a tacked-on duet.) There's no tension in the phrase to match the accumulating tension in the pattern. The crescendo is full of lulls between the introduction of a motif and its structural integration. It makes no difference what steps the motif consists of. The larger units in the weave—the solos and pas de deux—are all very flashy and unconvincing, and there are intimations of hostility in the partnering, which seem to have no expressive purpose. What is *Fire* about? Does conceptualism yield a concept of fieriness? I could find no clue, either in the choreography or in the backdrop—an architectural drawing, by Michael Graves, of what could have been several incinerators standing about on a grassy plain.

—February 21, 1983

Choreographer Under Balanchine

When they were unveiled last fall, the New York State Theater's new proscenium and enlarged orchestra pit were very welcome by-products of the extensive acoustical renovation that had just been carried out. They really seemed to make a difference. The lowered proscenium—it had been dropped to a level some fifteen feet below the topmost ring of seats—sharpened the stage's focus and seemed to enliven the human scale of the performance. The musicians, no longer made to sit under the stage, projected a more balanced sound. But these changes quickly became unnoticeable. They didn't produce a new look or a new sound; they only corrected long-standing weaknesses, and one adjusts more quickly to comfort than to revelation. The renovated theatre was celebrated on opening night of the winter ballet season with a joint performance by the New York City Ballet and the New York City Opera. Each company did scenes from its repertory, choosing composers held in common. *Vienna Waltzes* inspired the two most effective transitions. Peter Martins waltzed Karin von Aroldingen through the Lehár episode, and singers followed with numbers from *The Merry Widow*, using the same set—Rouben Ter-Arutunian's "Maxim's." In the last-act trio from *Der Rosenkavalier*, the two women trailing in panniered skirts across the darkened stage paved the way for the entrances of the women in white in Balanchine's setting of the *Rosenkavalier* waltzes. The acoustical adjustments mattered less to the ballet than to the opera. If there cannot always be perfect orchestral sound at the ballet, there should at least not be noise. That house curtain that used to rise and fall with a sigh, like a freight elevator, has been silenced. But the First Ring's capacity as a whispering gallery has, if anything, been enhanced. I was sitting there for the *Rosenkavalier* scenes, and there was a sibilance all about, like—yes, ladies' skirts across the grass.

Peter Martins's appearance in this gala was the last I saw of him as a dancer all season. Ib Andersen took over for Martins in *Orpheus* as well as in *Apollo*, Joseph

Duell took over for him in *Stravinsky Violin Concerto*, *Robert Schumann's "Davidsbündlertänze,"* and *Union Jack*; Sean Lavery and Adam Lüders did his other roles. A back injury and the pressure of his mounting duties as ballet master—besides supervising the bulk of the rehearsals and the casting, he put on two premières—kept Martins backstage. Toward the end of the season, he several times partnered Suzanne Farrell in *Tzigane*, but I missed him and saw Andersen instead. A dancer like Martins does not easily pass out of the mind's eye. It is only now that the season is over that I realize how seldom he danced. Perhaps had his replacements been less vivid I would have missed him more. But the only bad patch was Andersen slithering up to Farrell in *Tzigane*, and he wasn't actually bad; it was just that only Martins succeeds in justifying the presence of a partner for Farrell in this ballet. From what Martins says about *Tzigane* in his recently published book, *Far from Denmark* (Little, Brown), it's clear why. *Tzigane*, created for the Ravel festival, in 1975, was originally to have been a solo for Farrell, with some girls coming in at the end. Martins felt he hadn't been given enough to do in the Ravel festival, and he was eager to impress Balanchine with his desire to work. He shot his way into the ballet. (He quotes himself telling Balanchine, "It's O.K., I'll come in with the girls and sweep the floor. . . . Don't worry, it will be good.") In effect, Martins shoots his way into *Tzigane* every time he enters; it takes that kind of frightening conviction to be effective in the role, and one can only surmise the weight of calculation that went into Balanchine's fashioning of the male role, based on Martins's desperate need to take part in what was—and still is—a tour de force for Suzanne Farrell. It makes sense that if he could perform only one role in the course of the season, it would be *Tzigane*.

The drama of *Far from Denmark*, which was written with Robert Cornfield, is made of a succession of little crises like *Tzigane*, in which Martins confronts Balanchine. The resolution comes when Martins persuades Balanchine of his seriousness as a dancer and his willingness to belong to New York City Ballet and believe in the value system it represents. (Martins had previously passed another crisis, agreeing to sign with American Ballet Theatre and reneging at the last minute.) The book ends with Martins, now a choreographer as well as a principal dancer, regularly and more or less happily turning out pieces under Balanchine's supervision and summing up what he has learned so far. Because Martins takes himself for a disciple and because he began his discipleship at a relatively mature age, he has much to tell us; *Far from Denmark* becomes the first book on record to describe the growing pains of a choreographer under Balanchine. It is also worth reading for other reasons, of course. Martins is good company. The book's "voice" is remarkably unguarded, and as it ranges over a variety of personal and professional topics, seemingly holding nothing back, we may be reminded of another voice—August Bournonville's, in *My Theatre Life*. Martins—candid, generous, gregarious, inquisitive, yet firmly in control of himself and his views—sounds a lot like the paternal Bournonville. Perhaps it's the Danish temperament, but he even strikes notes of moral severity, not unlike the reformer Bournonville:

But when I choreograph I search for what is really right, what is the best and clearest and most truthful. I avoid any big applause-getting moments unless they are required, I avoid imposing any extraneous effects, and I get furious when the dancers start acting up in my ballets.

I see that I've become outspoken about my profession, for now I feel some real urge that comes from my deepening commitment to dance, to see that standards are raised. I want to make dance a better-functioning profession, both artistically and organizationally. I am sick and tired of this pathetic inadequacy I am seeing: I'd like the audience to be alert to fakery, I want inadequate and weak ballet masters axed if they can't cut it.

Martins seems pretty sure that he can cut it. His confidence is seen, too, in the fact that he never feels a need to explain or defend his choice of dancing as a profession. He lived in a country that thinks nothing of letting little boys grow up to be dancers. Not only that—there were musicians and dancers in his family. He had the benefit of training from childhood at the Royal Danish Ballet school, and for years he won ballroom-dance trophies on the side. (That explains his special prowess in *Vienna Waltzes*.) Martins brings the immensity of this cultural background to his job as ballet master. He has an institutional understanding of what it takes to make dances and dancers; he doesn't have only his own career to draw on. In this respect, he's so far ahead of any American choreographer of his generation that it's indecent; only Baryshnikov, at Ballet Theatre, has comparable authority.

But none of it would matter if he didn't also have talent. After the production of *The Magic Flute*, first for the School of American Ballet and then for the company, I think there can be no doubt of Martins's talent. It was this piece, a reconstruction of the 1893 Drigo ballet, that won him the appointment as ballet master. It was danced again this season, with a largely new cast, and for the fusty kind of thing it is it came up as crisp and fresh as new lettuce. Even the fustiness was fun. Last year, Martins made the Stravinsky *Concerto for Two Solo Pianos* for Heather Watts—his best choreography for her—and showed what he could do with a right-up-to-the-minute contemporary subject on a large canvas: in this case, sexual tensions in an over-civilized society. Neither of these ballets is a masterpiece, and neither of his new ballets is, either, and it may be that Martins will go along in this gratifying fashion for some time, showing "what he can do"— showing flashes of brilliance, even—but not making a great deal of difference to the art of choreography. That is not a bad prospect. Martins's work has been essentially investigative, and one feels his compulsion to work through a phase until certain questions have been settled in his mind. So far, watching his work and guessing which questions are unsettling him this time has been fascinating.

It is unlike Martins to mistake the measure of his material. But in *Delibes Divertissement*, the first of his premières this season, he got off on the wrong foot and never produced the ballet he seemed to have set out to make. I think he may have underestimated the fantasy of the Delibes music (selections from *Sylvia*) and what it takes to maintain a grip on it. Balanchine's Delibes ballets look like breezy tossed-off affairs, but they—*La Source* in particular—contain a tough core of thought. It's in these impalpable little "filler" ballets of his that Balanchine's mastery is most elusive. Martins tries to create some substance for his dancers (Watts and Jock Soto) in the pas de deux and succeeds only in making pointless fancywork. He avoids clichés in the ballerina's variation (the famous pizzicato one) but in doing so turns it into another string of pitfalls for the dancer. How, Martins must have been asking himself, did Mr. B. create so much interest to such bland music? How, indeed. You sense Martins's relief the minute he gets away from this deceptive blandness and into the more exotic portions of the score. Soto and four girls have a number (Pas des Ethiopiens) that Martins handles with little dartlike touches of character color, and things come alive again in the coda, which has some of the bacchantic surge of Balanchine's *Walpurgisnacht Ballet*. *Delibes Divertissement* is another piece that was first done for S.A.B. students, and it was put on by the company this season as a replacement for a Robbins première. It probably shouldn't be looked at too closely. But just because it is so clearly a picture of Martins trying to conjure his way out of a bind it compels you to look—look and think. Nothing Martins has made is dismissible.

The other new ballet is full of ideas, too, but most of them work. Set to Rossini chamber music, it's Martins's best-made dance suite since the *Sonate di Scarlatti* ballet, of 1979. In his book, Martins says that he originally named that ballet *Giardino di Scarlatti*, but that Balanchine vetoed the title, saying it sounded like an Italian restaurant. And Martins goes on to relate what else Balanchine had to say about titles: "Balanchine pointed out to me that I hadn't begun the ballet with a garden party in mind, and that if I had, the whole work would have been different. Maybe, he said, you would have choreographed it differently and shown us a garden. As it was, I was misrepresenting the piece, smothering it in an alien notion." Well taken. But the notion that a ballet is nothing but a literal representation of its music is also alien. Balanchine has been getting by with this suggestion for years, and Martins, following suit, calls his Rossini ballet *Rossini Quartets*, meaning that the music consists of two sonatas for string quartet written (at the age of twelve) by Rossini. But to follow literally the course of the music would be to indulge in music visualization, and neither Balanchine nor Martins has ever done that. What they have done instead is to fit a choreographic plan over, around, and through the music so that an effect of mutual support is reached. And one doesn't see quartets of dancers in *Rossini Quartets*—one is far more apt to see duos, trios, and sextets. In fact, *Giardino di Rossini* would be a lot closer to the experience of the ballet, because we do see something like an eighteenth-century formal garden in the choreography's clustering ensembles and ambient paths. The floral bloom of the women—Farrell plus Judith Fugate, Elyse Borne, and Lisa Hess—is especially sweet. And there is even a garden set—the one by David Mitchell that was used for the "Dance in America" videotaping of *Bournonville Divertissements*. One can see that Martins is heading for Balanchine-Mozart terrritory here, and also that, compared with Balanchine-Delibes, it's safe ground. He creates an impression of profusion and symmetry, a meticulous sense of line and ornament, a harmony of scale and impetus. The three ladies of the ensemble and their partners—Daniel Duell, Jean-Pierre Frohlich, and Kipling Houston—are all brightly featured. There may be an overuse of canonic movement in these sections, but, by and large, Martins's invention flows whenever these dancers are on the stage. If he had been content to make a Rossini sextet, he might have had a perfect, unimpeachable, and rather useless little ballet.

But Martins poses questions. He wants to explore the shadowed paths—the metaphysical side of the Baroque. He brings on Farrell and her partner, Lüders, and right away the little ballet threatens to crumble. Martins's choreography for Farrell is a question within a question; he gets carried away with his investigations of her technique. He asks her for a wide assortment of her awkward graces, but he doesn't combine them into a portrait—he trails them through the ballet like the pieces of a puzzle. We can feel his excitement over her, yet it's the technical mechanics of her style which keep exciting him, not the illusion that they can create. And although we see what Martins wants of her—the whole possibility she offers of strange proportion and mysterious connection to the scene before us—we don't see him do more than indicate that possibility. To his credit, Martins doesn't take Farrell and her impact for granted; he really works at trying to integrate her and Lüders with the rest of the ballet. But in order to achieve integration Martins would have had to take a giant step artistically—from the invention of steps to the dramatization of forms.

Martins tries various strategies of integration, and even on the level of incident they don't make sense. For example, the little ritualistic passage whereby Lüders exits, leaving Farrell with the women, and then, after a brief adagietto that carries the linked-together group across the stage, Farrell also exits, taking one or two dancers with her and admitting others, who join whoever is left in a pas de trois. The first time the ritual happens, it's Duell who joins Borne and Hess; the second time, it's Frohlich and Houston who join Fugate—the trios are mirror opposites. But whether Farrell takes with her one dancer or two, male or female, seems sheerest happenstance, and, in fact, we don't even see that she takes anybody with her; people just leave at the same time. So the ritual has no magic. Farrell isn't the catalyst of change that she might be, and Lüders—who seems in a hurry to abandon her—isn't her agent, as he might well be, too. The invisible film that binds all the dancers in the Andante of *Divertimento No. 15*, as partners succeed partners in wave after wave—does it take the genius of Balanchine to create that? In another passage, Lüders partners Farrell while the three other men hover on the sidelines. And hover is all they do; one wants to see them pulled organically into the pas de deux long before they compose an escort for the principals as they exit. Martins appears to be contradicting his own intentions. There's a similar contradiction in *Delibes Divertissement* where the principals are twice pulled apart by the corps, as Giselle and Albrecht are by the Wilis. And *then* Martins has them come together and dance, as if (as in *Giselle*) the tension had been resolved. But there was no tension there in the first place. Can one make decorative filigree out of what once was drama? When does incident become pattern and pattern metaphor?

Perhaps the biggest question for Martins, and for Joseph Duell, another capable young choreographer working in the company, is to what extent Balanchine's own answers to these questions are adduceable as models, as precedents, and as a license to proceed. In Duell's *Création du Monde*, the flashing surface of a ballet is created. Duell has duplicated Balanchine's stylistic manner and mode of address, but he hasn't tapped through to the process by which Balanchine arrived at his manners and modes. Martins is aware of this subterranean process; in his book he talks about locating the "central pulse" of a piece of music—its "structural bones and impetus." And that, to be sure, is what the process means to Balanchine. But Martins's work so far hasn't shown a great sensitivity to individual pieces of music precisely in the way that Balanchine's work does show it—in the evolution and progression of a distinctive imagery, different in each ballet. One suspects that in Balanchine's case questions about incident and filigree and metaphor don't even arise; once he's broken open the music, he has all the answers. One suspects, too, that Martins's gifts as a choreographer are much more compartmentalized than Balanchine's—that he can compose lyrically and he can compose dramatically, but all the possibilities in between, which Balanchine has explored time and again, may be closed off. Balanchine has made drama—great and exalted drama—from purely lyrical and formal elements, but that doesn't mean it's the only goal of choreography.

Although *Rossini Quartets* conceals most of its problems behind a very smooth and appealing façade, it still comes out strangely shaped: the perfect sextet foundation supports the folly that the material for Farrell and Lüders becomes as Martins tries to take it farther. (He takes it so far that the coda, in which all the components of the ballet should gather and rhyme and rest, looks like a scramble.) The first time I saw the piece, Farrell, for all the tricky balancing acts she has to perform, looked as if she weren't doing enough. By the end of the season, she was plumping out her role—not with added tricks but with finer and more suspenseful tact in continuity, threading one event to the next. Lüders did the difficult partnering very well. A pity his most outstanding dance passage stands out because it is overchoreographed. (Overchoreographing is a tendency Martins falls into now and then. But, he reports in the book, Balanchine has already warned him about it.) Some observers like to point out that Martins doesn't make the ballets that, from the way he dances, you think he'd make. His celebrated reserve onstage doesn't, I guess, prepare people for the brightness and tenacity of his work. But from his earliest days with N.Y.C.B. Martins' unique quality—he had it especially as a partner—was patience. If you rule out of that attribute any suggestion of passivity, it's what he shows now as a choreographer. He is going to keep asking questions until he is satisfied.   —*March 7, 1983*

Doe, a Deer, a Female Deer

Dance Theatre of Harlem spent its annual City Center season piling up revivals from the four corners of the earth. It revived, to list just the main offerings, de Mille's *Fall River Legend* and Lichine's *Graduation Ball* and Balanchine's *Square Dance* (the old version, with the caller) and—most improbable choice of all—Nijinska's *Les Biches*. Maybe the directors think that these dated pieces are appropriate training vehicles for young dancers. The company, handsome as ever, *is* younger these days, and greener, especially in the men's division. In any case, dealing in back numbers seems to have become house policy. D.T.H. appears to be trying on every style of ballet in the warehouse, just to see how it looks. How it looks in the dances, that is; the ballets are invariably redecorated. I attribute this to another house rule: visual design is carefully adjusted to skin color in every production. In the case of a famous décor, such as Benois's *Graduation Ball* or Laurencin's *Les Biches*, the new costumes and scenery are modelled on the original, retaining what is notable and necessary (the yellow dresses and the uniforms in *Graduation Ball*, the stinging sapphire blues and cloudy pastels in *Les Biches*) and eliminating restrictive references (Laurencin's fair-skinned does and demoiselles). Otherwise, artistic direction is color-blind, as it should be. If there is such a thing as an international repertory, black American classical dancers have as much claim to it as white ones.

And, in fact, it was only the poor lighting (endemic to this company) that spoiled the authentic twenties-summer-resort look of *Les Biches*. John C. Gilkerson's palette did a good job of warming up the pastels without blurring their delicacy, and the dancers in their plumed hats and taffy dresses looked ready to pose for Carl Van Vechten's camera. But visual credibility goes only so far. Apart from its good looks and scrupulous sound (the Poulenc score was given with its seldom heard choral parts—one voice for each part), this was a puzzling *Les Biches*. But then it is a puzzling ballet.

Les Biches (*The Does*) is worth reviving as a historical document. One of the handful of surviving works by Diaghilev's only woman choreographer, it is as intensely feminine a ballet as the *Polovtsian Dances* was masculine, not only in the quality of its experience but in its attitudes. Nijinska satirized fashionable Parisian society, and her satire is curiously estranged—neither cold nor envious but almost scientific in its scrutiny and in the bluntness of its conclusions. She presents a flock of women, silly for the most part, and only three men, who are even sillier. The point, though, is that the men are monolithic stud-athlete types, immediately boring, while there are various ages and conditions of women—some that had never been seen before on the ballet stage. *Les Biches* (which can be translated *The Darlings*) could well have been a woman choreographer's revenge on a century or more of female stereotypes in the ballet. But Nijinska doesn't seem to have had anything on her mind except representing, to Poulenc's music, the highly artificial characters she saw around her. The diversity of female types—they include an ensemble of tumescent young girls, a flamboyant Older Woman wrapped in pearls and waving a cigarette holder, a somewhat enigmatic brooder, and two inseparables in gray, whom Cocteau compared to the female lovers in Proust—was Nijinska's idea (she did not work from a scenario), and it was, in 1924, highly provocative. Misia Sert and Chanel, close friends and Ballets Russes eminences, were involved in the preparations for the ballet and may have lent some of their personal flair to Nijinska's formulations. The result was another of Diaghilev's scandalous successes. The audience claimed to recognize itself in the ballet, and most reviewers characterized the entire work—dances, décor, and music—in terms of an atmosphere that these elements shared in creating: some indefinable compound of elegance and poignance and ambiguity. Those terms have clung to the ballet ever since.

Looking at the Laurencin designs, one begins to be captivated by the legend of *Les Biches*. Listening to Poulenc's music, one begins to believe it. But, watching the ballet, one doubts whether the magical atmosphere ever existed or whether, if it existed, it could have lasted as long as people say it did. As late as 1946, Poulenc wrote that *Les Biches* was "a ballet in which you may see nothing at all or into which you may read the worst." And he went on to make what, in years since, has proved to be the most ambiguous of all comments on the ambiguity of *Les Biches*: "In this ballet, as in certain of Watteau's pictures, there is an atmosphere of wantonness which you sense if you are corrupted but which an innocent-minded girl would not be conscious of." The trouble with the D.T.H. production is that it is innocent-minded, even puritanical. Any latent ambiguity in the dance of the two friends or in that of the Older Woman and her muscle-bound companions is blanked out or smothered in wholesome laughter. But beneath this misinterpretation lies the bare truth: there is simply not enough (left?) in Nijinska's dances to be ambiguous about. The ballet was reconstructed for D.T.H. by Juliette Kando, from Benesh notation, and staged by Irina Nijinska, the choreographer's daughter. The two previous productions I saw had Bronislava Nijinska's own supervision and were nebulous to a point of inanity. One could only conclude that by that time (the sixties) the essence of Nijinska had evaporated.

Clearly, this is what has happened to the most famous character in the ballet, the enigmatic young woman who dances the Adagietto all by herself, in a short blue velvet tunic and white gloves. The brevity of the tunic—it comes to the top of the thigh—does not tantalize as it once did, and the épaulé poses and stalkings on point have lost their unique potency. (I kept seeing, superimposed on Nijinska's images, flashes from, of all things, Ruthanna Boris's *Cakewalk*.) Yet La Garçonne, as she is sometimes called, is at the center of the ballet's mystique. One still reads that this figure "may be" a page boy (whatever that is) and not a woman at all, and that *that* "may be" the point of his/her duet with the principal athlete. Is there anything quainter than the androgynous glamour of the twenties and thirties? Even if we could still believe in it, there is nothing of androgyny in La Garçonne's movements. Rather, there's a melancholy, a strained introversion, which we identify with a certain kind of faded chic. The bisexual image of the Blue Girl (as Nijinska preferred to call her) may have been suggested more by the way Vera Nemtchinova, who originated the part, looked in it and in the costume than by any strict intention of Nijinska's. No one I have seen in the role has looked markedly different from D.T.H.'s Virginia Johnson, who is coolly beautiful and remote. (Johnson unaccountably adopts a hard makeup with, I thought, a suggestion of whiteface, but it may have been the lighting.) The character, all artifice, was doomed to fade back into the iconography of the twenties, which spawned her. A forerunner of Garbo, she's as invisible to us today as the dangerous "androgynous" Garbo—lost, like the sweet "androgynous" Laurencin, to the annals of fashion and old perfume ads. Why does the mystique continue? The music, for one reason. And Poulenc's own enthusiasm for Nijinska's choreography was strong from the start. In a letter to Diaghilev, he wrote of one rehearsal in which things happened on the ballet's blue couch that would be remarkable today if one could only see them. The fact that one can't suggests either that Nijinska edited them out or that Poulenc was seeing things that weren't really there—a possibility he himself admits. The further fact, though, is that the reputation of *Les Biches* is built on the testimony of Poulenc, Cocteau, and legions of the suggestible. The ballet is a Rorschach test: Look, and you may see. The only thing you may not see is an inkblot.

In the Nijinska canon, *Les Biches* corresponds to Nijinsky's *Jeux* (as *Les Noces* corresponds to his *Sacre du Printemps*). Where her brother's ostensible subject was sport, Nijinska's is fashion, and both ballets are also about sex. Yet when Nijinska mentioned *Les Biches* in statements and interviews it was always to discuss formal matters—steps, positions, choreographic style—and to stress her allegiance to classicism. The D.T.H. program contains a typical quotation. Nijinska's way of talking about her ballets and those of her brother reflects the modern fixation on form; it leads us to think that whatever it was in *Les Biches* that aroused fascination was produced by pure and absolute dance. The bony dance structure—a divertissement without a plot—keeps us from seeing that *Les Biches* is not that purely expressive a ballet. Nor is it the porous Fokine kind of ballet which dance-actors can interpret. The studied, self-conscious moves and poses are intended to speak for themselves, but in contemporary performance they are no longer inhabited by meaning. When Nijinska predicted that her "choreographic discoveries" would be absorbed into the main body of classical dance, she was in a way prophesying the death of *Les Biches*. We no longer see what the critic A. V. Coton meant when he called the pas de deux an "arch comment on the rigors and difficulties of pure-line classical dancing." Nijinska's impurities ("phases of violent and harsh lifts and a final phase of acrobatics in which the female is supported at shoulder height in full extension whilst the Athlete struts proudly") have become common usage. The draining, by time, of meaning from movement creates an irremediable central emptiness that must be faced by anyone who thinks to revive this artifact of the golden twenties, with its glorious, undiminished score.

A few blocks south of the City Center, where the Harlem dancers work themselves into a tizzy in their charming *Schéhérazade*, lies the current revival of *On Your Toes*, with its pseudo-*Schéhérazade* ballet *Princess Zenobia*, originally created by Balanchine, and revived by Peter Martins with the addition of a pas de deux that really is a feat of see-it-or-not invention. The supported adagio, danced by Natalia Makarova and George de la Peña, is precisely that "arch comment on . . . rigors and difficulties" described by Coton. For those familiar with such things, the contrivances and convolutions are a joke, but they're so evenly delivered that those who don't get the point don't miss it. Martins's pas de deux is a generalization of ballet's absurdities; it doesn't really have anything to do with *Schéhérazade*. What follows is an approximation of Balanchine's gagged-up finale, in which somebody is always out of step. Here the joke is unmissable, although *it* has nothing to do with Fokine's ballet, either. A few exotic backbends and prances and a few tons of beads and satin pillows suffice for *Schéhérazade*. True, it is no longer a very plump target, but then it isn't being seriously aimed at.

The satirical objective of the show and, it seems to me, its whole dazzle are concentrated in the person of Natalia Makarova, who makes of herself a delightful figure of fun. As a dancer she seems to be working in second gear, but she has so much energy and radiance as an actress that we don't need *Princess Zenobia* to establish her, or even *Slaughter on Tenth Avenue* to bring her performance to a climax. Makarova has always known how to maximize her material. (She once danced a celebrated Blue Girl in London, which I would love to have seen.) She understands that the part of Vera Baronova, technically a Russian ballerina, is really that of a thirties-Hollywood-movie screwball, and she plays it silky, pettish, and sly, with shrieking Lyda Roberti–Isabel Jewell outbursts. (With her blond thirties fringe, she even looks like Isabel Jewell. With her thick Russian accent, she sounds like Akim Tamiroff.) Makarova reincarnates the great movie tradition of beautiful and funny women. She fits so snugly into the heart of this thirties show that when she has to dance the ballets, which come from another world, she seems to be behaving with unreasonable respectability. (But it's better than if she turned them into camp.) *Slaughter* is a mixture of ballet and vaudeville-style apache dancing; it's very much an American Ballet product, and the costume designer has obviously looked at old George Platt Lynes photographs. In the two striptease dances (which have been altered to accommodate her) and in the seduction pas de deux, Makarova is almost disconcertingly straight. She's also made up a little too tartily. She may be mistaking the heavy-breathing, limb-flinging sexy acrobatics for real drama. The second pas de deux, in which she stops the bullet meant for the hero, is more her meat. It, too, has been slightly rearranged to take advantage of her boneless legato style.

Martins, in charge of all these adjustments, manages them without a break in Balanchine's style, even though he cannot have seen much more of *Slaughter* than a few performances of the 1968 New York City Ballet revival, and had to entrust the actual work of reconstruction to two City Ballet dancers, Susan Hendl and Susan Pilarre. The new version differs from the 1968 one not only in the choreography for Makarova but in a few narrative particulars, such as having the warning note delivered to the Hoofer by a waiter, who makes a special entrance, instead of by the undead corpse of the Strip-Tease Girl, lying in full sight on the stage. The note, of course, warns the Hoofer that he will be shot from the audience at the finish of his big dance. Lara Teeter, who performs this role, seems to have been cast on the strength of his all-American looks. He's too big and stolid a partner for Makarova, and not a good enough dancer to fill out a role that made Ray Bolger a star. For me, the part of the Hoofer is identified with Arthur Mitchell, who danced it in 1968 opposite Suzanne Farrell, and who soon afterward founded Dance Theatre of Harlem. When Teeter started tapping in circles, knowing each tap could be his last one, I thought of Mitchell and the way he built tension. Teeter's circling is too slow, and the terrified reprises taken to stay the assassin's bullet lack the ever more desperate ingenuity that in Mitchell's performance made them funny.

Ballet was new to Broadway in 1936, but in 1983 tap dancing is more of a curiosity than ballet. Perhaps it's a sign of the times that the star of today's *On Your Toes* is a ballerina, while the male lead's contribution to the tap dances is either tepid or nonexistent. The title number, which pits tap pyrotechnics against ballet ones, suffers from the nonparticipation of the Teeter character. But Donald Saddler, who devised all the non-ballet dancing in the show, solved the problem by blending the opposing factions into an ensemble blockbuster very much like the one Balanchine created for the 1938 film *The Goldwyn Follies*. How many people it has taken to replace Balanchine! He's even had to replace himself.

—*March 21, 1983*

Bad News

The cast of Merce Cunningham's *Quartet* is four dancers (Helen Barrow, Karen Fink, Judy Lazaroff, and Rob Remley) plus Cunningham himself. Whatever this has to do with the scoring of David Tudor's sound accompaniment— Tudor's title is *Sextet for Seven*—need not detain us. What matters is Cunningham's relationship to his dancers. He has told us before (notably in *Rebus* and invariably in his Events) that he stands behind them and a little to one side— that his position as a dancer is no longer the leading one. When the curtain goes up on *Quartet*, he's alone upstage left, standing with his head and torso inclined to one side. And he doesn't move around much in the course of the action; he holds his territory, advances, retreats, becomes briefly involved with the others in ways that seem unsatisfactory, and leaves before the end. You are not likely to miss anything he does, not only because of the distance between him and the other dancers but because of the closeness: for all that he now abjures broad movement and intricate footwork, he is very much a part of what they do. Some Cunningham pieces give us a full exposition of Cunningham movement. *Quartet* is one of those with a restricted palette. Though it ranges from Cunningham's personal minimalistic gesture to the more expansive, space-devouring activities of the group, the gradations in size, speed, and force combine with the variations in shape and direction to form a series of tonal clusters. At times, the movements of Cunningham and the group are actually the same; more often, they're architecturally related, the way a cupola is to a Victorian mansion. Something of the same relationship between Cunningham and the group occurred last season in *Gallopade*, but whereas *Gallopade* is a wild comedy of eccentric movement *Quartet* seems to center on a tragic perception of human behavior. The amazing thing is that both pieces—both the comedy and the tragedy—appear to have been developed by Cunningham from the same strain of rhetoric.

A recurring movement in *Gallopade* is the jeté ouvert in which the body is thrown from side to side while it hangs forward in a crouch and the arms and head waggle absurdly. The open leap is missing from *Quartet*, but the shape of it is constantly there, as the dancers crouch in low fondu, their arms either spread out or retracted like folded wings. When they do leap, it is apt to be in a variant of this position, with one leg bent under and the other held straight out in front. The sharp predatory profile of this image is characteristic of *Quartet* and as different from the profile of *Gallopade* as a hornet is from a squiggling worm; yet one image might plausibly become the other by metamorphosis. (If you have difficulty seeing how, think of Cunningham's material as a block of wood, with *Gallopade* becoming *Quartet* where the grain gets darker and less knotty.)

There are other motifs in *Quartet*, related and unrelated to this central one. The oddest are those groupings in which bodies are sandwiched or trapped, seemingly, in revolving doors or nested one inside another in optically baffling ways. There's a crouch within a crouch within a—But we can't quite tell: all we can see is that a man seems to have caught a two-headed woman on his lap. These images, accumulating between periods of stillness, are what give *Quartet* its unsettled atmosphere. Typical Cunningham passagework—swift chaînés, long leaps and runs ending in a headlong flat fall—roils the atmosphere still further. But the specific emotional turbulence is provided by Cunningham's performance—by his gift for extremely legible yet impalpable effects. In dramatic terms, his role seems to be that of a bearer of bad tidings—a Tiresias or a Cassandra. But his message, so precise of utterance, is obscure. With sharp flicks of his arms, hands, and head, he's a man sculpting in powder. When he darts ineffectually toward the others, then away, his hands flickering distress signals, he's all emanation; no wonder they don't pay him much attention. Without the edge of panic that Cunningham gives it, *Quartet* would, I suspect, be a less involving piece, though still a disturbing and, in terms of craft, a remarkably concise one. I must also give Tudor's score and Mark Lancaster's sombre lighting their due in creating the mood I have described. The sound, low-pitched throughout, at one point brought in a thunderstorm with sluicing rain, but most of it was as indecipherable as Cunningham's message. One heard, almost subliminally, voices speaking over crackles of atmospheric static—a sound that seemed to put the people onstage in outer space. A buried civilization, perhaps, with one lone signalman prophesying doom.

The other première of the Cunningham season at the City Center was of the stage version of *Coast Zone*. (A film version was shot earlier this year.) This is more comprehensive work, arranged in the form of a dance suite and enlisting most of the company in a demonstration of the versatility of Cunningham technique—particularly in allegro. As sheer dancing, it is one of the pleasantest experiences Cunningham has created recently, and the large cast seemed exhilarated by all that it did. Despite the addition of several good women dancers, the company is still dominated by the men (and the men are dominated by Chris Komar, whose authoritativeness looks nearly as lunar, at times, as Cunningham's own), but the imbalance didn't show in *Coast Zone*.

The Hamburg Ballet opened at the Brooklyn Academy of Music with its production, by John Neumeier, of A *Midsummer Night's Dream*. It was a gala opening, attended by the Lord Mayor of Hamburg and a large German delegation. A lobby exhibit of photographs extolled the commerce and culture of Hamburg as well as its ballet company. A *Midsummer Night's Dream*, which has also been mounted by the Paris Opéra, has been called innovative. Here are its innovations: Titania, Oberon, and Puck double as Hippolyta, Theseus, and Philostrate, master of the revels. The mortals are placed by the designer, Jürgen Rose, in a Napoleonic imperial setting; the fairies, wearing white tights and skullcaps, are in a frost-white forest. Hermia and Lysander are played straight. Helena and Demetrius are comics; she is not tall, but she wears glasses, while he is a soldier, forever saluting. The music for the mortals is by Mendelssohn, the music for the fairies by György Ligeti. The rustics cavort to a mechanical organ that plays folk songs and light classics—von Suppé, that sort of thing. When the lovers get mixed up, Helena loses her glasses and Puck puts them on. He also puts on a funny hat, hangs upside down from trees, and climbs a ladder from the stage into a box full of patrons. There are various kinds of dancing: knockabout-acrobatic for the comic lovers and Puck, dinner-club adagio for the straight pair, Glen Tetley modern for the fairies, and courtly-classical for everybody when the lovers get married. This is a something-for-everyone-bring-the-family staging. At the wedding, the rustics do Pyramus and Thisbe as an extended slapstick mime scene: the hit of the show.

Most of Neumeier's ideas would serve just as well—or ill—in a production of the play (and often have). A dance lover doesn't have much to work with. The choreography shows a superficial command of genre and never answers the question why Neumeier should have tried for so many contrasts in one ballet. The connections implied by the role-doubling aren't worked out in the action, and from the way the lovers maul each other in the forest it's impossible to believe they could be presented at court, let alone married there. The Germans in the audience were receptive to these complaints; one needed to see the all-Neumeier repertory to see the real Hamburg Ballet, they said. But the choreography in the other ballets turned out to be as cosmetic as it is in the *Dream*.

Bach Suite No. 2. As a choreographer, Neumeier seems to be wearing glasses, too. He always reveals what he's been looking at. Here it's the Paul Taylor of *Aureole* and *Airs*, but where Taylor's phrasing is compressed, Neumeier's is constricted, lacking logic and momentum. It is impossible to tell how he hears the music. The Bach suite, like most of the music used in the Hamburg repertory, is on tape, and pickets from the musicians' union are at the Academy's doors. But if there had been no music at all it wouldn't have made much of a difference.

Vaslav. Another Bach experience, set to piano selections (played live) and vaguely alluding to the legend of Nijinsky, whose diary speaks of a projected Bach ballet. Fittingly, Neumeier has made a schizophrenic piece. A female ensemble engages in footwork that appears to exercise Nijinsky's preferences in the matter of full point versus demi-point. This craftsmanly debate is laid aside for an extended male solo that seems intended to be a portrait of Nijinsky in his madness. Derivation: Hans van Manen with lashes of Béjart.

Mahler's Third Symphony. The music *has* to be on tape; what pit orchestra could support this conception of a ballet? Neumeier uses the whole symphony and pads it out with a section danced in silence. His dramatic program is not Mahler's: the first movement depicts the growth of the Nazi war machine (young men change from white tights to khaki), and the rest deals in dreamy pictures of boys and girls together. Neumeier's youths and "angels" are Mahlerian inspirations who closely resemble the personae of Kenneth MacMillan's ballet to *Das Lied von der Erde*. But the mixture of glossy heroics, visionary pining (the dancers do a lot of standing and staring), *Winds of War* nostalgia, and homoeroticism is Neumeier's own. He wanders so far from the music that when Mahler quotes a Spanish folk song (the famous jota aragonesa of Glinka's First Spanish Overture) he appears not to have heard it. (He must be wearing earplugs along with his glasses.) The portion of the ballet that is danced in silence is an agonized pas de trois that Neumeier dedicates to John Cranko. Cranko, Nijinsky, Tetley, MacMillan . . . For Neumeier, choreography is a pipeline to other choreographers. It's a notion that clashes oddly with another of his theories, which is that big music and big sounds make big ballets. After the Mahler superballet, I thought it best to avoid the setting of the Bach St. Matthew Passion (on Palm Sunday, yet, and with the choreographer as Christ). Is there no limit to this Bachomania? This Mahleritis? Neumeier has now done four of the Mahler symphonies. Yet no composer is as important to him as the brotherhood of choreographers. Belonging to this select band allows one to take liberties with music. No true choreographer fears to tread on the St. Matthew Passion or to combine Mendelssohn and Ligeti.

Composers are only sound men. Unmusicality, a liability and a curse throughout his profession, seems to be a point of pride to Neumeier. He's the Prometheus of unmusical choreographers.

Once one understands the place of music in Neumeier's repertory, one sees why he's so curiously unvigilant in matters of theatrical scale. The only ballet in which the music does *not* diminish his choreography is *Legend of Joseph*, to Richard Strauss's ballet score originally composed for Nijinsky. Strauss's music is on the right scale for dancing, and because it has nothing on its mind but Joseph, even though Neumeier's Joseph is a male prostitute equally available to Potiphar and his wife the drama flows with a semblance of theatrical vitality. This ballet *looks* like a ballet. For what it reveals of a great composer's understanding of the proportions of dance theatre, the music is worth reviving (and comparing with Prokofiev's *Prodigal Son*). Neumeier's choreography is a string of clichés. Judith Jamison, making a guest appearance as Mme. Potiphar, did them ample justice, and she also showed her form as a veteran dancer—something she doesn't often do nowadays. It was while watching her on a stage full of younger dancers that I began to see another failing of Neumeier's—his inadequacy as a director of dancers. (*The Encyclopedia of Dance and Ballet* cites "the flair with which he develops his dancers" along with "the originality of his treatment of music and plots" as the reason for Neumeier's great reputation in Continental Europe.) If his movement looks small and infirm, it isn't just because of the out-of-scale music; it's because of the technical insufficiency he accepts from his dancers. Neumeier doesn't demand strong, solidly centered movement that radiates out- ward. He loves big leg gestures; you'd think he'd want the legs lifting from inside the lower back instead of from somewhere underneath. He loves pirouettes, but his dancers are so weak between the waist and the thigh that they can't carry their center around even once without squirming. (One of my visual memories of the Hamburg Ballet is of a million pirouettes around a twisted axis.) Flaws like this make minor blemishes of the inconsistent turnout and unworked feet that one also sees. Without a center, it isn't possible to dance expressively. But with a reasonably good figure and enough physical daring to get through the acrobatics one can do imitation dancing. It's all that Neumeier's choreography calls for.

Strong technical criticisms of a similar nature can be applied to every other European company that has appeared so far in the Brooklyn Academy's Ballet International series. And the standard of choreography has been as low. The misery is reciprocal: the dancers aren't made to extend themselves by the cho- reography they're given to do; the choreography is uninspired because the dancers are dull. Companies with a lot of rehearsal time and little to rehearse always make a fine impression, but uniformity of appearance shouldn't be confused with style, and little things neatly done shouldn't be confused with good schooling, as they were in the case of the Basel Ballet. This was the most wistful of the visiting companies, with its repertory of Brand X ballets and *Giselle*. The timidity of the Norwegian National Ballet, which brought us a single work, by Tetley, was offset by the calculated craziness of the Cullberg Ballet, of Sweden, which set *its Giselle* in a Goiterville ruled by the inmates of a mental asylum. The Dutch National Ballet was comatose, as usual—is it the world's most boring dance company? The Basel presented the series' most talented dancer—Martin Schläpfer, who has the greatest natural elevation I have seen in years. But Schläpfer's form badly needs tending. It was sad seeing numbers of Americans in the Europeans' ranks. Many had had good initial training; some had left promising careers in this country to go abroad.

Company regimen, good or bad, sets its seal on dancers. A sound regimen can make unfinished dancers appear better than they are. The week of the Hamburg's opening also saw a local appearance, at Lehman College, by the Dayton Ballet—Dayton, Ohio. This is one of our oldest and most respected companies, but it has weathered its forty-five years on a modest scale. It doesn't enjoy a glittering reputation or strong financial backing. It has two or three very good soloists; it isn't packed with great dancers. But what Dayton has got—and what the European companies I have been seeing have not got—is strong artistic direction based on a knowledge of and a pride in dancing as pure expression. The European companies all seem to be trying to present dancing as a delectation for non-dance-minded audiences. In Dayton, one can see such ballets as Stuart Sebastian's *Stage Struck*, which at first seems to be a delectation—a backstage view of a ballet company with a lowly corps member who dreams of dancing the Swan Queen—and turns out to be a genuine dance experience. I've seen few ballets, in fact, in which a fixed contemplation of dance on so many levels was as real a possibility as it is in *Stage Struck*.

Sebastian has mounted a complex, two-act spectacle on his slender, corny little story. The aspirant gets her chance: she goes on and finishes the première when the ballerina foolishly lets herself be detained backstage. But before the big moment comes (and, amazingly, we don't see it coming) Sebastian takes us through company class, repertory rehearsal, dress rehearsal, and then through the première, which happens to be a A *Midsummer Night's Dream*, with its impromptu substitution of one Titania for another, and its aftermath, in which the ballerina's heart breaks to think of the role she has lost. And we can believe it, because all through *Stage Struck* we have been watching the operation of a regimen that persuades us that ballet, for every one of these dancers, is a poetic reality, not an unregulated fantasy. Sebastian, who wrote his own scenario, has staged it to a musical potpourri; he uses Mendelssohn's music for the première, but also snatches of *Swan Lake*, and whole chunks of Saint-Saëns, Ibert, Roussel, Debussy, and others. His finest achievement as a craftsman may be the rehearsal sequence, in which he fabricates a repertory of ballets in several different styles, as well as a work in progress, without once opening a breach in continuity or invoking the method of some other choreographer. His tumultuous *Midsummer Night's Dream* ballet does have a Bottom who goes about reading a book, much like Armand in Neumeier's *Lady of the Camellias* for the Stuttgart Ballet. With the Hamburg fresh in mind, I couldn't help taking this figure to be a satire of Neumeier, the heavy thinker. Sebastian, the fluent and musically intelligent director-choreographer of the Dayton Ballet, could not be more unlike.   —*April 11, 1983*

Theatre as Truth

Why is the new Paul Taylor–Alex Katz ballet called *Sunset?* It could have been called *The Park* or *Red Beret* or *Summer Leaves* (a pun), or, if the title had not already been used, *The Girls in Their Summer Dresses*. A sunset is not part of Katz's décor; Jennifer Tipton's lighting does not imitate one. It is the time of day in which the events of the ballet take place, not so much in real time as in remembered time—time in the abstract. But the ballet doesn't have the sunset glow of memory; it has the chill of an actual experience on which the light has died, leaving the meaning of the experience suspended. And the feeling of suspension in the observer is perfectly pleasurable; we don't want to disturb it with explanations. Yet we can't deny that some part of the pleasure we feel comes from having, already, enough complexity of emotion to deal with. It's not just a feeling of being sated; it's a feeling of being sated and off balance. So the experience haunts us. There is some kind of trouble going on here—something unique, which the events of the ballet sharply qualify without naming. It calls out to be named, and there is no name. Under the circumstances, *Sunset* is as good a title as any.

Most of the pleasure we take in dance is purely private and has for sanity's sake to be defended from scrutiny—our own as well as others'. But usually this pleasure doesn't ask to be defended. With *Sunset*, it does. Taylor and Katz have done more than make a piece filled with inscrutable sensuous-kinetic allure. They've taken our awareness of this allure and made it a condition of comprehension. What goes on inside us as we watch *Sunset* is normally the commotion that attends our responses in retrospect, and that's why, in retrospect, the ballet makes trouble for us. Thinking back on it is like probing a sore tooth. The sensation of the performance can dimly be re-created in memory because it sinks in deep from the start—it's like memory to begin with. We start with some soldiers in a park, whiling away the last hours of what probably was a weekend pass, and then the girls come in. The fact that the piece has a dramatic situation—that it isn't *pure* dance and therefore a comparatively pure memory—seems to me a masterstroke. Just the banality of it is a joy. But right away we are thrown off balance by the soldiers' unrecognizable uniforms: army fatigues with shoulder patches that we can't read, and red berets. Then, there's the park itself. We see what must be a lookout promontory, but only a corner of it. The scenic view is cut off by a screen of Katz foliage—dabs of aqua and green—bordered by a metal guardrail. The screen meets another, taller one to form a sharp upstage angle; on this are painted more dabs, with the pattern ending where the treeline meets a patch of blank sky. Katz has thus walled off the back and one whole side of the stage, leaving the dancers no way in or out but stage left. Such a drastic modification of stage space might be expected to create a drastic effect. In fact, it looks modest and comfortable; the adventure of it dawns gradually as Taylor lays out his own modest bombshells.

When the curtain goes up on the men lounging by the guardrail, the whole stage picture has the disarming angular intensity of an Alex Katz painting; it is a natural scene from his special point of view. (It has the same selectivity that makes him paint only the upper story of a house, for instance, or a lakeside vista from behind a tree trunk.) And Taylor accomplishes the kind of miracle we hardly ever see in the theatre. He brings the naturalness and strangeness of this vision to life, and he even moves it through several levels of meaning and changes of tone without sacrificing its intensity as an image. The piece continues to look like an Alex Katz painting all the way through. The final pose—the frieze of women in their white summer dresses standing by the rail while another girl holds a beret that one of the soldiers has left behind—is another beautiful picture, and a complement to the first one. The movement of the ballet between these two images is motionless motion; nothing really seems to be happening but the rippling of a surface. Taylor achieved something of the same magical stasis a few years ago in *Nightshade*, his piece based on Max Ernst's collages in *Une Semaine de Bonté*. The violent stresses of Ernst's Surrealism immobilized Taylor in a churning whirlpool of discontinuities. The new Katz ballet (which will be seen only three more times before the end of Taylor's run at the City Center) has the same circularity of design but also a bland and benevolent calm. It's a contemplative rather than an obsessive stasis. And things connect. Beneath the sweet, dreamlike surface, there's the conclusiveness of a social commentary. The agreeable dance manners of the piece are drawn from the social manners of the men in uniform. The elaborate listlessness and nonchalance they assume as a mask for loneliness are casebook attitudes. So is their behavior when the girls enter: without shifting their chewing gum, they become tense as young bulls. The moment has almost a generic fatalism, and the women are just women of the genre—nice city girls, as in *Fancy Free*. But in another minute the action diverges from genre ballets about servicemen, and diverges so significantly that it almost seems to be commenting on theatrical as well as social stereotypes. The women catalyze the change in the men; they themselves don't change (although they may be beginning to when the curtain falls). Taylor is very clear: this is a piece about men and men's responses to women.

Taylor has often shown us the power of his men dancers. It's unlikely that Christopher Gillis, Thomas Evert, Kenneth Tosti, David Parsons, Elie Chaib, and Daniel Ezralow have ever before set off the vibrations that they do here, in their awkward military uniforms. The boxy shirts and the belted pants with pockets that stick out give the wearers a kind of lumpish virility that prepares us for the situations they get into. Becoming involved with the women (Kate Johnson, Lila York, Cathy McCann, and Karla Wolfangle) releases a flow of reactions that the men don't seem to have under full control. Now and then, they lurch into dream situations, and we bob along on a tide of male subjectivity. At other times, the action is as prosaic as a street conversation. The littlest woman (York) is lifted and swooped through the air, more to the men's delight than to hers. Gillis makes a special moment of gallantry out of carrying her on his shoulder, and the others love bouncing her around. When she climbs over a mountain formed by their obliging backs, Gillis assists her, holding her by the hand, and at one point his hand clasping hers is between her legs. The climb, besides, is precarious; York doesn't attempt to disguise it. She doesn't make an issue of it, either, or of that indecorous handclasp. If we get the feeling that she's not too happy playing the part of an adorable little thing, it's no more than a shadow brushing the sun. Feelings like this come seldom. The women are happy with the men, and happiest of all with Chaib, who lets them pamper him and carry him about. (Unlike York, Chaib revels in being manipulated.) The others pair off to mutual good effect. One soldier (Tosti) is left out of the mating ritual, and his predicament pulls the ballet farthest from its pleasant prosaic center. Taylor has Tosti lie flat downstage during Chaib's idyll and appear to spy on it. This bitter moment is enlarged subsequently by Tosti's wrenching body lifts and slides on the floor. He's so much the odd man out that he almost falls out of the style of the piece. But the moment of near-expressionistic bravura passes, and, in one of Taylor's most tactful transitions, Tosti is restored to the amicable world we now know he doesn't belong to.

The finest of all Taylor's transitions occurs late in the action, during a dance for Kate Johnson and the six men. The absence of heat from this dance puzzled me at first. Johnson is the most elegant and the most demurely provocative of the women, and I was expecting some climactic development in the drama. But Taylor is already beginning to draw the men and the women apart—the day is ending. Johnson is there among the men, but she's not on their minds. They begin to form soldierly rows around her, and the neutrality of the arrangement persists when she is joined by the other women. At the end of this passage, the men take off their hats impassively in a farewell gesture. Then they march off in formation (dropping one hat), wanting clearly as much to be where they are going as where they have been.

The things we take away from *Sunset* for the sake of conversation and criticism are the least interesting things about it. Whatever the piece "says"—about women as a part-time need of men, or about the fatuity of male assumptions in regard to women, or about love versus duty, honor, and country—is inconsequential beside the shimmering ambiguity of the vision it holds before us. Emotionally, no moment is unmixed, and the continuing delicacy and subtlety of the piece trains us as we watch it. A simple response is impossible. The short way of saying this is that *Sunset* invents a new realism in the theatre. Taylor and Katz have taken the measure of the emotion we invest in the transitory phenomena of dance and extended it to transitory phenomena in the real world. Edwin Denby, reviewing the première of *Fancy Free*, recognized the ballet as "a superb vaudeville turn," but he also could write, "Its sentiment of how people live in this country is completely intelligent and completely realistic." *Sunset* derives from painting rather than from vaudeville; it, too, is a serious document of the way people live. You can study it for the changes that have occurred in human nature in the last forty years—or, rather, in our stageable perception of human nature. Still, the fact of change isn't as important as the motion of it. *Sunset* changes before your eyes.

Taylor's choice of music is oddly inspired: Elgar's "Elegy" and "Serenade" for strings. The dying embers have never seemed so nobly plaintive. In the Tosti episode, the music is interrupted by a tape of the cries of loons. This may seem unbearably sensitive to someone who wasn't there. And Taylor's choice of Handel for a new pas de deux to be danced this season by guest stars Suzanne Farrell and Peter Martins may seem unbearably predictable: the "balletic" Taylor of *Aureole* and *Airs* strikes again. In the event—a one-time-only performance at a benefit for the Taylor company—the new duet took an inevitable rather than a predictable course. Taylor had proposed steps that were a composite of his style and his guests', and Farrell and Martins were like filters for Taylor's compounds: they transformed his choreography into something more than an experiment. So *Musette* (to a section of the Concerto Grosso Opus 6, No. 6) came off an achieved work of art—the equation balanced. Experiments can be dangerous. Mikhail Baryshnikov's appearance at another benefit, a week later, was the sort of thing that appeals to the technician in us and to a kind of secret sadism, too. Baryshnikov danced along with the Taylor company in *Images* and tried mightily to look as if he belonged there. To have been successful he would have had to change as completely as Jekyll into Hyde. But what purpose is served by the extinction of Misha? Dancers of Baryshnikov's sophistication can always show us something; they can magnify elements of an alien technique even as they fail to encompass them. That's why— besides the effect on box-office—these "gala" experiments go on. But unless they are genuinely collaborative, like *Musette*, they are educational at best, sacrificial at worst.

Taylor's other new piece is *Snow White*—really *Snow White*, with all the ingredients of the fairy tale in place, but (and here is the catch) recounted in a blue streak, as if by a tired daddy eager to get the job over with before the ballgame comes on. It's *Snow White* in speed-writing. This daddy misremembers what he doesn't telescope ("And then the prince comes in—or no, not yet. And what was it the mirror said? Forget it"). In spite of himself, he gets carried away with the dwarfs, of whom there are only five (". . . Grumpy and Dopey and, uh, never mind"). These guys, you recall, were forever singing about their work, and so here they are, the busiest workers on view, bustling about in a pack, turning themselves into scenery and props, lifting and carrying the principals, and, when the time comes, ripping the stuffing out of the witch with a vengeance that suggests what a hard day daddy's had at the office, what a very hard day. All the action is cast, of course, in inimitable Taylor body language. The prince is a stick, the witch waves her talons, Snow White is—well, you know. And the dwarfs! Not only do they do all the work, they do it squatting or doubled over. And at top speed.

Snow White is performed stage-within-a-stage style, on a small white floorcloth flanked by two white-and-gilt plaster columns, replicas of the Moorish decorations on the proscenium of the newly renovated City Center. David Gropman, the designer, must have been reminded of old palatial movie theatres. Cynthia O'Neal's costumes for Ruth Andrien as Snow White, for Elie Chaib as both the prince and the witch, and for Evert, Parsons, Ezralow, Tosti, and James Karr as the dwarfs are modelled on the Disney movie. A Bad Apple, danced by Karla Wolfangle in a devil-red bodysuit, is a pure-Taylor frill. The commissioned score, by Donald York, flicks the action along with Stravinskyan ostinatos. It is a straight-forward piece of theatre music, for a chamber ensemble, and never once gives the joke away.

I was bewildered, appalled, and ultimately charmed by the Los Angeles Ballet (at the Joyce). I was never bored. John Clifford, the choreographer, specializes in cheeky pastiche. In *The Young Apollo*, Leto gave birth by opening her legs in a V, and Apollo sprang through it. In *Afternoon of a Faun*, the choreography veered between Nijinsky's stylizations and Jerome Robbins's naturalism. Clifford seemed to want imaginary afternoons with real fauns in them. He is partial to inelegant lifts and excessive and brash effects of all kinds. The Faun pulled a veil the size of a bath towel through his crotch. In *Rhapsody on a Theme of Paganini*, an ensemble display piece, the stage was plunged into silhouette so often that it was a question whether Clifford intended to show off his dancers or hide them.

No need to hide these dancers. Clifford's artistic direction imparts sound dis-cipline and a passion for performing. And the new dancers he has acquired since the company's last local appearance, in 1980, strengthen it enormously. A number of the new women are tall and large (their size makes some of the inelegant lifts inadvisable as well); it says much for Clifford that he is able to present them as classical dancers, not as Vegas showgirls. Perhaps the most promising is Evette DeMarco, who danced the Nymph in *Afternoon of a Faun* and the slow movement in the *Rhapsody*. She has the ineffable gift of perfect line. The star of *The Young Apollo*, and its obvious inspiration, was Damian Woetzel, fifteen years old, ad-mirably placed and trained, and already a dancer of power and distinction. As a showcase, *The Young Apollo* is little more than a sketch, but it is a telling one. Woetzel has a seriousness and a restraint remarkable in a young dancer. And it is remarkable of Clifford to have revealed those qualities when his own performing style is so different. There are several other good men in the company, but they tend to imitate Clifford's eagerness, and they are short in plié, which makes them look flighty.   —*April 25, 1983*

Loyal to the ℛoyal

The opening program of the Royal Ballet's week at the Met may have looked like a tribute to Frederick Ashton. It actually was a tribute to New York in line with the current Britain Salutes New York exhibitions of British art around the city. *Enigma Variations*, *Voices of Spring*, and a world première of a new ballet—all by Ashton—saluted New York's idea of the Royal Ballet, which is that it is Ashton's company. The idea persists in spite of the fact that Ashton retired as director in 1970; the last full-scale ballet that showed him working productively in association with the company was A *Month in the Country*, in 1976. That Ashton is or should be in charge is a harmless enough fantasy—fun, even, especially when Ashton is around to take curtain calls. He's right when he says he has always been appreciated in New York. This time, the ardor he commanded from his subjects—stepping up the applause with bow after bow, silencing it with a wave of his hand—was like that for a deposed king. It almost seemed as if the audience hoped to vote him back in power and have the dear old Royal we used to know restored. Ashton has become a choreographer for special occasions, the Royal's laureate. The ballet he produced on this occasion—named V*arii Capricci*, after its music, by the late William Walton—played up to the audience's fantasy and at the same time dispelled any possibility of fulfilling it. Beguiling rather than captivating, outspokenly trivial, it nevertheless starred Antoinette Sibley and Anthony Dowell, who were the ruling young principals for most of Ashton's directorship (while Fonteyn and Nureyev were the ruling seniors, billed as guest artists), and its style harked back to an even earlier period. It was to be expected that as a guest choreographer Ashton would lose touch with the company sooner or later, and V*arii Capricci* bows gracefully to that inevitability. It's neither the old nor the present-day Royal that we see here—merely Sir Frederick summoning some old ghosts and setting them in motion. It's one last fling one more time: one other gaudy night.

The program was rounded off by Glen Tetley's *Dances of Albion*, an American's view of the Royal Ballet—or, rather, an English view of an American's view. Tetley's career as a choreographer was established under European auspices and, in England, by Ballet Rambert under the regime of Norman Morrice, who now heads the Royal. Since Tetley's ballets have become ubiquitous, it is necessary to keep these origins in mind. The Royal management undoubtedly thought so. It only remained for the audience to discover, if it could, what Tetley had done in dances of Albion that made them any different from dances of Stuttgart or Tel Aviv or Amsterdam or New York. Not only are Tetley's products ubiquitous and interchangeable (they have probably contributed more to the homogenization of style than any other influence on world ballet), not only are they long-winded (*Dances of Albion* is stretched over *two* scores by Benjamin Britten), choppily constructed, narrow in range, and arduous in expression, but they are almost always gloomy. Is this a consequence of Tetley's oversolemn taste in music? The two Britten scores are the Serenade for Tenor, Horn, and Strings and the Sinfonia da Requiem—an elegy and a dirge. Tetley is the kind of choreographer who draws imagery rather than impetus from a piece of music. I have a feeling that if one could turn off the sound of Tetley's ballets they wouldn't be so bleak. But they'd still be relentlessly torturous and full of those images—crucifixions and the like—by which Tetley strives for emotional substance. Perhaps the very laboriousness of his style dictates the funereal tone. Though *Dances of Albion* was subtitled "Dark Night Glad Day," it was Dark Night that prevailed.

Enigma Variations, unseen here since its début season, continues to exert its genteel charm. The fascination it once held, which lay in Ashton's attempt to deal in nonexpressionistic terms with the mental states and feelings of a range of characters, hasn't exactly faded. The ballet still "works," but now it works like a superb mechanism inside a bell jar. One responds to a preserved spontaneity rather than, as in 1969, to the pressure of the life that Ashton recorded. Certain performances are inevitably missed, but Derek Rencher is still there holding things together as Elgar, and the brio of the ensemble in the mime scenes is admirable. Ashton's effects are so modestly achieved it's easy to lose sight of the precision of his method and the grandeur of his intent. Paul Taylor's new work *Sunset* is like *Enigma Variations* in its meditative calm and subjective flow; it's interesting, too, that Taylor chose music by Elgar.

Varii Capricci is modest both in intent and in accomplishment. It fairly shrinks beneath the outsize, overheated David Hockney décor that was provided for it. Hockney has designed inventively for opera, but his colors are too vibrant and his forms too active for ballet. He flattened the *Sacre du Printemps* that Jean-Pierre Bonnefous choreographed for the Metropolitan Opera's Stravinsky triple bill; here he does a cerulean swimming pool beneath an orange-and-crimson sky, and the pool has whitecaps in it. When the dancers are in the air, they are apt to fade into the pool like a flock of shrimp. Hockney's landscape is said to have been based on the garden of the Walton villa in Ischia, which is where Ashton sets the action, and the ballet is also dedicated to Walton, whose music has furnished six Ashton ballets. The first of these, *Façade*, is directly commemorated in the roles for Sibley and Dowell, which are updated versions of the Débutante and the Gigolo. She reclines on a poolside chaise, guests gambol, he crashes the party, and in an instant the two of them are together again. Sibley, who returned to the stage a couple of seasons ago after four years in retirement, looks fit and performs with no loss of edge, but the ballet is Dowell's. The exotic character he plays is called Lo Straniero and is strange indeed. He wears a black Presley pompadour, black glasses, and a black shirt with puffed sleeves, all of which seem to reflect an idea of contemporary punk chic. But when he walks he rolls his hips lazily, like a lounge lizard entering a boudoir. Even stranger is the corps of four

couples, who in their Ballet Russe tatters reflect no kind of chic—neither Dowell's
nor Sibley's. (She wears a thirties-style chemise overladen with pleats.) A damaging
comparison with *Façade* comes in the dances Dowell does alone and with Sibley,
which are straight light-classical dances with marginal links to his character. These
are in their own terms deft and pleasing dances; coming from Ashton, they could
hardly be less. But the ballet makes no comment. Ashton has seen his job as the
reuniting of a beloved team, and he has acquitted it in an atmosphere congenial
to him—the atmosphere created by Walton's music and fond memories of what
that represents. Perhaps it was a mistake to put him together with Hockney, of
whose world and kind he seems to have no knowledge. When Ashton is being
decadent—when he decorates the stage with seated or kneeling dancers stretching
their necks and ankles—he evokes a Firbankian languor. Hockney's decadence
has a naïf element—it's contemporary fauvism. Dowell's punk is half in Hockney's
world, half in Ashton's. One can only sympathize with the costume designer,
Ossie Clark, if in his attempt to clothe this ballet he got a little confused.

The occasion for *Voices of Spring*, a pas de deux set to the Strauss waltz, was
the Covent Garden *Fledermaus* of 1977. It, too, is a trifle—one of Ashton's chiffon-
and-rose-petals affairs—and seemingly deserving of a less earthbound performance
than the one given it at the Met by Merle Park and Wayne Eagling, its original
cast. It's good to see the Royal again in Ashton choreography, but what a peculiar
evening! One imagined the whole loyal and loving audience going backstage
afterward to meet the dancers, like the Royal Family, and murmuring, *not* like
the Royal Family but like E. F. Benson's Lucia, "My dear, aren't we getting
vecchio." I sat through the Tetley tedium twice, simply because the changes in
casting allowed some of the younger dancers onstage (and the length of the piece
kept them there quite a while). I saw Lesley Collier and Bryony Brind in the same
part, and I learned nothing from it. In an Ashton ballet, they'd be as unlike as
any two dancers in the company could be. But Tetley's turned-in choreography
doesn't project dancers as individuals on an opera-house scale.

The second half of the Royal's run was devoted to *Mayerling*, the three-act
ballet by the company's principal choreographer, Kenneth MacMillan, which was
being seen for the first time in New York. It is dedicated to Ashton, and now that
it has passed five years in repertory and lost some of its shock value the relationship
of MacMillan's style to Ashton's becomes more obvious and the dedication makes
a new kind of sense. Like *Enigma Variations* and, to some extent, *A Month in
the Country*, *Mayerling* tries to grasp invisible meanings and put them on the
stage without succumbing to the fraudulence of expressionistic gesture (in which
meanings are preassigned to movements). Among MacMillan's ballets, *Mayerling*
has a limpidity of progression that sets it apart; it really does explain why its two
principal characters want to kill themselves. The explanation may have nothing
to do with the historical characters the story is based on, and it is not something
that can easily be recounted in words. MacMillan makes the Prince Rudolf–Mary
Vetsera love story a kind of paroxysmic Liebestod; sex and death crystallize in a
union of dance metaphors. And this poetic crystallization occurs against a back-

ground of purposeful prose continuity. At times, the very prolixity of *Mayerling*—the leisurely paced court scenes, the obligatory set pieces for minor characters—weighs against its ever achieving its goal. MacMillan doesn't launch the fatal love affair until the end of Act II; until then, we have plenty of time to dissent from the scripted meanings he seems to be trying to impose upon the action, such as that Rudolf suffers from syphilis or that he embraces revolutionary politics. These aren't things that can be said in dance. But part of the reason to see *Mayerling* is that it's a gamble. A greatly talented choreographer is taking risks, some less calculated than others. His success is in doubt until the very last minute—until, in fact, the Act III pas de deux in which the suicide pact is sealed (and which has become known to jeerers as "a girl, a guy, and a gun"). But if you've stayed with him that long you've already taken the measure of MacMillan's courage.

The other reason to see the ballet is, of course, the performance the company gives it. Brilliant as always in mime, brilliant in the dance arias that carry the story—this was the Royal at its best. It says much for the current strength of the company that a complex role like that of Countess Larisch, Rudolf's procuress—a role in which Merle Park continues to triumph—can also be taken successfully by a younger dancer, Genesia Rosato. Nineteen-year-old Alessandra Ferri is the best Vetsera I have seen since the role's originator, Lynn Seymour, whom she resembles, not only physically—in the shape of her legs and the high arch of her points (which are emphasized in the choreography)—but in the combination of headlong impulsiveness and implacability which makes us see Vetsera as Rudolf's dark angel. Rudolf himself is a study in pathology. Wayne Eagling's miming skillfully conveys the monster that lurks inside this weak, twisted man. His dancing in the soliloquies, when he acts out his torments, is persuasive; it is less so when Rudolf is in public and must put on a princely front. Eagling's classical dancing is not his strong point (the role was made on David Wall), but the company's lapsed standard in academic classicism offers him nothing to aim for. In *Enigma Variations*, the presence of Sibley and Dowell, master academicians still, pointed up this general failing. In *Mayerling*, the dance diversions, which MacMillan had set with Ashtonian clarity, were spottily done. This falling off and MacMillan's increasing commitment since *Mayerling* to expressionistic forms are surely not coincidental, but which came first? MacMillan's aesthetic, it now seems clear, is both an extension and a refutation of Ashton's. Somewhere along the line, this once great classical company took a turn that has made even its casual admirers restive. Precisely where and how this turn came about I cannot say, but the road passes through *Mayerling*.   —*May 9, 1983*

The following was written for the "Talk of the Town" department of The New Yorker *and appeared in the issue of May 16, 1983.*

Balanchine

George Balanchine died at four o'clock on the morning of April 30th, a matinée day. The audience filing into the lobby of the State Theater that afternoon passed between two giant sprays of white lilacs, white roses, and lilies of the valley. A color photograph of Balanchine taking a curtain call had been hung in the display case. Except for TV camera crews at the stage door, there were no other signs that anything had happened. The program posted beside the box-office windows was unchanged: Jerome Robbins's *Mother Goose* and *The Four Seasons* and Balanchine's *Kammermusik No. 2*. Leslie Bailey, the New York City Ballet's press representative, was standing in a corner of the lobby, looking pale but composed. "Jerry Robbins offered to cancel," she said, "but we felt we couldn't disappoint the children who would be coming." Mikhail Baryshnikov arrived, wearing a dark-blue suit and dark glasses. "I had to come," he said. "I woke up early this morning, in a panic. I thought I must be late for something. I started to get up, thinking, I'm late, I'm late! And I couldn't go back to sleep." Lincoln Kirstein, co-founder of the New York City Ballet, passed swiftly through the lobby and stopped, noticing Baryshnikov. The two men embraced without speaking. Then Kirstein headed backstage.

Upstairs at the bar, Bob Ross, the bartender, talked about Balanchine drinking his celebrated vodka toast to the memory of Stravinsky and saying, "In Russia, we drink to the health of the guy that died." Ross went on to say, "Mr. B. was quite a belter. I served him here all the time—not vodka but Scotch. He liked boilermakers. One time, he said, 'Have one.' We clinked glasses, and he downed his in one gulp. I did, too. Then I had to pretend to be very busy under the counter. My eyes were watering. Smoke was coming out of my ears. But he didn't turn a hair."

The audience that was settling into its seats was the standard Saturday-matinée audience—grandmothers, small children, no critics—on whom Balanchine would frequently try out new casts unannounced. In place of the usual pre-performance din, there was subdued chatter. Only a few musicians were warming up in the pit. Then the house went dark, and Kirstein stepped before the curtain, holding a hand microphone, and began speaking, hoarsely but distinctly. "I don't have to tell you that Mr. B. is with Mozart and Tchaikovsky and Stravinsky," he said. "I do want to tell you how much he valued this audience, which is like a big family that has kept us going for fifty years and will keep us going for another fifty. The one thing he didn't want was that there be an interruption. So there will be none. Think of yourselves as the marvellous, supportive, cohesive family who understands—" Here Kirstein was drowned out by a loud electronic wail. He lowered the microphone and continued, "—who understands the family that's about to perform now."

Hugo Fiorato, the white-haired conductor, appeared on the podium, and after a brief orchestral prelude the curtain rose slowly on the first scene of Robbins's *Mother Goose*, which shows the dancers, in practice dress, standing or reclining about the stage, surrounded by the scenery and props of a dozen other ballets in the repertory. It was a perfect illustration of Kirstein's reference to "the family." One of the dancers, having the inspiration to act out the tales of Mother Goose, reached into a wardrobe trunk, pulled out a cavalier's plumed hat (from *Harlequinade*), and clapped it on his head. In an instant, as the other dancers were pulling out more hats, the creased old garden backdrop that has done service since City Center days was rolled down. Then Sleeping Beauty entered, skipping rope, and the show went on.

On that weekend, there was more Balanchine activity in the city than there would have been on any other weekend of the year. Not only was the New York City Ballet playing at the State Theater and *On Your Toes* on Broadway but the School of American Ballet was giving its annual workshop performances at the Juilliard Theater on Saturday and Monday, and on Monday night American Ballet Theatre was opening at the Met with a program featuring Baryshnikov's revival of *Symphonie Concertante*, a Balanchine ballet that was introduced by School of American Ballet pupils thirty-seven years ago. The stir of dancers in and around Lincoln Center was intense. And their emotion united them, perhaps, as never before. Wherever one looked, there seemed to be dancers meeting and embracing wordlessly. At the Juilliard Theater, the students who would be dancing on Saturday evening began dress rehearsals at ten o'clock that morning. They rehearsed two Balanchine ballets they had probably never seen—*Valse Fantaisie* and *Western Symphony*. Many of them had never even seen Balanchine, except from a distance, having grown up at the school in the years when he was following a curtailed schedule under close medical supervision. Like the rest of Balanchine's organization, the students had lived with bad news of Mr. B. almost daily since last November, when he entered Roosevelt Hospital. Now, on the fatal Saturday, they worked with their teachers as if it were any other day, and the rehearsal went smoothly. The only voice to be raised was Robert Irving's, repeatedly admonishing the student orchestra not to watch the stage. That night, at eight o'clock, the performance went on after Kirstein, flanked by Jerome Robbins, Peter Martins, and John Taras, made another brief speech from the stage, thanking the audience for "this school and your support of it." Kirstein continued, "We know that this night George is probably teaching the angels to tendu. The *angels*, who don't need to rehearse."

Kirstein also spoke to the Saturday-night audience a block away at the State Theater, and he would appear onstage at the school performance on Monday night, reassuring the audience each time of the continuity of the Balanchine tradition and, each time, wearing in his lapel the silver lyre pin designed by

Balanchine for the Tchaikovsky Festival. On Saturday night, the closing ballet at the State Theater was *Symphony in C*, conducted by Gordon Boelzner before a packed house. Suzanne Farrell and Peter Martins appeared in the great adagio and finished to a storm of applause. They took two bows. They took a third. Then, as the audience began to demonstrate, they ran off and did not return for another bow. In the finale of this ballet—surely the most exhilarating finale ever devised by Balanchine—there comes a moment when the profuse invention of the choreography clears away like mist and the stage turns into a classroom, its three sides lined with young women doing battements tendus while the four principal ballerinas compete like dervishes in the center. In this moment, at once the simplest and the most complex moment in the ballet, Balanchine seems to be outlining both his dream for American ballet and the foundation necessary to achieve it. Then, the vision having been disclosed, the happy dazzle of invention returns, mounting and mounting until, with an abrupt flourish, it ends. This time, the dancers took call after call from the standing, shouting audience. It had been a performance that Balanchine, had he been backstage running the curtains, would have been glad to acknowledge as extraordinary.

A lifelong communicant of the Russian Orthodox Church, Balanchine died the day before Palm Sunday, on the feast of the resurrection of Lazarus. At the funeral, Bishop Gregory Grabbe pointed out the coincidence in his eulogy, and he went on to praise Balanchine as a devout Christian who had prepared himself for death. The Cathedral of Our Lady of the Sign, at Ninety-third Street and Park Avenue, was overcrowded; the funeral service was long, and the humid air was thick with the scent of flowers, incense, and hundreds of burning candles. When the service ended, shortly after noon, the candles were extinguished, and for an hour or more the mourners filed by the open coffin, some pausing to kneel, to kiss the ribbon printed with a prayer which lay across the forehead, to kiss or touch the hands, or to leave a flower. Some chose just to pause and pass on. Among those who approached the casket, one by one, were great and famous dancers—dancers young and old—whom Balanchine had nurtured. The beautiful little faces were crumpled with grief. The crowd overflowed onto the staircase outside and into the courtyard, two stories below. As the church emptied, it was impressive to see six generations of ballerinas descend the stairs. Many were weeping. Some children of *Nutcracker* age wept, too, though they were too young to have known the man—only the legend. The mass of mourners dispersed; a few hundred lined the stairs or joined the crowd that had gathered on Ninety-third Street. At length, the closed coffin appeared in the doorway, was lifted, and, accompanied by the tolling of a bell and the chanting of the cathedral's small choir, was borne along the balcony, down the stairs, through the courtyard, and out onto the street, there to be placed in a waiting hearse and covered with a blanket of gardenias. It was the ending of *La Sonnambula* in reverse. As the cortege rolled away, heading toward Long Island, where the burial would take place, it was impossible not to think of the ballets in which Balanchine staged his own death. Besides *La Sonnambula*, there is *Orpheus* and *Don Quixote* and

Robert Schumann's "Davidsbündlertänze" and, most awful and explicit of all, his setting of the last movement of the "Pathétique" Symphony. And there are dozens more in which the fact of mortality is held out to us not in sorrow or anger but in the calm certainty of transcendence. If the readiness is all, then the Bishop was right, and Balanchine died a happy man. It was only that his dancers and his audience could not bear to let him go.

The Legacy

In the first week of life without Balanchine, it was good to have New York City Ballet to go to, and especially good to have so many performances of great works like *Divertimento No. 15* and *Concerto Barocco* and *Symphony in C*. All honor to the dancers who performed so gallantly in such trying circumstances. Because of them, the darkest week in the history of the company—in the history of ballet in America—was not also a desolate one. Ballets don't exist unless they are danced; to see Balanchine's danced at such a time by his own company was to have the best possible assurance that they can endure as his monument. Which of them are masterpieces is a question that we do not have the luxury of deciding. Let posterity make the choices. For the moment, it is more important to know which are most perishable and therefore in need of closest attention from those now in charge of preserving Balanchine's repertory. Of the three I have named, *Divertimento No. 15* strikes me as the most finespun, the one most likely to snap under the strain of insufficient rehearsal or inadequate casting. Even when the dancers are good and are well prepared, things can be set wrong with a flick of an indifferent conductor's baton. In contrast to the *Divertimento, Concerto Barocco* is hewn from rock, yet it, too, has its vulnerable points. Overscrupulous and unmusical execution such as one sometimes gets from other companies that perform this work makes its marble surface gritty; in the long cantabile phrases of the pas de deux, lapses in stamina open fissures that Balanchine did not intend.

Concerto Barocco was made, along with *Ballet Imperial* (now called *Tchaikovsky Piano Concerto No. 2*), for a tour of Latin America in 1941. As companion pieces, they present balanced views of Balanchine's roots in imperial Russian ballet and of the flowering of the new ballet in America. *Concerto Barocco* could also have been called *Ballet Imperial*; New York is the Empire State. This small ballet (ten women, one man) to the Bach Double Violin Concerto has the epic power of some such new colossus as the Manhattan of the thirties. Power, cruelty, exhilaration (the colossus rising) are offset by baroque scrollwork and unexpected bursts of jive (the colossus as habitat). As in those black-and-white photographs taken by Walker Evans or Berenice Abbott from the tops of skyscrapers, one sees detail and depth with contrapuntal clarity. "It amazes me," Balanchine said, "that some people never notice the tops of buildings."

It is difficult, seeing these ballets just now, to avoid thinking of them as landmarks in time—as milestones if not masterpieces. The conjunction of *Concerto Barocco* and *Symphony in C* on many of the past fortnight's programs repeated the historic first-night bill of New York City Ballet in 1948, at the City Center. (The middle ballet was *Orpheus.*) *Symphony in C*, another architectural marvel, had been unveiled the year before in Paris, under the title *Le Palais de Cristal*. Balanchine, reviving an early composition of Bizet's, staged it on commission from the Paris Opéra. So successful were the Balanchine evenings in Paris that he was urged to stay and assume control of the Opéra ballet. He might well have been tempted—it was the prize post in Western ballet. Balanchine returned to America. The following spring, instead of new triumphs at the Opéra there was *Orpheus* at the shabby City Center. As for the Bizet ballet, it has come to symbolize not the Paris Opéra but New York City Ballet.

Balanchine is widely and justly ranked with Stravinsky and Picasso. Unlike them, he lived and worked in New York and chose to consider himself a New Yorker. The city furnished him with inspiration right through to *Who Cares?* and *Stravinsky Violin Concerto*. Belatedly—not until the sixties—it provided a showcase theatre and a home for the School of American Ballet, which was Balanchine's first enterprise in partnership with Lincoln Kirstein and the foundation for all the others. To function properly, New York City Ballet and the School of American Ballet must be mutually dependent: the school feeding the company new dancers; the company, through its choreographers, feeding the school new ideas of dance style. (Balanchine also liked to say that style comes from the stage to the classroom, not the other way around.) This ideal exchange has not been consistently maintained; for one thing, Balanchine's new ideas were not always readily assimilated, even by his company. But in the school's annual workshop performances the soundness of the system proclaims itself. The reciprocal process works on a day-to-day, nonapocalyptic basis.

The school performances this year, as always, offered a range of work. Besides the Balanchine *Valse Fantaisie* and *Western Symphony*, revived by Suki Schorer, and the Bournonville pas de deux from *Kermesse in Bruges*, Act II, revived by Stanley Williams, there was a selection of Morris folk dances from England, staged by Ronald Smedley and Robert Parker, of the Royal Ballet School. Even in a country-dance minuet or a four-hand reel, there is such a thing as correct style; indeed, the more elementary the form the more exposed are the basic principles of expressive dancing. In this respect, the S.A.B. students were better exponents of minimalism than some of our professional postmodernists. The new ballet on the program was a setting, by Helgi Tomasson, of dance music by Messager, mostly from the opera *Isoline*. Tomasson has done one other work for the school; his *Ballet d'Isoline* is by far the more successful. The more ambitious, too. Tomasson hasn't yet found a personal style; his choreography keeps saying "Not by Balanchine" much the way the Messager music keeps saying "Not by

Delibes." But the ballet is a skillful, confident, even venturesome piece of work. The House of Balanchine is turning out to have more rooms than one may have supposed. *Ballet d'Isoline* will be produced by the company, and there'll be more to say about it then, especially if it is revised. At the moment, it is strongest in the ensembles and male variations, weakest in the pas de deux. Here the choreography loses its grip on the music and meanders. A male quintet is the high point; Tomasson seems to have exercised recondite aspects of his own formidable technique as a soloist. The pride of the workshop series was the group of young male dancers who were featured in Tomasson's ballet and in the Balanchine pieces. It is unusual to see so many good boys in one year. But the level of achievement was a high one over all.

The fresh young performing in *Valse Fantaisie* and *Western Symphony* made me want to see both ballets in repertory—*Western* with its long-missing third movement restored. The version of *Valse Fantaisie* was the later one, choreographed in 1967. It shares a few steps with the 1953 version, but it is a different ballet. In expanding the male soloist's role Balanchine seems to have drained off much of its poignance. Once a ballet about a man and three women, *Valse Fantaisie* became an extended pas de deux—actually, two pas seuls—with a backup group. The first program announcements by the school erroneously gave the ballet's date as 1953. Maybe next year. There are not many other ballets retired by Balanchine which would be worth restoring to active repertory. *Gounod Symphony* would be, but not *Clarinade* or *Variations pour une Porte et un Soupir*.

Symphonie Concertante was unaccountably dropped in 1952 and forgotten for thirty years. When American Ballet Theatre revived it from dance notation last winter, one could only be grateful for the recovery of a lost treasure. But the performance seemed wrong then, and after two viewings at the Met this month it still seems wrong. The principal roles, arranged to follow the violin and the viola of Mozart's concerto symphony, are still being danced by Cynthia Gregory and Martine van Hamel with the concern for trivial technical perfection and the unconcern for dynamic shading and musical transparency which marred the première performances. They were followed by Susan Jaffe and Magali Messac: same irrelevant display of technique, same unmusicality. If Gregory and van Hamel, senior ballerinas with ironclad performing styles, were miscast, their juniors were miscast and misguided. Jaffe was plainly taking Gregory for her model, while Messac's virtues were never meant for Balanchine. Stiff where they should be crisp, weak where they should be soft, persistently on the beat and off the music, all these ladies danced as if they thought Balanchine and Mozart were a more concentrated version of Petipa and Minkus. Patrick Bissell, the cavalier in the first cast, seemed to know better but not to have passed his knowledge on to his successor, Ross Stretton. After four months of breaking in, A.B.T.'s noble experiment in resuscitation looks very much like a failure.

The questions that arise are: (1) Does the failure reflect incapacity on A.B.T.'s part? or (2) Is there something the matter with trying to revive a ballet as complex as *Symphonie Concertante* from notation with no other memory aid and no authority on hand to settle all-important issues of style? The main issue, which has to do with regulating the shape, pulse, and flow of the dance phrase in relation to the musical one, seems never to have come up.

(1) Incapacity. A.B.T. has long possessed a Balanchine jewel in *Theme and Variations*, and would on occasion perform it to the hilt. I saw some wonderful *Themes* as recently as a year ago. This ballet stems from the same creative period in Balanchine's career as *Symphonie Concertante* and *Symphony in C*, and although it is set to Tchaikovsky, and not Mozart, it supplies clues to Balanchine's musical thinking which could have been pertinent to the reconstruction of the unknown Mozart work. But the two ballets as staged come from two different worlds. And, as if to create the widest possible contrast between them, A.B.T. has revised its production of *Theme and Variations*, substantially reconceiving the ballet in the process. The stage is dark; the pas de deux is now a nocturne. The slow tempo doesn't make it more romantic; the legato attack only blurs and sentimentalizes the beautiful dance poem that Balanchine was able to create while contriving an ingenious simulation of adagio effects for an allegro technician, Alicia Alonso. The ensembles have been touched by the same martinet's ruler that prods the corps of *Symphonie Concertante* into its lifeless precision routines. The two ballets now look more alike rather than less—they're *both* un-Balanchinean.

Baryshnikov is presiding over a new Ballet Theatre—one in which every corps member performs impeccably. A clean style is always pleasant to see. But scrubbing away impurities isn't enough to make dancing interesting. I am sure Baryshnikov knows it. He is assembling a dream repertory of works by Balanchine and Merce Cunningham and Paul Taylor and Twyla Tharp that *do* make dancing interesting, but in completely different ways. A mixed repertory has ever been Ballet Theatre's policy and ever an impractical one. No company in the world could master all these styles at once. Ballet Theatre excels in *Push Comes to Shove*, which Tharp created on commission (and keeps restudying). It is credible in *Airs*, a piece that was begun by Taylor on A.B.T. dancers. But its version of Cunningham's *Duets* suffers because ballet dancers aren't trained in Cunningham methods of torsion and attack. Drawing ballets from here and there is chancy even when choreographers are commissioned. When works are appropriated, they are bound to be misrepresented no matter how carefully they are coached. Unless, of course, they're dead works—so old no one remembers how they should be done. Is *Symphonie Concertante* a dead ballet?

(2) Notation. No known system records the synchronization of steps to music with anything like the precision it takes to dance Balanchine. Ballet Theatre enlisted several Balanchine associates in its preparations, and at one time or another Tanaquil LeClercq, Maria Tallchief, and Diana Adams were invited to have a look. (LeClercq, who originated the "violin" role in a student performance, in 1945, and danced it in repertory opposite Tallchief or Adams, had never seen the ballet before—she'd always been in it.) Even for the remarkably retentive memories of dancers, thirty years is a long time. The Mozart ballet that replaced *Symphonie*

Concertante in N.Y.C.B. repertory in 1952 was itself forgotten after only four years; Balanchine largely re-created *Caracole* when he gave it again, as *Divertimento No. 15.** That loss was made good. Still, what wouldn't we give now for a notated score of *Caracole* (or *The Figure in the Carpet* or *Transcendence* or *Cotillon*, and so on back through time)? Isn't it reasonable to suppose that style can be reconstituted once a text exists? Or, inasmuch as Balanchine style *is* the text, wouldn't a reconstitution by the School of American Ballet or New York City Ballet have a better chance of success than one by American Ballet Theatre? Probably. But Balanchine thought his ballets were for the world, not just for his own dancers—he gave them away free. (In a moving opening-night tribute to Balanchine, Baryshnikov said, "Mr. B. doesn't just look out for the company across the plaza. He looks out for us and for all companies.")

The ultimate issue then becomes what Balanchine is in the world's eyes—the dance world's, I mean. Has he taught it to dance Mozart? And what of the audience? The eye- and ear-filling experience that is a Balanchine ballet—that is any Balanchine ballet—simply isn't being delivered in the monochromatic rotework of *Symphonie Concertante*. Yet the audience applauds; the company has a hit. I think the applause would be much greater if the ballet were done right, but I've seen too many imitation-Balanchine pieces go over with audiences to believe that accuracy genuinely matters. Audiences are perfectly happy to applaud the most inane "abstract" ballets, particularly when they offer the agreeable sight of dancers in tutus demonstrating classical decorum. *Symphonie Concertante* began life as a student piece, and it does reflect the regimentation of the classroom, with its lessons and drills. Performing the ballet, Tallchief has said, "was like taking your medicine every day." The hygienic spectacle that is A.B.T.'s version may reflect *some* classrooms. Not Balanchine's.

New York City Ballet maintains the world's largest active repertory, but it has never hesitated to retire pieces for long periods, because Balanchine would be there to remind the dancers how to do them. (And it was how rather than what that concerned him; he was inclined to forget steps.) If the pieces no longer served, he would replace them. His whole operation as a ballet master looked so easy that up until the last decade of his life Balanchine was taken pretty much for granted. The absence of ego in his work and the protean forms it took tended to make people think they were responding not to one man's genius but to the genius of his medium. The artist disappeared into his art. When I came to New York, as a college student in the fifties, the first theatre I happened to see was a performance of New York City Ballet—a company I knew about only because it had been featured in *Life*. I saw *Symphony in C* and thought it one of the natural wonders of New York, something in no way extraordinary except as ballet itself was extraordinary—and New York, too. On the way out, I heard a man greet another man whom he obviously hadn't seen for a while. "Oh, I couldn't miss

---

* *Postscript 1987:* The extent to which *Divertimento No. 15* is or is not a remake of *Caracole* is a matter of some debate. Lincoln Kirstein includes *Caracole* in his list of lost Balanchine ballets (*Thirty Years*).

Symphony in C," said the other one. "It's my bread and water." That made sense to me, and since I was eager for caviar and champagne, I didn't go to the ballet as often in those years as I might have. I missed *Metamorphoses* and *Opus 34* and *Roma,* and they have never been done again. I certainly didn't miss *Concerto Barocco;* with the arrival of *Agon* I became an addict.

In recent seasons, N.Y.C.B. programming has been going slightly overboard in the minor Balanchine; there are too many pas de deux and tin soldiers and Russian scherzos. A program in which Balanchine is represented only by *Swan Lake* and *Kammermusik No. 2* is one I won't attend. But what about five years from now? A few nights ago, when *Concerto Barocco* was put on in place of *Ballo della Regina,* I felt a qualm. What if we should never see dear little *Ballo* again? Who cares if it isn't great? The greatest Balanchine ballet is the one you happen to be watching. —*May 23, 1983*

Reflections on Glass

One of the commandments of choreography is that there shall be dances to music by Philip Glass. The primordial simplicity of Glass's music makes choreographers want to construct clean statements in space and time. Yet there's also a neutrality: the music has the capacity to reflect whatever the choreographer wants to do. Lucinda Childs's dances to Glass were austere and diagrammatic, seemingly a mirror of Glass's own methods of composition. Andrew DeGroat, who devised the bulk of dances for *Einstein on the Beach,* drew on the misterioso as well as the purely formal qualities in the score. Kathryn Posin set the same music as a hard-edged Dadaist drama. And the chain of possibilities—narrow but densely woven—is extended by the combinations and permutations that Glass keeps introducing as organic developments of his style.

In some of these developments, the sound is surprisingly conventional, with only a hairline separating the Glassian-organic from the non-Glassian-idiomatic. Such moments give us a glimpse of the obviousness in Glass's formulations and go some way toward explaining why, as John Rockwell says in *All American Music,* "people *like* this music." Glass not only reduces the process of composition to essentials; he also expands the process of enjoyment by playing up those trance-inducing elements in music which our teachers warned us about. The way to listen to Glass is to go with the flow, and when you do, the happy hallucination you get is that the music is yours, not his. This must, at any rate, be the experience that choreographers have when they start to deal with Glass's rhythmic units, which are numbing in their cubelike infinite progression. In his latest work for New York City Ballet, Jerome Robbins uses a Glass score; he even uses a modicum of the minimalism associated with Glass choreographers such as Childs and DeGroat.

The stage is hung with a plain beige sheet, lined like graph paper; most of the dancers wear practice dress and jazz shoes. It all has the look of some new, pristine adventure, yet what Jerome Robbins comes up with is a Jerome Robbins ballet. Exactly what the music ordered.

Glass Pieces is in three parts. The first two are built on selections from the CBS record *Glassworks*; the third uses the opening instrumental section of the opera *Akhnaten*, as yet unrecorded. As a Glass sampler, the pieces are well chosen. They give us hard- and soft-core Glass. But they also give us his strengths and weaknesses. "Rubric," laying down deep chords of steam-whistle-like sound over a burbling, pulsating accompaniment, is followed both on the record and in the ballet by "Façades," a smooth and serene intertwining of two melodies, one wavering, one steady. "Rubric" and "Façades" are the most seductive tracks on *Glassworks*, and for Robbins they work together as classic audience psychology—stir 'em up, quiet 'em down. "Rubric" has radical heat and energy, while "Façades" lingers on the borderline of convention. The pounding drums of the *Akhnaten* excerpt, to my ear, cross that borderline and end deep in jungle-movie-soundtrack territory. And the extended finale that Robbins has devised to that music is the weak part of the ballet. He doesn't give in to the convention—he can't, because of the peculiarly restraining rhythm—yet he's uncomfortable with the alternative, which is to pretend that Glass is being as pure as he is in "Rubric."

Like the rhythm of rock, Glassian rhythm is static; as movement, it takes you everywhere and nowhere. Its sensibility is Eastern; its mode is ritualistic. To a Western romantic like Robbins, rhythm is abstract or anecdotal. He succeeds in making anecdotes of "Rubric" and "Façades": he tells us the story of the music. "Rubric" opens pell-mell with a nondescript horde of dancers walking—barrelling—around the stage in various directions. Into this rush-hour mêlée drop two ballet dancers (assemblé descent), to be lost in the swarm, then recovered in time for a brief pas de deux in conventional ballet syntax. The horde returns, and two more aliens arrive, clad like the other two in Milliskin tights and toe shoes. The four of them are together in a double duet, then the horde fills the stage again. The filling and emptying of the stage, the arrival of the aliens (three pairs in all), their disappearances and reappearances—all this fits perfectly with the alternating strands in the music. The traffic pattern occurs four times, with slight variations each time; by the last repeat we see quite clearly that the process could go on forever, at which point everything stops and the scene blacks out.

Choreographers of Glass's generation (he was born in 1937) don't try to explain the peculiarities of his music—they just accept them. Older choreographers may see the music's strangeness as a subject in itself. For Robbins, the fact that the music is sunk in a ritualistic mode means that a story can be constructed about it—a story that seems to tell us something of the impervious, aimless rushing about we do in our lives, never stopping to notice the wonders in our midst. In "Façades," the ritual is again double-stranded. One melody oscillates like the path of a moonbeam on the surface of a lake, and the other melody spans it in slowly shifting single-note progressions carried by the high winds. Robbins translates the slow melody into a floating, rather mindlessly beautiful pas de deux for Maria Calegari and Bart Cook, while the all but motionless oscillation becomes a line of shadowy figures inching along in profile at the back of the stage: the piddling continuity, as it were, of daily life. Robbins doesn't ever mix the two motivic strands (though Glass does); his pas de deux could have been done for any other ballet. But then his point is that the wonderful events in life are different in kind from the ordinary events. They may interpenetrate, as in "Rubric," but custom prevents us from seeing this. In "Façades," beauty is enclosed in an entirely secret realm. Calegari and Cook at one point run to the line of figures and break through it; it goes on as if they'd never touched it. Yet it's the humdrum background, not the ravishing foreground, that one wants to watch. Robbins's minimalistic choreography includes about a dozen steps, all as tiny as the inchworm shuffle that gradually carries the line off, and the way the minutiae accumulate, with a sidestep or a kneel or a pause added for every repetition of the sequence, makes a hypnotic spectacle. In *Akhnaten*, Robbins's motifs spread beyond the two parallel strands he's worked with up to now, and he again fills the stage, this time with prancing contingents of boys and girls. You can feel him trying to break out into abstract rhythm. All that happens is a series of devices for modulating and containing the force of Glass's rhythm; Robbins never does succeed in inflecting it.

As dance music, Glass's compositions call up ancient associations not only with Oriental (specifically, Indian) ritual dance but with old ballets like *La Bayadère*. It is also head music, and, as such, conspicuously a product of the sixties, that era of drug-incited revelations and rock ecstasy. The hallucinogenic power of Glass's music is directly attributed by Rockwell to the sixties drug culture; what marijuana revealed, he says, was a "new way of hearing things," which "profoundly affected the way we made, heard, and judged all music." None of this matters or has to matter to Robbins and his Glass ballet. The fact that a choreographer of his stature chose to involve himself just now with Glass's music set me pondering the whole Glass phenomenon. And *La Bayadère*, revived once more this season by American Ballet Theatre, seemed a more than ever relevant link to that phenomenon and to the consciousness of that generation. Philip Glass and *La Bayadère* have both transcended the sixties, of course. With his own ensemble, Glass performs in high-decibel rock clubs and is a major figure on the art-rock scene as well as on the concert and opera scene. It seems to me that as a composer for dancers he has done something very like what Delibes (in *La Source*) and Minkus (in *La Bayadère*) did—namely, filter the ethos of the East through popular Western idioms. For Delibes and Minkus, the idiom was the waltz, as intoxicating in its day as rock was in the sixties. *La Bayadère*, set in India, describes the travails of a Hindu temple dancer. She dies, and her Nirvana is (as Ted Shawn would have predicted) in three-quarter time. It is also a paradise of grand-scale minimalism. This vision of infinity, the "Kingdom of the Shades," is beheld by the hero in an opium trance. A key element in the choreography is ritual repetition, which also marks the work of Glass and his colleagues in music, theatre, and dance. It only remains for *La Bayadère,* a work of capital significance in ballet, to take its place on the fever chart of the American sixties. That was the decade and the climate of its Western début and first Western revival, and the repercussions are still being felt. —*June 6, 1983*

Baryshnikov Among Sylphs

Men used to perform high cabrioles with the torso held erect. Since Baryshnikov, nearly everybody does them with a backbend. "He *lay* in the air" has replaced "He *sat* in the air" as the way most people would describe the look of the step. Baryshnikov's version complements the leg action with a resistant drag in the upper body; the tight high clasp of the legs pointing forward becomes the active principle, the languid arc of the back the reactive principle, and the combination fastens our attention on the whole body, not just on its lower half, as it passes through space. The completeness of the image involves a contradiction; a synthesis of oppositions is one of the chief means by which dancing acquires sophistication of expression. Another is amplification through excess. Everyone is talking about the step Baryshnikov does in his latest role, choreographed at American Ballet Theatre by Twyla Tharp: he lands from a double air turn in deep plié in fifth position. Dancers have done this before, landing in second. Baryshnikov's unwaveringly perfect pinpoint descent is an extension of his normal double tour: the normal landing in demi-plié is pushed beyond its functional limit into a new area of audacious demonstration. The excesses that a great virtuoso is capable of are extended: as he has jumped higher than anyone else, now he lands lower. And Tharp has found other, more subtle variations on Baryshnikov's technique, which don't depend on excess *or* synthesis but instead express the simple defiance of propriety which has always enlivened her approach to classical choreography. The barrel turns that he does so beautifully—so high, so even, so uniform in their off-center pitch—appear here fleetingly in a startling "corrected" version, with a straightened body that makes the backward tilt of the spiral even more precipitous. And Baryshnikov sailing into the teeth of disaster looks casually down over his shoulder.

Tharp gives us Baryshnikov as he is today, not as he was in 1976 in *Push Comes to Shove,* and not even as he is when he currently performs that ballet. The changing imperatives of *Push*—the unsettling shift from a rag to a Haydn symphony, the ballerinas rushing this way and that, the corps in continual disarray— no longer find Baryshnikov pretending to be at their mercy. He now meets the tactical switches Tharp has devised with a nonchalance that is twice as funny as his former bafflement. When he springs to terrier alertness ("Ready when you are, A.B.T.!"), it's not to keep up with the other dancers; it's to go along with the gag, like Jack Benny. Tharp, monitoring the production over the years, has modified it so that it clicks along cracking its jokes out of the side of its mouth and in general keeping itself attuned to the throwaway style of its star. (Other dancers in Baryshnikov's role have been strained and frantic but not ineffective, because push *has* come to shove—it never really has in Baryshnikov's case.) It may be that observing Baryshnikov's change of style in this part gave Tharp the material for the portrait she draws of him in the new piece, which she calls *Once Upon a Time*. She no longer sees him as a brilliant interloper trying to fit himself into the scheme of American ballet; instead, he's a reflective figure steeped in the tradition of Russian ballet, pursuing its chimerical sylphs down one hopeful path after another. The role is analogous to Baryshnikov's in real life as he tries to shape the direction of American Ballet Theatre and at the same time be its greatest star. In this duality, as Tharp defines it, lie the makings of a dilemma. She doesn't say what path, if any, leads to the future; she leaves Baryshnikov in the pose of the Romantic poet, hungering after his visions. But in the wonderful role she has given him she suggests that he himself fulfills our hopes, at least for the present.

Tharp sees in the new Baryshnikov a consummate master of subtleties, but, as in the great solo in *Push Comes to Shove*, he is still a dancer who moves with the speed of thought—whose moves *are* thought. We see him ruminate, argue with himself, light up with the flash of an idea, and become obsessed. We see him knock off and just kick things around. The brain wave becomes hyperactive whenever the Ballerina is near—the One who becomes the focus of his obsession. But Deirdre Carberry doesn't tease or taunt her pursuer in classic Romantic-ballet fashion; elusiveness is simply her nature. Carberry and her three sister sylphs—Elaine Kudo, Amanda McKerrow, and Nancy Raffa—are the only other dancers in the cast, and in the immense gloom of the Met stage (as Jennifer Tipton lights it) they are conspicuous little phantoms, drifting in and out on toe, clustering prettily, evaporating or appearing suddenly in a far corner with hallooing, decorative arms. Except for a few small Tharpian deformities, their choreography keeps to classic patterns of sylphhood; they are "the ballet," while Baryshnikov is "the ballet master." There is in *Once Upon a Time* no *actual* ballet to watch—it's in gestation. That may be why Tharp has made it only twelve minutes long (it was originally performed under the title *The Little Ballet**), and why she doesn't close it with a traditional ensemble number; the vision just peters out—but not before Baryshnikov executes one of his most breathtaking evolutions, from a grande pirouette to a kneel. And it may explain why the girls are costumed not in tulle tutus but in the pinafores of Russian women students of the last century. Baryshnikov dances in slacks, a shirt with rolled-up sleeves, and a loosened tie—all in shades of gray. The music is by that most representative of Russian conservatory musicians, Glazunov, who composed the last authoritative works of Petipa. The academy casts its shadow forward through time. Had Santo Loquasto, the costume designer, also done a set, it might well have shown the façades of Theatre Street

---

* *Postscript 1987:* Tharp reverted to this title for the following season and has kept it ever since.

getting a face lift. Tharp's selections from *Scènes de Ballet* and *Raymonda* are in the idiosyncratic spirit of the whole ballet. The music is all soft and lustrous, with flowing rhythms—waltzes, mainly, and none with too high a color. Within this self-imposed adagio format, Tharp sets bursts of allegro working to inner rhythms. She gives us the dynamic contrasts of a traditional ballet suite without stopping for set pieces; everything happens within the flow. Baryshnikov's pas de deux with Carberry is interwoven with his solo, which runs from end to end of the piece.

The continuity has a stream-of-consciousness drive. Looking at Baryshnikov, you find that nothing you think about as you look at him is irrelevant. The portrait of him in *Push* incorporated real-life gestures that Tharp had observed in rehearsal. Here he's a maturer, more intently focussed artist, less interested in trying things on (the symbol of novelty in *Push*: the derby hat) than in divesting himself of habitual, known effects. For him, dancing is a science. He sees himself with cold scrutiny; he lends his talents to projects with the objectivity of a Pasteur experimenting upon himself. Discipline for him is not what it is for other dancers, nor are their goals his. Competition is unreal. He consolidates strengths in order to be able to dismiss them. Such a dancer may make a good director. But transcendence is one thing, divination another. Twyla Tharp—who as a dancer-director knows something of what being Baryshnikov must be like—casts him in *Once Upon a Time* as a man of vision, which may be just what Baryshnikov isn't. There are undertones of Balanchine in her portrait. Perhaps it was Balanchine whom she and Baryshnikov were thinking about when they worked on the ballet. *
Anyway, he's there, pre-eminent among the shades of Petipa and Fokine and Nijinsky and Merce Cunningham and whoever else comes to mind when you ponder, as the ballet encourages you to, its subject and its author in the full consciousness of their collaboration.

Baryshnikov's malleability occasionally invites abuse. It's easy to think up excuses for another of his new numbers, executed by the San Francisco choreographer John McFall; maybe McFall only intended to relate Baryshnikov to the boys of the company the way Tharp relates him to the girls. But McFall's contribution (which has a title cuter than Tharp's—*Follow the Feet*) isn't rooted in anything we see in Baryshnikov or know about him. It pretends that he's an aging kingpin about to be toppled by a youthful challenger, Robert La Fosse. (The transcendent phase he's in now makes Baryshnikov's style all but nonexistent as a goal for the other male dancers.) Again, Baryshnikov goes along with the gag, but McFall can't do much with the idea of a competition, so he substitutes a mock competition—a woodenly whimsical affair with more struts, snits, and curled pinkies than there are in *Les Biches*. And Baryshnikov can't do anything with *that*. What he does do is underplay the implications of the movement, so that even though there's no real contest going on between him and La Fosse,

---

* *Postscript 1987:* The double air turn into grand plié fifth mentioned at the beginning of this article was a favorite step of Balanchine's, given in class. In his choreography, it appears in the solo for the leader of the men's regiment in *Stars and Stripes*—sometimes.

there's not much else going on, either. It takes Baryshnikov's gift of subtlety to be able to underplay without underdancing. But then Baryshnikov—the soul of honor when it comes to giving the choreographer full value—would never think of underdancing. Other dancers don't have the luxury of choice that he has, but when Johan Renvall dances the role opposite Ronald Perry the two of them automatically are let off the hook, because Renvall is white and Perry is black, and the audience may decide it's seeing a ballet-camp version of Nick Nolte and Eddie Murphy.

In *Giselle*, Baryshnikov underplayed again, muting his performance in deference, I thought, to the now highly erratic Gelsey Kirkland. But what I took to be underplaying in *La Sylphide* in deference to Erik Bruhn and the novice ballerina Cheryl Yeager was, I learned later, Baryshnikov dancing with a slight injury. Bruhn was playing the mime role of Madge, the witch who puts a curse on the hero for the flimsiest of reasons. Whether played by a man or a woman, Madge is more credible as the means than as the cause of James's destruction. James, by venturing into the spirit world, destroys himself. But it is now common practice to inflate the role of Madge, and the foolish scene, rivalling Walpurgisnacht, in which she and her fellow-witches prepare the fatal scarf is seldom deleted. Bruhn, who some years ago revised Harald Lander's production for A.B.T., has now staged a new version. He restores the original musical arrangements used by Lander and by the Royal Danish Ballet; the production sounds truthful once more. As Madge, Bruhn looms over it like the force of destiny. Shambling barefoot through the ballet in his gray Medusa makeup, pulling every string in the plot, he turns a convenient minor character into James's nemesis. The whole production is scaled up to match this august conception. The room with the fireplace is now a great hall bulging with heraldic devices and ancestral armor. Effie and her friends are in frilly Empire dresses and pantalettes, a triumph of period accuracy over practicality. Those skirts are not easy to dance a Highland fling in. Desmond Heeley, the designer, repeats the worst feature of the current Danish production (in which the women wear kilts): he places the staircase against one of the side walls of the stage, making it hard for the audience on that side to see what is going on there. His forest, though, is beautifully done—by itself as complete a stage picture as when it is filled border to border with corps de ballet. There are one or two charming mechanical effects. There should be more—more faces appearing among the trees. The finale, in which the Sylph is raised to unthinkable heights, is managed with a dummy. *La Sylphide* is a gentle, modestly scaled piece; it is not *Giselle*. What Heeley's first-act frills and Bruhn's bombast conceal is the simplicity of James's home life and the sweetness of it, which sickens him and drives him into the forest to satisfy his immortal longings. And surely the pain of nostalgia at the end, when the wedding procession passes by, is punishment enough without the omnipotent Madge decreeing that the wretch! must! die! At a second performance, Baryshnikov danced peerlessly but less passionately than he has in the past; Yeager is as yet a dutiful Sylph and not an inspiring partner, and Kenneth Schermerhorn conducts with a laggardly beat. In the forest scene, Baryshnikov does his usual double air turns, landing stock-still, rocketing off again in the opposite direction, and smiling. Madge was played zestfully and without bluster by Ruth Mayer.

It is good to see Martine van Hamel back on the New York stage, but not so good to see her in *Torso*. About all that can be said for her role in this stiflingly solemn Jiří Kylián pas de deux is that it is centered in the upper body and has a minimum of footwork. Van Hamel can perform it without fear of exacerbating the injury that put her out all last season. Kylián's plastique has no way of showing a continuing synthesis of oppositions. The stretch principle in his choreography is infinite, like Silly Putty. I don't know who van Hamel and her partner, Clark Tippet, are supposed to be in *Torso*, but technically they are bores, doing the movement equivalent of yammering until the curtain falls. Except for the Tharp piece, A.B.T. hasn't had much luck with premières this season. Peter Anastos's *Clair de Lune* came out last year, when I could manage only a glimpse of it. This season, I saw it with two casts, and it confirmed my impression of a real advance for Anastos, who only a few years ago was known chiefly for his comedy ballets and a few years before that was known solely as the Trockadero's mistress (Olga Tchikaboumskaya) of revels. The surprise of *Clair de Lune* is not that it's serious choreography but that it isn't more aggressive serious choreography. One would think that making a big turn in his career would have prompted Anastos to a grander pronouncement. The piece is a pas de deux using the four sections of Debussy's *Suite Bergamasque,* and the choreography has the virtues one would wish for this music—freshness, classical restraint, rhythmic suppleness. It also has a fullness of phrase that in Magali Messac's performance became powerfully evocative. Looking like one of those chaste nymphs who adorn the front of the Paris Opéra, she took me into the music and its era—the era of Mallarmé's writings on dance. (Anastos, with his acute historical sense, may have intended the very thing.) La Fosse was her sturdy partner. At the finish, as "Clair de Lune" began, the dancers stood decently still, gazing out at a dark sky. Comparisons with Jerome Robbins's Chopin ballets, which Anastos used to parody, would seem inevitable, would even be useful, but the reviews haven't mentioned Robbins. Apparently, Anastos still isn't being taken seriously enough for that. The fragility of *Clair de Lune* does not indicate a fragile talent.

At the first two performances of *Once Upon a Time, Symphonie Concertante* was on the bill. With Susan Jaffe and Cynthia Harvey being partnered by La Fosse and with Schermerhorn conducting, the performance was hit-or-miss, a little sharper than other performances have been but basically uncomprehending. With Paul Connelly conducting the same cast, things were still chancy, but the ballet began to come through. Jaffe had stopped trying to hold balances at every opportunity; Harvey seemed actually to be listening to the music. The tension of Balanchine's phrases could be felt at least part of the time, and when real blanks occurred they seemed more likely the fault of the script than of the performance; some of the steps appear not to have made it onto notation paper in the first place.

All this suggests that with proper coaching and some reweaving here and there Ballet Theatre could yet make *Symphonie Concertante* happen.

—*June 20, 1983*

Postscript 1987: There has been no change in A.B.T.'s performances of *Symphonie Concertante*.

Paging Mr. Astaire

When his epochal series of films with Ginger Rogers ended, in 1939, Fred Astaire seems to have taken a vow never again to become involved with a dancing partner to the extent that he had been with Rogers, and in the long course of his subsequent career he never worked with the same woman more than twice. A late exception was Barrie Chase, with whom he made a number of successful television specials. In the movies, he made sure that there was no Fred-and- combination. He had started out in vaudeville partnering his sister Adele, and it had been Fred-and-Adele all through the big-hit years of the twenties. He had survived her retirement only by going into the movies, whereupon he found himself teamed even more prosperously with Rogers. He survived Rogers by ruling entangling alliances out of his career, and for a long time the decision showed itself not only in the relatively unserious and uncommitted character of the duets he performed with other women but also in the women themselves. In *Broadway Melody of 1940*, he has a buddy relationship with Eleanor Powell. In *Second Chorus*, he spends hardly any time alone with Paulette Goddard (a nondancer), and he dances with her only once. The two women in *Holiday Inn*, Marjorie Reynolds and Virginia Dale, are like stand-ins for some real partner who never shows up. But somewhere along in here he has a fling with Rita Hayworth, who was then in the full vigor of her youth and beauty. Moreover, she knew how to dance, having been trained by her father, the Spanish dancer Eduardo Cansino. But, whether because her style was too flamboyant for the easygoing Astaire or because she was too young for him or because his bias against forming another team made him keep his distance, they aren't a great match. She glows and he enjoys it, but their partnership is what Edward Everett Horton in *Top Hat* calls "a *passade*," and nothing more. The dance that the two of them do to "I'm Old Fashioned" in their second film, *You Were Never Lovelier*, is about as far from the kind of thing Astaire did with Rogers as he could get and still appear to be keeping a beautiful woman company. It's neither a flirtation nor a seduction nor yet a rapturous lost-in-each-other dance (like "Smoke Gets in Your Eyes" or the "Waltz in Swingtime," to name two of Astaire's other Jerome Kern numbers); it's a getting-acquainted dance—lightly social with a pleasurable veneer of romance. Astaire, who believed in building numbers out of plot circumstances, drew on the character that Hayworth plays and on the song that Kern and Johnny Mercer had written for her: she's an old-fashioned girl who loves the old-fashioned things. (She certainly didn't *look* old-fashioned, but the Gibson Girl fantasy of Hayworth continued in *Cover Girl*; *Gilda* was far ahead.) Astaire also drew on the shape of the song, which within narrow limits grows more and more expansive, as if it were being carried away with its own emotion; then it catches itself up to end decorously, though not quite as decorously as it began. His choreography is not one of his most distinctive compositions, though it does have his customary wide-ranging rhythmic variations, including a rumba that reminds us of the film's Argentine setting and of Hayworth's antecedents, and it leaves a clear implication that, when you see it in context, lifts the whole movie. "She may be old-fashioned," it says, "but she can swing when she wants to."

The fact that "I'm Old Fashioned" doesn't mean a great deal out of context and isn't gilded Astaire (on *You Were Never Lovelier* his collaborating dance director was Val Raset, with whom he never worked again) hasn't kept Jerome Robbins from choosing it as the basis of his second new work of the season. The ballet starts with a piece of film giving production credits while we hear Nan Wynn, who dubbed Hayworth's voice, singing "I'm Old Fashioned" on the sound-track. Then comes the Astaire-Hayworth dance, which takes place on a terrace before some French doors. Maybe Robbins thought that in choosing a comparatively unforceful and uncelebrated example of Astaire's work he could better isolate those elements which make Astaire a master, much as one might choose to illustrate Balanchine's mastery through the "Waltz of the Flowers" rather than *Agon*. Twelve hours were spent studying "I'm Old Fashioned" on videotape, interviewers were told, with Robbins claiming that at the end of that time he still hadn't seen everything. If we are to take him literally, the "I'm Old Fashioned" project comes to sound like one of those deliberately obtuse investigations in which scientists force-feed themselves information available to any schoolchild. When Robbins says he paid special attention to the way Astaire sets steps "on, over, or against the music," we wonder if he thinks of "on, over, or against" as options that were simultaneously present in Astaire's mind at every moment in the construction of the dance, so that microscopic scrutiny of Astaire's movements would reveal some sort of system by which he chose the "right" option, and, perhaps, enable others to choose it, too. I do not know; I only guess at the reason for the almost immediate evaporation of the Astaire factor once the film clip ends and Robbins's variations begin.

First, Robbins restates his theme by having Judith Fugate and Joseph Duell present the film choreography step for step in enlarged and elaborated ballet terms and with Fugate on point. We understand that we're going to see New York City Ballet in a ballet, and not in a literal emulation of Astaire's personal dance style. But we should also understand that to Robbins New York City Ballet is its own theme—a legend approximately equal in size and lustre to Astaire—and that

Robbins would not be Robbins if he didn't try to bring Astaire's system and style together with the aggregation of systems and styles which is New York City Ballet. Or, perhaps, what with Balanchine and Robbins both having on repeated occasions acknowledged their regard for Astaire, it's not so much a matter of bringing the two great emblematic forces together as of revealing their compatibility. Naturally, this compatibility would express itself on a plane above and beyond that of technique, so in a sense the little translation of the "I'm Old Fashioned" duet into a ballet pas de deux is irrelevant. Yet, having fixed the terms of revelation, Robbins does not go on to reveal anything. As I watched the ballet, my mind seesawed between the possibility that Robbins took the Astaire factor for granted in anything danced by N.Y.C.B. and the likelihood that no, he didn't take it for granted, he thought it demonstrable—only something was preventing him from demonstrating it. Robbins's variations on Astaire plus N.Y.C.B. are accompanied by Morton Gould's variations on "I'm Old Fashioned" plus various other musical themes that it is possible to associate with N.Y.C.B. through Robbins. In analyzing the song, Gerald Bordman, in *Jerome Kern: His Life and Music* (Oxford), notes that in essence it follows a theme-and-variations development—ABA^1A^2—"all played out in a range of just over an octave." Presumably, Robbins and Gould hear this, just as Astaire must have, but Astaire's use of a concise format for a concise melody isn't appropriate for a thirty-minute ballet. Gould has to add other factors, and in the course of twelve numbers we find him working out an equation between Jerome Kern and Jerome Robbins. We get the Leonard Bernstein factor—"I'm Old Fashioned" as revealed by flashes of *West Side Story* and *On the Town*. Meanwhile, Robbins seems to be pursuing the subliminal connections of his videotape sessions, now and then making a few overt references of his own. A double sextet does variations on *Who Cares?*, which is Balanchine's treatment of Astaire. Bart Cook does a rumba with body slaps that recalls both the rumba of the Third Sailor in *Fancy Free* and the Astaire solo in *You Were Never Lovelier*, which may well have inspired it. He also does the sissonnes from the man's solo in *Interplay* (the ballet to a score by Gould) which were inspired by Odette's variation in *Swan Lake*—the references build up layer upon layer. This layered consciousness is very N.Y.C.B. It is the dancer's version of race memory—this knowledge that thousands of patterns persist in whatever seems new or strange. In *Who Cares?*, Balanchine was able to link Gershwin to Astaire, and himself to both and to Petipa, too. But in the process of connection you saw exactly what the popular tradition shared with the grand tradition in dance. Robbins's process of connection resembles more a sentimental reminiscence; he thinks back to times when popular and grand really did share something, and by evoking those moments he hopes, perhaps, to create new ones. The Astaire connection may once have been real for Robbins—a real incentive in his work—but he doesn't re-create that reality in the new ballet. And, with Gould prodding his (and our) memory with past triumphs, he also seems to be piling up credits he hasn't earned.

Robbins's variations are at their wooziest in the duets, only here the problem is less a failure of connection to Astaire (or to Hayworth) than a failure of connection to the dancers who perform them. Kyra Nichols and Sean Lavery have a jivy pas de deux built mostly around the bump-and-bow business that occurs between Astaire and Hayworth as they make their exit through one of the French doors. But the purpose of the second Nichols-Lavery pas de deux and both of the long pas de deux danced by Heather Watts and Bart Cook escaped me, and I think it's because Robbins is using the dancers to serve whatever Astaire-related point he has in mind; he's not serving his dancers first—releasing *their* capacity to make the point for him. Watts and Cook, Nichols and Lavery look miscast or out of focus. Joseph Duell dances a solo that reminds us of his good performance in *Fancy Free* while Gould summons up *On the Town*. Duell has the creamiest of the six principal roles—short but effective. (Fugate's role, limited to the theme and the finale, is just short.) It's Duell who leads the cast in the penultimate number, a fugue that set allusions to *Fanfare* and *Goldberg Variations* rolling across the stage. Robbins divides the corps into segments and the segments into pairs and has them repeat the bump-and-bow routine all over the place. In the film, this routine occurs when Astaire and Hayworth try to get through the door at the same time and go into a rigmarole of courtesy, referring us to the "old-fashioned things" of the song. Robbins uses it as abstract gesture and as a gateway to the finale. Again we see the film sequence, this time with the image enlarged to cyclorama proportions and with the stage full of dancers dressed in versions of the tuxedo and black ballgown worn by Astaire and Hayworth. The orchestra takes over the soundtrack, and the dancers take up the original dance, pausing now and then to gaze up at the screen. Robbins is good at smash finales. The implication here, though, that he has portrayed the chemical change that turns the company into Astaire's descendants isn't deserved. The "I'm Old Fashioned" ballet is a Robbinsfest that need never have invoked Fred Astaire in the first place.

Fred Astaire is one of the few artists who worked in Hollywood of whom it can be said that their careers measured up to their talent, and it's a rare year that passes without some form of tribute to him. There have been movie and television compilations, critical studies, record reissues, testimonial dinners, and awards of every kind. There have also been tributes in dance. Robbins's ballet is unique in attempting something more than the usual pastiche, which is usually terrible. What madness to think that by putting on top hat, white tie, and tails and doing a tap dance with a cane you can be Fred Astaire. A few weeks before the Robbins première, Les Grands Ballets Canadiens played the City Center with a ballet called *Astaire*, which employed the songs, together with like-sounding arrangements and orchestrations, of several of the thirties films. The choreographers, Brydon Paige and John Stanzel, alternated between pastiche and direct transcription, with predictably dire results. Astaire's dances are inseparable from Astaire and the women he partnered. They do not constitute choreography for other dancers to copy or material for other dancers to redefine. They are artifacts created on film, the imprint of a moment. Choreographers who want to "do Astaire" have to come up with new material that's just as good, and they hardly ever manage that. The big chorus dances in *Astaire*, although some were on point, were really no different from the big production numbers in the films—the ones we sit through waiting for Fred and Ginger to dance. The solos and duets, especially those which incorporated Astaire's own steps, were embarrassing. Astaire was impersonated, if that is the word, by Stanzel, a bumptious soul of some sixty winters; "Ginger Rogers" (whose name, for some reason, was not mentioned) was the company's red-headed ballerina, Jerilyn Dana, wearing near-facsimiles of Rogers's gowns. To crown the tackiness of the whole production, the sound—music, taps, spoken introductions—was entirely on tape. What can be the purpose of a piece like *Astaire* in ballet repertory? "Repertory" to Astaire addicts means a collection of film images. "Performance" means rewinding the film and watching the image again.

The lessons one learns from watching Astaire don't go out of date, but as the popular song-and-dance tradition he was part of recedes, the import of those lessons may change. Primary and secondary considerations, primary and secondary effects may be confused by a generation unfamiliar with the dance manners of Astaire's day. If you were brought up in the age of television, you may have trouble distinguishing between the moods Astaire created and the attitudes he adopted. I recently read the opinion of a member of the TV generation that the "Let's Face the Music and Dance" sequence in the Steve Martin movie *Pennies from Heaven*, inelegant as it was, at least conveyed something of what the dances of Astaire and Rogers meant to audiences during the Depression. But did it? The movie makes such a cosmic fuss over the number, you wonder why it didn't win ten Academy Awards for 1936 plus a commendation from the Legion of Decency for forestalling suicide. The Steve Martin movie looks at Astaire-Rogers with the eyes of our own time, and it misses the point. Robbins has other fish to fry; his ballet is *beside* the point. But in that uncanny way he has of being exactly abreast of the zeitgeist, not a step behind or ahead, he also sees Astaire as the eighties see him—with a clear vision of his greatness but with no particular insight into his tradition. Days after I saw the Robbins ballet, I was bothered by one detail—a detail of Astaire's that Robbins had made into a motif. Did Robbins really think the bump-and-bow nonsense was important enough to justify the amount of quotation he gave it? Or did he know it wasn't important and quoted it because, as the outstandingly conventional moment in the dance, it let him feel free to quote—it would resist charges that he was attempting one more god-awful pastiche? There's still another possibility: Robbins throws in the bump and bow (sometimes only the bump) so as not to lose that portion of the audience unsubtle enough to be wondering where Astaire is in all this. Robbins seems to divide the audience into those who know a primary from a secondary Astaire effect and those who don't, and he baffles both halves. But he is a baffling artist. When he talks to the press about Astaire's musicality, surely he knows he's talking primary Astaire. There's not a choreographer working today who wouldn't benefit from studying this aspect of Astaire's art. But one doesn't make a science of it. A primary poetic instinct can only be wondered at as a kind of inspiration or appropriated as a guide to taste. You can't learn "the Astaire method," but you can learn what to avoid, what *not* to do. And you can learn, I think, from his sense of drama and story, his attention to what can only be called the meaning of the dance. In his simplest devices, he expresses a meaning. With him, the bump and bow has the full value of a convention invoked for its own sake and the further value of bearing out an idea about a girl and the song she sings. If Robbins had been as cognizant of Kyra and Heather as Astaire was of Rita and Ginger, maybe he'd have given us what at the outset of the piece he promises: a ballet in the Astaire tradition.

Tommy Tune, in *A Day in Hollywood/A Night in the Ukraine*, devised the cleverest tribute to Astaire (and Rogers) I have ever seen: he captured the style—but only as much of it as could be shown from the knees down. (*My One and Only*, Tune's current show, is a revamping of an old Fred-and-Adele vehicle, but, so far as I can see, it has nothing whatever to do with Astaire.) The most *touching* Astaire tribute I can remember was a quiet moment in an earlier Broadway musical which showed a boy dancing out a private fantasy in an alley. It was the "All I Need Is the Girl" number from *Gypsy*, directed and choreographed by Jerome Robbins. —*July 4, 1983*

Signs and Portents

Maria Calegari is one of those tantalizing untypable dancers whose advent makes New York City Ballet the most phenomenal ballerina breeding ground in the world. Calegari's repertory just now includes roles that have probably never before been covered by the same dancer: second pas de trois in *Agon*, Ricercata in *Episodes*, Choleric in *The Four Temperaments*, the "angel" in *Serenade*; she does *Swan Lake* and the *first* movement of *Symphony in C*; in addition to the roles she originated in *Glass Pieces*, *Gershwin Concerto*, and *La Création du Monde*—roles in which she's as glamorous and aloof as a forties movie star—she dances Suzanne Farrell's role in *Rossini Quartets*, Sara Leland's in *Symphony in Three Movements*, and Violette Verdy's in *Dances at a Gathering*. That's about as broad a range and as improbable a composite image as one can have, yet the complete Calegari may still be waiting to be exposed. In nearly every one of these parts, she reveals some vital new facet; she fills out the steps in a way you hadn't expected, calling on deeper reserves of strength or larger powers of comprehension than could have been inferred from whatever you saw her in last time. Calegari doesn't just take a role, she claims it. She gives apparently definitive performances in her oddball range of parts, but she herself eludes definition. Looking at her, watching her move, you wonder where it all comes from, and she keeps you guessing even about basic characteristics. Is she short or tall, delicate or strong, fiery or cool, dramatic or lyrical, adagio or allegro? A few things are clear: Calegari is thin (very). She has coppery red hair and exceptionally pale skin—so pale, in fact, that her moods seem to inhabit a spectrum of paleness: she can look hothouse or ice-cold or bled-out, as if skim milk ran in her veins. The pallor—a quality she shares with Farrell—is a part of her presence, but it isn't the color of her energy. (It is with Farrell. In her prodigious youth, Farrell's whiteness had a metaphysical impact, like the whiteness of the whale.) It may actually prevent you from seeing her energy. And her turnout is such that in poses en face or écarté she almost loses a dimension, she's so flat. But when she begins to move that flatness disappears. Calegari is one of the most plastically alive dancers in the company.

Her performance in the *Agon* pas de trois is the best I can recall seeing since the original one, by Melissa Hayden, but where Hayden gave the fast movements a fine slamming brio and the slow ones a sinuous play, Calegari gives them all a continuously liquid classical articulation that, without blurring the contrasts, blends them with meshlike intricacy. It's the same dance, more tightly knit. The "Spanish" solo, with its insistent contrapposto, is a good place to see Calegari's angular limbs and trunk acquire solidity and shapeliness. But while she steps into high relief the dance remains mysteriously veiled, its accents now lightly, now forcefully punctuated, its torsions strict or less strict, its continuity a supple twisting weave flecked with nuggets that catch the light. In Spanish-dance terms, she might be Argentinita, whereas Hayden was closer to Carmen Amaya. Calegari could probably stand to gain a few pounds. The bony clavicle, the bony knees under a classical tutu, and the drawn, heavy-lidded prettiness of the face prepare you for Pre-Raphaelite languor, not for incisive expression and baroque richness of plastique. "Plastique" is an old-fashioned word to apply to a Balanchine dancer, but that's the point. In Balanchine's company, there are many brilliant executants of steps; Calegari is also a brilliant executant of shapes. When, in *Agon*, she does a step done by the men—a backward lunge-kick braced from the heel—she shows the toughness and curtness of the step and also the mechanism of it. The elastic expansion of the kick as it pulls back from the heel is related to the wonderful effect she achieves when she strikes an arabesque: you see her simultaneously stretching and holding the shape. She doesn't "lock"—doesn't stop stretching once the shape has appeared.

Working for Balanchine, most dancers learn to show a keen moment-by-moment musical responsiveness. Calegari, by the constant vivacity of her sense of design, expresses something more. "Plastique" becomes not only the clear statement of bodily gesture in space and time but the clear sense of that gesture as part of the architecture of a whole ballet. In *Symphony in Three Movements*, she has a dual role as the athletic "American" of the first movement and the introverted "Oriental" of the second, dancing a cryptic, jasmine-scented pas de deux with Jock Soto. Calegari keeps the tension of the duality running throughout the duet, tightening her body evasively or releasing it in gestures of broad compliance. Balanchine could have cast two different women. The fact that he didn't poses no mystery to Calegari, and his ruminations on the ballet's subject, which is the Second World War (the war at home, the war in the Pacific), become that much clearer. In *Serenade*, the Calegari arabesque appears like a bow drawn taut above the fallen body of the heroine, and it keeps its full-out stretch as the man invisibly turns it full circle, once, twice. This exalted moment never fails to impress an audience, no matter who executes it. Calegari shows us why it's great. Her arabesque is every arabesque anatomized—the arabesque as a sign of the infinite. It's odd to think of Calegari as she used to be some years ago, with her hyper-extended joints and too pliant back. She was baroque in a way she couldn't control—she flopped about. Now she's magnetic. The gift she is developing—rare indeed—is the ability to show the way movement works in everything she dances.

Maria Calegari attained principal-dancer status this past year. Valentina Kozlova and Leonid Kozlov were granted it upon entering the company this spring. They were given a handful of roles, which they danced commendably on the whole. Kozlova has the small head, wasp waist, and long legs of the average New York City Ballet dancer. Her thighs are full but the hips are incompletely turned out—not lifted away from the thighs, like N.Y.C.B. hips—and the force of her pointwork doesn't flow from the articulation of her legs. She was trained in the Bolshoi tradition of neoclassicism, which is thought to have features in common with Balanchine; there, however, hyperextended knees would seem to be orthodox, and the placement of the pelvis against the spine is markedly non-Balanchine. Her husband is the male model of a Bolshoi technician; his dancing is buoyant, large, unreproachably clear: a plain, gray style. Like most Bolshoi men, he tends to sink his weight into his hips and thighs; this drops his center of gravity to about a foot below that of the Americans and Danish-Americans of N.Y.C.B.'s male wing. The disadvantage to the Kozlovs of appearing in Balanchine's choreography in the midst of Balanchine's company is obvious. Their best joint appearance was their first, in the Fall section of Robbins's *The Four Seasons*. Stylistically, the choreography is hospitable to Russian-trained dancers, and Robbins helped them out some more with a few adjustments. The patented star performances they gave weren't unseemly, but though they tried not to repeat that style of performance in their other Balanchine-Robbins roles, they are all too evidently used to their own kind of stardom. Kozlova, cast in the new Helgi Tomasson ballet, performed diligently and effectively at first. As her confidence grew, she took on more and more of an official Bolshoi presiding-officer manner. Even for dancers trained in compatible schools, it takes two or three years of breaking in at N.Y.C.B. for the company style to take hold. Adam Lüders and Ib Andersen, products of Copenhagen's Royal Ballet, are good cases in point. Andersen, who joined N.Y.C.B. in 1980, is just now becoming assimilated, and he—like Baryshnikov in the season of 1978–79—was rushed through role after role in what Balanchine used to call the Strasbourg-goose treatment. The sparing use of the Kozlovs and the indeterminate results of it at the season's end left open the question of why they had been hired in the first place. A look at the company roster reveals a shortage of ballerinas in active service. Some of these women have been put out by injury;

some, past their prime, are just fading away. The cadet ranks are full, but no real ballerina candidate has emerged since Calegari. Can it be that the great ballerina breeding ground is going fallow? Right now, all one can say is that the shortage is acute, and Kozlova is a long-term proposition at best.

The burden of vacant roles fell most heavily on Heather Watts, who throve on it. Being the workhorse of the repertory seemed to stimulate her; she danced almost nightly for nine weeks and was always fresh. Watts can be underrated just because she is so dependable; some of her performances this season went beyond valiant repping to reveal an interpretive flair. She was especially brilliant in the lighter Balanchine. In the effervescence of *Donizetti Variations* and *Who Cares?* (as the girl who dances "Embraceable You" and "My One and Only") she found a kind of momentum. Watts is always a pleasure to see in pirouettes and jumps. The entrechats with upflung arm in *Donizetti*, the retirés sautés in "My One and Only," and the whirling finale (the "Merrill Ashley" coda) were festive moments that branded themselves on the eye. But in the course of a variation or a pas de deux she has a tendency to coast—to stop dancing and fill in with indications about the point of a passage. Watts always knows the "story" of the dance; she isn't always able to project it steadily. Nevertheless, things happened for her this season. They happened for Ib Andersen, too: new hunger, new range had come into his dancing. He also seemed newly centered; the flyweight quality is disappearing, and with it the little-boy look that made him an inappropriate partner for big women. He paired beautifully with Watts in *Donizetti Variations* and with Stephanie Saland in *Robert Schumann's "Davidsbündlertänze."* In *Mozartiana*, he supported Farrell as if the pas de deux were a dialogue between the two of them—which it is.

Vacant roles in a repertory this size allow for plenty of experiments, and some have to fail. Saland was wonderful in *Davidsbündlertänze* but not in the Symphony of *Episodes*. Elyse Borne was charming in another role vacated by Sara Leland, the Explosions Polka of *Vienna Waltzes*. But those of us who had seen Leland and loved her randy Belle Watling quality will always miss her. A very big "but" must be lodged against the casting of David McNaughton, Katrina Killian, and Gen Horiuchi in classical roles. These are maverick talents—dancers with the kind of physical and technical equipment which one would more reasonably expect to see in character or specialty roles. (Along with some other more promising dancers who are also being featured—Nichol Hlinka, Stacy Caddell, Lisa and Alexia Hess, Susan Gluck—they make up a sizable influx of short people; it's as if the company were experiencing an attack of the tinies.) The surprise performance of the season was turned in by Sean Lavery, cast against type in *Who Cares?* One might have expected the technical perfection—indeed, one winced at it only last winter—but where did this loose and lighthearted song-and-dance man come from? *Who Cares?* did no harm to Lavery's technique; his dancing was as pure and his partnering as courtly as ever. What it did do was take the starch—that stiffly conscious *classique* quality—out of him and open up his personality. Lavery must be one of the few male dancers who can grin right out at the public without appearing to be trying to put the make on us. His breakthrough is an individual triumph. But it is also part of the new performing spirit that the company has been showing for the past year. Nearly all the ballets I have been mentioning— *Who Cares?* and *Donizetti* and *Vienna Waltzes* and *Davidsbündlertänze* and *Symphony in Three Movements* in particular—have been good not just because of one or two dancers but because of everyone in the cast. And this ensemble spirit or morale is new; it isn't a quality I have associated with New York City Ballet (or with any other ballet company except the Royal of England). The fact that one can now talk of esprit de corps at N.Y.C.B. means, of course, that the company is reacting to Balanchine's passing with a burst of conviction. It is eager to prove itself anew in all departments. Tomasson's *Ballet d'Isoline*, which is very much in the Balanchine-divertissement tradition, was given a company première of massed might. Farrell, partnered by Peter Martins, brought dramatic tension to the ballerina role. Peter Frame led the male quintet. Robert Irving, with his special tenderness for French theatre music, conducted the Messager score. Scenically, it was a two-chandelier ballet. The tutus and tunics were by Ben Benson in his favorite shade of blue (Ben blue). Tomasson may fulfill the hopes that have been pinned on him, especially if he can continue to choreograph, as he has here, sparkling innovative classical dances for men. This could lift the general level of male technique in the company to parity with the female level, and *that* would make it the highest in the world.

Tomasson has been an invaluable interpreter of the Balanchine repertory for something over a decade, and, to judge by *Ballet d'Isoline*, he has stored up a great deal of information. When he joined the company, Balanchine had just about completed the run of great roles which were interpreted and inspired by Edward Villella. With Tomasson, as with Martins and the Danish dancers who followed Martins into the company, Balanchine explored a new range of brilliance. The standard in male dancing became softer, more plangent and romantic. This is a generalization, of course; there are aspects of Villella's roles and of earlier roles created for other men which exemplify those values. But the culmination of Balanchine's explorations in the seventies was the development of a masculine style as light, fluid, and complex as the style for women. Tomasson's solo in *Divertimento from "Le Baiser de la Fée,"* Martins's solos in *Duo Concertant* and *Chaconne*, and Andersen's in *Mozartiana* removed the last traces of squareness and percussiveness from male dancing. As a solution to the problem of technical limitation, they were far more plausible than the attempts of dancers like Rudolf Nureyev and Anthony Dowell to raid the female technical vocabulary, and they were beautiful compositions as well. But Balanchine did not worry about more than one man—one virtuoso—at a time. Tomasson's male quintet, which is of a daring complexity and musical refinement, proposes that the new style become a group endeavor, and it's an exciting prospect.

Some of the troubles that American Ballet Theatre has been having in its long season at the Met—underfull houses, unenthusiastic or negative reviews—can be laid to the effects of the labor dispute that put the dancers out of work for nine weeks last fall, disrupting company schedules and causing the cancellation of at least one major production. The Met hasn't helped by charging forty dollars for every seat in the orchestra. But most of the problems stem unavoidably from the general condition of ballet in the eighties, which is not favorable to the kind of institution that A.B.T. is. The fading away of the star careers that supported the company through the boom years of the seventies hasn't been balanced by the rise of new stars from within the ranks. That is because A.B.T. is fundamentally a showcase and not, like New York City Ballet, a breeding ground. (That N.Y.C.B. should now be facing a shortage of ballerinas in addition to its perennial shortage of men may be an index to the scarcity of talent in the eighties.)

Mikhail Baryshnikov took over the direction of Ballet Theatre with the intention of raising technical standards of execution in the corps and strengthening middle-rank soloists. He has done both those things. He also promised to promote talent from within the ranks instead of bringing in outsiders, but he has not been able to make stars of the likes of Susan Jaffe, Cheryl Yeager, Robert La Fosse, and Peter Fonseca. His great successes have been Magali Messac and Patrick Bissell, who are often featured together and who are now the brightest dancers in the company after Baryshnikov himself. The Baryshnikov policy has not affected the A.B.T. star pattern nearly as much as the critics suggest. The careers of Cynthia Gregory, Fernando Bujones, and Gelsey Kirkland are sad stories of great talent sacrificed to unworthy notions of stardom, and the sacrifice—self-willed in all three cases—was under way before Baryshnikov stepped in. The top of the roster shows the usual quota of reliable soloists, hot performers, and public favorites; these people may be valuable, but they don't carry a company. There is the grand Martine van Hamel, who even if she had been dancing at her best this season could scarcely have provided the company with what it needs most—a partner for Baryshnikov. And where else would a partner come from? The few alluring young ballerinas who have turned up around the world are unavailable; their companies cling to them like pearls beyond price. It is suggested that Baryshnikov bring in guest stars in the bad old A.B.T. tradition, to prop a sagging box office. Again, whom could he bring? Stars are not what they used to be. The international scene is a pretty desolate one. The Ballet National de Marseille, which will follow Ballet Theatre into the Met, has never before played Lincoln Center and has been persuaded to bring in, as guests, Natalia Makarova, Rudolf Nureyev, Richard Cragun, and Patrick Dupond, all of whom appeared at their peak with A.B.T. in the flush years. Predictably, the only excitement will be caused by the Paris Opéra's Dupond, who is still at his peak. The years of glittering peripatetic stars are over, and companies like A.B.T. are being forced to cultivate their gardens in economically uncongenial times.

The panacea urged upon Ballet Theatre in the old days (by me, among others) was more and better coaching. The standards in the nineteenth-century classics were being set by the Royal Ballet and the Russian companies; A.B.T., then the only American company to attempt "the classics," lacked the proper style. Today,

A.B.T. has a staff of coaches of the best pedigree; the Royal and the Kirov are both represented. However Yeager in *La Sylphide* and Jaffe in *Giselle* may have looked, they did not look uncoached. But they failed to deliver. The starlet system at A.B.T. isn't working out because the plum roles don't seem to mean anything to these girls. Jaffe is really astonishing; she doesn't look uncomfortable in the star spot, like Yeager, yet she has no idea what she's there for—no imaginative grasp of the material, no capacity for expressive movement (as distinct from the striking execution of steps), no sense of identification with the character. The performance is rotework of a kind I don't think I've ever seen before. If Giselle herself called Jaffe up during the Mad Scene, she'd get a busy signal. And Jaffe is as abstracted in modern works. In Robbins's *Other Dances*, she appeared to be concentrating not on what she was doing but on what she would do next; her main worry was making a performance come off. Her partner, La Fosse, was just as mechanical. It's strange to see two strong young dancers throw away opportunity like this. But stranger things have happened at Ballet Theatre.

In a smart move, Baryshnikov revived *Three Virgins and a Devil*, the old Agnes de Mille piece. It comes to little more than a sketch, recalling some chic revue of the forties, but Baryshnikov doesn't need a partner in it. His role, which is that of the Devil seducing souls, is fat and silly, and his performance is pure Mack Sennett. He can twitch, cringe, beg, plead, snarl, wheedle, prance on tiptoe, gallop apace, round corners on a hopalong foot, or fall over stiff as a plank and pound the ground, sobbing, to his heart's content. He can thrash his tail, fiddle his fiddle, cuddle up to his victim, sniffling, gulping, batting his big blue eyes. Maybe for a few minutes he can even forget Ballet Theatre and its malaise.

—*July 18, 1983*

The Waves

Eadweard Muybridge can be regarded as the first dance photographer, so *The Photographer*, a theatrical production about Muybridge with music by Philip Glass, a composer much associated with dance these days, could be expected to have a conspicuous dance element. The piece had its première a year ago in Amsterdam. This fall, the Brooklyn Academy of Music produced a second version, commissioning choreography from David Gordon, who had already done a Muybridge study starring his wife, Valda Setterfield. With Setterfield and the rest of Gordon's group taking part, and with a few further commissions—book by Robert Coe, who has been a dancer and a writer on dance, staging by the avant-garde director (and former wife of Philip Glass) JoAnne Akalaitis, costumes and scenery by Santo Loquasto, and lighting by Jennifer Tipton—the whole package sounded promising.

The Photographer/Far from the Truth, as the production is called, was planned in three parts: a play followed by a concert followed by an extended dance scene. In the event, only the dance scene and the concert (played to a show of the photographs) evoked the spirit of Muybridge. The photographs, their splinters of human motion projected rapidly on a vast scale, spoke for themselves. Glass's music spoke of similar microscopic transitions within larger linked units. And Gordon's movement for actors and dancers bore eloquent witness to the static and dynamic principles of both the photographs and the music.

Muybridge's work has a strange beauty, weird and serene, like some nineteenth-century American painting, and it has the exhaustive range of a nineteenth-century science. Whole bodies, the shock of discovery still fresh upon them, are scrutinized in numberless activities; also, a legless man, in the kind of motion available only to him. Women show themselves naked in their everyday roles; they are not artists' models but laboratory specimens. (One, who seems to resent this, hides her eyes and her genitals.) Time has turned the photographs into works of art, but Coe's conclusion—that Muybridge's pursuit of scientific truth was illusory—seems harsh and forced. If there is a moral in Muybridge's work, it isn't that photography is "far from the truth"—it's that no one photograph can be *the* truth. The very pluralism of his exposures testifies to his skepticism on this point. But because of the turmoil of his private life—finding that he was not the father of his wife's child, he sought out the real father and killed him, went on trial, and was acquitted—Muybridge becomes a fit object of condescension, a man whose uncontrollable passions belied the pretensions to objectivity in his work. Coe's Photographer is just another repressed Victorian.

The only thing that prevented the banality of this idea from sinking in as readily as it might have was the chaos of Akalaitis's staging. She devised so many busy variations on Coe's "paradoxical" theme that her embellishments became an end in themselves. Every scene dripped rhetorical gingerbread, some of it organic (Mrs. Muybridge and her lover, grappling on a couch, pantingly recite strictures from a Victorian book of etiquette), some not (phantom choruses enter, wheezing, hissing, bearing candles). The only sensitive note in all this was the décor. Loquasto's designs, beautiful and disturbing, were in that vein of surrealistic Victoriana invented by Max Ernst. But in the dance scene his costumes took on the touching veracity of Thomas Eakins's paintings. (It's appropriate that Muybridge's people, clothed, should look like Eakins's; the two men, who felt a kinship, collaborated on some technical experiments.) Going from the swollen scale of the photographic projections to David Gordon's dancers was one of the evening's bumpier transitions, not improved by Akalaitis's stratagem of five silken banners crumpling to the floor. (We had to wait while stagehands cleaned up.) The difference between Gordon's calm assurance and the opinionated, cocksure tone of Coe-Akalaitis was even more noticeable—it amounted to a break in style. The play's cast of characters had been portrayed by actors and dancers; Gordon retained the whole cast, along with the character references and bits of the action, so that one saw, amid the populous comings and goings, incidents from the play repeated or repeated with a twist. Mainly, though, he created a Muybridge panorama that had nothing to do with the Coe-Akalaitis section.

In its volubility and propulsive flow, its careful spacing, and its changes of speed and density unpredictably timed to the music, this was one of Gordon's most admirable technical achievements. His crowd scene isn't composed of the usual marching automatons one gets with Glass's scores; I would compare it favorably with the crowd in *Petrushka*. Nor is his Muybridge the wild-eyed fanatic that he was in the play—he's a sober figure immersed in the movement around him, a man now lost in the crowd, now standing apart and observing. Gordon reminds us of the humanity of the artist and his subjects, and without trying to mimic the photographic sequences he brings to life the various catalogues of movement and behavior. Even the "Muybridge solo" that Valda Setterfield performs here—an extension of a 1972 piece—is not a sequence in Muybridge's terms but a series of distantly related or wholly unrelated poses drawn from various parts of the canon. Setterfield, who earlier had taken two speaking parts (the more amusing one as a fervent lady lecturer), performs this virutoso dance in the midst of the crowd, standing in a shallow pool of water. The water echoes the arc of her movements in the air (splashing water, crystallized by high-speed photography, was one of Muybridge's minor themes) and plasters her Grecian tunic to her body; she comes to look like a nymph in a fountain. Wild yet composed, the solo builds a counterpoint to the casual, more unconscious grace of the mass dance of men, women, and children that encircles it; it's the perfect "artful" contrast to the dance of life—the image of paradox, one feels, which had eluded Coe and Akalaitis. In their view, art and life exist to rebuke each other. Gordon's art, uncontumacious and clear-eyed, is based on life studies.

The Photographer/Far from the Truth opened the Brooklyn Academy's current avant-garde season, and, along with some other events in the series, it will be sent on a tour of American cities next spring. Not all these programs, which the Academy bills under the general title Next Wave, are exclusive Academy commissions. Trisha Brown's *Set and Reset* springs from a mixture of funding sources; Lucinda Childs's *Available Light* originated under the auspices of the Museum of Contemporary Art in Los Angeles. But, wherever they come from, the main Next Wave events are alike in attempting collaborations among leading members of the avant-garde—choreographers, directors, composers, visual artists, sculptors, architects. *The Photographer/Far from the Truth* was one attempt that didn't come off. *Set and Reset* was one that did, in the special sense of a present-day Merce Cunningham collaboration—the contributions of the artists involved (Brown, Robert Rauschenberg, and Laurie Anderson) were independently effective. At times, there seemed to be collusion between Brown's choreography and Anderson's music, but I wouldn't swear to it. In any event, one saw a technologically impressive video installation by Rauschenberg and then one saw a pleasant concert of dance.

It began with an image from Trisha Brown's past—one in which a dancer, borne horizontally along by two stagehands, appeared to be walking on the back wall of the theatre. The entire concert up to *Set and Reset* had been a retrospective of Brown's work, and by evoking the long-gone days when she used to walk on walls (with the aid of a harness) Brown seemed to be setting the new piece in the context of previous phases of work, suggesting, perhaps, that she was moving on. Indeed she was. *Set and Reset*, a suite of dances for Brown and her company, was novel both in quality of movement and in specific kinds of moves. The dancing was looser, with more dynamically varied phrasing; it had a rhythmically keener edge. And the partnering was astonishing. Much of it involved supported air work but not lifts. People would be yanked out of the air as they leaped, or their momentum would be suddenly stopped by a catcher who hadn't noticeably prepared the catch. At one point, Brown caught hold of the edge of one of the wings (which Rauschenberg had made of clear plastic), and her extended body was swung around it, remaining visible on both sides. The ragalike music, its beat marked by the clanging of a fire bell, added to the urgency and breathlessness of the dancing. But though a lot of new things were happening in the choreography, it didn't, to my eye, accumulate more depth of expression than Brown usually shows. Part of the problem is that Brown's dancers are carbon copies of their leader with none of her zest and intricacy. Part of it lies in the curiously flat-footed technique. With no relevé to speak of, too much attention is absorbed by the upper body, and there's too much torsion trying to take the place of a clearly multidimensional bodily technique. Brown's style—her whippet-fast transitions, particularly—seems designed to be seen close to. On opera-house scale, it can look hasty, indistinct, and monotonous. The lack of proper scale is a general drawback now that postmodern dancing is moving into large theatres. In Brown's concert, the many feet of unused cubic space were partly diverted to Rauschenberg's décor. Still, the dancing didn't transform what was left over into a reverberant field of action. None of the Next Wave choreographers have managed to use the big Brooklyn stage in this way. The scale of David Gordon's Muybridge scene was measured more by his use of actors and his commitment to an over-all picture consistent with Coe's play than by considerations of space in the abstract. Only Setterfield—ironically enough, rooted to the spot—was granted the opportunity for all-out radial movement and seized it.

As for Lucinda Childs, the question of space didn't arise in *Available Light*, not only because here, too, a set intervened (Frank Gehry's jutting platform on packing-case supports, the effect of which was to pocket the dancers in separate cubicles of air) but also because defining large-scale space is simply one of a long list of things Childs can't do. The excessive frailty of her technique undermined *Mad Rush* as well as *Available Light*. These two pieces, presented together in Brooklyn, were plainer and fancier versions of the same thing: Childs and her dancers facing the audience, performing their "See Spot run" movement sentences. Sometimes the dancers switched to a diagonal; sometimes only a few performed while the others stood and waited. The two works are distinguished mainly by their composers—Philip Glass running through his gridlike patterns in *Mad Rush*, John Adams bathing *Available Light* in oceanic, dramatically suggestive sound, some of which recalled famous dance scores. Childs's minimalism these days consists of a scattering of basic ballet steps, to which she assigns a mystique of legibility. In fact, nobody onstage seems to know for sure how the steps are done. Spot can run, but he can't turn like *that* and call it a pirouette. I don't think I'm imposing an irrelevant standard. The dancing just isn't what it seems to want to be—delicately modelled, surgically clean. It's mechanically inexact and theatrically anemic. Childs has always had her fixations, and ballet steps may as well be one of them—she's as high on her feet as Brown is flat. But Childs's adaptation of ballet has no inner core. When she's finished, you feel as if you'd heard a whole opera sung falsetto by a church choir.

—November 14, 1983

Americans from Abroad

Love Songs, presented by the Joffrey Ballet, works very hard at affronting the audience, and, in fact, part of the audience at the Joffrey's opening in Los Angeles last spring *was* affronted; the other part applauded demonstratively. In New York, the piece plays to a different public—one whose sensibilities have been conditioned by the Joffrey's trendiness. *Love Songs* has to do with women's anger. It's a suite of dances, mostly solos and duets, that focus on women, and because it uses a lot of flailing paroxysmic movement that doesn't make the women look attractive some observers concluded that its intentions were anti-feminist. That, I think, is giving the choreographer, William Forsythe, more than he deserves. He may well lack sympathy for the women he depicts, but his manner of depicting them is so inflexibly violent that it couldn't express a viewpoint if it wanted to. The ballet has nothing to say about women except that they are angry; it takes a theme that has persistently resounded in the media and exploits it on the most reckless mediainflamed level. *Love Songs* (the ballet is subtitled "Side One—Old Records" and uses a score consisting of songs recorded by Aretha Franklin and Dionne Warwick) is as shallow and self-celebrating as *Astarte* and *Trinity* and all the other Joffrey ballets that have plugged into the audience's awareness of and identification with media issues and pop fashions. These productions don't deepen our understanding of the issues and the fashions; all they do is inform people that the attitudes circulating throughout our culture can also be found at the ballet—they're a come-on.

The Joffrey attracted a new audience with this kind of product, and it has held on to the more serious-minded by offering two other kinds of product: revivals of famous old ballets and premières of works by new—radically new—choreographers. Although its reputation was formed by the salable sensational novelties, the company actually keeps three repertories in balance, shoring up its pop image on both sides. In a single evening, the Joffrey can attract three publics—the balletomanes, the avant-garde, and the media-aware, just-curious-about-ballet crowd. The problem is that these publics swiftly tire of one another. In the end, it's the people for whom a company must reflect what they read in the papers and see on television who remain the Joffrey's steadiest customers. After a season or two, these initiates may move up to Fokine or over to Laura Dean, but they can still feel connected to their original impulse by the publicity about "ballet booms" or the newsworthiness of avant-gardists like Dean. And, as the Joffrey faithful can move from one repertory to another, a Joffrey choreographer can appeal to more than one public. It happens that only one—Twyla Tharp—has ever done so successfully. *Deuce Coupe*, her Beach Boys ballet, fed the company's early-seventies preoccupation with the youth cult and was at the same time a wild and witty, genuinely novel piece of work. Ten years later, we have Forsythe regaling us with the sex war and doing it in an idiom that is transparently Tharp's own—one that embraces her Joffrey period (not *Deuce Coupe* so much as *As Time Goes By*) along with her current essays in movement terrorism. Forsythe's version of Tharp is highly simplified, to be sure, and is colored throughout by his ballet background. He likes the cliché of long runs ending in a split jeté quite as much as he fancies the Tharpian off-balance twist-pirouette in low arabesque, and he doesn't pass up the opportunity to make the women's pointwork look as painful as Cossack toe-dancing. Still, a Joffrey audience can justifiably murmur, "It all comes from Twyla."

The fact that Tharp herself never used her vocabulary politically, the way it is used here, is irrelevant. It's interesting—a sign of the times—to see idiomatic Tharpisms turning up as normative expression in a Joffrey protest ballet. It would have been more interesting to see these usages absorbed by a choreographer of means (as Paul Taylor absorbed certain usages of Martha Graham's). Forsythe lacks fluency—he's all short, sharp thrusts, blatant jumps, loops within loops within whorls that maunder unstoppably—and he lacks scope. A short plumpish girl does the first flailing solo and is followed by a long lanky girl doing much the same thing, with no modification in shape or attack; later a young hopeful girl dances against the grain emotionally, but the movement keeps to the same repetitious pattern. In the two pas de deux, the men are brutal, and the single male solo is just the tables being turned: observed by a woman (as the women were observed by men), this man grinds his pelvis, lashes into his turns with the same pent-up fury as the women, and ends with a by now predictable gesture of contempt toward the watching lover. The Joffrey dancers work as conscientiously as they did for Twyla Tharp, even though the movement makes them all alike. Tharp investigated movement; Forsythe incorporates results of those investigations. I'm not suggesting there's anything illegitimate in that—the growth of the art, after all, depends on a steady process of incorporation. And Tharp isn't the main influence on *Love Songs*. I only wish that she were—that Forsythe, an American-born choreographer, could show himself closer to the roots of the idiom he has tapped here.

Forsythe's "school" isn't really American dance. Though he's a former Joffrey dancer, he established himself as a choreographer in Europe, working for companies like the Stuttgart and the Netherlands Dance Theatre, and his sense of characterization and continuity has Jiří Kylián stamped all over it. *Love Songs*, his first production for an American company, is an adaptation of a ballet originally done in Munich. The New York première was followed by *Offenbach in the Underworld*, an Antony Tudor ballet nearly thirty years old. The Joffrey acquired it in 1975, and this year it acquired a third Kylián work. The simultaneous presence of Tudor and Kylián did not make the aesthetic that they are said to share any easier for me to see. The coincidence of the Tudor and the new School-of-Kylián Forsythe showed that if any aesthetic connection existed it has now broken down. The hard-driving Joffrey dancers are scarcely the ones to resurrect the Tudor, which even when new must have seemed unreachably nostalgic—a softer, more imaginative remake of *Gaîté Parisienne*. But in the can-can episode these dancers are exactly right. As English alehouse doxies (which Tudor's can-can girls inescapably are), they romp through their drills, giving themselves over to different effects of gracelessness and sluggishness and abandon. The subtlety under the coarse theatrics is Tudor's imprint; it makes the whole routine into a drama larger than its motive in the show. Here are women for whom the emotion of anger and its release in movement are only a starting point, and here is a standard of craftsmanship which once informed the Anglo-European dance tradition and seems now to be dying away. Tudor was really saying something about these women; it wasn't a great utterance, but it made *Love Songs* seem pipsqueak protest indeed.

There was also a Joffrey commission, *Square Deal*, in which Forsythe continued his assault on the audience and confirmed—if, after *Love Songs*, confirmation were needed—that his primary interest really isn't dance. *Square Deal* uses dancers as facets of a cubistic configuration involving lights, voices, sound, words, and non-words. There's a set composed of portable screens on which headlines are fleetingly projected, and the action jerks along in discontinuous fragments punctuated by blackouts. At first, it all seems to be a parody of the cuteness and smartness of the avant-garde, but the parody gets swallowed by Forsythe's apparent need to prove himself cuter and smarter. Irony is a weapon aimed at the audience, never at himself. The scenario, which doesn't develop and doesn't become clear, appears to revolve around the creation of the piece we're seeing, and Forsythe has his mouthpieces onstage deliver running critiques, such as "It's a blend of the new realism and the old artifice," as if this were what the audience is thinking and aren't we fools. Tactics like this are too cheaply abrasive to administer the shock of the new. Another mistake was to set the whole piece, thirty-five minutes long, in terms that work only for the first five minutes; *Love Songs* has the same defect. Even a choreographer who is a nag at heart should know better. *Square Deal*, this season's daring new work, was probably meant to antagonize New York the way *Love Songs* antagonized Los Angeles, but all it garnered was a few boos and a weary round of applause. The fastidious technological effects with which the piece was equipped deserved a great deal more.

Carolyn Carlson is another American choreographer who has made a name working in Europe—mainly at the Paris Opéra, and now at La Fenice, in Venice. With her company from the Fenice, she made her local début, at the Brooklyn Academy of Music, dancing an evening-long piece called *Underwood*. The set suggested an American pastoral scene; the Italian voices that called out from time to time suggested it was not to be taken literally. Perhaps Miss Carlson was going back in her mind to Oakland, her birthplace; perhaps there is an insane asylum in Oakland like the one portrayed on the stage, where women run about in their slips and try to dump each other out of rocking chairs. Or perhaps Miss Carlson is interested in the Theatre of Exorcism, in which a great many American women choreographers have run about in their slips casting off emotional burdens. One spends the evening at *Underwood* slipping from one vagary to another: Where are we now? What doing? What's in those boxes? Who's that in the rocking chair? One seeks clues to a puzzle, and one is wrong to—these are only formalist conceits. The Theatre of Exorcism blends with the Theatre of Ritualism and grows quainter. At any moment, the simple mad folk on the stage may erupt into squads of robots doing one step over and over hard on the beat, for all the world like the step done just last week at this very theatre. Nobody here but us postmodernists catching the Next Wave.
Underwood is constructed out of two—at least—incompatible systems of movement. The implication that there is a repetitious ritualistic content in expressionistic dance and an emotive force in the plain ritualistic walking, stepping, and running of radical anti-expressionistic dance is not unfascinating, but Carlson's amalgamation of the two systems is highly indecisive. Sometimes she just appears to have settled arbitrarily on one system for instituting dramatic meanings and another for taking them away. Which does which is a toss-up; this choreographer puts *all* terminology in doubt. In Act II, she comes out in a floppy straw song and sings a hat.
A former Nikolais dancer, Carlson still performs for the most part in a style that keeps the extremities in play with no noticeable motivation from the center of the body, and her long thin limbs and long thin torso make a further spectacle of the style. As *Underwood* goes on, she becomes more and more isolated (the other dancers are far from capturing her movement) and more and more fraught with possibilities, but she stays fraught. She has made what in old-fashioned modern-dance terms would be an Ophelia piece. The bouts of minimalism, the ritualistic pieties, the chopsticks music—all that is Ophelia's new clothes.*

—December 5, 1983

---

* *Postscript 1987:* I know now what I didn't know then—that Carlson had picked up a lot of her ideas from Pina Bausch, whose blend of Ritualism and Expressionism was the hottest thing on the Continent.

A Balanchine Triptych

Balanchine used to deny that he wasn't interested in male dancers; when he said "They are very important as princes and attendants to the queen, but woman is the queen," it was, he insisted, because of the woman's greater technical capacity. A woman can do more; consequently she makes more demands on a choreographer. Balanchine reiterated the point three years ago in an interview in Paris. "It is easier to make dances for men—they jump, they turn. A woman is more complicated, that is the only reason they are a priority." Maybe so for other choreographers, but for Balanchine? One gathers from his ballets that Woman would have been queen in his universe whether he had been able to design a step or not. Pressed to explain what special pains he took with his ballerinas, he resorted, typically, to metaphor. "They are fragile like orchids. You have to know exactly how much sun, how much water, how much air and then take them inside before they wilt."

A full-evening Balanchine ballet called *Flowers* is not unimaginable, nor is one called *Horses* or *Birds*—images more or less conspicuously floral or equine or avian are strewn throughout his repertory. In 1967, the three-part ballet called *Jewels* was made, and it is still unsurpassed as a Balanchine primer, incorporating in a single evening every important article of faith to which this choreographer subscribed and a burst of heresy, too, to remind us that he willingly reversed himself on occasion. Edward Villella was then as much a priority as the ballerinas who composed the original cast—Violette Verdy, Mimi Paul, Patricia McBride, and Suzanne Farrell—and so, in between "Emeralds" and "Diamonds," we have "Rubies," with a smashing male role, more than prince or attendant, at its center. The exception proves the rule about technical capacity; only a man who could do the things that Villella could do would have deflected Balanchine from his preoccupation with female dancers. Still, there the role stands, in lonely eminence, flanked by male roles that are virtual definitions of the consort and the cavalier. These men are not just links in the chain of jewels. They are active presences, courtiers of rank and sensibility, and they are the means by which Balanchine focusses our thoughts on the women and creates a setting for them. The men embody the choreographer's point of view; those who partner the ballerinas in "Emeralds" and in "Diamonds" are what Balanchine's male dancers often are—stand-ins for Balanchine himself. But the roles are so beautifully differentiated—lover and poet in "Emeralds," knight in "Diamonds"—that they can be interpreted as fully as the more richly developed jesterlike Villella role in "Rubies." And *Jewels* includes a fifth principal male role—that of a youth in "Emeralds" who dances between two young princesses in a pas de trois and whose choreography gives opportunity to any soloist of mettle. (The original soloist was John Prinz, then the company's most promising male dancer.) Designed as a company showcase and as an introduction to Balanchine, dressed in glittering costumes and scenery, christened with a real title hinting at a pretext if not a plot, *Jewels* remains New York City Ballet's most powerful box-office attraction after *The Nutcracker*. The audience is told in three ballets a great deal about Balanchine and what he stands for; it is *not* told that he disdains male dancing—on the contrary.

As a popular hit, *Jewels* has had to withstand charges of expediency. Balanchine, newly settled at Lincoln Center and needing to lure an unaccustomed public, had contrived the theme of jewels to link three unrelated non-story ballets. Actually, couldn't you call any three Balanchine ballets *Jewels* (or *Flowers* or *Horses*)? It's true that *Jewels* isn't about jewels. Although Claude Arpels is said to have originally suggested the mining and cutting of gems as a scenario to Balanchine, the geometric dazzle connecting classical ballet and precious stones could have occurred to anybody. (A less facile connection to Oriental carpets was made several years earlier in *The Figure in the Carpet*.) Even as a metaphor, *Jewels* doesn't quite work. By 1967, Balanchine's style had evolved beyond the kaleidoscopic manipulation of strict classical forms for which he was chiefly known. He was less interested in the chiselled severity of footwork than in the weight and shape of the body as it posed or plunged in cubic space. "Rubies" and "Diamonds" both take their stylistic cues from the bravura of their stars, which was as much curvilinear as rectilinear, while "Emeralds" is a floating island, its softness of contour an anomaly in Balanchine's repertory then and now. Yet "jewel" imagery is not neglected; it depends on where you sit. From high in the house, the loops, strands, and pendants that emerge in the changing patterns of the corps may be distinctly seen in all three ballets. The weakest choreography of the evening is the section that comes the closest to foursquare geometrical precision—the opening of "Diamonds," set to the second movement of Tchaikovsky's Third Symphony. From orchestra or first-ring level, it is boring to look at—a plodding ensemble waltz that lasts forever. Seen from above, it shows you diamonds, diamonds, diamonds. This is Balanchine as Busby Berkeley, thinking up ways to eat up space on the large new State Theater stage. The sparkling footwork throughout *Tchaikovsky Piano Concerto No. 2* is more properly diamantine.

Balanchine took his titular metaphor seriously enough, but he took even more seriously another kind of imagery—one that seems to have come to him from the imaginary world of ballet. For Balanchine, who inherited it from Petipa, it is not only a feminine microcosm but an actual stage world. "Emeralds" and "Diamonds" are each a conflation of *Swan Lake* and *Raymonda*; they bring back the medieval pageantry and chivalry of those ballets, complete with their glow of post-Wagnerian mythomania. "Rubies" is a sharp (not to say malicious) commentary on the anachronistic survival of the myth into the twentieth century; it's the New World—Stravinsky, jazz, America, sexual equality—pitted against nostalgia for the Old. Both "Emeralds" and "Diamonds" are about queens and the courts they rule; in "Rubies" the royalty is like that in a deck of cards; and it is all part and parcel of the toy kingdom of ballet. The leading male roles in all three ballets are Maryinsky stereotypes, but what Balanchine does with them is something else again. It's as if he'd taken the male cast of a late Petipa ballet and used it as the framework of a new architecture. Here in "Diamonds" is Siegfried-Florimund-Jean de Brienne. There in "Rubies" is a contemporary Bluebird. In "Emeralds" we have a Siegfried, a Benno, and a Florestan. Amid these reverberant depictions, the female roles assume the substantiality of a continuing lineage stemming from the Maryinsky and beyond the Maryinsky, for what was the late-Petipa era of Russian ballet in Petersburg but a revival of the era of Romantic ballet in Paris, with its Gothic inspirations? The roles in *Jewels* are made of memories of memories. They are also, of course, living portraits of their originators as they were in 1967, and though this makes them difficult to keep in repertory their archetypal connections insure that something is left over when the originators are gone. There is probably no ballet more closely identified with Suzanne Farrell than "Diamonds," and Farrell's performances of it this season seemed to set on it the ultimate seal of ownership. Yet when Merrill Ashley took it over, it became intelligibly another construct. The pas de deux without Farrell can still be performed as an Odette fantasy (with hand-behind-head poses reminiscent of Raymonda); Ashley handled this aspect extremely well. And without Farrell's all-absorbing presence it was easier to concentrate on the structural ties that make *Jewels* a true triptych.

The choreography's binding theme is walking. The walking on point that is done in the most memorable pas de deux in "Emeralds" reappears with a different emphasis in the "Diamonds" pas de deux, but it is recognizably a theme that bridges the evening's three sections. In "Emeralds," the walk is paced to the pulse of the music; it follows the turns and twists of a melody that gives no hint of how it is to end. It is as a dance virtually patternless; nothing occurs in it that might call forth a consummation, and so it is as an image virtually motionless, too. It wanders on, beat by beat, until, to a sudden sighing cadence in the music, it passes away into the night. Balanchine is not often given to such stylization, and for him to keep the dance so still is also unusual. He even has the dancers underline the regular beat of the walk with stop-motion poses of their limbs while they're standing still. The consequence is that we pay closer attention to the music, but the music, which is indeed beautiful, does not entirely explain a choreographic treatment that for Balanchine verges on pedantry. Fauré's score was written to accompany a French adaptation of *The Merchant of Venice*, and this Nocturne was heard under Lorenzo's speech to Jessica about "the sweet power of music." "Mark the music," says Lorenzo, and Balanchine does—literally! (I believe the stylization of the dance also derives from the somewhat stilted conceits in the Lorenzo-Jessica love scene a page or two earlier—the lines beginning with six repetitions of the phrase "In such a night.") Some years after the première, Balanchine added to his choreography for "Emeralds" another pas de deux and an epilogue the effect of which introduced a fatal symmetry but also enlarged and integrated the ballet's images. The braced and straining arabesques in the new pas de deux become in the epilogue a linked series of such arabesques spread like an ornamental chain across the back of the stage. We see the necklace one last time before it dissolves into fragments to be folded and put away for good. The music for the dispersal is Mélisande's funeral march from Fauré's *Pelléas*; it ends as the choreography has reverted to walking steps for the three cavaliers, now bereft. On a final note, they kneel in tribute to a vision lost in time.

Balanchine followed Fauré's musical pattern in the portions added to "Emeralds," just as he had throughout the ballet, but he ascribed his own meaning to the pattern, and that is the procedure he seems to have followed all through *Jewels*. The heraldic horns in the Fauré link up with the mournful French horns in Tchaikovsky's symphony, and we hear the horns the way we see the walking—as a motivic element in the structure of the work as a whole. (In "Rubies," the horns are heard in the brassy whoops of a neoclassical jazz score, and the walking becomes running and prancing.) In "Diamonds," when Farrell walks on point she stretches her feet in a slight pawing motion and we hear a horn call. The echo seems to come from way back in the forest of "Emeralds"—from that wonderfully youthful pas de trois and its air of freedom, of an outing in the woods, perhaps a hunt. (The young man several times extends one arm to lift the two women in light sautés—like a trainer testing two mares in dressage.) Hunt scenes from old ballets rise up invisibly to reinforce that sound and that image, now tranferred to "Diamonds," but Farrell's "Odette" wears no plumage. Rather, she flexes her long feet, places her delicate points on the earth, and arches her neck like a white steed—like the one, in fact, she gives us in a pawing, head-tossing passage in *Monumentum pro Gesualdo*, the ballet to Stravinsky's setting of sixteenth-century madrigals (in which, as it happens, Balanchine also uses a necklace construction). And when she bends her head low and stretches both arms out above a forward extension of her leg, "horse" passes into "unicorn," and the "hunt scene" becomes an allusion to the unicorn tapestries in the Cluny Museum. Farrell is both the lady and the unicorn, and in a sense she's the hunter, too, on the scent of her own mystery. (A passing reference to the unicorn, symbol of virginity in medieval iconography, may have been what Ivanov intended in one of Odette's signature poses in the second-act pas de deux, but the way it is usually done it looks more like a stork. The pose is deleted in Balanchine's version of *Swan Lake*.) The long "Diamonds" pas de deux is really a monologue; the man is privy to secrets the woman reveals to herself. That, at any rate, is how I read it when it is danced by Farrell and Peter Martins. Its relation to the walking pas de deux and the two intensely private "Mélisande" variations in "Emeralds" seems to me unmistakable.

One could parse Balanchine's language for further correspondences; I have named only the most obvious. But even a casual glance at *Jewels* shows it to be composed not of three unrelated ballets but of two matching panels and a flagrantly dissonant middle panel, which, however, keeps a connection with the two others by extending and upending their formal logic. Without "Rubies," Balanchine must have reasoned, *Jewels* would be a bland evening. By way of describing the ambiguous but compelling logic of abstract ballet, our greatest dance critic, the late Edwin Denby, used to like to cite a line of Mallarmé's about poetry that is made up "of reciprocal reflections like a virtual trail of light across jewels." "Rubies" refracts instead of reflecting; it does its job in the total scheme of things, and it may be the evening's masterwork.

Balanchine carried out his tripartite scheme to the music of three different composers. It is the music that determines the instant-by-instant progression of his choreography, its accent and impetus; and the music is what gives the evening its pleasing symphonic shape—a broadly flowing andante prelude, a red-hot scherzo, a maestoso finish. If I had to guess how the piece was made, I'd say that Balanchine worked backward from the pas de deux of "Diamonds" and from the scherzo that follows it, in which Tchaikovsky burrows into the magic forest of Mendelssohn's *A Midsummer Night's Dream*. As we saw in the pas de deux, Balanchine makes it a tapestry forest, but basically it's the same forest that he planted with Fauré's help in "Emeralds." Music is widely supposed to be the beginning and end of Balanchine's concern with expression. *Jewels* shows how effectively he could use music to pursue concerns of his own.

This season's performances of *Jewels* saw a new décor, by Robin Wagner, consisting of three different diadems hung on the backcloth and a false proscenium enclosing each ballet. The idea, more discreet than the old careless opulence, seemed to be a jewel box. The graduated arches behind the proscenium bothered me at first; by the second performance I had ceased to notice anything but the dancing. There was new casting in some of the principal roles, the most successful being "Emeralds" with Maria Calegari in the walking pas de deux and Carlo Merlo, Alexia Hess, and Shawn Stevens in the pas de trois. These were also Peter Martins' last performances of "Diamonds." He now retires to devote full time to his duties as a ballet master-in-chief. In "Diamonds," as in *Apollo, Symphony in C, Duo Concertant, Concerto Barocco, Other Dances,* and *The Nutcracker,* Martins exhibited for the last time, alas, his magnificently limpid, unshowy style in dancing and his incomparably tender partnering. Is there another man in ballet who can bring glory to a ballerina merely by the rapt attention he gives her and the amount of space he creates around her? The audiences who saw him off with ovations will miss him no less than will Miss Farrell, Miss Ashley, and Miss Watts. As a dancer, Martins has always been a winner; his victories have looked almost too easy. But if his gifts were lavishly bestowed he has been their wise custodian. In his years with New York City Ballet, he grew immeasurably as an artist. Placing himself in Balanchine's service, he rose to the kind of stardom that makes him, in his turn, master of the art and the one who must now set the terms of it for the next generation. A loyal knight, he has earned the prize. The enchanted kingdom is in his keeping. —*December 19, 1983*

Mark Morris
Comes to Town

Curly-haired, androgynously handsome young dancer-choreographers who look like Michelangelo's David have been a feature of the dance scene for some time. Unlike the shaggy hippies whom they replaced, they can be found in ballet as well as in modern dance, in Europe as well as in New York and other American cities. They seem to have come in on the wave of seventies glamour—unisex, it was called then—that is now at flood tide among the young. It's a look I can do without, and I wouldn't be bringing it up except for the fact that Mark Morris, who closed the fall season at Dance Theater Workshop, has that look without the aureole that puts me off. Morris is a serious choreographer. He has talent, and also, along with his self-awareness, the self-possession that makes the androgynous-youth look stand for something besides dime-store narcissism. Actually, he does sometimes make it stand for that, but it's a precisely identified attitude—one can smell the popcorn in the air.

Morris, whose ringlets are brown—not blond, like the other michelangelini—has some of Sylvester Stallone's droopy-lidded sultriness, but he's saved from absurdity by toughness of mind. He doesn't use his soft, pretty-boy looks on the audience. He doesn't flash camp messages with his eyes, or messages of any kind—not even when he does a turn in drag. The meanings are all in the movement. From up close, which is how you see him in D.T.W.'s loft theatre, his eyes while he dances are blind with fatigue; they have the permanently bruised look of insomnia. And he dances with insomniacal energy. His large, wide-hipped body, his big legs and feet are all over the place, lunging, clomping, skittering. Every movement is clear and precise, yet bluntly delivered; strong, yet with a feminine softness. Even the big Li'l Abner feet are never rough. Prepared to laugh at the drag act, the audience is silenced by the lack of imposture in it. It isn't an act; it's Morris declaring an aspect of his nature as matter-of-factly as the Japanese *onnagata*—female impersonator. It's impersonal impersonation. He defuses dangerously gaudy material by shaping it into a dance that presents itself—presents *dance*—as the true subject. In the second of two concerts, he performed a companion piece in a business suit, discarding jacket and vest as he entered. The differences in the quality of the movement were in structural, technical, and musical details, not in sexual ones. Morris turns the transsexual chic and the frivolous passions of his generation into pretexts for dances. He's committed to his time and place, he seizes on the theatricality of it, but he doesn't try to be anything more than a good choreographer and a completely sincere theatre artist.

Morris works in the time-honored tradition of the modern-dance choreographer who breeds a company and a repertory entirely out of his own dance style. His performing background includes ballet, modern and postmodern groups, and folk dance. His dances, among which solos number far less than pieces for large and small ensembles, blend all these influences into an indefinable Mark Morrisian brew. His own physical versatility is the model for the group (seven women, six men), but he doesn't set up unfair terms of competition. Much of his choreography is plainly set out, and all of it is musical. The sharp musical timing gives the dancers another standard to aim at; they aren't lost if they can't move just like their leader. But they have to be able to handle radical dynamic changes (Morris shows more variety here than any five other choreographers his age) rung on a restricted range of steps. Not easy to make so little count for so much. Morris's inflections of a single step or his combination of many steps in a single phrase are a real test of virtuosity. He sometimes loads a phrase beyond his dancers' capacities—requiring them, for example, to fall splat and spring erect on one count. But Morris is a witty taskmaster who can make a virtue of sloppy recoveries. His invention is at its richest in the exigencies that come about through having to create choreography for other people. *Bijoux,* his solo for the small, light, and agile Teri Weksler, filters her style sympathetically through his own. I was able to see only a first-night performance of this piece, when Weksler was slightly less in command than she usually is. The music, a suite of nine brief songs by Satie, was on tape. Live, it might have exerted less harrowing pressure. So musical a performance—such musical choreography—needs accompaniment that breathes. The occasional impression of steppiness I get from this and other Morris pieces is an effect of density created from limited means. He really doesn't have a lot of steps, and, though he may not think so, he doesn't need them—neither does Paul Taylor. (Morris's combination of musicality, sprawling energy, and sparse vocabulary may remind you of Taylor; to sharpen the resemblance, Morris also has a flair for comedy. But his originality defeats comparisons.) In another Satie piece, he reversed the proportions of *Bijoux*: instead of many brief packed solos for one dancer, a woman, he created, to the music of *Socrate,* an extended slow-moving frieze of discontinuities for six soloists, all men. Draining his line of the high-contrast dynamics that gave it shape, color, and texture, Morris offered us the nothingness of steps. *The Death of Socrates* was a parched and static vista peopled by boys in Greek tunics. As a picture, it had life and thought; its intentions were clearly stated. But as a dance it was inert.

What does Morris do that's funny? Well, he always includes one or two mime pieces to pop music on his programs. I like them less than his dances, particularly when they're accompanied by country songs with long spoken inspirational texts. Audiences find these semi-captioned displays of Morris's hilarious. I prefer the Thai or Indian numbers, where the expostulatory gestures chatter alongside incomprehensible ditties and aren't upstaged by a corniness already familiar and complete in itself. Best of all are the pieces that blend mime and dance, and the best of *these*—Morris's "masculine" solo and *Dogtown*—are both funny and unfunny. In *Dogtown*, done to the quizzical songs of Yoko Ono, Morris actually makes dogs. He contracts his palette to a few crouching, crawling, prostrate forms interspersed with frisky leaps, usually by one dancer upon the unsuspecting rump of another. But the amazing thing about *Dogtown* is that it doesn't operate literally. The dogginess of it all is a continual shadowy implication in movement as finely drawn and cunningly interlocked as the pattern on an ancient Greek jar. In the title number, the rhythm of forms is so beautifully controlled that it wins laughs from the sheer electricity of its timing. It's the *design*, not the subject, that becomes funny.

This mastery of mimetic implication in the logic of forms is a mark of wisdom as rare in choreography as musical mastery. No other choreographer under thirty has it; the few of those over thirty who have it have been great. Like musicality, it is a gift, and it appears right away. (No use waiting for those other bright young choreographers to get the idea through observation or experience. If the things that root their art in life are not instinctively understood, they are not understood at all.) Morris comes from Seattle, where he will return later this year to teach at the University of Washington. His first New York concert was held in 1980. I encountered his work two years later, and the wonderful effrontery of it still hasn't left me. Nothing in his biography, training, or performing history explained how he could have come by such technical sophistication. This year's concerts show him using and flexing his technique with even greater assurance. *Canonic 3/4 Studies*, a parody of human beings in ballet class, is one evolutionary step beyond *Dogtown*. In its investigation of three-quarter time and in nearly every other way, it is an improvement on 1982's *New Love Song Waltzes*, the piece that most of Morris's admirers love best and the one that stunned me with its precocity. Seen again this year, much of it seemed too big and splashy for the Brahms liebesliederwalzer it was set to. It remains Morris's purple ballet, his moment of excess before the reining in that signifies the start of true growth. Next to *New Love Song Waltzes*, *Canonic 3/4 Studies*, to an arrangement of ballet-class tunes, appears cautious, but it is the more secure piece by far—less in need of contrapuntal commotion and shock effects to keep the audience in a state of excitement. (During an adagio in the Brahms, a body is dragged backward across the floor, right over another body, which is lying there prone.) One of the "studies" has two women being alternately lifted by one man in minimal arcs that zip back and forth and forth and back. Like *Dogtown*, it is the kind of number that, once seen, is never forgotten.

There *is* a kind of cautiousness in Morris's current work: he tends to make each piece a batch of exercises or lampoons that don't quite add up to a complete entity with a point of view (though the suite *Dogtown* comes close). Instead of a conclusion, he reaches an arbitrary cutoff point. It is obvious that he is still learning, but it is also obvious that no one is teaching him. His "technique" is something he was born with. The raw gift of choreography may be the most individualizing of all gifts to experience. Those who possess it are enclosed in a kind of sanctuary. No word or sound contaminates the freshness of their language, and dance language as we have known it—old academic or anti-academic usage—falls from their bodies like rags. In its place are new sights, which we perceive with a thrill of recognition. The Mark Morris experience is like nothing else in dance but quite like a lot of things outside it—especially in the streets and shops of lower Manhattan. I imagine that the younger you are the more of these things you recognize. For me, Mark Morris is a dancemaker and a spellbinder. That is enough to make him transparently a symbol of his times.   —*January 2, 1984*

Midnight

In addition to listing Baryshnikov as co-choreographer of *Cinderella*, American Ballet Theatre bills the ballet in name-above-the-title style as "Mikhail Baryshnikov's production." Since Baryshnikov is the undisputed artistic director of the company, the ballet could not possibly be anybody else's production, but Baryshnikov's regime has come under criticism lately from the board of trustees, and there is some speculation that Baryshnikov, in taking full responsibility for a costly production (one million plus) that may not reflect the board's idea of artistic policy, is paving the way for his departure. (He offered to resign last summer, when the board dismissed his administrator, Herman Krawitz, and was refused. He still hasn't withdrawn the offer.) But *Cinderella* is not at all the disaster that is predicted by this interpretation. The première performances, which took place at Kennedy Center, in Washington, over the Christmas holidays, revealed a lively, abundant show, distinguished in design and staged with a conviction and security of effect which increases through all three acts. Still very much a work-in-progress, it is already a success with the audience. If Baryshnikov really is looking for an excuse to leave, he may find that by the time it reaches New York in the spring *Cinderella* will have only strengthened his position as director.

Cinderella, to Prokofiev's music, is the first original full-evening ballet in A.B.T. history. That is, unlike *Swan Lake, Giselle, La Sylphide, The Nutcracker, Don Quixote*, and *La Bayadère*, it is in no way modelled on a production created for some other company. It is also a story ballet, in the fullest and most serious sense, which means that in presenting it Baryshnikov and his co-choreographer, Peter Anastos, are working against the grain of modern ballet aesthetics. Almost nothing in *Cinderella* can be described as absolute dance. It is either mime or character dance or, at the very most, classical dance that refers to and impels some narrative element. The choreography tends to lessen in interest the closer it gets to absolute classicism, as in the Seasons divertissement or in the two pas de deux and two variations for Cinderella and the Prince. In these instances, though, it could be the music leading the dancing astray. Prokofiev himself seems not to have believed in the need for a Seasons suite. His music is grumpy and disobliging, and its placing in the score, right at the point in Act I when the Fairy Godmother appears and starts her transformations, kills the drama just as it is beginning to build. And what induces Cinderella to watch this un-germane, quadripartite allegory being staged on her doorstep? Is her charity still being tested? No matter how good the choreography—here it is quite good—we wouldn't blame her if she decided her godmother was a crazy lady, excused herself politely, and got back to her pots and pans. The big Cinderella-Prince dances are almost as inopportune—part of a format rather than part of the emotional development of their relationship.

Having to deal with these structural defects in Prokofiev's score makes a hard job of choreography harder. It should surprise no one that the means of telling a story in its precise dramatic gradations eludes the choreographers from time to time—less when the story is comic than when it is romantic or lyrical. As performers, both Baryshnikov and Anastos have excelled at comedy, and they are so far from being sentimentalists that they may unintentionally dry out the sweet, juicy effects the story needs. Just now their gravest miscalculation in regard to sentiment is the Apotheosis, in which, as the music conjures up an infinity of blissful reconciliation, we see all the silly and cruel folk—the ugly sisters, the courtiers, the hairdressers—step out of character and surround the lovers in a final tableau. The ballet gives us this collective absolution of the baddies without first having given us Cinderella's triumph over them. Moments earlier, recognized by the Prince, Cinderella immediately dances a long and unaccountably private pas de deux with him. But, as any child knows, it isn't enough for Cinderella to be glorified in the Prince's eyes (or, as the pas de deux would have it, for the lovers to be glorified in each other's eyes). For justice to be done, there has to be a *public* moment in which the heroine's true worth is acknowledged. *Cinderella* is a proletarian revenge fantasy, not a political morality play, like *The Sleeping Beauty*.

This sin of omission is compounded by the failure, at the ball, to show the Stepsisters' reaction to Cinderella's transformation. Could one guess that the ballet was composed, in 1944, with Ulanova in mind? In fact, the star of the A.B.T. production is not Cinderella but the Prince. It must be said that this prince is a real character and a highly attractive one—sexy, debonair, impatient of ceremony, and so full of life and high spirits that he's impossible to keep up with. The heroine, too, is likable and spirited, not mopey or pious, as Cinderellas usually are, but once he has entered (downstage, with everybody upstage, looking off in the wrong direction), her story, her psychology, even her choreography all become somewhat vague. Baryshnikov has not yet danced the Prince—a role obviously designed for him—or any of the other roles. The fact that the ballet is a hit without him is an encouraging sign. But the Prince's choreography, filled with overwhelming bravura steps, is too difficult or too idiosyncratic for those who do dance it (Patrick Bissell, Kevin McKenzie, Robert La Fosse, Ross Stretton, Danilo Radojevic), and it makes the demure Fonteynish choreography for Cinderella look weak tea indeed. (The Fonteyn link is to her Aurora, and is one of several unwarranted references to *The Sleeping Beauty*.) The three (out of five) Cinderellas I saw all had trouble being big and bright enough. Cynthia Harvey carried it off best, in a most musical and romantic partnership with McKenzie.

The choreography's other sins of commission are all sins of superfluous invention. I was puzzled by the presence of a Stepmother who careers about in a wheelchair; of a group of beggars at the cottage door (only the one who turns out to be the Fairy Godmother counts); of a Masked Lady in Act II who isn't needed until Act III; of inscrutable Denishawn figures in long white wigs who herald Cinderella's appearance at the ball. To those who know Anastos's work with the transvestite Trockadero Ballet, the sparing use of the Two Stepsisters, who are, of course, in drag and on point, may come as a surprise. Act I gives them plenty to do, and one expects them to pop up more often in the ball scene. One hopes, too, that Anastos and Baryshnikov will eventually do the roles themselves, and set the business and the timing, and get the laughs in the first act that the sisters aren't getting now. Such roles need to be defined in performance by comedians working as a team. In the three performances I saw, the milder of the two sisters was done promisingly by Thomas Titone, whose makeup made him look like Alice the Goon. The other one was played by three different dancers, none of whom could work up much of an act with Titone.

The ballet's setting is the France of the ancien régime, which is where the Russians have always placed it. Santo Loquasto's scenery and costumes, whether on the near or the far side of caricature, sustain a look of opulence. He has designed a number of breakaway sets, the best of which is a cottage kitchen with steaming kettles and other working contraptions. (Cinderella in a moment of rebellion stuffs the laundry in the oven, and the whole hearth glows in satisfaction.) He has heard the sardonic strain in the score (the strangely savage relishing of masquerade and scariness which makes Prokofiev's ball not quite a nice place to be); the ponderousness, too. A Merchant's palace, visited by the Prince in the third act, is everything one might wish for a production of *Le Bourgeois Gentilhomme*; its hideousness is delicious. For reasons I cannot fathom, all the mobile sets are placed against permanent hangings that enclose the stage in what looks like tessellated aluminum foil—a very curious effect, and one that deprives Cinderella's world of a horizon. Loquasto's ideas are not polite, and some of them will be controversial, but ballet décor is seldom as fantastically real as the best of what he has done here. It is hard to accept the dark lighting, by Tharon Musser, which gives the whole production a wrathful look. In Washington, the gilded ballroom set was gratefully applauded when the curtain went up on it, but because of the lighting it already seemed to be giving off the sulfurous smell of the calamity that would strike at midnight.

In the second and third acts, the production finds its style, and though the choreography, too, has its *noir* aspect—midnight revellers in grotesque attire menace the heroine as she tries to leave the ball, and the mysterious Masked Lady is mistaken by the Prince for his lost love—its prevailing tone is neither heavy nor perverse. The Masked Lady, who seems to have stepped out of a Balanchine ballet, is a peculiarly effective creation. All the more reason to reserve her till the third act, when she works her wiles and when her appearance has been prepared for by the midnight revellers. Another Balanchine memento occurs in the opening steps of the Dancing Master's lesson, which are quoted from the opening of *Theme and Variations*. The most striking homage is paid to Frederick Ashton, when the Seasons dancers mass to form the coach that bears Cinderella off to the ball—an image not from Ashton's *Cinderella* but from his *La Fille Mal Gardée*. Quotation raises thoughts of comparison—good thoughts. The bubbling ballroom ensembles, the four feckless aides-de-camp who turn up in this act, and the episode of the oranges, in which the Stepsisters have their innings, are things that stand up very well against Ashton's choreography without in any way resembling it. Act III stages the sequence, which Ashton didn't stage, of the Prince's travels in search of the owner of the glass slipper, and it is inspired from start to finish. A galop repeated three times speeds the Prince, with his four aides puffing behind him, from one adventure to another. In the first, he meets the Merchant's three awful daughters, each of whom tries to make the shoe fit. Next, he is seduced by the Masked Lady in a lovers' trysting place. Finally, he is pursued by the entire female population, like Buster Keaton in *Seven Chances*. All this is carried out in dance terms (pas de quatre, pas de deux, round dance), and the technical polish of each number and of the sequence as a whole could not be improved upon. It ends charmingly, with the Prince stumbling into Cinderella's cottage, sinking down exhausted, and at once falling asleep. Ballet Theatre's *Cinderella* is now as close to realizing its goal as the Prince is to his in that scene. Provided it does not fall asleep at the last minute, the production should survive its trials and reach as happy an end.

Baryshnikov is dancing most beautifully these days in choreography by Twyla Tharp. Last year's Glazunov piece has now reverted to its original title, *The Little Ballet*, and has gained an extra solo for Baryshnikov—a waltz from *Raymonda*. In that ballet, it is a ballabile—a big group dance. As done here by Baryshnikov, with exquisite retards and renewals of impetus, it has the quality of ballabile in the original sense of the word, which was "danceable." With an excellent partner, Elaine Kudo, Baryshnikov also performs *Sinatra Suite*, one of Tharp's flights into luxe vaudeville. Sinatra sings wryly, and the two dancers scrap and tumble like models in an Avedon ad. He sings wistfully, and they coil in erotic knots. Kudo has glamour with an air of brazenness; she can take anything Baryshnikov can dish out. But in "One for My Baby" he's alone in the spotlight, thinking about her, savoring their best moments, shrugging off their worst. Baryshnikov's solo is a soliloquy. No dancer is more eloquent. No actor, either.

—*January 16, 1984*

Closed Circuits

Paradise, an evening-length dance drama by Karole Armitage, separates itself all too easily into two halves. The dance half is stylish, sure of itself, lucidly performed by Armitage and the six other dancers in the cast. The dramatic half, which runs concurrently, is performed by two non-dancers who stalk with frozen faces and mulish persistence in and out among the dancers, impaling them with glances and forcing on them "story" situations of total opacity. We can't just brush aside the two pests and enjoy the dancing. We can try—they are offstage for long periods—but we're haunted by the suspicion that pure-dance meanings aren't what we're here to see. The choreography, which *seems* organized in abstract concert-suite form, may *really* harbor ulterior meanings that relate to the absent duo and whatever story they're part of.

For a generation or more, our most progressive dancers have lived by the rule of purity which lies at the heart of modern expression in the arts. The historic shift to non-representationalism—"A poem should not mean but be," etc.—has been the principal factor in the emergence of dance as an art. In the other arts, reaction sets in when liberating developments have run their course. But a reaction against pure meaning in dance threatens the life of the art. Young choreographers who may wish to restore a story element are handicapped by their youth. They have no direct knowledge of the various storytelling forms that were legitimately employed by choreographers earlier in the century and no sense of the peril to the art when these forms became reductive. Postmodern reaction—if that is what choreographers like Armitage and Jim Self and Charles Moulton represent—has rediscovered narrative, but it's in danger of turning dance back into illustrative gestures. That wouldn't be so bad if the gestures really were illustrative. As it is, they're uncommunicative—illustrative of closed-circuit meanings. Reluctant to give up the modern tradition, yet impatient to have something of their own, these choreographers launch themselves on a sea of contradictions. Armitage's direction is peculiarly unresolved. A gifted self-declared student of Cunningham and Balanchine, she makes dance movement of exceptional poetic power. Yet the course she follows in *Paradise*—she invents meanings out of the non-dance movement and pushes them into the dance like cloves into a ham—is completely uninstructed and unaware of its regressive tendencies. When I saw a preview of *Paradise* last summer, it was still incomplete, and its two-sidedness looked like something that would be fixed in due course. It hasn't been. Armitage seems to want very urgently to tell us a story that she has no means of telling, and the piece slowly strangles before you, a victim of inarticulate technique.

Armitage has been on the leading edge of radical experimentation in choreography ever since she presented *Drastic Classicism*, in 1981—an hour or more of frenzied classical dancing to a deafening rock score. The frenzy was carefully controlled, and the dancing emerged without a stain on it. Classical values that were flayed alive stayed alive. Armitage seemed to be self-elected to guide classicism through the straits of punk rock, punk chic, and whatever else the youth culture had to offer. She then went, like so many vanguard American choreographers, to Europe, where she executed several commissions and was duly lionized. Last year, she returned, ready to divest herself of the punk image and start something new. I think *Paradise* may be the story of that start. When I saw the preview, I was impressed by the way she had found to extricate herself from the dead end of *Drastic Classicism*. The new, nonviolent group choreography was a retrenchment and also an advance. It was "drastic" in a new way. Instead of stepping up the energy, Armitage redistributed it in "character" deformations of classical shapes and systematized these in a code of behavior. It wasn't exactly Expressionism; it was skewed classicism on the order of the earlier Cunningham. Armitage arranged these new terms in unpredictable causal sequences, and you followed her veering logic easily. For one thing, she used music, by Jeffrey Lohn, that—though no less excruciatingly loud than the music for *Drastic Classicism*—was much more clearly defined rhythmically. For another, she had recruited some extraordinary young dancers and rehearsed them minutely in the terms of the new dispensation. Their performance was remarkable. The slashing rhetoric of *Drastic Classicism* had been pared down to a fine set of vigorous discriminations, and this involved ambiguities of movement and posture which Armitage herself could not always keep under perfect control. The rhetorical assault on style had been muted, but aggression was still being committed everywhere one looked—with a scalpel, though, not with a cleaver. Meat-rack mayhem was out.

The refined deployment of her characteristic dance gesture still seems to me the best thing about Armitage's work in *Paradise*. The thought that such refinement could reflect the merely notional promptings of a scenario is disturbing but maybe not altogether defeating—of Armitage's promise, I mean. Notionalism does defeat *Paradise* as a work of art. As an exorcism of the punk image, it probably has great meaning and value for Armitage and her associates. In reviewing *Drastic Classicism*, I wrote that she had handed classicism over to the dark powers. *Paradise*, with its skulking Satanic interlopers, is like a literal enactment of the struggle for the soul of classicism. I'd rather not think that's what it was about; the implication is that Armitage is banking too much on a mystique. But there's her success as the punk priestess to think about, too. She only just got back to New York and already she's a prime candidate for a cult.

The audience was a dream audience. It came early, filled up every seat in a rickety, uncomfortable house (the La Mama annex), watched the dancing with rapt concentration, and applauded long and lustily at the end. The bludgeoning by Lohn's band it took in good part; it probably could have done with more. It poured adulation on Armitage and her dancers, on Lohn, on Muriel Favaro and John Erdman, who played the two evil ones, and on Charles Atlas, who designed the lighting and the imaginative low-budget costumes (fatigues, rubber gloves). How sodden the spell that descends on her who alone of all there present does not understand what the hell is going on. A month earlier, there had been a rapturous reception for Nina Wiener's *Wind Devil*, a work that I found even more obscure than *Paradise*. And a month before *that*, in another part of the Brooklyn Academy but in the same state of bafflement, I had sat through Carolyn Carlson's *Underwood*. I can name other mystifying events for the same period. Not all of them are intransigent blanks in memory. What one cannot understand one can still enjoy. Deborah Hay's concert at the Dance Theater Workshop in December was a good example of the Edifying Obscure. It built outward in serenely inscrutable layers from Hay's own inscrutable but marvellously authoritative performance, and, watching it grow, I wasn't bored one second.

You think the experience of dance surely can't get more rudimentary than that: watching something grow. And yet most dance concerts I attend fall below this threshold of irreducibility. Nina Wiener makes exquisitely polished phrases for herself and her group. She makes them long and large and fine, and she keeps them flowing from one pinpoint connection to another, and builds them into undistractedly clear sequences and the sequences into episodes and the episodes into acts. *Wind Devil* was in two acts, both of them consisting of dancing from end to end and both of them exactly alike in effect. What I miss in Wiener's choreography is progression—progression within the phrase and progression in the process that binds the phrases together; I want a cumulative rather than an additive experience. And if there are other-than-dance motives I want to know about them. I don't expect explanatory program notes; choreographers no longer write them. The fact that Nina Wiener felt compelled to write a program note for *Wind Devil* is in itself interesting. This is what she wrote:

> *I wish to explain to the audience how my company is involved in the creation of a dance. I begin a dance by teaching my dancers core phrases which express the emotions and concepts of the dance. Then I design problems for the dancers which alter the material in different ways—producing variations on the core phrases which I tailor to the needs of the dance and of the individual dancer. Many of these variations are integrated into the finished piece in different forms, so that the dance in some ways reflects the personalities of the dancers. For their individual and communal contributions to this work and for their willing spirits, I wish to thank them warmly.*

Nina Wiener is a bridge from the seventies to the eighties. The working method and the communal ethos that she subscribes to belong to the seventies. The word that leaps out at you—the word that signals the transition to the eighties—is "emotions." "Phrases which express the emotions" is an amazing formulation, coming from a choreographer like Wiener. "Phrases which *secrete* emotions," I might have expected her to say, or "phrases which *may* secrete emotions." The way most seventies choreographers would see it, the phrases themselves must first of all be technically sound. If emotion leaks out, well and good, but that is of no concern to the choreographer initially. In actual fact, Wiener's phrases are unemotional. The emotional barometer in her work is regulated by energy levels, by attack (staccato or legato), and by facial expressions (smiles or frowns). The phrases are longer or shorter but exactly the same in the kinds of tension they encompass. They don't attenuate or thicken. They don't make a drama of the distance they travel from their original impulse. So we see adagio phrases that don't build an adagio variety of effect. We see them made-to-order, releasing only one kind of effect, over and over. It's bouncing a ball against a wall as opposed to bouncing it toward a partner and having it come back to you a new ball. There is much to admire in Nina Wiener's work. It is impeccable. It is mannered, but the mannerisms are not unpleasant. It is scrupulously performed by attractive-looking people. Though much of it is appealing to the eye, none of it makes so much as a dent in the consciousness. Instead of growing and growing, it just keeps on going and going.

A farmhouse set by Judy Pfaff added to the impression that more was happening in *Wind Devil* than a suite of dances. The overexuberant colors and details were too much for the dancing to carry. It's hard to know how much in the way of décor choreography of this kind *can* carry. Just as Karole Armitage may have intended not drama but atmosphere, Wiener may have wanted to convey not emotions, precisely, but the fragrance of emotions. But atmosphere and fragrance are not to be equated with imprecision. Armitage is lucky to have Atlas designing for her; he makes the tentativeness and confusion of *Paradise* look like subtlety and provocation. Atmosphere appears as a result of particularization—of small but definite strokes.

The same is true in choreography. The other afternoon, in Balanchine's *Raymonda Variations*, I saw Carole Divet open her leg to second and fold it shut, at the same time bringing her wrist with a finicky gesture to her breastbone, and I caught the parlor fragrance of some long-ago young-girl-with-fan. The image was sparklingly immediate, as real as the girl who had produced it. And it had blossomed not out of the blue but out of the quality of tension between two aspects (développé/port de bras) of a single phrase. Divet's moment was only a flash, but it was enough. One or two flashes like this can light up a whole work.

—*January 30, 1984*

Schubertiad and Sinatraspiel

Peter Martins's new ballet is about young people, young emotions; it is about that time in life when we aren't sure who we are and hope to find the answer in another person. The seeking of partners, the choosing of partners, the changing of partners—this is Martins's subject. He makes it seem as solemn as the sealing of pacts, and for the better part of an hour he keeps a half-dozen or so young stars of the New York City Ballet caroming off each other while we in the audience try to gauge the suitability of the combinations. At the end, when all the choices have been made and the curtain falls, the partners are posed standing dubiously apart from one another. We aren't sure they've chosen wisely, and neither are they.

The note of skepticism has an undertone of practical truth. In the day-to-day operation of a ballet company, "right" casting may be as much a gamble as it is in life. The dancers who pursue each other through the piece are the same ones we've seen teamed in other ballets in the repertory, and our knowledge of how they have worked together influences—and is influenced by—the way we see them here. Are Maria Calegari and Sean Lavery really perfect together or does the perfection seem a trifle bland? Could (should) the vibrancy of Kyra Nichols and Joseph Duell be transferred to other ballets? Martins plays off predetermined images to a certain extent: Nichol Hlinka is eager, Stephanie Saland and Ib Andersen are insular (they get together), and Bart Cook and Heather Watts seem not so much to be enjoying a new equation of energies as continuing the relationship they have in Jerome Robbins's ballets. Like a novelist who has read his E. M. Forster, Martins uses round and flat characters. But the realism of the piece does not lie in the dancers' identities. It lies in the passing states, emotions, unpindownable significances that arise as the field of choice narrows and the dancers are more nakedly exposed in their will to perfection, their need to seek wholeness in one another's arms. The subject, one may say, is dancers' lives both in a literal and in a nonrestrictive metaphorical sense. Beside the ballets by Balanchine or Robbins that present this same duality, Martins's ballet seems remarkably worldly. No matter how we look at it—whether we see dancers pairing off or lovers bonding for all eternity—the dynamic process is the same, the poignancy is the same, the complications are almost the same. Martins has composed a Romantic ballet in a spirit of empiricism which the Romantics themselves might recognize. His dancers live and move and couple in a world of sentimental experience governed by the mutable chemistry of human relations—by elective affinities.

The ballet takes its form and its title, A *Schubertiad*, from the musical evenings held in private houses by Schubert and his circle during the eighteen-twenties. (Goethe had published *Elective Affinities* in 1809.) Gordon Boelzner is the onstage pianist, playing the twenty-three dances of the first scene from an alcove in a Biedermeier salon. (With his round face, rimless glasses, and full ruff of hair, Boelzner even looks like Schubert; only James Levine could look the part more.) The alcove changes to a pavilion in a garden, and we hear two impromptus (Opus 90, No. 4, and Opus 142, No. 4), followed by the Fantasie in F Minor, Opus 103, which was rendered in the initial performances by the ballet orchestra, in an arrangement by Paul Schwartz. The dancers—men in cutaways, women in adaptations of period dresses and hairdos—are guests at the party. Schubert pours out his écossaises and ländler, his valses nobles and sentimentales. Martins's choreography is for ballet dancers, in ballroom scale, and it is effortlessly seductive. The dancing, by turns frolicsome and serene, grows more brilliantly competitive. We begin to see who goes with whom, and in the garden scene we see these attachments explored at length.

Balanchine's *Liebeslieder Walzer* was also in two scenes. The shift from the ballroom to the theatrical arena accomplished a dramatic heightening of scale and intensity which Martins tries to duplicate, with one great difference: he also tries to keep before us the possibly provisional nature of the attachments. Not until the end of the ballet does he settle all the options, and then it's with an implied question. In Balanchine's ballet, the matter of who goes with whom was decided at the outset; his couples never parted. But then Balanchine's interest was hardly ever in how couples came to be or came to stop being couples. His men and women move toward and away from each other, but except in early ballets like *Serenade* or ballets with a mime base (*Ivesiana, Meditation, A Midsummer Night's Dream*) their situation is fixed; they are how they are forever. In his second scene, Martins gives us two consecutive pas de trois which in Balanchine would be unthinkable: a man must decide between two women and then a woman between two men. The symmetrical reversal is not absurd as Martins stages it. The sexual geometry is engrossing; the second pas de trois (Nichols between Duell and Andersen) even imparts a suggestion of erotic fear and longing. From this peak Martins meant, I think, to bring his theme of partners to a summation by diffusing it throughout the rest of the cast. A good idea, much too leisurely executed. Where we need a synoptic compression of the theme and a quick finale, we get further development set to the twenty-minute-long Fantasie. The two characters left over from the two pas de trois (Watts, Andersen) are given mates (Cook, Saland), and in a passage reminiscent of standard Balanchine "symphonic" recapitulation all the other dancers from the ballroom scene are brought back and married off. The choreography is too decorous for the dark tones in the music and helpless against its repetitiousness. Worse yet, the suspense has dried up. The ballet is really over before the Fantasie begins.

Richly conceived, handsomely wrought, perilously overextended, *A Schubertiad* is also the most expressive declaration of independence from his mentor that Martins has yet made. *Liebeslieder* exists as a model to be departed from. At times, Martins seems to be concocting a deliberately messy forerunner of that great work, searching out choreographic motives that Balanchine didn't use and putting his dancers through the process of selection that Balanchine didn't depict, in order to see where it would lead. It hardly leads us back to *Liebeslieder*. A *Schubertiad* is Biedermeier Romanticism; it is daylit and pragmatic. Maybe, even if he wanted to redo *Liebeslieder*, Martins would be prevented by temperament. He can be sardonic but not dark. In the Fantasie, he doesn't come near the dark places in Schubert's psyche. He comes closer to mystery when he's dealing with his dancers.

A fundamental requirement of the piece, unevenly realized by the dancers, would seem to be acting. This is a vexed question at New York City Ballet. Emoting is taboo. But in a piece like A *Schubertiad* a neutral presence is death.

The demands Martins makes as a dramatist are modest enough: the dancers are not to impose characterization on the dancing but to carry out the character implications of the dances and the dance situations. When this kind of impersonal dance-acting is done successfully, it dissolves the problem of effects and how to get them, leaving only a sense of completion of incident. Apart from its suite of ballroom dances, the most impressive achievement of A *Schubertiad* is the "story" of Kyra Nichols and Joseph Duell. Duell becomes a performer of force in this ballet, and he creates a muscular, saturnine figure. The quality is not overtly sketched in anything he does; it's a matter of tone. And we're given to believe it is the secret of his appeal for Nichols. In one of the ballroom dances, as he lifts her on his back he bends forward with the thrust of a buffalo, and she clings contentedly. In the garden pas de trois, he seems to have this lunging power bottled up inside him. Duell's role is a little like the one Martins made for Jock Soto in *Concerto for Two Solo Pianos*. (In both ballets, the men are rivals of the elegant and fluent Ib Andersen.) Nichols's character is completely unexpected. Role after role—most recently a consummate *Raymonda Variations*—confirms that, for all her speed and variety, her great quality remains stability. Physically, she is solid-state, lilke a marble colt, and her marmoreal looks never melt or flow—not in legato, not even in the white heat of high-velocity allegro, which is one of her specialties. The changelessness is proof against the myriad changes of her dancing—it's a gift of grandeur. There's nothing intractable about Kyra Nichols, but nothing quicksilver, either. And Martins casts her as a mercurial tease. If she didn't understand her part as well as she does, she'd look miscast.

Federico Pallavicini, a new designer, contributes a pretty baroque room with high windows. His garden is a mite tropical for Vienna. Chenault Spence chose to key his lighting to the colors of the set rather than to the time of day, so this Schubertiad seems to start at 4 A.M. The piano in the alcove-pavilion is not amplified, and the sound is muffled in some parts of the house.

Frank Sinatra records may not seem much of a basis for serious choreography, but in *Nine Sinatra Songs* Twyla Tharp has made them work excitingly for her and her superb company, now performing at the Brooklyn Academy. The dance style is ballroom-acrobatic, and it's very different from her original, rather arty approach to this music back in 1976, when she and Mikhail Baryshnikov worked together in a duet called *Once More, Frank*. The three songs she used then—"Somethin' Stupid," "That's Life," and "One for My Baby"—are represented in the new ballet, along with "Softly As I Leave You," "Strangers in the Night," "All the Way," "Forget Domani," and "My Way." ("My Way" is used twice, in two different versions.) It's certainly a mixed bag. Tharp hasn't tried to separate the connoisseur's Sinatra from the Vegas brawler, and in that I think she's been true to the nature of her material. In pop music, one can flash from the shallows to the heights without warning. Tharp confronts what Sinatra stands for in all its aspects (though when we get to the "dooby dooby doo" section of "Strangers in the Night," she lifts the needle; there does seem to be a limit to her tolerance). She emerges with something like a panorama of Middle America in middle age. The generation that came of age in the fifties probably knows Sinatra best. It spans his bobby-sox era and his ring-a-ding-ding and Paul Anka and Stephen Sondheim eras, and it was one of Tharp's most perceptive decisions to set "My Way" both times as an ensemble dance instead of as a duet. The graying masses have throbbed to this valediction ever since Sinatra first recorded it. As staged by Tharp, with first three, then seven couples wheeling and sweeping across a stage lit by a turning silver ball, it has an anthemic power.

Oscar de la Renta's ball gowns are fifties-ish without being archaic, and, with the exception of the one for Sara Rudner, which looks like two bibs hanging back to back, they aren't examples of egregious chic; they're what wives and girlfriends might reasonably dream of wearing on New Year's Eve. The great Rudner is also given the most labyrinthine acrobatic choreography—a tortuous series of slithers, blind leaps, upsy-daisy lifts, and ass-over-heels floorwork, to "One for My Baby." With excellent support from John Carrafa, Rudner makes it all lyrical. (When Tharp devised her spinoff *Sinatra Suite* for American Ballet Theatre last year, she gave "One for My Baby" to Baryshnikov for a solo and used some of the Rudner material for his "That's Life" duet with Elaine Kudo.) The sexual frankness of Tharp's choreography may surprise people who haven't seen exhibition disco recently. But the discos know nothing like Tharp's wit. Her roughhousing is as tautly controlled, as systematically applied as her boffo effects. The two tactics come together in Song No. 8, "That's Life," when Sinatra sings "Pick myself / Up and get / Back in the race!" and a supine Shelley Freydont is yanked to her feet by degrees, one yank per beat. The audience starts to yell, because nothing as brutally obvious and as funny has happened up to that moment. Then Tharp tops it by having Freydont hurl herself through the air at Tom Rawe *before* he has quite finished putting on his dinner jacket. He makes the catch: uproar.

Nine Sinatra Songs hits the audience very hard—it can barely keep still. Nearly every number is met with groans and giggles at having these old family albums brought out and plumped down right in front of everybody. Even if you haven't grown up with the songs, the mixed emotions they induce are apt to make you slightly queasy. Tharp toys with the audience's susceptibilities, but she doesn't take undue advantage. The straight numbers are perfectly straight. "Softly As I Leave You" is a gliding and flying exhibition-style number, arranged for Shelley Washington and Keith Young. "All the Way," more intimate and romantic, is performed by the tall and beautiful Amy Spencer, with Raymond Kurshals. As for "Strangers in the Night," it's a militant tango done by a mock-serious, straight-backed team, Mary Ann Kellogg and John Malashock. In the up-tempo division, we get two surprises. The newest and youngest-looking woman in the company, Barbara Hoon, dances "Somethin' Stupid" in puffed sleeves with Richard Colton and captures the essence of dopey Junior Prom ecstasy. "Forget Domani" is

Jennifer Way and William Whitener wagging their heads roguishly and practicing their flamenco—the essence of dopey middle-aged escapism. I wouldn't care to choose among such riches, but when I think back on *Nine Sinatra Songs*, "Forget Domani" is the one that makes me smile.

Technically speaking, the main interest of the piece is its adaptation of professional ballroom dances. Tharp has dissected the style with her usual care. Her tango parody is a knowledgeable one. Her aerial work in "Softly As I Leave You" is a beautiful development of exhibition heroics. There's a whole stack of dance manuals—as well as a few cruise brochures—behind "Forget Domani." Even the roughhouse has its model in the knockabout ballroom acts; it's crème de l'apache. Like Peter Martins, who is a former ballroom champion, Tharp knows how to feature the women without shading the men. In another area of technique, her work here can be admired for its resourcefulness in setting steps to long vocal lines and chunky ones, to rigidly regular rhythms and overplangent orchestrations. Although the spectacle of the ballet seems utterly familiar, people never actually danced to Sinatra records. Tharp's choreographic line is like a wide silk ribbon winding through the plush of the ballads. When I first heard of her Sinatra project, I wondered why she wasn't using a virtuoso jazz singer like Mel Tormé, whose way with a pop song strikes me as more nearly equal to her own methods than Sinatra's. Possibly there would have been too even a match—silk on silk. As it is, *Nine Sinatra Songs* joins *Sue's Leg* and *Baker's Dozen* and *Eight Jelly Rolls* on the Brooklyn bills as a masterpiece of Americana.   —*February 13, 1984*

Tharp Against Tharp

"Yes, but what is it about?" I didn't hear that question voiced at the Brooklyn Academy of Music while the Twyla Tharp company was there in its enormously successful three-week run. I didn't hear much of anything but applause—applause every night from sold-out houses, and every bit of it deserved. *Nine Sinatra Songs*, an instant classic, was so popular that extra performances had to be added. The three other new pieces were completely different and completely different from each other, and were also hits. To have asked what any of them were *about* would have been like asking the Goose That Laid the Golden Egg for a side order of bacon. Actually, only *Bad Smells* explained itself the way the Sinatra piece did, and, considered purely from a dance point of view, it struck me as the least interesting of the lot. As theatre, it had quite a bit to say about media interference in our lives. The only bit of décor was a movie screen, hung up front. Seven dancers, got up horror-movie style in gray, rotting skin and clothes, socked out the tight, high-voltage phrases that Tharp has been using lately. The movement, chock-full of energy, never seems to break out of the dancers' bodies and reach us; instead, it implodes. The trouble with the piece is not this disturbing, perverse, unreleasing movement but the difficulty we have in watching it. A video cameraman (the dancer Tom Rawe) darts constantly between us and the action, and we see what he photographs being projected on the screen overhead, some of the time upside down or sideways. You'd think that the terse, locked-in movement would photograph well in closeup. It doesn't. The dancers' choreographed grimaces are magnified, but the bodily configurations are obscure. The big and terrible event that is evidently taking place—Raymond Kurshals in a savagely dominating role appears to be destroying Mary Ann Kellogg—is one thing on the stage and another on the screen. My mind was shredded trying to synthesize the two channels of information, and I found I couldn't comfortably watch just one, either. *Bad Smells*, which takes place to a blitzing Glenn Branca score, was made in 1982. An all-video version of it was seen in Tharp's *Scrapbook* film. In a rehearsal about a year ago, I saw an all-dance version; Rawe went through his moves, which are carefully programmed, without his camera. It seemed to me then the most aggressive piece Tharp had made—a real flattener. On the stage, it becomes a chunk of curiously deflected raw sensation. It's all about itself— about things of horror and how the reporting of these things keeps us from experiencing them. A parable of the electronic age? Unmistakably, though to achieve it Tharp has had to sacrifice some fascinating choreography. The meaning of *Bad Smells* is not in the dancing but in the production.

Another piece I had expected to be more aggressive was the one that is called *Fait Accompli*. Here again the choreography was less important than what the production made of it. And it was very peculiar choreography. In her pre-première interviews, Tharp had spoken of death, dying, concentration camps, war, bombs, plane crashes. A lot of publicity had been given to the fact that she now takes a daily boxing lesson before her ballet class. Boxing and other kinds of gymnastics are visible in the short, choppy movement executed by groups of squarely planted dancers. But not bombs or planes or death camps. Santo Loquasto, who designed the leprous rags in *Bad Smells*, dresses everybody in plain black shorts and tops. The implosive movement style (the energy seems to be sucked out of the ground, as in some forms of break-dancing) resembles *Bad Smells* without the violence. Tharp seems to have cut any lingering strands of elasticity, so that transitions become a problem. The way she solves the problem—by layering contrapuntal groups and phasing one rhythmic unit into another—is a technical feat of great elegance.

With no ongoing arc of movement and no legato (until the end), the piece jerks around like a punch-drunk fighter whose reflexes have been demolished, and yet it has momentum. It spreads and flows. The first half becomes a study in negative will. Tharp, by denying herself the use of her normal equipment, forces new compositional methods into being. The choreography is choral but not communal. The dancers do not partner, handle, or even touch each other; they jerk and convulse in isolation and much of the time in unison. Furthermore, this strangely desolate, strangely monosyllabic Tharp choreography moves mostly toward and away from us, hardly ever into or out of the wings. Those exits and intrusions that light up the edges of the stage in her work are absent here—the wings are off-limits. I've often thought that Tharp's wingside technique was like quick cuts to closeups in the movies. In *Fait Accompli*, when she does move to a closeup it's in the standard way—star supported by chorus. The star is herself, and in the second part of the show she is partnered by five of the eight men lined up behind her. The emotional implications of these partnered episodes are hard to avoid, not because of what they contain but because we've been cued to feel emotion. Tharp may even have eliminated partnering from the earlier section so as to weight its use here with a very special dramatic meaning. But she doesn't tell us very much. The men are by turns challenging, sensual, sweet, and goofy, and they're all blurrily seen; if this is an autobiographical survey, it's a noncommittal one. The main point—that the heroine is left alone—is not really a point. It's an opportunity for a solo. This is a kind of twitchy rumba, and it's pure Tharp, but its context is not so pure. The personal, "confessional" material is clouded by standard theatrical usage. Perhaps the oddest of the many odd developments in *Fait Accompli* is the fact that the first half, with its simple, blocklike movement, its exclusion of stylistic trademarks, and its devious near-invisible continuity, is very unconventional Tharp but looks *more* conventional than the second half, in which she reverts to a standard framework.

The pleasure of the piece, for me, lay in the way it was made—Tharp's reversing her technical habits almost completely and still drawing us into a pattern of expectation. For others, *Fait Accompli* seems to have functioned like a giant Rorschach test—no two interpretations are alike. What is it about? Why, pollution, urban anxiety, sexual warfare, loneliness, the end of the world. Everyone who has seen the piece remarks on the extraordinary lighting, by Jennifer Tipton, and it's from Tipton's shafts of light, beamed straight down from an exposed bank of floodlamps, that the work derives much of its suggestive power. The dancers of Part I move in and out behind this curtain of light. At one point, they are bathed in clouds of steam, like the athletes in the morning mist of Leni Riefenstahl's film *Olympia*. For the second section, danced by Tharp and the men, Tipton switches to dark burnished cross-lighting, which reinforces the solemn Germanic tone, and when Tharp walks alone upstage at the end, the darkness ahead of her is pierced by a row of lights at ground level, which look like footlights. Make of it what you will, it has to be *some* vision of glory. The fiery Wagnerian beauty of it all is so impressive that we may lose sight of how little is actually being said in the choreography or else attribute a sacerdotal meaning to its extreme asceticism. Tharp's choreography usually teems with suggestiveness. I prefer that to the recessive doodling she does in this superspectacular production.

And I prefer her working with music rather than with the kind of thudding multilevel sonics that David Van Tieghem provides here. (One of his levels sounds much like Alwin Nikolais; another is a sophisticated form of rap music, bringing in police sirens and bulletins from our newsroom.) Tharp seems to have arrived at a point of virtuosity in which outdoing herself—ever her main objective—

means confounding herself, with every work becoming a criticism of every other. Her four new pieces this year present stark contradictions in choreographic content, as if defying us to believe that the same person made them all. *Nine Sinatra Songs* is ballroom pop, *Fait Accompli* is postminimal minimalism, *Bad Smells* is orgiastic postminimal minimalism—Tharp's own *Rocky Horror Picture Show*. The fourth new piece, *Telemann*, is a classical ballet. I marvel at this aesthetic range, I applaud it, and yet I wonder: is it enough that the subject of a piece be its maker's ambition?

Telemann, done to the Concerto in E Major for flute, oboe d'amore, and violin, starts out a perfectly charming, diverting little piece and ends up a mad game of Ping-Pong between Tharp's baroque sensibility and Telemann's. The choreography is filled with irregular spacing and counting so brilliant it outdazzles itself—it outwits wit. Part of the problem is that Tharp, who may be compensating for her dancers' lack of polish in classical technique, has committed them to feats of timing they can't always bring off. The final section is so excessively busy that it's musically nontransparent, like a Merce Cunningham piece danced to a Paul Taylor score. But another problem is Tharp's motive for the ballet. There is no reason in the world for it to have been made. Baroque manners are a mask the dancers assume (as opposed to the ballroom manners, which they wear as unselfconsciously as their own skins, in the Sinatra). *Telemann* would probably be better danced on point by a ballet company, but it would still leave us wondering what Tharp wished to say by it other than that she can do this kind of thing.

Usually, when Tharp uses music she creates an imagery greater than what can be accounted for by her skill in manipulating a score. This imagery always looks unpremeditated, and I would guess it is largely unconscious. From the unbidden pictures that arise in *Eight Jelly Rolls* and *Sue's Leg* and *Baker's Dozen* and "The Golden Section" of *The Catherine Wheel* and *Nine Sinatra Songs* we deduce the nature of Tharp's subject. Or if "subject" sounds too hard and formal for this very elusive process of hers, let's just say we grasp an imaginative continuity that corresponds to the music. We go someplace in our minds with Twyla, and that someplace is both in and out of this world. If *Telemann* had the imaginative continuity of *Baker's Dozen*, it would tell us things no other classical ballet has told us. But Tharp's power of evocation has been defeated by her ferocious competitiveness. It's not only Tharp against Telemann, it's Tharp against herself.

—*February 27, 1984*

Visualizations

In Alwin Nikolais's new piece *Persons & Structures*, the curtain goes up and you see at the right of the stage what looks like a phone booth covered in white cloth. The cloth goes up and there's a two-story glass box mounted on metal legs about a foot high. Inside the two cubicles are two men, one up and one down, who look completely naked and who squirm uncomfortably. The cloth comes down and a moment later goes up again, and this time two men are crammed together in the top box and two women are below. The cloth cover keeps rising and descending all through the piece, which is set to one of Edgard Varèse's most disquieting compositions, the *Poème Électronique*, and we never lose our dread of what we will see stuck and writhing in there. The content is always different; once it's just one man on top with an empty box below him. Inside the boxes, the people are either desperate to get out or determined to perform; they do slow tumbling acts, displacing each other with enormous difficulty. In the meantime, the stage is full of background and foreground motion. Numbers of dancers are constantly crossing behind the box, which is open at the back, and, of course, some of them get in and out while it is draped. Perhaps to divert us, the foreground action consists of a sequence of dances. I shall have to see the piece again to say what these were like; after the first one, a pas de trois in which two men lifted a woman between them by pressing their heads against her rib cage (her feet dangled in the air like a doll's), I stopped looking. That box was too fascinating.

Nikolais has often shown a flair for the freak show, but these spectacles of his seldom sustain themselves beyond the first few minutes. A good example is *Gallery* (1978), which the Nikolais company was also presenting this season (at the City Center). It's "gallery" as in "shooting gallery." A row of fluorescent green skulls floats in black air. Pop, pop, and they disappear. They rise and sink, they change places, they appear in clusters, but soon enough we've seen it all, and Nikolais isn't able to renew our interest. He also is surprisingly careless with the mechanics of his illusions. In the same piece, two clowns come out wearing bags that have a clearly defined illuminated front and a black velvet back. This makes convincing two-dimensional plastic shapes in the dark, and when the clowns take their feet off the ground the shapes contract to squiggling blobs in the air. But if Nikolais is so concerned to keep that two-dimensional front before us why does he have the clowns turn sideways again and again, exposing their "nonexistent" rears? Although the dance goes on and on, we never again can see the original illusion. Some essential part of the Nikolais spectacle is constantly being undermined by imprecision or by laxity in planning and development; we wonder why he is showing us these things. And sometimes in the more horrific numbers there seems to be a reluctance to go the route—an emotional holding back, as if the dispenser of these grim and grisly treats wanted us to see him as really a harmless old fuff who wouldn't hurt a fly. In another of the new pieces, *Liturgies*, two men carry a third (Joy Hintz, the shortest woman in the company, made up as a little bald man), who hangs between them on a pole. There are ropes tying the third figure to the pole, but if you think you're going to see anything made of that you don't know Nikolais. The whole apparatus drags its unexamined possibilities around the stage a few too many times and vanishes. In another section, he experiments again with a rope and a hanging body and again goes nowhere. The man is either a terrible tease or a self-satisfied conjurer whose least soap bubble must be preserved for posterity.

The boldness and the succinctness of *Persons & Structures* therefore come as a surprise. Nikolais doesn't shrink from the logic of the pattern he has set in motion, and he even dramatizes it. When the people outside the box rush to it and flatten themselves against it while the ones inside peer out, they instantly double the emotional power of the image, which has been steadily rising. It's as if they, too, were helpless animals. The dancers don't act this moment; they state it and trust us to respond. This trust is something I'm not used to in Nikolais's work. The lack of drama in so many of his pieces had made me see him as a displaced person—a fine-arts designer with no great theatrical appetite. Infinitely delicate and painstaking with his designs, he has often directed with a heavy touch. His dancers not only act, they overact. Not content with being clever, they are also cute, forever capping some tricky bit with a dead stare out front, prompting our reactions. When they play for laughs, they play for keeps. (The same pedantic humor was seen in Debra McCall's recent revival of the dances of Oskar Schlemmer, the director of the Bauhaus theatre workshop and a forerunner of Nikolais. Form followed function, all right, and fun *had* to follow form.) In the new piece, the pathos is greater for not being pushed out at us. Nikolais's theatre sense here has a leaping, charged quality I'm also not accustomed to. Maybe his using another composer's score instead of having to compose one of his own helped him find a dramatic focus. The costumes, too, which effectively imply total nudity, were inspired by another designer, Lindsay Davis. *Persons & Structures* is a most untypical Nikolais production, yet it's the production many of us have long wanted from him—the piece he has often promised but never quite delivered. He builds it to an unforgettable climax. The last time we see them, both of the boxes are filled to bursting with bodies—a jumble of hands, feet, faces. The rising cloth that reveals this horrid sight keeps on rising and uncovers a man standing erect on top. Before we can decide how he got there and who he is, the scene blacks out and the piece is over.

Nikolais's theatre has lately become less illusionistic—concerned less with costumes and props than with the exposed bodies of dancers dancing. When he makes a nifty piece of choreography these days (like the opening of *Liturgies*, which churns out a great froth of insect visualizations, from beetles to centipedes), his conceits are likely to be purely anatomical. The company is trained to this kind of expression, and it's no longer as good at disappearing into the décor as it used to be. An old piece like *Noumenon* (1953) loses its point, because the dancers, who are completely enclosed in stretch fabric, let us see, in between the triangles and pentagons and trapezoids and whatnot, the outlines of *persons*, and the intent of the choreography is that we not see this until the very end, when the fabric falls about the heads and shoulders of those within, defining them as so many draped but unmistakably human statues. Looking at the older pieces in the current repertory—three out of four were revivals from the fifties—I was struck by how often they seemed to require (as much of their audience as of their maker) a hermetic concentration on form and no interest in the real world. We are seldom taken beyond the manipulation of design elements into an understanding of where the design impulse comes from. In Nikolais's work then and for a long time to come, a decorative object that looked like an onion or a trumpet was never used to remind us of onions or trumpets, because, I suspect, references of that sort were thought to be at best utilitarian and at worst anti-art and just too Disney. Though Nikolais's abstractions may have corresponded to the mood of the fifties—particularly to the ethos of some Abstract Expressionists—their lack of resonance makes them look pointless and trivial today. Whereas Disney (to invoke the archfiend of those years) has started looking really bright and consequential. Right after a Nikolais matinée, I saw *Fantasia*, which was playing just across the street, and I kept thinking of Nikolais—of his affinities with Disney and his lack of interest in them. In the Chinese dance in Disney's *Nutcracker* episode, the dancers are mushrooms with coolie hats. Everything you see and think about because of what you see is intended to be there, and the impudent associations (China, dope, mushrooms, trance) are sweetly sent up by the innocence of the music. The same thing happens on a slightly lower level in the Arabian dance, only here it's the visual image that sends up the music. The parody of the classic belly dancer (she appears in both the Ivanov and the Balanchine productions of the ballet) in the form of a guppy wearing lipstick and mascara is not apparent unless you know *The Nutcracker*, but you don't have to know it to enjoy the ineffable rightness and silliness of the image and the brilliance of the choreography, which in a series of fishtail twists and turns captures amazingly the slumberous and sinuous movements of belly dancing. It even adds an exit no dancer on any stage could duplicate—a zigzag flick too fast to be seen as more than a blur that leaves a dazzle of bubbles behind.

The worst part of *Fantasia* is the dull opening—a display of fireworks and some wisps in the sky which look like UFOs, set to the Bach-Stokowski Toccata and Fugue in D Minor. This is a watered-down version of designs submitted to Disney by Oskar Fischinger, the German avant-garde filmmaker. The compromise seems to have dishonored everyone concerned. As music visualization, this overture to *Fantasia* is surpassed by the Waltz of the Flowers, with its whirling leaves, its glistening, pollen-skirted Toumanovas, its snowflakes, and its ice-skating Tinkerbell. The sections of the movie that work best are, as one might expect, those that are set either to ballet music or to music that has a visual conception built into it, like *The Sorcerer's Apprentice* or *Night on Bald Mountain*. The Arcadian clatter that goes on to Beethoven's *Pastoral* was originally meant to be accompanied by Gabriel Pierné's *Cydalise et le Chèvre-Pied*, a two-act nymphs-and-satyrs ballet first presented by the Paris Opéra in 1923, with choreography by Léo Staats, and starring Carlotta Zambelli. Extracts from *Cydalise* became a staple of the light-concert-music repertory. Had Disney gone through with his plan to use this score, he might have made a more seemly spectacle, but then generations of schoolchildren might not have been introduced to the Beethoven who is reflected in the lordlier aspects of Disney's creation. That business of Zeus rolling over in his cloud blanket after his thunderstorm of a tantrum has died down is wonderful, and the further business of his fishing out from underneath him a stray lightning bolt and tossing it casually to earth (where it detonates, an echo of the dying storm) is *really* wonderful. I venture to say Beethoven would have loved it.

I first saw the film, which was originally released in 1940, about twenty years ago. It seemed to me not nearly as bad as people said, and I thought the Stravinsky episode was actually exciting; but on the whole *Fantasia* impressed me as a film made for children by children. It used to be fashionable to praise the comedy portions—especially the still hilarious ostrich-hippo-alligator-elephant ballet to Ponchielli's *Dance of the Hours*—and deplore everything else. Stravinsky's animadversions on the use of his *Rite of Spring* seem to have been more anti-Stokowski than anti-Disney. Leopold Stokowski, who not only conducted the soundtrack of the film but collaborated with Disney on the production, made some cuts in the *Rite* and changed the order of some of the sections. The scenario, of course, was completely different, but since the original scenario is regularly abandoned in productions of the ballet nowadays, that seems no great violation. Between them, Disney and Stokowski almost manage to persuade us that Stravinsky's music is about the creation of the planet Earth, the emergence of sea and animal life, the appearance and disappearance of the great reptiles (the tyrannosaurus seems to have been inspired by King Kong), and the formation of the continents and the topography of the earth as we know it. The real problem is that this story has no place for the final cataclysm that in the ballet accompanies the Sacrificial Dance of the Chosen Victim, so Stokowski cuts this music and substitutes an ending of his own, for which Disney's artists provide some rather inconclusive, dun-colored views of the planet from outer space. (Too bad they didn't know about the blue-and-white marble.)

The strength of the *Rite of Spring* sequence—the strength of the film as a whole—is the appositeness of the music and the movement. The visualization of the *Rite* is apposite in *scale* to the music; the visualization of the *Pastoral* is not. Part of the enduring charm of the *Dance of the Hours* is that Disney murders music that deserves to be murdered. (And probably had been already. Burlesques of Ponchielli had to have been standard practice on the vaudeville circuits for years.) He murders ballet preciousness and ballet conventions right along with it, and for accuracy's sake he employed Irina Baronova to model the steps.* For

---

* *Postscript 1987:* Besides Baronova, who posed for the ostriches, Disney employed Tatiana Riabouchinska (hippos) and David Lichine (alligators). Charles Solomon, the animation historian who sent me this information, adds: "The future Marge Champion also appeared in reference footage, doing poses and steps for the hippos and ostriches. The films of Marge Champion were preserved by her former husband, animator Art Babbitt, who drew the dancing mushrooms and thistles in *The Nutcracker* as well as the sequence of Jupiter with the thunderbolt. . . . The other reference films have, alas, been lost." According to the Disney director T. Hee, "We hired a corpulent, wonderful black actress named Hattie Noel, who was not a ballet dancer, to dance like a hippo for us, so that we could study the big flow movement of the body. We had a dancer here to show her the steps and then I would show her certain routines we marked out on the floor of the sound stage and tell her she would have to go there and pirouette here, and then we shot her doing it. She wasn't a dancer, but she was an actress, and she was marvellous. And then there was another girl who *was* a ballet dancer. She was a very tall, very ostrich-like girl and she loved doing the burlesque of the ostrich for us." (Quoted in *Walt Disney's "Fantasia,"* by John Culhane, Abrams, 1983.)

some of the choreography and at least one of the sets he was indebted to Balanchine's staging of the "Water Nymph Ballet" in the film *The Goldwyn Follies*. In December 1939, while Balanchine was in Hollywood (probably for *I Was an Adventuress*), he visited the Disney studio along with Stravinsky, and the two men had their picture taken with Walt Disney and T. Hee, a director of the Ponchielli sequence. In the picture, they are handling small plaster models of the stars of that sequence, and Balanchine is grinning like a boy. Though Disney never had him under contract, it's likely that he did have Balanchine's support for the project as well as some indirect assistance.

What appears appallingly out of scale in *Fantasia* is the treatment of the conductor. Stokowski is most often seen silhouetted against the blaze of a thousand suns. Conducting, as always, without a baton, he subdues his legions of musicians and molds music out of thin air. It's the Führer conception of the conductor, but in the end *Fantasia* transcends this unwelcome reminder of thirties cultural propaganda. It gives us Mickey Mouse conducting the elements in *The Sorcerer's Apprentice*—a deliberate satire of Stokowski. Then it gives us a less ingratiating and possibly less conscious parody in the towering bat-winged devil who dominates the revels in *Night on Bald Mountain*. *Fantasia* is a big enough movie not to be dragged down by its inequalities and its gaffes in taste. It is big enough to parody itself—to suggest that the play of forms within forms is, after all, finite, but that it is anarchic, too. Thus, an omnipotent conductor is both Mickey Mouse and Satan, and the lascivious alligators who swoop down on the hippos in the *Dance of the Hours* are the pterodactyls of the *Rite* in disguise.

Fantasia is now being shown with a completely rerecorded soundtrack, synchronized to Stokowski's and conducted by Irwin Kostal, and with the addition of a foreword dedicating the reissue to Stokowski's memory. It is not at all the naïve movie I remembered.   —*March 12, 1984*

Three Elders

Radical ideas, if repeated long enough, become traditional ideas. They don't even have to be widely imitated to lose their original eccentric force. This season at the City Center, the Merce Cunningham company marked its thirty-first year. Cunningham's philosophy of movement has been more extensively adopted than his actual language of movement, yet that language—one might call it a protestant classicism, with its grammar of dissent—no longer seems strange. It has become traditional to Cunningham, and we accept it along with other formerly disconcerting features of his canon, like the relevant-irrelevant sound. Everything looks so sanely irrational on Cunningham's stage that we can fail to notice new peculiarities when they creep into the work. Some of the recent pieces seem organically connected, as if they were segments of a larger, ongoing work or variations on a theme. It's easy to see these connections when they're imagistic, as in *Quartet* and *Gallopade*, and when they fall into discrete patterns, as they do in those two works. But then there are the non-imagistic works—*Trails* and *Coast Zone* and *Pictures*—which haven't a clearly defined "closed" structure and simply progress from one thing to another until the curtain falls. I don't suppose that Cunningham has never used linear progression before, but I doubt if he has ever used so much of it at one time. Because nothing appears to repeat or return in these dances, they are all but impossible to grasp as entities.

In *Pictures*, the newest piece, some of the dancers fall into poses and hold them while the others keep moving, but these poses are all different and completely contradictory in their makeup—sometimes strikingly arranged, sometimes beautiful, but more often unresolved or off balance. Whether the stopped action has any intelligibility as a pose seems a matter of luck, like a snapshot taken at the right time. And the meaning, if any, is purely formal; these aren't images in the poetic sense, and they have no cumulative power. But they do give us handholds—literally points of rest—that keep the flow of movement from dissolving into chaos before our eyes. I can imagine a younger Cunningham who would have relished such a dissolution. But *Pictures* is a gently inquisitive work; at first glance, it doesn't seem to be up to very much at all.

Pictures may have evolved from *Coast Zone* (1983), which may in turn have come from *Trails* (1982). *Trails* is a succession of entrées in which no fewer than two and no more than five dancers are on the stage at one time. (There are ten dancers in all.) The entrées are fairly long, fairly virtuosic, and they build. But they do not build one upon another, there is no climax, and once the piece is over you realize that it is centerless. *Coast Zone*, similarly constructed for twelve dancers, seems not only centerless but spineless. Each event lasts less than a minute and is wiped away by the succeeding event. The structure is so restlessly episodic that it seems to be all transitions. Cunningham even breaks up the one constant factor: the dancers who keep running in and out suddenly about halfway through the piece change into other dancers; one cast is wiped away by another. I believe this happens in *Pictures*, too; it contains all the dancers in the company, and a most effective entrance late in the action is made by Cunningham himself. Once the dancers come on, they tend to stay on for long periods; my memory is of a stage almost constantly full of various kinds of slow-winding activity. Cunningham comes close to Chinese landscape painting.

The other of the season's new works, *Inlets 2*, is a new version of an older piece. Cunningham has created new choreography from the same material, deleting his own role in the process. He has also deleted the Morris Graves décor, but not the John Cage score, which sounds like a faucet dripping in a bucket, then like a campfire. These noises and some vivid animal imagery are all I recognized of the *Inlets* of 1978. The soft-edged sectional design and the quietly unfolding moods were closer to *Pictures*. Both in *Inlets 2* and in *Pictures*, the choreography employs doubling devices—people sharing a phrase by performing it in unison or in canon or splitting it between them—in a marked way I don't recall seeing before in Cunningham's work. But the more I see of his work the more unfamiliar it looks. The chain-smoking phase he seems to be in now, igniting one dance with the tip of another, emphasizes similarities in his work that were probably there all along. It also reproduces the essential Cunningham experience on a new plane. Out of what first seems to be undifferentiated spectacle themes appear, objectives appear, and continuity assumes familiarly strange proportions.

Orientation can take some time. Luckily, even people who are dissatisfied with Cunningham's current way of working agree that he could not find a better designer than Mark Lancaster. Lancaster, too, works in a serial format, and he restricts himself to the tights, shirts, and leotards that come in boxes. The fresh colors he dyes these garments, though, hold their fascination all through a piece. In *Coast Zone*, he uses lavender, purple, orange, and aqua in various combinations. In *Inlets 2*, his colors under the sombre lighting are all but unnamable; I made out ochre, brown, plum, gray, and mustard. *Pictures* has shirts in slate blue ranging through slate gray to charcoal and black. These are worn with Prussian-blue trousers. When, during some of the prolonged poses, the colors are inked out— Lancaster also does the lighting—the stage picture goes into silhouette, and the cyclorama glows pearly white.

There is a characteristic moment in all Jerome Robbins's best ballets which I can't help looking for in each new ballet he does. It's the moment that crystallizes the secret of the ballet's excitement—that reveals the innermost workings of Robbins's gift. Invariably, it's a tiny thing, like the way the girl drops her head just as the boy begins to lift her in *Afternoon of a Faun*,* or the moment when the cast of *Moves* (which New York City Ballet will revive this spring) appears, sinks into fifth-position plié, and extends a line of tendues forward along the floor. Those small gestures are kernels—a discreet academic emphasis in which a quality of sentiment is contained, essential to the whole ballet and to Robbins's aims as an artist. In *Dances at a Gathering*, the moment comes when the partners in the Opus 42 waltz stand hand in hand with their backs to the audience and do a string of relevés passés and sautés passés. At this moment, they are good little ballet students striving their hardest to please some stern invisible teacher, and Robbins seems to open his heart to them and to us. In its simplicity, this passage is diametrically opposed to the clever lift that comes a moment later and is applauded by the audience. *Dances at a Gathering* is filled with clever lifts, clever exits, clever choreographic schemes that never fail to impress us. The plain old relevés passés, coming at such a crazy moment in the music (Chopin seems to

---

* *Postscript 1987:* I make too much of this "tiny thing" in what follows. The dropping of the girl's head as the boy lifts her in *Faun* is something I remembered seeing often enough to think it was part of the choreography. Apparently, it isn't. But the emotional implications I attribute to this moment are present in other moments that *are* choreographed—for example, the contraction of the girl's body as the boy holds it prone in the air, or her sudden whirl into pirouette coming to rest on the boy's extended arm, a reflexive move that surprises both of them.

be rushing his coda, like a child saying his prayers in a hurry to get out of church), have a disproportionate grandeur, a beauty of aspiration by which in a single flash of recognition we come to know, judge, and accept the ambition that lies at the heart of the whole ballet.

Robbins's greatest ideas are nearly always revelations of the commonplace. He gives us something we've seen a million times in the one form in which we think we've never seen it before. He's able to do this, I think, because he's an outsider who came to ballet relatively late and for whom tensions and barriers as well as the most magical correspondences exist between ballet's fantasy world and real life. When Robbins is expressing familiar things in ballet terms, as in *Fancy Free* and *Interplay* and *Faun* and *The Cage* and *Moves* and *Dances at a Gathering* and *Mother Goose*, he has a quality of insight like no other choreographer's. No one else gives us these flashing nuggets that all by themselves light up in memory and reactivate whole ballets. It's because alone among major choreographers Robbins has *ideas* about ballet; he conceptualizes while the others move. And he's at his greatest when feeling out the implications of a brilliant conception. When the girl drops her head in *Faun*, she turns away from the direction of the lift and also, we feel, from her usual self. For once, she doesn't look into the mirror (which is to say out at the audience) to see the effect of a movement, she feels it inside. She yields as a woman, not just as a dancer, to the boy's hands on her body. And yet the turning of the head in one direction while the body sails in another is only classical logic; the movement that looks so intimately revealing could have been taught. The gesture calls up the whole disturbing mood of Robbins's ballet because it crystallizes the ballet's discovery of a correspondence between realism and artifice—a correspondence that it was Robbins's genius to arrive at as if it were a natural coincidence, and not something derived from a study of the Nijinsky original. In Nijinsky's ballet, the dancers move in profile, with the feet going straight ahead, either parallel or one behind the other, and the torso twisting to the front. Why they do that is still a question, but in Robbins's *Afternoon of a Faun*, which is about contemporary dancers in a studio, if we think about Nijinsky we find that Robbins answers the question on his own terms. It's because dancers are self-absorbed beings who are always looking in a mirror. Nijinsky's profile stance is modified by Robbins to fit the preoccupied behavior of dancers who, even as they hold and caress each other, constantly look away into a mirror. It's faces front all the time—no getting away from it. If Robbins is proclaiming that Nijinsky's Faun was a direct descendant of his Narcissus, he is persuasive. His ballet is the best critical essay that has ever been composed about *Faune*; it shows conclusively how, by invoking a commonplace of *his* time (what Lincoln Kirstein calls "the Maryinsky's 'Egyptian' style"), and investing it with a novel tension, Nijinsky could have brought off his 1912 explosion. And, of course, the Robbins version is in its own right a masterpiece, which we have admired for more than thirty years.

Last season, Robbins returned to Debussy and the Greek nymphs of Debussy's (and Nijinsky's) period. In its dances for eight women, *Antique Epigraphs* even revived Maryinsky profiling. But this time Robbins had no comment to make. It was merely a pretty world that he showed us—one uncertainly situated in time. Was this the Greece of the Belle Époque, was it the Greece of early American modern dance, or was it the historical, unimaginable *Greece*? The ballet suggested a little of all three. Florence Klotz's gauzy long shifts, cinched under the breasts, made the dancers look heavy—an effect Robbins may have intended (to judge from the weightedness of his choreography) or, then again, may not have (to judge from the toe shoes he had the dancers wear). Sadly, this indecisiveness, which comes from the lack of a vivifying, controlling idea, is typical of Robbins's work these days. If he—and Klotz—had come right out and said that these women were suffragists *imagining* themselves Greek, the ballet might have had some flavor.

Robbins and Merce Cunningham are in their middle sixties. Martha Graham will be ninety in May, and she, too, is still producing—at least, her company is still producing, with her advice and consent. As part of the birthday-year celebration, it announced a production of *The Rite of Spring*, to be presented at the State Theater, in costumes by Halston. I went expecting nothing more than a glimpse of the thinking that had allowed Graham to say in press conferences that she was returning "to hallowed and terrifying ground." I assumed she meant the terrain of *Primitive Mysteries* and *El Penitente* and *Dark Meadow*, although some press releases had her saying what could not easily be believed: "Dancing the role of the Chosen One in the 1930 revival of the Nijinsky ballet was a turning point in my life." (It was Massine's, not Nijinsky's, choreography that was being revived, and Graham's clashes with the choreographer on that occasion are still legend.) No, by "hallowed and terrifying ground" I hoped that Graham was speaking of her own turf, on which she would now erect not—preposterous expectation— another work of art but perhaps a sign or two of her understanding of the primitive rituals of the Southwest. I imagined her dusting off old notebooks and reading aloud to her dancers; these notes would, of course, be similar to the anthropological jottings in *The Notebooks of Martha Graham*, published a decade ago.

And she may well have given readings, and she may have dictated every gesture in the rehearsals and supervised every stitch of Halston's costumes. The results are still as trifling as we had every reason to fear they would be, and they are inauthentic besides. The outlines of Stravinsky's libretto are vaguely impressed upon a locale that could be Santa Fe, Samoa, or Haiti. The Chosen One, topless in a black sarong, is trussed up in thick white cable, then immediately untrussed. She thrashes and dies under the Shaman's gorgeous cape. More cloth is flung down, and that's the rite. Even if the rhythms of the music were deployed in the choreography, even if the dancers were stronger than they are, the ritual drama of catharsis could not occur, because the Graham technique—that supreme instrument of theatrical catharsis—has now faded to the point of ineffectuality. The only note of authenticity is an occasional reminder of old Graham dances: in the relationship of the Shaman and the Chosen One there are echoes of St. Michael and Joan of Arc, and some of the choral episodes recall *Dark Meadow*.

I suppose it is something that a production as large, long, and expensive as this can actually be put on by a woman in her ninetieth year. That it is devoid of content will not disturb people whose knowledge of Graham's work begins with her Halston period. Older pieces on the program do not show it up, since there's scarcely anything left of them. It used to be that only those in which Graham herself formerly danced were being misrepresented. Now, because of lobotomized performing, we're losing works like *Seraphic Dialogue* and *Embattled Garden*— works that Graham never appeared in. The stage of the State Theater, twice too large for such pieces, does its own job of burying them. In *Primitive Mysteries*, the dancers had to take about fifteen steps to get from the wings to the center of the stage. Because they exit and re-enter so many times, *Primitive Mysteries* became a piece about walking. (It was, however, the most scrupulously rehearsed of the old works.) The audience was justifiably puzzled by these curiosities. As soon as the curtain rose on an *Andromache's Lament* or an *Acts of Light*—pieces made on a big scale in the eighties and furnished in posh fabrics and gilt—you felt the atmosphere change. These new synthetic products have nothing to say, but they project. People relax and start to applaud. The worst is *Phaedra's Dream*, in which Phaedra and a male rival (designated The Stranger) compete for her stepson Hippolytus. It carries the anonymity and the bombast of the eighties to a new level of violation. The action, which takes place in Noguchi's old set for *Alcestis*, is filled with a kind of coarse realism—lurchings and couplings and evil stares—that I have never seen before on Graham's stage. I'd thought nothing could be worse than the caricature of Graham exercises which appears in *Acts of Light*—all preening postures and flaccid dynamics. *Phaedra's Dream* is worse than a distortion—it's a sham.   —*March 26, 1984*

Slouching Toward
Byzantium

All dances have an inner time and an outer time. The outer time is the tempo of the steps, usually set by the music; the inner time is the rate at which meanings accumulate. A slow-moving dance can develop an amazing impetus in its internal logic. The great classical adagios from Petipa to Balanchine are all much faster— and seem to last longer—than the time they take to happen. If the impetus is timed exactly to the speed of the music in an adagio, the dance will drag. But to know how to time dance impetus correctly you have to understand all the variables it is made of—qualities of scale and pressure and momentum and repetition— and understand them, too, from the audience's point of view. The choreographer has to be able to see continuing configurations, just as we do, and he has to know their worth as an image of human experience. The idea that a human image springs from planned disparities in timing is very different from the idea that it can be imposed. The difference is sharply illustrated by a piece of Paul Taylor's— the *Duet from "Lento"*—that is on the programs this season at the City Center. When he made the duet, in 1964, Taylor didn't have the sense of inner and outer time that he has now; his interest was all in the ingenious involvements of the man's big body and the woman's small one as they make shapes in space, and the shapes are all timed to the steady beat of a largo by Haydn. The dance is a monolith, with no quickening inner drive. We can't care about all this "caring"; it doesn't look real. Nowadays, though Taylor makes slow duets that are much more interesting, he still doesn't specialize in them. He's much more inclined to extend his mastery of inner and outer time to whole pieces. In *Sunset* he builds a high-velocity drama behind an almost static façade. The actual velocity of *Mercuric Tidings* is belied by its unmercurial imagery. This helter-skelter piece may be the fastest that Taylor has ever created, and its inner consistency is as calm and smooth and unchanging as the surface of a pond. It's this consistency that Taylor celebrates as he prods the dancers along at top speed and sustains and sustains and sustains that calm at the center of the whirlwind.

Different again—very different—is Taylor's newest piece. It's neither slow with a fast inner tempo, like *Sunset*, nor fast with a slow inner tempo, like *Mercuric Tidings*. It's fast inside and out. It's also compulsively watchable from start to finish and very nearly incomprehensible. Before I try to describe it, let me say that I saw three performances and pieced things together afterward, often revising a previous impression. A description seems to nail down meanings. Barring some obvious passages like the opening half of the first scene and the whole of the second scene, the happenings I describe are only things I thought I saw when I came to think about them later. Normally, Taylor's meanings hit me and expand inside like dumdum bullets. This time, I wasn't sure I was being hit at all.

Taylor calls the piece ". . . *Byzantium*," after Yeats's "Sailing to Byzantium." As an inscription he uses the poem's last line—"Of what is past, or passing, or to come"—and he divides his choreography into three corresponding sections. "Passing" comes first. The scene is America today. The dancers are young Americans in jeans and shorts and sleazy dresses, and they're galvanized by sexual energy, bounding along in fever heat, doing wild disco dances, leaping and twisting one at a time or writhing en masse on the floor. Taylor's attitude, as always when he shows us lewd-and-lascivious, is dispassionate. The point this time is that everyone flails away individually, in alien rhythms, without taking on anyone else. The writhing clump on the floor is made up of couples who grope each other indiscriminately. One boy seems to have turned into a robot against his will. (Or maybe he's a prisoner of rigid beliefs—the meaning isn't clear.) A girl, completely isolated, offers a cry of protest. But both boy and girl are seized and swallowed up in the mass shuffle. All this movement passes across the front of the stage—it's literally a passing parade. Before the crowd disappears, however, one tall woman makes a solo crossing followed by a young man bearing an ecclesiastical banner; like the robot, she assumes a rigidly beatific pose as the crowd lifts her and carries her away. The "icons" may be Taylor's notations on the survival of belief in a secular—no, a profane—society. These people are so crudely self-gratifying they profane their own bodies. The religious images, fleet-ingly seen, are all that connect this scene to the next, "Or Past," which is different in every respect. The lights come up on four figures ranged one behind another staircase fashion in the deep center of the stage. Linked close together, never unlinking, they tilt this way and that like the fingers of one hand. They wear silk chasubles of purple, blue, green, and magenta; the drapes, the little bald heads, the stylized hands recall the ranks of saints stacked up in Byzantine mosaics. They are also birdlings in a nest, opening their mouths skyward and being fed from above. The play of arms and hands, with palms extended stiff or curved with beaked fingers, is birdlike. One thinks of the Holy Ghost, of Holy Communion. This scene, with its monocellular development, unfolds in "Or to Come" into a spectacle of big-scale unison movement. The four priests preside over metrical drills performed by the inhabitants of a futuristic golden city, who wear gold-mesh versions of the first scene's 1984 sleaze. In this scene, which brings Gibbon and Orwell together with a clash like a pair of cymbals, Taylor is at his most ambivalent. The authoritarian drills, in which the dancers stomp out contrapuntal rhythms, are also an expression of group ecstasy, of blissed-out perfection. But—to quote from the Yeats poem that may really have inspired Taylor—"Things fall apart; the centre cannot hold." If this is the New Byzantium, as Byzantium was the New Rome, it is strangely similar to the Old America of hedonism and anomie. Or is it? The piece ends with fanaticism sliding into anarchy. Or does it?

Taylor's technical virtuosity these days approaches a kind of genial cynicism. He's always fun when he's tossing himself weird challenges: he works with the utmost seriousness, and yet he's cockily self-confident, letting chips fall where they may. He expends a tremendous amount of technical muscle on ". . . By-zantium." But he's not just using his technique for the hell of it; one understands that he wants to say something, too, and that this something stems from convictions to which he has already given a great deal of thought. In ". . . Byzantium" he isn't going for one of those unpremeditated utterances that glimmer in the cross-fire of music, décor, and dance. Not that the unpremeditated Taylor—Nightshade is the current extreme example—lacks conviction. But having one's thoughts or-ganized by one's material is different from having them carried by unexpected confluences in unforeseen directions, and Taylor doesn't often risk the totally unforeseen. Nor does he often speak from prior certitudes. I don't want to ex-aggerate the a-priori aspect of ". . . Byzantium" or to make it seem—because it is a baffling piece—that Taylor is out to tease us with cryptic meanings. The point is that ". . . Byzantium" is neither one of the "dark" pieces that he occasionally dredges up out of precognitive musings on a subject nor one of those more common miracles of his that jell somewhere along the way and give us both the Taylor who seeks and the Taylor who divulges meaning. Watching these pieces—they range from Nightshade to Sunset and Runes and Cloven Kingdom—is a little like overhearing Taylor talking to himself, constantly questioning his material and trying to catch himself unawares. The provisional quality that emerges from this inquiring process is without slipperiness. Like the great dancer he used to be, Taylor can throw himself far off balance without losing his center.

". . . *Byzantium*" represents a different sort of Taylor adventurism. It seems as schematic and sealed as *Le Sacre du Printemps (The Rehearsal)*, which isn't being done this season, or *Big Bertha*, which is (on programs with ". . . *Byzantium*"). But it isn't nearly as adroit as those two pieces; the parts that are supposed to lock together don't quite fit—the pattern doesn't come clear. This time, what's provisional about the work is the very idea of a scheme, and that's the thing that is never in question in the *Sacre* piece or in *Big Bertha*. The Scheme, by enclosing with ever tightening logic a whole series of incongruities, is what gives those works their incomparable dreadful fascination. In ". . . *Byzantium*," the Scheme is given to us sequentially, in three movements, and not even when the ballet is over are we in possession of all the pieces of the puzzle. In *Big Bertha* and the *Sacre*, we are given all the pieces at once, and we watch in astonishment as Taylor fills in his picture. In ". . . *Byzantium*," we have a triptych and—what is almost as unusual for Taylor—a musically nonpropulsive, sonically atmospheric score: three orchestral pieces by Edgard Varèse. (Strange to think that this most perplexing Taylor work could have been induced by the Varèse centennial.) This music allows Taylor to do just about anything he wants to do—it even lets him impose a rhythm when he needs one. And the triptych, which lets him deal with one part of his subject at a time, postpones the effect of incongruously juxtaposing contemporary America and "the holy city of Byzantium." We don't know where we've been till we know where we're going. William Ivey Long's costumes and David Gropman's scenery furnish the necessary associations. (Gropman's strips and panels suggest the Stars and Stripes, then mosaics and marble walls.) The piece left me feeling that I understood the separate sections and the connections between them well enough, but I wasn't satisfied that all Taylor's cards were on the table. Somehow, in using these materials he's playing with less than a full deck. Varèse's glittery metallic turbulence is right for the *idea* of Byzantium, but it doesn't keep Taylor going places; he has to provide his own incitements. This means that when we get an inkling of what's going on we may get it only from the choreography, not from the choreography working together with the music. It also means that Taylor, with so little to pace him or to force him to recapitulate, goes too far too fast.

This happens in the third scene: right at the last second the authoritarian structure looks about to topple, but how this comes about I can't say. There appears to be a lone dissident among the citizens of Byzantium ("The best lack all conviction"), and there's a tall, thin, gold-robed idol—a Pope or an Emperor—who's borne aloft and speaks in inscrutable gestures and *seems* to be a false prophet and actually is played by the woman who in the first scene crosses the stage in front of the ecclesiastical banner. When an indiscriminate orgiastic clump of Byzantines rolls across the ground upstage, it even seems that there's going to be a return to the beginning. Taylor stops short of this, and I don't think he succeeds in planting the cyclical idea. We have to infer it from the logic of incident. That other, fantasy logic has escaped his control. ". . . *Byzantium*" winds up a self-propelled piece with an inner rhythm so fast it's incoherent.

And yet such is Taylor's power of incantation that I would be happy to see it all again. In effect, it's like sitting through a fiery sermon filled with obscure language that is nevertheless rhetorically compelling. Sitting through *Nightshade* is like tapping into somebody else's nightmare; you *know* there's no understanding it. *Nightshade*, which is disembowelled Victorian pornography, is being revived this season with one role recharacterized. Raegan Wood dances the same steps that Carolyn Adams used to do, but she's costumed as a child in a frilly pink satin dress. The revision deepens the lurking tone of prurience; it also changes the balance of forces in the drama. Carolyn Adams wore African primitive dress and played a kind of nature spirit reminiscent of Rima the Bird Girl. When she perched on the shoulder of Elie Chaib, who wore—and still wears—a black net face mask and wild witch-doctor hair, she seemed to be his familiar. Raegan Wood seems to be part of the crazy white polite society whose repressions churn through the piece; she becomes another of Chaib's intended victims, like the ever prostrate white-skinned blonde danced by Karla Wolfangle. And the change brings the underlying comedy of the piece closer to the brackish surface. When *Night-shade* was first done, five years ago, it appeared to be an abstract dance drama, bizarre but perfectly serious. Perhaps it was the Victorian costumes that made me think of Martha Graham's *Deaths and Entrances*; perhaps it was the random, inexplicable character of the action. Taylor does have a talent for abstract drama, but in *Nightshade* its organizing principle is aleatoric. The Graham ballet is, or was, great *symbolic* drama. (I speak without reference to the shabby production given by the Graham company last month.) Its outcome, arranged to coincide with the climax of Graham's own performance, was controlled and aimed at from the beginning. I'm not excluding the possibility that Graham's performance, which I saw only once, contained an aleatoric element; and the Graham repertory certainly has its share of dream logic. But Taylor's repertory, seen this year so soon after Graham's, does not look as closely connected to hers as it once did. Without a doubt, he rather than Graham herself or any of her other heirs is the choreographer who has moved Graham theatre ahead in the second half of this century. However, it takes an unusual Taylor piece like ". . . *Byzantium*" to point out the affiliation.   —*April 9, 1984*

The Regions in Brooklyn

This year, the School of American Ballet is fifty years old; George Balanchine, whose idea it was, would have been eighty. Toward the end of March, Pacific

Northwest Ballet made its local début at the Brooklyn Academy. It is the newest of the many companies that are being raised around the country on a foundation of Balanchine's teachings, and, as its Brooklyn performances proved, it is also one of the strongest. In only seven years, two former New York City Ballet soloists, Kent Stowell and Francia Russell, have managed to build a company in Seattle that can put on an easeful and glowing *Chaconne* with two different casts. The only other regional company that does *Chaconne* is San Francisco Ballet, now fifty-one years old. Pacific Northwest Ballet has thirteen other Balanchine works—in Brooklyn it also danced an adventurous *Four Temperaments*—and a third of its thirty-one dancers come from the School of American Ballet. But it also has a school of its own, which is already turning out dancers. Boys as well as girls are impressive; some of the girls are special. The school has a nice line in tall, swift blondes with slim, strikingly accomplished legs and feet. Balanchine cultivated the type; here it seems to grow wild.

Chaconne brought on nearly the whole company and all the blondes. In the prologue, nine supers lent by the School of American Ballet appeared as the muses. The production, staged by Rosemary Dunleavy, is a replica of New York City Ballet's, with costumes by Karinska. Dunleavy has allowed minor adjustments in some of the more difficult steps—for example, a modified fondu in the attitude held by the secondary soloist as she pirouettes, catching her partner's hands behind her back. In a company that is already trained in the basics of Balanchine style, such adjustments do no harm—are, in fact, barely noticeable. The two principal roles were danced in a mixture of styles that reflect European as well as American training. Irena Pasaric, from Yugoslavia, imposed orthodoxy on the Farrell role, dancing with brio but without risk. Wade Walthall launched himself gamely in a rougher, smaller-scaled version of Peter Martins's steps. Walthall studied at S.A.B. and performed with European companies. Two days later, I saw the part done by Michael Auer, a Viennese who studied at the Vienna State Opera and has performed in other American companies. Auer is taller, rangier, and easier than Walthall in the solos, but he does most of the élancé steps conventionally upright, without the space-spanning avidity that defines them. Deborah Hadley, American-born and bred, was his ballerina and would probably be ballerina material at New York City Ballet. Without being Suzanne Farrell, she was entirely Balanchinean, and her *Chaconne* was rich in rhythmic intelligence, in plastique, in dynamic variety.

These are incipient company virtues. They bolster the Balanchine "look"—the open backs, the high, fully energized legs, the speedy toes with the body's weight centered right over them. Though technical standards are not uniformly modelled on Balanchine's, everyone moves expansively, with fluid positional changes and clean multiple pirouettes. And everyone phrases musically; at least, everyone did here and in *Dumbarton Oaks*, an elegant, sporty piece in the Balanchine-Stravinsky vein, devised by Stowell. The choreography is full of dangerous, amusing accents that carry one along despite a loss of momentum toward the end. Stowell's *Pas de Deux Campagnolo*, to Verdi, is less musically acute, and his *Ravenna*, to Rossini, is far less so. The first of these two "Italian" pieces evokes the whimsical style of another of Stowell's mentors, Lew Christensen. *Ravenna*, overlong, overpopulated, and overactive, never decides whether it wants to be simple and folksy, like *Napoli*, or ironic, like *Donizetti Variations*. It is broken into many featured bits, so that everyone gets a chance to perform. As a company showcase, it tells you everything about the dancers except how well they can sustain the intelligibility of classical continuity—only the Balanchine works tell you that.

Stowell is a conscientious, unfocussed choreographer, far from dull. The scarcity of academic-classical choreographers good enough to challenge his dancers must be apparent to him. So must the necessity of keeping a balanced repertory. *Ramifications* and *Lento, a Tempo, e Appassionato* are not by Balanchine or Stowell, but that is all that can be said for them. Rudy van Dantzig's clammy sentimentalities in the first piece and Vicente Nebrada's gaudy acrobatics in the second are the kind of thing that does not extend but only undermines the prestige of a classical company. Understandable in its way in Stowell's commissioning of *Cascade* from Lucinda Childs. (Childs had worked with ballet dancers of the Paris Opéra.) Named for the mountain range outside Seattle, *Cascade* is the standard Childs cross-weave of faintly differentiated steps going on until the music (*Octet*, by Steve Reich) stops. The fact that the steps are done on point, in optimum scale, and with a precision that keeps the distinctions between them clear ought to make a difference, but it doesn't. It's just another one of the distinctions-without-a-difference that I find Childs's work to be full of. Like van Dantzig and Nebrada, Childs gets more value from the company's dancers than she gives, but even these good dancers can't give expression to material as limited as this.

Francia Russell's version of *The Four Temperaments* has the old finale, with the Temperaments assembling but not melding in the pumping-heart image that Balanchine created in 1977. I thought I preferred the old choreography until a sudden blank in the middle of the stage made me see otherwise. In the Theme section, the performance was not as smoothly filled out as N.Y.C.B.'s, but it was a live interpretation, not a memorization of things done at N.Y.C.B. That goes for the rest. The way Adam Miller danced the Melancholic variation underscored its links to Apollo's solos—something we should be able to see more often and think about. (Not that the links show Apollo to be melancholic, or Melancholic to be Apollonian; they show Balanchine to be economical.) Miss Pasaric made a sincere attempt at the style of Sanguinic, and Walthall was persuasively exotic and self-absorbed in Phlegmatic. The brightest performance was Lucinda Hughey's Choleric. One of the homegrown tall blondes, she's willowy but fleet, with amazing control in intricate allegro steps, and she restores details to the role which have been missing at N.Y.C.B. for years. Can there really have been gargouillades in Choleric as well as in Sanguinic? It makes sense in a ballet in which all steps recur and all systems are nourished by a common bloodstream. It's good to be reminded by a whole new company how commonsensical and gutsy Balanchine's choreography is, and how beautiful it makes dancers look when they open themselves to it. This company would rather not be known as a New York City Ballet satellite; it has ties to San Francisco Ballet, too. Above all, it wants to develop a style of its own. Well, that is what it is doing. But until it can find choreography to match its standards in schooling it would do well to cling to Balanchine. There's nothing the matter with being a satellite to the right planet.

At the other end of Flatbush from the Brooklyn Academy, Brooklyn College also books American ballet companies. This spring, it began an arrangement with Atlanta Ballet which will present this oldest of regional companies locally at least once a year. Longer seasons than the customary single weekend would also be welcome; the company gets to do only one program. This year, though, it did bring its own orchestra, under John Naskiewicz. (Pacific Northwest Ballet had its music director, Stewart Kershaw, conduct the Brooklyn Philharmonic.) Only one score, consisting of New Wave jazz, was on tape.

In the Atlanta Ballet one sees the same strong classical foundation as in the Pacific Northwest company—Robert Barnett, the artistic director, is also a former Balanchine soloist. But he enforces a more academically cautious approach to performance. Everything is clean and correct in Barnett's *Arensky Dances*; the dancers come on sedately two by two and show steps as if to a critical drillmaster. In the jazz piece, Lynne Taylor-Corbett's *Appearances*, they cut loose, but only to strut and pose like fashion models. *Palm Court*, by Peter Anastos, gives them a real chance. Meetings and perambulations in a palm-bedecked hotel salon lead to a suite of palmy-days dances: waltz, mazurka, rag, czardas, and so on. These are done to teatime favorites played by the salon orchestra. A scenario (by David Daniel) links the dances and hints at the ballet's genre. Anastos's choreography is absorbingly varied in shape, tone, and accent, and the dancers responded willingly but incompletely. They danced, but they did not perform. Besides their fine training, the Atlantans have a natural reserve, a kind of soft-spokenness, that is very winning; it's a feature of their style. But inhibition is not stylish. That thread of a scenario seemed to get in their way; even the broadest generic conceptions—like Yesteryear, the Continent, Young Officer, Merry Widow, Deb— were left to the imagination of the audience. There were some exceptions. In the czardas, Radenko Pavlovich's furtive and impassioned gestures as he tried to seduce Mia Monica were very funny, but her lack of reaction deflated the joke. The czardas is exceptional because it asks for mime. Most of the numbers are straight dancing, and straight classical dancing at that—the genre flavor is in the timing. Shannon Mitchell, Michael Tipton, and Lorita Travaglia in the ragtime trio caught the point. The others—handsome, talented dancers—were all too stiff.

Anastos is one of the few academic-classical choreographers who are willing to free-lance. It seems that every time I go out to Brooklyn College to see a visiting company I see one of his ballets, and each is better than the last. *Palm Court* is a richer, more stimulating piece than *Table Manners*, which the Cincinnati Ballet did last year. But *Table Manners*, in which social manners and dance manners are compared, had lovely things in it, among them a "Pygmalion" pas de deux with the man arranging the woman's poses as in a game of statues. Anastos is an in-demand choreographer in the regions because he works considerately with dancers. I think he may have overestimated the abilities of Atlanta Ballet simply because as an institution it has been around so long. It is at the moment a very young company; its thirty-nine dancers are relatively inexperienced. In the upper echelons one finds more dancers with foreign training; there's a foreign-native ratio very nearly the same as in Pacific Northwest Ballet. Some half-dozen members of the Atlanta's foreign contingent are Filipinos, including two of the four principals, Maniya Barredo and Nicolas Pacana. He is a seasoned stylist in the Baryshnikov mold; she is a skilled, somewhat flashy technician. Though Pacana is the softer, more ingratiating performer, neither dancer personifies the company's style, and their American opposite numbers, Susan Clark and Michael Job, have yet to arrive. It's impossible not to feel positively hopeful that they will—that Atlanta's great days are just around the corner. An example of what the company can do now is the production of *Paquita* set for it by the European choreographer-coach Hans Meister from his studies at the Kirov. Barredo and Pacana led the cast, but the show belonged to the soloists and the corps, all female. Assimilating Petipa at an early stage is the job of any classical organization. What these young women showed was something rare and truthful: that the essence of Petipa is feminine, and femininity is—or used to be—the canonical essence of the classical dance. Not that this *Paquita* looked old-fashioned. It managed to renovate old-school classicism and yet preserve the charm of antique steps. The quaintness that clings to the ballet's technique is something the dancers feel comfortable with, and though I'm a little uneasy about that, I realize it may be a condition of progress. Nearly every woman who had a variation danced it with freshness and individuality. There rest the hopes of the future.

Equinox, a new piece, crowned the Paul Taylor company's exciting season at the City Center. Taylor has been using Romantic music lately—here he uses Brahms's Quintet in F Major, Opus 88—and his dance architecture is changing. It's as if architecture and ornament were becoming ambiguously fused. As you watch a piece, it's more difficult to distinguish between what is essential to the plan and what only colors and decorates it. So the ballets present a lively challenge to one's powers of perception and everything in them becomes interesting. *Equinox* makes me think of an Edwardian tennis party with undercurrents of strained eroticism. At times, the erotic tensions are in the foreground, but even then they have the aspect of formal play. The formality of the piece relates it to Taylor's "baroque" ballets, which have music by Bach and Handel and Boyce. But these are comparatively plain structures. *Equinox* is one of Taylor's pleasant and deceptively placid-looking formal gardens. Enter, and look out.

Linda Kent and Kate Johnson are the two principal women in it. Johnson is a newcomer to the company who immediately established her place and captivated the audience. Kent has been there since 1975 and is just now coming into her ascendancy. They are both small women, but Johnson's movement has the voluminous, round and full tone that is normally found in larger women, while Kent is flat and knobby. Johnson's role in *Equinox* gives her a long solo that shows the beauty of her legato phrasing and sets her apart from the others—makes her more sensitive, more of an idealist. She ought to be the heroine of the ballet. Kent is used mostly in slow acrobatics; I don't recall that she has a solo, and in one of her protracted backbends Taylor chooses to highlight not the backbend but the way Elie Chaib reaches up from the floor to support her. I don't know why it is—I've never particularly liked Kent's dancing—but both times I saw the piece it was Kent I remembered when it was over. Something about the way she has been projecting herself (or maybe not trying to project herself) this season, combined with the strange new structural emphasis in Taylor's work, seems to have brought her to my attention and made her haunt me.   —*April 23, 1984*

The Search for "Cinderella"

Mikhail Baryshnikov has brought his *Cinderella* to the Metropolitan after a four-month break-in tour. Box-office has been pretty much what it was on the road: big. The most expensive production in the history of American Ballet Theatre, *Cinderella* has already recouped its costs four times over. Baryshnikov achieved this success without dancing in the ballet himself. Apparently, the public has trusted him to put on a show it wants to see—a show called *Cinderella*. But is *Cinderella* a hit? Hits in ballet are not made of money. From the moment that *Cinderella* was announced, Baryshnikov's artistic prestige was on the line, and now that the financial returns are in, it still is. The out-of-town critics wrote reviews balancing the show's flaws and merits. In New York, the press was mostly negative, and also captious, inattentive, unjust. Baryshnikov doesn't consider himself much of a choreographer and has said so. The New York critics seemed determined to take him at his word and go him one better: he's not only not a choreographer, he's a vandal. His victim is the beautiful, beloved fairy tale of *Cinderella*. He and his accomplices, Peter Anastos and Santo Loquasto, have drained the innocence and the magic out of it and turned it into a heartless burlesque.

In mounting such a line of attack, the critics have made two mistaken assumptions. One is that the ballet they want is the ballet Sergei Prokofiev wrote. (Does the public share that assumption? We shall see.) The other is that Baryshnikov and company have deliberately set out to undermine the romantic and sentimental values of the fairy tale. Prokofiev's ballet, written in Stalin's Russia during the forties, is not a conventional, sweet storybook romance; it is a brooding, disjointed affair. The domestic scenes are broad farce; the court scenes are farce and satire; and the love scenes are emotionally overscaled, as if by exaggerating their passion Prokofiev could make Cinderella and the Prince transcend a world they obviously don't belong to. The out-of-this-world aspect of the love duets has its negative reflection in the ballroom music. Cinderella's home life isn't bad enough; her social life is characterized by sour tunes and clashing tonal colors. The sinister "fate" music builds out of the ballroom waltzes in such a way as to suggest that the heroine is imperiled by the society she finds at court, not by her own forgetfulness. Prokofiev's musical imagination in *Cinderella* is to my mind livelier and less neurotic than in *Romeo and Juliet*, but at times he seems to be casting Cinderella and the Prince as star-crossed lovers. The crescendos in the love duets are so huge they run the risk of alienating Cinderella from her own aspirations. Love on these terms isn't something she has dreamed about—it's a whole new reality, troubling in its size and importance. But then going to the ball isn't wish fulfillment. What girl could hope for happiness as the princess of this crass, petit-bourgeois kingdom, with its dinky little court? And doesn't Prokofiev's sarcasm infect the love duets? Listening to the score several times over at the Met, I found that what used to seem full-throttle emotion sounded more like bombast: a dream of pure love is inflated with hot air. The producer of *Cinderella* has no choice but to go along with it, hoping by some ingenuity of staging and choreography to convey a sense of grandeur and poetic isolation. The Baryshnikov production doesn't do this; its effects are too modest. But it isn't trying to drain the ballet of romance—only of pomposity. If Baryshnikov does in fact undermine the spirit of a fairy tale, his chief accomplice is Sergei Prokofiev.

Prokofiev affronts the child in us who wants to see Cinderella enter the same beautiful world of privilege her sisters are part of. The sisters are ugly, and so is their world. As an alternative to materialistic greed, the scenario proposes the wealth of nature. Birds, flowers, the changing seasons are represented in a divertissement presided over by the Fairy Godmother, and Cinderella goes to the ball not as a social-climbing impostor but as Rousseau's naturally good human being in search of a non-brutalizing environment. She doesn't find it. (The Fairy Godmother should have known that, but she's naïve.) Instead, Cinderella finds another child of nature—the Prince—who, even as she, has miraculously escaped environmental conditioning, and the two of them are united in the starry idealism of a world to come. This fatuous moralism is what passes for a fairy tale in Prokofiev's version. Half the time, he doesn't seem to believe it himself. The Western version of *Cinderella*, with its practicality, its fantasy of social conquest and revenge, and its vindication of the individual, can't be imposed on the Soviet fable without considerable sleight of hand. If Cinderella is made to dream of love and beauty and good times and to find them all at the ball, then Prokofiev's satire of a corrupt society is out of place. If she doesn't find these things at the ball, there's no point in her going there in the first place, especially when she's given no moment in which to awaken from her delusion. We're supposed to believe in a differently motivated Cinderella, purer than the one we know. Baryshnikov and Anastos, who together choreographed the ballet, have been criticized for making Cinderella the scullery maid too cheerful. She dances contentedly with her cat instead of moping by the hearth. Taxed beyond endurance by her stepsisters, she stuffs their dirty laundry in the oven. I find this conception of the heroine the one instance of compatibility between the traditional and the Soviet versions. A Cinderella who doesn't accept her lot meekly yet doesn't waste time repining is sturdy enough to resist worldly temptations. She'll marry the Prince not because he's the Prince but because she loves him. She'll deserve the title of Princess because she really is one and knows it. (Actually, she's Mary Pickford, whom Russians of Prokofiev's generation adored.)

The Baryshnikov-Anastos-Loquasto production doesn't want to change the Soviet *Cinderella* so much as it wants to make it more agreeable. I wrote about Loquasto's décor when I reviewed the première in Washington last winter. Little has changed, though Tharon Musser's lighting has been redone to give off warmth. The aluminum-foil backdrop that stays in place for all three acts was the one feature of the set which I didn't understand then, and I still can't understand it, even though now in the second act it has a coppery glow and in the third act it is punctured by stars. Of course, Loquasto's designs are the first thing you see, and they are anything but sweetly pretty; they're in fact the key to the ideological style of the whole production. How to satirize luxury without violating standards of good design or insulting the taste of the audience: that was the problem, and Loquasto has handled it gracefully for the most part. He has received little credit. Nearly every review has either commended the production's Trump Tower opulence or bridled at "glitz." The problem faced by the choreographers was no less difficult. Inexperience, impatience, unruliness show in their work. But not bad taste, cynicism, profligacy, lack of intelligence. If anything, Baryshnikov and Anastos have been too intelligent, too tasteful. In the Ugly Sisters' scenes in Act I, their touch is light, but the pacing is slam-bang, as if buffoonery were something that needed to be got through as quickly as possible. In this respect, the production is light-years away from the Frederick Ashton–Robert Helpmann scenes in the Royal Ballet's *Cinderella*. These were deliberate, unhurried clowns, and funnier for it. They were also two distinctly different people. A.B.T.'s Sisters are different, but not different enough. At this speed, they can't get much character distinction out of the dressing up and primping scenes. Instead of being fussy and fastidious as only female impersonators can be, they're nervous, squalling prima donnas too much of the time. Yet they dance well; the pas de trois with the Dancing Master is a real business of getting up on point and into arabesque. We'd like to see more of the Sisters at the ball—there's a place for them to pop up in the mazurka— but Baryshnikov and Anastos rein them in. They don't even let us see what the Sisters might make of Cinderella's appearance as the belle of the ball. (If they don't recognize her, we ought to see that they don't.)

In a story ballet, story points have to be brought out at every opportunity. Not enough happens at this ball, and what does happen tends to be underplayed. When, for example, the Sisters enter, one of them falls down the stairs. Huffily, she refuses assistance. Then she notices that someone else is wearing the same gown she has on. Two blows before she even gets in the door! The trouble is, the audience sees only the first blow. It's a performance slip of a kind that occurs often. We don't really register Cinderella's dreaming in the first act—she takes so little time over it. The moment is there in the choreography; it's up to the dancer to frame it—a closeup, as it were. Earlier, Cinderella's scene with her father is just roughed in. There are no mime details to convey that the picture he shows her is of her mother, that it *is* a picture, and not a mirror, and so forth.

The production gives us a conception of Cinderella but not a living character. This may be one reason we forget about her so quickly when the Prince comes on in the second act. Suddenly, he takes over, and it becomes his ballet. As in *The Sleeping Beauty* and *Giselle* (as Baryshnikov plays those classics), love transforms a playboy. There are few things in the ballet more genuinely romantic than the Prince's single-minded search through the kingdom for the owner of the slipper. I suspect that if this production is gratefully remembered it will be for its handling, witty as well as romantic, of a sequence that is usually cut. The Prince visits the home of the Bourgeois Gentilhomme, where he is besieged by three rapacious daughters, in waltz time. He goes to the garden of *Le Nozze di Figaro*, Act IV, where he has an assignation with a Masked Lady who he hopes is Cinderella. (The ploy is no more cynical than Siegfried's mistaking Odile for Odette.) These conceits that, perhaps undeservedly, relate Prokofiev's ballet to other works of art are effective in more than one way. They give Loquasto relief from the cottage and the castle. They suggest that there's some further dimension to the world of folly and wickedness evoked by the ballet. The idea is not that Prokofiev's satire is on a level with Molière and Beaumarchais but that it's in the same tradition. Has any other production of the ballet been as generous to the composer and his librettist? Ironically, Baryshnikov has had to be generous at Prokofiev's expense. The music that was composed for the travel episode, a trashy montage of exotic scenes, has been replaced by waltzes from *War and Peace* and the film *Lermontov*, which were written at about the same time as *Cinderella*. The fact that this outstanding sequence is an interpolation tells much about the production and its struggle to come to life. The fact, too, that it is an episode in which Cinderella does not figure.

Cinderella and her purity place a great strain on the narrative of the ballet, particularly in the overblown love duets. How shall they be danced? The solution has usually been to import the content of a climactic pas de deux in some other ballet. Ashton's choreography is based, none too persuasively, on *The Sleeping Beauty*. The Konstantin Sergeyev production for the Kirov went right along with the music's suggestion that the lovers were really Romeo and Juliet. In a recent version for the Chicago City Ballet, planned around Suzanne Farrell, Paul Mejia spirited in touchstones from several Farrell roles choreographed by Balanchine. Baryshnikov and Anastos go so far as to switch the order of the duets in Acts II and III, putting the more pompous one last (it sounds as if Cinderella were marrying Alexander Nevsky), but the choreography is vacuous. The woman's role has no repose but also none of the drive that Farrell's Cinderella had or Irina Kolpakova's in the Sergeyev production. We are told no story in these dances, nor can we make one up while we watch. A chance to set up a story is missed in Act II by having Cinderella and the Prince declare their love as soon as they meet. They waltz in and out among the guests, and the dance subsides in a pretty tableau, with the ensemble framing the principals, already deeply in love. They ought really to be only on the threshold; the big pas de deux that comes up a few minutes later brings them over. Prokofiev's pattern here is very much on the lines of Romeo meeting Juliet at the masked ball, contriving to find her in the crowd and dance with her, and only gradually disclosing his fascination with her (not his love—that comes in the balcony pas de deux). By the time the lovers in *Cinderella* get to their all-alone-in-the-night pas de deux, they've already said it. This isn't why the pas de deux is empty; this is why it would take much better choreography not to *seem* empty. The third-act pas de deux is now preceded by a scene in which the Prince unveils Cinderella before her tormentors and they react with appropriate amazement and mortification. The story is thus rounded off and the lovers can be alone to display their technique at no cost to verisimilitude.

There are other such improvements and at least a half hour's worth of deletions. Cinderella's solos are less tepidly Fonteynish. (I accused the choreographers of attempting a link to Margot Fonteyn's Aurora. Ashton attempted it first.) I question the wisdom of retaining an unidentifiable entourage for Cinderella in the ballroom scene. Who *are* these daughters of Denishawn wafting about the premises? What were they to Cinderella in Act I? Why don't they attend her in Act III? An apotheosis has also been left intact in which, to the sweetest music in the score (which the composer marked "Amoroso"), all the characters of the ballet assemble and parade about an empty stage till we get the point that they're no longer characters—the story is over. Like all such built-in company calls, this scene makes the actual curtain calls anticlimactic and puts a damper on applause. But Baryshnikov and Anastos also seem to be offering an image of collective redemption. Are they saying that (1) a hypocritical, ostentatious society doesn't anathematize the individual after all or (2) we can only wish that it didn't? However you take it, it's strange to see a ballet company simply walking or standing still without a single révérence or port de bras. It's daring, but then much about this production is daring. They really should be calling it *Zolushka*—Russian for *Cinderella*. After all, *our* Cinderella isn't in the ballet, and Ballet Theatre happens to have nobody who can make us think so. Maybe the right ballerina could sweep up all the contradictions and soar to glory. There are things that could be done to make the production more worthy of her, should she ever be found. It could be made more dramatic, but it could never become a sweet, simple fantasy. That is not its style.   —*May 21, 1984*

Love-Song Waltzes

Among Balanchine's masterpieces, there are those which are especially prized—not only admired but loved. It is easier to name the ballets than to define the qualities that have earned them this special affection. *Apollo* is loved in a way that its great descendant *Concerto Barocco* is not. I never saw *Cotillon*, but from the way people still talk about this lost ballet of the thirties I recognize it as one of the magically affecting ones, with thematic connections to *La Valse*. It might be supposed that people are more deeply moved by ballets with a story or the circumstances of one, but *La Valse*, though extremely popular, isn't adored and *Divertimento No. 15* is. Balanchine's variety is such that one cannot even put together a theory of what makes people love some of his ballets and only revere others. And his complexity makes it impossible to understand more about the ballets that seize our hearts. They are no more simple, no more explicable, than the others; they are not necessarily warmer or more benign; they are not a genre—*Apollo* is not a "ballet of the sentiments." The lyrical tenderness of *Divertimento No. 15* or of *Serenade* involves something deeper and darker than a play of sentiments, and sometimes it seems that what beguiles us is the mystery that lies behind such seemingly guileless creations. Balanchine is never more inscrutable than when he's wearing his heart on his sleeve. All we can say about these most seductive, most enchanting, most lovable ballets of his is that they stir the feelings in some unfathomable way.

When people talk about *Liebeslieder Walzer*, the hour-long ballet on Brahms's two song cycles, they use almost confessional language, but they also use words like "strange," "haunting," "ineffable." The same adjectives are often applied to *Serenade*, which may be the most beloved Balanchine ballet of all. As dance compositions, *Liebeslieder Walzer* and *Serenade* are lucid, robust, filled with exhilarating invention. But I think the quality that makes them deeply involving emotional experiences comes from something other than sheer dance invention; it comes from happenings that Balanchine's imagination sets up and converts into dances. There exists a kind of raw material that is integrated with the dance pattern, absorbed by the technical language, without ever losing its identity as Balanchine phenomena. I think of the moment in *Serenade* when five girls, holding each other around the waist, form a line and pick their way downstage, one arm lifted to shield their gaze. Later in the piece, a line of girls linked in the same manner bourrées laterally to the center of the stage and kneels; immediately another line, facing the first, appears from the opposite direction. A "phenomenal" moment has been integrated and made to produce a pattern. *Serenade*, set to Tchaikovsky's Serenade for Strings, was Balanchine's first ballet in America. It is easy to imagine him contriving these simple reflexive movements to show inexperienced American dancers how the meagre technical vocabulary they then possessed could be used to build interesting and consequential events on the stage. When, in 1940, Balanchine added the fourth section (the Tema Russo) to the three he had made in 1934, he began it with five girls standing in a row who slowly slide to the floor; each then turns her head and offers her hand to her neighbor. The organic process was continued. This continuity was so important to Balanchine that he made a little ceremony out of the offering of the hands; he didn't just relink the dancers. From the deliberate way the heads are turned and the hands are extended, and from the way the end girl, as deliberately and as graciously, offers her hand to empty space, we can tell that the dancers are saying "Let us go on with *Serenade.*" Pattern is everything.

The Élégie, which Balanchine placed last, broke the pattern. It presented a new and virtually self-contained process and a new movement language—made up almost entirely of pure phenomena. Its link to the previous sections was its opening image: a girl had fallen once before; now another girl is lying in the center of the stage. The ballet continues with what appears to be a drama enacted around the fallen girl. At the end of this brief drama, she falls again, this time in a man's arms. As the man holds her body low to the ground, she rolls over between his hands and dies. Timed to hushed chords in the music, the final collapse and the stillness that follows stun us. In *Liebeslieder Walzer,* in the midst of one of the slow waltzes of the ballroom scene a girl is dipped far backward and held in the same position as the girl in *Serenade.* And, to the leisurely, hammock-like sway of the music, she turns herself completely over in the man's arms, just as if this were a normal thing to do in a dance. *That* stuns us, too. In its new context, the movement expresses a kind of logical continuity that we hadn't foreseen. But we had seen it before.

Serenade will be fifty years old on June 10th. It was given a commemorative performance last month by the School of American Ballet and is on this season's bills of the New York City Ballet. *Liebeslieder Walzer,* half the age of *Serenade,* is being danced again, in a new production, ten years after its last performance in New York. When the two ballets are placed together, as they were one Sunday evening, it is tempting to see cross-references. Offering the hand in *Liebeslieder* is part of the elaborate Victorian etiquette of the ballroom. When the men line up four chairs and the women sit there swinging their arms to the music, we see more pretty behavior, but the fact that the end girl is swinging her arm in the opposite direction, so that she turns toward as well as away from the three others, endows the whole sequence with a meaning that belongs to *Liebeslieder.* In *Serenade,* the end girl's gesture continues the pattern that has created the ballet and aims it into uninhabited space; it lets us see all five girls generically as dancers. In *Liebeslieder,* the end girl by going against the pattern makes her friends and her ballroom space that much more prosaically real.

Balanchine had used the chair business in *Cotillon.* The gesture of shielding the eyes had occurred in that ballet also, in the passage called "The Hand of

Fate." It crops up constantly in Balanchine; it's in *Liebeslieder*. Like the gesture of turning and offering the hand, it probably has its origins in Slavic folk-dancing, but whether Balanchine is quoting a convention or expressing a meaning of his own is not always clear. It isn't clear in *Liebeslieder*, where it becomes almost an emblem of the ambiguity that runs deep throughout the ballet. The gesture of shielding the eyes, performed in a duet by the male partner, seems more conventional when the ballerina is Valentina Kozlova; when it's Kyra Nichols it's as if there were something about her the man didn't wish to know—something sorrowful. In a later waltz, one of those that chill the air of *Liebeslieder* with an impalpable melancholia, the woman "dies": she falls back full length and is carried for several measures by her partner. Yet this moment doesn't recall any of the other swooning falls in the ballet, and it is related only distantly to the "death" in *Serenade*. It's really a *Liebeslieder* phenomenon. *Liebeslieder* has its own organic process, its own dazzling pattern. When we see a woman, clasped by a man, roll completely over, we're more apt to be reminded of the ingenious way another woman ducked out from under a man's arm in an earlier waltz. The snug fit of the women in the men's arms and the easy, surprising things they manage to do there give us a cozy picture. Unlike the communicants in the Orphic mysteries of *Serenade*, these are real women, with big feather beds and servants; they revel in the *Gemütlichkeit* of their salon world. More than any other Balanchine ballet, *Liebeslieder Walzer* is a depiction of manners, but most of the conventional side of that subject is dispensed with in the first ten minutes. After that, it's manners raised to the level of metaphysics. In another of the duets, a woman reclines peacefully on her partner's arm while he hunches over her with his other arm shading her body like the wing of a bird of prey. It's Balanchine in his E. T. A. Hoffmann mood. He loved the charged-up morbid atmosphere of German Romanticism—so much so that, in spelling out his characters' destinies, he created ambiguities. One wonders what he thought of these comfortable young aristocrats: were they half in love with death or just telling ghost stories?

Because we have lost many more significant early works besides *Cotillon*, we will never know how Balanchine's poetic language came into being. But he lived and worked among us long enough to have established his methods of communication. We saw how he adapted this language of his to widely differing musical scores, to exigencies of repertory, to particular dancers. His three great waltz ballets are remarkably unlike each other. *La Valse* is about waltz intoxication, vertigo, and death. *Liebeslieder* is about love. *Vienna Waltzes* is the lore and repertory of the waltz. Of the three, it is *Liebeslieder*, and not *Vienna*, that is the most compendious. These "love-song waltzes," each no more than two or three minutes long, give us the complete anatomization of three-quarter time. Enlarging its subject through the scrutiny of detail, the choreography is never inflexible. It finds polkas and mazurkas buried within waltzes; it performs endless adagio variations on the waltz lullaby. It is a dictionary of movement, with more lifts in the second scene than in all the rest of Balanchine. The variety of *Liebeslieder* is a consequence of the intensity of *Liebeslieder*. In its concentration and intricacy, the ballet surpassed everything that Balanchine had done up to that time, except *Agon* and *Episodes*. It may well have been the pointillistic Webern scores for *Episodes* that conditioned Balanchine's musical technique for *Liebeslieder*, and the succession of unthinkable events in the *Agon* pas de deux may have given him the idea of a duet marathon. Yes, *Liebeslieder* stirs the feelings; it is sensuously, at times voluptuously romantic, and yet—one does not speak of Balanchine's art without speaking paradoxically—it is austere. If he had made it any other way, it would not touch the heart at all.

In the slightly deranged climate created by the Stravinsky and Webern ballets of the fifties, the idea of making a dance to an hour of lieder, all of it in waltz time, did not seem impermissibly mad—just mad enough. There are two books of the Brahms songs, composed five years apart. The first book has eighteen numbers, the second fifteen. Four voices sing, accompanied by four-hand piano. Four couples, in ballroom dress of Brahms's period, dance the first book of songs. The curtain drops and there is a pause. The second book is danced in ballet costume and point shoes; the doors of the ballroom set are thrown open to the night, and the moonlight streams in. Brahms's text was lyrics of dance songs that had been translated into German, of no value as poetry. The choreography pays as little attention to the words as in *Who Cares?* (where they are not sung). For the last song, which is a setting of Goethe, the stage is cleared, and as the music is being performed the dancers return to listen. Gradually, the ballroom recovers its former aspect, with flickering candles and lighted chandelier, and we see that the dancers are dressed as they were in the first scene. When the ballet was new, much was made of its tour-de-force aspects. Balanchine followed Brahms's song sequence exactly. He staged only about a quarter of the numbers as trios, quartets, or double quartets; the rest are duets. He did not try to create drama by switching partners among the four couples. He did not assign special characteristics to the couples. All the drama was to be created by the instantaneous materialization of dance shapes out of musical sounds. All the couples would be at various times merry, sad, tragic, poignant, mysterious, young, old. Part One would be domestic, Part Two theatrical, but—and here a major point has been overlooked in the excitement over the change in atmosphere—neither part would be more or less fantastic than the other. The Balanchinean mixture of fantasy and reality prevails in both sections of *Liebeslieder*, as it does in all his other ballets. Just as he shows us ballet form in social dancing and social dance in ballet, he gives us fantastic emotions in "the ballroom" and heightened realism on "the stage." Everything becomes lighter, higher, larger, and more transparent in Part Two, but the intensity of the love relationship continues, the same as before. Balanchine presents love between men and women not as the signed-and-sealed pact of the traditional pas de deux but as an adventure—open, discontinuous, and unpredictable—and he implies that it is most magical when it is monogamous.

Liebeslieder is the grand apotheosis of the Balanchine pas de deux, and it is fertile territory for any student of Balanchine's view of women. The four women who hold the ballet together are like four planets revolving around each other; the four men are satellites. Originally, the ballerinas were Diana Adams, Melissa Hayden, Jillana, and Violette Verdy—a balanced cast that has been miraculously duplicated in Suzanne Farrell, Patricia McBride, Stephanie Saland, and Kyra Nichols. A second cast, consisting of Maria Calegari, Heather Watts, Judith Fugate, and Valentina Kozlova, is smaller-scaled and more evenly toned. In fact, when the ballet began I thought I was seeing four sisters, but soon contrasts began to emerge, and the joys and sorrows of *Liebeslieder* poured forth. In both casts, the women dance wonderfully and are wonderfully partnered. Out of the whole group, which includes two different male casts, only Farrell and McBride have danced their roles before. We cannot help seeing them through the lens of *Vienna Waltzes*, in which Farrell dances the *Rosenkavalier* sequence and McBride re-creates an image of Fanny Elssler. Farrell's *Liebeslieder* role is much lighter, and she compensates for it by playing young. For McBride, no adjustment is necessary; she has grown back into the role but not past it, and she's as exciting to watch as Farrell. The most interesting casting had Nichols and then Kozlova in the Verdy part, to which Balanchine assigned the darkest fantasy as well as some passagework of extraordinary difficulty. It is the Verdy character who "dies" and from whose imminent doom her partner averts his eyes. When Kozlova dances the role, the fantasy is just that—an illusion projected with a touch of coquetry. It's "What if I were dead—would you miss me?" Verdy also played a gifted self-dramatist, whose emotion was no less real for being insincere. With Nichols, though, the tragedy is real. She sees and accepts her fate. She *is* going to die. The success of a revival is measured as much in roles joltingly reinterpreted as in roles smoothly sustained. Nichols is an enlivening jolt. So, in another way, is Kozlova, whom I had expected to see in the relatively uncomplicated role done by Saland or Fugate. New to the company as well as to the ballet, Kozlova has an "accent" that, like Verdy's, is becoming in this part. She resembles Verdy slightly, and Saland, who gives a lovely contralto-toned performance, resembles Jillana. Calegari is far more than a Farrell substitute, and so it goes. What other company could double-cast four such varied and distinguished ballerina roles, reviving after ten years the glow they had when they were new? The choreography was reconstructed by Karin von Aroldingen, who danced the Adams-Farrell role and who has staged revivals in Vienna, London, and Zurich. The remodelled State Theater is a more hospitable setting for the ballet than it used to be, both visually and sonically. The handsome new silver-and-rose ballroom was designed by David Mitchell after a room, which Balanchine is said to have admired, in the Amalienburg pavilion at Nymphenburg, in Munich. The musicians are Jeananne Albee and Gordon Boelzner at the piano, and Karen Huffstodt (soprano), Cynthia Rose (mezzo), James Clark (tenor), and Scott Reeve (bass). The music sounded better to me than ever before.

The revival is also a tribute to Barbara Karinska, who died last year, six months after Balanchine. The pale satin *Liebeslieder* ballgowns and the tulle shadows of those gowns which appear in Part Two were among Karinska's most beautiful and original creations. Like the choreography, they are reproduced in every detail.

—*June 4, 1984*

Life Studies

David Gordon's pieces, dancier and less verbal than they used to be, are fascinating in their devious logic. The new, expanded dance portions are not interludes intended to relieve the spoken portions; they're parallel constructions that soak up the content of the speeches and redistribute it in abstract form. Not that the abstraction is immediately recognizable; at first, you just look and listen delightedly.

Parallel composing in words and movement has been Gordon's method for some time. As a general rule, the intelligibility of movement takes a lot longer to grasp than the intelligibility of words, and one way he has dealt with the disparity is by playing with common everyday speech patterns, using puns and non se-quiturs, and stringing them out casually in rhythmic sentences that slow down thought, bend it, or trip it up. "I hate the word 'out,' " a Gordon character will remark. "It's everything 'in' isn't." A long monologue plays on the colloquial use of "go" for "say." "He goes 'Move over.' I go 'Hold it.' He goes 'Hold what?' I go 'Very funny.' I go 'Ha ha.' He goes 'I'm going.' I go 'Go.' " Lately—in *TV Reel*, in last year's *Trying Times*, and now in *Framework*—Gordon has been experimenting with different qualities of impetus in dance movement. He now has three or four speeds, from the near-stasis of contact improvisation (or its simulation) right through to straight lyrical dancing. He has also developed with the designer Power Boothe a kind of portable décor that is flexible; a Masonite panel or a picture frame made of wooden strips can be different things at different times. It is this highly operative, integral décor that gives *Framework* a controlling metaphor as well as a title.

Framework is an evening's discourse on the way we compartmentalize ourselves as social beings. The panels and picture frames are objectifications of the alien-ation, confinement, or conventionalized rapport that we feel in our daily relations with fellow-workers, lovers, and friends. They objectify good feelings, too, such as closeness in marriage, but the prevailing tone of *Framework* is wry, and its theme of manipulation, at first amusingly plaintive, darkens gradually to end the evening on a note of desperation. Manipulation isn't only a function of the décor. It's a requisite in dancing, where it functions as the inverse of dependency. The choreographer manipulates and depends on his subjects; partners manipulate and depend on each other. Added to the social picture that Gordon gives us—the absurd behavioral patterns, the pressures, the distractions—these purely formal biomechanical situations, played out to the pounding of rock records, take on a certain psychological realism. Gordon is careful not to press meanings on us, but he does keep attacking. It's as if his manipulation theme acquired its malign shadings as a corollary of his versatility.

Gordon has expanded his technique and his subject matter at the same time. He's no longer content to expose the surface ambiguities of limited movement. Moving more, he sees more. In the manifold machinations of *Framework* he sees tokens of the subtle monstrosity of human relations. And since he seems to be adducing evidence from his own life—the life of a harried, hardworking artist— we're invited to see him as part of the monstrous scheme and, ultimately, when he trudges slowly, slowly across a stage filled with indecipherable hubbub, a victim of it. There may be something too notional in all this. When an artist's theme is what it is simply because of the number of ways it finds to express itself, the artist may feel that he hasn't chosen it—it has chosen him. He feels trapped, while we in the audience want to rejoice in what looks to us like a virtuoso performance. The last word in *Framework*, an unspoken pun, is Gordon saying "I was framed." We're showered with droplets of self-commiseration. There was always a moralizing taint to the earnestness with which postmodern dancers went about their anti-technique revolution. I don't think David Gordon believes that technical sophistication is corrupting. But the self-deflating ending of *Framework* may be the last vestige of postmodernist morality in his work.

The emotional ending is surprising, because nothing about *Framework* is facile. The piece, which was produced at the tiny Bessie Schönberg Theatre at Dance Theater Workshop, will be seen later this month in Cambridge. At the Loeb Drama Center, the plan is to stage the deflationary ending with the addition of a giant collapsing frame descending from the flies. This would account for the protractedness of the ending, but would it justify the emotion? *Trying Times* had an epilogue in which Gordon went on trial for his presumption as an artist. These endings are like last-minute apologias; they may reflect Gordon's wish to dominate our reactions to an even greater extent than he does already. Not many choreographers can sustain a whole evening as well as he can, on the basis of his own invention. His collaboration with Power Boothe is a happy one, and Boothe himself may be the best thing that has happened to dance since Jennifer Tipton. But his contribution to Gordon's work has Gordon's sensibility stamped all over it. The boards and frames of *Framework* (which first appeared in *Trying Times*) sound like clichés until you see how Gordon has used them. In the first of several long pas de deux, Gordon and Margaret Hoeffel put a frame against a board and keep the two moving between them like a sliding door. They slip the frame ahead and step into the opening, close it up, and step in on the other side. This develops into variations, no two alike, in which they take turns setting and eluding traps, supporting each other's weight on the board, or disappearing behind it. The "board" pas de deux is offset, in the second act, by a "frame" pas de deux, in which Gordon holds a frame for Valda Setterfield to step through as she executes a fluid adagio in classical style. In neither case do the man and the woman touch.

The nature of the relationship in the first duet is defined by the way each perceives the other's "space." In the Setterfield duet, the frame is her barre, her home, her Platonic halo. Possibilities multiply and crisscross. It is the hoop that her husband the choreographer puts her through even as it is the image of his adoration.

Like every other David Gordon piece, *Framework* teaches us how to see it. It is a total system discharging interior meanings. But it is also a view of real life. We recognize the times and the customs, the clothes, the postures, the lingo. The music sounds as if someone backstage had turned on the local rock station and let the dial drift, so that wisps of Chopin now and then float above the beat. Gordon keeps the dualities so delicately balanced that we can be lulled by the formal beauty of the piece into ignoring signs of its double life. When, at some point in the action, the dancers pause and sum up "the story so far," we're startled, because so much of the action has been abstract. Are these dances staged to look like social rituals or are they social rituals staged to look like dances? The content seems at all times reversible, and though the suggestion of a "story" is partly ironic, it is serious in its urging of a non-insular, non-relativistic point of view. In fact, the spoken synopsis turns out to be a completely acceptable literalistic interpretation of the borderline drama of the piece. ("Margaret and David had a falling out," etc.) For a moment, we get to see things in the "framework" of a story, then back to the mirror world. The wonderful "I go 'Go' " monologue, vivaciously delivered by Susan Eschelbach to five other dancers as they group themselves around, behind, and beneath a panel (a table, a door, a bed), seems to open up another story. Whether or not it is one depends on how you read the pas de deux of Eschelbach and Paul Evans which immediately follows. Gordon is a collagist. Many of his dances and set pieces (like Eschelbach's monologue) can be lifted out of context and combined with new material to make a new impression. The pleasure we get from Gordon's work is the pleasure of synthesis. The integrity each new piece has is always a surprise. We go to see how the collagist's beads and shells and feathers and pinwheels will work this time and what new things have been added to the collection. For me, the outstanding novelty item in *Framework* is a group dance that goes to the song "Fresh." A sextet that frequently divides into three couples, "Fresh" has a momentum unlike any other ensemble that Gordon has done; it keeps on unrolling itself like surf as the dancers spin, dive, re-dive, tumble, shove, and toss each other into the air. Then, with a shift into slow motion, it seems to plunge underwater and go on travelling. This five-minute dance, which ends the first half of the show, sums up many of Gordon's movement motifs; it's awash with seashells and pinwheels. It's exciting—new and old at the same time—and somehow I think I'll be seeing it again.

If Gordon is a collagist, Douglas Dunn is a draftsman who keeps sketchbooks. His sketches are admirable; each has a life, a secret of its own, a brilliantly opportune idea that seems to lead the eye. The trouble is, Dunn's ideas don't extend themselves for more than a few seconds; they keep erupting, ever new. While we long to scan a landscape, to see large configurations develop and details recede, Dunn keeps showing us page after page of motifs. There used to be a fidgety, short-winded quality in his movement. The newer numbers in his recent concerts at the Joyce showed very little of this. In *Elbow Room*, Dunn's phrases have lengthened, and they've never been more beautifully formed, more inventive than they are in *Pulcinella*. But they are still fragments. Dunn originally staged the Stravinsky score on commission from the Paris Opéra Ballet. The New York production has a drop cloth, by Mimi Gross, showing a sunbaked Bay of Naples, and an array of crumpled white silk costumes, also by Mimi Gross, that suggest a down-at-the-heels commedia-dell'arte troupe. There is no plot. The dances ramble along in the disorderly fashion and with the diffuse impact of a street festival. Stronger continuity could have made the image a valid one, but though Dunn's phrases are set on the music they have no adhesive power, and forty minutes is too long a time to deal with fugitive impressions.

Dunn himself is a gifted dancer and a highly civilized artist. His too assiduous imitations of Merce Cunningham's performing style are an obstacle. A former Cunningham dancer, he was also a member, with David Gordon, of the choreographers' collective known as the Grand Union. His style is nervous, sensitive, refined, but inconsistent. Some steps in a sequence are perfectly pronounced, but others are tentative, so that the clarity of the connection keeps breaking down. Gordon, who lacks Dunn's phrasemaking talent, is technically cleaner and more precise, and he seems to have learned more about sustaining effects from those improvised Grand Union evenings than Dunn did. As a choreographer, Dunn remains a soloist, and he heads a company of soloists, augmented for the Stravinsky ballet. He danced a frazzled, hallucinated Pulcinella. Karole Armitage made a guest appearance doing odd, violent, high-tension solos that seemed to relate more to her own work than to Dunn's.

I also saw at the Joyce two programs by San Francisco choreographers. Brenda Way's choreography, which I had not seen before, struck me as energetic but crude, and I found nothing to admire in her costumes or lighting. Margaret Jenkins's pieces aren't much on the production side, either, but the fertility of the movement ideas makes up for this. In *First Figure*, and even more in *Max's Dream*, I was held by a succession of ideas mounted in long, full, rhythmically taut phrases. *Max's Dream*, suggested by images from Max Ernst, was something in the surrealistic line; the choreographer wandered among her dancers wearing a tuxedo, her upper body encased in a huge cabbage rose. What the dancers did was more penetratingly eccentric, more Ernstian: a woman was inserted head downward through the arms of an embracing couple; a woman dove down a man's back into the wings. Partners holding each other by the hand swung apart and together in wide, whipping loops. Jenkins likes to counter flowing big-scale body movement with small staccato gestures of the head and arms; here these looked like the manic chattering of puppets.

There was live music (by John Geist) brought all the way from San Francisco by the Kronos Quartet. The Joyce, a converted movie theatre, has no pit, and uneasily accommodated musicians in groups. The theatre was planned for dance, but its inordinately wide stage creates problems for choreographers. Even so, it is not cheap to rent. It has become a showcase for solidly established, old-guard American dance companies and foreign companies with subsidies. The loft-generation choreographers who have been carrying on in the uncompromising tradition of American modern dance are, for the most part, still in their lofts, hoping for an invitation from the Brooklyn Academy. Dunn's and Jenkins's concerts were the first serious choreography and serious dancing I had seen at the Joyce in the two years of its existence.

The version of the *Paquita* Grand Pas Classique that Natalia Makarova has staged this season for American Ballet Theatre is better than the one Makarova and Company presented four years ago on Broadway. The adagio is now done with the complete participation of the corps; the interpolated pas de trois is gone. The difference amounts to an architectural restoration—I won't say "of a monument," because the result lacks structural integrity in the two principal roles. A fragment, then, on the scale of a monument. And watching *Paquita* is very much like walking through a building. The female corps comes on in symmetrical formations of four at a time, then two, then eight. The ballerina enters in their midst through a kind of portal. The male soloist walks down a diagonal corridor, steps behind the ballerina, and supports her in an adagio. To a broad, slow melody, she arches her torso, tilts this way and that, deploys a leg forward, back, and to the side, and turns repeatedly on one spot. Tipped low to the ground in arabesque, she becomes a study in cantilevered weight. During this, the corps revolves and repositions itself at intervals, buttressing the ballerina's line, echoing her poses. From the main rotunda of the grand adagio we move through a colonnade: six solos, of which the man takes one. I could have wished for a more interesting assortment, with less repetitious brickwork. (The Kirov, which indirectly furnished this choreography, has heaps of interchangeable variations lying around labelled "Petipa-Minkus.") Suddenly we step down a flight of entrances and exits and out the back door. The ballet is ending the same way it began, but twice as fast. There's a whirl of fouettés by the ballerina—a fountain—and a final assembly like a low, arched gate. The curtain descends like a portcullis. Your souvenir is the damnable tunes of Minkus, which echo in your head for days.

Paquita has a Spanish flavoring; parts of it turn up regularly in *Don Quixote*. The Ballet Theatre casts do each variation so slowly and with such definition you could write down the steps. The spice of Spanish dancing doesn't enter into it. The gruel of pedagogical discipline does. This, too, comes from the Kirov—this methodical step-by-step concentration. It puts the dancer under a microscope and magnifies every technical flaw. The Kirov dancers, who have grown up with the method, are able to do more under exposure than the Americans, who, I'm afraid, will always look like students. As for the principals, it's no longer news that Cynthia Gregory can turn six inside pirouettes unsupported or that Fernando Bujones overjumps his entrechats. Exciting the audience is their job, and that's what their choreography is about. When Martine van Hamel and Patrick Bissell take over, it is rather a waste. The claptrap star routine doesn't bring anything exciting out of them; they need real parts. And in the *Sylvia Pas de Deux*, André Eglevsky's staging of Balanchine choreography, they get them.   —*June 18, 1984*

Guest in the House

It has been a season for collaborations between choreographers. Baryshnikov and Peter Anastos did *Cinderella* for American Ballet Theatre. Jerome Robbins and Twyla Tharp created a piece for New York City Ballet. The precedent for the Robbins-Tharp partnership, however, undoubtedly occurred in 1959, when George Balanchine invited Martha Graham to join him in presenting an hour-long work to Webern's music. The union of the ballet master and the modern dancer was a historic occasion, even though it wasn't really a union. The two choreographers worked separately with their own dancers; *Episodes* came together in performance. The Robbins-Tharp ballet is a real collaboration. But then it was a far more feasible project than Balanchine-Graham. It might even symbolize the changes that have come over American dance since 1959. Our idea of classicism has broadened, thanks largely to the genius of Balanchine, and American modern dance has outgrown the expressionistic stereotypes of its founding generation. It is possible to think of Duncan as a classicist and of Nijinsky as a modernist. Twyla Tharp is now an establishment figure, a choreographer of classical ballets, while Robbins, with works like *Watermill* and *Glass Pieces*, declares himself an enthusiast of the avant-garde. This season, he revived his *Moves*, subtitled "A Ballet in Silence About Relationships." It was made the year of *Episodes*, and Robbins may think of it—and may mean us to think of it—as an anticipation of *The Fugue*, Tharp's three-part invention, which is also danced in silence. *Moves* is still a very solid and satisfying piece, especially with the "relationships" unobtrusively outlined, as they now are by the New York City Ballet dancers, but it is not central to Robbins's work the way *The Fugue* is to Tharp's; for him, silence is another problem licked, like the music of Philip Glass. Tharp, for her part, has been homing in on New York City Ballet for some time. No one has worked harder to deserve a commission; no one could be worthier of one. Her *Bach Partita*, executed last year for A.B.T., is an N.Y.C.B. ballet in disguise, an essay in baroque classicism, and an appropriate contribution to a repertory that lacks *Concerto Barocco*, *The Four Temperaments*, *Agon*, and *Kammermusik No. 2*. Her side of the collaboration with Robbins has its share of tributes to the man who was their joint mentor, but she has not tried to reactivate her Balanchine mode. As an outsider, and as the only prominent woman choreographer to work with the company since Ruthanna Boris, she represents no one but herself. If New

York City Ballet lacked anything, after all, it lacked Twyla Tharp. Now it has her, and it also has a wonder of a new ballet.

The chosen music is the twenty-five variations and fugue written by Brahms on a theme by Handel. The music has strange humors in it, which a modern orchestration, by the British composer Edmund Rubbra, italicizes, and which the combined wit of Robbins and Tharp italicizes in boldface. The variations aren't attributed, so we have to guess who did what. This makes a fascinating puzzle; after an obvious opening section by Robbins and after Tharp has staged an obvious entrance, the pace gets faster and the guessing gets tougher. The large cast is divided into two ensembles and two pairs of principals (Merrill Ashley and Ib Andersen, Maria Calegari and Bart Cook) who are dressed by Oscar de la Renta in simple costumes of turquoise for Robbins and kelly green for Tharp. The device of concealed authorship keeps the ballet from being an outright competition, and it also ignites a spark of madness. Not only do the dancers keep changing sides but some group numbers are divided, with one choreographer taking foreground, the other background, action. Other variations are executed by one, with the other passing through or peeping in. There's at least one duet that seems split down the middle. I wouldn't put it past Tharp and Robbins to have impersonated each other's style now and then or choreographed different steps of the same dance. (The alternate phrases in a double solo suggest both options.) It all builds to a glorious pouring mass of bravura entrances for the entire company, which drains away into the wings only to start rising again in the fugue. Decorum prevails in the end. Against the seething tide and somehow abreast of it, the four principals pose, their arms sedately linked.

The ballet has a remarkable stylistic unity, but because excess is a part of Tharp's makeup (and caution is a part of Robbins's) it seems to be more her ballet than his. The constancy of the pressure in the ensembles—it hovers at a point just this side of pandemonium—is Tharpian, and the group textures have her unmistakable viscosity. There are such Tharp trademarks as women being lifted with their legs worming in the air, or being cartwheeled over men's heads or dragged in splits across the floor. The fury of activity that Tharp alone seems to have provided occasionally creates the impression that two cooks are one too many, but even as we recoil the music opens a hungry maw and is sated. Most collaborations between choreographers run the risk of mutual deference, which ends in anonymity and an unaccomplished or underaccomplished ballet. Was this the problem in *Cinderella*? Was it what plagued Robbins's attempts to choreograph with Balanchine *Pulcinella* and *Le Bourgeois Gentilhomme*, or were those ballets simply uncongenial assignments, which, undertaken by either man, would have turned out badly? (Balanchine revised *Pulcinella* by himself and it still didn't work.) Robbins seems to have envisioned *Brahms/Handel* as a steeplechase of a ballet, with Tharp as the rider beside him. (She had created a *Brahms/Paganini* for her own company.) So extravagant and crazy a piece hasn't been seen on the State Theater stage since *Union Jack*. But *Brahms/Handel* is not a stunt. I think a stranger who knew nothing of Robbins and Tharp and the wherefores of this piece could tell that someone has been at pains to make serious choreography for brilliant dancers. Strategically, the piece resembles other game-plan ballets of Robbins's, such as *Interplay* and *Fanfare*. The melding and then the separating of the Blues and the Greens at the end of the fugue recall the fugue at the end of *Fanfare*, only with gale-force winds behind it. Robbins has followed through on the provocativeness of his idea; it's been tastefully handled, but it hasn't been tamed.

The choreographers seem to have used the talents of Ashley, Andersen, Calegari, and Cook as supreme tests of their skill, and they keep topping each other. Ashley's role is her best since *Ballo della Regina*. Acrobatic rather than allegro, it unleashes her Amazonian intrepidity. She races along with gangs of men and dives head first into their midst. Returned to herself, she speed-slides away, un-catchable. Numbers of men support Calegari also, but as a queen on a float. This is Tharp's homage to Balanchine, devised as the formal entrance of the Greens. With Calegari held aloft, the cortège incorporates images from *Serenade*, "The Unanswered Question" (from *Ivesiana*), and Lifar's entrance in *La Chatte*. Calegari's softness and plasticity complement Ashley's steel-spring bounce; their duet in canon makes the point neatly. The nimble Andersen is as elusive as a German elf, and Cook, looking like a boy again, is especially fine in the various court and country dances with which the piece is studded. These are all happy dancers, and this is choreography they cherish.

One could say the same of *Bach Partita*, and one would have to add "but don't perform often enough." Ballet Theatre is doing its utmost to keep up what may well be the hardest ballet it has ever danced, but although it's a shining hour for Cynthia Gregory, Martine van Hamel, Magali Messac, and their partners Ross Stretton (or Fernando Bujones), Clark Tippet, and Robert La Fosse, repertory conditions militate against its becoming a completely comfortable one. In N.Y.C.B. repertory, certain ballets feed certain other ballets, and the style for such a piece as *Bach Partita* is in the dancers' bones. In A.B.T. repertory, it's anomalous. Not even *Push Comes to Shove* prepares the dancers for it. I noticed that after La Fosse danced the role that Tharp had choreographed for Baryshnikov in *The Little Ballet* his performance in the Bach piece became twice as bright. (So did Baryshnikov's own performance; La Fosse was very good.) But no such possibility exists for anybody else. The solution is to keep digging into the material of *Bach Partita* when every temptation exists to trim it to more negotiable limits.

Tharp has taken the five movements of the celebrated unaccompanied Partita No. 2 in D Minor for violin and set on them an enormous, whirling, weightless ballet. Besides the six principals, the hierarchical cast includes seven pairs of demisoloists and sixteen corps women. These are forces that fly before you like the wind. The single violin, with its multiple voices, effortlessly supports them all. I find a great deal of pleasure in watching *Bach Partita*, but most of it lies in Tharp's ingenuity—in the subtlety of her calculations, the ease of her logistics, the daring with which she approaches an all but insuperable task. Despite the titles of its sections (Allemande, Courante, Sarabande, Gigue, Chaconne), the great Partita is not to my ears dance music that can actually be danced. In setting a ballet to it, Tharp tries to breathe flesh and blood back into matter that has become spirit. Her attempt to bring off this tour de force lays bare the structuralist who lives inside the choreographer. You can follow (not too easily on the Met stage, I grant you) the spread of the harmony in the spread of her groups and trace the rise and fall of melody, its subdivisions, inversions, and renewals. To watch *Bach Partita* is to see musical process revealed. But though Bach's passion was in his process Tharp's diagram succeeds in capturing passion only when it registers some seismic configuration of Bach's or contradicts Bach completely. In the best part of the piece, the women's dance in the Chaconne, sixteen corps women whom we have never seen before whisk through a scene so buoyant that they add nothing to it but the shock of their appearance. Then men come on to partner the women, and Tharp has an attack of Bach madness akin to the madness of *Brahms/Handel*. The contrapuntal variety is such that four or six ballets seem to be going on at once. Katzenjammermusik! It's a sweet moment while it lasts. *Bach Partita* is ravishing but finally too sane and methodical a piece to love. The material it is made of is quite another matter. Were I a dancer, I would long for it every day.

This ballet was Tharp's formal notice to the world that she is a classical *academic* choreographer. There are no dance neologisms among the steps. (There is one extraordinary lift in which Messac slides her leg straight up La Fosse's chest and, holding a split in the air, cartwheels over backward.) Tharp's grasp of academic form is beyond question, but more interesting is her talent, evident everywhere you look, for seeing movement in a new light. What she sees seems to solidify in some special way; it becomes tactile. When a dancer in the midst of a line of déboulés is grabbed by the shoulders and turned back to front, it's as if she'd become a piece of living sculpture we can feel with our hands. Tharp has now done four pieces for A.B.T., and they were given a special evening this season. Baryshnikov danced *The Little Ballet* and *Sinatra Suite* back to back. In one, he is Russian, romantic, classical; in the other, he's American, insolent, pop. The perception that these two pieces can be done for a single audience is an inspiration he shares with Tharp. *Push Comes to Shove* expresses the same duality: Baryshnikov starts out dancing a rag and ends up in a Haydn symphony. On the Tharp evening, Danilo Radojevic performed the role and was interrupted at the last moment by Baryshnikov, who came on to lead the choreographer out for her bow. How has it happened that Tharp, who is not herself a classical dancer and was never part of any ballet company, now choreographs these amazing pieces for the reigning ballet dancers of our time? In thinking over this question recently, I was forced to reconsider some of the events that I began this article by citing.

When *Episodes* was first done, critics said that Graham's section looked old-fashioned, while Balanchine's looked new. The two camps seemed to have switched sides. Actually, modern dance under Merce Cunningham had already adopted the new dispensation. Ballet or modern, the emphasis in choreography was now on dance over drama. This emphasis and the equally widespread acceptance of daily ballet practice by dancers of all persuasions healed the ideological division between ballet and modern dance. This still didn't mean that modern-dance choreographers could work productively with ballet companies, and we had a slew of hopefully ecumenical ballets by choreographers like John Butler and Glen Tetley to prove it. Soon the rift reopened, along lines drawn by music—its use, non-use, or misuse. Compared with the old cleavage, this was the San Andreas fault. Perhaps it was only natural that once dance began aspiring to the condition of music—non-programmatic music, I mean—music itself should become an issue, and pro-music modern-dance choreographers like Paul Taylor and Twyla Tharp should gravitate toward the ballet companies. Taylor, it will be remembered, was the one Graham dancer to work with Balanchine in *Episodes*. He became a kind of apprentice to Balanchine, and even learned certain roles, though he never went so far as to perform them. Tharp joined the post-Cunningham generation of "silent" choreographers after a spell in Taylor's company proved to her that she needed to deal with other issues in choreography besides music. She reverted to music eventually and has never looked back.

When, at the beginning of the sixties, Taylor found his form in musical choreography, he defied avant-garde notions of dance as an independent art. But modern music had already ostracized dance. What Webern's music in *Episodes* seemed to say was that the next logical phase was silence. When Twyla Tharp reverted to music a decade later, the issue had been pretty well disposed of by the rise of structuralism in music, in painting, and in the choreography of Twyla Tharp. Structuralism was non-expressionistic; it dealt with process. Its elements are still there in Tharp's aesthetic. But she has nothing else in common with the choreographers who were led back to music by the structuralism of Philip Glass, Steve Reich, and other new composers who share their Asian sensibility. For those choreographers, the best music is that which makes the fewest demands on a movement idiom that cannot sustain too much variety. Tharp, meanwhile, revels in baroque complexity. She always has. Her musical taste is rooted in the classical tradition of the West—in Bach, Handel, Haydn, and Mozart. Most of the technical problems she faced during her nonmusical phase had to do with dancing in unconventional places—gyms, art galleries, city streets and parks. The reorganization of stage space is a factor in her work, but it isn't fundamental to it, whereas the crypto-musical *The Fugue* became the cornerstone of her company's repertory. Tharp's sense of baroque design operates with or without music. The more I see of her work, the more I am persuaded that it is this sense, and not just her musical skills, that has enabled her to operate within the complex movement idiom of modern ballet. Those musical skills are formidable, of course, and without them Tharp couldn't have moved from being the most interesting post-Cunningham choreographer to being the most interesting post-Balanchine one. She would just have been the most interesting post-Cunningham choreographer to work for the ballet.

To some people, that is what she still is; and Peter Martins, who inherited many of Balanchine's duties, is interesting only because he's there. Martins, who was trained in one of the great ballet academies of the world, has known from boyhood things about the art and science of ballet that Tharp has been able to teach herself only recently. Tharp, on the other hand, represents the improvisation that stands at the heart of the creative tradition in American dance. As Balanchine well knew, that tradition was not to be found in the ballet, but to modern dance he preferred the Broadway of Jerome Robbins. (Robbins himself preferred the ballet.) He couldn't have anticipated how things would turn out this spring, only a year after his death: modern dance makes a crossover bid, Mr. Broadway is there to make it good, and the academy fructifies.

Peter Martins's new ballet is also to Bach—the Suite No. 3 in D Major plus selections from the Suite No. 4, the last of which, "Réjouissance" ("Rejoicing"), gives the ballet its title. It is dance music, evoking Lully's ballets and inciting Martins to an extended exercise in company style, excellent to begin or end a program with. This is another ballet with six principals heading a tremendous cast. Suzanne Farrell is the regnant ballerina partnered by Joseph Duell and flanked by Valentina Kozlova with Adam Lüders and Lourdes Lopez with Leonid Kozlov. Below them, there is the junior school, all female, divided into courts for the three principal couples. Six male courtiers complete the ranks. Martins's choreography has grandeur without pomposity. Its subject is the eighteenth-century fantasy of innocence which gave such radiance to baroque manners and to the ballets that commemorated them, Balanchine's above all. Balanchine concluded his Webern ballet by returning, through a Webern transcription, to Bach. A quarter of a century later, *Episodes* is still being danced and the newest Bach ballets play across from each other at Lincoln Center. *Bach Partita* is German baroque, *Réjouissance* is French baroque. Martins's ballet is not the more audacious but it is the more nobly bred, and in Farrell's performance the more limpid and serene. When the curtain goes down, it's with a sense of flags snapping in the breeze, flying regimental colors, saying, "Look, we have come through."

—*July 2, 1984*

Bad Smells

I happened to see *Amnon V'Tamar* the week Pina Bausch's Dance Theatre of Wuppertal opened its local engagement, and the night it closed I saw *Take-Off from a Forced Landing*. Martine van Hamel was making her début as a choreographer for American Ballet Theatre with *Amnon V'Tamar*, and it wasn't an auspicious one; I don't suppose the ballet will be around when the company comes back to town. *Take-Off from a Forced Landing* was a dance-and-dialogue drama by Dianne McIntyre, which played a few performances at the Joyce without attracting much attention. Ordinarily, I'd refrain from mentioning either of these events, on the ground that their amateurishness places them beyond serious discussion. But the truly otherworldly success of Pina Bausch's troupe at the Brooklyn Academy brings a new meaning to the word "amateur." To the aggression of those who have not the means of doing what they aspire to do but do it anyway Bausch adds the utter nihilistic certainty that no such means exist. This truth then becomes a joke to be shared with the audience, and the show goes on in a kind of pretended nightmare of decomposition. Nothing happens, and it happens over and over again. Anything follows anything. The tone of confident directionlessness is carefully designed. Bausch hasn't a smidgen more technique than van Hamel or McIntyre, but, unlike them, she's willing to strike attitudes over the fact, and she has found an audience that takes the attitudes for art.

Of course, it was van Hamel's stature as a ballerina that entitled her to a conspicuous and extensive première. Maybe, since she has taste and a flair for arranging plastically interesting steps, she'll do a real ballet one day, and that will give us something to measure *Amnon V'Tamar* by. But how do you deal with a Biblical sin-and-sex epic—a cliché of a subject to begin with—that can't make its characters' identities clear or define anything that happens between them? The title, in Hebrew, means *Amnon* [the son of David] *and Tamar* [his half sister]— not *Amnon Versus Tamar*, as one might suppose from some of the action. When the curtain rose, the title characters were onstage with two other characters— whether David and Bathsheba or David and Jonathan, the friend of David's youth, I can't remember—and van Hamel was giving us involvements and "conflicts" before she'd even stated her premise. I couldn't straighten out much of what went on in Dianne McIntyre's piece, either, but at least it was based on an original idea—a tribute to the choreographer's mother, who was one of the few black women to get a pilot's license in the forties. She wasn't able to make a career out of aviation, but the experience of flying planes, we are told, caused her to raise powerfully motivated children. Dianne McIntyre attributes her own career as a dancer to her mother's example. In *Take-Off from a Forced Landing*, flying is identified with dancing and with overcoming handicaps; it's a metaphor for transcendence. In the best scene, the company of six dancers takes a flying lesson in the form of a dance class, translating into dance exercises such instructions as "Taxi into the crosswind" and "Reverse controls and sideslip." McIntyre, who plays her mother, moves with the attenuated strength of Carmen de Lavallade, but her dancers look like beginners, and they use too many big, wide, ecstatically imprecise movements. Although their spirits soar, their style remains grounded in the generalizations of religiose modern dance. Yet it probably wasn't the wooziness of the technique that caused the piece to be overlooked so much as it was the upbeat attitude expressed in the flying imagery. A black woman artist who does jubilation dances and whose message is "Keep your nose on the horizon" is as unfashionable as a ballerina who makes Biblical costume dramas.

Meanwhile, out in Brooklyn, the Bausch company was the height of chic, a resounding hit with the fashion-conscious. Nothing could have better served the current depressed mood of fashion than these glum, despondent dabblings in theatrical Dada. The visual effects echoed fashion-magazine layouts; the politics did, too. If Pina Bausch had staged McIntyre's piece, the flying dances might have represented drug highs and all those black girls who wanted wings would almost certainly have been given their revenge on the male white world. Pina Bausch plays right into feminist paranoia; besides the ritualistic amateurism, it's her most consistent theme.

In the Louise Brooks movie *Diary of a Lost Girl*, a sadistic matron in an orphanage makes the girls spoon up their soup to a metronomic rhythm. The rhythm of a Pina Bausch piece is obsessively regular. Bursts of violence are followed by long stillnesses. Bits of business are systematically repeated, sometimes with increasing urgency but more often with no variation at all. At every repetition, less is revealed, and action that looked gratuitous to begin with dissolves into meaningless frenzy. *Café Müller*, which opened the Bausch season and set the pattern for it, is thirty-five minutes long and feels ninety; its subject is duration, and repetition is its only device. The café—apparently it is meant to resemble a real place—seems to be the canteen of a mental hospital. A small cast of inmates gives us intermittent doses of violent/apathetic behavior while a woman who may be a visitor scurries noisily about in high-heeled shoes. Music from Purcell's operas drifts over the loudspeakers, doing its best to solemnize the goings on. *Café Müller*, with its thin but flashy shtick, is a how-to-make-theatre handbook. It enshrines the amateur's faith in psychopathy as drama. Bausch herself is in it, entering the set at curtain rise and remaining onstage throughout. A thin, spectral figure in a nightgown, she is also sightless, and she creeps along a wall and huddles in the dark until the end, when she staggers dimly downstage and starts bumping into the furniture. It takes a considerable ego to cast yourself as a pathetic, sightless, wandering creature. When I saw Bausch playing the blind princess with the sad smiles in the movie *And the Ship Sails On*, I thought she was a typical piece of hammy Fellini invention. But Bausch evidently sees herself as this wan, wasted Duse; the blind-seeress act is perfectly in keeping with the inverted romanticism of her theatre. There have been numerous clinical analyses of Bausch's Theatre of Dejection; they're beside the point. Bausch may have her hangups, but basically she's an entrepreneuse who fills theatres with projections of herself and her self-pity. Since there's nothing between us and her—no mediating dramatic rationale, no technique to transfigure and validate raw emotion—we think that she's some-how authentic, that her suffering, at least, must be real. She *can't* be just a little girl acting po' faced. Bausch's power lies in having calculated audience voyeurism to a nicety, and those sad smiles have a way of curling up contemptuously when it comes to her favorite theme of men and women. In Bausch theatre, men brutalize women and women humiliate men; the savage round goes on endlessly. The content of these bruising encounters is always minimal. Bausch doesn't build psychodramas in which people come to understand something about themselves and their pain. She keeps referring us to the *act* of brutalization or humiliation— to the pornography of pain. It's what we came for, isn't it? Presumably, the superficiality of it all is what allows the Wuppertaler Tanztheater to call itself that;

dance is something it hardly ever shows us. (One of the great jokes of the season was the choice of this supremely unathletic company to open the Olympic Arts Festival.)

When the Wuppertalers do dance, they're strangely inhibited. They usually begin by standing in place and stretching and swerving the upper body this way and that, their hands locked over or behind their heads. They don't move their feet much except when they run, and then it's usually pell-mell. But it seems they only run in order to halt. Either they halt stymied (by banging into something or somebody) or they halt dead, feet planted apart, eyes cast down, as if they'd suddenly realized they were violating the ground by running over it. The run motifs and the halt motifs are used in Bausch's version of *Le Sacre du Printemps*. Running in herds (the Tribe) is opposed to running alone (the Sacrifice). The catalogue expands as the piece goes on: sweating, heavy breathing, clammy bodies slapping against each other, peeling wet clothes from clammy bodies. We'd already seen these motifs in *Café Müller*, but there the stage was completely filled with little black tables and chairs, and in the *Sacre* it's covered with packed-down dirt, like a camping ground or like a Peter Brook set. Bausch's covered floors have become famous, and I imagine the clinicians really do have something to say about this need to fill the floor end to end and wing to wing with objects or foreign substances: dead leaves are used in *Bluebeard*, live grass in *1980*. Another aberration—or perhaps it is an extension of the littering compulsion—is Bausch's use of sets with walls and ceilings that completely enclose the stage picture. For someone in search of dance theatre—or, indeed, theatre of any kind—all this is just so much window dressing, and it's of the same order of unpleasantness as everything else. By getting sweaty dancers dirty, the earth floor adds an element of yuck to *Sacre* which the other pieces don't have, but the dead leaves and the grass are bad enough: they made the Brooklyn Academy, which isn't air-conditioned, smell like a stable. Naturally, you don't dance on such stages.

In spite of its yuckiness, the *Sacre* remains in memory as the only tolerable Bausch piece. But if the Stravinsky score sets limits on her tendency to maunder and repeat, it also amplifies and energizes her theme of female persecution. This must be the tenth or twelfth *Sacre* I've seen in the past five years. Every one but Paul Taylor's has used the score to whip up an excitement the choreography could not have sustained on its own. Bausch's version, which is about ritual murder with no reference to fertility, has no more feel for the rhythms of the score than Martha Graham's version did, earlier this season. In the Sacrificial Victim's dance, it reaches its wit's end long before the music runs out. If Bausch has a choreographic technique that she disdains to use in her "theatre" pieces, here was the place for it. But she produced a run-of-the-mill *Sacre*. The only moment of tension—I found it agonizing—came when the choice of the Victim seemed about to settle on one of the little fat girls in the company. The Bausch troupe contains quite a few members who don't look like dancers and are none too prepossessing physically. They look their best in *1980*; the women dress up and comb their hair and put on makeup, and even the men seem civilized. When the whole cast of eighteen comes on like a chorus line, snaking through the audience and grinning in all directions, we can see that they mean to be likably batty, but then they go on to do vaudeville turns and little skits reminiscing about or reverting to their childhoods, and they're corny and tiresome. The casting is so determinedly egalitarian (everyone gets a chance to bore you) and the material is so clownish or so literally childish (actual children's games and songs, actually played and sung) that the fact that some, if not all, of these reminiscences are biographical has no weight. And why is it that everyone seems to have had a sad childhood? Because everyone belongs to the Theatre of Dejection, that's why. 1980, named for the year it was first put on, suggests what life in the Bausch company must be like: *Animal House* with weltschmerz.

The Theatre of Dejection builds down from the Theatre of Absurdity and the Theatre of Cruelty and other manifestations of the sixties; the cycle has come back to the raw pulp of abuse it started with. It is hard to believe in mental-asylum metaphors twenty years after *Marat/Sade*; in audience-involvement techniques fifteen years after the Living Theatre; in bleak despair, in the prankishly surrealistic, in monomaniacal simplicity, and in all the affectless contrivances of avant-garde fashion which Bausch puts on the stage after two full generations of American modern dancers have done them to death. She is a force in European theatre, and perhaps that explains everything. (It explains quite a bit of Carolyn Carlson, an American choreographer now working in Europe, in the European mode. In exchange for the dirt floors Bausch has from Peter Brook—who probably got *his* from Gurdjieff's headquarters—Bausch gives Carlson madwomen in lingerie.) To judge from the Eurotrash that has poured in on us in recent seasons— a partial list would begin with all those terrible ballet companies that preceded Bausch into the Brooklyn Academy, and include Brook's *Carmen*, Maurice Béjart, Jiří Kylián, and Patrice Chéreau's *Ring*—there is not much resistance to such a force.

I can't say I was surprised by anything I saw done by the Wuppertal Dance Theatre, but there was one element I was surprised not to see. Bausch's publicity has exaggerated the amount of scandal and salaciousness in her work. Some mild ribaldry, some rather unappetizing nudity are all she has. As a theatre terrorist, she gets her main effect by repetition. People throw each other against the walls not once but many times. Women are caught in a sling and swung round and round and round not once but many times. Men are undressed, paraded naked, and smeared with lipstick not once but so frequently and maliciously that the point reverses itself: the worm turns once too often, and Bausch's vengeance becomes seemingly that of a woman who not only has hated to expose herself for male delectation but has feared to. Body shame is a subtheme of the female-exploitation theme. In *Café Müller*, *Le Sacre du Printemps*, and *Bluebeard*, the women most of the time wear filmy slips without bras, which makes them look like a bunch of sad sacks, and they use a characteristic Bauschian gesture: they hang their heads and let their hands creep up the front of their bodies, lifting the garment exhibitionistically as they go. Skirts are sometimes lifted without implications of shame but never with implications of pleasure, and it's typical of Bausch's males that they show no interest whatever. It's typical, too, that when they strip they have nothing to show *us*. I was unable to hold myself in the theatre for more than an hour of *Bluebeard*, the most concentrated of Bausch's feminist tirades, and an hour and a half of 1980 (which was four hours long), but I should be surprised to learn that Bausch was able to turn out one credible, attractive image of masculinity. Having made women look worse on the stage than any misogynist ever has, she is under no obligation to men. —*July 16, 1984*

"Giselle, ou La Fille des Bayous"

Dance Theatre of Harlem, at the City Center, has done its first full-length classic: *Giselle*. The first act is set on a Louisiana plantation, with a white porch and white barns overhung with Spanish moss, and with a black farm girl betrayed by a rich landowner's son, also black. The second act takes place in the bayous. Like some other D.T.H. transpositions, the production is pictorially and emotionally so satisfying that we gladly excuse a few implausibilities. And, anyway, what are a few more implausibilities in *Giselle*? The music isn't what you'd have heard in the American South of a hundred and fifty years ago, but then we listen to the score of *Giselle* less for its local color than for its melodramatic and sentimental efficiency. The only passage of music and dance that seems wrong is the peasant pas de deux, a traditional interpolation that takes its flavor from folk-based steps. In the context of this "Creole" production, the effect is the reverse of what it usually is: instead of two field hands showing off to the local gentry, the dance seems to be displaying imported Paris finery—the steps themselves look gentrified. (Maybe a few tambourines banged on the sidelines à la Bournonville would reinforce the intention.) There are some implausibilities the production would be better off without. The fine folk for whose benefit the pas de deux is danced: shouldn't they all be invited by Mme. Berthe to sample the scuppernong? Instead, as in the traditional production, a meagre glassful is doled out to the two kingpins while their "court" stands about stiffly. On this point and on several others concerning the manners of Act I, I agree with Deborah Jowitt's review in the *Village Voice*. Albert's sword is sheathed in a gold-headed cane, but it's hardly the mark of caste that Albrecht's sword is. And why, confronting Hilarion, should this same Albert grope for a missing sword at his hip when he doesn't carry it that way? The staging, by Frederic Franklin, makes almost no concessions to the new setting, and thus passes up several good opportunities to reinvigorate a stereotype.

According to copious historical notes provided by the company, caste among the free blacks in the Louisiana of the eighteen-forties was determined chiefly by the number of generations a person could count up from slavery. Though Giselle, whose mother was born a slave, is three rungs lower than Albert, the difference between them is not so great as the difference between a peasant girl and a duke, and a Giselle who goes mad and kills herself when it turns out her fiancé is engaged to the belle of Plaquemines Parish is insecurely motivated unless it can be shown that she's unbalanced to begin with. Or pregnant. The pregnancy-of-Giselle theory has long been entertained by some students of the ballet. It's the real reason, they think, that Berthe keeps cautioning her daughter against dancing. I doubt if anyone has actually played out this interpretation on the stage. Yet, unlike a related theory—that Giselle has lost her virginity and is "ruined"—it is playable; it is something that can be shown as well as known. (And shown simply, with no more clinical detail than "weak heart"—Giselle's usual condition, though not in this production.)

Carl Michel, who compiled the historical background of this version and designed the sets and costumes, and evidently was very much a moving force, achieves his greatest coup in the second act, with Albert being poled through the swamp in a flat-bottomed boat toward the tomb of Giselle looming through the wisteria. (It is set above the ground, Michel tells us, like most Louisiana graves, because of the high water table.) The scene recalls the river Styx with Charon the ferryman—an image appropriate to a ballet whose libretto parallels the descent of Orpheus and his encounter with the bacchantes. The whole second act moves in the heavy dead air of "Thanatopsis." There would appear to be a tomb for Myrta, too, with her statue mounted over it like a civic virtue, grim in crown and sceptre. Instead of ballet skirts, gray tattered shifts are worn (Giselle, the novice, is in white), with an effect of shrouds, like the draperies in Pavlova's production. Michel has omitted nothing. But his colleagues have. The lighting (by Shirley Prendergast) is weak in those atmospherics which should startle the villagers at the beginning of the act, and totally negligent when dawn arrives to save Albert from the Wilis. Act II is a ballet d'action from start to finish, not the abstract ballet with a few set pieces of narration which we are used to seeing. Franklin's staging of the choreography is routine. Beyond those set pieces, it rationalizes none of the action from a dramatic point of view; it omits the travelling in Myrta's travelling arabesques, has her declaim the same mime speech over and over, has Giselle enter before Albert is finished praying for her to do so and then fudges the steps she performs on entering, has Hilarion enter, chased by Wilis, before the stage is clear, and has the women push him so sedately up the line and off you'd never guess he was being thrown to the crocs. Franklin also poses his Wilis with their hands fanned out behind their backs, as if indicating the waist wings their costumes don't have. The gesture is a throwback to ancient productions in which the Wilis were flown on wires. But why should they have flown? These women are the undead—creatures of the earth, not sylphs of the air. (They're called Wilis in the program, by the way; the term derives from a Slavic word for "vampire" and is probably too indelibly associated with the ballet to change. Myrta's two lieutenants are called Miseries.)

The two casts of principals are quite different and are thoughtfully balanced. Virginia Johnson, delicate and dutiful, is paired with the forceful Eddie J. Shellman; Stephanie Dabney's fervor is modulated by Donald Williams's reserve. All of them dance better than they mime, perhaps because the direction makes so little of its chances dramatically. But Cassandra Phifer is one of the best Berthes I've ever seen; she mimes colloquially. Lowell Smith and Keith Saunders both do a dignified, manly Hilarion. Theara Ward is Bathilde, in a top hat wound with a veil, a wing collar, and a riding habit with a full white skirt; she looks ravishing but acts unassertively. (Michel, who also composed biographical sketches of the ballet's characters, may have put her off with his suggestion, unnecessary to the action, that Bathilde is capricious and hard to figure.) Ward is one of the company's striking assortment of big, handsome women. Her counterpart in Act II is Lorraine Graves, who plunges bare-legged through the role of Myrta and fills the stage with untrammelled power. Graves is so beautiful in arabesque it's a shame to deprive her of those voyagées. She heads a corps whose collective performance is the triumph of the production—huge in scale, avid in attack yet plangent in rhythm. Dabney's Giselle reflects the corps's voracity, and she has some marvellous impulsive moments. Bolting from the wings into the supported temps levés en arabesque, she actually brings off the illusion of displacing her partner's faltering strength.

Agon, the Balanchine ballet, was danced as a curtain-raiser, and I'm sorry to say that it's no longer the shining, taut Agon we used to see this company do. Taut has become stiff; formerly elastic phrases have hardened, fractured, and been rejoined in odd places. The mock-ceremonious manners of the piece are exaggerated. Ward and Shellman are physically magnificent and technically able in the pas de deux, but their timing is gauche and the moves are all out of shape. Ward has a quality of excess that's exciting. It's not the dry stylistic exaggeration we see in other dancers—it's sheer anatomical abundance flowing in all directions, not all of which are appropriate to Balanchine's choreography. A good coach could edit the flow, but for the moment I'm almost glad to see it bursting out; it distorts Balanchine, but not as much as it defeats the rigid controls on expression now being imposed on the dancers in this and other classical ballets. The imposition is carried out, I am sure, in the name of discipline, and I don't know what to make of it. It's both benevolent and hurtful. It energizes a wonderful Wili corps in Giselle but tightens the life out of Agon. Dancers seem caught in a vise— encouraged to dance on a generous scale but also with a prissy correctness. Attending D.T.H. these days can be a bewildering experience. It's exuberant— flamboyant, even—one night, dauntingly respectable the next. Respectability is not the worst of virtues, but it's no substitute for elegance. There's a lot of talent in this company being made to mind its manners too much of the time.

—October 22, 1984

Strangers in the Night

At the bottom of every national art form lie the tea leaves of a culture, but you have to know the culture to read their meaning. What Butoh, or "dark soul dance," is all about I must leave to the experts on contemporary Japan. From what I have seen of the work of a few local practitioners, notably Eiko and Koma, it is clear that Butoh is an aesthetic rather than a school of movement.* And now the visit to the City Center of Sankai Juku, a troupe of five Japanese dancer-mimes, suggests that it has ideological, even political roots. (In fact, as the experts point out, Butoh had its origins in nuclear-protest activities in the sixties.) The performing style of Sankai Juku has a strong mystical cast; the five dancers, all male, with their shaved skulls and white body makeup, their slow writhings and soundless screams, seem to be members of a cult. They inhabit the same theatre of shock and devastation and they use some of the same procedures as Eiko and Koma, but they don't produce anything like Eiko and Koma's primordial and unimaginable sagas of pain—their imagery is more pampered and insular, and this is so despite the fact that they acknowledge the natural world as their primary source of inspiration. Well, I find more in early Pilobolus. Sankai Juku doesn't seem as interested in the forms of fishes or birds as in penetrating to some inner state of fishhood or birdhood, and the moment of contact is not always a legible one that we can share. To those not already enrolled in the cult (or willing to be), Sankai Juku is only an exotic disturbance—far too lethargic to be exciting.

This lethargy was the last thing I had expected. I had heard about the sensational aspects of the performance—nudity, bodies hanging upside down, horrendous imitations of cripples and mutants. The reviews seemed to reel from a pounding assault on the senses. It's true that Sankai Juku pounds, but, like some routine horror movie unloading its effects, it just keeps hitting you and then stalling until it finds something to hit you with again. The waiting in between gives you time to notice time, and one of the things that occurred to me was that it wasn't the slow time of classical Japanese theatre—it was slowed-down time. Instead of a pace dictated by events, we had a dribbling of events over vast expanses of time, a constant dissipation of tension, and a deadening of what few lines of communication lay between us and the mystical process unfolding on the stage.

* Postscript 1987: Since this was written, Eiko and Koma circulated a letter denying any connection to Butoh and pointing out that since 1976 they have been New Yorkers who periodically teach workshops in their own technique, which they call Delicious Movement. In the Fall 1986 catalogue for Movement Research, Inc., the course taught by Eiko and Koma is listed as "Introduction to Delicious Movement: The aim is to present oneself as if naked and existentially to give birth to the inexpressible."

The company was founded in 1975 by Ushio Amagatsu, who remains its director, choreographer, and master mime. The slack pacing and the preciousness are undoubtedly his fault, but he is also responsible for the high moments of the evening, one of which opens *Kinkan Shonen*, the troupe's signature piece. Dressed like a schoolboy in cap and short pants, covered head to foot with white flour, mouthing silent syllables in a cavern of silence, he suddenly topples over backward, slamming the floor with such force that a white cloud rises from his clothing. Later, he reappears, knees under his chin, as a midget, rocking from side to side in a shapeless gown. The bodilessness focusses our attention on his face, which laughs, cries, and speaks the same soundless sentence over and over in an agony of repetition. Each repeat is uncannily exact, and the shifting of gears between emotions is accomplished with perfect control. In the final scene, a rectangle of blue sky opens on a blackened stage, and Amagatsu hangs there head down, twisting first in silhouette, then in blazing light. I wish I could say that everything about his performance revealed the precision and physical audacity of these high points. But except for that last image, which gradually brought the show to a close, Amagatsu's great moments were all vitiated by what followed them—the schoolboy gobbled mounds of rice and sent up more white clouds, the midget grew tall and pranced about in a skirt dance. These contrivances struck me as clumsy attempts to sustain transitions in what should have been a sequence of events horrible in its randomness, inexorable in its flow. But the discipline that would have motivated it all aesthetically wasn't there. What we got was one damn thing after another.

Persons to whom "Dancing in the Dark" is a ballad by Arthur Schwartz and Howard Dietz and not a record by Bruce Springsteen will be pleased to hear of a new dance company called American Ballroom Theatre, which just made its theatrical début at Dance Theatre Workshop. The four couples who make up the company are all of Springsteen's generation, and they perform the old dances to the old tunes with an ease and a zest and an accuracy that bring them alive again. The sensibility of American Ballroom Theatre is what might be called neoclassical eclectic. The traditional step patterns of the foxtrot, the lindy, the rumba, and so on are revived and invested with a new vitality based squarely on the energy and the imagination of the dancers who perform them. We see *real* dancing—not dancing that's been depersonalized and embalmed by overconscientious reconstruction. I hate to watch young people reverently revisiting the past or trying so hard to score points in traditional competitions that they overscale the steps and flatten the dynamics. American Ballroom Theatre gives the dancers room to entertain themselves. And it entrusts them with the key to the life of these dances: differentiation. The dancers as they move keep differentiating particles of rhythm, of pace; they keep the shape of a step moving and changing and catching new lights; they make you see that the fun of discriminating among fine details is the whole fun of dancing.

Personalization is an aspect of differentiation founded on rhythm. Another aspect is founded on simple knowledge of the field. In American Ballroom Theatre many strains are joined and evoked by implication: the Savoy, Roseland, the Harvest Moon Ball, the Latin hot spot, the dinner club with the specialty act whirling in a spotlight, the intimate revue with the wisecracks, and the big jazzy stage show with squads of exhibition dancers trucking in front of the band. For such a panoramic sweep to succeed, there has to be a measure of specialization among the dancers, and there is. Pierre Dulaine and Yvonne Marceau, who are the company's artistic directors, are an exceptionally elegant acrobatic-adagio team, whose lifts (and descents) are prodigious without being arduous. Gary and Lori Pierce are the more lyrical, John and Cathi Nyemchek the more bravura of two exhibition-dance pairs. (The Nyemcheks, shorter and more chunkily built than their colleagues, are glittering stylists; they brought down the house with their quickstep to "Anything Goes," and they reprised the head-to-head circuit of turns in "The Carioca" with a manège of barrel turns wrapped in each other's arms.) Then, there are Wilson Barrera and Margaret Burns—handsome, unstereotyped Latin dancers. But all the dancers are handsome; and all of them do the complete repertory—that's what makes them a company. That, and the choreography of John Roudis.

Ballroom dancing is a salon art, hard to expand in theatrical space. These days, we see it mostly in movies or on ice; the medium does the job of expansion without destroying the intimacy of the style. Roudis began his dancing career in vaudeville in the twenties, and his staging has the nimbleness and musical fluency of a golden era. In the American Ballroom Theatre performance I was interested to see how the elasticity of the dancing kept adjusting space-time ratios, and how Roudis followed through on that, shifting the focus from one couple or one dance to another, separating and reuniting couples, splintering numbers into segments, and in general applying whatever theatrical tactics seemed natural and useful to the form. The result was a show that opened up on its own terms. The stage at Dance Theater Workshop was actually too small for it.

A more serious impediment was the musical soundtrack, which consisted mostly of pop records. The records were fine, but they kept forcing the transitions between numbers into awkward holding patterns. This is a problem for the new company to iron out. I can't see that it has much else to worry about. It is personable and talented. It has a unique identity and (if the reception at D.T.W. was any indication) a waiting audience. It encourages individuality in the dancers, yet the style is firmly centered on the standards of exhibition ballroom dancing. Roudis, who has worked with professional ballroom dancers for the last thirty years, doesn't comment on the form, as Twyla Tharp does in *Nine Sinatra Songs*, and the few times he ventured into additional material I thought he was wrong to. The swirling bullfighter capes in the "flamenco" section were particularly distracting. And in what classy boîte of yesteryear would a male dancer have been permitted to play his partner's bottom like a bongo drum? Yet the tango, the waltz, and the foxtrot were full of the romantic sexual attitudes of the past, openly proclaimed. I don't object to them when they're part of the dance, but sometimes the dances were encased in the kind of fervent sentiment one doesn't see anymore outside of Dracula movies. There's no need of it. American Ballroom Theatre is saying that classical social dancing is still good to see and do; one doesn't have to strike poses.   —*November 19, 1984*

Championship Form

Mark Morris didn't call his Brooklyn Academy of Music concert "The Modern Dance Till Now," though he well might have; the three numbers on the program took us from Bennington through Judson to Morris's own era in ninety minutes (with intermission). When it was over, it seemed as if Morris, in summing up his tradition, had placed himself in charge of it and could now take it wherever he liked. He's the clearest illustration we have, at the moment, of the principle of succession and how it works in dance: each new master assimilates the past in all its variety and becomes our guide to the future. In dance, the present is the only known tense, so the spell cast by a Mark Morris is the illusion of a perspective—seeing the past and the future simultaneously contained within the present, seeing Then as Now, Now as Forever. And within this perspective there is the no less fascinating spectacle of Morris's own evolution. I felt that *Gloria*, the earliest work on the program, was not quite the whole Morris, yet it has things—a musical score, for one, most sensitively treated—that the latest piece doesn't have. And it is a kind of modern-dance compendium in itself.

The rhetorical style of *Gloria* is in the main a recapitulation of an early pietistic phase in modern dance which has actually persisted in the work of Alvin Ailey and some others. Set to Vivaldi's Gloria in D, the choreography is full of the sky-sweeping arms, canting torsos, and ecstatic, relevé-triggered spiralling "falls and recoveries" that were dear to the heart of old Bennington. But the piece is also a postmodern testament: there is the odd gesture, the convulsive accent, the mild strain of dissonance; one person shoves another, hands grip crotches, a whole bunch of people fall to the floor and crawl forward on their bellies. If the "uplift" movement recalls at times the puritanical fervor of Doris Humphrey (at other times the unction of Ailey), it also hints at the radical simplicity and frankness of Paul Taylor. But the breezy impenitence of it all summons up the robotic era, just past, of motiveless motion and druggy dissociative gesture typified by such choreographers as Laura Dean and Andy DeGroat. These echoes appear not as a nice neat set of discrete evocations but as a scrambled-together cacophonous mass of material. Maybe to Morris the past is all one piece of goods, and it could be that what I see as a historic survey (the religiosity of the thirties generation superimposed on the ritualism of the seventies, or the other way around) is only his response as a choreographer to a certain kind of music. He danced for several seasons in the company of Hannah Kahn, who sets pleasantly anachronistic joy-of-dance movement to classical music. Like Morris's, Kahn's technique is highly kinetic, and she uses the same kind of wide stance, broad upper body, and round, full phrasing. But I find no adventure in the dances and no musical feeling to compare with his. Morris also danced with Dean, who was possibly a more potent influence. At all events, he hasn't turned out a pastiche. The fact that he has made a very successful new version of a modern-dance staple shows that an instinct for the new can coexist with a taste for the perennial. (This may seem a cliché, but count up the "new" choreographers and see how many there are to whom it actually applies.) Even if Morris was as conscious of his past in making *Gloria* as I was in watching it, I think his impulse must have been to make it as if no one had been there before him. I also suspect that, seen at an earlier stage of his development, *Gloria* (which is in fact a reworking of a 1981 piece) would have been the evening's high point—the event that revealed *the* Mark Morris. It wasn't this time, and not because the two newer pieces were without doubt the weirdest to be seen on any stage this season.

Behind the weirdness, Morris has a lot of common sense. The second work on the program was a twenty-minute solo that he performed himself. Twenty minutes is a long time for a solo, but not for this tour de force. Morris had adapted to his own purposes classical Indian dance forms, which with their typically protracted time sense and repetitive structures have inspired a whole body of avant-garde music and dance in America; even as he danced, *Einstein on the Beach* was being rehearsed in another part of the building. Yet *seeing* Morris in the guise of an Indian classical dancer was something of a shock. He appeared in a loincloth, with his shoulder-length curls unbound, and with his palms and the soles of his big feet anointed with red paint. These trappings were assumed quite unaffectedly; the dance turned out to be a personal variation on Indian dance themes, no more ethnological than the music of Philip Glass. Yet Morris's performance was as far from the minimalism of Glass, Steve Reich, and their attendant school of choreography as the real, rich, endlessly nuanced ancient art of India is itself. In those twenty minutes, Morris established two points of connection with the past. First, he is the link, missing until now, to the mid-seventies and the cult of Eastern music and dance which began flourishing then. Second, he transcends cultism and becomes himself a connection to the original source material—becomes, indeed, a kind of corrective to the cult. Instead of a score by Glass or Reich, Morris uses a tape of "O Rangasayee," a raga by Sri Tyagaraja. M. S. Subbulakshmi, who sings on the tape, has a soft, supple, velvety voice, and Morris produced movements that are a mirror of her inflections, even of the texture of her sound. Some of his movements—the warrior stances, the one-legged Shiva-like poses en face with cocked knees and angled arms—are traditional; others appeared to be freely invented, though close enough to the tradition to seem part of it. (If there were an indigenous modern dance in Southern India today, it might look like this.) In what he attempts here, Morris evokes another tradition—that of Ted Shawn and his dances of the Orient. Shawn, however, Westernized his models; one can't imagine him performing a twenty-minute raga or, if he ever did, observing its structural pattern. In one section of *O Rangasayee*, Morris does about fifteen repeats of a passage on the diagonal, which he varies occasionally with lateral sorties at the rear of the stage. Every time—every single time—Morris repeated the diagonal sequence, it was different. He followed a basic pattern: holding himself in profile, he would back upstage in small, delicate emboîtés, then abruptly about-face and walk the rest of the way squarely erect, waggling his head. Whirling and continuing to whirl, he would come back downstage in a wide-striding crouch. The sequence was a loop, and as one watched it one saw shortened and lengthened phrases, phrases thickened or attenuated, accent shifted, attack altered. But one saw these things with one's second sight; primarily, the experience of the passage was a purely rhythmic pleasure with incidental pleasures along the way. The head-waggling, for instance, became ever more mysterious, the emboîtés ever more delicious (Morris would vary the depth of his plié and the drumming of his feet as they travelled upstage). The catch step that resumed the emboîtés became—like the metal clasp on a necklace—a small event in itself, unwearyingly familiar, to offset new sparkles in a constantly changing configuration.

In his bearing, Morris has a relaxed and powerful physicality. He's voluptuous but not narcissistic. He gives the impression of dancing for his own pleasure, but without vanity. Not a small man, he's not all soft edges, either. Previous solos of his that I've seen have played on his androgynous quality, but *O Rangasayee* went beyond them all in its reconciliation of masculine and feminine aspects in his dancing. It excelled, too, in its labyrinthine rhythm and its dynamic use of antithetical energies (stasis-kinesis, abandon-control). Reconciliation of opposites was, in fact, the solo's poetic theme. East and West, tradition and the avant-garde as well as sexual ambiguities were brought to new harmonious resolutions, and it was done through the manipulation of abstract dance forces. In the solos in last year's New York concerts, Morris had shown himself to be a remarkable personality, with a sense of form and a flair for self-presentation. The solos were awesome, and afterward you wondered, Who is this guy? After *O Rangasayee*, I still wonder at Mark Morris's mystery. But that he is one of the world's marvellous dancers I have no doubt.

Somewhere in his being, Morris is a philosophy major. Last year, he gave us a piece on the death of Socrates; this year, it's *Championship Wrestling After Roland Barthes*. The basic point Barthes makes in his amusingly pedantic essay "The World of Wrestling" is that wrestling is not a sport but a spectacle; it belongs to the theatre, and, like the theatre, it deals in "the intelligible representation of moral situations." Morris doesn't present a morality play. Since, according to Barthes, wrestling already is that, Morris focusses on the details of the way wrestlers look and act; he uses wrestling as a dance spectacle. The result is very different from Johanna Boyce or Molissa Fenley attempting to present sports as dance, and it's different from the various sports ballets, in which sports can't really exist. There is no tennis in *Jeux*, no skating in *Les Patineurs*. But everything about wrestling exists in *Championship Wrestling* except the actual clouting of the opponent—no one gets bruised. As a parody, the dance is practically one on one with its subject. Even point-scoring can be eliminated, because, if Barthes is right, what matters in wrestling is not the excellence of the contestants but their participation in a universal drama—"the great spectacle," as he puts it, "of Suffering, Defeat, and Justice." Wrestling (like dancing) has no hidden code of meaning; what you see is all there is to it. Ergo, on with the show.

Morris designed the piece for ten members of his company, five men and five women, and he has men fighting women as well as women fighting women and men fighting men. He doesn't try to make any of it beautiful; it's all as indefensibly stupid as it is in the arena, only—because of witty staging and impeccable comic timing—a thousand times funnier. The clinches, the body blows, the crashes to the floor are as finely engineered as the mayhem in vintage Tom and Jerry cartoons. In the most outlandish sequence, two antagonists supported by two teams are maneuvered against each other in slow motion. On contact, each delivers a blow— in slow motion. One punches the other's head precisely ten times, is punched back, and by dozens of grappling hands is turned head over heels slowly and excruciatingly, over and over and on and on. Herschel Garfein, the composer, has provided a half-documentary, half-cartoon score, filled with crowd noises and electronic whammies. The dancers, men and women alike, take their macho poses and hunker around with brute authority; they manage to look svelte and squat at the same time. As the lights go down, they are lying all over the stage, slapping the floor with their hands in order, as Barthes says, "to make evident to all the intolerable nature of [their] situation."

The Mark Morris Dance Group ended the choreographers' series in this year's Next Wave Festival, which is how the Brooklyn Academy bills its programs of new or newish non-mainstream music and dance. Previous entrants—Meredith Monk and Ping Chong, Remy Charlip, Elisa Monte, and Bill T. Jones and Arnie Zane—were presented in the Opera House; Morris was in the big cold cave on the second floor called the Lepercq Space. He not only defeated the disadvantage; he put on a show that in idiomatic range, technical command, and audacity of vision eclipsed the competition and, for the first time this season, justified the series' title.

New York used to see a great many more visiting Spanish dancers than it does now. In the fifties and sixties, it was nothing for a Spanish company to play a three-week season on Broadway. Antonio Gades was the last great Spanish dancer to make a New York début; that was in 1964, and since then the torch has been carried by a thin trickle of soloists, none of them stars, booked into out-of-the-way houses. But business may be picking up. Gades returns with his company to the City Center next month, and last month we had the brilliant María Benítez for a week at the Joyce. Benítez is herself a sign of the changing times—a non-Spanish-born Spanish-dance artist whose authenticity is beyond question. The undisputed Spanish-dance star of the fifties and sixties was José Greco; in terms of box-office power he may have been the greatest of all dance stars until the advent of Rudolf Nureyev. The fact that Greco was not Spanish but an Italian (raised in Brooklyn) was held against him by the purists, and during the palmy days of the Spanish touring companies his was often accused of trumpery. María Benítez, born in Minnesota, has an American Indian mother and a Puerto Rican father. She studied and toured in Spain, and in 1972 formed her first company, María Benítez Estampa Flamenca. She has appeared in New York before—I last saw her in Brooklyn, in 1979—but never with the impact she had last month at the Joyce. And with her during the week, appearing as a guest artist, was José Greco. Greco's waist has thickened (he is now sixty-five), but the line of his back is still iconic, and he lifts and braces his knees like a stallion. Benítez dedicated her season to him, in thanks for having broken the Spanish-by-birth barrier. In a program note, she wrote, "It is very easy to make a personal, private statement of admiration, but it is a tremendous joy to make this statement public." And she danced with him in the romantic *Nobleza Andaluza* and in the rousing flamenco finale.

The current Benítez company is a reconstituted group, talented and attractive but not a completely integrated ensemble. Young Rosa Mercedes danced a firm and springy eighteenth-century-style solo hampered by the overfull cut of her costume. Pablo Rodarte and Timo Lozano performed solidly as contrasting studies in masculine vigor, the one impetuous, the other more restrained; neither is as yet the partner Benítez requires. Opening night started shakily. Not until the star's first solo, which caught the house, did the company relax; then everyone performed with spontaneous warmth. The dancers are sunny, with an offhand elegance; they don't spoil the seductiveness of Spanish dance with hard work and pomposity. Benítez's strictness and intensity have always been impressive but just a little scary. She's a mellower performer now, with a calm that draws you in. Her solos had some wonderfully suspenseful Kabuki-like moments, and in the dances with Greco she was exhilarating—gracious, enveloping, at every moment plastically vivid and responsive. There was good music, too, by the two guitarists and the singer, Luis Vargas, who went right along with the amiable spirit of the evening. The only miscalculation was the inclusion of a perfunctory dance drama in which Benítez was caught—physically—between her husband and her lover and stabbed by mistake. As soon as that happened, the curtain rushed down, the clouds parted, and the sun came out again. —*December 17, 1984*

Experiments

The Tap Dance Theatre of Gail Conrad represents a kind of post-romantic view of the art of tap dancing; it says that tap needn't always be genial and naïvely optimistic and high-spirited, and that its survival into the eighties isn't an anachronism. Conrad's kind of tap dancing asks to be identified with new-wave forms of expression in music and pop-world manners; it seeks out other truths in the medium than the perennial ones, which no music is being written nowadays to support. I think those truths exist in the mechanics of tap and have always existed—Astaire alluded to them in certain of his solos which have an almost surly force—but they have the flavor of decadence about them. The post-romantic phase in tap is like the twilight of the Romantic era in ballet. By the time of *Coppélia*, the bright day of the immortal and ethereal ballerina had dimmed. The mechanics of pointwork had once reinforced an image of otherworldly grace; now, in *Coppélia*, they revealed something in the very nature of points that was not superhuman so much as inhuman—automatic and shrill. Historically speaking, metaphysical truth in ballet flowed from tragedy to comedy; in tap it flows from comedy (from, specifically, musical comedy, which is Gail Conrad's poetic point of origin) to tragedy—to the perception that all is not wonderfully well between the sexes and right with the world.

The question that Gail Conrad's theatre raises is not whether tap can sustain these perceptions; it's whether it can sustain them as a tap story—as a continually evolving cause-and-effect structure of meaning generating power and excitement from the discipline of the form. If I come away uncertain of the answer, it's because too much of what Gail Conrad is doing these days tends to separate the meanings from the form—to have tap be only a convention that contains some very loosely codified physical movement of a kind meant to convey the real significance of characters and situations. This auxiliary, quasi-dramatic modern-dance element is always in danger of pre-empting the tap monologues and duologues and choruses, but one almost wouldn't mind if it did as long as it could make *something* clear to us which tap could then go on to amplify and explain. In her most recent performances, at Marymount Manhattan Theatre, Conrad seemed to have got things the wrong way around. She glided from situations to hang dances on (her most effective tactic) into situation turns and twists that became events in themselves. While we puzzled over the nature of these events, the tapping dwindled into ineffectual expostulation or silence. She helped us out, as usual, with props and scenery and bits of soundtrack atmosphere, but these hints seemed always too few or too many, and her sense of costume was arbitrary as ever—usually the same basic outfits are worn from piece to piece.

Beyond the Bases, the most ambitiously atmospheric number, was the most obscure. A couple of baseball players meet a sunbather ostensibly for a picnic. They have tap-dance adventures instead. Then it rains, and three ghosts—girls dressed as baseball players—appear and keep appearing. Clearly, "baseball" and "picnic" are only allusions to a context. But Conrad means to do more than evoke long summer days and adolescent reveries. She lost me with those ghosts. They didn't fit into the picture I thought I had recognized, and they weren't integrated in such a way as to form a new picture. *Beyond the Bases* fizzled; it didn't turn sour, like another new piece, *Scotch and Soda*. This started as a challenge duet with sexual overtones and became increasingly and pointlessly argumentative. Working against the clichés of the form may create tensions, but one can't replace the stylized repartee of the tap duet with "real" dialogue without working against the *clarity* of the form. One might add that the challenge dance is a star turn. David Parker is an ingratiating performer and Kathryn Tufano an able technician, but neither has the virtuosity or the star personality to fill out the roles and make us understand what these two people are to each other. (They look mismatched, but that happens not to be a factor in the argument.)

Gail Conrad's success has been in collecting what she had to say as a witty and resourceful tap-dance choreographer inside theme plays (not narratives) that she writes herself. Her *Wave* (1981), which had to do with middle-class suburban values coming unstuck in the midst of a natural disaster, had a satirical theme that related admirably to the nervous, jittery appeal of tap dancing. One saw the hypothetical point of tap in *Mission*, a science-fiction fantasy created two years later, but here it was the production values that came unstuck; the parts of an intricately conceived jigsaw puzzle gravitated toward each other but never locked into place. In relation to scenic and plot elements there was too little dancing, too little of which depended on the features of tap. And that's been the problem with just about every other "story" piece Conrad has done. Her style is innately dramatic, but it's the style of dance-as-drama; it's not dance drama in the linear, sequential terms she's shown such a great interest in since *Mission*. Presenting tap dancers as characters can only be a ploy, after all, and Conrad is currently acknowledging that fact in her best pieces, which have little or no story frame. The Marymount Manhattan program opened with one of these pieces and closed with another—ingenious, relaxed, glistening tap toccatas in which Conrad herself performs as a member of the ensemble.

Drama, of course, is produced from contrast, which is a function of rhythm. When I say Gail Conrad is dramatic, I mean she's rhythmically prolific to a degree that promotes extreme possibilities of color and expansion in her material. It's easy to see how she has become interested in a storytelling tap theatre. Among the lively contrasts of the form as she pursues it, the liveliest is the one in her sensibility between her responsiveness to a contemporary pop style and her knowl-edge and love of tradition. She never ventures so far from the sunny side of tap that she becomes eccentric; the darker, harder tones present the sunshine in perspective. She never pretends that she and her company are other than white and middle class—or at times lower middle class, as in *Waterfront*, which seemed to me to be taking place in a fifties cinder-block tavern with a jukebox. The milieu of *Red Skies*, the closing piece, was a bit nicer—something like a campus disco. These distinctions of place and time may be just fancies of mine; there's no evidence that Conrad thinks numbers like these are anything but decompression chambers to ease us into or out of the real business of the evening. *The Racket* generally comes early in the program; it's an in-betweenish affair, with long, clearly elucidated and differentiated sections of tap held together by some nonsense about a mugging and two rival pairs of crooks seeking to do each other out of the booty. Even though *The Racket* is a theme play that reads very clearly (and is only thirteen minutes long), it's not a favorite Conrad piece of mine. Somehow, the patently artificial pretext betrays her into pertness and inconsistency. The vividness of the mugging (we see the victim spread-eagled on the ground with her dress over her head) clashes with the stylized "apache" swagger of the dancing, with the berets and raincoats and the air of Montmartre chic. And the payoff— the victim coming alive, gunning down the crooks, retrieving her purse, and then replanting herself face down as a lure for the next thief—raises more questions than it answers. It also seems a great mistake, a lapse in form, not to have the victim dance, especially since she turns out to be the controlling force.

Conrad's dance music, arranged by Ernest Provencher, is live, and it is support music, nothing more. In the days when she was availing herself of stock tunes and classical tags, she got more heft from a phrase. If only a tune would surface now! The skeletal, intermittent scores of Provencher are discreet, but they don't supply much impetus. Is it a coincidence that Conrad's scenarios started to thicken at the same time that she turned to custom-made music? Like John Curry, whose ice shows are a mite too jealous of ballet, she's trying to do things with the form that probably can't be done. And needn't be. Conrad's work in tap is more interesting than her ambitions for it.

The way to fulfill a commission is to make demands on yourself in behalf of the sponsor, giving him what he wants but hasn't asked for. American Ballet Theatre commissioned a piece from David Gordon; Baryshnikov's only request was that Gordon use a set. Gordon has done more—he's made a real ballet, as the audience kept saying wonderingly when A.B.T. staged it last month in Washington. He's taken a piece of classical music, John Field's Seventh Piano Concerto, and set steps to it that ballet dancers can use their technique on; the women are on point. Moreover, the choreography is distributed like ballet-company choreography, with a ballerina (Martine van Hamel) and a danseur (Clark Tippet) heading a cast of six demisoloists and a corps of twelve. There's an egalitarian spirit among the ranks, but the position of the ballerina is never in doubt. Where Gordon breaks the rules is in his treatment of stage space. He doesn't layer the ranks with the queen on top. He doesn't divide the stage into sectors of influence or open up dramatic depths; he simply doesn't see it as an enclosed arena at all. The choreography passes right across the stage, with the dancers—starting with a long solo trill for van Hamel—entering at the left and exiting at the right, and never crossing back. The entrées, set to the first movement of the concerto, have their own spatial logic. Instead of dramatizing a constant space, they keep negotiating with a fluid one, creating a select series of happenings almost all of which are completed before the next series begins. It will be interesting to see how this modest, debonair idea works on the larger stage of the Met when the piece, which is called *Field, Chair and Mountain*, is presented there this spring. At the Kennedy Center, it was like seeing pictures on a Japanese screen slipping across the stage.

The piece is about partnering. The six demisoloists are divided into three pairs, the corps into six pairs. In Part I, Gordon switches pairs about, combines them, separates them. He demonstrates partnering in pairs as a ceremony of mutual danger, tact, and courtesy; he shows a lift or a supported leap as an event with a clear impulse and a resolution; he shows a cluster of lifts and leaps repeating and reversing themselves in a web of consequence. In the second part (to the second and final movement of the concerto), he begins a new game—partnering with chairs. The folding chairs (he has used them before, in other pieces) are comic relief, but they're serious play, too. As the dancers swing themselves through and over the chairs, line them up, sit down or stand on them or suddenly change places, they put themselves through rigorous drillwork in three-quarter time. Pairs then conjoin over a chair, and the partnering begins again, repeating some of the permutations of the first part, with some of the same air of tender consideration. The climaxes start piling up in the ensemble work and then in the stars' pas de deux. Tippet partners van Hamel from a sitting position as she does chaîné turns around him; he promenades her as she carries a chair or they carry it between them; finally and unforgettably, standing high on her chair, van Hamel promenades on point, swinging a magisterial leg over Tippet's head.

For all its thin watercolor texture, there's a lot going on in *Field, Chair and Mountain*. The first object in the title, a pun on the composer's name, refers to a rock field that appears behind the dancers in Part I. Santo Loquasto designed it in accordion folds that open laterally as the dancers traverse the stage—a parody of the Japanese-screen idea in the choreography. In Part II, Loquasto contributes a backcloth depicting mountain peaks dotted with folding chairs. What with the Victorian laciness of the music, and the etiquette and the extremity of the choreography, this mad picture of Loquasto's, which appears in the final minutes, seems to release a fragrance of barmy gentility that permeates the whole ballet. *Field, Chair and Mountain* is the kind of folly that advances to the limits of frivolity on the strength of passion.

Ballet Theatre has also acquired Balanchine's *Donizetti Variations*. I saw it danced before the Gordon première by Marianna Tcherkassky and Danilo Radojevic, who hadn't yet worked out their approach to the principal roles. The ballerina role, one of the very few in the Balanchine catalogue which never once pay homage to the image enshrined by the Romantic era, is extremely difficult, especially the adagio portion. There's a tinge of perversity in the steps, which honor technique at the expense of beauty (Balanchine may have had in mind some of the armor-plated Italian ballerinas of the nineties), and it isn't the kind of technique that gets applause. The variations are more gratifying, but even these have a spoof element, which is matched in the principal male role. The characterizations in *Donizetti Variations* are so subtle that the ballet can be done straight. As in the A.B.T. performance (once the tricky adagio was over), it still succeeds. But then the more broadly drawn supporting cast—nine long-suffering, highly competitive dancers—steals the show.　　　　—*January 28, 1985*

Cheers for Kyra Nichols

In her Balanchine roles, Kyra Nichols looks like the Goddess of Reason, a paragon of classical discipline and refinement. In the two biggest roles that Peter Martins has choreographed for her—in last year's A *Schubertiad* and the new *Poulenc Sonata*—she's provocative and vexatious; she doesn't calm the audience, she stirs it up. And she's utterly charming. Not that she isn't charming in Balanchine. If he never got around to making a role for Kyra Nichols—a fact always to be regretted by followers of New York City Ballet—Balanchine did create a repertory in which her noble, pure, and sunny classical style could flourish. Nichols dancing Balanchine is an image of rock-solid perfection and contentment—it's Nichols at peace with herself. In Martins's ballets, she resembles more the warrior princess we had a glimpse of in one of her minor Balanchine roles—Hippolyta in A *Midsummer Night's Dream*. Stampeding her hounds through the forest, clearing the mists with a burst of fouettés, Nichols's Hippolyta ruled with an iron will and sowed danger and disruption in her wake. Martins capitalizes on those effects. Especially in *Poulenc Sonata*, he gives us a Kyra Nichols whose very presence unsettles us and fills us with fear and fascination.

The interesting thing about Nichols in this new ballet is that she's not an oppressive, overbearing character; in fact, she's not a character. Her role, which has her sweetly but persistently tugging at the affections of two men, describes a condition. Nothing happens to her that she does not make happen, yet she does not act, and the ballet is not in any workable terms constructed as a narrative. Martins, I think, means to objectify the drive that lies behind Nichols's perfectionism, and though we see the drive clearly enough, we don't see what it leads to. It goes in circles. The heroine seems to be a creature of formless calculation, and her two men (Christopher d'Amboise and Alexandre Proia) are similarly blind (although, like all male characters in Peter Martins's ballets, they're terribly well intentioned).

As a choreographer, Martins uses sexual triangles in a very strange way. He casts three dancers, but then he constructs a pas de deux, frequently to a two-piano score. Changing one of the partners from time to time gives everything scope and tension, but the situation is seldom inherently a triangular one. (There are some proper trios in A *Schubertiad*, but they're at best preliminaries to the main business of the pas de deux.) In *Poulenc Sonata* (for two pianos), he keeps alternating Kyra Nichols's partners, but only, it seems, to give her dance power more play. She does things in this ballet that I've never seen anyone do before—things like the unsupported multiple en dedans pirouette that several times swings open into a croisé devant extension; or like those wonderful peremptory leaps in which she flies, standing up, straight through the air into her partner's arms. And, along with these "mere" technical feats, there is the lyricism of her duets with the men—slow, deep-breathing duets of extreme tenderness and rich irony in which with all her strength of will she delivers herself submissively into the man's care.

Nichols is so meltingly lovely in these passages and Martins has designed them so carefully to fit the breathless nocturnal hush that recurs in the music that we read them as climactic passages in a dramatic context. But the piece turns out to have no more dramatic continuity than a Merce Cunningham "chance" piece. And Martins seems far less interested even than Cunningham in projecting a specific meaning. He isn't interested even if one emerges from the dance continuity. In this respect, *Poulenc Sonata* is a much more opaque piece than the one it structurally resembles—the ballet to Stravinsky's Concerto for Two Solo Pianos, which Martins made for Heather Watts three years ago. Although he takes great pains over the men's individual styles, blending them with the music so that Proia's handsome classical line and d'Amboise's flashy jazz patter seem part of the same ballet, Martins certainly doesn't develop any of the possibilities in Nichols's preferring now Proia, now d'Amboise. In fact, the several pas de deux she dances with these two quite dissimilar men are very much alike. In the end, I was forced to conclude that in relation to Nichols these men and their styles were meaningless—that what mattered was Nichols and *her* style, her drives and desires. Although Martins may be carrying on one of those choreographers' experiments to see how dramatic sheer dancing can be, I prefer to think of *Poulenc Sonata* as a ballet about someone who doesn't realize her own strength. It ends the same way it began, with Nichols alone, her arms blocking her face. The image says, all too plaintively, "lost." But then we've seen the wondrous self-possession with which Nichols becomes lost—seen her keeping her balance in a tempest, flying fearlessly blind into a man's arms, or just placing herself there and walking away a moment later. We think of the quiet deliberation with which she reclines on men's bodies or stretches her neck to bury her face in their hands. The role is one long controlled flight into dependency.

Martins, choreography's most prominent autodidact, has been working exceptionally hard of late on displaying the special abilities of his dancers. In *Poulenc Sonata*, not only does he build an entire ballet on the dominating, unaggressive performing style of Kyra Nichols; he provides d'Amboise with an impressive role and responds sensitively to Proia, a young French dancer new to the company. The piece fills a demonstrable need; it's not just another ballet. Two other ballets that were given premières this season, Helgi Tomasson's *Menuetto* and Bart Cook's *Seven by Five*, were prettily composed affairs of no particular consequence. They didn't lack merit; they lacked the analytical impulse that might have earned them a place in the repertory. Nichols appeared in the Tomasson piece alongside Maria Calegari. Two such distinguished and different young ballerinas ought to challenge any choreographer, but Tomasson only pointed out some of their specialties and told us nothing new about them. He did better with a pas de trois set to the titular music (the menuetto is the third movement of Mozart's Divertimento No. 17 in D), danced by two of the company's most promising young men, Peter Boal and Carlo Merlo, with the very competent Miriam Mahdaviani. As a choreographer and teacher, Tomasson may yet make a difference to male dancing in this country. He has just accepted an invitation to direct the San Francisco Ballet, long a masculine stronghold, and one that should prove hospitable to his gifts.

Poulenc Sonata is one of Nichols's few non-Balanchine roles that you feel doesn't just use up her energies. (Another is Robbins's *Other Dances*.) She was born to dance Balanchine. She's squarely in the tradition he adapted from the Russian academy, and she's superb in all those roles in which, mainly to Tchaikovsky's music, he commemorates the academy: the Russian Theme in *Serenade*, the *Piano Concerto No. 2*, *Theme and Variations*, *The Nutcracker*. *Raymonda Variations*, which Nichols does so beautifully, is in this same mode. In a different mode but in the same sparkling form she dances Sanguinic in *The Four Temperaments*, Polyhymnia in *Apollo*, and *Square Dance*. The pearl of her allegro collection is probably the lead in *Divertimento No. 15*; it's Nichols at her most glowingly impersonal. Nichols almost purifies choreography as she performs it, even choreography as clean as Balanchine's. She's at her best in roles that combine transparency and force. It doesn't matter whose role. Her *Walpurgisnacht* is completely different from Suzanne Farrell's. Where Farrell is wit incarnate, Nichols is reason inflamed. And the way Nichols performs Violette Verdy's parts in *Liebeslieder Walzer* and *Emeralds* accounts in large measure for the successful revival of those ballets. It takes exceptional strength and technical precision to dance Nichols's repertory. It also takes the heart of a lioness. I've watched Nichols with extra care ever since I noticed, in the fourth movement of *Symphony in C*, the thing of beauty she used to make of the double fouetté pirouette that ended in a drop to one knee—she'd bring the knee clearly and riskily à la seconde before tucking the leg back to a kneel. That was years ago. Nichols could have retired into her perfectionism and become faultily faultless. With her Madame Récamier looks, she'd have got away with it, too. Gradually, along with her precision, she developed urgency and a tantalizing style. Of all the ballerinas in the company who do *Stars and Stripes*, it's Nichols who brings off the crackling bravura comedy with the least amount of self-applause. But she rates ovations. She's a lioness who jumps through hoops and loves it.

Since they won't stop mucking about with *Carmen*, let them at least refrain from giving us any more of those horrid dance translations in toe shoes. *Carmen* ballets always seem to have a ballerina who slinks around stabbing her points in all directions and glaring at people from under her eyebrows. But while I'm grateful to Ballet Antonio Gades for not perpetuating these clichés in its current engagement at the City Center, I hesitate to recommend an evening that does less than might be expected to turn a dance version of the opera into a flamenco showcase. There is a great deal more to Spanish dancing than we see here; substitute pounding heels for stabbing toe shoes and you've just about got the dramatic measure of this *Carmen*. Ballet Antonio Gades is a vivid, disciplined company, but it is not rich in soloists. Only Gades himself, who dances Don José opposite Cristina Hoyos's rather stolid Carmen, is truly first-rate. But the show is really a monolith, exciting only when the chorus takes over the spotlight.

The rhythms are flexible, propulsive dance rhythms, and they're generated most of the time by the dancers themselves, clapping or beating time on tables and benches, or by the folk songs of the singers and guitarists. Bizet's music is heard only in taped snippets, and its elegance contradicts the raw vitality of both the live singing and the dancing. I take the contrast to be intentional. This is a production that deals in the legend of *Carmen* rather than in direct translation. And purely in dance terms I thought it succeeded in proportion to the distance it put between itself and scenes from the opera. The action takes place in a rehearsal studio with mirrors; the idea is that we are present at a series of rousing improvisations on the *Carmen* theme. But the ruse doesn't work. Rehearsal, workshop: whatever we take this event to be, it fails to engage us in the conflicts essential to the story. The movie version of this show had a wraparound story about dancers acting out parallel conflicts in real life. On the stage, this extra, *Pagliacci* layer is missing (and a good thing, too), but nothing else is introduced that would account for the keen interest the dancers all take in playing out a famous love affair. Balanchine is on record saying that *Carmen* can't be danced, because the tragedy of the central character must be explained in words. Carmen is crushed by a destiny that brings *"la liberté"* and *"la mort"* into fatal correspondence. So, one might argue, is the Swan Queen. But *Swan Lake* possesses a potent visual metaphor for *"la liberté,"* and *Carmen* doesn't.   —*February 18, 1985*

An American in Paris

George Balanchine's ballet to Gounod's First Symphony, unperformed for twenty years, has been recovered in a lustrous New York City Ballet revival. Why it was discarded has never been clear; Lincoln Kirstein, in his book on New York City Ballet, lists it among "losses regretted by those who prize delicacy of texture or quiet sweetness of expression." Perhaps the ballet was too quiet for audiences who heard resemblances in the music to Bizet's Symphony in C and expected a ballet as brilliant and exciting as the one Balanchine had staged to that score. Maybe now we can begin to appreciate the qualities that Kirstein mentions and to assign the ballet a place in history.

Gounod Symphony, which had its première on January 8, 1958, is the forerunner of *Emeralds* and *Le Tombeau de Couperin*. In the chronology of Balanchine works, its nearest antecedent is *Scotch Symphony*, especially the last movement, with its steadily unfolding choral symmetry. The great stage and the spectacular corps de ballet of the Paris Opéra were the direct inspiration of all these works. Balanchine himself acknowledged the influence on *Gounod* of a Paris Opéra classic, *Soir de Fête*, choreographed in 1925 by Léo Staats to excerpts from Delibes's *La Source*. Balanchine could have seen it in the twenties, when its star was Olga Spessivtseva, and again in 1947, when he was a guest choreographer at the Opéra for six months. It was then that he produced, as *Le Palais de Cristal*, his ballet to the Bizet symphony. The inception of New York City Ballet the following year called forth the American production, retitled *Symphony in C*, and after that Balanchine kept a Paris Opéra wing in repertory, consisting of his own impressions of Opéra style. These he usually set as full-scale pieces to French music, but not always. *Scotch Symphony* is by Mendelssohn; so is A *Midsummer Night's Dream*. *Chaconne* is the Paris Opéra of Gluck's day. *La Source* is a small-scale divertissement to Delibes's music, as is *Ballo della Regina* to the music of Verdi. The quality that all these Opéra pastiches hold in common is femininity. Sooner or later, the stage is flooded with women. *Walpurgisnacht Ballet*, the only other Gounod piece in the company's repertory, says it all, both in its pulchri-tudinous finale and in the dances that come before, which barely permit the passage of the single male in the cast. In *Gounod Symphony*, Balanchine uses a corps of twenty women and ten men. The regnant ballerina has a cavalier who partners but seldom dances.

Gounod Symphony is a companion piece to *Symphony in C*, deliberately chosen as such. Besides the creative challenge of distinguishing between two closely related pieces of music, besides the undoubted pleasure of having a sumptuous new exhibit to add to the Opéra wing, the making of *Gounod* served Balanchine with a polemical purpose in his ongoing struggle for acceptance. Reviewing the première of *Symphony in C* for the *Times*, John Martin had written, "Mr. Balanchine has once again given us that ballet of his, this time for some inscrutable reason to the Bizet symphony." The charge that all his ballets were alike was the biggest weapon in the arsenal of Balanchine's critics. There weren't many people around who were prepared to concede that the ballets looked alike only because, as Martin later came to admit, they were so unlike anybody else's. By creating a completely different work—different in expression, different in rhythm and contour, in style and spirit—to music that matched the Bizet score in its basic strategy and formal progressions, and even in some of its features (the fugue in the second movement, the droning bass in the third), Balanchine was hoping to respond to his critics, refuting the charge that he had no choice but to repeat himself. He was making a little musical lesson out of his twin Bizet-Gounod ballets—a lesson that began in the perception that, though they dealt with similar material, the two symphonies were differently conceived, by two different musical intelligences. (Bizet had, in fact, closely studied Gounod's symphony before, at the age of seventeen, writing his own; being Bizet, he had achieved fresh and distinctive results.) I think Bal-anchine was also saying that no true musical intelligence repeats itself without meaning to. Not even Sousa, whom he regarded as America's Offenbach, ever composed two marches exactly alike. To bolster his point, Balanchine made *Stars and Stripes* that same season. He began his choreography to the title march with an extended quotation from the opening of *Pas de Dix*, a Glazunov suite he had recently made to selections from *Raymonda*. In that ballet and in the "Stars and Stripes Forever," he had the dancers enter with the identical steps. One can almost hear him murmuring to himself as he set this up, "See, I'll repeat myself on purpose and no one will notice." And no one did. He proved that the same steps set to different music are different in effect, just as in *Gounod* he proved that he was not compelled to treat same-sounding music in the same way.

The closer one looks at *Gounod Symphony* and its auspices, the more it appears to be part of a campaign. Balanchine was interested in making his style in ballet the American style. To do this, he would have to persuade the public that an authentic American dance tradition existed on which he—and he alone—could build. He had for years fought the inclination of Americans to regard ballet as ever and exclusively Russian. (Kirstein complained that "balletrusse" was one word.) He seems to have projected the winter of 1957–58 as his make-or-break season. And he included in it *Gounod Symphony*, a ballet most observers of his career have tended to look back on as something knocked off in between preparations for *Square Dance*, *Agon*, *Stars and Stripes*, and a major revival of *Apollo*. The new ballets weren't designed with the sole intention of displaying Balanchine's versatility. Their apparent differences were transcended by the common aim of clarifying and forwarding American classicism. Yes, it was a campaign; Balanchine even used the word to designate the separate sections of *Stars and Stripes*. And, to a great extent, this campaign of his succeeded. The links between the two Stravinsky ballets, *Apollo* and *Agon*, were noted at the time. Those between *Square Dance* and *Stars and Stripes* were strengthened by Balanchine's use in the former ballet of a caller to holler out square-dance combinations while the dancers executed classical steps and figures that were actually derived from seventeenth-century dance forms—a cultivated version, in other words, of the steps and figures of traditional American country dancing. In a subsequent revival, the caller was removed, and *Square Dance*, set to string music by Corelli and Vivaldi, emerged more specifically linked to the old court dances that had inspired both *Apollo* and *Agon*. Balanchine's message to his 1957–58 public was succinct. *Apollo* predicted the classical style that he would develop in America and consolidate in *Agon*, *Square Dance* demonstrated the Americanism of classicism, and *Stars and Stripes* outrageously celebrated it.

Where did *Gounod Symphony* fit in all this? The conclusion then and for years to come was that it didn't fit and wasn't meant to. The historic season of 1957–58 is on record as one in which Balanchine, exercising his powers to the greatest capacity ever seen, abundantly and irrefutably made the case for American ballet and for himself as its master, and still found time to write a love letter to the Paris Opéra. But why should Balanchine have chosen to do so much at once? If he had wanted to, he could surely have put off work on the outré Gounod ballet to the next season. He'd still have been the most versatile choreographer of all time, and the piece might have won more of the critical attention it deserved. True, he held a commission from Paris. But *Symphonie*, as the piece is called there, wasn't staged by the Paris Opéra Ballet until March 4, 1959. The ballet was done a year in advance because, as I see it, Balanchine *wanted* it included in the American season. His creative juices were stimulated by the other works he was doing and the connections among them, which extended to *Gounod*. Moreover, as soon as the season ended, the company would leave on a five-month Asian tour, and Balanchine would not be going along. Even if he were to go, his time would be taken up with official functions and the exigencies of the tour; he would not be able to rehearse a new ballet. Those creative juices were already flowing in the direction of a spectacular tribute to the French classical tradition, and he simply couldn't wait.

The relevance of *Gounod* is easier to see now than it was then. Its splashiness and prettiness (which relate it superficially to *Stars and Stripes*) may have concealed the formal integrity of a scheme based firmly on the music. Gounod planned all four movements around dance forms that he drew from the same Baroque sources that underpin the music of *Apollo*, *Agon*, and *Square Dance*. The first movement of the symphony is a gavotte, the second a bransle (metrically resembling the bransle gay in *Agon*), the third a minuet, and the fourth a rigaudon that opens with a pavane. Balanchine's choreography is a free fantasy on those models; he doesn't evoke court dances, as he does in *Agon* and *Square Dance*. He probably had in mind the Paris Opéra as an institution with the Baroque as its unique heritage. He envisioned a stage fully dressed and filled with women and their consorts, all reposing in clusters as symmetrical as the flower beds in the Luxembourg Gardens, then launching themselves in profuse demonstrations of *la danse d'école*. Every man in the corps has two women to support. What that leads to—two lines of women, each holding a balance as a line of men crosses between them; repeated instances of this, with variations, until finally the lines link together and dissolve in a maze—must be seen to be believed. Kirstein has likened the ballet's imagery to the ornamental gardens of Versailles. Then, there are the quasi-military formations—diagonals, wheels, and so on—that are the mainstay of spectacle in any large megalopolitan theatre. At one point, the lines form up so as to suggest the radial spokes of the avenues leading from the Arc de Triomphe. (Balanchine didn't have quite enough dancers, but you get the idea.) Throughout the ballet, there is a witty tension between grandiosity of scale and daintiness of detail, between frivolity and *gravitas*. Like America, France has a lively vernacular dance tradition; when the gavotte of the opening movement changes into a galop, the dancers burst into the emboîté hops associated with the cancan. Balanchine, to whom coincidences mattered, would have been interested to know that Offenbach opened his Bouffes-Parisiens in 1855, the year of Gounod's symphony; *Orphée aux Enfers* was produced there three years later. Probably he did know it, just as he knew that Sousa (who was born in 1854) played in Offenbach's orchestra when the French composer toured the United States. The second number of *Stars and Stripes* is "French"—the girls do an entire cancan routine in the coda. So Sousa and Gounod are made to exchange a salute to Offenbach, because of whom, as Balanchine once said, "Americans walk fast." The American march was driven by French tempos.

Ballets created in the same moment bear a watermark that time makes plain. All through *Gounod* are traces of things done in *Square Dance* or *Stars and Stripes*. We recognize in the blocky evolutions of the corps and in the lavish use of canon a phase in Balanchine's work which was soon to close. The long pas de deux of the second movement is notably short of wind; the adagio phrases that Balanchine would demand of his ballerinas in the sixties—phrases unthinkably fine and invisibly linked—are starting to blossom in *Gounod*, not in the pas de deux but in the pavane danced by the corps. The only quotation from *Symphony in C* I have been able to spot occurs in that pas de deux, in the sequence of slow finger turns in piqué attitude lengthening into piqué arabesque. On each ara-besque, the ballerina pauses in profile, just as she does in the Bizet adagio, but without bending her supporting knee. The omission of this detail and the very different musical context make the passage new. Other mementos of the Bizet ballet are written into the role of the corps and are all but buried beneath the myriad elaborations to which Balanchine subjects them. The stately entrance of the ballerina in the Bizet second movement is here done en masse; the Bizet's "country reel" is expanded into the swarming maze of the Gounod's marvellous allegro vivace finale.

The original première of *Gounod Symphony* marked the tenth anniversary of *Symphony in C* (another reason Balanchine may have been eager to get it on early). Martin, by then a supporter, was a *Gounod* enthusiast. Edwin Denby, to whom the revival is dedicated, wrote of the "autumnal richness of *Gounod Symphony*, hovering over a stately score, its steady four-bar phrases punctuated in thirty thousand ways, all correct." This hints at a regularity in the music which Balanchine had to find ways of overcoming. Other critics, less admiring, found the piece overambitious, both too large for the City Center stage and too difficult for the dancers. The ballet was given during N.Y.C.B.'s first year at the State Theater, then it made way for *Brahms-Schoenberg Quartet*, which, though not its equal, covered the vast stage without being too hard for the corps to dance. Since then, the company has matured; it handles with authority the slow parades and promenades that Balanchine made for it a generation ago on faith. *Gounod* always belonged to the corps. Originally, the third movement was danced entirely by groups. Balanchine, after a season or two, inserted two entrées for the principals, and these are the only parts of his choreography that have been lost. Peter Martins made new choreography that passes for authentic Balanchine. The rest of the ballet has been staged from a choreographic script of her own devising by Vida Brown Olinick, who in 1958 was Balanchine's ballet mistress, and who also staged the Paris première. (*Gounod* has long been defunct in Paris; *Le Palais de Cristal* was recently revived.) Besides Mrs. Olinick's script, the company had only a silent 16-millimeter film of the corps in rehearsal and the principals in performance. Maria Tallchief and Jacques d'Amboise danced the 1958 première. Tallchief's place was soon taken by Diana Adams (who was in the record film), then by Allegra Kent. Most of the company's ballerinas had their day in *Gounod*; Violette Verdy, now a teaching associate, is especially well remembered. All the current performances have been danced by Merrill Ashley with Sean Lavery. Ashley is at a peak of strength these days, and she has kept on expanding artistically. In the season's single performance of *Symphony in C*, given on opening night, she danced the adagio with fresh musical insight and fullness of phrase. But in the Gounod second movement she has problems finding the right punctuation for the four-bar phrases Denby spoke of—problems that have kept her, despite Lavery's excellent partnering, from bringing the long dance to a climax.

Karinska's costumes have been retained, with subtle modifications. The Degas cut and coloring of the women's dresses, the old-gold brocade of the men's doublets are still exactly right (though the ballerina's tutu should be fuller). A new décor, by Robin Wagner, depicts an indoor arboretum with glass walls and a vaulting glass roof. The crystal palace that was Balanchine's original metaphor for the Paris Opéra was a hothouse for the nurturing of delicate plants. In *Gounod Symphony*, he was showing the American public how classical ballet flourishes in an institutional setting. In its initial season, it was at once the most old-fashioned and the most forward-looking of the four ballets. It was the ballet that tied together past and future, and said, "See what happened in Paris? It can happen here."

—February 25, 1985

Getting It All Together

"Welcome to Pilobolus," the voice on the loudspeaker says before every performance. And this intelligent, imaginative company really does exist in a world of its own creation, one to which we were carefully displaced, on each of three programs presented at the Joyce, by the opening work—a *Bonsai*, a *Ciona*, or a *Mirage*—which told us what Pilobolus is and does. The metaphors sparkled, the acrobatics delighted, and when the metaphors were produced by the acrobatics— by the extreme extension of physical wit—Pilobolus was at a peak of expression. Next would come a solo (Moses Pendleton's *Momix* or Jonathan Wolken's *Pseudopodia* or Alison Chase's *Moonblind* or *A Miniature*) that told us that the Pilobolus ethos is roomy enough to accommodate individual variations, however eccentric (Pendleton), abstract (Wolken), or whimsical-experimental (Chase). Another solo, extracted from *The Empty Suitor* and performed by its creator, Michael Tracy, shows Pilobolus's links to the new currents in circus and mime performance (the Pickle Family Circus, jugglers like Michael Moschen and the Flying Kara-mazov Brothers, clowns like Bob Berky and Bill Irwin). There would also be a duet—a deliberate trifle, like Carol Parker and Peter Pucci in their impressions of the big-band era, or else something madly improbable, like Pendleton's *Stabat Mater*, danced by one figure in a hooded monk's robe and another on stilts. Through all this part of the show, Pilobolus maintained its good humor along with its customary style of casual contrivance. But in the second half things took a turn.

Program A: *Return to Maria la Baja*. In front of the audience, Robert Faust, a tall, powerfully built man, rummages in a trunk. He pulls on a skirt, clamps something on his head, then backs upstage, bent over. When he straightens up, he's wearing a mask with a mop of long hair. Faust is a woman of inhuman strength. He reaches behind him, seizes Lisa Giobbi, lifts her slowly over his head, and lowers her onto his lap. Later, this girl, who is manhandled and raped, and whom we see dangling in the air like a doll, carries him around the stage on her back. These are effects that only dancer-mimes can bring off, and this version, by Alison Chase and Robby Barnett, of "The Incredible and Sad Tale of Innocent Eréndira and Her Heartless Grandmother," by Gabriel García Márquez, brings them off all too easily. The piece is a coldly methodical conception that gives you nothing to react to but shocks. I could make no sense of the drama, which is about a child who is sold into prostitution by her grandmother, and which is depicted as a series of atrocities ending with the murder and decapitation of the grandmother (the mask with the hair comes swinging out at us, hanging from the murderer's arm like the head of Medusa), but on some mechanically theatrical level the piece is effective. I enjoyed the smooth performing of Faust and Giobbi even as I wondered why we'd had to watch them dress up or why Giobbi's post-rape scenes had to be so consciously pathetic. Barnett appeared as various rapists and murderers; I enjoyed watching him as much as ever even as I tried to figure out why his accomplices, all male, were played by Carolyn Minor. (The travesty impersonation doesn't jibe with the travesty impersonation of the grandmother.) I admired the masks, the costumes, the lighting, and the immaculate timing of each horrific event even as I winced at the unleavened grimness and the third-rate surrealism of it all. When Pilobolus loses its humor, it loses its grip on style, too. *Return to Maria la Baja* is an attempt to produce a narrative, using characters and continuously consequential action—something the company is not known for. Pilobolus pieces tend to be agglutinations; one happening follows another in a more or less logical sequence, with little concern for tempo and climax. This piece not only doesn't dispense with the episodic structure and with all discontinuity (the action stops for a passage of mask-twiddling); in its pursuit of violence and horror, it bypasses the dream logic that has always characterized Pilobolian fantasy. It's too literal a nightmare—it runs on a monorail of luridity. The only element of fantasy is the transsexual casting, and that isn't enough. For the first time at a Pilobolus performance, I found myself thinking of other companies that do this sort of thing better—the Royal Ballet, for example, with its clinical-grotesque pieces by Kenneth MacMillan. And I tried not to think about the only other atrocity piece dominated by an oversize female I've ever seen: *Big Bertha*, by Paul Taylor.

Program B: *What Grows in Huygens' Window*. Actually, this isn't so bad. An

Alwin Nikolais–type costume piece, it was designed by the choreographer, Jonathan Wolken, in collaboration with Kitty Daly, who has designed or constructed the bulk of Pilobolus's costumes for the past ten years, and who must be the greatest unsung designer in the business—unsung, I suspect, because she produces unobtrusively perfect results in a variety of styles. Here the dancers wear big downward-curving hats, and tent dresses beneath which they manipulate sticks with hands on the ends, so their arms seem twice as long. The costumes are activated to suggest changing shapes, and then—the Pilobolus touch—they give birth to their wearers. The lights fade as the "mothers" rock their "babies." The title is an enigma. (Huygens was a seventeenth-century Dutch mathematician.)

Program B also featured *Tarleton's Resurrection*, in which two churls (Peter Pucci and Michael Tracy in medieval togs) play nasty tricks on each other. Some of the jokes are good, such as the fistfight where the two stand apart, never touching, but reacting to the blows each deals in turn. On the whole, though, the piece falls into the art-clown category—the rear guard of the new movement in mime performance.

Program C: *Elegy for the Moment.* Conceived by Alison Chase in one of her misterioso moods, this traces the doings of a sexually ambivalent trio; there's a woman in one of Kitty Daly's clinging silk gowns, a man in a tuxedo, and a woman in a tuxedo. They all move to the morose hooting of a soprano, and they're lit so that their shadows loom on the backcloth. The lighting may be a technical outgrowth of the study in light that Chase presents in her solo *A Miniature*, but it's artistically regressive. *A Miniature* is a composition in swirling lights and darks, as elegantly turned as a sonnet, as turbulent as a painting by Munch. Taken separately, its effects (all of which are achieved by Chase with two hand-held flashlights) are nothing the world hasn't seen before. Taken together, they are theatrical magic. *Elegy for the Moment* is a loose bundle of ideas, none of them fascinating to begin with. Why are Piloboli hipped on violence and kinky sex? They made wonderful satyr plays in the seventies. Now they make these passionless orgies.

Luckily, all three programs ended with a lift. *Day Two*, the last of the epics of Priapean joy, and *Untitled*, the fable about the Victorian giantesses who give birth to their lovers, are Pilobolus classics that one can see again and again. Of the six pieces that were new to me, only *Stabat Mater* seemed close to that level. With its trompe-l'oeil opening, its strange amalgamation of the stiltwalker and the scurrying little priestess, its dashes of wild humor (the priestess rushing between the stiltwalker's legs, the stiltwalker dragging her by the cowl, her leaps that freeze in the air), it built what might have been a pat statement of repressed erotomania into something completely novel. As far as new directions go, the path seems to me to lie with Pendleton's recent pieces, which have a dance continuity and use music contrapuntally, rather than with the Chase-Barnett prose dramas to synchronized sound. The new talent in the company includes some very good dancers. Two of the best, Parker and Pucci, are also comedians of inspiration. When they come on to do their turn to big-band swing music, *Can't Get Started*, they look self-conscious and external, like students of the era who have discovered their characterizations—"bobby-soxer," "hepcat," "eager beaver"—in the attic. But their bodies are inside the music. Though it isn't really a dance (most of it is done sitting down), *Can't Get Started* swings.

As I look back over the season, it seems clear that when the agglutinated Pilobolus piece works it does so through a process of assimilation; its key element is montage. The piece fails when the ideas don't come together or when (as in *Return to Maria la Baja*) there aren't enough of them to create the friction and tension of montage. Sometimes there are too many ideas, and we get a kind of spillover; the second part of *Bonsai* and the middle part of *Mirage* don't seem organic to those pieces. But even a nutty lightweight duet like *Can't Get Started* works through montage. Its double-edged consciousness is a Pilobolian state of mind.

A performance of *Tchaikovsky Suite No. 3* at New York City Ballet this past season had Suzanne Farrell in the "Élégie" and Lourdes Lopez in the finale ("Theme and Variations"). Only a few years ago, the casting might have been the reverse: Farrell as the dazzling classical ballerina, and Lopez, with her dark, glamorous looks, as the elusive vision in the haunted ballroom—the woman who emerges from a line of women and fades back into it, leaving the man to dream on without her. The role is a simplified version of Farrell's role in *Meditation*—simplified dramatically and technically—and it was a natural one for her to take on in a season in which, because of injuries to two of her partners, Adam Lüders and Joseph Duell, she was losing performances. (Her partner in the "Élégie" was Alexandre Proia.) But it really isn't a Farrell role. Not only is it relatively undemanding but the fact that it is danced in unblocked slippers means that a major portion of her technique goes unused, and at this stage in Farrell's career, when her repertory is diminishing anyway, we want to see that technique of hers in full play as often as possible. Farrell off point is still a great dancer—she proves it in the first half of *Liebeslieder Walzer* and in *Vienna Waltzes*—but in a pure "glamour" role, like the "Élégie," with no technique to it at all, she's neutralized.

Farrell was the first ballerina in our time to announce herself to an audience wholly through her dancing; she made no appeal on the basis of personal charm, acting ability, or resemblance to a known ballerina type. Her technique was and is the definition of her personality. Lopez is very much a type; she reminds me of the ballerinas of the forties who had large dramatic faces and moonlighted in the movies. She's a very beautiful woman for whom classical technique has as yet nothing like the expressive force that it has for Farrell, and in the "Theme and Variations" she seemed as anonymous as Farrell did in the "Élégie."

Lopez is strong and talented, and she wasn't miscast, yet the beauty she brings onstage isn't amplified and dramatized by her dancing. Her gifts were apparent from the minute she turned up in a School of American Ballet workshop, in 1973. She graduated into the company the following year (along with Maria Calegari, Kyra Nichols, and Judith Fugate); last year, she was made a principal dancer. Lopez has never sought to trade on her looks, and while I can't help feeling that she might have come along faster if she had, I also feel that she habitually dances with less than her full impact. Looking at her feet in "Theme," I saw carelessly loose fifth positions wherever the choreography calls for airtight ones—for example, in the soutenu turns that are practically the role's signature step. Narrowly based footwork is more than just a technical nicety, a sign of good workmanship; it's a hallmark of Balanchine style. Not only in this role but throughout his choreography, it is the chief means by which the moving image of a woman is given focus and distinction. Lopez's beauty is soft and doelike, and sometimes I think she keeps her base wide in order to further soften her image; in other technical respects she's as punctilious as Merrill Ashley. Ashley-style enunciation with Spanish consonants—that seems to be what she's aiming at. It's much too modest, too general a goal. Maybe, though, if she tried closing her fifths as tightly as Ashley does, she'd look more herself. Cleaner technique can only make her a more individually beautiful dancer.

Technique is the key to distinction for men, too. Christopher d'Amboise can dance. Like his father, Jacques, he has natural elevation and ballon, a captivating presence, and a good ear. But his abilities are underrepresented by his technique, and he compounds that problem by trying to turn minimal and blurry technique into a style. He achieves distinction, but of the wrong sort; among the other male soloists he looks like a visitor from another planet. If Lourdes Lopez's face belongs to a past era, d'Amboise's whole style is an unwelcome reminder of the "real guys don't turn out" days. Ib Andersen is not greatly turned out, either, yet he has built on his classical training to strengthen his technique. In the past year, he has become more accurate in his leaps, more imposingly calm, and more musically fluent, all at the same time. Opposite Lopez in "Theme" (it was a double début), he gave a forceful performance in a notoriously difficult role.

With Sean Lavery (and in the absence of Lüders, Duell, and Helgi Tomasson, who has now retired), Andersen has taken over most of the first-dancer roles. Jerome Robbins put him and Lavery in his new piece, *Eight Lines*, where they appeared with Calegari and Nichols—golden girls for two golden boys. Robbins's choreography never explained why he needed such high-powered talent or what he heard in his music, by Steve Reich. Occasionally, there'd be a mettlesome dance passage or something that corresponded visually to a musical event, but by and large Robbins made no attempt either to build on the virtuosity of his performers or to follow the music's process. And there didn't seem to be any other conception behind his rather desultory choreography. Robbins, in his indecisive way, is a montage artist, too. Looking this season at *Piano Pieces* and noticing the veering course he pursued in constructing each variation—heading one way, breaking off, starting over, breaking off, and so on—and noticing, too, how the result invariably met with storms of applause, I began to think that Robbins's choreography is not the progression of moments I have always looked for but a collection of moments. When Heather Watts appeared in the Barcarolle, she got the most applause of all, because she understands how all the moments add up—

or, rather, how they don't add up. Watts is the perfect Robbins dancer; she makes his indecisiveness and evasiveness seem purposeful. Nichols and Calegari are also in *Piano Pieces*; next to Watts they look weak. And Robbins casts them and not Watts in his new piece.

Farrell still dances *Meditation*. She gave a performance of it on closing night, Lüders managing to partner her for the occasion (a benefit given by the dancers for their emergency fund), and the experience was one to set beside the astonishing performances of *Chaconne* and *Tzigane* and *Walpurgisnacht* she had already given us this season. It's hard to believe that this slim, young-looking Farrell will be forty this summer. By never trying to outpoint her former self, by concentrating on uncovering new riches in her roles, she has found the secret of perpetual youth. To the loss of athletic power she responds with heightened plastic sensitivity and musical discrimination. In two back-to-back *Chaconnes* she gave two different performances, one separating and dramatizing the components of the role, the other emphasizing their structural continuity. And she's still very strong, although her presence has become sweet and light, almost mothlike. She has always been the wittiest dancer alive, but in this new condition of impalpable strength spirituality enters in; wit becomes a beatitude.

A major event of the season was Darci Kistler's return to the company after a two-year absence. She danced several performances of *Afternoon of a Faun*. All of them had the exuberance, magnetism, and sheer animal energy that one remembered, but the last one, on the benefit night, had subtlety and discretion as well. Afshin Mofid, one of the company's young lions, was her perfect partner. —*March 18, 1985*

The America of Choreographers

Phrases, a new work performed by the Merce Cunningham company, begins with the full company of fifteen dancers clustered together, facing the audience. There's a dispersal, and soon we are watching a cast of eleven, divided into three, three, three, and two, performing the same steps. This is as big as the piece gets, and the force of unison movement (offset by one or two small variations in direction) becomes something the dancers intermittently refer to but never quite recapture. *Phrases* is a big-scale piece that seems to yearn toward intimate, contrapuntal effects. There are often two dances going on at the same time; say, a quartet upstage, a trio down. This then becomes two trios echoing each other imprecisely—not mirrors but counterparts. *Phrases*, one of Cunningham's great, chuntering group-upon-group pieces, lacks the relentless concentration of *Torse*;

its diffusiveness reminds me more of *Landrover* or *Exchange*. It is constantly building and demolishing itself, yet its foundation—the dance phrase—is never imperilled. Late in the action, the phrases become end-stopped, and the rhythm begins to oscillate in stop-and-go, statement-and-response patterns. Just before the end, the choreography shakes off this reflexive accent and starts to gather momentum. The dancers are covering the stage in a wide, swinging loop step—so attractive!—when the curtain falls.

Phrases is a thick set of pages torn from the Cunningham encyclopedia, but I'm not sure that, of the three new works given this season at the City Center, it makes the best introduction to Cunningham. For *Phrases* you have to have the appetite that comes of watching other, more tightly organized pieces in the repertory and following their unpredictable flow. *Phrases* rambles on, but these other pieces have a very mysterious magnetic core; the secret of their momentum is unguessable. What makes *Duets*—a succession of pas de deux—function as one unbroken line from start to finish? What gives *Pictures*, which keeps stopping at seemingly arbitrary points to form static images, its tensile strength? The action of *Doubles*, a new piece, looks as lazy and unplotted as that of a summer afternoon; what keeps it from falling apart I cannot imagine. Yet the connectedness of it all is unmistakable. The discontinuities (or so they appear) are all strung on the same thread.

"He has a boyish delight and trust in Things: there is always on his lips the familiar, pragmatic, American 'These are the facts'—for he is the most pragmatic of writers and so American that the adjective itself seems inadequate; one exclaims in despair and delight: He is the America of poets." So might Randall Jarrell, writing on William Carlos Williams, have described the man who is the America of choreographers. Cunningham's respect for the facts has colored his modernist sensibility with the convictions of a classicist. (And has helped make America the commodious haven for classical dancers that it is now.) He has no use for hidden meanings. "For me, it seems enough that dancing is a spiritual exercise in physical form, and that what is seen is what it is." The first thing one sees in *Doubles* is Catherine Kerr or Patricia Lent (the piece, designed for seven dancers, has two almost completely different casts) standing alone in the middle of the stage performing the kind of scrupulous, slow-motion développés and sustained balances that one might see in class. This is discipline as observable phenomena and as ritual—the dancer's daily ordinance. The slowness of the movement carries the eye from one incident to another: the mobilization of the thigh in développé, the tiny shift of weight that recenters control in equilibrium. This quality of clean-limbed power and clear detail is characteristic of the entire piece. We sense the pleasure of things accomplished for pure discipline's sake, and we sense, too, the existence of forms and objects moving beneath the surface of routine. I don't mean that the shapes and poses are evocations, though the boys in their rearing and bucking leaps, the girl who lies down and turns up her face like a sunbather—these say what they say. It's a more tenuous connection in moods and in the timing of events and their displacement by other events that makes us believe in

Doubles both as a formal progression and as a picture of reality. Twice the stage empties completely; mysteriously, the drift of things continues. Cunningham manages it all without languor, without irony, without even those small touches of the irregular and the exotic that composed the "fugitive" atmosphere of *Summerspace*. Yet one thinks of *Doubles* in the same breath as *Summerspace*. It is perhaps an urban pastorale—Central Park rather than Arcadia. It is grittier, less ceremonious than *Summerspace*. But ceremony, "spiritual exercise," is the occupation of both pieces.

Though they often perform the same steps as the men, the women of Cunningham's company have a quaintly bred, collegiate look, while the men are untamed, impulsive, even feral. (This suggests that whereas the women try to do the movement objectively, the men look to Cunningham himself as a model.) The two interpretive styles are vivid in *Doubles*, where they seem to fit in with other sets of contrasts to make up a total dynamic configuration. The good thing about Cunningham, of course, is that he can deploy a pattern unpredictably. These sets of contrasts (such as stillness/motion, staccato/legato, alertness/indolence) aren't stuck together; they are variously combined. There can be passive and active stillnesses, for example. And Cunningham can use sectors of the stage dynamically. One thinks of the two women who make a gradual upstage cross and later make another cross downstage in the same disparate manner, each in her own way, pacing or swaying gently, while the action continues around them. These women are the only dancers in the piece who do not have a solo, a fact that seems organically related both to their sentinel-like crossings of the stage and to the individualized ways in which they cross it. The five solos are the heart of the piece. Each seems wonderfully shaped to the talents of the dancer you see doing it. (The double casting of the roles accounts for the title, which might with equal accuracy have been *Singles*.) Within the range of masculine or feminine style, each dancer finds his or her own quality of emphasis.

Ideally, a solo should be a process of self-realization for the dancer who does it. It is one of the hard truths of classicism that the more stress dancing lays on the self, on personal vanities and habits of expression, the farther from self-realization it gets. Cunningham hasn't made it easy for his soloists, particularly the men. The three male solos, which are split into nonconsecutive segments, are constructed of viselike imperatives, and they're not so dissimilar in material as to bring out easy distinctions in the men's individual styles. No, the material makes these men brothers (just as the double casting makes them twins), and, like real brothers, they have to fight for an identity. The curious result of this pressure is that each dancer has been brought to extend his range surprisingly. Chris Komar and Alan Good, normally opposites, are made to trade virtues: Komar becomes larger, less febrile; Good's lankiness acquires shape and tension. In the thrusting off-center leaps that are one of the choreography's motifs, Good really throws his body in two directions at once, and without buckling in the middle—he bends in the air like a sapling. Neil Greenberg has often seemed too eager, even violent; in the Komar role he is steady, composed, precise. If there is one principle of attack common to all these roles, it is élancé. It is a revelation to see Greenberg's blunt power in élancé next to Good's lyrically attenuated version next to the more naturally dartlike force of Komar or Robert Swinston or Rob Remley. And in another recurrent step—the frisky low hop with one foot kicking up to the back—it is simply amazing to see the imprint of so many personal variations. Swinston and Remley (who are alternates) have unusually strong feet. They get to do a whole series of these low hops in place, and they charge the step with a pistonlike energy. Swinston gets an élancé shading into the hop, while Remley has the back kick of a mule. As for the women, Kerr and Lent, in their perfect placement and firm command of their outspreading limbs in adagio, are both wonderful to behold. Helen Barrow's responsiveness in repose makes her, too, a pleasure to watch, and one got to watch her, along with Good (their alternates had both left the company), in every performance. *Doubles* isolates its dancers and lets us see them away from the flux of group presentation. Cunningham hasn't made a piece like it in a long time. That he can do so now with two casts is an indication of the company's current strength.

Barrow's solo contains more pictorial elements than the other female solo, and in ensemble sections she is most often placed among the women, while Kerr (or Lent) is placed among the men. Also, Kerr (or Lent) is actually paired with one or another of the men, but none of the other women take partners. The peculiar atmosphere of many of Cunningham's pieces derives from unfathomable choices like these. And the choices of the designer, Mark Lancaster, are equally unfathomable. In *Doubles* he uses his familiar pants-over-unitard combination, and his color assortment is as bewitching as ever, especially in the men's costumes, where chalky tones of taupe, mauve, and blue are worn with chalky lemon-white pants. The image of those pants against the mauve cyclorama is so striking that you can remember the whole piece by it. And if you think the color is affected you're wrong. Coming back from the City Center one night, I saw lemon-white jeans walking ahead of me in the subway. Lancaster left Cunningham's employ last year. *Doubles* was his last piece. His place has been taken by William Anastasi and Dove Bradshaw, who are responsible for the sets, costumes, and lighting of *Phrases* and the third new piece, *Native Green*. In *Phrases* Bradshaw does a Lancaster-type layering job, beginning with solid-color unitards and covering them with sweaters, vests, and ankle-warmers as the piece goes on. In *Native Green* the dancers are in white unitards, with white overskirts for the women. These costumes, by Anastasi, are covered with speckles of pinkish-beige, and the cyclorama is a pinkish-beige speckled affair. It also has a diagonal line drawn across it, and the cyc for *Phrases* has two diagonal lines. None of this makes a more than fleeting visual impression or bears the slightest relation to the dancing. When, at the end of *Native Green*, the dancers suddenly pick up a rubber strip that has been lying at the back of the stage and manipulate it into an arch, it looks like a desperate attempt to bring unity to the choreography and the scenery.

The speckled look of *Native Green* has reminded some observers of *Summerspace*. The choreography, though, is nothing like that of *Summerspace*, and it isn't much like the rest of Cunningham, either. It is of standard opera-house design, frontal in focus, strong on diagonals. Its three couples (Komar and Barrow, Swinston and Lent, Good and Megan Walker) are together at the start of the piece, and they stay together, just like couples in a Balanchine ballet. But if the ground plan of *Native Green* is conventional, the steps are not. Cunningham's way with partnering dissents from the practice of classical ballet; he places the man more often at the woman's side than behind her, and has him support her by holding her hand rather than her waist. In *Native Green* Cunningham makes partnering jokes: in a supported passage, the women get themselves into awkward positions and the men switch handholds hastily, as if wondering whether grabbing a wrist or an ankle makes any difference; in several walking lifts, a woman's forward leg blindly probes the air ahead. When Cunningham does place a man behind a woman, it's usually to have him duplicate her movements, no matter how unlikely. She slumps in plié; so does he, right on top of her. The choreography of *Native Green* is full of a number of things: recondite waltz steps, classical postures from the Balinese dance, animal images (rolling heads, arching feline backs) from Cunningham's own bestiary. The mood of the piece is a nice blend of lyrical and antic. I say "nice" because is it is often hard to tell the two strains apart. Deadpan jokes come naturally to a man who believes in facts. But the piece is undeniably fun to watch. The audience had a very good time with it.

I saw *Phrases, Doubles,* and *Native Green* on the same program. The sound scores for all three pieces seem to have been indiscriminately commissioned. Mice raced through the wainscoting, animals gasped and died, caravans bearing shipments of marimbas blundered across pontoon bridges in the dark, whole cities were chopped to pieces by pneumatic drills, and the electronic equipment in the pit came down with gastritis. There should have been a sign over the City Center door: "If you have ears, prepare to plug them now." But what would the America of choreographers be without the America of crackpots?   —*April 1, 1985*

Modern Love

One hears so much about the death of romance in the relations between the sexes that whenever an artist manages to make a truly romantic work one has to ask where he got the material for it. Usually, the answer is that he got it from the past—the artist has produced a study in nostalgia. Changing sexual attitudes, it seems, are always imbued with a sense of loss. How can we really have lost something, though, and kept the appetite for it? The appetite for romance and all that goes with it—chivalry, the graces of courtship, the charm of intimacy— is in itself romantic. So is the idea that we have lost romance. The new piece with which Paul Taylor opened his season at the City Center is a romantic work about the loss of romance. Set to music by Wagner, it's a full-blown, surgingly lyrical piece that keeps the audience on edge, looking for the stroke of skepticism that never comes. Taylor is perfectly innocent here—as innocent as he can be. He toys with our feelings by not toying with them, and in the end he relaxes us and sends us away happy. The piece is called *Roses*, and he has put into it some of his best and most serious work in the pas-de-deux adagio form. What is more, without using devices, relying solely on structure and choice of music, he presses a series of philosophical points about romance and the way we view it.

First, structure. Taylor mounts a large composition for five couples, builds it to a climax, brings it to a close, and then introduces a sixth couple to dance alone while the others rest. The sixth couple, in white, adds nothing substantive to what the five couples, in black and gray, have already done; it adds a slight but noticeable difference of style and sentiment. At the conclusion of their duet, the two dancers in white retire into the group of black-and-gray couples, and the curtain comes down. Why did Taylor need this extra couple? (The audience is more than ready to applaud at the conclusion of the ensemble section.) And why did he place it at the end rather than at the beginning? Why did he prefer a slightly anticlimactic diminuendo effect to what might have been seen as a perfect crescendo in theme-and-variations form? The answers are in the music. If Taylor had used the white couple (Cathy McCann and David Parsons or Kate Johnson and Thomas Evert) at the start of the piece, the music for the duet, an Adagio for Clarinet and Strings composed in the eighteen-twenties, would have compelled him to build *forward* to the music of the Siegfried Idyll, which accompanies the ensemble section. Instead, he builds backward, contradicting the chronology of the two pieces of music and the chronological implications of their respective musical idioms. In the Adagio, the clarinet voices a Bellini-like melody over the strings; it might almost be a transcription of an actual Bellini aria. (Wagner was a great admirer of Bellini, but this Adagio, credited to him in the Taylor program, is now thought to have been composed by the clarinettist H. J. Baermann.) When this bright, linear, florid music *follows* the Siegfried Idyll, with its plushy texture and revolving chromatic progressions, we seem to move backward in time to another era and another range of sentiment. Thus juxtaposed, the two scores do not just form a meditation on two periods of Romanticism spanned by Wagner; they also provide the basis for a Taylor essay in retrospection as, in his staging, the manners and sentiments of one epoch give way to those of a previous epoch. Taylor even suggests that it is a natural thing for the sexes to revert to the imagination of an earlier age—that romance is always nostalgic. We in the audience, watching his dances for "1870" lovers, are displaced onstage by these lovers when they themselves settle back and contemplate the "1820" lovers. (But as romance is always nostalgic, so there are no period steps in these dances—only straightforward, muscular Taylor choreography.)

Romance seeks an ideal image and turns to the "perfection" of the past. The point is worth making; it may even be true. It is, to my mind, the answer to why *Roses* is designed in that peculiar way. But it isn't the answer to the spirit of the times, which keeps crying out that romance is dead. There's a sense in which romance *is* dead for us today; its token representations within the culture don't reverberate the way they used to—the fragrance of roses is faint, even suspect. What seems to have happened since the seventies is that relations between the sexes have been so politicized by the excesses of the women's movement and by the male reaction to those excesses that when love is shown without a political slant it looks old-fashioned. The self-consciousness of *Roses* is attuned to this development, but it's really a reaction to another development—one that poses a continuing problem for any artist, and particularly for any choreographer, who is drawn to the subject of love in our time. The different stimuli we used to employ to let the vicarious or anticipatory pleasures of romance roll through us— namely, popular music, the musical theatre, the movies, dancing cheek-to-cheek— have all dried up, for reasons that have nothing to do with the sexual revolution. Still, their decline strikes with dull force at the expression of romantic sentiment. Choreographers have to work without the musical impulses that used to come from the depths of our culture. Taylor, whose company is now celebrating its thirtieth anniversary, has only recently begun to address this problem. Besides *Roses*, he has turned out two other studies of love between men and women, to scores by Brahms and Elgar. The Brahms (*Equinox*) has a gentle Edwardian glow. The Elgar (*Sunset*) is staged as an episode of the recent past—around the fifties or early sixties, to judge from the women's dresses. But Taylor has carefully enclosed the action in a frame of memory, which activates a distinct mood not of nostalgia but of sorrow. *Sunset* is about things—small and fateful acts—that acquire meaning only in memory, and the fact that it is not here and now endows its image of sexual relations with a special poignancy. Taylor could have used music closer to us in time, but he could not conceivably have found contemporary music of such transparent sympathy and remorse. And therein, I think, lies the problem of all contemporary "romantic" choreography. There is no dance music being written to support it. On the one hand, *Roses* eases out of the problem by implying that our natural mode of association with romantic love is anachronistic. On the other hand, by using nineteenth-century music Taylor is doing just about the only thing a choreographer can do. Lovers whirl on, on the stage as in life, but the music of their exploits is that of another age.

Taylor's choreography is musically so limpid and so instinctively buoyant that when it takes on a score of the dimensions of the Siegfried Idyll it has to look a little undernourished technically. Wagner's harmonically complicated slow-moving tides are, if they are to support any dancing, more suited to the technique of classical ballet, which, unlike barefoot modern dance, can sustain a long musical line. There are passages in the Siegfried Idyll that seem to call out for the flow of pointwork and the arrested flow of balances on point. By and large, enough, Taylor's dances do sustain the pressure of the music, and in the most exhilarating way—by making us aware of the challenge involved. Taylor turns the chromatic unrest of the music into a kind of dancers' relay, passing the focus from one couple to the next. Relaxing from their play, the dancers slide to the floor and nestle, enveloped in the shimmering warmth of what Wagner intended as a birthday salute to his son Siegfried and perhaps also as an ode to domesticity. The "Bellini" dance strikes up another kind of acquaintance with music; it is as elaborate and improbable as an acrobatic-adagio act in a hotel ballroom. In a way, it is, I think, meant to reveal the nineteen-thirties to our eyes just as the music reveals the acrobatic bel-canto style of a century earlier. William Ivey Long's costumes reflect the duality of Taylor's conception. The black satin gowns for the women of the Siegfried Idyll are modern (like the gowns in *Cloven Kingdom*), but billow with a suggestion of hoopskirts. Under Donald York, the orchestra plays the chamber version of the Idyll with shining clarity; Anand Devendra is the fine clarinet soloist in the Adagio.

In 1960, Balanchine made Brahms and love duets fashionable with *Liebeslieder Walzer*. In 1969, Eliot Feld paid a fledgling choreographer's tribute to *Liebeslieder* with his *Intermezzo*—three couples in Karinska-style nineteenth-century costumes dancing to selections from the piano music of Opuses 39, 117, and 118. He is now presenting (at the Joyce) *Intermezzo No. 2*, with the same number of couples wearing similar costumes and doing similar things to the music of Opus 76, plus more of Opus 118 and one extract from Opus 119. It is an odd work for Feld to have produced—a virtual self-parody. His company is no longer the refined group of dancers he had in 1969, when I was moved to describe *Intermezzo* as "the most brilliant piece of work by an under-thirty choreographer since Paul Taylor's *3 Epitaphs*." It may be that the blowsy and heavy-handed *Intermezzo No. 2* is a reflection of the declining technical abilities of his dancers. The saddest thing about it, though, is its sacrifice of a poetic vision to the creation of a patented, pretested success. Whatever Feld originally meant to say in *Intermezzo* about Brahms and love and dancing he evidently no longer remembers. In the *Intermezzo* of the eighties, the subject is Feld's own tactical virtuosity in licking the genre a second time. I say that the virtuosity is limited by the dancers' comparatively meagre abilities, but it is constrained even more by the showoffy choreography.

A generally good rule when you have little to work with is: Do less. But one must know what to do less of. Since Feld apparently can't trust his women's point technique, he keeps them flying about in the air in lifts, lifts, and more lifts. This throws the emphasis squarely on the lack of footwork the ballet suffers from. The women do *all* their beats in lifts, none in jumps, and they're so overpartnered they become physically mute—undistinguished puppets dangling from the men's arms. Women who have no fate apart from that wished upon them by their masters are a poor subject for a "romantic" ballet. There were too many lifts in the first *Intermezzo*, too, making it in places mechanistic and overdriven, but it did have women with feet and with heads of their own; it even gave one of them a solo. I don't think the effect of subjugation is intended; it's an unhappy consequence of the labored, compensatory technique that Feld applies—his liftomania. But the style of the sequel also suggests that *Intermezzo* has now taken the place in Feld's mind that *Liebeslieder Walzer* had in 1969. The greatest tactical departure that Feld made from Balanchine was to characterize his three couples as bravura, lyrical, and comic. *Intermezzo No. 2* repeats a formula that was a mistake to begin with. Brahms did not write funny music. In the original version of *Intermezzo*, nothing was played for laughs. The gagged-up version became traditional, however, and now Feld forces a gagged-up duet into the sequel for no reason other than that he did it the first time. Certainly for no musical reason do we see two dancers lurch through a waltz clutching each other blindly. I can't think why Feld had to produce a second ballet whose net effect is to undo nearly everything that is still good in the first one. It may be, though, that the seeds of destruction were there in whatever made him start playing for laughs in the seventies.

Karole Armitage, who has done more than any other choreographer to combine theatrical dancing with the sounds and sights of avant-garde rock, is still doing it. Her latest concert, to which she gave the title of a physics equation, $-p = \frac{\partial H}{\partial q}$, consisted of an extended pas de deux based specifically on the theme of love—"the complex tensions of love's romance, eroticism and emotional unrest," to quote the flyer put out by Dance Theater Workshop. I went to see the piece and was not disappointed. Armitage has dropped most of the inscrutable symbolism that disfigured *Paradise*, the last work she showed in New York. With Joseph Lennon, she danced the long pas de deux as a series of legible physical events whose dramatic overtones were clear. At first, the dancers were two extroverts, performing with exaggerated flair as if before an audience in a huge theatre. Gradually, they grew more intimate, dancing as if for each other. But the implicit theatricality of everything they did precluded any effect of real intimacy. This I took to be the main point of the evening; whether as "lovers" or as "dancers," these two were always on. They didn't contribute much more than that to the lore of the pas de deux—their "erotic" number was essentially a variation on Nijinsky's *Faune*, and later they added variations on the *Agon* pas de deux—but they certainly put on a colorful and engrossing show.

Armitage, who wore five-inch spike heels when she was not on point, danced with astonishing force and indifference to gravity. She spent much of the evening off balance, bending toward and away from her partner like a flame-tipped sprite with a tallow center. She did bumps on point; then, reversing her terms, she did slow grands battements in those stiletto heels. She is a comedian whose act—annihilating the image and the propriety of classicism—is more amusing each time I see it. Part of my enjoyment comes from the strain Armitage places on definitions. Is she a real destroyer of classicism or a brazen hussy with a primpingly *classique* manner? Someone truly interested in destroying classicism would need to conduct more raids on its technique than Armitage does. Armed with her discontinuities of step and gesture (which she derives from Merce Cunningham), anatomically gifted, she can dance all night without showing you a single phrase, yet her prodigious scale and equilibrium and her conscious theatricality are enough to carry you along. She has evolved a *theatre* of dance with herself at the center.

But it isn't all about Armitage. An Armitage evening is also a fashion parade, a light show, and an art-rock concert. She is open to the influences of her collaborators, who are in turn open to the horrific, the kinky, the gorgeous, the new. Charles Atlas, her regular designer, provided the current show with a series of costume changes, using the conventions of punk chic in the style that has become his alone. He takes standard dancewear, dyes it culturally deprived colors like orange or turquoise, mixes in some harlequin blacks and whites, and adds a few comic-book touches (Spiderman boots and gloves, for example). It's so simple, and it looks great on dancers. Atlas also did the lighting for $-p = \frac{\partial H}{\partial q}$ at its première, earlier this year in Grenoble, France. The lighting designer at D.T.W., Phil Sandström, achieved some striking local effects. At one point, the door at the side of the stage was opened and Armitage danced a solo in the path of light from the adjacent lobby.

The music at Armitage concerts is always loud enough to take the skin off your face. This time, David Linton and Conrad Kinard played an amplified percussion score by Linton. It began with a blistering gong stroke and went on, with breaks, for fifty minutes. Toward the end, the two musicians, who wore white tie and tails, came off their platform and began putting on an act of their own. A moment later, the side door opened again, and Armitage came in stiltwalking and bearing a huge round frame while Lennon approached from the opposite direction encumbered by a large *square* frame that had religious pictures fluttering from it. But for these lapses into total anarchy and inscrutability, the evening was all one solid gesture. Armitage is not for everybody, and there are those who see her as symptomatic of the cynical, pranksterish spirit of the times, if not as the spirit of the times itself. Working with Atlas and Jeffrey Lohn, the composer of *Paradise*, she has recently completed a film for WGBH, as yet unseen. It was made in Providence, Rhode Island, my hometown, and I can hardly wait. It's called *Romance*. —April 29, 1985

Postscript 1987: Jeremy Bernstein wrote to say that Armitage's title was not a physics equation but possibly an attempt to render Newton's Law (force equals mass times acceleration). In any event, the title was changed, and the piece is now known, for equally mysterious reasons, as *The Watteau Duet*.

"Romeo" Revived

Reading Lynn Seymour's autobiography, *Lynn*, is probably not the best way of getting in the mood to see the Kenneth MacMillan ballets that American Ballet Theatre is now presenting at the Met. The roles of Juliet and Anastasia, which

MacMillan created for Seymour, are being performed by dancers of another company tradition and another generation; the impulse that motivated Seymour and MacMillan in the sixties is missing. And the self-scandalized, confessional style of the autobiography, published last year in England, is different from the way dancers tend to write about themselves here. Merrill Ashley in *Dancing for Balanchine* writes about roles and steps; *Lynn* is more like a celebrity memoir. Seymour doesn't tell us as much about the creative process she shared with MacMillan as about the vicissitudes of her friendship with him, and the strain that developed between them doesn't quite explain how, after a string of successes with Seymour, MacMillan could have gone ahead and created the ultimate Seymour role—that of Isadora Duncan in his ballet *Isadora*—without her. Seymour doesn't seem to have any idea of the part she and MacMillan played, separately and together, in the artistic fortunes of the Royal Ballet; to her (or her amanuensis, Paul Gardner) it's all personal history, and no item is too intimate to be left out.

When Seymour gets to the *Romeo and Juliet* chapter, we expect some account of the impact on the London ballet world of the Bolshoi production, starring Ulanova. The Royal tried as late as 1963 to acquire this very production before commissioning a new version from a house choreographer. One imagines how all the prestige garnered by the Russians must have weighed upon MacMillan as he started work. In sheer physical terms, too, the Bolshoi version was of a tonnage to daunt the most experienced choreographer. MacMillan, at thirty-five, was creating his first full-evening ballet. But there's no mention in the Seymour book of the Bolshoi. In her account, the main impression on MacMillan was made by John Cranko's post-Bolshoi production in Stuttgart, where Seymour had been invited to dance Juliet, and by Franco Zeffirelli's staging of Shakespeare's play for the Old Vic. Zeffirelli's (in film form) is probably still the best-known version of the play. The Cranko and MacMillan versions of the ballet have been trouped around the globe, rival classics that have withstood every attempt—and there have been numerous notable ones—to dislodge them from the repertory. What this means is that every year more people see *Romeo and Juliet* as a ballet or as a film than as a play. This wouldn't matter so much if the ballets really were classics and if the movie really was Shakespeare, but the movie is almost as much a ballet—or an opera—as the dance productions are; Zeffirelli cuts the text and substitutes camera action. And in the ballets the text isn't Shakespeare—it's Prokofiev.

The Russians had paid their respects to Shakespeare by pantomiming their way through the music; they tried to hold on to the meaning of the language by dancing as little as possible. Cranko saw the necessity of substituting dance for mime in the obvious places; he modernized the lovers' pas de deux, picked up the pace of the other scenes, and produced a faster, lighter, and younger *Romeo* than the Bolshoi's. But he also vulgarized the material and miscalculated most of the dramatic suspense in the score. His third act, encompassing the potion scene, the funeral, and the lovers' suicide, is a crude sketch compared with MacMillan's—crude and, in the final moments, incomprehensible. Juliet discovers Paris's body *after* she discovers Romeo's. Cranko has arranged the anticlimax so that she can stab herself with Paris's dagger, Romeo having used his to stab himself. (Romeo's not taking poison, as he does in the play, is Cranko trying to cover for the lack of a scene showing where the poison came from.) The comparative accuracy and simplicity of MacMillan's treatment are, like all the rest of his comparatively accurate, comparatively simple production, the result of a finer musical sense. His staging tells the eye what Prokofiev's music tells the ear, not only in point of incident but in point of tone. Cranko's version suffers from Cranko's inveterate unmusicality. Although he converts mime passages into dancing, it's an athletic, unlyrical kind of dancing. The poetic seriousness of the music is not of a consistently high order, but that doesn't excuse Cranko's Broadway zip. He was, in this work and throughout his career, the master of pop ballet. It's fitting that in this year of *Romeo* revivals his version should have been chosen by the Joffrey Ballet—the company committed since its beginnings to a pop image.

As many other choreographers have shown, it is no use trying to do the ballet without the scenario that Prokofiev followed. But this scenario, conceived by the Shakespearean director Sergei Radlov and prepared twice over with the assistance of two different choreographers, is a dramaturgical nightmare. Nothing is condensed or converted into ballet terms; every turn of plot is faithfully retained until we get to Romeo's exile, whereupon the plot is simply thrown out. Though MacMillan's ballet has the dignity of weight and scale appropriate to the score, it isn't drastically dissimilar to Cranko's, and its finesse runs thin over the same cracks in the plot that troubled Cranko. Friar Laurence is a noncharacter who emerges from his chapel like a clockwork toy to administer marriage vows and potions. Besides the two leads, only Mercutio makes a plausible dance character. His duel with Tybalt (implacably a mime role) has the high contrast of Errol Flynn's movie duels with Basil Rathbone. The duets, the duels, and a background of marketplace hubbub are about all a choreographer can hope to sustain. Both Cranko and MacMillan bring on Rosaline as a character (although only MacMillan gets anything out of the lute music that Prokofiev wrote for Romeo's serenades to her). The ballet needs her. But does it need Lady Capulet's violent demonstrations of grief over Tybalt's corpse, which strongly imply that the two have been having an affair? Here is one plot element the ballet *adds*, and it commands our attention at the wrong moment—just as Romeo realizes that he is banished. It's his tragedy, after all.

Cranko retained such hallmarks of the Bolshoi production as the Pillow Dance at the ball and Ulanova's breathless run along the front of the stage to the apothecary and back. MacMillan has the Pillow Dance without the pillows, and he minimizes the run in favor of a now equally famous scene in which Juliet sits motionless on her bed, gazing out at the audience, while the orchestra conveys the turbulence of her emotions. MacMillan's tendency to underplay moments like this matches neither the Italian verismo of the Zeffirelli production nor the operatic mime of the Bolshoi. He uses stillness again at the start of the balcony pas de deux, when the lovers, separated by the whole distance of the stage, simply stand and stare at each other. The histrionics are all in the dancing. In the marketplace scenes, he cuts down on the opera-house filler by introducing a village wedding—a device that Zeffirelli had also used to parallel Romeo's new-found happiness as Juliet's husband. The Mandolin Dance is performed by the wedding attendants, and in the A.B.T. production the acrobatic principal role is taken by Mercutio. But the filler is there nonetheless—Prokofiev wrote tarantella music by the yard. Where Cranko choreographs a giddy festival with pushcarts, lanterns, and fruit flying back and forth, MacMillan has three whores warring interminably with the good women of the town. It is all as impossibly tedious as any opera spectacle, when the supers are trying to get some color into this thing. And it is aggravated by the inability of American dancers to act. The Joffrey dancers manage well enough with the callowness of Cranko's conception. But in the A.B.T. crowd scenes the dancers look as if they were trying to hide from the audience, and they automatically regularize every movement. When MacMillan stages a passeggiata in the square with the low-lifes mimicking the affectations of the nobles, one half of the dancers are walking like this and the other half are walking like that. No attempt is made at individual variations. The flatness of the effect extends to the supporting roles. The A.B.T. casts have a good Mercutio in that winning performer Gil Boggs. The rest try hard but they don't project. Susan Jones wears too much padding in her costume to register the emotions of the Nurse. Kathleen Moore wears less, but she, too, misses the moment when Juliet, forced into an engagement to Paris, ostracized by her parents, turns to her nurse for advice. Juliet doesn't even get a response.

In the Joffrey performances at the State Theater in March, only David Palmer as Mercutio had dimension. Cranko's first Juliet was Carla Fracci. He revised the production and cast Marcia Haydée. His model seems to have been the waif played by the aging Ulanova, but Haydée looked more like the wallflower heroine of old musical comedies like *Good News*, and Richard Cragun was her big, handsome football-player Romeo. The twosome I saw at the Joffrey, Patricia Miller and James Canfield, were true to type. Seymour as MacMillan's chosen Juliet brought Anna Magnani–size passions to her love scenes and her defiance of her parents. She stabbed herself and died with her legs spread, Romeo's head resting on her thigh. Christopher Gable matched her in impetuosity, and his virility and athleticism were free of jock overtones. In both London and New York, the Royal's first cast was Fonteyn and Nureyev, who in adapting themselves to roles made on two other dancers showed their class as stars. The ballet sealed their fame as a team; in turn, they made it a box-office success. In spite of what Seymour says in her book, she wasn't cheated of her reward either in applause or in critical esteem. If her imprint on the role is blurred, that's because no one else has been able to dance it and act it just her way. Neither of the two Juliets I saw at A.B.T. reminded me of Seymour—or of Fonteyn, either. MacMillan, now with the company as associate artistic director, has evidently allowed his American Juliets (there are six of them) to find their own interpretations, just as the Royal ballerinas did. Susan Jaffe was a shy Juliet who went gaga over the glamorous Romeo of Patrick Bissell and gradually became dependent on him.

But Jaffe was unable to summon the hysteria of dependence that could have made all the last part of the ballet credible. Amanda McKerrow was able not only to do that but also to suggest a precocity of feeling that let her see into the tragedy ahead. When she discovered Romeo dead, she stood for a long moment quietly looking down at him. It was a stroke that brought to a natural resolution the stillnesses that are written into the role. McKerrow's dancing was even more impressive than her acting. She is small but not short, delicate but not waiflike or mousy. Her pulled-out limbs, quick feet, light runs, and lofty jump make her by nature a fantasy character. She doesn't have that Ballet Theatre flaw of dividing the impulse of a movement between the upper and lower body—she's all of a piece, and her element is the air. With her partner, Robert Hill, she did low, trancelike lifts, her feet brushing the floor in tremors; in leaps she appeared to fall from the heights into his hands.

Both *Romeos* are given in replicas of their original sets and costumes. Jürgen Rose's designs for Cranko are accurately and effectively reproduced. Nicholas Georgiadis's more resplendent designs for MacMillan are rendered dully in sepia pinks and browns, with yellowish lighting. Both sets have a second story, but Georgiadis's has staircases, and they make a great difference to the choreography. (Too bad the two levels of the set aren't used in the duels.) The A.B.T. performance is long, with stage waits that, in the last act, encourage walkouts. The Joffrey gets you out sooner, but you have to endure the jerky rhythm of Cranko's staging, and when he's done you haven't been anywhere. In a logy performance, the MacMillan can appear rich, handsome, and dead, but the Cranko is intrinsically slick, light, and foolish. What the choice finally comes down to isn't maturity of conception, or talent, or even stage wisdom; it's quality of mind. MacMillan is better company.

I have never seen a piece by anyone, anywhere, like Paul Taylor's *Last Look*. Basically, it's one of his visions of damnation, but it's an extreme statement even for him. The other works it reminds me of are *Churchyard, Dust, Private Domain*, and (quite specifically) the opening scene of *". . . Byzantium."* But those are all resemblances of atmosphere. *Last Look* moves in a way that cannot be related to any other piece: it twitches and thrashes and flails; it is one long series of spasms. Taylor has used "natural" movement before. Here the absence of any clearly defined dance movement suggests that he has reached some impasse of expression. For the enormity of the things he has to say, steps fail him.

The piece, which had its première at the City Center, was designed in collaboration with Alex Katz, and it is Katz's set, as usual, that establishes the terms. This consists of seven mirrored triangular boxes stood on end in an irregular grid pattern. The boxes, about as tall as the dancers, cut the stage into fragments, so that we're no longer looking at an abstract space—we're looking at a real place, a room. Furthermore, it is a closed room. The entire cast of nine dancers, onstage at the beginning, is there at the end; nobody ever exits. The sense of confinement is overwhelming. These people are penned together, and as the piece goes on, and their quivering and shuddering become more and more agitated (it's as if they were being electrocuted through the floor), we realize that there's no way out, no escape from the walls, the mirrors, the glaring lights, the bodies underfoot.

In the same instant that we take in this pressure cooker of a set, we take in the costumes (also by Katz). The women are in longish satin wraparound dresses with sharp lapels and cummerbunds; some wear jewelry. The fashionable retro look is easier to deal with than the men's dull-green shirts and pants, which look like uniforms. Because of the women's outfits and the mirrors, I saw the "room" as a disco, and the impression persisted despite the sound of the music, which was very far from the sound of disco. It was, in fact, a sound that drenched the terrible frenzy onstage in pathos—a sombre, brooding, deeply mournful orchestral threnody in which one heard, now and then, strains from *La Valse*. Donald York composed this music on Taylor's commission, and Taylor may have requested the reference to *La Valse* and meant to remind us of the inscription on the score: "We are dancing on the edge of a volcano."

Ravel, in 1920, sensed an impending social crisis. Taylor is precise about the nature of the crisis he evokes in *Last Look*. When his dancers are not writhing uncontrollably, they are staring at themselves in the mirrors. Susan McGuire and David Parsons perform a nominal pas de deux; the furtive postures, the narcissistic caresses tell us that in fact each is masturbating. Later, Parsons dances a reckless, convulsive, onanistic kind of solo, returning again and again to the mirror. Throughout the piece, the only allusions to formal dancing that crop up are to the waltz (woozy, out of control) and the frug. Of course, nobody ever takes a partner. Hell is not other people so much as it is the space other people take up. Parsons dances his solo in about six square feet of space. At the end, the image with which the ballet began—a heap of bodies—is painfully rebuilt, body on body, with one woman clawing her way to the top of the heap.

Newspaper accounts of night-club fires always include the ghastly detail of the bodies piled up at the exits. *Last Look* may not be the luxe vision of the apocalypse that Balanchine offers us in his *La Valse*, but it scares us more. It is the holocaust of small souls. —*May 13, 1985*

Bournonvilleana

Abdallah is a Bournonville ballet in three acts with an Arabian Nights plot. The title character is a poor shoemaker who does a good deed and is given a magic candelabrum, which he lights, one candle per wish; it makes him a rich man with a harem. The slave girls who dance in an elaborate second-act divertissement are kin to the bayadères and péris, the dryads and sylphs of various nineteenth-century vision scenes. The queen of the harem, Palmyra, is contrasted with Irma, the decent heroine. The contrast in types was a convention of the Romantic era. But, unlike Effie and the Sylph in *La Sylphide* or Gamzatti-Nikiya in *La Bayadère* or (the ultimate polarization) Odette-Odile in *Swan Lake*, Irma-Palmyra is not an idea rooted in the dynamics of the plot. Abdallah's love for Irma isn't seriously tested, and nothing's at stake when he becomes rich and sodden. And when he lights the forbidden fifth candle and the harem goes up in smoke the loss is only temporary.

Abdallah treats the issues and stereotypes of Romanticism almost too lightly to sustain its length. Then, too, the plot has its confusions. The grateful sheikh who is Abdallah's benefactor is an inscrutable figure, pushing the story now this way, now that. There are peripheral characters whose function is unclear, and when, in the third act, Abdallah enters the real world of wealth, presided over by the sheikh, it turns out to be no different from the dream world to which he was transported by the magic candles. In fact, two characters from the dream world—Omar, the pudgy master of the harem, and Sadi, a slave boy—are unaccountably present in the third act. The ballet, produced by Bournonville in 1855, was not a success, and after three years it was permanently dropped from the repertory. Hans Beck, who became director of Denmark's Royal Ballet fifteen years after Bournonville's death, took fragments from *Abdallah* and inserted them, slightly rechoreographed, in his expanded version of the Master's *Napoli*, Act III. These interpolations were all the world knew of *Abdallah* until early this year, when the entire ballet was reconstructed by Ballet West, in Salt Lake City. I am guessing that the unstable plot was what brought about the failure of the original production; my guess is based on the Ballet West version, which I saw on tour, at the Kennedy Center, in Washington. It is faithful, for the most part, to Bournonville's libretto. But I wonder if Bournonville's own production was as unserious. Ballet West uses the plot almost as a decorative element. It makes next to nothing of the notion, advanced in the libretto, that Irma is a noted dancer of the region (the alternate title of the ballet was *The Gazelle of Basra*) and Abdallah makes her shoes. When she is restored to him in the third act, she is veiled, and he recognizes her by the shape of her foot. It is a moment that Ballet West beclouds. But then ballet plots can go on just so long, especially in our day. The reasoning behind the production is all too understandable: Damn the plot, on with the dance.

But why Ballet West, and not the Royal Danish Ballet? And why *Abdallah*? Bournonville produced, by his own count, thirty-six original ballets. Seven have been preserved by his home company. It happens that the first production of *Abdallah*, in Copenhagen, was notated by Bournonville with more than usual care because he planned to present the ballet in Vienna later the same year. (Similar circumstances in the creation of Balanchine's *Gounod Symphony* made possible its recovery by New York City Ballet last winter.) These notes, written into a rehearsal copy of Holger Simon Paulli's score, were preserved in the Royal Library in Copenhagen along with the orchestral parts, the original ground plans and costume designs, and several drafts of the libretto. Yet another draft was acquired at auction by Bruce Marks, the artistic director of Ballet West, and, enchanted by the ballet's combination of exoticism and naïveté, he earmarked it for revival. Marks, a Bournonvillean, is the only American to have performed as a principal dancer with the Royal Danish Ballet. In 1966, he married the great Danish ballerina Toni Lander, and a decade later she joined him at Ballet West. The company was one of the enterprises of the Danish-American Christensen brothers; it was formed in 1963 from the ballet department begun by Willam Christensen at the University of Utah. Under Bruce Marks and Toni Lander Marks, the Danish connection was strengthened with productions of Bournonville ballets and of Harald Lander's *Etudes. Abdallah* is not the first time a "lost" ballet of Bournonville's has been revived in America. In 1983, another transplanted Dane, Flemming Flindt, put on *The Toreador* for the Dallas Ballet—the first production since the late-twenties Copenhagen revival starring Harald Lander. But *Abdallah* had never been revived. Ballet West's may be the first attempt to produce Bournonville straight out of the archives, from the documents of Bournonville's own time.

The set-and-costume designer, Jens-Jacob Worsaae, obviously had the best of the deal. Nobody knew exactly how the ballet was supposed to look, so he was free to invent. He has used modern devices to effect the mechanical transformations common to the nineteenth-century stage. His painted backdrops are unlabored period pastiche, and they probably make the ballet look better than it did at its première, when Bournonville was forced to use scenery from other productions. The starry gardens overhanging the harem are, one feels, just what Bournonville would have wanted, and so are the pantalets worn by all the women—even the slave girls—under their tutus. But if Worsaae worked unhampered by modern-day accretions, how must the lack of a performance tradition have affected the choreography? How clear, how extensive was Bournonville's choreographic script? Toni Lander, who had the task of translating it, described it in a program note:

> The score for two violins had Bournonville's own handwritten (in French) notes of steps and actions in the ballet. But, of course, not every step has been written down. It looks as though Bournonville just made a few notes for himself so he could remember a phrase, and sometimes very little is written. Occasionally, steps were impossible to read, and at times nothing is written.

So Toni Lander had to invent, too. She did so confidently, she wrote, relying on years of experience in Bournonville, on body instinct, and on her imagination. She had the help of the Bournonville authority Allan Fredericia and of the dancer Flemming Ryberg; the staging and the mime were fleshed out in collaboration with Bruce Marks. But it is Toni Lander to whom this production owes its existence.

In *Abdallah*, there are more dances in proportion to mime than was Bournonville's custom. Apparently, the Viennese audience loved to see flashy dancing, and Bournonville was trying for a hit in Vienna. The first act contains the women's extended pas de trois that went into *Napoli*. The second act, by far the best, has large-scale choral dances for men and women, variations for Palmyra and two attendants, a comic set piece for Omar and Sadi, a scarf duet à la Sylphide for Abdallah and Palmyra, and a festive waltz coda. Abdallah disposes of old friends in a pas d'action ending in a drunken galop. In Act III, set in the sheikh's court, the story is cut short by one of those "Let's everybody get married" gestures from the sheikh, and one of those lopsided Bournonville dance suites ensues—a pas de quatre involving two sons and two daughters of the sheikh, and Irma, who must for some reason choose a mate. In the grand finale, the courtiers join the reunited lovers and the pas-de-quatre principals. Everything ends symmetrically, but at some cost to the integrity of the score: the same music is played for three entrées in a row.

Paulli's music has a familiar ring elsewhere in this act, too, either because, like the first-act trio, it has been incorporated into other ballets or because it was traced over by Paulli himself. The composer of *Kermesse in Bruges* and *Konservatoriet*, of parts of *Flower Festival in Genzano* and *Napoli*, and of five other "lost" ballets besides *Abdallah*, Paulli seems to have been to Bournonville what Minkus was to Petipa—someone who could be called on to repeat a certain number of effects dependably from one piece to the next. There is nothing in *Abdallah* that lies outside Paulli's range as we already know it, and nothing in the range of the dancing that lies outside Bournonville's. This is as true of the second act, which seems the least plundered, as of Acts I and III. In the second act, the range of music and dancing is at its widest, not because there is more going on in the dances but simply because there are more kinds of dances and the variety has a certain sweep in relation to the plot. In themselves, the dances express very little. They don't move the plot ahead or expand poetically upon its meanings. They don't comment on the setting. (The only bits of ethnic color are in the stomping dances of the male ensemble, irremediably Nordic.) This neutrality, of course, is what makes the dances interchangeable, capable of being moved not only from place to place within the ballet but from this ballet to another. (Think of transferring dances from the Persia of *Abdallah* to the Italy of *Napoli!*) The choreography is not so much repetitious as it is dramatically innocent. It looks true to the standards of its period, whereas *A Folk Tale*, from the same period, looks in comparison like a twentieth-century ballet. (Which, owing to its longevity, it partly is.)

Toni Lander has given us scrupulous authenticity. Though there are several little pas de deux, they tend to be double solos, with a minimum of partnering; there is no supported adagio as we know it. The dances are technically sound, musically adroit—Bournonville to the core. If they tend toward sameness, or if we seem to have seen them before, that may be because there is nothing more to be discovered in the archives. When first Nureyev, then Makarova and Baryshnikov began mounting their productions of *Bayadère* and *Don Quixote* and *Paquita* for Western audiences, we didn't know that the first burst of revelation would also be the last—that soon we'd be witnessing the strange phenomenon of reshuffled Petipa. It was, perhaps, the moment to concede that as far as Petipa was concerned the nineteenth century was over; it had been sacked of its treasures. With *Abdallah*, we could be reaching the same point in the Bournonville legacy. The relics may continue to flow, but the revelations probably won't. A *Folk Tale*, in the Bournonville-centennial production of 1979 (Worsaae is now redesigning it), was the *Bayadère* of the Danish repertory. There can't be another like that.

Toni Lander was Ballet West's principal teacher, and the conscientious way the dancers performed their long and taxing roles was a credit to her influence. The second cast—William Pizzuto as Abdallah, Lisa LaManna as Irma, and Mary Ann Lind as Palmyra—though not as pretty and colorful as the first, danced and mimed with more precision. Bruce Marks was a genial and elegant Sheikh Ismail, and the orchestra was conducted—a bit relentlessly—by Varujan Kojian.

Bournonville did not number *La Sylphide* among his original works; it was an adaptation of the Taglioni ballet, though with a new and better score, commissioned from Herman Løvenskjold. *La Sylphide* quickly became the masterpiece of the Danish repertory. Its dances are responsive to character, locale, incident; it is a genuine ballet d'action. And it is the quintessence of Romanticism. The hero's illicit desires are depicted with overwhelming expressive force. We know there is no reconciling this ideal world with the sleepy country life and its bourgeois comforts; along with James, we become swallowed up in visions of unrespectability. A new production that the Pennsylvania Ballet brought to the Brooklyn Academy drives James into the Sylph's arms and then forward to his doom with breathless speed and urgency. The staging, by Peter Martins with the assistance of Solveig Ostergaard, is modelled on the Copenhagen production. Its modesty and air of controlled panic are preferable to the inflated scale and the melodramatics of the current American Ballet Theatre production. But there are some mistakes. Susan Tammany, the designer, does a nice simple country cottage, but then she lets herself go in a violently stylized forest scene. The snaky lines and inflamed colors seem intended to express the widest possible contrast to the staid domesticity of Act I, but in the Romantic view Nature and Supernature are beguilingly intermingled. This isn't Romanticism, it's Expressionism.

I suppose there are some who would say of the dancing that this isn't Bournonville, but I find the big and bold style a refreshing change from the needlepoint of the strict constructionists, especially in Act I, where the rough-hewn phrases in the reel and the broad leaps and choppy footwork of the men's dances (based on Scottish folk steps) match the plainness of the setting. These are farmers, after all. The Pennsylvania's men were uncommonly good at the style and comfortable with the mime. William DeGregory's clean line and firm delivery made him a bonny James. Marin Boieru, a dark and moody James, forced his attack unnecessarily. He has ample power and, when he relaxes, a strong presence; he also has a superlative jump. The women were less secure than the men. Tamara Hadley and Melissa Podcasy were pictorially charming but much too corporeal and forthright as the teasing, amoral Sylph, and their dancing lacked definition. Both might have profited from a few classes with Toni Lander, one of the great Sylphs of modern times. Lander combined ambiguity of intention with clarity of step, and there was something uncanny in her ability to change position in midair. A light flick and there she'd be, completely re-formed: head, arms, hands—perfect. Like the Danes, the Pennsylvanians use both women and men in the part of Madge the witch. Robin Preiss and Edward Myers alternated in the performances I saw. The role is not aggrandized, as it is at Ballet Theatre, but at the end James seems to expire at Madge's feet, even though the program note says that his lot is to be "left with nothing, forced to wander aimlessly, dreaming of his Sylph."

As a curtain-raiser, the company performed a long, ambitious, and pointlessly difficult new ballet by Richard Tanner to Schumann's Eighteen Symphonic Etudes— keyboard music that needs dancing as much as, say, Beethoven's sonatas or the Goldberg Variations. Tanner arranged it as a partnering sweepstakes—couples rushed about and got themselves into ever more innovative predicaments (with the men often blocking the women from view)—and the shape of the piece was so amorphous that not until the end could I tell how many couples there were. Most of the company's ranking dancers were in the ballet, working hard to make something of it, and many ranking dancers from other companies sat in the audience watching. Not, I hope, with envy.

The Pennsylvania company, which I haven't seen in a while, is dancing very well under its new director, Robert Weiss. It's a common belief that good dancers are a dime a dozen and only good choreographers are rare. How lovely if the dancers of every company were of Pennsylvania Ballet calibre. And are choreographers the only creative geniuses in the business? Some weeks ago at the Joyce, I saw a couple of performances by a company new to me, Garth Fagan's Bucket Dance Theatre. Fagan's choreography was extremely limited, but Lord, what dancers! The texture of their movement was like deep pile velvet. This little-known group from Rochester must be the best Afro-Caribbean–modern dance company now performing, and while I long to see the dancers in good choreography, there's no denying that Fagan, who trained most of them from scratch, is someone extraordinary—a teacher whose powers equal those of all but the best choreographers around.   —May 27, 1985

The Fire This Time

The revival of Firebird by New York City Ballet brings back a famous décor, by Marc Chagall, and a famous piece of choreography—the role of the Firebird as set by George Balanchine for Maria Tallchief. Chagall's designs, originally executed in 1945, are among his most successful works for the theatre. His enchanted forest has an iridescent glow that matches the colors in the music, and there has never been anything in this repertory—or in many another—to equal the impact of the vibrant ruby reds in the throne room when, to the spaced hymnlike chords of the finale, the curtain rushes up and reveals them. There are also two frontcloths painted with themes and motifs from the ballet and from Chagall's imaginary world; these have not lost their fascination. Chagall's fantasyland and Balanchine's choreography were not created together, and there has always been a degree of tension between them. Balanchine in 1949 took over the décor from its owner, S. Hurok, and staged within it a likable but disconcertingly whimsical and modest little ballet. The staging expressed not a personal vision so much as the lack of one; Balanchine appeared to be saying that this wasn't, of course, *his* ballet—it was Fokine's and Stravinsky's, and now it was Chagall's, too. The only part of the show that seemed to interest him deeply was the ballerina role, but even the Firebird, even in 1949, was not a Balanchinean conception. Chagall's view of this mythological creature takes several forms; Balanchine ignored them all and presented Tallchief straight out as a virtuoso ballerina in a flame-red tutu. This was also the conception embodied in Diaghilev's revival of 1926, with the Gontcharova sets and costumes—the revival repudiated by Fokine. Fokine saw his creation (which had had overtones of the bayadère) reduced to a "ballerina stereotype." Balanchine, however, filled the stereotype with new content. The Firebird of the fifties danced steps that could never have been imagined in 1926. In Tallchief's depiction, the element of fire was conveyed by bravura—by qualities of force and speed in her technique, of intensity in her temperament.

In 1970, Balanchine redid the ballet as an extravaganza, with new choreography, enlarged sets, and costumes based by Karinska on Chagall's drawings. One of these, showing the Firebird in a short gold tunic with panniered wings jutting from her hips and a little cockade trimmed with a spray of feathers on her head, inspired the costume for Gelsey Kirkland. Her dances were filled with dainty beats and with jumps of all kinds, notably gargouillades. Balanchine was evidently searching for something different from the demonic strength he had found in Tallchief; he wanted an airy, impersonal, twinkling Firebird. I don't think he got it, but in any case the Kirkland version of the role was soon eliminated and a whole new set of characteristics was introduced. The dancer (Karin von Aroldingen) was now tall and statuesque. The costume was a long gown of mottled blue-and-white silk with big white wings sticking out of the shoulders and a train trailing behind. It was another Chagall inspiration, but it was not a dance costume, and comparatively static choreography was designed to accommodate it. When Kyra Nichols took the part, she was given an all-gold version of this confining outfit. "The Firebird," said Balanchine, "is *zhar*: incandescent, gold, like the sun." And that was his last word on the subject.

The music for Balanchine's ballet is the "ballet suite" arranged by Stravinsky, some seventeen minutes shorter than the original score. The current production includes the Firebird's waltz variation (she goes straight into it on entering, without first crossing and recrossing the stage, as in the Fokine version), her pas de deux with Prince Ivan, and her long solo in the Lullaby—all this in the Tallchief choreography of 1949—together with the Scherzo and Round Dance of the Maidens, the monster scene, and the finale, all from the revival of 1970. What with Stravinsky's musical cuts, the ballet resembles more than ever the *Highlights from "Firebird"* that it always essentially was. The monster scene has choreography by Jerome Robbins in his best musical-comedy tradition—lively, detailed, satirical. At its height, the Firebird appears, thrown upward from the center of a huddling group and holding high the sword with which the Prince will kill the enchanter Kastchei. As the music continues to build, she makes her exit in a circle of ever-higher split jetés. This passage was created for Kirkland; Tallchief's exit was a streaking series of déboulés. The original Balanchine version followed the original Fokine in making the Firebird the only character who dances on point. As a magical benevolent being, she opposes the magical evil being Kastchei, who at the sound of the climactic ostinato in the Infernal Dance rises onto his toes and scuttles sidewise in diabolical bourrées. In 1970, the Princess and the Maidens were also put on point. It makes a difference in the spirited Scherzo but none whatever in the grounded steps of the Round Dance. (Is this the reason, perhaps, that Balanchine's 1970 Round Dance is less inspired than his 1949 one? With no apparent motive, he appears to have changed it for change's sake.) The fact that the Princess now appears on point, however, strengthens her identification with the Firebird and suggests a duality similar to that depicted in the two-headed Bird-Bride creature who appears on Chagall's first frontcloth. And the duality is borne out at the end of the ballet, when the cast takes its bows and the Prince is flanked by the Firebird, in her flame-red costume, and the Princess, in her garnet-and-ruby velvet gown. If you are lucky, you see Lourdes Lopez as the Firebird and Hélène Alexopoulos as the Princess—two handsome brunettes of Chagallian sensuousness. What it all means, though, should not be thought about too deeply, at least from Balanchine's standpoint. If the Firebird and the Princess are "sisters," surely it's because all the women in every Balanchine ballet are sisters. His work is innocent of psychology, and he has always been uneasy with symbolism. For Balanchine, ballet deals in hard reality: what you see is what you get. Interviewed by Nancy Reynolds for the book *Repertory in Review*, he came down heavily on the idea of *Firebird* as a ballet: "Right from the beginning, it didn't work. You can never make it convincing that the ballerina really is fire—she's just a dancer in a red tutu."

The two characteristics that are immediately striking in Tallchief's role are its variety and its womanliness. The dynamic variety of the pas de deux—the push-pull oppositions of the bird's struggle with her captor, the taut and then the loosened, relaxed line of her poses as she coils about him—is derived from Fokine. But the rhythmic drama of these dynamics seems to me pure Balanchine: the way the tensions shift to the music, following it like light in a dark tunnel. A sharp turn, a convoluted one, a spasmodic one may be followed by a full recovery on balance; a delicate flutter is the preamble to a direct rush. Then, there is the wide-ranging vocabulary. The bird's strategy (for it is she who dominates the pas de deux) is devious, "Oriental"; step by step, she pits her strength and cunning against the man's. The step that does it best, for me, is the lunge on point braced by him from behind. This pose, with the legs in profile and the torso turned front, seems to *say* "strength and cunning." It's related to the wonderful moment that comes when the bird is completely lulled and bound over to the man—when, again standing on point and braced from behind, her arms intertwined with his, she slowly and deeply bends and straightens both knees together, moving her body in a languorous S-curve. (And isn't *that* related to the "Oriental" pas de deux in *Symphony in Three Movements*?) A couple of times, the bird flies at the Prince, feet first through the air, like a deadly projectile. Another time, held by one hand, body arched and fully extended in a split, she is swung around and around by him in a huge circle. These acrobatic-adagio effects, souvenirs of the night clubs that New York was then full of, are what Balanchine would have called "calculated vulgarity." The instant or two of flashiness that they supply are immensely invigorating to the ballerina's classical demeanor, like the rippling "Hindu" port de bras that Balanchine also gives her at one point. If the Firebird is not made of fire, perhaps she is made of mercury. She is many beasts, shapes, and colors. She is bird but also cobra and jaguar. She is woman, not girl, and for this reason we may see the encounter with the young Prince as a sexual one, providing for him a rite of initiation, for her a lesson in tenderness. In his subsequent revisions, Balanchine steered away from the "woman" aspect of the Firebird; he may have felt that he had closed that chapter with Tallchief. The Firebird was only the most spectacular of the roles that Balanchine made for her—roles that in many instances were reconceived versions of the canonical ballerina roles. Tallchief was also Balanchine's Odette, his Sugar Plum, his Sylphide, his Raymonda. She was "woman in ballet," and she became herself the ballerina archetype of her generation.

The Firebird's choreography is still difficult. The balance is often off center, with the upper body canted far forward or backward over the points. Step follows step without pause in a continual, scrolling Art Nouveau line. It doesn't look old-fashioned—not when one thinks that it is now nearly as old as Fokine's choreography was when it was made. Lopez, the ballerina who fits into it best, was given one performance, impressive in every way but somewhat too cautious. She needs to show more freedom of accent, more relish. Joseph Duell was a strong and serious Ivan. He understood the naïveté of the character and only once failed to project it—in the monster scene. The production was directed by Robbins; Violette Verdy, Rosemary Dunleavy, Francisco Moncion (Tallchief's Ivan), and Tallchief herself all had a hand in the reconstruction. The Firebird costume, beautifully cut, with a small tutu, was supervised by Dain Marcus.

As the Raymonda of the fifties, Tallchief appeared in *Pas de Dix*, a reduced version of the Hungarian suite in Act III of *Raymonda*. In the seventies, Balanchine did this one over again, too, creating a longer and grander work and using a full complement of the forces that are traditional to the ballet. *Cortège*

Hongrois, also revived this season, gives us Balanchine's mind at work on pre-existing material that he obviously cared for a good deal. He didn't have to reckon with alien and intractable conceptions or with painters' images that clouded his vision. As always in his after-Petipa pieces, his method is clear-sighted and touched with divination. *Cortège Hongrois* has a corporate bulge and sheen. It's the most "Maryinsky" of his various versions of these third-act dances; some of it even evokes the Kirov, and pointedly, too. I am thinking not of the overblown pas de deux (the resemblance to Kirov Petipa is here quite unconscious, it seems to me) but of the grand adagio, which is done from start to finish by eight ensemble couples in unison. Kirov practice (reflected in the Baryshnikov version at American Ballet Theatre) has the adagio performed by the principal couple in concert with the eight couples of the ensemble. The difference isn't a major one; it's just Balanchine's way of announcing that *his* ensemble doesn't need stars fronting for it. Another, more important difference is his insistence on up-tempo performance; there are none of those frozen-on-the-brink relevés-passés so dear to the hearts of A.B.T. ballerinas. But N.Y.C.B. might well relax its vigilance slightly in the ballerina's czardas variation; it was so brisk the night I saw it that Kyra Nichols couldn't get any mileage out of its meandering phrases or much contrast out of its terse ones.

Among other revivals—if by "revival" we mean the return of a work that has been out of repertory two years or more—we have *La Valse* and *A Midsummer Night's Dream*. Unlike *Firebird* and *Cortège Hongrois*, these are pure Balanchine ballets; though *La Valse* may derive from *Cotillon*, which had a book by Boris Kochno, and though *A Midsummer Night's Dream* has a book by William Shakespeare, we have no doubt that it is Balanchine who has created the poetic worlds we enter. And how securely he shapes those worlds, defines those characters, directs their destinies. I suggest that people who know Balanchine only as a master of abstract ballets study his work here and see for themselves what a great storyteller he was. I have my reservations about the way certain of the male roles in these ballets have been cast, but male casting has become a general problem in this company, and meanwhile there can be nothing but praise for the performances of Nichols and Suzanne Farrell as the heroine of *La Valse*, for Maria Calegari and Darci Kistler as Titania, and for Judith Fugate and Stacy Caddell as Hermia. But Hermia's solo is becoming too gestural and losing dance momentum. And what about that second-act set? It's as ugly as the Chagall throne room is beautiful.

Did the Chagall era of set design know something that we don't? Ballet Theatre's revival of Antony Tudor's *Dim Lustre* (1943) includes the original décor by Motley. This should have been interesting; instead it looked like a page torn out of a fashion magazine of the period. Chandeliers are painted in white dots on a borscht-colored background; floating in front of it are ballgowns and tuxedos in solid colors like écru and coral and apricot and maroon. The principals are in white. As for the choreography, it's so notional that it would have driven Balanchine crazy (and maybe did, when he had it in repertory back in the sixties): the lead couple at a ball keep having blackouts and going back into the past. The irregular timing of these flashbacks in relation to the episodic score (Strauss's *Burleske*) is the chief point of interest for me. The flashbacks themselves are like movies I'd rather not see again. Come to think of it, so is the whole ballet.   —*June 10, 1985*

Postscript 1987: I now believe what these comments on *Cortège Hongrois* begin to suggest— that it is Balanchine's definitive statement on *Raymonda* Act III and a much better ballet than I ever gave it credit for being in the past. It was done again the following season in a series of transparent performances. Nichols not only conquered the czardas variation, she gave a new and authoritative shape to the "overblown" pas de deux. To top it off, the School of American Ballet workshop, in the spring of 1986, scored one of its major successes with a production of *Cortège*.

Singular Sensations

Gen Horiuchi holds his leg up in second on the stage of the State Theater and starts turning. You look at the fully extended leg; it has the impact of a fully extended finger. Horiuchi, the shortest dancer in New York City Ballet—the man who does miniature grands battements and miniature grands jetés—is in the midst of his miniature grande pirouette. After about five or six turns, he whips the leg in and turns some more, on momentum—seven, eight, nine, *ten*, and he keeps on going. The pirouette is perfectly centered and balanced; when he finally finishes, braking to a smooth halt in fourth, arms flung wide, a big grin on his uptilted face, the audience roars. You might want to roar right along, but though you've seen the pirouette you haven't felt it; none of its force has reached you. Horiuchi's feat, like all his dancing, has no power of kinetic transference—it is purely visual. At five feet two inches, he's the Mighty Mouse of the company— not only its shortest dancer but its most glibly proficient. Horiuchi can sustain longer virtuosic sequences with less evident strain than anybody else, except maybe Ib Andersen. Yet he's inarticulate. Steps pour out and evaporate. Seconds after a Horiuchi performance, it's hard to remember anything about it but quantity— the number of turns or jumps or beats. It's hard to care that Mighty Mouse, who has just been promoted to soloist, may have already set the house record in turns.

Audiences love small, gutsy dancers, and they love male dancers who look like children. Horiuchi looks like the doughty lad he really must be. Trained by his father in Tokyo, he was fifteen when he won the Prix de Lausanne, seventeen when he got into New York City Ballet, in 1982. Yet he never dances as if he were the underdog out to prove himself, and until his latest role, made for him by Peter Martins, he didn't try to win us by being adorable. He just danced, with that phenomenal fluency of his and that dismaying lack of scale and weight and consequence. Martins may be trying to break up the gnatlike monotony of

Horiuchi's dancing by giving him a lot of quirky, amusing, individual things to do and seeing to it that he shines out in competition with two other young dancers, Peter Boal and Michael Byars. (The ballet is a trio for boys, a male counterpart of the trio for girls that Martins made some years ago and named *Eight Easy Pieces*, after the piano scores by Stravinsky. The new trio uses the same music, orchestrated, and is called *Eight More*.) Boal and Byars are also slightly built, but they seem to tower over Horiuchi, and not just because they're taller. Their bodies are classically proportioned; they can produce the long lines of classical ballet. And though Horiuchi can't produce those lines, the fact that he can parody them appears to fascinate Martins. The antic bits written into Horiuchi's role are a parallel to his dancing: they're a parody of humor. The jokes are the obvious kind—pretending to fall, pretending to collide with the others or with the proscenium—that Horiuchi, with his lack of spontaneity, can pull; but that doesn't make him a comic. And the easy advantage he's given over Boal and Byars is unfair to two genuinely accomplished dancers. As "the little guy," Horiuchi is an audience pet no matter what he does. He is something the company has never had before—a specialty act. If he poses a challenge to a choreographer, it is unmet in *Eight More*. Martins just takes the occasion to endorse audience favoritism.

I used to blame Horiuchi's tonelessness on his size. If he were bigger and encountered more resistance from the space he moved though, maybe his maddening proficiency would look more like virtuosity. He's so little and limber he seems to slip through the air on overgreased joints. But Horiuchi's dancing is unreal because in addition to being tiny it's divorced from any visible imaginative impulse. Horiuchi is effective in the toy world of *The Nutcracker*, and in the third movement of *Stars and Stripes*—a role that calls for unmodulated fortissimo stuntwork—he's very good and very funny. The qualities that serve him here cut him off from the repertory at large.

Mel Tomlinson, who also dances in a vacuum, is Horiuchi's opposite in every other way. He's tall—over six feet. He has a skimpy technique, which he compensates for by fine-tuning his presence and looking emotionally fraught. With his snaky, wire-taut musculature, he exaggerates the dynamics that Horiuchi leaves out. He's all texture; every move, though it be nothing more than the twitch of an eyebrow, reverberates. Well, this is technique of a sort. Trouble is, it doesn't go far in New York City Ballet repertory. Tomlinson, who joined the company about the same time as Horiuchi, is almost as isolated. And he gives closed performances filled with cherished, memorized effects, all quite as bad as, and very similar to, the singsong rotework of Horiuchi. Tomlinson came from Dance Theatre of Harlem, and so far the biggest roles he dances are the two that he used to perform with that company—*Agon* (Pas de Deux) and *The Four Temperaments* (Phlegmatic Variation). He does an assortment of character roles, the latest being Kastchei in *Firebird* and Death in *La Valse* (to which he brings his penchant for evil guises) and Theseus in *A Midsummer Night's Dream* (to which he brings some decorative postures). As with Horiuchi and those perennial guest artists the Kozlovs, one feels he's being cast not so much because he's right for a role as because he's under contract and needs something to do. The Kozlovs, despite one or two individual successes (hers in *Liebeslieder Walzer*, his Ivan in *Firebird*), are as far as they ever were from assimilating the company style. In certain Balanchine ballets—*Symphony in C* and *Swan Lake*—they even negate it. But at least they have a style of their own, and their dancing gives us something to look at. Horiuchi and Tomlinson represent nothing so reasonable as an alien or alternative style. The whole insular, bizarre operation they're being indulged in is anti-style and decadent at its core. It represents the separation of personality from performance.

As long as Christopher d'Amboise is given roles like Oberon in A *Midsummer Night's Dream*, there will be some justification for Leonid Kozlov. Not that Kozlov could do Oberon; his Bolshoi technique is all wrong for the role. But so is d'Amboise's all-American slapdash technique. In terms of company style, d'Amboise, who was brought up in the School of American Ballet, is as much an alien as Kozlov. Balanchine would often cast dancers against type, hoping to stretch them. As a stretcher for d'Amboise, Oberon is more like a torture rack. The role, created for Edward Villella, is one of the climactic attainments of Balanchine style for men. The fact that so far it has eluded every one of Villella's successors is a judgment not on its intractability but on the failure of the company to breed dancers who are up to its demands. What's hard about Oberon? It requires a dancer who can combine noble bearing with infernal speed. As a classical (not a character) role, it is the equivalent of Balanchine's great innovative roles for women—roles that put American ballerinas in the forefront of twentieth-century dance. This season, the search for Oberon seems to have been called off. We had a choice between the eye-glazing Horiuchi and the maverick d'Amboise; in other words, no choice. Both gave facile, two-dimensional performances of the choreography; the formerly marvellous Scherzo was a succession of flat pop-up pictures (Horiuchi) or smudged sketches (d'Amboise). And both looked foolish. When Horiuchi—a full head shorter than Jean-Pierre Frohlich's Puck—went behind Titania's pink shell to push it downstage, he disappeared completely. D'Amboise's easy jump and his tap dancer's ability to cut steps at high speed got him through the part. But even if he had had the right technique he'd still have been miscast. Underneath d'Amboise's Americanism there's an authentic American spirit, which, in a becoming role (like Melancholic in *The Four Temperaments*), strikes a note of homely lyricism rare on the ballet stage. The brio of Oberon—not to mention the Greek chiton and gilt wig—is utterly foreign to such a spirit.

Because its roles allow more latitude for interpretation, A *Midsummer Night's Dream* is a more conspicuous magnifier of trends than most Balanchine ballets. This season, it was the company fever chart. The casting of Oberon wasn't the only low point. I've mentioned Tomlinson's Theseus. There was also Frohlich's Puck, outrageously playing to the gallery. There was the surly Demetrius of Peter Frame and the hammy Lysander of Daniel Duell. Florence Fitzgerald couldn't manage all of Hippolyta's choreography. But Fitzgerald performed honestly; it was the men who wrecked the show. And it is the male wing of the company which now threatens it with stylistic anarchy. We also saw a restrained and romantic Demetrius done by Afshin Mofid and a warmhearted Lysander by David Moore; as Puck, Victor Castelli put dancing ahead of mugging. Were they right or wrong? Is New York City Ballet to become a company like American Ballet Theatre, which has traditionally offered the wares of individual artists without requiring them to adhere to a company style? Is there in fact a double standard at N.Y.C.B. (which does not prevail at A.B.T.), permitting the men to display extremes and disparities that would never be tolerated in the women? Not long after the disastrous *Dream* performances, Baryshnikov was interviewed in the *Times* about changing directions at A.B.T. (The two companies played side by side at Lincoln Center.) He referred to Balanchine's "moral point of view toward the theatre" and said he had tried to learn from it. Ironically, the morality that is at the heart of Balanchine's style is being questioned by practices in his own company at the very moment that Ballet Theatre is becoming less eclectic artistically and more homogeneous in its presentations. The "new" Ballet Theatre, with Baryshnikov, Kenneth MacMillan, and John Taras running it, could become a livelier challenge to N.Y.C.B. than it ever has been.

With Baryshnikov relatively inactive as a dancer this season and with Patrick Bissell in a slump, the male standard at A.B.T. was upheld by Kevin McKenzie, Ross Stretton, Robert La Fosse, Johan Renvall, and Gil Boggs. The depth of casting required by the new production of *Romeo and Juliet* brought forth a number of new talents. But Ballet Theatre has never had any difficulty attracting talented male dancers, whereas N.Y.C.B. has had to contend with its reputation as a women's company. And, what with the retirement from dancing of Peter Martins and Helgi Tomasson, there aren't at the moment enough pure-water classicists among the male soloists there to act as inspirations to the young. Andersen and Castelli, Sean Lavery and Joseph Duell have been the season's heroes. Duell, who takes on straight partnering assignments and mime roles as well as a variety of dance roles, brings honor to the male echelon every time he sets foot on the stage. Among the newer men, David Moore has distinguished himself. He has the vernacular appeal of Christopher d'Amboise without the incongruity of appearance or style which poses problems for d'Amboise. (In type, d'Amboise resembles the Neds and Wilburs who hung out behind the auto-body shop in J. R. Williams's cartoons.) Though Moore isn't a virtuoso, he has a sensitive and supple technique and a mind that communicates itself at every moment to an audience. He happens to be the one nonexotic among the young men who are currently moving into prominence—men like Mofid and Jock Soto and Carlo Merlo and Alexandre Proia. (Boal and Byars, who are right behind this crop, are exotic in a different sense. With their identities as yet undefined, they give the impression of having been incubated in ballet studios.) Each of these men has something unique to offer, but each seems to be as diffident as he is talented. Perhaps it isn't diffidence—perhaps it's confusion. They may be looking at the disunity in the ranks just ahead and wondering what's wanted of them. The answer, of course, is where it always is: in the ballets. When Merlo danced his first performance of *Valse-Fantaisie* this season, he looked as if he didn't know what a deceptive "little" ballet it was; he ran out of steam halfway through. By the time of his last performance, he'd learned to pace himself and was beginning to develop an authoritative, even an exultant, account of one of Balanchine's trickiest roles, not unlike Oberon in its propulsion and continuity.

Merlo's ballerina in that performance, Melinda Roy, took the part for the first time and danced it with a soft strength and a large intelligibility. There is a sequence of grands battements ending in cambré poses on point; Roy filled the stage with it. Then she took off in flying pas de chat changing to low temps de flèche with a cambré crest. The connection between the two sequences—between leg gestures à terre and en l'air, between two backbends (cambré)—was clearly shown; it was a lucid demonstration of how shapes blossom from steps. As for the pas couru–grand jeté steeplechase—a test of the dancer's ability to match size with speed—I have never seen it more beautifully done. On the same program, Melinda's sister, Leslie Roy, brought a delicate incisiveness to the "Valse Mélancolique" of *Tchaikovsky Suite No. 3*. And Merrill Ashley came on at the end, in the "Theme and Variations," and performed miracles of transition in speed and shape and scale, one after the other: a breathtaking display, even for her.

Yes, they are amazing, these women. I wish I felt more grateful to Martins for his *Valse Triste*, in which Patricia McBride's ravening Irish looks and fluid adagio style are effectively exploited; though it's a deftly constructed dance, it leaves no clear impression as a drama. In a similarly sombre and nebulous vein, Jerome Robbins has made *In Memory of . . .* for Suzanne Farrell. Starting with last season's *Poulenc Sonata*, for Kyra Nichols, and counting *Valse Triste*, this is the third piece in a row made by Martins or Robbins in which the ballerina seems to be in mourning or preoccupied with some deep sorrow or inner condition. There'll be more to consider in the Robbins ballet after it has had its official première.   —*June 24, 1985*

Postscript 1987: Some of the jokes are gone from Horiuchi's role in *Eight More*. Tomlinson was cast in the "Five Pieces" in *Episodes*, partnering Hélène Alexopoulos. He surprised me with a subdued, accurate performance. Leonid Kozlov has become a reliable actor and partner, Soto continues to strengthen his gifts, and Boal has developed steadily. Mofid left N.Y.C.B. and La Fosse joined it. Bissell recovered from his slump (again). And on February 16, 1986, the sterling Joseph Duell jumped from a fifth-floor window and killed himself. The loss was one of the most tragic in the company's history. Tribute is customarily paid to the level of accomplishment and quality of dedication of the deceased. In Joseph Duell's case, the eulogies were true.

Opus Posthumous

In 1935, Alban Berg interrupted work on *Lulu* to write a violin concerto in memory of his close friend Alma Mahler's eighteen-year-old daughter, who had died of infantile paralysis. By the end of the year, Berg himself was dead (like Lulu, he died on Christmas Eve), and the world took his memorial to the dead girl for his own requiem. However, George Perle points out, "what the world did not know was that Berg had *planned* the Violin Concerto as a requiem for himself as well as for Manon Gropius—that he had taken advantage of the inherently ambiguous character of programmatic expression in music to conceal an alternative and equally authentic programmatic conception beneath the one that he had offered to the public." Perle goes on to cite extensive internal evidence, which reveals Berg's alternative program to have been concerned with his own mortality and to have contained references to his first love, a servant girl who bore him a daughter, and to his last—not his wife but Hannah Fuchs-Robettin (who was Alma Mahler's sister-in-law). Hannah's presence is expressed much as it was in the Lyric Suite—through numerological elements and musical ciphers. In the closing Adagio, the transfiguration of the dead girl is depicted in a traditional chorale with Bach harmonization and other, more cryptic touches, in which Perle discerns Berg's message to Hannah that he would be united with her in eternity. The belief in eternity recurs in Berg's work. The Concerto is "dedicated"—his words—"to an angel." It is not a sentimental inscription. One thinks of Countess Geschwitz's dying cry: "Lulu! My angel! Let me see you once again! I am near you, remain near you for evermore!"

Perle's essay, extracted from his book on Berg's operas, is printed in the New York City Ballet program book as a note on the score for Jerome Robbins's new ballet, *In Memory of . . . .* If Robbins's ballet also contains a hidden program, it remains his secret. Ostensibly concerned with the life and death of Berg's Manon in the most symbolic terms (Robbins's portrait bears traces of Anne Frank), the ballet takes on additional programmatic weight by the casting and use of Suzanne Farrell. But instead of constituting an alternative, "hidden" program, the presence of Farrell and, even more, her performance, which recapitulates and extends the adagio aspects of her performances in Balanchine's ballets, displace the Berg-derived program and all but capsize the ballet.

In Memory of . . . has those three dots because Robbins wants Berg's meditation on youth and love and then on death and eternity and love's transcendence—wants the full value of all that to support his commemoration of Berg's period (Program 1) as well as his commemoration, through Farrell, of Balanchine (Program 2). He, too, wants the richness of ambiguity that Perle says Berg took advantage of in programmatic music. But programmatic statements in dance as well as in music have to be stronger on their primary level of meaning than on their secondary, or they simply fail to be art. The level of meaning that Farrell brings to the ballet may have been intended to be nothing more than subliminal reinforcement of a theme; it turns out to be the theme itself. In Robbins's choreography, which is the first he has ever created for her, Farrell both does and doesn't look the way she looks in Balanchine's ballets, and she's more powerfully expressive when she does. Robbins hasn't masked this power—he has let Farrell be Farrell. But the power doesn't flow full strength until midway in the piece. Up to then, we have a conventionally beautiful, fairly docile Farrell embodying Robbins's conception of such a young woman as Berg might have known, whose untimely death coincides with the brutal sacrifice of her generation to totalitarian conformity and tyranny and war. We see Farrell in a pale-rose dress escorted and presented by a young man (Joseph Duell); we see them among other young people—first the girl among other girls, then her and the boy among young couples at a waltz party. The darkness of the harmony under a ländler-like folk song, the pallor of the lighting (by Jennifer Tipton), and the vast, mottled obscurity of David Mitchell's Jugendstil backdrop add to the impression that we are in Vienna between the wars. (There is no evidence as yet that Berg was thinking about Austria's fate in the Concerto, but he wrote letters at the time expressing his feelings of devastation and homelessness.) And we see the crowd of young people, including the boy, make a unison exit in a pointy-toed robotlike walk, leaving the girl alone with a sinister male figure (Adam Lüders). It's at this point—the struggle with Death—that Farrell overwhelms and supplants her "character," or, rather, transforms it: becomes the heroic Farrell we know from *Meditation* and *Don Quixote* and *Chaconne*. It's not that she appears invincible; she remains vulnerable as fear and resistance change to calm resignation. But the pas de deux with Death takes place on or near the expressive heights of those Balanchine ballets, and there is nothing else in *In Memory of . . .* to match it.

Robbins recaptures the excitement of Balanchine's discovery of Farrell's gift for expanding dance logic, and he knows how to squeeze the logic for extra thrills. In one passage, he has Farrell, bent low on point as if she were about to kneel, pivot in deep fondu to face her partner, then gradually unfold the other leg a hundred and eighty degrees into arabesque penchée. He revels in her voluptuous wide-swinging, off-balance promenades, her ability to control their sweep to the musical phrase with the merest touch of her partner's hand. But he doesn't show how any of this becomes holy. He gives us Farrell as a theatrical icon but not Farrell as a metaphor. His vision of eternity isn't a commanding one, and he seems much less secure than Berg is (or Balanchine would have been) in the conviction that his heroine goes straight to Heaven. Farrell is seen reigning over a leaden Limbo in as blank and featureless an apotheosis as was ever set before the God of Good Endings. In the final moment, she is lifted between her co-stars down a long diagonal toward the light, and on each lift she pedals in the air. Farrell makes something serene and grand of this moment, which could have come right out of a Jiří Kylián ballet. But the spirituality she projects in other ballets doesn't radiate; her translation into "angel" is largely a matter of letting down her hair and putting on a thin white dress.

It happens that Balanchine had planned a Berg ballet for Farrell as long ago as 1967. According to Robert Craft's diary (published in *Retrospectives and Conclusions*), it was to have been to the *Lulu* Suite and to have dealt not with Lulu but with Salomé. There was talk of the project again in the seventies (what a John the Baptist Baryshnikov would have made!), but after Balanchine fell ill it was never heard of again. I think that by taking on Berg and Farrell together for the first time, Robbins is making a conscious, and perhaps even a conscientious, choice. It's interesting that he chooses to present a "sacred" Farrell to Berg's music where Balanchine would have presented a "profane" one; interesting, too, that in much of what he creates in the first half—the slightly hallucinated "frame of memory" atmosphere, the mawkish camaraderie of the waltz party, with its klutzy "folk" motifs, the premonitory dead-woman lifts, in which Farrell hangs full length, parting the air with her hands—he is closer to the drear expressionism of Anna Sokolow than to Balanchine. One of Sokolow's most acclaimed pieces is *Lyric Suite*, tenuously set to the Berg score. *In Memory of . . .* betrays a similar tenuousness. The Concerto's contours are not hard to follow in dance, its rhythms are actively engaging, and something theatrical can be made of its program(s). But the music's depth cannot be penetrated choreographically—at least, Robbins doesn't demonstrate that it can. When Farrell leaves the stage on Lüders's arm and Robbins begins filling it with seraphim (corps members in white leotards) preparing the way to the next world, the transparency of his choreography disappears; the light that had been coming through it from the music is completely blocked out, and it never returns. It's as if Farrell were Robbins's filter; without her he seems lost. The spiritual deadness of the last scene is related to its musical unease. Robbins can't do much with a Farrell stripped of her virtuosities; he mostly has her stand or walk around, tentatively offering her hands to the other (lost?) souls. As the ballet sinks to a close, he strums away at his ambiguities. But Robbins's ambiguities have a way of diminishing into mere perplexities, and he adds one more in the final seconds. Why, if this is Life After Death, do Duell, the boyfriend, and Lüders, the Death figure, return as Farrell's porteurs? Even more of a conundrum: Where would they all be without her?

We have had the curious experience this season of seeing at long range, on the vast stage of the Metropolitan, the work of David Gordon, which we normally see at close range, in the intimate downtown loft theatres where postmodern dance was born. Gordon's pieces for American Ballet Theatre and Dance Theatre of Harlem were very human-scale and very low-pressure; they were conceived in terms of the easygoing, non-specialized movement that is his hallmark. He also used the basic ballet vocabulary, because it is a ballet dancer's basic means of locomotion, but he did not compromise his style in order to execute big opera-house commissions. The question raised and answered by *Field, Chair and*

Mountain (the A.B.T. piece) and *Piano Movers* (the D.T.H. piece) was whether Gordon's style of dance can be fruitfully produced on opera-house stages. I think it can, but probably not on the Met stage. This house is much too big for any kind of dance to be seen comfortably, and it defeats the anti-spectacular appeal of Gordon's work. But, for all its size, the Met is a beautifully focussed theatre; provided you do not sit too close to the stage, it lets you judge the formal relations a piece has without becoming involved in them. Of course, it's better to become involved; the picture you take away from the Met may be clearly focussed, but it's almost always of something you'd like to see developed someplace else.

Field, Chair and Mountain looked better at the theatre where I first saw it—the Kennedy Center, in Washington. At the Met, its long first half became crowded and indistinct in the section where the corps is intricately engaged in close-quarter partnering—the most involving section of the ballet. The oddest aspect of the staging—the calculatedly shallow perspective and the left-to-right flow of the action—gave surprisingly little trouble at the Met. When the piece was programmed with Antony Tudor's *The Leaves Are Fading*, one saw that Tudor had also used this "Oriental" flow-of-time idea, and that he, like Gordon, had misjudged the audience's ability to concentrate on intricacies of partnering and other small differences in so many consecutive or simultaneous pas de deux. The Gordon work is like the Tudor, too, in being all adagio in effect; the allegro passages that each contains do not change the quality of its vitality. Gordon's piece, though not as beautiful, is more robust; and, of course, he has taken care to create a kind of anti-dance spectacle for the second half which joins his elegantly populist aesthetic to the practices of ballet and uncovers a secret sympathy between them. *Field, Chair and Mountain* came across, even at the Met, as a play of delicately juxtaposed forces on a common ground of eccentricity. The sight of Martine van Hamel balanced in full-point arabesque atop a folding chair was one of the season's indelible images.

Gordon's work has changed a lot in recent years; his pieces now tend to consist of non-dance or semi-dance movement more or less closely timed to music. The music is recycled, just as segments of the movements are. John Field, the composer of the score used in *Field, Chair and Mountain*, was also heard in previous and subsequent pieces. Gordon planned to add Field selections to his Thelonious Monk score for *Piano Movers*, but he changed his mind (and reshaped the piece) when Dance Theatre of Harlem switched its New York engagement from the City Center to the Met. The all-Monk score consisted of five taped solos, including " 'Round Midnight" and "Ruby, My Dear." With its sparsity, its dry wit, its unpredictable "wrong" harmonies and variations in rhythm, the music proved to be a perfect counterpart to Gordon's style. The piece unrolled in twin ribbons of sight and sound, but at too even and deliberate a pace. Gordon's preference for moderate speeds—nothing very fast or very slow—is showing up more now that he's using music as an integral element, and this had a slightly glazing effect in relation to Monk's suspended chordal progressions. (Not until midway in the third selection did Monk lay down a beat.) The D.T.H. dancers—seven pairs and one odd man out—seemed to be performing in a colloquial trance. They did not-the-lindy and not-the-shim-sham in this not-jazz jazz ballet; they did not-exactly-classical steps, too, and they looked happy about the whole thing.

Gordon is evolving his own Beowulfian classicism. His "steps" in *Piano Movers* weren't ballet combinations but the spins, pivots, tilts, falls, and stretched positions that classicism has enhanced into a system. We had seen some of this kind of material earlier in the season in the opening work of a concert presented by his own group, the Pick Up Co., at the Joyce. *Offenbach Suite* was set to the Suite for Two Violoncellos—early academic stuff that doesn't sound like Offenbach—and it was one stage lower in the evolutionary scale. The dancers were not all completely turned out; their arabesques were a little stiff. The performance, clean but without polish, was closer in spirit to the ironic attitude that Gordon has always held toward his work—work in which art and the consciousness of art are presented together. Perhaps Gordon was asking himself how much farther technically he could afford to go before this consciousness disappeared. The outstanding moment, for me, was a passage that seemed out of keeping with the primitive charm of the piece as a whole. It was a short adagio in which Gordon repeatedly lifted Valda Setterfield, revolved slowly, and returned her to the floor. The pose she assumed as he held her—legs crossed, one arm around his shoulders, the other cocked behind her head—was unvarying, but he never lifted her the same way twice. The tiny variations, the slow revolutions as if on a pedestal, turned the two of them into living sculpture. Here, Gordon seemed to be saying, is technical perfection, in its own way as pure and absolute as what the ballet companies present. But Gordon is not satisfied to be a miniaturist, and he knows he's not a virtuoso. In between lies a range of skills and choices. Entering mainstream dance in mid-career, Gordon is finding his level.   —*July 8, 1985*

Institutions

We have feet, two of them, although it is the fantasy of certain dance forms to pretend otherwise. Classical ballet keeps removing one foot from the ground or both together, as if to suggest that the classical dancer's element is other than earth. In tap dancing, the body has multiple feet covering ground; in flamenco, its compressed bipedal force drills to the center of the earth. But the triumph of bipedalism is in social dances like the waltz and the tango. Here the illusion is of four feet pretending to be two. The waltz, with its three-beat phrase, makes a drama of balance. Weight is continually suspended, as if it could somehow be abolished, leaving us free to float. The tango, in four beats, offers no such incentive to keep moving. As an image of destiny, it is tragic rather than poignant, a dance in which we confront our mortality, luxuriate in it, but do not transcend it.

More than any other Latin dance, the tango exalts sensuality and sexual energy. But its eroticism—that cruel, insinuating grace made famous in thousands of theatrical portrayals—has been much exaggerated. The tango is a magical, captivating dance, as capable of laughter and sociability as it is of deep erotic emotion. Its variety was the subject of *Tango Argentino*, a show from Buenos Aires by way of Paris that appeared at the City Center for one week at the end of June and set off an uproar at the box office. That there already exists a sizable audience in New York for this kind of entertainment was one surprise. Another was what happened when word got around: the theatre had to throw open its second balcony.

Strictly speaking, *Tango Argentino* was a concert, not a show. Number followed number with nothing in between; there were no frills or diversions. The only spectacle was the tango, flowing like a river through endless permutations, provocative and discreet, hot and cool, riotous and austere. The dancers were all professional ballroom-style dancers, and they worked most of the time in teams. Each team had its own style and repertory, evolved from a common base. Some of the basic steps were familiar; many were not. The most unfamiliar, because censorable, aspect of the tango is the use of legwork to involve partners below the waist. Men and women alike do slow ronds de jambe that sweep along the ground and invade the leg space of the partner, or rapid ones that whip the air, pausing for an instant as the legs hook together. Since it's the so-to-speak legless tango that has been approved for worldwide popular consumption, it was something of a revelation to see this leg language in fully developed form—to see how articulate and graceful, how sensual without being salacious it is.

Tango Argentino was unstintingly first-rate in every department. Four *bandoneones*—Argentine accordions—poured their hoarse, corrugated sound into some thirty compositions, elegantly arranged against a background of strings. The format for the dances was a historical survey conducted without a shadow of pedantry. It began with women in bustles and men in flat-brimmed hats and white silk scarves meeting in a spotlight. All the costumes, from the chemises and tuxedos of the twenties to modern-day ballroom dress, were strikingly beautiful; the colors were black, white, gray, or silver. The designers, Claudio Segovia and Héctor Orezzoli, were also the producers of the show, which explains its exceptional unity of taste. For the twenties segment, the choreographer Juan Carlos Copes staged a tango drama about a girl from the slums who, seduced by a local bravo, ends in a brothel where tangoistas of every type, including a lesbian madam, await her. Amazingly, this vignette is played wholly for its dance values and gets away with it, reaching a kind of metallic perfection that stands apart from yet blends in with the rest of the show's style.

The tango is said to have originated in the working-class districts of Buenos Aires toward the end of the nineteenth century. Whatever it may be to the world, to Argentines it is a national art form, and it is a song as well as a dance. The singers in the show, uniformly spellbinding, were mature, substantial-looking folks who sang inconsolably of shame and pain and despair and plain bad luck: "When you want to put the last bullet in your pistol into your head, it won't fire." The greatest of all tango singers, Carlos Gardel, has been dead for fifty years and is still a national symbol. His most famous line, uttered in a movie, is "My life is a bad script." A current idol (to judge by the audience's response), the venerable Roberto Goyeneche, came on late in the evening and sang three songs in a row. The last: "Life is an absurd wound." These bitter pills of tango philosophy are dispensed as nuggets of wisdom, and toward the end of Goyeneche's seminar I began to gag. The songs are the raw heart of the tango, and the dances are its heart's blood, racing through the body, hot with life.

The show *Singin' in the Rain* is better danced than the movie—quite a feat, considering that dancers on the stage don't have the advantage that movie dancers have of attacking a number in installments, splicing the results from different takes, and post-syncing their taps. We can make the comparison because "Fit as a Fiddle," "Moses Supposes," "Good Mornin'," and the title number are staged exactly as they were in the film; only "Good Mornin' " is abridged. But although Don Correia and Peter Slutsker and Mary D'Arcy have the stamina and technique that Gene Kelly and Donald O'Connor and Debbie Reynolds didn't have, or didn't need in order to get through their dances, all but one of the quoted numbers fail to come across with the vitality they have in the film. The exception is "Fit as a Fiddle," and it works because the choreography is clever and funny in its own right and because in the movie it was done on a stage, as the vaudeville act of the two hoofers played by Kelly and O'Connor. The other numbers need the distinctive interpretation that the movie's stars brought to them or they need movie space, movie fluidity, movie effects.

Take Kelly's solo in the rain, a signature number if there ever was one. A less literal alternative would have been to stage it not as a solo but as an extension of one, with a shadow chorus reproducing "Kelly" over and over and resonating through the theatre like the memory that Kelly in this number has become—"imprinted," as Brendan Gill said, "on the brains of nearly all living Americans." I like the movie more as a comedy than as a musical, and more as an institution than as a comedy. Every time I see it, I feel the thrill of the hit that Kelly's big solo already was, right there on the set while it was being filmed; I can almost see its status escalating over the years from hit to classic to myth. And it was this feeling of escalation that I wanted from the stage show even more than I wanted the number itself. In Gene Kelly's era and before, when movies were the No. 1 mass medium, the escalation would sometimes take place almost immediately. Astaire became in an extraordinarily short time a myth who *behaved* like a myth, dancing with multiple images of himself or of Ginger Rogers. In one of Kelly's very first movie solos, "Alter-Ego" in *Cover Girl*, he danced in double exposure. Instant myth. Before Astaire and Kelly there was Mickey Mouse, and before that there were Méliès and Keaton, optically reproducing themselves to spectral effect, and long before either there was Harlequin and his millions—of Harlequins. Movies, with their techniques of replication—with their instrumentality, which *was* replication—broadened to infinity the mythological implications of popular theatre.

The metamorphosis of hits into myths used to be faster, but now it goes deeper. The culture has interiorized show-business success stories to such an extent that shows like *A Chorus Line* can be produced and can run for ten years without a star. Indeed, starlessness is the whole point of *A Chorus Line*. It's the musical of the Me Generation: everybody in it is Gene Kelly. What, then, is the point of reviving *Singin' in the Rain* on the stage in the post–*Chorus Line* era if it is not to commemorate a show-business myth? Beside that myth, the actual content of *Singin' in the Rain* is insignificant, and anyway it belongs inseparably to the movie that was made in 1952. But it is the actual content of the movie that we are faced with in the stage show, which has been choreographed and directed by Twyla Tharp in a spirit half reverent and half remedial. She inserts her own choreography, for the most part, in those places where the movie fails to shine; namely, in its satires of the big production numbers of the early-sound period. She replaces the fashion show to "Beautiful Girl" with a medley of the classier types of stage acts— toy-soldier choruses, acrobatic adagio teams, and the like—that lent their miscellaneous energy to such movies as *Hollywood Revue of 1929*, the first M-G-M film to use the song "Singin' in the Rain," with the cast in slickers. Tharp's reconstructions are a little too lovingly detailed to be forceful as satire, and they accumulate without building to a climax. Just how or why these acts worked or failed to work in the talkies is a point that gets lost in the scrimmage, but it is a larger point than can be made by choreography and staging alone. The book, adapted by Betty Comden and Adolph Green from their screenplay, doesn't set up the number; it doesn't give us any sense of the eager amateurism and messy experimentation of the era beyond those scenes that were in the movie—Lina Lamont being wired for sound and slipping out of sync. We get those scenes all over again. The beauty of the screenplay was the way it presented the comedy of early sound from the technical viewpoint of the movies. But that era saw clashes between the stage and the screen which were just as fateful as those between the silents and the talkies. A *Singin' in the Rain* properly written for the stage would have presented some of its transitional cacophony from a different angle. Too much of the burden of translating the movie into a stage show has been assumed by Twyla Tharp. There's a glimmer of inspiration when, during Lina's elocution lessons, the cast breaks out in an elaboration of "Moses Supposes" which expands her agony into a communal seizure. It's like the beginning of the "Rain in Spain" number in *My Fair Lady*, and it might have been expanded still further, into a general distemper affecting the entire movie industry.

Staying so close to the movie means too many short numbers and not enough scaffolding for the big ones—especially those not in the movie. The other monster number, entirely devised by Tharp, corresponds to the "Broadway Melody"– "Broadway Rhythm" number, wherein Kelly as a young hoofer arrives on Broadway and works his way up to hoofer's paradise, which in 1952 meant a ballet with

Cyd Charisse. Along the way, there were references to movie history—Kelly's Harold Lloyd glasses, an iniquitous den with a George Raft gangster flipping a quarter, and Charisse in a Louise Brooks hairdo. (I get this number mixed up in memory with the movie's opening, which recounts Kelly's rise to stardom; it's also easy to confuse with the "Girl Hunt" ballet in *The Band Wagon*.) But there wasn't a single reference to the French-revolutionary setting of *The Duelling Cavalier*, the doomed silent work-in-progress which Kelly and his pals were supposed to be saving with the songs and dances that *this* number represents. We got Donald O'Connor explaining how it was all going to work—the hero, in a modern setting, is brained and wakes up in the eighteenth century—but we didn't get the follow-up, possibly because the explanation was really another of the movie's in-jokes. Just nine years before, M-G-M had released *DuBarry Was a Lady*, with a similar plot, and with Gene Kelly in the smallish role of a duelling cavalier called the Black Arrow. The Tharp version corrects the movie's failure to tie the number in with *The Duelling Cavalier*; French peasants, we are told, can dance, can be risqué, can be anything you want them to be. We even see the end of the finished movie—now *The Dancing Cavalier*—on a screen, with all the characters gathered in a tableau, singing "Would You?" But the number itself, though it blazes with energy, is as much a farrago as the Kelly number it replaces. Dancers in eighteenth-century costumes frolic in the countryside, clog-dancing, tap-dancing, anything-you-want-dancing. Then the scene changes, as it does in the movie, to a low dive, and while a singer (Laurie Williamson) wails "Blue Prelude" Correia dances a sexy pas de deux with Shelley Washington, this production's Cyd Charisse. A fight breaks out, surrealistic figures glide by on roller skates, and finally, as if exploding from the pressure of non sequiturs, comes the climax: the whole cast erupts in a killer rendition of "Broadway Rhythm" ("Gotta dance!")—still wearing eighteenth-century dress.

Even the raptest admirers of the movie *Singin' in the Rain* admit that its climactic production number is its weak point, but Tharp has done a remodelling job that heightens the weaknesses—the abrupt switches in locale, in mood, in style—as if those were the things she liked best or thought intrinsic to movie choreography. Throughout the show, she has kept hold of the scene-by-scene content of the movie; here she throws out the content but reproduces the form—a kind of freewheeling permissiveness that wasn't so much intrinsic as endemic to movie choreography in the fifties. Two years after *Singin' in the Rain*, the whole business was sent up in "Somewhere There's a Someone," the song Judy Garland does in her living room in *A Star Is Born*.

But Tharp's killer number, misguided as it is, has some of the clotted fantasy and furious intensity of her ballets. (Its starting point may actually have been something envisioned for *Amadeus*.) And this production of *Singin' in the Rain*, misguided as *it* is, is still a lively and pleasant show. If you put it beside *42nd Street*, for my money the only other lively and pleasant show on Broadway, you see that a movie musical becomes a stage musical chiefly by having been one at heart. Gower Champion, the director of *42nd Street*, subtracted the camera from

Busby Berkeley's dances, and they promptly reverted to the extravaganzas they had been in the theatre. Champion showed that Berkeley's qualities of excess, illogical logic, wit without humor, and variation without variety worked just as legibly on the stage. The show became a success by putting an ironic distance between us and the urgency of the plot—not a hard thing to do. (As Pauline Kael has written, "It's surprising how organic the clichés once were.")

But the show of *Singin' in the Rain,* besides being hung up on the movies, has no irony—not even the irony with which Comden and Green originally viewed the scene they wrote about. Kelly's wonderfully fatuous, self-adoring movie actor is gone. When Correia's Don Lockwood dances "Beautiful Girl" with a bevy of fans (a number not in the film), he's much straighter than Kelly would have been, and he's no match for Lina, the only nasty person in Hollywood. Twyla Tharp softens Hollywood in the twenties just as she neatens up the connections between *The Dancing Cavalier* and the climactic production number. A child of the fifties, she grew up in an era when the cynicism of musicals like *42nd Street*—every man has his price, all a woman wants is to be kept—had been muted on the stage as well as on the screen by the dictates of family entertainment. With Comden and Green, those witty high-school kids, she has made a pretty, cozy, childish show—one that may actually suit the current mood of innocence regained better than *42nd Street* or *A Chorus Line*. In a season whose greatest musical hits have been *Big River* and *The King and I,* it deserves to be noticed.

—July 22, 1985

Hard Facts

Natalia Makarova retired from dancing the other day. To those for whom her glory years really began in 1970, when she defected from the Kirov Ballet, the career seems all too short. Yet fifteen years is a long time for a dancer to have been a star—especially a dancer who had already reached the age of thirty. Makarova's career in the West was a triumph against the odds. She never did accumulate the new personal repertory she must have hoped for, and no one's career better illustrates the fact that a ballerina without new choreography to amplify and specify her powers has no modern vocation to speak of. Though Makarova modernized her technique, her style was focussed on the nineteenth-century classics, and it remained what it was when she left Russia. That she succeeded in imposing her style on American versions of those classics is a testament as much to her personal qualities as to the quality of her training. And when she applied her personal qualities to the modern repertory as she found it (at American Ballet Theatre and then at the Royal Ballet and other European companies), so strong was her impact that her influence and originality are unquestioned. But the inevitable decline of physical powers is easier for a dancer to face if she has a personal repertory. Then she can, from intimate acquaintance with her roles, readjust and even recompose their more troublesome features, and no one (or almost no one) will be the wiser. Makarova's last "vehicles" came from the hand of Roland Petit and were increasingly trivial—already adjusted downward, so to speak. And Makarova looked increasingly ineffective in them.

Dancers of Makarova's calibre don't usually fade away. They're out there performing for all they are worth, and then, the next season, they're gone. They know how to conceal the evidence of the chronic injuries that are wearing them out. But finally there is the kind of injury that skill alone cannot reach. A dancer who is injured beyond hope of recovery and still performs goes from day to day, dancing a little better or a little worse, all depending on the state of injury, on the role, and also, if the dancer is a ballerina, on the partner. Dancing takes on the aspect of a game of chance. (Makarova, after Petit's *Blue Angel* ballet, must have decided that on this level the game was not worth playing.) It is a precarious existence, and the pain is too frightful to think about, but it is less precarious the more one performs—at least, that is what I have always heard. Performing under extreme pressure of this kind, with adrenaline a temporary buffer against pain, actually enlarges the possibilities of performance. One can't know in advance, by rehearsing, what one will actually be able to do. How much technique have I got left? the dancer asks. Is the glass half empty or half full? Different performances and different ballets can give different answers, and some answers are encouraging. All this explains why certain dancers are still onstage at a time when even their most fervent admirers wish them off it. They may—these diehards—be feeling a thrill in sheer performance that isn't coming through in their dancing.

Dancers used to have longer careers. Danilova, Markova, Ulanova, Fonteyn, Alonso danced into their fifties. Kolpakova, a contemporary of Makarova's who never left Russia, is still dancing at fifty-two. But the Western ballerina repertory has changed in the past twenty years. Today's dancers must meet steeply increased technical demands, and that takes a toll on longevity. Men may partner when they can no longer dance. (Jacques d'Amboise's last role, created in 1980, was as Suzanne Farrell's partner in *Robert Schumann's "Davidsbündlertänze"*; he performed it till 1984, when he retired, having been a star for thirty years.) But male endurance is measured by virtuoso standards, and—thanks to Villella, Nureyev, Martins, Baryshnikov, and their heirs—these, too, have climbed astronomically since the sixties.

Baryshnikov, at thirty-eight, is having to contend with the unpredictable effects of a knee operation. If the press gave dancers the same coverage it gives athletes, the public would now be hearing as much about Baryshnikov's knees as it once heard about Joe Namath's. And there would be daily bulletins on Suzanne Farrell's hip joint, the condition of which colors her every move. But these matters aren't covered even in the dance press; they're either taken for granted or thought to be too personal. Balanchine did not like his dancers discussing their injuries with the press, and no management is going to start making pre-performance announcements of the infirmities among the cast (although this is commonly done for singers when they are suffering from colds). But when injury becomes a dancer's condition, and the dancer is Farrell or Baryshnikov, then some sort of recognition is in order. Farrell and Baryshnikov are national treasures; dancing—to distinguish it for a moment from choreography—is the great theatre art we in America know today largely because of their contributions to it. So it is natural that what affects their performance should concern us and should lead us to consider the broad question of dancers' responsibility to their art.

I thought I detected a note of bitterness in some of the local press commentary on Baryshnikov when he had to withdraw from A.B.T.'s New York season last fall; it was nearly as if he'd injured himself on purpose to frustrate New York. Baryshnikov customarily gets a resentful press except when he's performing— either dancing or acting. The general feeling is that he has failed in the job of artistic director, and he is criticized for having inflicted policies on A.B.T. that are against its grain ("There are no stars"), when in fact it is the times that are against A.B.T.'s grain. Baryshnikov has made mistakes; so has Peter Martins at New York City Ballet. But the critics who consider Martins a failure haven't accused him of anything. New York City Ballet has become something of a sanctuary since Balanchine's death; no bad news is ever spoken. The silence about Farrell's injury is falsely conceived homage to a great dancer. I think we see more of what she is doing when we know that she is doing it under great stress. And there is simply no way to speak about her current performances of her classic roles without referring to the disrepair that may in fact be the final consequence of the physical forces that enabled her to undertake those roles in the first place. How serious it all is only she can say, just as only she can know, with that second sight which many performers possess, how much of the problem is visible to the audience. What one can see is that Farrell has lost a certain amount of extension and rotation in her right hip; the super-high battement is gone, the great arabesque no longer appears as regularly and as flowingly as it used to. But when you have subtracted these undeniably famous and precious attributes from Farrell's technique there is still a lot left over. Her timing, her flexibility, and her inspiration, which have always allowed her to expand beyond prediction the possibilities of performance at the moment of performance—these qualities are still there and are rising to support her now.

Lucky for us, because Farrell, even more than Baryshnikov, represents a line of creative thought. Watching New York City Ballet these days, you sense that the combination of her example and Balanchine's vision is very much on its mind. It is possible to see Farrell's example in the consistency and purity with which all the most talented of the company's ballerinas and younger soloists have been dancing since Balanchine's death. Merrill Ashley, Maria Calegari, and Kyra Nichols, among others, have actually gotten better, and while some of this improvement is attributable to Martins's direction much of it is simply infectious suggestion. Several of Farrell's most personal roles have been passed around— *Chaconne*, *Walpurgisnacht Ballet*, and the Rondo alla Zingarese in *Brahms-Schoenberg Quartet*. Calegari even did *Mozartiana*, relieving Farrell a few seasons ago in Saratoga, and this season she took over the Farrell role in the *Davidsbünd-lertänze*, while Farrell went into the more domestic Karin von Aroldingen part, opposite the ravaged Schumann figure, danced by Adam Lüders. (Calegari's partner was a noncommittal Leonid Kozlov.) The colossal span of the Farrell arabesque was replaced by the equally iconographic V-shaped arabesque of Calegari—it was like seeing the Winged Victory where for years we had had the Arch of Triumph; but the singularity, vitality, and daring of the Farrell character (who may represent Schumann's muse) were successfully captured in Calegari's dancing. As "Clara Schumann," Farrell will take some getting used to. Right now, with her old performance fresh in memory—fresher than anything she has been able to get out of her new role—there seems to be a resemblance rather than a contrast between Wife and Muse which forms the dramatic fulcrum of the ballet. But this has its fascination, and there is no question that Farrell understands her new part and projects it faithfully. Nichols, new to the Rondo in *Brahms-Schoenberg*, filled out the steps with a hardiness that put the role over; she excelled in the sheer exuberance, scale, and precision of her dancing, whereas Farrell, who did the part herself this season, relied, more effectively than you would think, on bravura presentation—the single element missing from Nichols's performance. Greater than individual achievements, though, is the new cohesiveness of the principal women. Roles that were unique to Farrell have become (with her consent and co-operation) a common birthright. Everybody shares; there isn't only one "Farrell successor." As a group, the ballerinas are closer than they have ever been to achieving the unanimity of style which, along with diversity of physique, was a primary Balanchine objective.

Farrell is not alone in what she is still able to show of the accomplishments of a senior ballerina. Patricia McBride is right there beside her. McBride was never the company figurehead that Farrell was from the start, and she isn't responsible for so large and crucial a segment of the repertory, although she, too, has the incomparable advantage of special roles that Balanchine either tailored or retailored for her. She is physically and stylistically unorthodox—something that was less easy to see in the days when physical diversity among the ballerinas was more extreme than it is now—and she has an unorthodox method of rendering her old parts: she secretes herself in a "through" current of energy and lets it (and a good partner) carry her. The method—if that is what it is—works, but, compared with last year's *Liebeslieder Walzer*, the McBride of this year's *Brahms-Schoenberg Quartet* is noticeably more recessed. McBride is a few years younger than Makarova and a few years older than Farrell. Now that her technique is fraying, we see how deep her strength lies. It is the kind of strength that Balanchine relied on to reshape the ballerina repertory. And as we watch McBride and Farrell maneuver inside their roles we see not only strength but the imagination that also played a part in the process. In *Brahms-Schoenberg*, which was made in 1966, both ballerinas are actually recapitulating and commenting on their roles in dance history.

But the most critical lesson to be learned from these two artists is the importance of performing. Darci Kistler, injured on the threshold of a major career, was off the stage for nearly two years. Now that she is back, she hardly ever performs, although she is scheduled frequently enough. And she is missed. It's my impression that her cancellations are the most deeply felt and hungrily discussed by the subscribers. To this large and loyal audience, Kistler's absences really matter. And the mystery that surrounds them—the company, of course, says nothing—has given rise to a lot of talk about permanent damage and a career destroyed. The more hopeful frame a picture of Kistler cautiously nursing her ankle back to health, reacquiring body tone, reviewing her old roles, testing out new ones, and in general composing herself for the great day when she claims her rightful place in the hierarchy of stars. But that picture becomes impossible to believe in once one actually sees Kistler perform. The day is manifestly here. No one who moves like that can conceivably be the victim of a disability grievous enough to keep her sequestered; nor—another dire rumor—can she have lost her appetite for dancing.

But Kistler continues to tantalize us. After twice dancing a role in *Divertimento No. 15* in the pre-*Nutcracker* season, she cancelled both of her appearances in *Brahms-Schoenberg Quartet*, in which she was scheduled to dance the Andante with Jock Soto. Then she cancelled *Nutcracker*. When she finally got on, in the next-to-last of the *Brahms-Schoenbergs*, she'd been off the stage for eight weeks— enough time for the clouds of suspicion to have regathered. On she came, dancing with a transparent ease and a plenitude of being that dispelled all doubt. Her dancing still has the unmistakable plushy texture of youth, and it is sophisticated dancing, too—dancing that summarizes and extends meanings, that clears a space for itself. And Kistler has the wonderful extra gift of making her audience happy. Why isn't she making us happy more often? Aren't the long vamping-till-ready periods offstage bound to dissipate energy that should be used up in performance? The trauma of injury in a young dancer can affect the direction of the career. In Kistler's case, it seems to have deepened an already marked commitment to long and careful preparation. She has been back a whole year and has yet to find a satisfactory ratio of rehearsal to performance; eight weeks in the studio to ten minutes on the stage simply isn't professional dancing. The example of Farrell is just now in extremis, but it shows that if a ballerina's first obligation is to her art, not her ego, then she must perform, because the art of dancing is perfected, if not actually discovered, in performance. Then, there are such things as company morale and audience gratification. The repertory needs Kistler, and the audience needs reassuring that she's not just a guest artist. I have the feeling that for Kistler a performance is a precariously held-together illusion each separate second of which must be predetermined and delivered in a set form. Performance then becomes something to be endured, a pleasant ordeal like holding your breath under water. Yet when Kistler dances she looks utterly spontaneous. Is this, too, a dreamed-up effect? Gelsey Kirkland had the same look of spontaneity, and she held to the same overfastidious methods of preparation, and her career, the single most promising one of the seventies, was over before the end of the decade.*

* *Postscript 1987:* It wasn't the drugs. Drugs may actually have prolonged Kirkland's career.

I don't say that Kistler is Kirkland all over again; I say that a provably bad method cannot be made good even if every other factor in the equation is different. One would prefer that, with the repertory she stands to inherit, Kistler spent more time in the world where it was made. For now, she's our dreaming princess of the eighties.

The revival of *Brahms-Schoenberg Quartet* this season was the first since the proscenium arch of the State Theater was lowered a few years ago. That alone would have improved the look of the piece, but it also has the benefit of new scenery, by David Mitchell. It is the third of the company's large-scale revivals since Balanchine's death. The first two were of *Liebeslieder Walzer* and *Gounod Symphony*, both of them ballets that are related to *Brahms-Schoenberg*. In a 1961 interview, Balanchine had expressed the opinion that "Brahms won't do as an accompaniment for dancing, except for the waltzes." (He had made *Liebeslieder* the previous year.) Schoenberg's orchestration of the Brahms Piano Quartet in G Minor may have changed his mind. The choreography for the Intermezzo, a long duet broken by solo entrées and sections for a female trio, is derived from *Liebeslieder* and the complicated partnering technique explored in that ballet. *Gounod Symphony* comes to mind in the third movement, with its deployment of a large corps de ballet behind a single couple and its continual metaphoric development of group configurations. It may have been the initial failure of *Gounod* at the State Theater which prompted the making of *Brahms-Schoenberg*. The ballet was designed to fill up the stage and present the company in a historic perspective. *Gounod* evoked the grandeur of Paris, the Opéra, and the dance academy of France, but with its one principal couple and its singleness of intent it appeared small. *Brahms* seems to be about Vienna and the Viennese rococo spirit: it sweeps through palatial boulevards, gracious gardens, through convolutions of mood and atmosphere, and ends in a gypsy whirlwind. Each of the ballet's four movements is led by a different set of stars, and each is self-contained, a problem for a designer. Mitchell gives us the Schönbrunn Palace seen mistily from the air, then from ground level. A scrim rises, disclosing a room in the palace with gray looped curtains, globe chandeliers, and gray square-cut columns edged in gilt and set at an angle. For the Intermezzo, the looped curtains are lowered to the floor, blocking out the palace view. It works beautifully except for the gypsy finale, when the palace, which stays in place, again becomes irrelevant. In a ruminative program note on the Vienna of Brahms, Schoenberg, Balanchine, and Mitchell, Mindy Aloff tells of an additional Mitchell drop, which we don't see, depicting "a sunset world, with flame and fire . . . in the manner of Kokoschka's landscapes from the Twenties." Karinska's costumes, in their original palette of pink, rose, beige, and gray, are unchanged.

Brahms-Schoenberg Quartet is one of Balanchine's more curious constructions. Its vagaries (based in the music) are not easy to follow, and its plumpness of contour is not easy to like. But the choreography is a tactical feat, and the dancers have wonderful things to do. There were frequent cast changes, with several dancers taking more than one role. D'Amboise's part in the Rondo was zestily performed by Sean Lavery or Joseph Duell; Nichols and Calegari both created images of beauty and refinement in the somewhat featureless first movement; and Jock Soto made a fine impression dancing the Villella role in the Andante.

—February 3, 1986

The Dreamer of
the Dream

Roland John Wiley's *Tchaikovsky's Ballets* (Oxford) is a good companion in a season when, *The Nutcracker* just past, we have Sadler's Wells Royal Ballet touring its recent production of *The Sleeping Beauty* while talk goes on of a possible Kirov *Swan Lake*—the St. Petersburg version restored—this year or next. Wiley is an American musicologist with a strong interest in dance. He discusses all three of Tchaikovsky's ballet scores in detail, and describes first performances, covering both the original and the revised edition of *Swan Lake*. His scholarly equipment includes knowledge of the essential languages—Russian and Stepanov choreographic notation—and he isn't afraid to do primary research in the archives, just as if no one had been there before him. When Wiley tells us that certain facts are missing from the record, he isn't just passing on a supposition, he's looked for them. But he sometimes doesn't explain why certain evidence is missing from his own record—why, for instance, there is no chapter on Delibes's ballets and the possibility of their influence on *The Sleeping Beauty* and *The Nutcracker*. (Tchaikovsky came to know *Coppélia* and *Sylvia* only after he had written *Swan Lake*.) Wiley's sense of background is unusually rich. He writes vivid accounts of the theatres, audiences, and critics of St. Petersburg and Moscow, of the "specialist tradition" in ballet composition, and of *La Bayadère* as an example of it; and he fills in the long gap between *Swan Lake* (1877) and *The Sleeping Beauty* (1890) with a history of the Imperial Theatres and the reforms of their most brilliant intendant, I. A. Vsevolozhsky. All very necessary. But comparisons and contrasts between the making of *The Sleeping Beauty*—a watershed in the history of the art—and the making of *Swan Lake* are a little shortsighted. Tchaikovsky himself compared *Sylvia* favorably to his first ballet; the inference is that had he known what Delibes knew *Swan Lake* would have been different. And what of the developments that took place in Tchaikovsky's work in the same thirteen-year period? What can we make of the *dansante* quality of so many of his non-theatrical compositions? In the symphonies and, especially, in the orchestral suites, we hear future Balanchine ballets as well as intimations of the great Petipa ballet to come.

There really isn't enough Tchaikovsky in *Tchaikovsky's Ballets*. But on the ballets themselves Wiley's performance is first-rate. He knows how to illuminate musical procedures in a way that makes the ballets come alive as theatre. And his work has already had an effect on current theatre practice. Peter Wright, who produced the Sadler's Wells *Sleeping Beauty* before Wiley's book was published, depended greatly on Wiley's researches both for his *Nutcracker*, presented by the sister company at Covent Garden, and for his new *Swan Lake*, to be presented in 1987.

It is tempting to read Wiley's chapters on *The Sleeping Beauty* as a corrective to the Wright production. Wright is not the first producer to impose interpretation on a ballet that needs none; nor is this the first time he has done so. When the Covent Garden Royals brought their medieval *Beauty* here in 1970, I reviewed Mr. Wright as Mr. Wrong. I still think he's wrong, even though his current production (1984) is cast in the proper time frame (seventeenth to eighteenth century). And, having seen his new, Wiley-influenced *Nutcracker* on tape (a Thorn EMI/HBO videocassette is available here), I believe that Mr. Wright will go on being wrong about Tchaikovsky, no matter how many accurate period details he incorporates. The only thing that has changed since 1970 is the reason for attacking the unmusical Mr. Wright in the first place. Then he spoiled the perfect picture being created by the dancers. Now he's the whole picture—there's nothing else to see. The production issues I'm about to raise wouldn't matter nearly so much if either *The Sleeping Beauty* or *The Nutcracker* were as beautifully danced as it deserves to be. Beautiful classical style creates its own meaning and is capable of vanquishing any number of misguided production ideas. But the dancing at Covent Garden these days is horrid, and at Sadler's Wells it is somewhat worse. I visited the latter company's *Beauty* twice in Brooklyn (at the Academy of Music); with a complete change of cast, it was no better the second time. The plain fact, which has been plain now for almost a decade, is that English classical style has fallen into provincialism and self-parody. It hasn't just failed to keep up with American or Russian classical style; it has failed to keep up its own standards. The temper and transparency that English dancers could show in the fifties and sixties have declined into wooden affectation. The pellucid musical phrasing of the great ballerinas, from Fonteyn and Beriosova to Sibley and Seymour, has become blank routine. The men of the company display more brio, but no complementary rigor. There's no shortage of gifted, willing dancers, but their shabby schooling denies them range and force of expression. It's a sad spectacle, and I don't wish to dwell on it. (British dancing does bring one quality to *The Sleeping Beauty* which American productions never get: stylistic unity. But all this meant in Brooklyn was that everyone was bad in the same way.) What British custodianship of the Tchaikovsky classics amounts to is an insistence on non-dance values—theories of interpretation and visual design and fancy renovation—and a willingness to spend money on them. And even these things it gets wrong.

Of the three ballets, *Swan Lake* is the most difficult to mount in four-act form, because Tchaikovsky's intentions are not always clear. *The Nutcracker*, in two acts, is the most problematic; it was, as Wiley says, the most ill-starred of all

Tchaikovsky's works. It is *The Sleeping Beauty*, strangely enough, which is—or should be—the easiest. To understand why the most popular of the ballets are hard to produce and the greatest but least known (because prohibitively expensive) all but produces itself, we have to do some compare-and-contrast work in the Wiley manner.

The main difference between *Swan Lake* and *The Sleeping Beauty* is that in the earlier ballet Tchaikovsky is teaching himself to write ballet music and transforming ballet music at the same time. In the later one, he demonstrates an enlarged perception of what a ballet score can be: not only a serious dramatic structure but a self-enclosed, self-illuminating world, each of whose parts carries some charged relationship to the whole. Like *Swan Lake*, *The Sleeping Beauty* is based on a central image, but Tchaikovsky has by now found a way to fill the entire score with insights into and permutations of this image. Large sections of *Swan Lake* are enigmatic and diffuse; it is a noble, baffling, enrapturing work. If your knowledge of it was, like mine, acquired piecemeal, starting with the second act and then moving on to this and that portion of the other three acts, you probably found yourself thinking time and again, So this, too, is *Swan Lake*! The extended terrain is fascinating. But further excerpts from *The Sleeping Beauty* only give you more *Sleeping Beauty*. Listening to the score in sequence, you go deeper into its mysteries, and you also experience the pull of its momentum; the wonder of how such a thing can exist at this depth may be the greatest mystery of all. In *Swan Lake*, the central image (Odette and her eternal separation from her mortal love) does not permeate the ballet; it is isolated within the ballet, and it is mobilized in the continuity between Acts II and IV. But *The Sleeping Beauty* is all forward movement, all imperceptible change. Drop the needle at any point in a recording and you know exactly where you are. The light that shines on Aurora's birthday is not the same as the light on her wedding.

The construction of the ballet is appropriate to a story the major—the *only*—events of which (the casting of the spell, the lifting of the spell) are separated by a span of a hundred years. As Wiley notes, the story is essentially static; the outcome is never in doubt. By analyzing aspects of the score, particularly its harmonic structure, Wiley shows how Tchaikovsky imbued the story with theatrical elements (activity, expansion, suspense) while retaining the static purity of the central image. *The Sleeping Beauty* is true music drama, and every note of it can be staged. Wiley doesn't actually declare *Swan Lake* unstageable, but he refutes arguments that the music is continually responsive to the libretto (without, however, saying what it *is* responsive to). He persuades us that it is "a score of carefully chosen tonalities," yet in the end the purpose of these tonalities is elusive. Tchaikovsky may have wanted to secure a harmonic unity against the whims of ballerinas and ballet masters, but "the coherence provided in the score by tonality is not so much recondite as subliminal." Producers of *Swan Lake* have to do quite a bit of mind reading. And they do, they do.

The Nutcracker shares with *The Sleeping Beauty* a glowing central image—that of the beauty of civilization at its peak—and it shares with the Carabosse sections of that work and with *Swan Lake* a dark phantasmagoric strain. The coexistence of bright vision in the second act with dark dramaturgy and grotesquerie in the first drives some producers of *The Nutcracker* to invent explanations. Wright's current production is driven to conclude that the vision is not that of the child heroine but that of the eccentric inventor Drosselmeyer. Wright has an ally in Wiley, who besides unearthing some of the original Ivanov choreography contributes a program note saying that Tchaikovsky links the two disparate acts by means of key and sonority and that both are connected to the characterization of Drosselmeyer. But then Wiley goes on to claim what he does not claim in his book—that Drosselmeyer is therefore the hero of the ballet, and that the vision of Konfitürenburg (the Kingdom of Sweets) is not something he conjures up and passes on to the children but his alone. And for Wiley this idea of Wright's "brings the story of *The Nutcracker* into the province of adult thought." A most peculiar adult, this Drosselmeyer who dreams of Candyland. The Royal Ballet's Konfitürenburg is designed and costumed (by Julia Trevelyan Oman) so as to lose all association with the various sweets who inhabit it in the traditional version; even so, it is a confectionary world, and Tchaikovsky created it that way. When adult emotion does enter the story, in the form of the adagio of the Sugar Plum Fairy and her cavalier, the Wiley of *Tchaikovsky's Ballets* hears nothing but the simple descending octaves that make up the melody, and the musicologist in him recoils from this "default of inspiration." He is much closer to the mark in an essay published separately, in the journal *Dance Research*, in which the eight descending octaves are identified with a phrase from "the *panikhida* (a funeral service) of the Russian Orthodox Church"; namely, "*I so svya-ty-mi u-po-koi*"—"And with the saints give rest." Out of this piece of information Wiley is able to construct a resemblance between Sugar Plum and Tchaikovsky's beloved younger sister Sasha Davydova, who died, after many years of illness, while he was composing the score, and a further resemblance between Konfitürenburg and Kamenka, his sister's estate, where he had spent happy days entertaining and being entertained by her seven children. When the descending octaves are heard in the adagio, it is for the second time; they had first announced the arrival of the two children in Konfitürenburg. It isn't necessary to associate Uncle Drosselmeyer with Tchaikovsky and make him the dreamer of the dream, as Wiley does, in order to see that for the composer of *The Nutcracker* Konfitürenburg is at certain moments more than "a children's utopia"—it is Paradise itself. The great descending octaves are the doors of Paradise opening for poor little Sasha.

The method of deducing meaning from an analysis of tonalities, which Wiley employs throughout the book, can lead to confusion as well as revelation. The lengths to which Wright goes to perpetrate the notion that Carabosse (the evil fairy in *The Sleeping Beauty*) should enjoy equal status with the Lilac Fairy (the heroine's godmother and the giver of all good) probably had their origin in the fact that Tchaikovsky identifies Carabosse with the key of E minor and Lilac with E major. They are sisters but not, Wiley cautions, look-alikes—not Odette and Odile. In Wright's version, the destiny of Aurora is the subject of a protracted struggle between Good and Evil. In the orchestra, though, there is no struggle; Aurora's destiny is resolved in the Prologue the moment the Lilac Fairy countermands Carabosse's prophecy. Wright has Carabosse hanging around during the second act, determined to have a showdown. She doesn't give up until the kiss of awakening is actually bestowed. It is all Manichaean farce, played to music that denies that any such dualism could possibly exist. The idea that Carabosse holds power equal to that of the Lilac Fairy is carried out with a kind of nutty logic in Act I, when the presenter of the lethal spindle turns out to be not Carabosse in disguise but a genuinely innocent little old lady who is dragged off to the executioner's block. (Carabosse actually can control Aurora's fate, you see, so she needn't turn up as she used to in the first act, poking spindles out of a long black cloak. But if the malefactor is not to be Carabosse, then why is it an old party in a black cloak?) The designer, Philip Prowse, makes Carabosse and Lilac all but identical figures, one in black and one in white or silver-gray. They are both mime figures, and so Lilac's lovely waltz variation and all her dances in the Prologue are performed by an interloper—the Fairy of Surplus, presumably. The casting of Carabosse with a woman instead of with a man *en travesti* I find less offensive than the idea of a Lilac Fairy without lilacs; she wears neither the flower nor the color, and there are no lilacs amid the foliage that she raises to cover the slumbering castle. Without that little symbol, a whole train of association gets bumped off the track: springtime, youth, Aurora, the dawn of life, renewal, Renaissance, the bright morning of civilization.

Carabosse is indeed a principal character; to misunderstand her function is to set in motion a series of misunderstandings that disfigure the ballet. If Tchaikovsky had meant the two fairies to continue their duel in Act II, he would have retained their key associations from the Prologue. But his meaning is exactly what Wiley says it is: "Carabosse is no longer a threat at this point; E major is no longer necessary as an antidote to E minor." So the Panorama, so richly suggestive, as Wiley remarks, of the world of the Lilac Fairy, unfolds in G major ("the key of resolution"), Lilac appears to the Prince in D-flat major, and the action eventually works itself around to a triumphant conclusion in E-flat major, the principal key, significantly, of Act II. And Carabosse's function is clear even apart from the tonalities. Wiley doesn't analyze scenarios with the diligence he applies to scores. If he did, he might not have written that "as a theatrical work the story of *Sleeping Beauty* is unusual" in that its outcome is revealed early by means of a prediction, which is then fulfilled. The figure of Carabosse is patterned on Madge, the witch in *La Sylphide*. Denied a place in the hero's wedding celebrations, Madge not only predicts his ruin but actively brings it about—a little too actively in some productions. Not letting Carabosse help fate along deprives the story of what little tension it has. And it has just enough. The cosmogony of the ballet is such that Florestan's realm may be tilted temporarily from its axis, but it cannot remain off balance for a hundred years—the Lilac Fairy sees to that. The whole idea of balance lost and regained is expressed in miniature in the overture. What the staging should tell us is that the world of the Lilac Fairy, which we visit in the second act, is the spirit world and may not be threatened by another spirit, however evil she may be. The world that the Lilac Fairy guards, however, is mortal and vulnerable. Philosophically as well as musically, *The Sleeping Beauty* is an advance from *La Sylphide*; it represents a world held in balance by divine force. In that respect, it is an advance, too, from *Swan Lake*. The ballet it most resembles is *Giselle*, where a divine force is palpable, whether the production centers it in the power of the cross or in the love that Giselle bears Albrecht from beyond the grave. Was it this connection, I wonder, which caused Balanchine to observe, in that charming but insufficient book of interviews called *Balanchine's Tchaikovsky*, that *The Sleeping Beauty* is "the best of the old ballets, second only to *Giselle*"? Certainly he can't have meant musically!

The stageability of *The Sleeping Beauty* is often attributed to the controlling vision of the ballet master Petipa, whose collaboration was not available to Tchaikovsky on *Swan Lake*. Wiley thinks Tchaikovsky often disregarded Petipa's instructions, which were none too specific to begin with. (Full texts are included in appendixes. However, Wiley also includes a statement by the first Aurora, Carlotta Brianza, testifying to the composer's behavior in rehearsals: "Tchaikovsky met the wishes of the ballet master halfway, shortening, supplementing, and changing the music according to the dances.") The value of Petipa's preliminary instructions may have lain in the mere fact that they existed; the composer only needed to be made aware of certain demands and constraints for his imagination to do its work. Vsevolozhsky commissioned the score and, as designer and librettist, drew up the picture of a fantasy Versailles which served his collaborators as inspiration. For Florestan's realm, parallels were found in Baroque arts and manners. A musician of the dance could have imagined no greater Golden Age than that of Lully and Rameau. A choreographer needed no better incentive than the chance to invoke the spirits of Camargo and Sallé, Angiolini and Vestris. The result was a masterpiece of world theatre, a ballet that both celebrates the birth of the classical tradition as we know it and symbolizes its endurance. Aurora is the reigning symbol: the world's first ballerina, Dance itself, born on a May morning in France, put to sleep by the deadly ministrations of the Paris Opéra, awakening to a Russian spring. Petipa's choreography is also a succession of choice tonalities. But the true and irreplaceable author of the ballet, Wiley leaves no doubt, is Tchaikovsky. It is he who tells us why *The Sleeping Beauty* is a ballet and not an opera. *Swan Lake* might be unsatisfactory as an opera, but it is not unimaginable as one; it has its Wagnerian side, and some of its love music was originally composed for an opera that Tchaikovsky abandoned. But *The Sleeping Beauty* is Tchaikovsky's dream of ballet, its storied and privileged past, its perishability, its prismatic technique and human radiance.

In his *Dance Research* article, "On Meaning in *Nutcracker*," Wiley uses the Russian word *duma* to describe the vision of Konfitürenburg/Kamenka which he attributes to Drosselmeyer/Tchaikovsky. *Duma* means something between daydream and meditation: it allows fantasy to penetrate reality; it dissolves rational distinctions between what is real and what the imagination feels is true. More than any other composer, Tchaikovsky understood ballet as a happening out of this world and time. Each of his ballets is an extended *duma*, is both irrational and sane, and is, however personal its auspices, immediately the possession of whoever hears it. There were other good dance composers before him and after. But Tchaikovsky discovered the consciousness of the medium. In his music, time is space, sound is shape, thought is deed. Listening, we see, we touch, until we hardly know whether it is the tympani we hear or the hammering of our own hearts. *—February 24, 1986*

Postscript 1987: On the matter of Carabosse, Donald Sidney-Fryer wrote to say that my comparison of her to Madge in *La Sylphide* "generically . . . hit the mark," but that Vsevolozhsky and Petipa, who "*together* created the libretto of *The Sleeping Beauty* . . . would have been inspired by Perrot's grand fairy ballet *La Filleule des Fées* (Paris Opéra, October 1849), and rather directly so. Perrot produced the ballet in Russia for the seasons of 1849–50 and 1850–51, first with Elssler and then with Grisi, the original [heroine] Ysaure. In this earlier 'Manichean farce' the cosmogony is askew, and Carabosse's theatrical ancestor, the Black Fairy, is actually more powerful than the other (good) fairies, who must *beg* the Black Fairy to have pity on Ysaure and to allow her lover to recover his sight so that the lovers can be reunited. Yelena Andreyanova played the Black Fairy, and her success seems to have almost equalled that of Elssler as Ysaure. Marius Petipa was certainly in the ballet company at the Bolshoi Theatre (in St. Petersburg) at this time, and apparently was a kind of understudy to Christian Johannson, who played the lover of Ysaure. Petipa had a phenomenal memory for choreography. Surely he would not have forgotten Perrot's magisterial *féerie?*—nor yet the powerful character of La Fée Noire?"

As Mr. Sidney-Fryer suggests, the evidence linking *La Filleule des Fées* and *The Sleeping Beauty* is fairly conclusive. Ivor Guest doesn't mention *The Sleeping Beauty* in his book *Jules Perrot* (Dance Horizons, 1984), but the link is self-evident in his description of the action of *La Filleule des Fées*. And he records the objections made by a contemporary Russian critic to the philosophical "error" in the plot of *La Filleule*—objections with which the makers of *The Sleeping Beauty* would seem to have been thoroughly in agreement.

The critic, Rafail Zotov, wrote that "the power of evil was conveyed too strongly." He went on: "Let evil exist as an inevitable sign of human weakness, but it must always be weaker than good and order. Let evil do harm, let it even triumph momentarily, but this must be by means of mysterious machinations and not through the prevailing of a greater power. Good should be clearly victorious without having recourse to a humiliating appeasement to evil. The choreographer ought to have created his *dénouement* so that the evil fairy is finally defeated by the good fairies and compelled to slink away in shame."

In Town and Out

May 30th, New York City Ballet. Balanchine's choreography for Paul Taylor, which formed the penultimate part of the Webern ballet *Episodes*, is presented for the first time since 1961, when Taylor himself last danced it. A six-minute solo of enormous difficulty, it has been reconstructed by Taylor from his own notes. Peter Frame, of New York City Ballet, is the performer, and his physical resemblance to the Taylor of the early sixties creates a flash of recognition as he walks out from the wings. Tall, with brawny musculature and fair coloring, Frame looks like the same kind of uncomplicated, bland, good-natured guy that Taylor so deceptively seemed to be, and he has a soft, easy way of moving; you can see why Taylor chose him for the part. But he isn't the demon of articulation that Taylor was. The point of the solo—it closes a gap in the logical development of the ballet—is clearly made, but the *points* whereby it exercised its dreadful and absolute anarchic power are unexpressed.

The Taylor solo, composed to the Variations, Opus 30, was Balanchine's most radical statement of the knotty extremes to which Webern's music reduced the human body. It followed the Concerto, Opus 24, in which Allegra Kent had with her own incomparable aplomb set logic on its ear. And the section that followed Taylor was a complete break in continuity—an abrupt return to order by way of Webern's arrangement of the Ricercata from Bach's *Musical Offering*. Taylor just this season staged for his own company a setting of the *Musical Offering*, and he used the Webern Ricercata. There may have been more than passing references to Balanchine in his choreography. Like *Episodes*, Taylor's *A Musical Offering* is a pure-dance discourse on modern dance and its evolution or derivation from earlier dance forms. Taylor's forms appear to originate in primitive dance, and they come out roughly Germanic or Denishawn-anthropological in inspiration. Balanchine begins and ends with images of the classic court dance; his subject is less the generic modern dance than modernism itself. Though *Episodes* was made to stand by itself, it can scarcely be forgotten that the original production was a joint presentation by Balanchine and Martha Graham, whose mentor, Louis Horst, taught a then influential course in the court dances of the Renaissance. Only after Graham had performed *her* Webern ballet (on a Renaissance court theme: Elizabeth Tudor and Mary Stuart were the main figures) did Balanchine offer his, clearly intending its five sections as a kind of progressive atomization à la Webern of traditional classic dance, beginning with the Symphony, Opus 21, in which we see an Alice in Wonderland treatment of the Elizabethan court, and culminating in the Variations, Opus 30, and their exposition of dance energy as a thing by and for itself, with no regard for sense or sentiment. High-concentrate phrases begin and end invisibly, explode like crystals, sprawl and scatter, shrivel and retract. Peter Frame parses this material tidily, finding verbs and sentence structure in every outburst of actionless action. (With Taylor, there seemed to be no points of stability but his two blazing blue eyes.) He is reassuringly solid, and the solo passes off cleanly, twice as long, in effect, as it ever was before. As a Balanchine construction, it relates to the *Variations* of Stravinsky performed exclusively by Suzanne Farrell; it is choreography for a special dancer, indivisible from that dancer's performance. And the Taylor choreography is more special yet in that it is full of Taylorisms, which he consciously or unconsciously contributed. It might have been better to have had a Taylor dancer in the part—more in the historic pattern, too. (Taylor was at the time one of Graham's dancers.) But this is to presuppose an accuracy of which current Taylor dancers aren't capable even when they dance Taylor's old roles in their own repertory. One could make the case that Balanchine's choreography for Kent was just as personal to Kent, and that without her the Concerto loses much of its force. The facts are that Balanchine elected to preserve the Concerto without Kent but not the Variations without Taylor. This isn't to say that the revival of the Variations is an outright failure; only that, while such a revival can complete the explication of Balanchine's ideas in *Episodes*, it can't embody them—can't make *Episodes* happen again as a totality. With Frame in Taylor's part, Samson is back shaking the temple, but it doesn't fall down.

June 1st, the Kirov Ballet. If you never saw Taylor or Kent in *Episodes*, you may not miss them, and if you have never seen Altinay Asylmuratova you may not suspect the things that can still be done with ballerina style at the Kirov. The company possesses formidable technicians in Chenchikova, Kunakova, and Te-rekhova. It is not that they lack beauty or delicacy. It is that once you have seen Asylmuratova the technique exemplified by these other women looks like mere efficiency servicing an expressive ideal that is hopelessly out of date. Today's Kirov is led by dancers who perform a pointlessly amplified, coarsened version of the style of a generation ago—the style of Kolpakova and Makarova and Sizova. Asylmuratova dances on the huge scale currently in vogue but without distorting the old values, and she brings to them her own quality of poetic illumination. She would have been a wonder among wonders then; now she is just about all the company has got. Some impressive young soloists, male as well as female, who were seen on the recent American tour did not diminish her singularity. She's what Kirov style these days wants to be all about, and I emphasize the word "Kirov." The company's technical strengths and weaknesses reflect its years spent in isolation from any but the most trivial Western influences. The technique on which it has raised Asylmuratova is not what I or many other Western observers would have wished for her, and the methods of promotion and presentation from which she suffers cannot be defended by claims of seniority. At twenty-five, she is still being passed over in favor of older and mightier ladies at the top. Still, she stands out, and I have the impression that Oleg Vinogradov, the current director, does what he can within the caste—and casting—system to give her every op-portunity.

Today, on this hastily scheduled matinée at the War Memorial in Trenton, she performs again the scene from *Esmeralda* I first saw her in, four years ago in Paris, and the magic floods back. Memory does not play tricks in dance—not on this level of experience. I note that her presence has ripened. Aside from that, she is the same phenomenon of lucidity she was then, with the same ability to evoke known excellences in her art and startle with unknown ones. She wins an ovation and is whisked away. The program, a combination of miniatures and repertory extracts, follows the pattern of Paris: in general, the older the chore-ography, the better, and the better the dancers look. The modern stuff, which includes two excerpts from Vinogradov's newest ballet, *The Knight in the Tiger's Skin*, is ghastly, but it is balanced by fragments of reconstructed Petipa, Ivanov, Saint-Léon, and Fokine. All the principal dancers on the tour manage to get on in one capacity or another. Zaklinsky, Asylmuratova's husband, is confined to partnering Terekhova in the Act II adagio from *Swan Lake*. The spotlight falls on two other young men, Lunev and Vicharev, who weren't in Paris, and who represent the rising male generation—for this tour, anyway.

I get back to the city in time for the evening performance of New York City Ballet. It's another world. *Divertimento No. 15*, the Mozart ballet, gets one of those serenely bright, tenderly true performances it has benefitted from all this season; the stars are Ashley, Calegari, Hauser, Kistler, and Saland, partnered by Lüders, Castelli, and Frame. *Divertimento* used to be an elusive masterpiece— too difficult, it seemed, for mortals to perform. Not anymore. How strange that Balanchine's dancers are more conscious of his principles and more willing to put them into practice now that he is gone. Perhaps it is only family psychology: defy the father while he is alive; when he is dead, keep his laws.

In contrast to the fragile *Divertimento* comes the indestructible *La Valse*. There cannot be a bad performance of this ballet. That may be one of the reasons *La Valse* has always ranked, in my mind, as less than great. It is dancer-proof, surefire, and somewhat suspect if by "surefire" we mean that it trades on cheap effects. But so is *Giselle* surefire, and *La Valse* may be one of those ballets that (like *Giselle*) both typify and transcend the fashions of their period. The mood of irony that used to cling to *La Valse* doesn't seem so insistent these days, and it's unimaginable to me now how I could ever have viewed it, as I seem to have done in the sixties, as a piece of camp. Saint-Georges, the librettist of *Giselle*, was approached by the ballet's author, Gautier, with instructions to arrange a "pretty death" for the heroine. This so that they could go ahead with Act II and the graveside dances that are the raison d'être of the ballet. Posterity has taken the frivolously morbid *Giselle* more seriously than its makers did, and something like the same fate may be in store for *La Valse*. Although who knows? Balanchine could have been completely serious.

June 4th and 5th, the Kirov Ballet in *Chopiniana*, *La Bayadère*, and *Paquita*. You have to be pretty agile to see Asylmuratova on the American tour. She did one unscheduled *Swan Lake*, in Los Angeles. In Philadelphia, she was replaced, unannounced, in the first performance of *La Bayadère* by the egregious Mezentseva; people went home thinking they'd seen Asylmuratova. Here at Wolf Trap, the program lists the same two names for Nikiya in the Shades scene of *La Bayadère*. It is Asylmuratova who actually appears, and who appears again in the repeat performance, the next night. But that first appearance is such a surprise that she is well into the adagio before I can believe that it is she. If she startled me before, she shocks me now with this image of an obdurate, implacable Nikiya. She is not spiritual like Makarova, grand like van Hamel, or refined like Fonteyn; and she isn't hard or icy. She's simply a killer beast, warm-blooded and deadly.

Berezhnoy, her excellent partner, seems to cower when he kneels before her in homage. She never sees him, but as she lifts a long arm on high the hand relaxes, and we know she can forgive. The idea of a wrathful Nikiya is, of course, to be understood in the context of the complete ballet, which I hope to see on the Kirov's next visit. But who has ever performed the ballet like this? What Shade, no matter how provoked, would have risked the staccato sweeps of the arms, the fierce attack on élancé, the hard-edged dead stops in fifth plié that characterize this Nikiya? And what other Kirov ballerina, having drawn so clear a picture, would erase most of it in the next performance? Here she was again, implacable as before, launching her fine high split–grand jeté in second position, and landing in tight fifth with the same unnerving pounce. But the rest of it—the overemphatic firm stops and staccato attack—was gone; she had softened her delivery without changing her characterization.

With her large, rangy frame and small, sleek head, Asylmuratova strides like a Bengal tiger through the role of Nikiya. It's as much a triumph for her as *Le Corsaire* was for Nureyev twenty years ago; she even has the ease and rapacity of motion that Nureyev had. One could wish that she also had Nureyev's or Makarova's version of the *Bayadère* choreography. But she is the most musical of the Kirov's ballerinas, and she uses her musicality to create effects that aren't in the steps—for instance, the big, bouncing lifts that the Kirov performs without leg beats to mark the accent. She makes the crest of each lift higher and wider, and you hear the up-up-up in the music as if the beats were there. Kirov-style musicality, which I generally find uncongenial, I find refreshing in her. And she's exceptional in yet another way—the way she takes her bows. In contrast to company custom, Asylmuratova's curtain calls aren't even grand; she comes straight out of character and looks girlishly eager and happy. At the peak of the applause, she will take fifth position on point, fling up her arms, and lift a wide, smiling face to the gallery. Since it is a face of shattering beauty, she could probably limit her appearances to this one pose and still be a star. But Altinay Asylmuratova is a dancer, one whose range has yet to be presented in full to the American public. We may hope for the experience soon.

So as not to seem too starstruck, I will add the names of dancers who also impressed me. Chistyakova, Sitnikova, and Ayupova, who danced the Three Shades, seem to be the best of the under-thirty generation. Terekhova, superbly strong and clean in a *Paquita* variation, continues to be the fairest of the senior ballerinas. Young Lunev was the most pleasing of the male dancers; he did wonderfully soft split jumps and sissonnes in the pas de trois of *Paquita*, that lumpiest of Petipa grab bags. The *Bayadère*, which looked so shabby in Paris, has regained its form. (It was *Chopiniana* that seemed drab this time.) The corps's descent to the stage is not straight down a ramp but around a corner and then down. Each dancer faces the public as she lifts her arms, and is immediately supplanted in that pose by another dancer. The silhouette then switches to profile and dips into arabesque. This entrance, probably improvised for the tour, had the grand effect of highlighting not the ongoing port-de-bras/arabesque sequence but the fact that there were numbers upon numbers of Shades to perform it. You saw the first port de bras, then instantly another one right behind it, and another one, and so on. Infinity appeared in a flash.

June 6th, Pennsylvania Ballet. A new production of Balanchine's *A Midsummer Night's Dream* should look better on the stage of Philadelphia's Academy of Music than this. The standard Hays-Karinska décor, which has long needed replacing in New York, is reproduced, none too kindly. (Another change in attitudes toward Balanchine involves his visual taste, universally criticized while he was alive. Now when a company acquires a Balanchine ballet it almost invariably takes the costumes and scenery, too.) Staged by Richard Tanner, the production goes pretty far toward cementing the conversion of the witty lovers' quarrels into low comedy and the elegant Puck into a stock buffoon. But Melissa Podcasy is a charming, twinkly Titania, and Jeffrey Gribler has the toughness and resilience that are built into Oberon's choreography. He and Marin Boieru both dance the roles of Oberon and Puck, and I am told by a company spokesman that I have come on the wrong night. But Boieru, directed away from the boisterousness that marks his portrayal (and in which he himself does not believe), could be a fine, feline Puck. And on another night I might not have seen Tamara Hadley and William DeGregory in the second-act pas de deux. The cantilena line of the adagio, which is as perishable as anything in *Divertimento No. 15*, comes through intact.

June 7th, Martha Graham Dance Company. The first member of the cult of Ruth St. Denis was evidently St. Denis herself. In *The Incense*, one of her earliest solos, the self-mystification is of a near-stifling order. Revived this season by the Graham company along with two other Denishawn solos, it gives us a picture of the nebulous foundation on which Graham was forced to base her art. *Serenata Morisca* is a woman's solo, devised by Ted Shawn, that Graham herself danced many times. It is robust, professional, nothing more. *Tanagra*, an early attempt at choreography by Graham, is some business with a veil, very much in the Denishawn mode. But, like the name "Denishawn," it is a perfect synthesis, combining the mystique of St. Denis with the professionalism of Shawn. Graham's theatre sense is beginning to operate. Then, in *Lamentation*, the functional veil becomes a functional tube of stretch jersey, and we have one of the key Art Deco theatre works of the thirties. The last of the solos is *Frontier*, with Noguchi's fence. It is 1935, and the Graham persona is fully pronounced.

The company had earlier in the season revived *Heretic*. Five minutes long, it is a study in theme-and-variations form for a female soloist and group. The history books call *Heretic* (1929) a breakthrough, and it may well have been. In it one can recognize a cell of the living organism that we know as *Primitive Mysteries* (1931). But only one cell. The real question is how, from such morose and monolithic constructions as *Heretic* and *Lamentation*, Graham could have broken through to the configurations of *Primitive Mysteries*. The revival of *Heretic* was staged by Yuriko. It is to be regretted that with her services on hand, and with the company back on the hospitable stage of the City Center, an opportunity was missed to bring back Graham's most significant early piece.

June 8th, New York City Ballet. *Piccolo Balletto* is Jerome Robbins working in a Balanchine vein. With its Stravinsky music (the "Dumbarton Oaks" concerto), its theatre-auditorium set and its costumes in Easter-egg colors (Santo Loquasto, designer), and its playful, inventive choreography, the little ballet is reminiscent of *Danses Concertantes*. But there are other reasons to like it besides that. It is good to have Robbins back in a sunny mood after two gloomy in-memoriam pieces in a row. *Quiet City*, which was given earlier this season in tribute to the dancer Joseph Duell, was Robbins at his most sentimental. Its hero was Robert La Fosse, formerly of American Ballet Theatre, and La Fosse dances the lead in *Piccolo Balletto* opposite Darci Kistler. The two go well together. Robbins blesses this star marriage with the kind of image-building roles that he fashioned for Farrell and Peter Martins in *In G Major*. The audience buys it, and so do I.

The matinée begins with *Mozartiana*, danced by its original cast: Farrell, Ib Andersen, and Victor Castelli. Robert Irving conducts, and things happen. Farrell, who now dances a small selection of relatively untaxing roles (she had done *La Valse* and *Slaughter on Tenth Avenue* earlier in the week), performs her choreography in *Mozartiana* on a reduced scale but with no loss of detail: a luxurious performance. The two men are fine, the four other women are fine, the four little girls are ecstatic, and the ballet ends in a festive calm.

This evening, Balanchine's choreography for *Swan Lake* is given with a new set and new costumes by the French artist Alain Vaes. I had liked Vaes's quasi-surrealistic backdrop for Jean-Pierre Bonnefoux's *Shadows* a season or two ago, but not his ashen hilltop for Martins's *Songs of the Auvergne*. *Swan Lake* is another striking bit of quasi surrealism—a great Gothic vault dripping with icicles and, in the distance, a deep-blue fjord (not a frozen lake) rimmed with mountains of ice and pouring mist. To the playing of the overture, the dummy swans enter on their track—a white queen and, behind her, a flock as black as jet. And the transformed swans who arrive on the stage are in full black tulle tutus with winglike panniers; only the queen is still in white. All this might seem too fanciful if Balanchine's thirty-five-minute *Swan Lake* were just the second act of the ballet. Instead, it is a composite of Acts II and IV, and as such it's like no other *Swan Lake* that can be seen. Balanchine prescribed the black dresses—he even ordered the tulle. And five years ago, for all the ballets of the Tchaikovsky Festival, he installed an "ice palace" setting of white plastic tubes. Ice-blue, swan-black, the glamorous new *Swan Lake* is to Balanchine's taste.   —*June 30, 1986*

Nureyev and Baryshnikov:
Paris and New York

One of the most extraordinary features of Liberty Weekend, its prelude and aftermath, was the visual barrage of images of the Statue of Liberty which the media put the nation through. We saw the statue day and night, from every conceivable angle; and yet no one seems to have commented on its quality as a piece of sculpture. Paul Goldberger, in the *Times*, said that it was good, but he didn't say why. An editorial—it may also have been in the *Times*—remarked on the dual aspect the figure presents: she seems to be striding forward from one perspective, firmly planted from another. But Liberty is nothing without her torch, and the torch would be nothing without the arm that lifts it—an arm the strength of which starts in the lower back and flows up through the shoulder. The gesture does not start from the shoulder any more than the branches of a tree start from the trunk. There is a lesson for dancers in this. Those who watch dancing can also learn something about supported versus unsupported gesture by comparing the statue with the myriad bad copies of it, which also flourished during the festivities. One of these bad copies has stood for years atop a warehouse across the street from Lincoln Center. The celebrations there included a two-week engagement at the Met by the Paris Opéra Ballet, and someone thought to place a viewing machine in the plaza, trained on the false Liberty and her unimpressively brandished torch. But she could be seen perfectly well, in all her cautionary glory, from the porch of the Met, where American Ballet Theatre ended a nine-week run just as the Opéra dancers were arriving.

The two companies are linked by the fact that each is directed by a defector from the Soviet Union's finest ballet company. To the Lincoln Center authorities, busy promoting July 4th and July 14th as a tandem occasion, it was a matter of the greatest significance that Rudolf Nureyev gained his freedom in Paris, while Mikhail Baryshnikov, soon after defecting in Canada, made his way to New York and has remained here ever since. In addition, Baryshnikov was set to be sworn in as a United States citizen on the eve of the Fourth, to receive, along with eighty-five other immigrants, a special award from the Mayor of New York, and to dance in one of the televised extravaganzas. (He danced the title number from Balanchine's Gershwin ballet *Who Cares?* A pas de deux, it featured Baryshnikov's partner, Leslie Browne, as much as or more than Baryshnikov himself, and he didn't choose, or wasn't give time, to follow it with the male solo to "Liza." But the choice was an appropriate one, nicely staged, with the two dancers meeting on the windswept stage on Governors Island and looking out, before beginning to dance, not at a painted drop of Manhattan but at New York Harbor, with the illuminated statue in the distance. And Helen Hayes, in her introduction, did not omit to remember Balanchine, another Russian immigrant.) As part of his regular routine, Baryshnikov danced with his company on closing night in *Giselle*—an American production of a French classic—and on the previous night, the night of the Fourth, Nureyev appeared as a guest with A.B.T. and danced in the same ballet. There was symbolism everywhere you looked. An official ballet gala was held at the Met, involving A.B.T. and Paris Opéra dancers, with Gene Kelly as host, and Nancy Reagan in attendance. By July, the theatres of Lincoln Center are filling up with tourists, and last month there seem to have been more tourists than ever, many of them French-speaking. The regular balletomane cheering sections were augmented by people for whom Nureyev and Baryshnikov were among the city's top scenic attractions and Baryshnikov was not only a famous dancer but a movie star. He has been a big success in the movies, whereas Nureyev has not, and it may be because in both of his movies Baryshnikov played a character based on himself. This, and not the fact that he is a better actor, lent him a credibility that Nureyev didn't have when he impersonated Valentino or played a violinist in that movie with Nastassja Kinski. Nureyev's instincts played him false in his movie roles; he did exactly the opposite of what he does on the stage. But so did Baryshnikov; each man made movies more appropriate to the other.

The closer one examines the two men's careers, the more dissimilarities appear. Nureyev was twenty-three when he defected, Baryshnikov twenty-six. But Nureyev was seventeen when he began studying at the Kirov. He was never the product of institutional care and training that Baryshnikov was, but he was strong-willed and self-reliant, and he overcame the late start. Both men were already formed as dancers at the time of their defections. Their careers in the West took shape as much from their abilities as from the opportunities offered them. From the beginning, Baryshnikov possessed an ease of assimilation that is still amazing. Time and again, we have seen him take on strange new roles and styles and penetrate them to the quick. Nothing in dance seems alien to him. Nureyev, on the other hand, does not sink himself into new roles so much as convert them into occasions for further appearances. One could say that it is the way of a star, while Baryshnikov's is the way of an artist, but there's more to it than that. Baryshnikov has assimilated America, while Nureyev, officially a citizen of Austria, remains independent, perpetually detached. Paris and the Opéra are where he hangs out.

The Franco-American gala closed with a special performance of *Push Comes to Shove*, arranged by its choreographer, Twyla Tharp, with Baryshnikov dancing his familiar role and being upstaged by three Baryshnikov clones in derby hats—Gil Boggs, Danilo Radojevic (both of whom now dance the ballet more often than he does), and Tharp herself. It was not the kind of audience that would have recognized Twyla Tharp in a derby or understood much of what was going on; it came to life only when Baryshnikov himself was onstage and when, at the very end, Tharp brought on Nureyev as yet another clone. Nureyev's role was only a bit, and he played it just right—stiff, comically bewildered. Still, you could tell that he *really* didn't know what he was there for. He kept twirling his hands helplessly, and he used a robot walk, as if the derby had turned him into Chaplin— it was his only concession to a style other than his own. Lest you think Tharp too radical a test of Nureyev's versatility, there was a moment earlier in the program when he and Baryshnikov were called on to appear in white tie and tails and escort Leslie Caron through one of those old-fashioned medley tributes to a lady star and her hits. It was little enough to ask of a great big sexy man like Nureyev, but he looked uncomfortable—with the situation, with the music, with the suit, maybe even with the lady. His lack of skill made him appear ungallant, but it's not that he's unwilling to cede the spotlight to someone else; it's that he simply doesn't know what to do outside it. He can't easily surrender the responsibility for the performance. His partnership with Fonteyn is legendary, but Nureyev still partners women the way he often tried to partner Fonteyn—manipulatively, competitively. He is one of nature's soloists, and in the course of the Paris Opéra season he proved it irrefutably. Alas, he was supposed to be so much more.

Nureyev can be overbearing onstage, but he has never lacked generosity toward other dancers. Much testimony exists to suggest that he genuinely admires talent and enjoys creating opportunities for it. When he was appointed director of dance at the Opéra, in 1983 (so the story goes), he immediately set about exploring the school's latest crop of dancers and speeding the best of them up the hierarchical ladder to the rank of étoile. Nureyev's road at the Opéra soon turned rocky, but of all his policies this was probably the most benign. Long before the Opéra Ballet opened its New York season (its first since 1948), the talk was all of the baby ballerinas Sylvie Guillem and Isabelle Guérin, and of Elisabeth Platel, étoile since 1981 and a pupil of the renowned Yvette Chauviré. There is no dance institution in the West quite like the Opéra; what the company lacks in artistic profile, the school makes up in prestige. Any consideration of the merits of Nureyev and Baryshnikov as artistic directors would have to begin with the fact that Nureyev has a school to draw on and Baryshnikov doesn't. (The School of American Ballet gives priority to New York City Ballet.) It's true that Baryshnikov doesn't have to contend with the internal politics and problems of discipline that make the Opéra Ballet a nightmare to run. But then the Opéra Ballet has to contend with Nureyev. He's not having the nightmare; he's part of it.

School or no school, I think it fair to say that Baryshnikov has made the most of what he has been given to work with; indeed, he has made more than the most. If there is a disabling factor in Baryshnikov's makeup, it's this tendency of his to overestimate talent or to confuse it with aggression. I confess to some confusion myself. I don't know whether Baryshnikov is deluded in his assessment of talent or whether his attitude is one of laissez-faire indifference; with an artist of his complexity, it's difficult to say. Through all his magnificent protean endowments as a dancer there runs a streak of submissiveness, which I think he must have inherited (along with the endowments) from Nijinsky, and though he's better at running a company than poor Nijinsky was, I wish he'd said no to some of what went on in the season just past—to Rouben Ter-Arutunian's effusive costumes for *Francesca da Rimini*, or, better, to the whole ballet. And Kenneth MacMillan's setting of Andrew Lloyd Webber's Requiem is even more inexplicable. John Taras, the choreographer of *Francesca da Rimini*, used to be with New York City Ballet before he joined Baryshnikov's staff, and his genteel, fulsome production is something that may well have been denied the light of day there (as part of the Tchaikovsky Festival, perhaps). But is there any reason to suppose that MacMillan could not have staged his latest anti-war, anti-death testament for the Royal Ballet? Despite the fact that Vietnam and Cambodia (for such seems to be the subject) are more in the American consciousness, it is British to the core, and the music, a Requiem Mass by the composer of *Jesus Christ Superstar, Evita*, and *Cats*, is the essence of mod spirituality. As is so often the case with MacMillan, the choreography is well wrought and the ballet is wrongheaded as can be. Admiration for his craftsmanship must struggle with distaste for his themes, which incorrigibly resist expression in dance.

MacMillan has been an artistic associate of A.B.T. for nearly two years without appearing ever to have left London. His chosen ballerina, Alessandra Ferri, is now Baryshnikov's most frequent partner, and her position is exactly the sort of puzzle I referred to a moment ago. Ferri's classical technique is modest. If she had been brought here by MacMillan to be co-starred with Baryshnikov in dramatic MacMillan ballets, that would be quite understandable. Her tragic intensity is suited to modern dramatic works, and Baryshnikov, though he has been dancing his classical roles flawlessly, may be thinking of quieting down somewhat and diversifying his repertory. He and Ferri look good together, but their most reliable vehicle so far has been *Giselle*. They didn't dance in *Requiem* in New York. Instead, Ferri did *La Bayadère*, in which she was outdanced by the other Shades (Amanda McKerrow, Christine Spizzo) and outclassed by her partner (Patrick Bissell). In *La Sonnambula*, with Baryshnikov, she showed what her tragic mask of a face and her strikingly shaped feet might be capable of with the right coaching, but she's not the figment of Romantic inspiration the ballet is about. Ferri's Sleepwalker, like her Giselle, is closer to the Dumb Girl of Portici than to the heroines of Romantic ballet.

The two other new works of the season, Karole Armitage's *The Mollino Room* and David Gordon's *Murder*, were more in line with what A.B.T. has become in the Baryshnikov era—a composite expression of the more vigorous trends in American dance. Armitage, for all her avant-garde deviltry, has a ballet background, and has held several ballet-company commissions (two from the Paris Opéra). It was only a matter of time before she got around to A.B.T. David Gordon has no ballet background at all, but, as things turned out, Baryshnikov seems to have got exactly what he wanted from Gordon and rather more than he bargained for from Armitage. *The Mollino Room* is overstuffed with ideas; half of them have to do with modern ballet choreography in the post-Balanchine era, while the other half rove through the terrain of postmodern aesthetics, trying to cover every development since Cage, Cunningham, and Rauschenberg. The ballet is hung with paintings by David Salle which depict plain objects like overshoes, coffeepots, and fishing reels, and is dressed, by the same artist, in play clothes, the majority of which are in curious, off-putting colors and shapes. Lurking in all this visual gimmickry is some kind of statement about the classic beauty of utilitarian or commercial design—hardly a new idea, and one, in fact, that the ballet's makers claim to have from Carlo Mollino, the Italian industrial designer. But the ballet's animating principle is montage. Everything in it—the overshoes, the play clothes, the sound score (made up of two movements of two different Hindemith chamber works plus a taped Nichols and May routine)—has been plucked from its normal context and reassembled or recycled or in some way made to serve a "new" environment. Even the dance steps, which Armitage has set for Baryshnikov and a mixed ensemble, have been uprooted from their classically sequential contexts and re-embedded in jagged new combinations. Intellectually, it all fits together. As an experience, though, *The Mollino Room* is arduous. It's like a giant music video trying its best to dislocate and stun us. The pattern of ideas doesn't come across in sensuous terms (which are the only terms that matter in ballet); instead of harmoniousness and integration we get a spectacle of cross-purposes. A pity, because on sheer choreographic merit the ballet deserves attention. Armitage, the hip neoclassicist, really shows her credentials in the fluidly controlled, incisive measures she devises for the group and its leaders (Leslie Browne or Susan Jaffe with Robert Hill). Her material for Baryshnikov is less effective; she isolates him from the group without giving a reason for his isolation. (It's his genius, of course, but he doesn't have genius steps, only hard ones.)

Last year, in *Field, Chair and Mountain*, David Gordon gave A.B.T. *his* ideas about the mechanisms and manners of classical dance. This year, he presented a straightforward comedy ballet, a parody of the PBS series "Mystery!" In *Murder*, Baryshnikov gets the juiciest mime role he has ever played, the large supporting cast gets an array of miniature character roles, and the audience laughs a lot. The décor is by none other than Edward Gorey. I loved *Murder*, but is it viable without Baryshnikov? (Johan Renvall's one performance came on a night when I couldn't go.) He does multiple characterizations, one of which, in ringlets and frills, suggests what *Camille* would be if it were danced by Karsavina. The only thing Baryshnikov's movie audience doesn't know about him is how funny he is. As for Gordon, *Murder* may not be a major achievement, but it is a true one. He has made a linear progression of events occur to a pre-existing musical score (the first movement of Berlioz's Funeral and Triumphal Symphony) without a moment's unseemliness, and that sort of thing is hardly ever done nowadays.

And then came the Opéra. Though its two weeks were studded with lavish productions and nightly changes of cast, the story was pretty much told on that gala program, when Nureyev led the company in his latest roundup of *Raymonda* excerpts. Though he forced himself mightily, Nureyev can no longer even intermittently conceal his physical decline. But that's no surprise—he's forty-eight years old. The real surprise was the impoverished classical style of the Opéra dancers. The bad things one had always known about them—the things that the

Nureyev regime, with its illustrious new stars, was supposed to have changed—were right there on the stage: weak lower backs, unworked turnout, careless feet. Lots of pretty faces, to be sure, and charming manners. The Paris dancers are virtuosos of charm. But the legs have no force. An à la seconde en l'air extension is like the arm on the false Liberty of West Sixty-fourth Street—stuck out from nothing. Fifth position is a mere formality. These failings don't necessarily reflect on the Opéra school. A poor company regimen can destroy the best training. Yet it's a question just what the French école is all about. During the season, a program of French dance films was shown at the Lincoln Center library. In one, billed as her homage to the French classical style, Maya Plisetskaya stood on a platform and waved her arms portentously. In another Chauviré demonstrated *The Dying Swan* sitting down. (And the younger dancer she demonstrated it to danced it as if *she* were sitting down.)

But even if the French used to be the greatest upper-body dancers in the world they aren't anymore. Those backs don't hold épaulé distinctions firmly enough. Head, neck, and arms are the most palpable part of the silhouette. The torso looks overbraced, with shoulders and hips rotating against an ungiving spine. There is no lack of energy. Despite their stylistic constraints, the dancers do move; they get into the air, and they aren't pert or sedate about it. But how strange to see a major company that doesn't want to release its energy expressively, by using the strength of the back to direct the deployment of the thighs. In short, by maintaining turnout. And how sad to think of Nureyev heading such a company—he whose turnout was so steadfast as to seem, in the early days, exotic. One of the great Nureyev numbers in those days, *Le Corsaire*, was rendered at the gala by Patrick Dupond and Sylvie Guillem in a manner that suggested their director to be Maurice Béjart rather than Rudolf Nureyev. Mlle. Guillem has a beautiful face, long legs, and loose hip joints; her high battement is a good trick. Her overarched feet are like Dupond's straining thighs—decorative, non-functioning vestiges of a style. Of course, the two of them tore the house down, but that morning's *Times* had quoted Nureyev as saying that Petipa keeps dancers in shape, and that's why he keeps Petipa in repertory; and these dancers are not in shape.

Nor are they likely to be *put* in shape by the choreography that Nureyev gives them. With every *Raymonda* he produces (the current version must be his fourth or fifth), he gets farther from Petipa. In this fifty-five-minute production, only the women's variations and the closing section of the galop are recognizable academic Petipa; the rest is Nureyev trying to be creative. A new and costly *Swan Lake* was disfigured by his insistence on dancing the tutor and the sorcerer as a dual role in imitation of Odette-Odile, thus reducing the prince to the status of a puppet. There have been many great ballet stars who took themselves for choreographers, but Nureyev choreographs as a star, in his own interests and from his own point of view. He lacks even the elementary theatre sense of Serge Lifar, the Opéra's ballet master until 1958. Lifar's *Les Mirages* was given a few showings. Weak as it was, it had professional finish; Lifar obviously knew how to use a stage and present dancers. If we ever thought him unmusical, we now have Nureyev, whose choreography actively defeats music. It was so obstructive in *Swan Lake* that I found myself nodding off while the orchestra sawed on. (Opéra standards in conducting defeat music, too.) And his bad taste turns a well-meant effort like *Washington Square* into an ignominious assault. Nureyev maltreats Henry James as much as Charles Ives, and he even abuses his good friend Martha Graham, whose vocabulary furnishes the choreography's principal motifs.

When you have two weeks to do six ballets and three of them are by a choreographer of staggering incompetence, one is by Serge Lifar, and one is a pastiche of Lully by a dance historian, you'd better have a good cover. The Opéra's cover was costumes. You couldn't see the steps unearthed by Francine Lancelot for *Lully: Quelques Pas Graves de Baptiste*, but you could feast on the costumes. The silks in *Swan Lake* glowed like stained glass. The sixth ballet was *Le Palais de Cristal*, done in colored costumes modelled on the original ones by Leonor Fini. Paired with *Washington Square*, it was intended as a salute, I think, to New York. But what the Opéra did to Balanchine's ballet (danced here as *Symphony in C*) was only a little less appalling than what it did, with Nureyev's help, to Petipa. The dancers tried hard, but they were performing, with inadequate technical means, a corrupt version of a masterpiece. In every movement but the fourth, there were major errors, gaps, and substitutions in the choreography, both in the principal roles and in the demisoloist and corps sections. The fourth movement had errors, too, but basically it adhered to the version that used to be danced by Balanchine's company at the City Center. The version called *Le Palais de Cristal* was created first, in 1947. When Balanchine restaged it in New York, he made changes and he continued to make them, but the Paris version cannot have been worked on by its choreographer after the fifties. It is quite a muddle, and nowhere more so than in the second movement, which encompasses one of Balanchine's greatest adagios. This was where he made the most changes; still, it was impossible to accept more than about twenty percent of the steps danced by Guillem or Platel at the Met as the work of Balanchine.

Baryshnikov has a certain dexterity as a choreographer but no great enthusiasm for the task, and for the most part he has abjured it. He's not especially interested in partnering or in teaching, and his dancing is sometimes so immaculate as to leave out the reason it is done. Baryshnikov is the Joycean disinterested artist as dancer. Nureyev is the compulsive, doomed, solitary hero. A decade older, he dances with all the motivation Baryshnikov leaves out. Baryshnikov's stance as a company director can be puzzling, but by and large his rule at A.B.T. is an extension and an enrichment of the resources of American dance. Nureyev and the Opéra are separate planets whirling in the same orbit. Each seeks what it needs in the other and, having found it, looks for not a speck more.

—*August 4, 1986*

Spanish from Spain

Flamenco Puro, the new show at the Mark Hellinger, is just what the title says it is: an entire evening of undiluted flamenco, presented without embellishment or commentary. For the New York audience, whether Hispanic or non-Hispanic, it is an evening of attentive looking and listening. The cast consists of seven dancers (four female, three male), seven singers, and six guitarists, all of whom are Spanish from Spain and many of whom are also Gypsies from Andalusia. To say that their knowledge of flamenco lies deep in the blood is to state a premise implicit in the word *puro*. And these performers do not compromise their art; they shake the dust of Andalusia in our faces. The printed program includes a glossary of song and dance forms which is none too helpful, and the English translations of the song lyrics only intensify their mystery. No matter; the show's staging makes everything accessible. It begins with handclaps and shouts (as in the opening of *The Three-Cornered Hat*), and the curtain rises with the whole company onstage, presenting its principal members one by one in brief solo turns (bulerías). The lights then go down, and the evening's few formal elements are introduced: one singer in a spotlight, followed by one guitarist, followed by three guitarists and three singers. By the time the dancers step out of the shadows, wearing austere gray costumes, the stage has been prepared by ritual incantation for ritual gesture.

Flamenco is to Spanish dance what the blues are to American jazz. The blues are incantatory, as Whitney Balliett was saying here the other week: "You can almost chant them."* So it is with flamenco; cante jondo, or deep song, is nothing if not soul music. And the distinction Balliett went on to make between blues singing and ballad singing—"The emotions in blues singing are primary, and the emotions in ballad singing are kaleidoscopic"—holds true for the flamenco of the Gypsies and the more objecfively developed salon style of Spanish dancing which is featured in other touring companies. The primary emotions of flamenco make it by nature a soloist's art, one that disdains the stylizations and accessories of a more sociably theatrical recitalist tradition. Pure flamenco dancing is done without castanets, without partners (in the sense of a pas de deux), and without formal choreography. It is autobiographical. The dancer is provoked to confession by the music; nothing comes between the dancer and his "song." (In *Flamenco Puro*, the proscription extends even to other dancers. Only once, in a number called "Tarantos," do we see two or more dancers moving together.) What happens, of course, is that as the evening goes on this radical concentration of means gives

* "Two in One," by Whitney Balliett, *The New Yorker*, October 27, 1986.

rise to kaleidoscopic impressions. Personalities blossom or contract, backgrounds are filled in, the range of the rhetoric starts to widen, and gradually a vista opens on the whole flamenco tradition: it becomes a metaphor of human fate. At least, that is the possibility which the evening holds out to us. The rewards of flamenco are a gamble. Its passions are spontaneous and dramatic rather than artful and lyrical. It is not meant to be served up in predictable form night after night. I think the producers of *Flamenco Puro* must have had this unpredictability in mind when they designed the program. After a leisurely progression of solos, to which we give the intensest scrutiny, they close with another bulerías, just like the first. But now as the performers step out one by one, we see them in the perspective of their art—we see how their art has transformed them, or else failed to. We see flamenco as a volatile process and art as a catalyst.

The producers, Claudio Segovia and Héctor Orezzoli, are the team who presented *Tango Argentino* last year. Segovia and Orezzoli are a new breed of producer; they may even be unique. They aren't living in the golden age of the art forms they present, and their concern seems to be with preservation—with isolating the essence of the art form's vitality even as the tradition that supports it diminishes and dies. (Their next show, significantly enough, is about the American blues tradition.) The tango was a revelation to American audiences; to Argentines it is a cliché perpetuated by middle-aged addicts. No one pretends that the flamenco clubs of Seville are bursting with talent; as if to prove the point, *Flamenco Puro* contains no outstandingly gifted dancers—no firebrands who ignite the art form and in effect re-create it. But if none of the dancers in the show are noticeably young and daring, none are licentious, either. With great talent there often comes violent change; the danger is that the art form will be re-created in the image of one all-powerful personality. *Flamenco Puro* is flamenco stabilized as much as possible; it is a picture of the forces that preserve the art against predatory star performance on the one hand and touristy reductions on the other. And in its solid, equable way it is exciting.

Manuela Carrasco and Eduardo Serrano would probably be stars in a more theatrically exploitative setting. Here they are the dancers who draw us the farthest into an understanding of the natural elegance of the style. Carrasco is a large, handsome woman with magnificent carriage. Blessed with a strong presence, she employs the widest plastic contrasts and in her footwork makes the biggest sound I have ever heard from a woman flamenco dancer. Though Serrano isn't a small man, his sound is comparatively delicate, and its tonal variety is astonishing. In pure flamenco, men and women dance the same steps, but one is hardly ever aware of the fact, so diversified is the style. The men tend to excel in line, the women, lifting Picasso arms, in plastique. Angelita Vargas and José Cortes are dancers of the same order of accomplishment as Carrasco and Serrano but less even in delivery. One night, Vargas was finely tuned but mousy; another night she was sensationally vivid, while her husband, Cortes, who can crackle with good spirits, was merely precise. Many of the performers in *Flamenco Puro* are related, and most have sobriquets. Cortes is El Biencasao (well married). El

Farruco is a vigorous older party, evidently legendary, who dances with a hat and cane. His two daughters, La Farruquita and La Faraona, seem to be the comediennes of the troupe—one sweet, the other salty. The first time I saw the show, all the women let their shawls down under their bottoms and ground away at the audience. The second time, only La Faraona chose to do this, but she was prodigious. (In recital flamenco, needless to say, this isn't done at all.) Moments later, we had the pearly soleares of Serrano (El Guito), which he dances against shadows of himself projected on the backdrop, and this was followed by Carrasco's version, in which, wearing a white gown and beautiful to behold, she seems to burst the skin of the style and dance out of herself, becoming for a moment rawly, even awkwardly sensual.

Flamenco Puro is a women's show. As in *Tango Argentino*, the musicians are the heartbeat of the performance. All of them are male except the singers Adele Chaqueta and Fernanda de Utrera, and these two flamenco matriarchs all but steal the show. When Fernanda de Utrera sings her soleares, she improvises the lyrics, and you seem to hear each stanza as it pops into her head. She comes on at a point in the evening when our concentration is at its peak. Nothing distracts us from her song, and if as we listen we are struck by the way the sense of it meshes with its sound and with the stress and intricacy of the dancing we have just seen, it may very well be because the flamenco experience is designed in this show to be grasped as an entity. Flamenco does have a systemic consistency; it is one language articulated in sound and spectacle. Segovia and Orezzoli have perceived this, and they've used marvellous stagecraft to bring out the mutually reflecting facets of the form. The simplest things interact—the ruffle on a dress, the rippling of a guitar—and seem to give off meaning. The *idea* of flamenco has never been so clear.   —*November 17, 1986*

Choreographer of the Year

This time last year, Mark Morris was at Dance Theater Workshop, straining its seating capacity (one hundred plus) to the bursting point. A few weeks ago, when the Morris company played New York again, in the Next Wave series at the Brooklyn Academy of Music, it was the Opera House's biggest draw of the season. Morris in the past year has become the most widely interviewed, most talked-about, and most commissioned young choreographer in American dance. He interests magazine editors as much as artistic directors, he attracts the musical as well as the dance public, and he holds connoisseurs of fashion spellbound. Between the D.T.W. and the BAM seasons, he showed New York a total of fifteen works. This doesn't include pieces that were part of his "Dance in America" television show, seen here in October, or the ballet for the Joffrey, which was given at the City Center the week of the BAM engagement. And Morris did a lot of work this year that New York hasn't seen: one other ballet commission; a special three-part evening based on Roland Barthes essays, mounted in Boston; two pieces for his company's début at Jacob's Pillow, last summer; and the "Dance of the Seven Veils" in a Seattle Opera production of *Salome*. All this in addition to his regular teaching commitments at the University of Washington, in Seattle (where he still lives). At the end of such a year, one might have expected a somewhat depleted choreographer to show up in Brooklyn. Besides *Marble Halls*, a Bach piece repeated from the D.T.W. programs, there would be two world premières, and one of these would be set to a piece of sacred music—Pergolesi's *Stabat Mater*—that is around forty minutes long. As it turned out, *Pièces en Concert*, to a suite of Couperin dances, was as fresh as anything he has done, and the *Stabat Mater* flowed out in a thick stream, the culmination of the grand and sombre series that includes *Gloria* and *Handel Choruses*. Mark Morris is still an amazing young man, and he was all there in Brooklyn.

Pièces en Concert is the kind of thing only Morris does, and *Stabat Mater* is the kind of thing only Morris does well. He's an innovator and a traditionalist, a satirist and a romantic, and one can never tell in advance what side of him will be presented in any given work or at any given moment in a work. The Couperin piece mingles absurdity and sobriety until they begin to look alike. The curtain goes up on a stage primly decorated with potted plants. Three people vaguely resembling eighteenth-century figurines come to life and dance a sarabande, then a courante, and so on. They use regulation deportment and nonregulation steps. Gradually, eccentric bits of timing and attack color the dance with a weird vivacity. As these different bits accumulate, a subversive logic takes over, yet the dance keeps moving with a specific exquisiteness through it all. The overstressed staccato attack turns into a passage about feeding birds, then into a passage about falling down, and soon we are in the totally unprincipled territory of pure slapstick.

How Morris (who is one—the silliest one—of the dancers) extracts the most laughs he can from this portion of the piece and then gets out of it and back to the unbroken porcelain calm of the beginning is a technical feat that I would think other choreographers could gain by studying, not only because of its psychological tact but for its delicacy in negotiating the Couperin music without violation. Impressive, too, is the way the absurdist tone arises so innocently from inside the dance—from Morris's shifting pauses and distributing accents with a kind of scientific detachment. In generic terms, the piece is an absolute novelty—a pas de trois that, for once, does not set up a situation wherein the two same-sex members (here Morris and Rob Besserer) are rivals for the affections of the other (here Susan Hadley); there is, in fact, no love interest at all. Perhaps the strangest thing about *Pièces en Concert* is that it seems to have been made with no preconceptions—not even a preconception of how funny it would turn out to be. It looks as if three Martians had come to earth, having encountered the spirit of Angna Enters in outer space.

Not everyone enjoys this sort of thing, and those who do are almost certain not to like *Stabat Mater*. Religious expression in dance so easily becomes sanctimony, I confess to a dread of it myself. But *Stabat Mater* isn't a piece of religious art. It's about religious feeling: specifically, the aspiration to faith and how people, especially young people, experience it in their lives. Even this much seriousness about religion may have been too much for the BAM audience, which gave the piece respectful applause and departed in relief. Maybe it was the triple dose of Baroque music that proved too much. Whatever it was, it was clear that Morris had not designed himself a safe success at BAM. His relation to the haute audience that patronizes Next Wave offerings had grown complex; he was certainly in that world, he was of it, but he was not in service to it any more than he would be willing to be the official standard-bearer of back-to-basics modern dance. *Stabat Mater* may be in an exalted Old Modern tradition, but it certainly doesn't look or feel anything like José Limón.

Morris is a true believer whose fidelity follows from his taste, especially in music. He can, for example, find and exploit the good in the fanatical style of Doris Humphrey. The first section of *Marble Halls* shows him doing it, but the piece as a whole salutes the Paul Taylor of *Esplanade*. In *Stabat Mater*, Morris reaches a kind of muscular effulgence that reminded me of Taylor's *A Musical Offering*. And though both pieces are episodic in structure, it was interesting to see Morris dispense with one of the things he does best—transitions—and invent a continuity by shifting his cast in silence between dances, stylizing the shifts so that each group of dancers runs on from stage left and displaces an equal number of dancers, who run off stage right. This happened over and over; as a device, it had something of the ritualistic power of the walks-to-place in Graham's *Primitive Mysteries*. But it also risked tiring the audience, and it points to one of the few weaknesses in Morris's command of choreographic technique, which is that once he has got hold of a structural device nothing on earth can make him let go. Usually, he derives structure from music and, as Taylor does, creates a correspondingly organic choreography. The tenacity of Morris's method has about it a marvellous integrity and sense of play, but there are times—the first section of *Esteemed Guests*, the ballet for the Joffrey, is an example—when he sticks too close to his musical spine, ignoring its free articulation, and ignoring, too, the possibility of expanding the dance's limits beyond structural equivalence. Morris actually comes close to such an expansion in the second movement of this ballet, when he brings off one of his headiest group transitions, converting a series of lifts into a series of poses. For a few moments, the ballet has a lyrical independence that feels like floating. Does this choreographer, whose sensibility is so Blakean, know Blake's proverb "Improvement makes strait roads; but the crooked roads without Improvement are roads of Genius"? His habitual use of Baroque music (*Esteemed Guests* goes to a cello concerto by Carl Philipp Emanuel Bach) may have improved his craftsmanship while straitening his poetic language. I make this suggestion mindful of works in the D.T.W. collection which were set to scores by Françaix and Shostakovich and were poetically expressive as well as structurally sound.

Having raised this objection to Morris's work, I should also point out that very few of his colleagues so much as acknowledge the structure of a piece of music or show any other kind of musical insight. The Joffrey chose to present, in the same season with *Esteemed Guests*, another piece to Baroque music by another young choreographer new to ballet. This was Mark Haim, whose *The Gardens of Boboli* showed talent and audacity. But it didn't show structural integrity, and it used music as a trampoline, in the manner of Gerald Arpino. The difference between Haim's ballet to Albinoni and Morris's to C. P. E. Bach was the difference between meter and rhythm, between rootless ingenuity and integrated invention. *Esteemed Guests* (who hands out titles at the Joffrey?) is not on the whole a success; it looks rushed and scrappy, and its central idea of a lone ballerina never gets pinned down. But Morris at least presents his credentials, and he makes us smile. I almost laughed at the allusion to Twyla Tharp in his two squirrelly female soloists and in his choice of Santo Loquasto for the costumes. *Esteemed Guests* comes at the same point in Morris's career that *As Time Goes By* came in Tharp's, and it is, with all its flaws, much the best new work the Joffrey has done since.

The adjective most commonly applied to Morris is "outrageous," and it refers to brilliant porno ballets like *Lovey* and *Striptease*, or to shocking fantasies of rape and repression like *One Charming Night*. Morris does have a taste for luridity, a taste for camp, and all the rest of that. But his most outstanding characteristic in these matters is his sense of balance. Outrage occurs in his work as a reflection of the natural order and what society has made of it. His sincerity can provoke some people to outraged reaction. Morris wears his heart on his sleeve, and nowhere does he do so more conspicuously than in his pieces with religious themes. But he's no less objective in these pieces than he is anywhere else. His great solo to an Indian raga, *O Rangasayee* (performed at BAM two seasons ago), had both ascetic rapture and sensual languor. Morris's personality seemed to merge with the dualities of classical Hindu dance. *Stabat Mater* is comparatively single-tracked; it's fleshy and glowing and hot with the sensual appetite of youth. Pergolesi wrote the music in the year he died, at the age of twenty-six; Morris turns it into a mirror of adolescent conscience. He sets his stage with three scrims, each with a cross; we see them sequentially, the first enveloped in crimson flames, the last pure white. The discipline of the choreography, formidable as usual, becomes part of the emotional texture. Bit by bit—the dance is in twelve parts—an imagery develops which is dumbfoundingly inchoate, like brutish statues being worked free of the marble that imprisons them. The simile comes from Michelangelo, and Michelangelesque or Blakean images recur in Morris's work. Yet shame, pain, ecstasy are here shown according to no known model. If there can be such a thing in dance as giving voice to the inarticulate, then Morris has done that thing. Once more, he has expressed the passions of a generation.

—*December 1, 1986*

Postmodern Ballets

Twyla Tharp has formed a new company—eleven replacements out of seventeen dancers—since her last New York season, three years ago. This time out, key performers like Sara Rudner, Jennifer Way, and Tom Rawe are among the missing, not to mention Tharp herself. And while Way and Rawe and Mary Ann Kellogg and Christine Uchida have returned to do one or two roles apiece, either as guests artists or as covers for the injured, Tharp has chosen not to appear in anything. All the more reason, then, to expect a difference in the way the company dances. But my first impression on opening night at the Brooklyn Academy was that Twyla Tharp Dance, as the company calls itself, was more like Twyla than ever. Men as well as women danced like her, stood like her, ran and walked like her. They seemed to have ingested her nervous system along with her dance style. I suppose this is normal enough for a company that is going through its first full-scale generational turnover. The new dancers are quite young—some are as much as twenty years younger than the founding members—and they're as pliable as warm cookie dough. The Supreme Founder has shaped them as she couldn't have shaped her peers, and, probably without meaning to, has instituted a whole set of personal mannerisms. In certain roles inherited from the company's other stars, the young ones take on the characteristics of those stars as well; Tom Rawe is uncannily present in Jamie Bishton's dancing of Rawe's roles in *Baker's Dozen* and *Nine Sinatra Songs*. But Tharp has also worked to give the newcomers latitude. All the girls are ballet-trained, and the two new pieces that Tharp has choreographed for the season include parts for women on point. There could be a collision in the making between the girls' schooling in classical technique and their impressionability in respect to style. But these are good, smart dancers. My guess is that as they mature they'll assert their individuality. They've already begun to shed the behavioral tics, and the season is still on.

But will they, in turn, give Tharp's choreography the new grounding in point-work which it seems to demand? In *In the Upper Room* (to a Philip Glass score) and in most of *Ballare* (to a double-piano sonata by Mozart), the passages on toe look inorganic and unexpressive. Points are a new and raw element in company choreography. Though Tharp has used them before, she has really succeeded only when the dancers have been other than her own—when they've been ballerinas with technical wisdom and years of stage experience. Tharp's own schooling was eclectic. (Her written script for *The Bix Pieces* opened with the line "I hated to tap-dance when I was a kid." She probably hated toe shoes even more.) As a choreographer, her technique has always been a zealously acquisitive one. She was the first of the postmodernists to work with ballet companies and to hire ballet dancers. She was the first to put an end to barefoot dancing, and she could be the first to acquire point technique and make something new of it. Her earliest use of points, in *As Time Goes By*, had a primitive charm that reminded me, at the time, of Nijinska. First danced by the Joffrey in 1973, this enchanting Haydn ballet is now in the Tharp-company repertory, and it retains its freshness. Tharp— or the ballet dancers she worked with—managed to blend elastically resilient pointwork with Tharpian dynamics. The gravitational pull of the body as it spun off center, the driving force of the legs were somehow enhanced; point technique seemed on the verge of categorical redefinition. This was integral expression, not the tokenism we see now in the Glass ballet, where the legwork is done on little stilts, and one feels no connection between the poised foot and the plunging instep or between the foot and the leg. And though Tharp's dancers are now all completely turned out, one feels no control from their turnout. In classical dancers, the impulse that ends in the pointed foot begins in the hip socket and radiates outward even when the step is turned in. I don't know why this is so; I only know that without clear motivation from the hip the foot on point looks like an Eleanor Powell novelty. It's a mysterious business, pointwork, and I don't doubt that Twyla Tharp will soon master it. There's distinct progress in *Ballare*. At first, the women seem to be doing nothing but bobbing and spinning in place or maneuvering from place to place. The movement looks constricted, not like that of ballet dancers or Tharp dancers, either. This goes on until the third section, when a synthesis occurs. Each girl has a solo that covers ground, and each looks natural and free. The piece ends happily, a real breakthrough. One is ready to forgive the crudity of *In the Upper Room*, where the points are only a means of advertising the newly constituted company and what it can do. (Just to make sure you get the message, the girls wear red socks and red toe shoes as part of their Norma Kamali costumes.)

Lincoln Kirstein's complaint about modern dance—that it is narcissistic and lacking in continuity—comes into your mind when you see a stageful of Twylas, and when you see them going up on point you may agree with his assertion, to W. McNeil Lowry in a recent issue of this magazine,* that modern dance has in fact disintegrated, because "the so-called post-postmodernists are all embracing ballet." Kirstein cited *Bach Partita*, created in 1983 by Tharp for American Ballet Theatre, as an example of the classical ballet's ability to absorb "bastard variations, mutations, conversions, perversions" and thus perpetuate itself, whereas modern dance cannot absorb ballet or perpetuate itself, because it is inherently anti-academic. In an article called "The Curse of Isadora," published a few weeks before in the Sunday *Times*, Kirstein located the fatal flaw in the democratic cult of self-expression. The moribund academy of her time left Isadora Duncan no other option, he wrote, and though she exercised it gloriously ("In dry seasons she poured rich wine"), her legacy was doom: "She certified modern dance with its dwindling succession." Kirstein has been saying these things for years. Why, on the eve of his eightieth birthday, with the School of American Ballet faithfully

The New Yorker, December 15, 1986.

nourished by private donations and government grants, does he still say them? Might it not be time for another essay, called "The Curse of Balanchine," in which it would be shown how the great choreographer created twentieth-century ballet and put it off-limits at the same time? He incorporated into the mainstream everything there was to incorporate—jazz, Bauhaus, twelve-tone music, American pop; yes, even the modern dance—and left the academy at a peak of virtuosity, with nothing further to express. Balanchine's progeny rework his accomplishments; they can honor his precedents, but they can add nothing to what he has said.

I gather that Kirstein thinks that reworking Balanchine is better than letting those whom he calls "dance dilettantes" get at his company. He seems to see academic training as a guarantee against anarchy and hazardous experimentation. New York City Ballet's latest première, Paul Mejia's *Sinfonia Mistica*, must therefore have been a bitter disappointment to him. Mejia, a graduate of the School of American Ballet, produced choreography that was not only hazardous but theatrically naïve to a degree that would have embarrassed an S.A.B. workshop production. It didn't use "the lexicon"—it didn't know how. Luckily, the company also presented this season two new ballets by Peter Martins, who may be said to represent the academy at its most purely and zestfully proficient. I like best those ballets of his which extend the dancers' virtuosity, so I liked *Les Petits Riens*, to Mozart's music, better than *Ecstatic Orange*, a big, boomingly hollow work to a minimalist-Stravinskyan score by Michael Torke, executed in Martins's Broadway-show style. The average age of the four boys and four girls in *Les Petits Riens* matches that of the dancers who have recently joined Twyla Tharp. The fact that Martins was able to hold these young people to the virtuoso standard he himself embodied as a dancer without having them mimic his dancing proves Kirstein's point about self-expression. But was it so very long ago that New York City Ballet was going through its spasm of imitating Suzanne Farrell, not only under Balanchine's very eye but seemingly at his behest? Critics were heard then to complain that Farrell was outside the classical tradition; now, at the moment of her retirement, they celebrate her centrality to the classical tradition as Balanchine has developed it. And who is to say that what Farrell gave Balanchine was not "self-expression"? But for her meeting with Balanchine, might she not have been another Isadora?

Farrellism was the last of Balanchine's great acquisitions. Today, the process of incorporation begun by that acquisition goes on, but invisibly, like the jazz in *Concerto Barocco* and the square dancing in *Square Dance*. I think the mistake many outsiders make when they look at Balanchine's ballets is to confuse Balanchine's language with neutral academic expression. Karole Armitage recently launched a new company on the strength of this confusion. I imagine she thought she was extending Balanchine's territory in her Webern-Stravinsky ballet, when she was really quoting or parodying him. Armitage, who had ballet lessons but gained her fame as a Merce Cunningham dancer, has taken to wearing toe shoes; she calls her company the Armitage Ballet, and her guest artists in her opening season at the Joyce were Stephanie Saland and Robert La Fosse. Without the sense these two dancers made of an Armitage pas de deux, the evening would have been chaos. Armitage has a more reflexive understanding of pointwork than Tharp does. With Armitage, points look self-conscious, but not artificial. (She herself looks a lot like Farrell in Béjart's choreography.) But she's doing what Kirstein accuses the dilettantes of doing—souping up her performance with ballet stylization. I can only assume that the skillful choreography she made for A.B.T. in *The Mollino Room* was the result of her working, like Tharp, with experienced classical dancers.

One of Balanchine's Louis Quatorze utterances might well have been *"L'a-cadémie, c'est moi."* His usages have become standard. His Baroque is *the* Baroque. He even thought up his own heresies, so in order to rebel against him a choreographer has to risk being completely incoherent. (Maybe this was Mejia's plan.) In *Ballare*, Tharp is not guilty of ballet stylization, or even Balanchine stylization; she's trying for straight classical expression in flowing white costumes (by William Ivey Long). Yet something—maybe the combination of pointwork and intricate Mozart piano music—throws off her rhythm. Can there be anything more difficult for a choreographer than making classical ballets in the Age of Balanchine? Kirstein is right: there is a void in American dance, and there has been a rush to the ballet, and it could be dangerous. In England, where there has not, until recently, been a native modern dance, a new tradition has been formed by blending English classical schooling with an aesthetic derived from Cunningham. The choreographer and company responsible for the blend, Richard Alston and Ballet Rambert, passed through New York on a North American tour. Compared with what is going on here, they are only moderately progressive, but they left the clear impression that it was still possible for dancers to take uncomplicated pleasure in their work. And they gave pleasure. The English dance delightfully, in three dimensions, with grownup manners. Alston doesn't duplicate the Cunningham formula for presenting dance; he uses sound and choreographs to its pulse. Or, less compellingly, he choreographs in silence. Sound, whether verbal or musical, is something more than aural décor; sometimes, as in *Java*, a piece to Ink Spots records, it's a text. *Java* is the kind of nutty confection I could happily live with. Its matching of movement to sound is so ritualistically precise I'm only sorry Alston didn't lay any comic stress on the Spots' own rituals—that same eight-bar vamping introduction, that same high tenor who sings the song, that same dolorous basso who speaks it.

So amiable, unstrained, and limply lyrical a piece as *Java* is unimaginable in the climate of American dance. And I can't imagine Alston or any of the other Rambert choreographers recycling their work, as Americans do, making it new, then more new. In *In the Upper Room*, not only do you see Twyla in just about everything the dancers do but you see the sources of her material—aerobics, karate, jogging, boxing, break dancing, and of course ballet—and you see them more clearly than in the 1983 piece called *Fait Accompli*, which used similar

material in a similarly striking format but used it less obviously and more ten-
dentiously. *Fait Accompli* was in two sections, one starring the company, the
other starring Tharp; it had a "crisis" subtext, a David Van Tieghem score, and
neo-expressionistic-cathedral lighting by Jennifer Tipton. Tipton more or less
reproduces her plot in *In the Upper Room*; as before, dancers enter and exit
upstage, behind a curtain of golden mist. Arranged in nine sections, designed as
a full-company vehicle without stars, *In the Upper Room* is unambiguously a
dance suite, and I had an almost intolerably mixed reaction to it. Just when I was
ready to dismiss it as designer choreography given a megalomaniacal production,
it would veer back to being genuine, and I'd rub my eyes and see that it was
probably closer to being Tharp's Olympiad than *Fait Accompli* was. It's also a
huge audience hit—a gift to the aerobics generation. Glass's music, with its tootling
ostinatos and keening strings, contributes exactly the supercharged atmosphere
that Tharp wants here, although it's easy to see why she has not collaborated with
Glass before. He sets a properly frenetic pace but builds no momentum; each
dance is pinned in its own gridlike cage of sound. Compared with David Byrne's
score for *The Catherine Wheel* (remounted this season in a streamlined new
production and in a smashing performance), the Glass makes almost no rhythmic
or textural demands on Tharp. And she doesn't seem to want them. Breaking in
a new company, holding the line at the box office, laying the groundwork for
artistic conquests of a kind never before seriously associated with her—these seem
to have been the priorities that shaped Tharp's current season. The Glass ballet
was a predetermined success; with it, Tharp reaches a new public and takes out
insurance for her experiments in classicism. Unlike *Fait Accompli, In the Upper
Room* will probably last a couple of seasons. As the piece in which aerobics are
made cosmic, as the proclamation of Twyla Tharp Dance II, it may not become
a classic, but who can deny its significance?   —*February 23, 1987*

Celebrations

Edward Villella

Villella. A name with the sound of dance in it, like some other names. A stair(e) is a step. So is Petipa (petit pas), the greatest nineteenth-century choreographer. His successor is Balanchine (balance, ballon-sheen, ballet). Villella, with those rebounding double ells, is a trampoline of a name. It belongs to a man whose *elevation in Tarantella* was an *elegant yell*; and whose bows afterward had the crisp modesty of his first name, Edward.

Edward Villella was in his physical person an event from the moment he first appeared, a new member of the New York City Ballet, in the winter of 1957. His first solo role was in *Afternoon of a Faun*. Jerome Robbins is said to have based the Faun on Villella as a ballet student and the image he called up of Nijinsky. I didn't see that début; my first glimpse of the newcomer was in another Robbins ballet, *Interplay*, that same winter. Villella was the boy in the orange sweater—not one of the leads—and I shall never forget him sailing backwards through space in the hugest jump I had ever seen and landing quietly in his place in the lineup. The jump isn't in the choreography; at least, when I see *Interplay* today I never notice it. So Villella must have exaggerated or otherwise transformed some commonplace traveling step to produce the sensational effect I have remembered for twenty-five years.

Exaggeration in a young dancer of extraordinary gifts usually precedes a period of great growth. From the wild, happy excess that characterized the twenty-one-year-old Villella to the achieved artistry of Oberon in *A Midsummer Night's Dream*, it is only five years. What a joyride those years were—the City Center years. For $3.95, the top price, one could sit in the orchestra and not see the dancers' feet or sit upstairs, where latecomers blocked one's view of the opening ballet, which would be *Serenade* or *The Four Temperaments* or *Divertimento No. 15* or *Apollo*. Villella danced in none of these except the last. By the time he made his début in *Apollo*, in the winter of 1964, he was a mature performer, famous throughout the world. He had described, in his own progress as a dancer, the course Apollo takes from raw expression to full command of his art. Yet Villella's natural qualities were always apparent and did not change. He continued to enlarge, transform, reinterpret elements of classical style. But his effects were no longer specialties; they were part of a continuous demonstration of extreme capacity in the service of a coherent vision. He had grown up to his talent.

If Villella's art was reflected in *Apollo*, his life was reflected in *The Prodigal Son*. Villella had emerged during the period of Rebels Without Causes in America and Angry Young Men in England, and he made his first major début on the brink of a turbulent decade, when the term "generational revolt" would come to describe a stock attitude of political protest. Villella's revolt in *The Prodigal Son* was without petulance. You saw passion in the headlong drive to destruction. You saw the true innocence and natural elegance of the soul that was imperilled.* All this Villella showed vividly and immediately. The last part of the ballet, The Return Home, was the part he worked on. Villella had bucked social convention to be a dancer; he had defied his parents for a number of years; to some extent, differing over goals and training, he defied his master Balanchine. The ballet *Prodigal Son* had been created by Balanchine years before, for Diaghilev's Ballets Russes. The Prodigal is largely a mime role, and Villella had to learn how to play it. It says much for his intuitive understanding of the subject that he was able from the beginning to move his audiences using so little of the flashy athleticism they were by now paying to see.

Balanchine let the rebel work his way into the part without supervision. Not until after the début did he call Villella to rehearsal. The dramatic aspects of the role were never defined; Balanchine would watch Villella do the crawl home and say something like "Think of Russian icons."

"That idea began to solidify the style for me," Villella has recalled. "It led me to find a new way of holding my head or stretching my neck. There was a way to stylize the head and the hands in a moment of pleading. The look became a quality for me."

Balanchine's laissez-faire attitude turned out to be a blessing to Villella. It released the dancer's initiative and touched off his imagination. The role of the Prodigal as we see it danced today (even by so redoubtable a performer as Mikhail Baryshnikov) has been very largely shaped by Edward Villella.

In those years, while Villella was becoming a star, Balanchine tended to use his prowess in high jumps as a feature of spectacular closing ballets. In *Symphony in C*, Villella entered flying. For years afterward, at precisely the same moment in the third movement, audiences would respond clamorously not only to the height of the leap and its perfection of form but to the illusion of sustained flight: Villella just seemed to keep on climbing and riding air the whole time he was on the stage. He also danced the "Thunderer" section of *Stars and Stripes*—who can forget him flashing his grin and saluting as he bounded between the ranks of leaping cadets?—and, until it was deleted, the bronco cowboy in *Western Symphony*. The male role in the first pas de trois in *Agon* was mocking and ceremonious, an offbeat part for Villella; he gave it a quality of force which it retains to this day. In the revival of *La Sonnambula*, Villella was a memorable Harlequin, a world-weary cousin to the elfin charmer whom he later incarnated in *Harlequinade*. And how delicious his Candy Cane in *The Nutcracker*—what crackle and zest as he vaulted through his hoop and shifted his weight in the air. While

---

* Villella conveyed this point with great precision in the pas de trois for the Son and his two servants which comes in the scene where they are greeted by the gargoyles. The delicacy of Villella's dancing here, stepping from second into wide fourths and turning in attitude, and then sweeping into sautés pirouettes à la seconde, was a great contrast to the near-brutal muscularity of everything that had gone before.

audiences roared, critics sighed with pleasure. Even more remarkable than the vigor of his dancing was its continuing clarity and solidity as it changed shape—mercurial changes, as it were, frozen solid and cold as crystal. Villella took clean bites out of the air.

The first role that Balanchine made for this dynamo cracked the demi-caractère mold that had been shaping Villella's style. The Prince of Lorraine in *The Figure in the Carpet* was a purely classical creation cast in the eighteenth-century image of Vestris. (Among the several coincidences in the careers of Villella and Baryshnikov is the fact that each danced a Vestris early in his career.) The ballet, an extravaganza featuring nearly every dancer in the company, was short-lived. My memory of Villella in it is chiefly of a beautiful and luminous presence, strangely tender and exposed. Conceived the season after the revival of *The Prodigal Son*, Lorraine was the Son's classical counterpart. Beneath the Baroque dignity of the one and the blunt expressionism of the other lay the same quality of intense emotion. These were a young man's roles.

Between Lorraine and the great role of Oberon, which came two years later, there intervened another ill-fated Balanchine ballet, called *Electronics* after its score, which utilized then-fashionable electronic tape. Villella was cast as a creature of fantasy, a kind of science-fiction satyr. There may have been elements here that led to the exotic *Bugaku*, which lay just beyond. I refer to elements of characterization. Other elements, relating more specifically to Villella's unique qualities as a dancer, are traceable from then on in all the roles that Balanchine was to create for him—roles ranging from Oberon to Harlequin in *Harlequinade* and from *Bugaku* to *Tarantella* and "Rubies." What I chiefly remember of Villella in these roles is his rhythmic power. Villella's rhythm was a combination of attack and volume; he could compress a phrase to pinpoints or explode it from the inside. The attack was often exciting in itself: the quick relevé, the short takeoff. It was like a sharp jab that vanished into something huge and cushiony—that absorbed its own shock. All the Balanchine roles for Villella would capitalize on his unrivalled ability to sustain enormous bursts of movement at peak energy. Compared to the way men danced in other ballet companies, there would be no time for preparations and recoveries between step-sequences; there would be relatively little emphasis on line and pose.

Though physically small, Villella danced on a big scale. Balanchine sometimes cast him small, the better to reveal his gift for detail. He envisioned Oberon, king of the elves, as Villella, an artist of changes. So Oberon became an emulative, procreative force of nature. In the Scherzo, where he was surrounded by dozens of beetle-like elves, Villella performed one of his richest, most intricate and mesmerizing dances, darting and skimming like a dragonfly crossing the surface of a pond. In the flash of a single variation, Balanchine's poetry transformed a buoyant, virile young man into an image of scooting iridescent intelligence. Villella's attack became insectoid: a sting.

There was something demonic about the individual qualities of speed, brio, stamina, and finesse that Villella possessed, but there was nothing demonic or inhuman about his presence. Villella was a real man, warm and open, and his personality colored everything he did. His Oberon was the sunniest of Sun Kings. I remember one of his exits that used to hit the audience like a joke—a high jeté-flip in which he reversed his pose and soared backwards into the wings. In another passage, he flew backwards at top speed, sitting on air and kicking air away like a tiresome footstool. This is an undying Villella image. (If a child ever asks you what it was that made Villella different, say "He could dance backwards.")

As Oberon, Villella mastered long passages of classical mime. In *Harlequinade* and "Rubies," the dance passages are saturated in character-color. "Rubies" may have been the closest to a full-length portrait that Balanchine ever made of Villella; it is also one of the few depictions we have in ballet of a fully sexed, civilized adult male. "Rubies"—so called because it is the second entry in a triptych called *Jewels*—used Villella's athletic stance to anchor an image of idiosyncratic masculine grace. (In college, Villella played varsity baseball and held the title in welterweight boxing for three years.) The other men in *Jewels* are cavaliers, poets, troubadours. Only Villella is non-romantic; he's jaunty, combative, debonair. He challenges as well as supports the ballerina. The role is infused with Broadway and circus and nightclub manners; its spiritual home is swing-time America. Villella's solos contained some superb comic moments. In one sequence, he pedalled about the stage, leaping and swerving ahead of a gang of men. In another travelling passage he seemed to play the piano mincingly before a sudden volcanic wind overtook him and he left the stage spinning with such velocity that you could almost see the air whizzing past his chest.

Villella partnered Violette Verdy and then, for many years, Patricia McBride. When Baryshnikov danced with New York City Ballet a few seasons ago, he inherited Villella's partner, McBride, along with Villella's roles. Baryshnikov is Villella's only possible successor; he has the timing, the punch, the virtuoso technique. Stylistically, of course, he is quite different. His assumption of the Villella repertory was largely a discourse on the differences in style between the American and the Russian classical schools and between their two greatest male exponents. (Strangely enough, the Villella role which fitted Baryshnikov best was in Robbins's *Dances at a Gathering*. Russian style was more easily accommodated by the American-born choreographer Robbins than by the Russian-born Balanchine.) When Baryshnikov left the company, the roles of Harlequin and the man in "Rubies" fell empty again. (Baryshnikov relinquished Oberon owing to injury; the Prodigal he took with him to American Ballet Theatre.) The ballets are done but without the Villella spark. One can add other roles to the "unoccupied" list: *Donizetti Variations*, Third Movement *Brahms-Schoenberg Quartet*.

I have left out of this memoir an account of Villella's performances away from New York City Ballet, even though I saw and was stirred by quite a few of them. Like everyone else who watched him on television, I was grateful to Villella for broadcasting himself to the millions, showing those who could not see it live what ballet was like, inspiring and encouraging who knows how many American boys to become dancers themselves. Television brought Villella his greatest fame.

But his glory as an artist lies in the ballets he left behind at his home company. The Villella repertory—both the roles he originated and those he assumed with special distinction—is the greatest corpus of ballets created for a male dancer in this century. When the final tally is taken and it shows American ballet in our time to have been largely a Balanchine production, there will be the honor roll of Balanchine dancers, name upon name. All those girls—and Edward Villella. —*May 1982*

Le *Mystère* Baryshnikov

He remains a classical dancer.
TWYLA THARP

"Genius" is a word commonly heard in discussions of the arts. Next to "defector," it is the word most commonly applied to Baryshnikov. It should not for that reason be discounted by those in search of the truth about this great dancer. Baryshnikov *is* a genius, even though everybody says so. He is, in my opinion, the only theatrical performer in the world today about whom that term may justly be used. Baryshnikov fits Samuel Johnson's definition of a genius: "a mind of large, general powers, accidentally determined to some particular direction." He is a phenomenally gifted man who happens to have become a dancer. That he did not become the world's foremost soccer player or concert pianist is an accident of fate owing to his mother's interest in ballet and the presence, in the Latvian school curriculum, of courses in folk dance.

Baryshnikov's genius is what sets him apart from even the greatest dancers we have seen, although it is important to note that he is not different from them in kind. The greatest dancers are born with the capacity to enrich their art, not merely their reputations. Some actually succeed in doing so, and most of these are women whose capacities have been explored by great choreographers in epochal roles. One thinks of Marie Taglioni in Filippo Taglioni's *La Sylphide*, of Carlotta Grisi in Jules Perrot's *Giselle*. In our time, there has been Suzanne Farrell in a repertory of roles created by George Balanchine. Baryshnikov has incarnated many different images, prepared for him by many different choreographers. He is the most protean dancer since Nijinsky. But like Nijinsky and like Vestris before him, Baryshnikov is largely self-produced. With or without benefit of choreography, he has generated shock waves that have swept the world of dance. By himself, he supplies the material for which ballerinas traditionally rely on choreographers— material which gives form and expressive meaning to creativity. This is not to say that he is immune to the disasters that can occur when choreographers fail him. And we cannot rule out the possibility of undreamed-of triumphs which might have been his if he, too, had had ballets made for him by Balanchine. But after twelve years in the West—years of discovery and exhaustive experimentation— Baryshnikov persists as an independent force, unique in stature, fertile in expression.

Baryshnikov, then, is the example in our time of the essentially procreative male genius in dance. Yet he is not another Nijinsky, still less another Massine or Lifar. For one thing, he abjures almost entirely the role of choreographer. It is easy to see how working in New York, which he calls "the city of a thousand choreographers and a thousand companies," could defeat any impulse he might feel to produce choreography in a formal sense. But a more compelling reason not to choreograph may be that he is not driven by a consummate ambition. Here is the greatest difference between Baryshnikov and all the others, great and small: though he may be possessed by a need to dance, he is not consumed by it. No white-hot flame burns in him, no unappeasable appetite for the stage. He will not die there, insatiable for applause or for whatever inner rewards performance holds. Baryshnikov is cool, very cool; he always has been, even when he first came bounding toward us with what the choreographer Twyla Tharp calls his "vast, naïve energy." Even then, one saw how that energy was framed by a ceaseless effort toward self-control and away from excess. For all his prodigious technique, Baryshnikov is never ostentatious, he is never eccentric, and he is no *monstre sacré.* His energy is spiritual as well as physical. In Baryshnikov's case, we must alter Johnson's definition of genius from "a mind of large general powers" to "a being of large general powers," but dancing is not mindless. It involves the participation of body, mind, and spirit.

At least, it does in Baryshnikov's case; we know because his every performance tells us so. What his performances do *not* tell us is how this undivided wholeness of expression can come about with no apparent involvement on the part of the personal Misha. The performances contain no self-explanations; it's as if the man who dances is somehow separate from the *being* who exists there on the stage. Where is the mortal man Baryshnikov? What motivates this impulse toward self-perfection? Where is the confessional element New York loves to see in every performer who ventures forth on its twinkling stages? Where are the revelations— the sweat, the sacrifice, the victimization? Where the naked need which only an audience can satisfy? Baryshnikov makes no concessions, no appeals; neither does he conceal himself. This is his mystery. This is why the most lucid classical dancer of our time is also the most enigmatic.

Baryshnikov in everyday life is a modest man with a sense of humor about himself. He would not have commissioned this piece if he knew I was only going to extol him as a genius, so I told him I would seek out his colleagues and co-workers and ask them to help me relate the man to the artist. From their answers I hoped to compile evidence that would enlarge my perception of the Baryshnikov mystery—add aspects to it, perhaps even furnish a key to the psychology, if not the mystery, of Misha.

For Twyla Tharp there is no discrepancy between the public and the private

Baryshnikov. The only distinction she countenances is between Baryshnikov as a classical dancer and Baryshnikov as the star of modern Tharp ballets like *Push Comes to Shove* and *Sinatra Suite*. As a classical dancer, Tharp says, Baryshnikov has worked toward a single goal of purity and control and ease.

"As he matures and feels his body changing," she goes on, "he finds more to think about during a performance. In certain ways, Misha's dancing has become less puppylike, less direct, and more self-reflective. Before I did *Push*, I spent four weeks with him just trying to figure out how he functioned. Misha at that time went to the limit of what a body can do. If he couldn't do a movement, that meant it couldn't be done by anybody anywhere in the world. I never saw a classical dancer with the strength in the upper back that Misha has. That's where his pirouette is, that's where the ballon in his jump is. How many classical dancers do you know who can walk around the room on their hands? He has that kind of strength in his upper back. But no matter how many unorthodox styles he tackles, he remains a classical dancer. Because that's where his discipline is."

To Kenneth MacMillan, the choreographer who is now associated with American Ballet Theatre, Baryshnikov appears as he does to many people—as "a very private person." "He doesn't confide in people," MacMillan adds. "I think the restrictions of his life in Russia made him curious, willing to experiment, to broaden his range. But they imposed inhibitions, too. He has a kind of cautiousness which I believe comes from having lived in a closed society. He doesn't even like to give his opinions of dancers and performances he's seen. He really opens up when he talks about dancing. He knows all about it, and he's a wonderful pedagogue. When I made *The Wild Boy* for him, I saw him as a force of nature. I believe there's a primitive side to Misha, an innocence under all the polish. He's often shocked by the way people behave in the West—the things they say, the vulgarity. Misha cannot be vulgar. Yes, he is very modest, a quality he shares with Ulanova. There's something Russian about it, a Chekhovian fineness. But no one else has that quality in combination with as many spectacular gifts as Misha has. He's the most poetic male dancer I've ever seen."

Baryshnikov is dancing these days with an Olympian detachment. When he takes curtain calls, he seems to withdraw from the audience's gaze—to become diffident. In conversation, he does something of the kind, falling every so often into a preoccupied silence. Then he seems not diffident so much as aloof.

Charles France is Baryshnikov's assistant and the man who is closest to him in his professional life. I asked France what Baryshnikov's silences signify. "He isn't being aloof," France replied, "and he isn't bored with you or depressed. We must remember that Baryshnikov's position is unique and that every day he must deal with untold pressures. He's not only a great and famous dance star who has reached the age when he might plausibly begin to think of retiring. He's not only the head of an important ballet company, responsible for the careers of ninety dancers. In the way *Swan Lake* is ballet, Misha is ballet dancing. He's a living symbol of dance in our era. He's expected to participate in all public causes related to dance. He has to be articulate in a foreign language. He is asked to read and evaluate movie scripts. These are very heavy demands and abnormal demands on a dancer. And Misha is sensitive to criticism, because he doesn't put his own interests first and take a don't-give-a-damn attitude. He's not one of these people who think they can part the Red Sea. He's not like Lucia Chase or Balanchine or Nureyev. Misha hasn't got the kind of ego that lets him ignore the world around him. And when he goes into himself in the middle of a conversation, it's probably because something has reminded him of some aspect of this existential dilemma of his."

Does Baryshnikov miss his homeland? France thinks he doesn't anymore. MacMillan thinks he does, deeply. Joseph Brodsky, the poet, is an old friend who knew Baryshnikov well in Leningrad and often reminisces with him about that beautiful city of classic perspectives. "We can go on for hours about this or that plaster relief or a courtyard we both knew," Brodsky says. "But there is a terrific sense of incongruity between the classical beauty of the place and the actual life behind those columns. Had Misha stayed at home, he'd be a ruin by now, both physically and mentally. Physically because of the bottle rather than because of overwork. Mentally because of that mixture of impotence and cynicism that corrodes everyone there—the stronger you are, the worse it is."

Nostalgia is clearly a complicated subject for Russians in exile. Brodsky is very precise. "In Misha's case," he says, "the past is a subject not for nostalgia but for a sort of cultivated love. The reason we dwell on that plaster curl or limb or on this shade of stucco is that we know we cannot return to the scene of crime, let alone to the scene of love. The only nostalgia to which Misha is still susceptible is the nostalgia which has set in motion a great deal of Russian art, especially in this century. Osip Mandelstam called it 'nostalgia for world culture.' For a Russian, this nostalgia is basically westward, because the West is where what's known as culture has come from. One who is so much engaged in the constant tête-à-tête with Art at its very seat can't be terribly nostalgic for one's hometown."

What kind of man is Baryshnikov? Brodsky summons up a list of adjectives: "Funny. Quick. Attentive. Very witty. He puns all the time, not in order to amuse friends but because he has a remarkable ear. He reads the way other people smoke: nonstop. It is as though he shields himself with a book against the illiteracy of existence. He also knows by heart more lines of Russian poetry than I do. Yet he constantly underestimates his intellectual capacity and believes that everybody else is better educated."

At times, Brodsky discusses his friend Misha in the same terms some of us would use to describe Baryshnikov the dancer. It is no surprise to hear that in private life Baryshnikov is "as lonely as he is intuitive." Or that "he has a terrific ability to absorb the new." Or that "he has a huge romance with Americana going."

"He adores his daughter," Brodsky adds. "The daughter is American, and by now so is he. That is to say, he is not any more Russian than Mozart was Austrian."

Mozart? My own favorite adjective for Baryshnikov's dancing is "Mozartean." Now Brodsky, searching for a way to communicate the essence of his friend's nature, says, "I think Mozart was like him. They share the birthday date, you know. I've never in my life met anyone else with this mixture of light and tragedy, of almost physical luminescence and tragic gravity made light. Several times, I have suggested to him that he choreograph Mozart's Bassoon Concerto. 'Write me a libretto,' is his usual reply. I never have done that. I think that all he has to do is walk onto the stage, turn on music, and start moving to it."

In *Murder*, a ballet made last winter by David Gordon, Baryshnikov plays multiple roles. First, he is a Mad Scientist who mixes a potion that destroys him. He is buried and rises again as a consumptive young girl—Camille in ribbons and flounces. She coughs her way to the grave and is replaced by a Master Spy, who dies in a duel. Finally, we return to the opening of the ballet, and Misha is the stagehand who is setting up the scene as the curtain falls.

Gordon is one of America's best postmodern choreographers. Baryshnikov's instructions to him were to devise the kind of ensemble piece he might make for his own company, and he, Baryshnikov, would play one of the roles. Gordon realized that he couldn't very well hide Mikhail Baryshnikov in the ensemble, so he combined most of the principal roles in *Murder* and gave them to Baryshnikov to perform in a series of quick changes. A parody of detective mysteries to begin with, *Murder* became a drama about reincarnation. It also became a portrait of Baryshnikov, presenting both the chameleonlike virtuoso and the unassuming Misha.

Gordon, who normally works on a small scale and a smaller budget, talks about the making of *Murder* as an adventure in the craft of theatre. "I was relying on the audience to recognize each of my genre scenes, and I came to trust absolutely Misha's sense of scale and timing. He seemed to understand everything about the kind of conventions I was trying to evoke. He understood the Camille figure as a character in the tradition of the Romantic ballet, and he played the type of ballerina who would have danced the part. Amazingly enough, this didn't emasculate him, and he was funnier than if he had tried to burlesque the part. All through the piece, he added little bits of business, not to get more attention for himself but to clarify a transition or a situation."

Working with Baryshnikov has permanently changed some of Gordon's ideas. "I used to have this postmodernist prejudice against elegant stage manners," he admits. "But with Misha, elegance isn't narcissistic or manipulative. It's a way of behaving normally on the stage. I was bowled over by the utter ordinariness of his elegance. Now, in my own performing, when I approach Valda [Setterfield, his wife and partner], I lift my torso, I lift under my arms, and I'm Misha. And I keep seeing connections between the way he does things and things in my own work. He's a very inward person, and so am I. He practices gregariousness. He's nervous before a performance—actually edgy and pale and unwilling to look you in the eye. Each time, just before the curtain went up on *Murder*, he would need reassurance from me that he was doing everything right. Imagine, the great Baryshnikov! Of course, the curtain would go up and there would be no sign of nervousness. His personal authority is tremendous. Working with him, it became clear to me early on that I was not only going to learn how to make this particular piece, I was also going to learn a tremendous amount about theatre. I thought I was pretty smart about theatre. But this guy is really great."

To a perceptive eye like Gordon's the everyday Misha is contained in the virtuoso Baryshnikov. By "the utter ordinariness of his elegance" we know the presence of a classical master. Like Mozart's, Baryshnikov's art is pure. It is ambiguous. It tells us everything and nothing about the life of the man who produces it. As the man grows older, the dancing becomes more selfless, more refined in its Mozartean transparency. What a Baryshnikov performance means we cannot say. It is as necessary and unremarkable as clean air, clean water, and light.   —*December 1986*

Edwin Denby

1

My introduction to Edwin Denby was his great essay on the Nijinsky photographs, which I first encountered in Paul Magriel's book. *Nijinsky: An Illustrated Monograph* (Holt, 1946) had been long out of print, but it was the only thing of its kind at the time, and I remember the mild stun it produced in my consciousness, like being hit on the head with a soft mallet. The Denby commentary, its centerpiece, was unique in giving us the mind of the critic together with the object it is fixed upon, and to read it with a selection of the photographs at hand (something one could not do again until years later, when Lincoln Kirstein reprinted the piece in his *Nijinsky Dancing*) was to be guided with an unerring precision toward a knowledge not only of Nijinsky's art but of all the beauty that dancing has to offer. It is not enough to say that Denby sees more than you do, or even that his eye acts like a corrective lens to your own, helping you to see more, too. He sees what you had not dreamed was there, as when he speaks of the thighs in a supporting pose with Karsavina in *Spectre*: "as full of tenderness as another dancer's face." He notices a "poignant duplicity of emotion" in the poses from *Faune* and *Jeux*. He looks at "the savage force of the arms and legs" in *Narcissus* and from this makes the thrilling deduction that "the hero's narcissism was not vanity, but an instinct that killed him, like an act of God."

On first reading Denby, I don't think I was moved as much by his perceptions as by the emotion that lay behind them. It certainly never occurred to me that this was the greatest essay on dancing I had ever read; Heaven knows I had read little enough about dancing. So little, in fact, that the wonders of Denby's prose impressed me as only natural and proper—the only way to talk, if one is going to talk at all, about the ballet. But the more closely I read, the more the words seemed to create their own drama in relation to the pictures. Who but Denby, after all, would have imagined what lay concealed there—those thighs, for example, or the hands in *Jeux*, "as mysterious as breathing in sleep"?

Then I found and devoured *Looking at the Dance*. I remember it was on the Second Avenue bus that I opened the book for the first time—"Second Avenue," as Denby was to write in a later volume, "where herds of vehicles go charging one way all day long disappearing into the sky at the end like on a prairie"—and read about *Apollo*:

Apollo is about poetry, poetry in the sense of a brilliant, sensuous, daring and powerful activity of our nature.

Denby was himself a poet, and it was as a poet that he wrote about dancing. *Looking at the Dance* may be the most universally admired book of dance criticism in American publishing history. As one who has spent years combing Denbyisms out of her prose, I can testify that it's also the most infectious. ("Wonderful, this dignity," I once wrote of Nureyev. "Wonderful and sad, too. . . ." Dear Edwin!) But those images of his that stick in the mind are quite beyond imitation. Who can forget "Miss Toumanova, with her large, handsome, and deadly face" or the "trees in the wind" passage in the review of *Concerto Barocco*? Nor can one escape the casual force of Denby the aesthetician. The idea that seems to me central to all his criticism, that "art takes what in life is an accidental pleasure and tries to repeat and prolong it," is so indirectly proposed *as an idea* that the exact wording has just taken me a half hour to look up in a book I thought I knew well. (You will find it in the essay "Against Meaning in Ballet.")

When *Dancers, Buildings and People in the Streets* was about to come out, I was invited to a party for Edwin by our mutual friend Bob Cornfield. By that time, I had launched *Ballet Review* very much under the sign of Denby. But Edwin didn't seem to take much interest in *Ballet Review* until one day he agreed to let himself be interviewed for our Fall issue in 1969. Alex Katz contributed a portrait for the cover.

My happy discovery on meeting Edwin was that he talked almost exactly as he wrote, so the fact that he'd more or less officially stopped writing dance criticism didn't mean that there could be no more Denby in print. But when I worked with him on the transcripts of our interviews, I began to see what had stopped his pen. He worried incessantly over every point he'd made in his recorded remarks, modifying, qualifying, refining his meaning until sometimes the point would start to get lost, whereupon I would try to coax him back to the original wording. Then he would demand a footnote. The tape recorder, he said, backed him into corners. But he rewrote and re-rewrote and still wasn't satisfied. I remember sitting in Edwin's loft into the early hours, snow whirling outside, while he delicately tore apart pages of incomparable commentary, asking himself, "Is this really true? Do I really mean that?" It was Edwin's great gift to illuminate the experience of subjectivity in watching dance, but he agonized lest he be even fractionally mis-understood.

Edwin never relinquished his interest in what was going on. To the very end his reactions were the keenest of anyone I knew and his need to ventilate them quite heartbreakingly apparent—the communicator in him never did die. (He once said that to write about dance one has to be interested in communication almost for its own sake.) I was often struck by how long he could remain at his post—by not only the hours he put in attending performances but also the weeks of meditation. Long after I'd filed a piece (filed and, as usually happened, forgotten it), there would come a call from Edwin, who'd been thinking. And he'd have worked the event I'd written about so deeply into the fabric of his consciousness that it was available to me whole and fresh once more. No one else could do this, and no one else would have been so patient with my reluctance to respond when the moment of his call found me tired or past caring. Edwin did me the exquisite courtesy of treating me like a colleague, but I don't think his comments were designed for me personally—I think he spoke that way to everyone.

Once, about the time of our *BR* interview, he analyzed a new ballet by a young choreographer in terms I'd never heard before. I knew he was talking "in the abstract" as only he could, and I was doubly alert, and I didn't understand a word he said. Edwin must have known this because he kept on and on, becoming, for Edwin, quite vehement. He was saying that this choreographer had no sense of how shapes changed their proportions in dancing; he was describing one of the elemental powers of ballet, as yet invisible to me. "You see, it's the thing of getting bigger or smaller," he would say, as if I were only momentarily failing to recognize something I knew quite well. A state of blank incomprehension is difficult to remember. If I knew that dancing could do this thing, I didn't know that choreographers could control it. And even after Edwin told me, I still didn't know. What I remember about this moment is my utter misery. It was during an intermission at the Brooklyn Academy. We stood at the back of the orchestra, getting bumped on all sides. It took me years to get what he was driving at that evening, and I got it at last only because he had insisted: it was important.

How many other dance critics must have a story like this to tell! Edwin spoke—and wrote—as if everyone saw things the way he did. His genius made us believe it was true.   —*November 4, 1983*

2

"The best dance critic living." That is what Edwin Denby, in 1940, called Serge Lifar. He thought Lifar, who had just published a book on Diaghilev, was good "because, first, he has the professional experience which turns dancing from a thing you buy readymade into a thing you make yourself. And second, he sees dancing with the eyes of intelligence, as an ordinary person sometimes sees a friend or sees the weather; sees and believes at the same time. 'The eyes of a poet,' people say who know what poetry is about."

If today those words sound more generous than exact as applied to Lifar, it is because they strike us as a good description of Denby himself. He, too, had been a professional dancer (in Germany before Hitler), and he saw with the eyes of a poet—so much so that "people who know what poetry is about" were more than likely to have noticed the resemblance between the dance critic of the bimonthly *Modern Music* and the image he drew of Lifar. Denby by then had been at the craft of dance criticism for four years. He had already written, in *Modern Music*, the pieces on *Noces* and *Faune*, on ballet music, on Balanchine's *Poker Game* and *Baiser*, and on Ashton's *Devil's Holiday* which would become immortalized in *Looking at the Dance*. He had addressed central issues in the work of Graham and Massine, identifying the qualities of pictorial tension which he found differently disturbing in each; and on Massine he had written one of the most luminous passages he would ever write: "As a pictorial arranger Massine is inexhaustible. But dancing is less pictorial than plastic, and pictures in dancing leave a void in the imagination. They arrest the drama of dancing which the imagination craves to continue, stimulated by all the kinetic senses of the body that demand a new movement to answer the one just past. Until a kind of secret satisfaction and a kind of secret weariness coincide."

This is the writing not only of a poet who sees but of a poet who feels, and who feels what we all feel. Denby gained from having been a dancer an incalculable advantage, but it is Denby the spectator who is the true artist of criticism. *Looking at the Dance*, the book that established his reputation as a critic, is very precisely named. Looking—perceiving with all his senses—is what Denby did. It is sometimes erroneously said that a School of Denby exists in American dance criticism. Schools are based on ideas and theories, and Denby's critical insight was a gift—his alone. The only idea he ever proposed (and it was more an article of faith than an idea) was that each of us should develop the critical insight he was born with. When he says that Lifar (read Denby) sees as an ordinary person "sees and believes," he is saying that the experience of dancing is a normal and subjective one—no special knowledge is needed in order to understand it—but also that this subjective experience is heightened by belief, by an unconditional acceptance of the truth of what one sees. Another way of saying it is that dancing appeals to the poet in us. But that still isn't all there is to it. Dancing is physical, a spectacle of grace in movement. The "kinetic senses of the body," more than the optic nerve, are what stimulate the imagination. I believe that Denby discovered these kinetic senses in his role as a critic, sitting there in the dark, and that the more he thought about it the more it seemed that kinetic excitement was what made viewing dancing a normal and subjective but by no means universal pleasure. Three years later, writing for the readers of the *New York Herald Tribune*, he arrived at a formulation both generous and strict: "To recognize poetic suggestion through dancing one must be susceptible to poetic values and susceptible to dance values as well."

This statement forms the cornerstone of *Looking at the Dance*, yet, because of the way that book was edited (it came out in 1949), it is extremely difficult to see how—by what cognitive process—the statement might have crystallized in Denby's mind. Not, in fact, until the publication, earlier this year, of a complete edition of the criticism was it possible to follow Denby's thinking as it evolved from one piece to another. The articles and reviews in *Looking at the Dance* were selected by the music and dance critic B. H. Haggin, who had championed Denby's work for years. Pieces written years apart were united under single headings—"Dancers in Performance," "Modern Dancers," "Dancers in Exotic Styles," and so on—and the entries within each category were not always reprinted in their original sequence. The internal logic of the book (devised, I take it, by Haggin) is admirable. In the opening section, "Meaning in Ballet," an amalgam of various magazine articles and what appear to have been Sunday columns from the *Herald Tribune* actually creates the impression that Denby had composed a primer in dance technique and dance aesthetics for the popular audience. (Of course, he had done just that, but not systematically.) Grouping scattered reviews on specific topics also points up the variety of the dance scene in New York in the forties and the variety of Denby's response to it. But though *Looking at the Dance* remains a classic, it gives us an Olympian Denby, whose most decisive utterances are as casual and unpremeditated as bolts from the blue. *Dance Writings* (Knopf), edited by Robert Cornfield and William MacKay, collects all but the most marginal critical work that Denby published, including the reviews and portions of reviews that were excluded from *Looking at the Dance*, adds some unpublished material, and presents the lot chronologically except where chronology would destroy some more significant order. Thus, although the *Modern Music* series (1936–43) overlapped for seven months the *Herald Tribune* series (1942–45), it does not do so here; all the pieces on Balanchine and New York City Ballet from 1946 onward appear in one section; and essays on matters unrelated to topical events appear in another.

The consequence of this new and complete presentation is the emergence of a Denby who is a more complex, more vividly real character than the deity of *Looking at the Dance*. We see him as a working critic and, when he joins the staff of the *Herald Tribune*, as a most improbably robust *hard*working critic. The dance calendar in those days was blank for long periods and insanely congested for brief ones; Denby filled out the year with ice shows, night-club acts, and Broadway musicals. He went to modern-dance recitals in hellish places; he reviewed the Rockettes. Constitutionally a frail man, he seemed to thrive under the pressure. During the fall ballet season of 1943, he filed fifteen pieces in October alone, and among these were two major essays and six reviews of collectible caliber. It is the opinion of Minna Lederman, the editor of *Modern Music*, that Denby's newspaper pieces, written to tight deadlines, are better than the articles he labored over for her; I agree with this—no finer body of dance journalism exists. But except for a few places here and there the *Modern Music* series doesn't seem labored, and there is no break in style when Denby takes up his newspaper job. If anything, he grows more precise, his tone becomes more intimate still, and his communicative zeal is palpable. Even in the most crushingly routine assignment he is a good reporter. The conscientiousness with which he reviews cast changes, program fillers, conductors, costumes, and scenery comes as a revelation to those of us who were bred on *Looking at the Dance*. (I remember thinking that these things couldn't have mattered to Denby, because he never discussed them. Well, he did.) In matters of opinion, too, there are some surprises. Ballets trounced in *Looking at the Dance* bob up restored by second or third viewings; a few personal reputations are sealed or unsealed. Normally the most benign of critics, Denby could be dangerous when provoked. Of Baronova's antics he writes, "She seems to want the title of 'Miss Ironpants.' " On the whole, though, fewer dancers than one might expect enter or leave the winner's circle. The famous portrait, verging on caricature, of "Miss Toumanova with her large, handsome, and deadly face," her "blocklike torso, limp arms, and predatory head positions" isn't radically altered by the addition of a few favorable comments, one of which—"When she dances it is a matter of life and death"—is reminiscent of a remark he'd made about Carmen Amaya: "She can dance as if nothing else existed in the world but dancing and death."

But Denby's Lifar turns out to have been a very different creature from what we had thought him up to now—chiefly an object of satire: "Poor Lifar. He looks older onstage than Dolin or Massine," and so on, in a vein of malicious sympathy that becomes openly derisive with a description of Lifar's pomposities in *Giselle*. But this was in 1950. In 1940, not only was Lifar the best living critic; he was also, of all the dancers of the prewar period, the one closest to Denby's heart. The passages on Lifar the dancer and Lifar the critic (both omitted from *Looking at the Dance*) are cast in the same terms. Lifar in performance has a naturalness

> *that goes beyond the gestures required, as though the character were as much alive as anybody living. As though on the stage, he seems to believe in the life that is going on outside of the theater in the present. He seems to believe that his part makes sense anywhere, that his part (in the words of Cummings) is competing with elephants and skyscrapers and the individual watching him. They all seem real at the same time, part of the same imagination, as they are really. There is something unprofessional about carrying reality around with you in public that goes straight to my heart.*

Denby seems to be in love. He is, as we never again see him, at a loss, fumbling for words. And he realizes how he must sound; his very next sentence is "This is the kind of criticism it is hard to prove the justice of; I wish we could see Lifar more often so I could try." The echo of Lifar the dancer in Lifar the critic is, I think, brilliantly illuminating, but it tells us more about Denby—about the qualities he loved and valued—than about Lifar. The echo of Amaya in Toumanova is also illuminating, but there Denby is talking about something he saw rather than thought he saw or hoped to see. He doesn't draw a parallel, and, indeed, none should be inferred. But he didn't strike that chord twice by accident.

Nor is "pictorial tension" coincidentally a problem in the work of both Graham and Massine. From *Looking at the Dance* you might be able to tell that this business of visual and kinetic suggestion was on Denby's mind in 1937 and 1938— the Graham and Massine articles are both from that period. But they're placed under different headings, and the Graham piece, in which Denby *first* brings up the matter, comes ninety pages after the Massine. In *Dance Writings*, it comes eleven pages before. Again, I don't wish to suggest a parallel, still less an "influence." But photographs from the past reveal conventions of the era that were invisible at the time, and dances of past eras may do the same, even though they were composed and staged under very different auspices. Nothing is harder to spot than the unconscious patterns that connect the work of contemporaries. Yet Denby's eye saw something—probably the only thing—in Graham's work that was like Massine's. That he didn't make a critical point of the similarity is immaterial. He may not have had the chance. Companies didn't perform, and critics didn't write, often enough in those days for such tight connections to be made. Or he may not, so early in his critical career, have completely understood the implications of what he saw, or may have thought them self-evident—who knows? And who cares? The test of a critic is not how many points he can clinch but how transparent he is; unless we can see through him to the way it was, it won't help to know what he thinks it means. As Denby says, "It is not the critic's historic function to have the right opinions but to have interesting ones. He talks but he has nothing to sell." For Denby, a critic is functioning properly when his readers feel free enough to have interesting opinions of their own.

Denby expressed these views on the job of the critic in 1949 (in an essay twice as long as it appeared in *Looking at the Dance*); he was by then the polished professional craftsman, the poet who became a journalist without losing his personal voice. It must have been with some misgiving that he forsook his privacy as a little-magazine critic for the public glare of a newspaper post. Newspapering is the most difficult work imaginable for a dance critic, and it was more so in Denby's day than in our own. The mood you were in when the curtain fell on *Pillar of Fire* was not the mood you had to be in to race to a typewriter and rap out a smart lead for the bulldog edition. Denby was exactly one year into the job, right in the middle of that congested 1943 season, when he had a mishap. He mistook Nora Kaye for Markova and wrote a glowing notice of the wrong ballerina. His apology was a characteristically elegant tribute to both ladies, but the episode embarrassed him profoundly; thirty years later, he still spoke of it. Denby, who'd had no journalistic training, was proud of his professionalism. Then, too, as a proponent of ballet at a time when most intellectuals preferred modern dance, he had an evangelical mission. Denby's supporters formed up against the modern-dance legions behind John Martin, of the *Times*. But it was more than ballet versus modern dance. Virgil Thomson, in his autobiography, speaks of the appeal of the city's two leading newspapers to "the educated middle class," saying that the *Times* "has regularly in its critical columns followed a little belatedly the tastes of this group; the *Herald Tribune* under Ogden Reid aspired to lead them. It did not therefore, as the *Times* has so often done, shy away from novelty or elegance." With Denby on dance (and he certainly did not neglect modern dance) and Thomson on music, the *Trib* was a juggernaut of opinion. Martin and Olin Downes, on music, were no match for it. One can imagine how Denby's enemies used his mistake against him.

Denby was a professional, but he loved Richard Buckle's monthly *Ballet*, because, as he put it when the magazine folded, it didn't make him feel like "a harried fellow-professional." After 1945, he never wrote for a newspaper again. He relinquished his *Herald Tribune* post to Walter Terry, who reclaimed it after the war, and for the next two decades he concentrated on his poetry, writing dance pieces more or less when the spirit moved him. Some of the critical writing from that period appears to have been motivated more by a wish to satisfy friends and editors who were friends than by a need to get things said. Still, the publication, in 1965, of a second collection, *Dancers, Buildings and People in the Streets*, revealed a Denby whose pertinacity of thought was undiminished. Only the sporadic nature of the pieces keeps us from making cognitive connections among them. Connections are anyway more a matter of tone. The title essay and its companion, "Forms in Motion and in Thought," were originally prepared as lectures to dance students, and it is to dance students rather than to the general public that one feels Denby is speaking in the fifties and sixties. Though the writing has a new, Jamesian density, the tone becomes more frankly confiding; he sounds like a man among friends and often writes as one, casting his reviews in epistolary form. It is a fair guess that the epistles were all addressed to Buckle, who published them. (It would have been nicer to be told who the "you" is, and where the "here" is in his letters from abroad.) But though Denby invoked the privileges of the form, he didn't abuse them. Far from writing for a coterie, as he was sometimes accused of doing, he was working to broaden access to the subject on its deepest levels, both for the reader and for himself. By the intensity of one's interest in dance one is made to feel a part of Denby's circle.

The editors tell us who some of Denby's actual friends were, and an imposing list it is: the poets Frank O'Hara, Kenneth Koch, James Schuyler, John Ashbery, Ron Padgett, Anne Waldman, Alice Notley, Ted Berrigan; the painters Willem and Elaine de Kooning, Franz Kline, Alex Katz, Red Grooms, Larry Rivers; the composers Virgil Thomson, Aaron Copland, Roger Sessions, John Cage; the photographer and filmmaker Rudolph Burckhardt; the choreographers Merce Cunningham, Paul Taylor, Jerome Robbins. This is the true School of Denby—his fellow-artists, with whom, as the generations passed, he had more in common than with the pack of inattentive children who were trying to become dance critics. Gentlest of men, he bore our presumption with angelic patience and never presumed, in return, to educate us. Rather, he just talked and listened as if we were his equals. The only piece of practical advice he ever gave me was when, at the end of a long ballet summer in the city, he found me staggering: "Get a beach vacation." (He also said that he used to prepare for Tudor's premières by downing a steak at Gallagher's, then going home and sleeping for two hours.) But Edwin by then was part of the intellectual history of New York; he belonged to that artistic community which had made New York in the decades after the Second World War what Paris was in the decades before the first one. He was the chronicler of the great New York dance renaissance of the forties and fifties. He witnessed Graham's peak, Cunningham's and Taylor's emergence; he saw Balanchine (whose work had first impressed him in Paris, in the season of Les Ballets 1933) consolidate his powers on his New York power base.

Looking back on years we never knew, it's easy to think "Bliss was it in that dawn," and yet the reality of life as Denby lived it was not magnificent. It was a life of cafeterias, cigarettes, and stale coffee, of dancers, buildings, and people in the streets. (And the dancers were starving.) Denby took all this as part of his subject. If, as Cornfield says in his introduction, he changed the way we talk and think about dance, it was a change that could not have come about in any other city in the world. The artificial character of life in New York turns the natural world into an abstraction, something for the mind to contemplate. That is why abstract art is so intensely true an expression of New York—it is nature lived as a value. When Cunningham revived his 1953 piece *Septet* this season, he brought back those long-ago New York summers, with their mental weather, their intent street-corner conversations about painting and dance. Denby muses on a Markova performance in 1952: "Her dancing was queerer than anyone had remembered it. A few days later, meeting a balletomane usually far stricter than I on the street, I asked him what he thought of her this season. 'More wonderful than ever,' he cried aggressively." Once, Denby runs into Cunningham; they talk about Markova, naturally, and Denby goes home and writes. In *Septet*, it is possible to see traces of Markova, also Graham, also Balanchine, and to sense the spiritual presence of Denby. The young Paul Taylor was a member of the original cast. Later, it was Denby who introduced Taylor to Lincoln Kirstein and then to Alex Katz.

On the night of July 12, 1983, at the age of eighty, Edwin Denby killed himself with sleeping pills. The notes he left were clearheaded, but his faculties were failing, and he was miserable in his dependency on others. His last published remarks are sad. They concern Balanchine, who had died two months before. Denby begins, ominously enough, with the revival of *Symphonie Concertante* by American Ballet Theatre, which had upset him. Then, as he had done so often in the past, he concentrates on what makes Balanchine different from other choreographers, but having to go through it all again (he is being interviewed for *Dance Magazine*) seems to dishearten him. You feel him near to desperation in the effort to be clear, as if it were a once-and-for-all-time effort, and he keeps underlining his remarks with "This is a rare gift," or "Few choreographers have known how to do that." He wishes that the ballets—"Balanchine's butterflies"— could be preserved, but he seems to think they won't be.

Dance Writings does not end on this note of anguish. The last piece in the book is the great analytical essay "Forms in Motion and in Thought," in the concluding pages of which Denby comes closer to capturing the dance experience than any other writer ever has, even his beloved Mallarmé. The dance is in his mind, a replay of something he's seen (undoubtedly by Balanchine), or perhaps something he's made up, and it is conveyed to us—such is his virtuosity—in three distinctly different phases of activity. First comes a description of how a classical ballet works, in writing that is entirely sensory, with no steps and no images, but so lucidly composed as to evoke continuous gestural force:

> But the action of a step determines the ramifications, the rise and fall of the continuous momentum. You begin to see the active impetus of the dancers creating the impetus moment by moment. They step out of one shape and into another, they change direction or speed, they erect and dissolve a configuration, and their secure and steady impetus keeps coming. The situations that dissolve as one watches are created and swept along by the ease and the fun and the positive lightness of it. They dance and, as they do, create in their wake an architectural momentum of imaginary weights and transported presences. Their activity does not leave behind any material object, only an imaginary one.

One of Denby's cherished beliefs about dancing had to do with the persistence of images as a key to comprehension. Dancing leaves behind "an imaginary object," "a classical shape," "a visual moment of climax," that goes on gathering force in the mind. From ballet in the theatre, then, he turns to ballet recollected in tranquillity:

> As you lie on the hot deserted beach far from town and with closed eyes recall the visual moment of climax, and scarcely hear the hoarse breathing of the small surf, a memory of the music it rose on returns, and you remember the prolonged melodious momentum of the score as if the musical phrase the step rose on had arrived from so far, so deep in the piece it appears to have been.

Finally, after all this so-to-speak disembodied language, he gives us an actual ballet in choreographic script and pictures, danced by cats and dogs on city streets. Every bit of it is wonderful. Here is one excerpt:

> And while cats one meets on different nights all like to follow the same adagio form, one cat will vary it by hunching her back or rolling seductively just out of reach, another, another night, by standing high on her toes as you pat her, and making little sous-sus on her front paws; a third by grand Petersburg-style tail wavings; a fourth, if you are down close enough, by rising on her hind paws, resting her front ones weightlessly on you, raising her wide ballerina eyes to yours, and then—delicate as a single finger pirouette—giving the tip of your nose a tender nip.

Only Denby's eye, only Denby's sweetness of wit, his deep understanding of the collusion of art and nature could have produced this incomparable fun. He left us a little too soon for friendship's sake. Still, his timing told us what we had known and feared to admit—that an era was really over. He had said his farewell years before, in the last poem in *Mediterranean Cities* (incidentally one of the few poems of his with a reference to dance):

> For with regret I leave the lovely world men made
> Despite their bad character, their art is mild

The seasons roll on. The music starts, the dancers appear on the vast stage and begin to dance, "creating the impetus moment by moment." And, moment by moment, it is as if nothing had changed since the days when we would see him there, gazing pensively out at what he helped to establish and would not have abandoned without cause.   —*April 13, 1987*

Index

Permissions Acknowledgments

A Note on the Type

This book was set in a digitized version of Electra,
designed by W. A. Dwiggins (1880–1956).
Although a great deal of his early work was in advertising,
Dwiggins later devoted his talents to book typography
and type design and worked with great distinction in both fields.
In addition to his designs for Electra, he created the Metro,
Caledonia, and Eldorado series of typefaces, as well as a number
of experimental cuttings that have never been issued commercially.
Electra cannot be classified as either modern or old-style.
It is not based on any historical model, nor does it echo
a particular period or style. It avoids the extreme contrast
between thick and thin elements that marks most modern faces,
and attempts to give a feeling of fluidity, power, and speed.

Composed by PennSet, Inc.,
Bloomsburg, Pennsylvania

Printed and bound by R. R. Donnelley & Sons,
Harrisonburg, Virginia

Binding design by
Claire M. Naylon